Edward-John Bottomley

Poor White

TAFELBERG

Tafelberg,
an imprint of NB Publishers,
40 Heerengracht, Cape Town, 8000
www.tafelberg.com

Cover by Michiel Botha
Cover photograph by Roger Ballen
Photos page 3, 138, 158, 174 by Nielen Bottomley
Text design by Nazli Jacobs
Typeset in Palatino

Printed and bound by Paarl Media Paarl
Jan van Riebeeck Drive, Paarl, South Africa

First edition, first printing 2012
ISBN: 978-0-624-05450-4
E-ISBN: 978-0-624-05803-8

For my father and brother

Table of contents

Author's note

This book makes frequent use of racial categories such as 'black', 'white' and 'coloured'. The use of inverted commas denotes the constructed nature of these terms and is meant to provide some distance from the offensive implications. In order to make it easier for the reader, however, the inverted commas have been done away with, but the labels should still be treated carefully. Racial categories have also been uncapitalised to indicate the many variations of each race, and to privilege none of them. Certain other historical terms such as 'native', '*armblankevraagstuk*' or 'poor white problem' have been placed in inverted commas once a chapter, after which the punctuation is removed to ease reading. These terms are (very often unfortunate) products of their time. The punctuation again indicates distance and, even unpunctuated, the terms should still be read as such.

Unless otherwise noted, all translations from Afrikaans are mine.

Introduction

This is the story of the greatest magic trick ever performed.

Whereas the lesser magicians of history – the alchemists of the Middle Ages and their modern counterparts in Las Vegas – were content with trying to turn lead into gold or making an elephant vanish, the magicians of Africa created an entire people from nothing.

With the sea-swept, dust-brushed land of South Africa as their stage, they brought into being a hardy race – a leathery group of farmers and hunters – and gave them a culture. They furnished them with songs and language. Dressed them in hats and bonnets. Gave them a history, a home and a country to call their own. They gifted them with white skins and straight hair.

But this was only the first part of the trick. As the people stood bowing proudly on the stage, the curtain came down. A drum roll, a flash, bang and a puff of smoke. When the curtain came up again, many of those on stage had vanished. And here's the impressive part: no one noticed.

It was only much later, after the magicians themselves had vanished, that people started noticing. Some of those who had vanished began to return and the people began to see that the others had never really disappeared at all. They had been there the whole time.

This is the story of how the magicians performed their trick. More importantly, it is the tale of why they decided to perform it. It is not the complete story. That would take many years and many books, but it is *a* story.

This particular tale ends, if it could be said to end, around 2010, when South Africa hosted the largest sporting event in the world and the eyes of the world turned once again to the young democracy.

More than 15 years after it held its first fully democratic elections, South Africa entered what some commentators called a 'second honeymoon' with the world. The attention resulted in something of a rediscovery of the country with the international press. The Reuters news service, for instance, was especially interested in the appearance of white poverty in South Africa.

In a country so defined by white privilege and the forceful upholding of white superiority, the appearance of acute white poverty was considered especially newsworthy. A Pulitzer Prize-winning photographer was commissioned to compose a photo essay on the 'new' white poor, which, after publication, was widely commented on both internationally and in South Africa. In an interview with *The New York Times*, the photographer, Finbarr O'Reilly, emphasised that white poverty in South Africa is 'not a new phenomenon, but the numbers seem to be more apparent than they were in the past'.[1]

It was not the first time *The New York Times* had reported on the issue. A decade earlier, the newspaper had run a similar story, in which it was noted that 'being a white man in South Africa used to mean having a steady job, a house, a car, a certain respectability. For an overwhelming majority of white men, it still does. But for an increasing number of whites, there are startling new realities.'[2]

In the Reuters article accompanying O'Reilly's photographs, it is noted that 'under apartheid, introduced in 1948, whites enjoyed vast protection and sheltered employment. The weakest and least educated whites were protected by the civil service and state-owned industries operating as job-creation schemes, guaranteeing even the poorest whites a home and livelihood.'[3]

The South African reaction to O'Reilly's photographs was mixed. The influential news website the *Daily Maverick* focused, for instance, on the problem of essentialising the poor along racial lines, but made no attempt to give historical context.[4]

This 'new' white poverty is taken for granted. Yet, in as much as these articles imply, or state outright, that white poverty in South Africa is a new phenomenon, or more acute now than ever, they are simply wrong. No mention is made of what happened *before* apartheid.

A curious form of collective amnesia exists with regard to South Africa's 'poor whites'. This amnesia is deliberate and has been constructed over years with the unspoken agreement of South Africa's ruling classes. Whites are specifically depicted as never having been poor, or certainly not poor in large numbers. In point of fact, however, during the first decades of the twentieth century, the 'poor white problem' assumed such proportions that it influenced the outcome of national elections. It was crucial when it came to standardising race relations in South Africa and in the eventual institution of apartheid. Far from being a new issue, the poor white problem was instrumental in the creation of an entire people and was crucial to their identity.

These people are the Afrikaners, those mostly Dutch descendants who formed the bulk of the poor whites a century ago and, it seems, form the bulk of the poor whites today. Between the 1880s and 1939, a series of natural disasters, wars and economic depressions plunged the Afrikaners into large-scale poverty. In 1916 the government estimated, for instance, that there were more than 121 000 poor whites.[5] By 1924 at least a quarter fell into the poor white category and by 1930, as the Great Depression started to take its toll, about 300 000, one-third of all Afrikaners, were 'absolutely indigent'.[6] Their numbers were never certain, however, and some estimates put the number of 'impoverished' whites at more than half the Afrikaner population by 1932. That is an astounding number. Less than a century ago, the Afrikaners were not known for apartheid or white privilege, their comfortable suburban houses with swimming pools, security alarms and potato salads/Sunday drives. No – less than a century ago, the Afrikaners were known for their poverty, as failed farmers and backyard dwellers.

The poor whites were, initially, mostly rural inhabitants, but with the discovery of diamonds and gold, the increasing industrialisation of South Africa saw huge numbers of poor make their way to the cities. These urban poor were crucial to how the state and the various governments made sense of the problem. The rapid growth of multiracial slums, especially in the mining city of Johannesburg, proved problematic for colonial authorities intent on upholding white prestige.

The poor white population, 1908–1932[7]

Year	Estimate	Proportion of white population	Proportion of Afrikaner population
1908	35 000	2.8%	5.2% (in South Africa)
			8.0% (in Transvaal)
1916	106 518	7.7%	14.3%
1921	120 000	7.7%	14.4%
1923	160 000	12.5%	20.0%

1924	223 000	13.8%	25.0%
1932	300 000 poor whites	16.1%	28.8%
	and 300 000 extremely poor	32.2%	57.7%

And even now their poverty haunts South Africa. The projects created and the political games played to win over poor whites played a large role in establishing the race relations and economic landscape of the modern country. The white poor of today are still glimpsed in the corners of society.

Men with old clothing leaning out of train windows, smoking and staring. Among stationary taxis hurling music at passers-by. In the bright glare of the sun. Glimpsed behind women proudly displaying the sheriff's badge of the Zionist Christian Church. Coca-Cola signs. Shoprite. The sweet, nuzzling smell of frying meat and baked air. '*Oom*, could I watch your car, *Oom*?' Doffing a cap, then sitting down again to stare at something far away. Rusting car frames in little yards. A dirty caravan. A small shack. A sparsely furnished white room. An embroidered sign reading '*God is Liefde*'.

In the evenings, neon glows above the street corners of the city. In the shadowy land beneath the Hotel 224 they hover, or talk, or smoke, or pray, or sleep in doorways. At a traffic intersection with a small, battered sign, poorly lettered. A poor black person in similar circumstances would elicit little, or cursory, sympathy. A poor white person in Rome or London would not be noticed. But in South Africa the sight causes a short, sharp pain in the chest. A mixture of directionless sadness and directed pity settles like a blanket over the observer. Why this reaction?

In his autobiography, Nelson Mandela ponders the same question:

> While I was walking in the city one day, I noticed a white woman in the gutter gnawing on some fish bones. She was poor and apparently homeless, but she was young and not unattractive. I knew of course that there were poor whites, whites who were every bit as poor as Africans, but one rarely saw them. I was used to seeing black beggars on the street, and it startled me to see a white one. While I normally did not give to African beggars, I felt the urge to give this woman money. In that moment I realised the tricks that apartheid plays on one, for the everyday travails that afflict Africans are accepted as a matter of course, while my heart immediately went out to this bedraggled white woman. In South Africa, to be poor and black was normal, to be poor and white was a tragedy.[8]

The story of the poor white problem is the story of their evolution from poor white to 'pure white' to 'white trash' and it begins in 1885 with the founding of Johannesburg and the long lines of poor stretching towards the city and its mines. It was not an Afrikaner problem – it was initially dealt with by the colonial British government overseeing South Africa. The poor whites created slums much like the overwhelmingly black townships of today and it was in these slums that they were defined and discovered by the state, which commissioned studies by various 'experts' to explain the new phenomenon. Later the poor white problem was deployed in the interests of racial superiority through tools such as segregation. The Afrikaner nationalists[9] were keenly interested in the poor whites and co-opted them into the ethnic imagining of the 'new' Afrikaner *volk*. After World War II, the state succeeded in solving the poor white problem, although to the enormous detriment of the other races, and the poor whites vanished from sight, hidden in enclaves of poverty where they were taught how to act as 'proper' whites. It is only recently, after the democratic elections of 1994, that the poor whites have again been noticed. But the world has moved on and the 'poor whites' have become 'white trash' – beggars, thieves and confidence men. Low-class, inbred, violent and drunk. Unworthy of charity and wasting any goodwill to come their way.

It is their story that is being told, but one should always be mindful that black poverty in South Africa was always, and is, much more serious. Any attempt to improve the situation of the poor whites necessarily disadvantaged black South Africans, culminating in their brutal repression under apartheid. A focus on the poor whites in no sense detracts from the injustices of a regime that was racialised from its colonial origins all the way through to the nationalist era. On the contrary, it is impossible to understand the historical subordination of black, Indian and coloured South Africans without hearing the story of their poor white counterparts and the construction of a white society in which non-white poverty was typically overlooked. Yet, the poor whites and the poor white problem were part of the materials used to build South Africa, as much as gold and bricks, diamonds and coal, and their tale – the story of that great magic trick – deserves to be told.

Discovering the poor

They found Alfred Francis[10] with some black women in a house at the lower end of town.

He worked as a teacher, of a sort, on a farm in the Cape Colony. Francis had been so poor when he sought employment as a schoolmaster that the farmer, Du Plessis, had to buy clothes for him. After a spell teaching the children to read and write, Francis stole a horse and headed for town, where the local police found him.

There were many like Francis in the Cape before the twentieth century. Men who had been sailors, perhaps, or had deserted from some army. They roamed the wide country between the mountains, looking for work as *meesters* on farms where the owners were unwilling or unable to send their children to the local school. The *meesters* were viewed as little more than beggars, stopping for a while to mend their shoes before the next rains came. If they were lucky, they found a farmer willing to employ them. Perhaps they stayed and taught the children what little they knew of letters and writing, and helped out with the farm work. They could sit on the steps of the little schoolhouse or church and stare out at the line of trees where the wind chased its tail. Perhaps the breeze shifted, and the rains came too early and they would steal a horse, or some bread, and make for the roads.

In those years there were reports of the 'lowest specimens of humanity' wandering the hills, eating roots, nearly naked. There had been depressions, when their numbers swelled, and the good times, when there were fewer of them walking beyond the towns. If they came begging to the outskirts of cities, or the little *dorps*, they would invariably abuse the charity shown them, people said, and in the morning be found drunk in disreputable streets.

Before the poor white problem, before the modern slumyards, there were the *meesters*. The poor, it is written, have always been with us.

Let us talk of empire – of the age of British expansion into the wild countries beyond their island fortress, when red masses were seen marching in the hills of Natal and the backstreets of Delhi. When great ships took to the waves, bearing the message of civilisation to the corners of the world. Where they docked the air trembled to the sound of thousands of polished boots marching in a murderous quickstep.

There the half-blood child of an English official and a Xhosa woman – symbol of conquest and of shame, abandoned by both parents, scrabbling in the hidden parts of the city. There the bodies of Indian protesters in Amritsar lying quietly as the wind brushes the sound of bullets from the air.

There the brothels glowing in the night. A discarded coat on a salon chair, stripes indicating high rank. The scent of perfume in the heavy evening air.

There the empire.

To take a closer look at history, to analyse our assumptions and reflect critically on what we find requires relying on a set of concepts – the lenses we use to spy on the past. One of these lenses is postcolonialism. In recent years, academics have been re-evaluating what is meant by the term 'empire'. Far from being an unstoppable monolithic force, the spread of empire is now conceived of as being far more haphazard, riven by internal contradictions, rivalries and conflicting agendas.

Much of this revisionist work has focused on the British Empire, envisioning it not as the single-minded focus of thousands of identical functionaries, but as an empire of humans, full of the chaos and clumsiness of our species. By the mid-nineteenth century it might be more correct to describe the result as an 'empire of beachheads and bridgeheads, half-conquered tracts, half-settled interiors, mission stations and whaling stations, barracks and cantonments, treaty-ports on the up and treaty-ports with no future'.[11] This does not mean underestimating the very real economic and military might of the empire – the sound of machine gun fire in the quiet of the Indian afternoon – but it does mean being more sensitive to the complex, multifaceted and human nature of such a 'project' – and to recognise that the business of running an empire was the result of continuous negotiation in the clubs of London and in the sweaty offices of administrators in Calcutta.

Broadening the concept of empire in such a way that we pay attention to shadows cast by the imperial dream is partly due to the rise of a particular form of academic study known as postcolonialism and its concern with the dissonance between the official history and the voices of the marginalised. Postcolonial studies begin with the assumption that the colonies – the business of dominating and occupying a foreign nation – had a profound effect on the colonisers as well as those they ruled. This effect was not simply economical, but cultural. The colonies created identities, marking those who lived there as forever changed – a foreign scent on the neck of an English society lady, a bowler hat worn by an Indian clerk.

Some scholars[12] have applied the ideas of postcolonialism to argue that the colonial identities of coloniser and colonised were constructed in relation to each other – both in the dominions and the metropole. In the colony the rulers had to adjust the outlook they inherited from their homeland to the new world they now inhabited. Colonisation made the English in South Africa or the Dutch in Sri Lanka culturally different from the countries they had left. These new arrivals experienced the rains over the veldt and the monsoon winds rushing in from the jungle, and this left them forever changed. The colonised – those who had seen the coming of the ships – also had to change. They had been fishermen or hunter-gatherers. Now they were servants and the world had become strange.

In the homelands colonialism had also reshaped identities. Markets flooded with exotic goods and foreign spices. Anticipated or not, those in colonial metropoles, such as London or Lisbon, were now conquerors. They had sailed into unknown lands and made them their own. They could not think of themselves as they had.

Other scholars[13] have taken this insight into the fluidity of identity by arguing that 'coloniser' and 'colonised' were never fixed identities, but categories that had to be continually renegotiated and reinforced. How does one classify the mixed-race children of British functionaries and 'native' women? The darker skin of these children marked them as different, but did it put them on the same level as those their parents had set out to colonise? And did the white poor who begged for food alongside the native Africans or Sri Lankans or Indians have the same racial status as the white shopkeeper? Classification was a blunt instrument in imperial hands, and its categories had to be constantly monitored as interests, tastes and societal mores changed.

After the ships had landed, the trading posts and government offices had been established and the flag hoisted high, the colonisers were confronted with a country foreign to them. Their children would grow up in a world vastly different from the one they had left, and the people they passed on the street were at first strange, then familiar to their eyes. It is here that our modern concepts of race, identity and governmental power were formed. Categories were forged, tested and discarded: 'The colonies . . . were underfunded and overextended laboratories of modernity. There, science's authority as a sign of modernity was instituted with a minimum of expense and a maximum of ambition.'[14]

The ideas of postcolonialism place an important emphasis on the colonies, and their contribution, economically and culturally, to the empire project. Yet despite the variety of colonies – for the British, places as diverse as Canada and Singapore – much of the attention has focused on only one place: the Indian subcontinent. Postcolonial scholars and commentators have, for one reason or another, given only glancing attention to the vast world outside the borders of India. There were few substantive conflicts against the colonised in settler countries such as Canada or Australia, yet the empire was formed equally in the mountains of North America and the tides of the South Pacific as on the battlefields of India (or South Africa).

'At best the overseas British have appeared in the guise of "pre-fabricated collaborators", copying the habits and consuming the products of industrial Britain in whose mould they were formed . . . Revision is certainly long overdue,' writes historian James Belich.[15] 'The dominions cannot be fitted into the Procrustean bed of "imperial collaboration". Nor can their contribution to British world power be treated as less important than India's.' Perhaps it is time to look beyond the slums of New Delhi and apply the lens of postcolonialism to countries where the colonisers came to stay, and which in time they began to call their own.

Belich argues that focusing on imperialism, on the conquest of nations and the subjugation of their inhabitants, hides a more important development – that it was the settler colonies like Australia, the United States and South Africa that had the most profound impact on the modern world, and not occupied countries, such as India: 'European empire dominated one and a half continents for a century or so. European settlement came to dominate three and a third continents, including Siberia. It still does.'[16] Imperialism washed the souls of colonised and colonisers in a terrible shade, staining hands, leaving slaves and widows and governors in its wake. Generations later, the embers of empire still smoulder in the heart of the world. Despite its impact, however, substantive European empire arrived late, and did not last very long. The true power behind the dramatic Anglophone expansion between 1790 and 1939, Belich concludes, was the settler societies.

Far beyond the factories and forests of Europe lay a settler colony that combined the features of both settlement and conquest like no other. South Africa was a huge, dry land where 'the bond of Empire was weaker and the strains on it much greater'.[17] Unlike other countries where the colonisers came to live, the British in South Africa were a significant minority in relation to native Africans, viewing themselves as an 'island of white' in a dark and dangerous sea, a view more common to smaller settler outposts, such as Kenya, Rhodesia or Ceylon. Equally important was that the British were a minority among the colonisers themselves. In South Africa the British came face to face with something relatively unfamiliar – a European colonial competitor jealously guarding the country for itself. The Dutch had been present in South Africa since 1652, and were firmly entrenched by the time of extensive British migration in the nineteenth century. The two groups had clashed since 1795, when Britain wrested the Cape Colony from the Dutch. For the next century, these nations circled each other warily, feinting punches, measuring reach, testing strength, until they growled and met in the Second Anglo-Boer War of 1899–1902. For more than 200 years the Dutch and British in South Africa have fashioned themselves in relation to one another – as Not-Dutch and Not-British – as well as to the indigenous black Africans, and they competed for control of the country through politics, economics and ideas.

The Second Anglo-Boer War, which was mainly caused by a struggle for the control of the Witwatersrand goldfields, is an emblem of the primary forces that shaped modern South Africa. In 1867 diamond deposits were found beneath central South Africa leading to a rush of the hopeful to the country, inspiring stories of glittering bird's eggs strewn across the countryside, easy fortunes for the desperate and the ambitious.

And then, 20 years later, the most extensive deposits of gold-bearing ore in the world were discovered beneath the Witwatersrand – the richest treasure in history. 'From 1886 the story of South Africa is the story of gold.'[18] Historian Charles van Onselen describes the years that separate the discovery of gold and the outbreak of World War I as a 'historian's dream':

> In little less than thirty years a republic founded on a modest agricultural economy was transformed into a colony boasting the world's largest and most technologically sophisticated gold-mining industry – a traumatic transition which was overseen by four different governments, punctuated by an attempted coup, and at one stage completely halted by a bloody conflict lasting two and a half years.[19]

Within 80 years South Africa leapt 'from a fledgling quasi-state to a surprisingly advanced industrial state... a process that took centuries in Europe'.[20]

The fortune beneath South Africa could make empires of nations and the vault was protected by nothing more than poor Dutch farmers more interested in raising cattle than ruling a world. The war would be over by Christmas. It took far longer than that.

Later, when the soft rains covered the corpses, tens of thousands of British and Boer troops lay sleeping forever beneath the stars. No one knows for certain how many black Africans perished. The conflict taxed the empire, leaving it stung and red-faced among the other European nations. As it raged, Britain committed nearly half a million troops against a total possible Boer force of 50 000. The Boers formed small bands of guerrilla fighters, stinging and stinging the impossible beast, only to vanish into the hills when the bodies were counted. To the world it was portrayed as a gentleman's war. On Sundays the combatants looked up from their trenches and peeked over their wagons to attend church and play cricket.

And yet – with a protracted, painful and expensive conflict ahead of them, the British committed to scorched-earth tactics, destroying the farms and families that resupplied the Boer combatants. The reek of burnt fields covered the wide country, the throats of cattle slit, bullets puncturing their soft flanks. Wells were poisoned. Fields salted. An entire agrarian economy now drifting on dirty winds.

It was a gentleman's war no longer. They took women and children, resettling them in vast refugee cities, which quickly became known by a new name: concentration camps. In total, more than 100 000 Boers and black Africans were interred in these camps where disease crouched on long legs to peer into tents, starvation stretched stomachs and snapped bones like dry twigs. Tens of thousands of Boer women and children died. No one is certain how many black Africans lay down beside them. More than 25 000 Boer men were exiled from their homes and sent to foreign shores. When it was quiet once more, the gold belonged to the British. The war impoverished an entire nation, shamed another and forgot a third, the black Africans. It tore a dark and furious chasm in the minds of those who became the Afrikaners, one that still glows late in the night.

English philanthropist Emily Hobhouse, who wrote about the conditions of the concentration camps, called it the 'terrible laughter of the Afrikaner'. The awful result of the scorched-earth policy had set Afrikaners laughing. Of the Van Graan brothers, who had both suffered enormous losses during the war, Swart records Hobhouse's words:

> One 'had seven little mouths to feed. He got seed potatoes from Repatriation for a promissory note, but the drought killed them. His brother lent him oxen to plough with, so he put in a little seed, but till it is ripe he has nothing to live upon. His beautiful house is in ruins, his blue gums all but two cut down, his fruit trees chopped.' 'But,' Hobhouse continued, 'how he laughed, and how his brother laughed.'
>
> Hobhouse further observed that 'like all the other burghers [Boer general] De Wet is laughing. If he did not, he says, he should die. It makes him

great fun. I do regret not being quick enough to catch all the Dutch proverbs which spice his conversation, nor the humour which runs through all the family talk – they speak so quickly.' In a rural hamlet in the Orange Free State, Hobhouse encountered 'a poor man', who – when she offered him some meal – said: 'I shall be so glad that I shall laugh without feeling any inclination to laugh.' In Pretoria, Hobhouse noted, the Boers 'say little and only laugh'. She concluded: 'There is getting to be something quite terrible to me in this laugh of the Boers which meets me everywhere. It is not all humour, nor all bitter, though partly both; it is more like the laughter of despair. We sit in a row by these stable walls and discuss every project possible and impossible, and then we laugh. Now and again the tears come into the men's eyes, but never into the women's except when they speak of children lost in the camps.'[21]

City of gold

With the country's mineral wealth secured, the massive effort required to excavate the treasure dragged a mostly rural South Africa into the industrial age, bringing hundreds of thousands to cities. Massive urbanisation brought pollution, desperate urban poverty and slum conditions into which the poorest were squeezed, breathing each other's air. In 1890 fewer than 10 000 Afrikaners (between 2 and 3 per cent) were urbanised. Less than 50 years later, 535 000 (50 per cent) lived in towns and cities. The centre of this accelerated modernity was the gold-bearing reef of the Witwatersrand, an area stretching about 60 kilometres from Springs in the east to Krugersdorp in the west. Lying roughly in the middle of the reef is Johannesburg, known colloquially in contemporary South Africa as *eGoli* – the city of gold. Founded in 1885, this shabby El Dorado was a blank slate onto which the colonial government could design the perfect colonial city according to its ideals of urban planning and racial order. The streets were laid out in a gridiron pattern – straight lines intersecting what had once been *veldt*. The new city's thoroughfares were well lit, wide and spacious to promote health and discourage crime.[22] Ideally, it would be a perfect colonial construction, spreading order, modernity and colonial values across the savage face of Africa. 'Like every colonial town, it found it hard to resist the temptation of mimicry, that is, of imagining itself as an English town and becoming a pale reflection of forms born elsewhere.'[23]

When the main reef was discovered, Johannesburg's population exploded from a mere 3 000 casual diggers to 100 000 permanent residents. By 1914, Johannesburg counted a quarter of a million residents. The city's municipal boundaries dramatically widened to accommodate its new residents – from five square miles in 1898 to 82 square miles just five years later. The newcomers were prospectors, entrepreneurs and fortune-seekers from as far afield as Australia, China and the US. In the heat of the gold rush, passers-by on the street could be heard talking in the tongues of Europe and Asia. In the heart of the city, a newcomer could be forgiven for thinking himself in one of the great capitals of the world. South Africans rapidly migrated from the countryside and the government began bringing in scores of cheap black labourers for unskilled work on the mines. The new city lived and died by the wealth beneath its surface and, in the same breath, so did South Africa. The mines were a crucial source of income for the state. In 1886, Johannesburg produced only 0.16 per cent of the world's gold output, yet by 1913 the output of the city's mines dwarfed those of its rivals, producing a massive 40 per cent of the world's gold.

Since it offered a relatively clean slate for urban planners, the city in many ways resembled a classically divided colonial city – 'high-standard, intensely regulated space for the colonial population, and low-quality, poorly regulated space for the indigenous population'.[24] The massive migration into the city from the countryside, as well as the large number of fortune-seekers from overseas, resulted in an acute housing crisis at the turn of the century. Consequently, Johannesburg developed some of the worst slum areas in the world at the time. Despite government efforts, the urban poor clustered in these slums, white and black freely mixing. These slums were 'liminal' spaces – hidden worlds guarding secrets, lurking on fringes, disturbing the proper order of things. The colonial ideal of a 'white' city physically separated from a 'native' one simply did not exist in the urban slums. Here poor Afrikaner women worked in Asian laundries and were glimpsed with Chinese husbands. Black pimps spoke of the gifts of their French girls. Mixed-race boys selling newspapers avoided the gaze of Chicago gangsters. Colonial categories of race and respectability had no place in the slums. These areas inevitably disturbed other colonisers, who called for their removal on grounds such as health and crime. Such places were dirty and dangerous, they said, and such mixing of white and black 'cried shame upon the Rand'. Separation was necessary in order to save the poor and settle the stomachs of decent folk. In such a way, slowly and unsuspectingly, the calls to bring order to the slums added volume to the calls for the establishment of formal racial segregation.

Yet little historical attention has been given to these twilight spaces of South Africa's poor. Although scholars have begun paying more attention to the margins of history, the story of Johannesburg is still very much a history of its captains of industry: 'It is almost as if by concentrating exclusively on the exploits of a small number of ruling-class actors the people could be ignored, and the city would somehow be endowed with a mythical collective past more becoming to its present role as one of the major finance capitals of the world.'[25] When the struggles of the poor and working classes are examined, it is typically in connection with the 1922 Rand Revolt, a semi–civil war, which brought home the danger of working-class frustration, and its threat to mine production. During the revolt, white mineworkers openly clashed with the state, occupying the poorer Johannesburg suburbs and firing upon soldiers. The government responded harshly, sending thousands of troops with the aid of tanks and artillery to crush resistance. The Rand Revolt, coming as it did on a world tide of socialist revolution, instilled a deep and abiding fear of class alliances in South Africa's elite. If they were pushed hard enough, the poorer classes might look past colour and violently make their voices heard. It was in the interests of the elite to make sure this didn't happen. In recent years geographers, historians and other interested scholars have begun emphasising the 'disorderly' nature of contemporary Johannesburg – the constant struggle between the poor and rich for the control of urban space,[26] a hidden war of attrition in which a victory is marked by an unoccupied square or the right to sleep undisturbed beneath a freeway. Despite this interest, however, the city's shabby history of mixed spaces and mixed races remains relatively unexplored.[27]

No less neglected in modern scholarship is the place of the Afrikaner in Johannesburg (outside of nationalistic history), and the role the city played in the development of Afrikaner nationalism. Johannesburg was symbolically important for the Afrikaners in a myriad ways. As Johannesburg was a capitalistic English city with no place for Afrikaner skilled or unskilled labour, Afrikaner success there was seen as a milestone in the quest for respectability. By conquering capitalism and carving out an established place in the city, the Afrikaners could look the English squarely in the eye. Despite being seen as an English city, by 1926 Johannesburg had the largest concentration of urban Afrikaners in the country, only eclipsed by Pretoria in 1960. For the first waves of urbanising Afrikaners, who formed the majority of poor whites in the city, Johannesburg led to something of a 'city shock'.[28] Employers usually spoke English, a language poorly understood by the Dutch descendants. Rural Afrikaners possessed few qualifications, were poorly schooled and had little experience of organised labour and trade unions. Employers of unskilled labour preferred black Africans, since they could be hired at a far lower rate than the Afrikaners were willing to accept. The Afrikaners struggled in the new city, many of them living in poverty, unable to make headway into the new century. The urban environment – and particularly Johannesburg – became something more than just a network of roads, factories and people. In nationalist mythmaking it became 'the city', a dark and foreign mass of towers, blacks and Englishmen, alien to the *veldt* and to the farm, but a crucial hurdle that the Afrikaners had to conquer in their search for a place in modernity. Speaking at the highly symbolic centennial celebration of the Great Trek in 1938, for instance, the National Party (NP) leader DF Malan put it succinctly: 'The armed struggle is over. That was the struggle of the Voortrekkers. A fiercer, deadlier struggle than theirs is now being fought. The battlefield has moved. Your Blood River is not there. Your Blood River lies in the cities.'[29]

The Afrikaner poor in the city had not suddenly appeared in the slums of Johannesburg, but were part of a broader issue in South African society – the so-called poor white question – that dominated social and political conversations in the first four decades of the twentieth century. Although white poverty had, of course, existed in South Africa nearly since its inception, the poor white question referred to a combination of events that resulted in unprecedented white and black impoverishment in South Africa. The poor white question was also viewed as a process –

a sinking of whites into poverty, dragging society with them. Poor white-ism was a machine that could not be turned off. It took in respectable whites and spat out the dangerous and impoverished poor. In their search for a means to disable the machine, the governments of the day set up various commissions to investigate white poverty, which they considered 'a process of impoverishment, with its sequels of moral and spiritual degradation amongst a section of the population that is of rural origin and Dutch-speaking, more particularly after they have abandoned farm life'.[30]

The trouble began in the countryside. During the late 1890s, a series of natural disasters, such as prolonged drought and the lethal cattle disease rinderpest, devastated farms. Impoverished Afrikaners known as *bywoners* lived a tenuous existence in rural areas, working as tenants on farms, helping out with the labour and perhaps owning a few cattle or sheep of their own. Afrikaners were slow to adapt to more modern farming methods and followed the Roman-Dutch law of inheritance, which forced the division of a farmer's property among his children after death. The farmer's sons, of whom there could be many, each inherited a part of the farm. Upon their death, their share would be further sliced up and shaved thin by their sons until a once prosperous farm became nothing more than a series of economically unsustainable plots of land – suitable only for growing some corn or grazing a cow. Yet the children stayed on the farm, able to draw on a cheap reserve of black labour from the surrounding countryside, seeing no need to become farm labourers themselves. School attendance was low, with many farmers seeing no need for their children to learn any skills beyond farming: 'An entire Afrikaner underclass formed on the farms, increasingly unable to feed their large families properly, many stunted in mental and physical development'.[31] In 1892, one school inspector noted that it was 'sad to see a class who were once land-owners, endowed by nature with greater possibilities than the natives, allowing their heritage to slip from their hands, and sinking into the class of unskilled labourers'.[32] This precarious state of affairs was finished off by the Boer War, which devastated town and countryside. The scorched-earth policy of the British left many farms unusable after the war. In the Boer republic of the Transvaal, for instance, 80 per cent of cattle and 73 per cent of the sheep were destroyed. *Bywoners*, and newly poor farmers, saw no choice but to try again in the cities.

From around 1910, poverty was increasingly viewed as an urban problem – a disease of the metropolis. The newly urbanised Afrikaners were out of their depth in the city, and struggled to find work, not least because the gold rush had seen thousands of skilled whites immigrate to South Africa take up positions in the city. The historian Hermann Giliomee points out that:

> . . . between 1875 and 1904 some 400 000 whites entered South Africa, more than the entire white population of 1875. Increasingly the Afrikaners, who began moving to the towns and cities in the 1890s, found that skilled and semi-skilled work, the professions and civil service positions were already filled by local or immigrant English-speakers. The British section had the advantage of better education, better skills and their command of English. Invariably they had longer experience of the cash economy.[33]

A series of economic depressions, particularly those of 1906–1908 and the post-war depressions of 1919, added to Afrikaner misery. In the second half of the 1920s, drought returned to the farms and persisted into the 1930s. A black cloud of misfortune clung to the Afrikaners. By the time of the Great Depression, the poor white problem had become a national crisis.

The Johannesburg and Witwatersrand area received the bulk of the poor whites owing to its size and the promise of employment offered by the mines. The gold-bearing reef dictated the geography of the working class of Johannesburg. As the reef ran east to west, it was chased by poor and working-class neighbourhoods, such as Jeppestown and Vrededorp, their pursuit made possible by the newly built railway lines that followed the reef. A line of Afrikaners intersected the city from Springs to Krugersdorp and onwards to Carletonville. This left the south, and especially the north, of the city to take on a richer character – where today the towers and office parks of Sandton and Bryanston are found.

It was in Johannesburg that the problem of white poverty was at its most visible – to the government, to the elite and to the black poor. It was here that the tensions caused by white poverty were strongest. Leaving aside the extensive economic concerns, poor whites disturbed colonial relationships in a society where national survival was a conversation topic at dinner parties.

In the salons of respectable society, South Africa was seen as a small beacon of white civilisation in an unknowable continent. The politician John X Merriman, in a letter to Afrikaner leader Jan Smuts in 1913, aptly expressed this: 'Above all we must constantly keep in mind that as Europeans we are but a handful in the face of an overwhelming mass of an inferior race.'[34]

In parliament, Merriman warned that white South Africa might go the way of other cultures and civilisations, other transient empires: 'The existence of the white race in Africa is by no means assured, and unless we mend our ways we may go the same way in the South that the Roman and the Greek, the Carthaginian and the Vandal did in the North.'[35] If white South Africans were not vigilant against the black man, if they were not constantly on guard, then centuries later, black civilisations would wonder at them in museums – a strange and violent footnote in the history of Africa.

While the very existence of poor whites was a constant reminder of how fragile white existence in Africa was, it was their position, and location, next to black Africans that caused the most anxiety. The poor whites in the Johannesburg slums lived 'side by side' with blacks.[36] The spectre of miscegenation – of interracial relationships – loomed ever large in the minds of South African doomsayers. 'In the already vulnerable settler colony of South Africa, poor whites were living, disturbing proof of the permeability of racial boundaries, thus they shocked the tenuous . . . ideological pillars of white supremacy.'[37]

'Poor whiteism' also had a distinct psychological dimension. It was not just physical, the experts said, it was also a matter of attitude. Nearly all of the official government investigations expressed their concerns at the perceived unwillingness of poor whites to do certain kinds of unskilled labour, which were labelled as '*kaffir* work'. The investigations fretted about poor whites' disdain for education and the unwillingness to do supervised work. Laziness, drunkenness, criminal tendencies and a lack of respect for racial boundaries were all described as cause for concern. These characteristics threatened the superiority of the white race. They undermined white prestige, pulling these impoverished colonisers closer to the level of 'white *kaffirs*'. As one witness told the Carnegie Commission of 1932, 'the educated Afrikaner feels with resentment and impatience that the poor white is a disgrace to his own people. "You feel, in a way, that they have let you down."'[38]

Whiteness studies

For the colonials and the later nationalists, 'whiteness' was therefore a central issue of the poor white question, a statement that needs some explaining. Whether they call them texts or icons or discourses, social academics rely heavily on abstraction. Concepts such as 'white prestige' and the 'boundaries of whiteness' arise out of the academic field of whiteness studies, which is the last, and most important, lens this book uses to study poor whiteism.

Concepts such as 'white prestige' rest on the basic assumption that, instead of being fixed, race is fluid. It can be constructed and assigned. This doesn't deny the fact that there is a physical difference in skin colour between someone from central Africa and someone from northern Europe, but argues that the closer you look, the more complicated things become. Would the child of the African and the European be considered white? Or the child of a European and an Asian? Assuming that child married a white European, what race would their child be? And after five or six generations of further white European marriage? What race we are is, to a very large extent, determined by those around us, and how we are viewed by others. It is in how we say certain words, how we hold our cutlery, where we spend our time. What race we are is a social construction. A mixed-race child in South Africa, for instance, would be classified into a separate racial group, as 'coloured'. Yet the same child, if born in the United States, would be classified as 'black'. The term 'white', as it is currently used, is actually a relatively recent construction, applied by Europeans to a wide variety of groups well into the seventeenth century. Portuguese conquistadors referred to the Arabs and Chinese as white. The Chinese thought of themselves as white – a colour associated with purity. Early European settlers described the Native Americans as white. The modern idea of what 'white' means 'seems to have emerged at the time of, and in response to, the emergence of European global hegemony and the, not unrelated, development of the biological concept of "race" in the late 18th century.'[39]

Consider the well-known case of Sandra Laing, a dark-skinned girl who was born to conservative white parents and grandparents during the apartheid era. Although she was initially classified as white, Sandra was later reclassified as coloured as she grew older and her skin darkened. As which race, then, was the state to classify her parents? Which race was she? Or consider the case of the 'pass-whites', who were born as light-skinned 'coloured' people but represented themselves as white to the outside world and lived in areas reserved for whites. 'Turning into a White was a long and complicated process, called passing for white. It often meant moving to another part of the country, where the aspirant White was not known as a coloured person, or moving to an area where it was possible to establish a "respectable" way of life. The pass-whites existed in the remotest boundary of the white race, in constant danger of being expelled from it. Conversely, it was dangerous for a dubious-looking white to be seen as a pass-white. Therefore it is important to examine how and on what grounds they were included or excluded from the racial category White.'[40]

Social construction theories are 'not intended to imply that race is a fiction with no material effects, but rather that racialised ways of thinking and the practices they inform have varied significantly from time to time and from place to place[41]'. Being white means different things at different times and places. Similarly, it follows that individuals and cultures can move in and out of, and also aspire to, whiteness. And here is the other crucial realisation – that 'whiteness' can be a quality. Being white in the eighteenth or nineteenth century meant better treatment, better living conditions, better pay, more respect. Being white in apartheid South Africa came with significantly more advantages than being black. Whiteness is not simply colour, or the lack thereof. It can have a quality; it can be aspired to; and it can protect and be protected. It can be in the thoughts of colonial administrators defending their society from perceived revolt, and in the minds of colonial housewives forbidding contact with the non-white domestic worker.

Whiteness gifted, and gifts, particular people with power – political, economic, social. One of the objects of studying whiteness is to determine the extent and content of that power. Historians such as David Roediger[42] have examined the ways in which the working-class whites in nineteenth-century America embraced the term 'white' – initially to define themselves as 'not slaves' and later modified the term to keep other groups from gaining the same power. Put differently, the American working class actively tried to make themselves more white. Other scholars[43] have looked at how European immigrants to the United States, such as the Irish and the Polish, aspired to and competed for the category of 'white' after being initially viewed as 'non-white'. The Irish were initially regarded by the English as something less than white. Not black, but certainly not respectable enough to be full members of the white race. The Irish were viewed as drunken, stupid and lazy. Newspaper and magazine cartoons from the period usually depict 'Paddy' with a darker skin tone – an idea that would be laughable today. Of course, the English could not call the Irish black. They were 'savage' or 'Celtic', but they were not white, and they could not enjoy the advantages that being white brings. And such racial classification is not limited to European nations. Race can be a 'cultural currency' that we exchange in order to advance ourselves. Race relations are, academically put, 'historical products of human activity . . . brought about by the concrete actions of human beings[44]'.

Race advantages one group over another by barring or granting access to resources – a whites-only bench, the right to live in a certain area. Belonging to the dominant group, the dominant race, has been a high-stakes game played over centuries – like the effort to fit in with the popular kids at school, only infinitely more dangerous and more damaging.

Bound up with the idea of race as a currency – something to be lost and gained – is a realisation of the tenuousness of whiteness, the shifting categories for membership, that the boundaries of whiteness are not fixed. This becomes especially clear when examining imperialism. As postcolonial studies have shown, there was never a unified imperial project with a single, all-encompassing purpose. The colonies of empire naturally differed in important ways from the home country in their conception of race. In the colonies, the agents of empire were suddenly confronted with a whole other nation or nations. They would have to live together, sharing the same country – something those at home had never had to deal with. The colonisers had to think long and hard about race, and the results of their decisions are with us still.

They did not have to make these decisions by themselves, however. Settler societies, such as Canada and South Africa, plugged into a global network of whiteness, marketing themselves as 'white men's countries'. Their policies were not developed in isolation, but reproduced and refined by way of global information networks of telegraph lines and newspaper headlines. Yet it was hardly that simple. If we apply the lens of postcolonialism to these 'white men's countries', we begin to realise that even the colonisers themselves were never clearly defined. They 'constructed imagined communities as deftly as the nationalist colonised populations to whom they were opposed'.[45] The colonisers had to process the strange world around them and retain a white identity that included mixed-race children, white prostitutes and black clients, criminals and poor. In the colonies, who was 'white' took on new meanings, was constantly changing and very different from the land they had left.

One of the ways the colonials maintained control over the societies they dominated was by 'identifying who was "white", who was "native", and which children could become citizens rather than subjects, on which were legitimate progeny and which were not'.[46] The colonisers were obsessed with miscegenation, white prestige and the protection of white women from the natives, and these obsessions were part and parcel of an on-going project of self-classification, of keeping wayward colonials, such as poor whites and prostitutes, from straying too much from their racial categories, from 'going native'.

In part, the logic was simple – weakening the white race endangered the overextended colonisers by bringing them on a level with those they had colonised. Once the illusion of control was broken, once the dominated began to see that the colonisers were not invincible, the colonised would rise up. Colonial blood would stain streets. The grand colonial project would come to a loud and violent end. In societies where the native population vastly outnumbered the colonisers, these empires needed all the true 'whites' they could get.

In South Africa, the colonial, and later nationalist, states had an important interest in keeping their citizens white. The enormous concern they had over poor whites, as opposed to the more extensive poverty of black Africans, arose partly out of a concern to racially re-inscribe white identity – to pick up those who had strayed and make them respectable, to recruit them into their ranks, to make them good whites by raising their living standards. The poor whites huddled on the margins of the respectable world – 'situated on the boundary between coloniser and colonised, they were . . . the marker of the limits of colonial acceptability'[47]. In the colonial imagination, transgression swirled around the poor whites – the sense of things not being as they should, the sense of boundaries crossed, the sense of certainties being disturbed.

Poor whites were seen as the most likely group to develop interracial relationships. They were most likely to work for, or alongside, other races; they were most likely to fall into drinking, crime and prostitution. The people of the fringes, of the backstreets and bedrooms, were another battlefield of colonialism, not because of their profession, or lack thereof, but because they demonstrated a disturbing willingness to defy the colonisers and undermine the entire project.

We should be careful not to use an examination of race and whiteness studies to project impossible motivations onto empires, nor to diminish the vast military and economic power of these regimes. But by looking at what was not said, at what was hinted at, we gain a far more subtle and complex, far more human, picture of empire.

Enquiries and experts

All the lenses are now in place – postcolonialism, settler societies, the complexity of South Africa and whiteness studies. Now we can turn our attention to how a state realises that it has an extensive problem with white poverty, and how it tries to understand the white poor.

For a ruling class to regard poverty as a national problem, it needs a reason to care. The existence of beggars and vagrants might be enough for churches and charities, but for poverty to be regarded not as a nuisance or a shame, but as a national focus, the ruling class needs to be afraid – of uprisings and revolutions – or it needs to see an opportunity for gaining more power. The state needs to 'discover' the poor in its midst. 'In South Africa this development occurred when the proponents of white supremacy concluded that a consolidated white group was needed to dominate the black majority.'[48] The existence of a class of unskilled and impoverished white people, whose loyalties were always unclear, stood in the way of such a consolidation. The black majority would not easily be dominated while the poor whites existed and so the poor whites became a problem that needed to be solved.

The first order of business, then, was to gather information about the poor. To understand and discover them. To this end, the state used techniques social scientists call technologies – maps, statistics, studies. In South Africa, various commissions were set up to investigate white poverty, which was intensively studied for more than 30 years, under both colonial and nationalist governments. To examine these commissions one needs to be sensitive to the context in which they were written – not just to racist and offensive phrasing, but to understand that the reports were products of their time and of the people writing them. Although their reports come across as coldly official repositories of facts, the commissions were influenced by their interviewers and witnesses, their overall direction and the political situation both locally and globally. Commissions are 'stories that states tell themselves'. They are stories with a moral, stories that recommend how to solve a problem. 'By definition commissions organised knowledge, rearranged its categories, and prescribed what state officials were charged to know. They . . . produced new truths as they produced new social realities.'[49]

As with any problem, poor whites first had to be defined and differentiated from other impoverished whites, such as tramps and beggars. At the turn of the nineteenth century, the European elite in South Africa were heavily influenced by how the poor were seen in Victorian England where the impoverished had been divided into the 'deserving' and 'undeserving' poor. The deserving poor had fallen into the slums because of the hardship of life. They deserved charity and, given the chance, would happily better themselves and become decent citizens again. The undeserving poor were the criminals, beggars and prostitutes – those who were poor by nature, who chose to be poor, and to live life at the lower order of things.

Poor whites as a specific type or class of the impoverished were not unheard of by the end of the nineteenth century. In all of the European colonies, concern over white poverty had intensified during the 1880s and 1890s, when it was connected to vague ideas of racial exclusivity and 'white' prestige. But the term 'poor white' probably originated in the American south during the 1870s when the desperately poor conditions of millions of whites were argued to be nearly equal to those of the recently emancipated slaves[50]. The poverty of these American whites was viewed predominantly as a moral problem – the white poor were lazy, lacked ambition and were ultimately the cause of their own poverty. The American poor whites were 'undeserving'.

The same period saw the development of social sciences and the rise of scientific racism, which argued that other nations were biologically inferior to Europeans. The combination of these views encouraged the idea that the underclasses were a sort of social disease – a natural but parasitical part of the human ecosystem that needed curing. Unless the right medicine were found, the poor would always be with them. These ideas resonated internationally. In the colonies European theories of poverty came up against more direct fears of race war and white survival. Conceptions of the 'moral' poor were mixed with theories of disease and race survival, and the end result was that the idea of poverty took on nearly cataclysmic overtones in the colonies.

In South Africa the most significant of the early investigations into poverty was the Transvaal Indigency Commission (TIC) of 1906–1908.

Historian Liz Lange argues that this commission 'did more than investigate the extent of indigency in the Transvaal. It established the existence of indigency as a question.'[51] The commission's report classified the South African poor along two main lines – those who were actually poor, and those who were 'so ignorant or lazy, and live life at such low standards, that they are almost certain sooner or later to find themselves in actual want'.[52] The first class included the disabled, the poor whites (whom the TIC described as not competent enough to do skilled or semi-skilled labour and unable to find work because of native competition) and the semi-criminal class known as 'the lazy and the vicious', who were 'unwilling to work, and existed as loafers and vagrants'. The second class, those who were not yet in actual want, had 'fallen behind in the march to civilisation', and were in danger of becoming poor whites after the slightest setback.[53]

The commission was unapologetically colonial, enthusiastically seizing upon the ideas of Victorian moral science. In a way, poverty was seen as a symptom of a diseased society, and its cure was to be found in the moral regeneration of the undeserving poor. The commission argued that 'the further creation of squalid, unhealthy and demoralising poor white settlements should be prevented' in order to 'protect the population from disease and to prevent the perpetuation of indigency and crime'.[54] The undeserving poor could perhaps be cured through labour camps, where they could be the 'moral, physical and technical patients of the state'.[55] The problem of the deserving poor was more troubling, however, and it is here that the colonial anxiety over the tenuousness of the white race in Africa is seen. Charity and relief work would not help, said the TIC. Poverty was 'almost invariably the product of lack of education or some weakness of character'[56] and the class had to be brought back into the fold through efforts to 'correct the weakness of character or to make good the deficiency in education or training'. The future of the white race, the commission argued, depended on the numbers of whites constantly increasing in relation to the natives. For the whites to increase, they needed to find employment, and if the deserving poor could not find unskilled employment owing to labour competition with the native, 'South Africa will at best be numbered among the countries which are owned and governed, but not peopled by the white races'.[57]

Consider for a moment of the people behind these statements. Just as crucial to the broader ideas that informed the commissions are the ways in which so-called 'expert witnesses' obtained their knowledge of the poor. Most of the investigations relied heavily on the testimony of those familiar with the field, and leant on a pool of experts on whose knowledge they could draw. These experts, and the commissioners themselves, were instrumental in shaping the state's knowledge of the poor and deserve specific consideration. Their expert views of the poor white problem were debated, drawn upon, cited, criticised, confirmed, elaborated and developed over decades – suggesting that the poor white was constructed in discourse as much as was found in reality.

The TIC was appointed by Lord Alfred Milner, then governor of the Transvaal, who staffed it with members of his so-called 'Kindergarten' – men he had hand-picked to serve under him. The commission was led by Lionel Curtis, Milner's secretary[58], along with Richard Feetham and Phillip Kerr. Feetham had been appointed town clerk of Johannesburg, but at the time of the commission was practising as a lawyer in the city. Kerr was attached to the Intercolonial Council and would later become Chief Justice of the Union of South Africa. The chairman was John W Quinn, who had been involved with the Rand Aid Association – a charity established by Milner with the help of the mine owners. The leaders of the commission were elite British colonials. They were lawyers and colonial imaginaries, who brought a Victorian moralistic conception of the poor and slums to their work.[59] Their experts held a similar world view. The moral experts were represented by the church, such as the Anglican Sister Evelyn and the Rev. D Theron of Fordsburg. FW Mills, the principal of the government school in Vrededorp, was an educational expert. The district surgeon for Fordsburg, Dr TB Gilchrist, testified on health, and Lieutenant Colonel Mackey O'Brian, Johannesburg Commissioner of Police, on matters of security. A small Afrikaner presence was visible in General Louis Botha, who attended the preliminary hearings, and the testimonies provided by JH Hofmeyer, leader of the Afrikaner organisation known as the Bond and later a government minister.

The experts brought before each of the commissions, and the commissioners themselves, were crucial sources of knowledge to the state, but, more importantly, they established how the poor would be viewed, and how they would be investigated. Their interests, networks and moral universes were important to the state's discovery of the poor. These experts chose what knowledge to include or leave out in their testimonies, and the commissioners chose what knowledge to include or leave out in their reports. The commissions established what the state would see when it looked at the poor.

The people behind the TIC had the unique task of defining poverty. In their meetings, in the unexceptional but comfortable rooms in which they met, in the larger spaces where they interviewed experts, the commissioners were busy defining a whole social group. It was no easy task. The commissioners struggled to reconcile the various conceptions of poverty with their own internal colonial mindsets. Where had all the poor come from, and did it mean something that so many of them were white? What did it mean for South Africa?

At the beginning of the twentieth century, white South Africa was grappling with a problem that would come to define it: what to do with all the natives. The natives were willing to do unskilled work for far lower wages than the whites, which, the commissions felt, pushed many Europeans into poverty because they could not find employment. Whites who were not trained for skilled labour were 'doomed to indigency' if they could not compete with blacks. 'In the Transvaal today the training ground of unskilled labour is monopolised by the native, who is thereby rapidly qualifying himself to perform the higher forms of labour, while the white South African is not being trained at all, or has to fall back on less efficacious methods.'[60] Before the twentieth century, the commissions said, impoverished whites found employment in, among other things, transport riding – trekking mechanical equipment and supplies by mule, ox or donkey from the coast, up the mountains and over the lonely interior of South Africa, into the hungry heart of Johannesburg. With the completion of the Cape to Johannesburg railway line in 1892, and three years later the lines to Natal and Mozambique, this work dried up and transport riding died a quick death.

Yet the commissioners were also told that the poor whites simply didn't want to work. A witness from Pietersburg complained that 'the majority of poor whites here are neither willing nor able to do a hard day's work as agriculturists. They have been accustomed to riding wood to the market, loafing about at home and hunting. They really do not know what it means to put in a hard day's work.'[61] According to JH Hofmeyer, this laziness was due to the legacy of slavery: 'Owing to historical causes the white population regards performance of rough labour under the supervision of a white man as the proper sphere of the native.'[62] He later added that ' . . . a great deal of harm has been done to white people in South Africa by the false idea that there is a certain class of work which is beneath his dignity for the white man to do'.[63] Dr. Gilchrist reported that 'a good many of those people are what are called the hopeless class – men who cannot and never will be able to obtain regular employment and keep it'.[64]

The problem was made all the more urgent because it was felt the 'natives' were quickly beginning to better themselves. 'A native commissioner was asked – "Are you in a position to say whether the desire for education is keener amongst the natives or the poor whites?" and replied, "Amongst the natives, from my experience."'[65] Surprisingly, considering what came later, the commission did not recommend instituting a colour bar preventing blacks from doing skilled work and securing higher wages than unskilled whites. According to the commission, this would only result in more unemployment among blacks and many whites being paid 'higher wages than they are worth'.[66] Yet something had to be done. 'There is no need for us to explain how important it is to the future of the white race that as many of the rising generation of townsfolk as possible should become skilled workmen,'[67] said the commission. It decided upon labour colonies for the 'undeserving whites', the vagrants and loafers. 'We think that the only way of dealing satisfactorily with this class is to make any form of culpable idleness an offence punishable with hard labour.'[68] The commission recommended a sentence of at least six months for infractions, such as sleeping on a park bench.

Notice here something that will become all the more important later on – the desire to remove poor whites from respectable society, from the eyes of the 'natives' and the decent classes. The idea was still rough and unpolished, and the commissioners struggled with the implications. If poor whites were kept on reserves, away from civilisation and in closer contact with native reserves 'they will surely sink to making a living by illicit liquor selling or by organising sheep or cattle stealing, by forcing natives to supply their wants or by other illegal means – they must be falling rather than rising in the scale of civilisation, and their children cannot fail to grow up with lower standards than those possessed by children brought up amongst other white children'.[69]

No, that would not do. 'The object of the government should be to concentrate the forces of civilisation so that they can support one another, and not allow them to be dissipated and overwhelmed in the mass of heathendom.'[70] To combat their becoming 'white *kaffirs*', the TIC recommended sending the deserving poor to farm colonies (an idea that would be refined over the decades). The commissioners expressed their admiration for the Kakamas settlement, a farm colony in the west of the country, which was founded by the Dutch Reformed Church in 1898. 'According to this system indigents are grouped together on the land under close supervision, and are taught how to farm and encouraged to acquire habits of industry. The colony is voluntary, and the inmates are allowed to remain only so long as they work and comply with regulations.'[71] As a last resort, if the farm colonies would not work, then the deserving poor should be given work on railways and relief works. It had worked in the past and, again, had the advantage of keeping the poor out of the respectable gaze.

Although the poor whites were initially viewed in a moralistic way, the commissions experimented with various racial theories to explain the sudden appearance of so many impoverished whites. A tempting possibility, especially for the transplanted colonials, was that poverty was caused by the environment in which they found themselves. The TIC heard testimony that the hot, dry climate of South Africa 'enables people to live upon the land almost without working at all' and that 'tends to encourage the growth of the class of poor whites'.[72]

This environmental view was the result of various academic theories that developed at the start of the twentieth century, which attempted to explain that the superiority of the European races was due to the climate they lived in. In *The Passing of the Great Race*, Madison Grant,[73] chairman of the New York Zoological Society, argued, for instance, that in their home climes the Nordic race 'flourish, do their work and raise their families'. If they moved to sunnier lands, however, 'they grow listless and cease to breed'. For Grant, this could be used to explain white poverty. 'In the lower classes in the Southern States of America the increasing proportion of "poor whites" and "crackers" are symptoms of lack of climactic adjustment. The whites in Georgia, in the Bahamas and, above all, in Barbados are excellent examples of the deleterious effects of residence outside the natural habitat of the Nordic race.'[74]

That also held true for South Africa. In his influential book *Civilization and Climate*, Ellsworth Huntington[75] argued that 'in South Africa the White men settled first in the regions most favourable from a climactic point of view and then pushed northward into worse conditions. Even the best parts of South Africa cannot approach England and Holland in the excellence of their climate. Hence the white settlers are everywhere at a disadvantage.' His vague reasoning for this was that 'when the white man migrates to climates less stimulating than those of his original home, he appears to lose in both physical and mental energy . . . it is only in adverse climates that we find the type of "poor white trash" developing in appreciable numbers.'

Environmental causes for white poverty persisted well into the twentieth century. In 1929, WB Osborn[76] published his theory that the very sunlight in South Africa was harmful to whites. Osborn argued that the sunlight in Africa was richer in ultraviolet rays and between seven and ten times more intense in Johannesburg than in London. His theory was elaborated upon to prove that the intense sunlight in South Africa was a significant factor in the 'physical and mental deterioration of the European indigents in South Africa'. The belief that African sunlight was harmful was not new by the time Osborn published his research and not unique to South Africa. It had been accepted as fact by colonials for decades. Dane Kennedy, for instance, tells the story of a colonial officer visiting an ailing doctor in the highlands of Kenya: '[The doctor] was in bed with a spine pad down the back of his pyjamas, a double terai hat on his head with another spine pad down the back of it – because the room, with a corrugated iron roof and wooden ceiling, was not "sunproof".'[77] According to Kennedy, 'other environmental factors, including high altitude, variable temperature, and the climactic conditions prevalent during certain months of the year, were suspected of contributing to European ill-health in the colonies ... The common theme joining these various concerns was a clear one: the physical environment of the tropics harboured mysterious and deadly danger for the white race.'

Another, and ultimately even more damaging, theory regarding white poverty that blazed briefly at the start of the twentieth century and gradually, mercifully, died out was eugenics: a theory that held that blacks were biologically proven to be inferior to whites. Although eugenics was never widely adopted in South Africa, it was influential at various stages during debates about poor whites. In the 1860s Francis Galton, a cousin of Charles Darwin, began investigating whether natural ability could be biologically inherited. In 1883 'eugenics' was coined by Galton to denote a science dedicated to improving racial 'stocks'. Eugenists proposed a 'scientifically derived' racial hierarchy of genetic fitness, with European whites at the top and blacks at the bottom. Using the ideas of evolution and incorporating the language of biology, eugenists believed that the high birth rate among the lower classes threatened the survival of the ruling classes. The reason for the poverty of poor whites was that they were degenerate. They were on a lower level of evolution than the middle and ruling classes, as proven by their perceived mental deficiencies and intellectual 'backwardness'. The constant increase in the number of poor whites threatened to lower the standard of the white race as a whole, dragging the race backwards on the evolutionary scale, towards the blacks and the monkeys. This was particularly frightening in South Africa where blacks were thought to already practice a 'primitive' form of eugenics by not allowing mentally or physically handicapped children to live, and keeping their stock strong as a result. Gloomy notions of racial decline, race suicide and the inevitable 'degeneration' of healthy white blood were constant themes in eugenic literature.

The historian Saul Dubow traces the appearance of the 'vocabulary of Social Darwinism' to South Africa in the 1870s, but argues that the ideas of eugenics only spread in the early twentieth century, with the appearance of several semi-amateur scientific associations, such as the Fortnightly Club, in 1907, and the South African Association for the Advancement of Science, in 1903. These associations were staffed by 'experts', such as members of Milner's Kindergarten, and eugenics was one of many theories sought to provide scientific justification for policies of racial segregation.[78] The popularity of eugenic ideas and eugenic language gradually intensified over the years, peaking in the early 1930s. By the time of the Great Depression and the resultant tide of poor whites migrating to the cities, concerns over the deadly blood of the poor whites led to calls on the state to limit the fertility of the degenerate members of the white race – and not blacks, as a superficial reading of South African history would imply. 'Already anxious about whites' numerical inferiority nationally and internationally, eugenists were convinced their race could ill afford erosion from within, and so they set out to curb the fertility of poor whites.'[79] This led to the establishment of a number of organisations concerned with limiting the fertility of the poor. Of these, the most eugenist in orientation was the Race Welfare Society, established in Johannesburg in 1930, where it provided contraceptives to poor white people.

Yet the eugenist calls to curb the spread of unfit whites were unsuccessful. Eugenics itself also eventually fell out of favour, largely due to its use by Nazi Germany. In South Africa, such ideas were difficult to reconcile with Afrikaner nationalism, as the majority of the poor whites were Afrikaners. Dubow notes that the prerogative to maintain white prestige meant that any association between white poverty and Afrikaner incapacity would be potentially highly problematic for future relations between Afrikaner and British whites.[80]

As the new century loomed over the mine shafts of Johannesburg and the open country beyond, the problem of the poor whites intensified and became a greater preoccupation of the state, especially as the white poor began drifting and settling in the cities. The various theories developed to understand white poverty could not disguise the lingering unease felt by the colonials as they gazed at the blacks labouring in the mines, factories and shops. To the colonials the simple truth was that every white who slipped into the muddy racial categorisation of poor white was a loss to the middle-class vanguard of colonial expansion. In 1894 Merriman, then Minister of Agriculture for the Cape Colony, made it clear: ' . . . the European race in this country [is] the garrison. They held the country in the interests of civilization, and in the interests of good government and general enlightenment to South Africa.' 'The question of the poor whites,' he said, 'was the most important ever brought before Parliament . . . it was impossible that these people could be left alone . . . The white population was in a minority in the country, and if their brethren were to sink into the slough as they saw them doing, it would be impossible for the rest to maintain their position of dominance.'[81]

In the end, the Transvaal Indigency Commission concluded that 'indigency is a problem for South Africa and not for the Transvaal alone. With its solution is bound up, not merely the relief of distress, but the future of the white race itself. If the poor white, instead of disappearing, continues to increase and multiply, it will be because the white race fails to hold its own in the ranks of labour in competition with the native.'[82]

The poor city

They came from the wide country to the new place stretching into the sky, bringing their few belongings and their wives with tired eyes. Perhaps they came creaking into the city on wagons, perhaps they drifted slowly from where they had been before, silently, and without much fuss, detaching themselves from the farms to haunt the long road to Johannesburg.

The cities accepted them with little grace, funnelling them into small areas full already with those who had come before, where little tin shacks glared at each other from across the dirty street.

The churches and government officials told each other stories of the people in those places, trying to goad themselves into action. They organised talks around tables, in halls, rooms, backrooms, parliament, streets, tents and living rooms. They organised conferences where they thundered at each other:

'A Boer and his family migrated to the city in search of

work,' the church official said. 'Every day he left the house in search of work, and came back every evening. And in the home Hunger stared at him like an unearthly being with hollow eyes, a monster which he feared more and more. And finally they had to surrender to the monster. His daughter took temporary work at the coolie across the street.'

In that year of 1941, the others who had gathered at the church conference nodded their heads, their eyes blinking in outrage. 'And so there are hundreds of them,' the church official said. 'Some walked back to their farms . . . but many did not have the courage to walk back . . . Here and there the woman did washing work for the coolie, because the man could not find work that day. And here and there the woman married the coolie, because he was the only person who was ever good to her. And somewhere else a woman saw the results of such unholy mixing in her own daughters who were yellow and black, and she could not be hard on them, because she had to live from them.

'And sometimes she stopped caring, because no one knew her there.'[83]

The problem of the 'poor whites', it was felt at the time, would not have been so frightening were it not for the situation in the cities.

Squatting like frogs in the corners of South Africa, the cities had an irresistible pull for the poor, who trekked there in droves to look for work.

Those in the government and the salons looked on, horrified, as their public squares and spaces, their inner cities, became home to the most disreputable classes. It was an invasion, in a sense. A pushing and probing of the established boundaries between the haves and the have-nots. Simply put, cities profoundly disturbed the nineteenth-century colonial world and proved one of the most persistent concerns of colonial authorities.

The cities were places of achievement and progress, of factories, avenues, high streets, dinner parties, tailors, doctors, order and invention. Yet cities were also dangerous. They were sites of crime, overcrowding, disease and decadence. More often than not, they were places of chaos, not order. To the Victorians, 'cities . . . were said to provide countless "places of darkness and concealment" for the fermentation of moral disease'.[84] Far away from London and Manchester, in the colonial margins, where the natural order of things was already strange, cities could be especially frightening.

It was the shadowy places within cities, the disorderly spaces of the slums and back alleys, that upset the middle classes most, concerned as they were with their lack of control over such areas. The most disturbing aspect of the slums was that they were, and are, mysterious. The slums of early Johannesburg and the townships of the present city are outside the public and official gaze. For the middle classes, they were places gazed at from a distance, accompanied by a shaking of the head and a shrug of the shoulders. To the Victorians, the slums and rookeries of London were the domain of chimney sweeps and orphanages, of vice and prostitution, of creeping smog and murder. In London there was 'a dark continent within easy walking distance of the General Post Office . . . as interesting as any of those newly explored lands which engaged the attention of the Royal Geographical Society'. Slums were 'anarchic, distant outposts of empire peopled by violent and primitive races'.[85] How much more anxiety must slums have created in the outposts of the empire, laden as they were already with racial fears and tensions? In South Africa, as the poor continued their long march to the cities, the fear of urban disorder framed the poor white problem.

How was the colonial government to deal with such amorphous neighbourhoods, which, by their very definition, were impervious to the gaze of outsiders? Part of the answer is that in order to deal with the slums, these sites first had to be defined and articulated. Cities are immensely complex human constructs, resistant to easy understanding, and managing a city necessitates simplifying the reality into residential zones and business zones, highways and parks. The state needs to 'arrange the population in ways that simplify the classic state functions of taxation, conscription, and prevention of rebellion'.[86] The colonial government first had to map the city into sites of work, recreation and habitation to bring order to colonial urban space.

Although it seems an easy thing to say that authorities have to define the spaces of a city in much the same ways that the poor whites were 'defined', scholars such as Patrick Joyce[87] and Mary Poovey[88] have devoted entire books to understanding this process. This practice is part of what the philosopher Michel Foucault termed 'governmentality',[89] and it is related to how colonial authorities tried to deal with the poor by paying close attention to where they lived. As sites of possible social unrest that destabilised the colonial imagination, the location of the urban poor, including problematic groups, such as criminals and prostitutes, were typically mapped out. This was inevitably a crude process. Colonial governments did not have the will to examine each and every house or tin-roofed shack in a neighbourhood before characterising it as a slum or destitute area. But defining an area as a 'slum' was a necessary step in order to facilitate their 'cleansing' through the relocation of inhabitants and the destruction of buildings deemed unfit for habitation.

Locating the poor white

The Afrikaners first came to Johannesburg in droves during the gold rush of 1886. Afrikaner farmers had long been scattered through the dry, wide country but never in any significant numbers. As in cities like San Francisco, the prospect of gold prompted a wave of migration that was virtually uncontrollable, and impossible for urban authorities to properly accommodate. These newcomers settled in ramshackle mining camps, living in or alongside their ox wagons, later constructing more permanent settlements of reed and clay, or living in prefabricated wooden and iron shacks. The sight and nature of these camps for many symbolised the breakdown of authority. Those used to more orderly cities would look out over the camps, at the hundreds of small tents, at the unwashed children, and shake their heads. The sounds of livestock and the clanging of tools would fill the air. The smell of cooking fires and sewage. It was difficult to imagine the government as being in control.

The city continued to grow at an astonishing pace as migrants from all over the world came seeking their fortune. A distinct city centre soon sprang up and by the 1890s high property prices meant that the mostly poor Afrikaners preferred land on the edges of the urban centre in areas such as Fordsburg, Jeppestown and Braamfontein. Home ownership among Afrikaners was rare – the overwhelming majority were only able to afford to rent.

In those days, before the war, the Afrikaner government of the Zuid-Afrikaansche Republiek (ZAR) still controlled the gold. They were sympathetic to the plight of the poor white migrants and miners among them, and supported the attempts of the poor to find a place for themselves in South Africa's cities. In fact, the ZAR's Volksraad sessions of 1897 revolved around an old soldier who had fallen into poverty and whose situation was compounded by having only one leg as a result of a war wound. The Volksraad's initially simple decision to grant him some land or money developed into a month-long debate on how best to deal with impoverished Afrikaners who had not recovered from the rinderpest plague. A Mr De Clereq said that, although he was very sympathetic to the soldier, the principle of the matter meant that in giving the man some land meant that they would soon be inundated with similar requests from other poor. A Mr Stoop angrily rebutted: 'Even should such a principle exist, when we can help our citizens, especially those ruined by the rinderpest, then I say let them come to us and we will help them.'[90] The Volksraad eventually decided in favour of buying the soldier a wooden leg.

New migrants who were unable to afford housing often squatted on government land until they were assigned a stand on which to live, in the same way that unofficial 'squatter camps' develop in modern South Africa, prompting the disgust of passing motorists. The Deputy Commissioner of Police for Pretoria told the Transvaal Indigency Commission (TIC) that 'these people were in the habit of wandering about from town to town, pitching their tents anywhere, and so force the government to grant them this land to settle on'.[91] It was impossible to drive the poor whites away, said the commission, 'because they had nowhere else to go to, and they were therefore given licences to live on the stands on certain conditions'.[92] The Pretoria magistrate, with an imagined sigh of frustration, said: 'I have come to the conclusion that the time has arrived to see that the poor wandering around our towns with their families have appointed for them a fixed place of abode. It is regrettable to see how these people without means take up their abode everywhere on government ground and put up tents everywhere in order to have a free place of residence.'[93]

This was the case in the area known as Brickfields,[94] close to the city centre of Johannesburg, where government licences for brick-making sites were cheaply had. These licences had the advantage of allowing for the rental of land. The appetite for housing in Johannesburg meant that the area soon turned into an active industrial district, with a large concentration of poor white families. Workers soon built homes on their brick-making land and, as news of the cheap land became more widely known, poor Afrikaners flocked to the area, ostensibly to work in the brick-making industry.

In and around the brick-making pits, the impoverished Afrikaners built their shacks and set up their tents, renting a small space to live when they could not obtain a licence. Since Brickfields was not designated as a residential area, however, there were no streets or areas for sanitation and the area soon began displaying slum characteristics. This was much to the annoyance of the government, which was flooded with requests to turn Brickfields into a residential zone.

In 1893 the government was forced to give way, and an area to the west of Brickfields was set aside for the settlement of the urban poor. The new district was called Vrededorp and incorporated land from the neighbouring Malaysian settlement. Yet the poor whites continued to come, filling Vrededorp and spilling over into the poor black and Indian districts. In the same year the neighbouring area of Jagersdorp (later Burgersdorp) was created to cater for the housing demand. These three areas, along with Fordsburg and the Indian township, formed the core of Johannesburg's Afrikaner white squatter camps before the turn of the century, and some retained their poor characteristics for many years after. In Johannesburg, this urban geography of slum areas and neighbourhoods represented the poor white problem in the clearest of terms.

It is difficult to find detailed information on where precisely the Afrikaners originally settled in Johannesburg, but, as Stals notes,[95] voters' rolls can shed some light, although they naturally take into account only those Afrikaners registered as voters. One of the most comprehensive sources is the Johannesburg Municipal Voters' Roll of 1922,[96] which shows that three decades after they had first come to the city, the majority of Afrikaners (69.5 per cent) were found in the south and west of Johannesburg. Here were the poorer white suburbs, with their Afrikaans names and disreputable people: Braamfontein, Fordsburg, Burgersdorp and Turffontein. Most of the Afrikaners in the west of the city were concentrated in one suburb: Vrededorp, which they had not left. A ridge of scrubby hills separated this area from the richer white suburbs spreading northwest from the centre, slowing Afrikaner expansion. Across the hills were found the English names: Auckland Park, Westdene and Melville.

Thirty years since their arrival, only 4.4 per cent of Afrikaners were still found in the inner city, where the planned suburb of Newtown had replaced the old Afrikaner area of Brickfields, and where high rents made accommodation for poor whites impossible. Afrikaners were also rarely found in the north-east of Johannesburg, which encompassed richer suburbs, such as Berea, Yeoville, Houghton Estate and Norwood – areas with a more Jewish or English character.

As the motorcar became an increasingly common sight in Johannesburg, and the city dwellers began their modern march to the outlying suburbs, the poor Afrikaners stayed behind, stranded by the lack of public transport between the far neighbourhoods and the mines or city centre. From the 1920s, however, many Afrikaners were able to commute into Johannesburg by train from satellite towns on the East and West Rand, such as Krugersdorp and Benoni.

Another decade passed and the poor were still no closer to finding better accommodation. When slums were demolished in one area, the shacks rose in another. A 1933 report of the Public Health Committee for Johannesburg noted that slum conditions for whites were prevalent 'in certain of the poor districts such as Fordsburg, portions of Jeppe and Doornfontein and Newlands'.[97] The first three suburbs were on the fringes of the city centre, where the Afrikaner poor had established themselves more than 40 years earlier. Newlands was in the north-west part of Johannesburg, where Afrikaners had always had a majority. The housing shortage and general growth of the city had finally pushed some of the poor past the Brixton ridge, which separated Vrededorp from the outlying suburbs. In the process new poor and working-class districts were established, such as Brixton, Sophiatown and Albertskroon. But by the 1930s the Afrikaners were firmly established in Johannesburg, and not all were poor. The areas north of the ridge, such as Melville and Linden, were the neighbourhoods of wealthier Afrikaners – the middle classes and opinion-formers. *The Star* newspaper reported in 1959, for instance, that 'just as the ultimate goal of every poor Jew living in Doornfontein is Houghton so, for some unknown reason, Afrikaners aspire to live in Linden ultimately'.[98]

Beyond the richer areas, where the city lost its momentum and came to a slow juddering halt in the countryside, the poor were again to be found. Too far from the city to be easily employed in the mines or in the factories, and too far from the farms they had left, the poor haunted the urban fringes. This marginal, semi-urban existence was not just an economic necessity: it was also approved of by many commentators. The Afrikaners were encouraged to settle here, away from the alienating influence of the city where it was thought their essentially rural values would remain uncorrupted. As one commission noted, 'In many cases the poorer Africanders from the country settle on the outskirts of towns, where land is cheaper, and possibly because the building regulations are less stringent . . . They have a freer and healthier life there; often they can cultivate gardens and keep a few animals.'[99]

As part of their efforts to control the influx of poor into the towns, the ruling classes encouraged the poor to return to the land, reasoning that the Afrikaners among them would have a better opportunity on the farms, as that is where their skills lay. 'People see the misery and poverty in which [the poor] live in the towns, and think that if only they could be put back on the land with its advantages of health and cheap living, the problem could be solved,' said the TIC.[100]

Various 'Burger Land settlements' had been created since the turn of the century in places such as Heidelberg, Standerton, Middelburg and Potchefstroom. In 1913, a commission suggested 'the establishment of labour and agricultural colonies, and relief works'[101], in much the same way that the TIC had suggested. In its report, the Unemployment Commission of 1921 'restated the seriousness of the poor white problem and proposed their resettlement on the land'.[102] The back-to-the-land approach was encouraged through the various resettlement schemes until the 1930s, when it became apparent that sending the Afrikaners to the farms accomplished nothing, as the poor whites had little to return to and, in the rare cases that they did return voluntarily, existed as 'indigent squatters on their own land'.[103]

During a time of frantic urbanisation, it was nearly impossible to stop the poor from seeking a better life in the cities. By the time of the Carnegie Commission in 1932, Afrikaner nationalists had realised that persuading the newly urbanised poor to return to the countryside would not solve the problem. JFW Grosskopf, one of the commission authors, noted that 'the rural exodus, especially, I can no longer hold to be mainly harmful; and to-day I should have the greatest hesitation in advocating "back to the land" as a promising expedient'.[104] In the same year the Unemployment Investigation Committee reported that 'except in a very few cases and under special circumstances, re-settlement of indigents on the land cannot be successful. The best hope for the great majority of the poor whites is that they should become unskilled labourers.'[105]

Yet the image of the city as a place of corruption and alienation for the Afrikaners remained strong, and this anxious discourse helped define who the poor whites were and prescribed where they would be allowed to live in the colonial city. Advocating a peri-urban existence kept the poor whites in the cities, but away from the slums and the disorder that threatened to corrupt, engulf and nullify them.

White slums and promiscuous spaces

To the colonials, the most terrifying aspect of the slums was the issue of race. The 'white slums' were a major driver of social and political commentary in South Africa. Yet concerns over white slums were often, and with little apparent contradiction, expressed along with fears about the white poor being forced to live cheek by jowl with other races, who were not merely also poor, but had a host of vices and corruptions as well.

Virtually from its inception and well into the middle decades of the twentieth century, Johannesburg proved incapable of dealing with the vast amount of people moving to the city. This led to an acute housing shortage, which contributed to the rapid creation of slum conditions and unsatisfactory working-class accommodation. In the first decade of the twentieth century, Johannesburg's slums 'were increasingly viewed as sites where misery, demoralisation and crime merged with miscegenation, thus embodying the worst fears of the colonial middle class'.[106] In 1910 Australian journalist Ambrose Pratt visited the city's slums, where he found 'a network of streets and lanes that cries shame upon the Rand. Dirty, mean little houses, broken almost impassable roadways, squalor extending for miles where poor whites, black and coloured people live in close proximity.'[107] On the streets were heard 'the clashing polyglot of a score of diverse foreign tongues' and 'white children, scattered through the murk playing in the gutters, picking up the words and vices of coloured scum'.[108]

As there was so little accommodation, housing prices skyrocketed, leading to drastically inadequate living conditions. At the turn of the century, the TIC was told that in the poor suburb of Fordsburg, where most of the houses were built from clay bricks or corrugated iron,[109] a three-bedroom house with a kitchen could be rented for £9 per month – nearly half the average wage of a skilled worker, and far beyond the means of the impoverished, unskilled and unemployed white. This meant that many families were forced to sublet and share a small house in order to afford the rent and, consequently, the slums nearly burst from the mass of humanity packed into them. A later commission noted that 'one of the evils of subletting of houses is that you have a family in every room and one room has to serve as a kitchen for the whole household, which is an impossible state of affairs and one which is very degrading and which makes for slum conditions'.[110]

As Johannesburg was the new capital of the mining world, and a budding New York, living costs increased along with housing costs. For example, the TIC noted that the cost of living was nearly twice as high in Johannesburg as in England. The wages paid to a skilled worker, however, were nearly three times greater than in Britain. A weekly skilled wage in Johannesburg was about £3, and in England about £1.

Comparison of weekly living costs and wages of a skilled labourer in Johannesburg and England, 1906–1908[111]

	Johannesburg	England
Food	21s 7d	14s 4.5d
Rent	10s to 20s	3s 6d
Sundries	6s 5d	3s 5.25d
Wages per week	£3	£1 to £1 5s

Note: Before the decimalisation of the UK's currency in the 1970s, 12 pennies (d) made a shilling and 20 shillings (s) made a pound.

Six years later, the Economic Commission of 1914 noted that rent made up half of a working-class family's expenditure, as rents were still more expensive than in England. According to the commission, 'the predominant cost of working-class housing in England is about 5s. 6d. per room per month including the kitchen which is there used as a living room. The cost in Johannesburg, including the cost of the same local services, and including the kitchen, which is seldom so suitable for a living room as in England, is about 24s. per month.'[112]

The white slums were a constant feature of Johannesburg throughout the twentieth century. In the century that the poor whites had been found, despised, pitied and saved, the places they lived in varied only in how hidden they were from sight. At the start of the century, a Mrs Faure of the Pretoria Benevolent Society told the TIC that 'the people live in the most miserable condition and are sinking in the social scale. There are no sanitary arrangements. They are most miserable, living huddled together in little tin shanties – married couples, young children and grown-up young people, all living together, sometimes in one little room or tent.'[113]

In the 1920s, some of the slumyards in Doornfontein were said to house over 300 people each, sometimes with as many as nine people sharing a room.[114] The image of the slums as unhealthy and damaging to whites grew stronger. A 1920 committee report noted that 'there is no question that the health of the people suffers, and suffers seriously, from such a state of affairs – physical and moral deterioration are the result, bringing with them disease and the evils of poverty, drink, immorality and crime'.[115]

Another decade passed, and in 1933 the City Council of Johannesburg further reported with dismay that 1 121 white families lived in 'unhygienic and overcrowded slum conditions'.[116] In a survey of the housing conditions of the poor in South African cities, the Carnegie Commission found that only 35 per cent of the houses were satisfactory (meaning large enough and clean). Of the rest, 23 per cent were too small, and 42 per cent were 'unfit for habitation'. In the same decade the editor of *Die Kerkbode*, the official circular of the Dutch Reformed Church, described the situation in anguished terms:

> A room which is shared by the mother and father, and even the children, is usually rented for between £3, 10s. and £4, 10s. per month. This room serves as bedroom, dining room and kitchen. The food for the family is cooked on a little Primus-stove. The laundry is done here, and often a sick man or child nursed. Can we as a *volk* allow our own flesh and blood to migrate to such hovels from the countryside?[117]

By the 1950s, *The Star* reported nearly 12 000 homeless whites living in Johannesburg, where the need for cheap housing resulted in property owners building shacks in their backyards, or converting rotting buildings and warehouses into rotting homes for the poor. The white slums had been with Johannesburg from the start, from the colonial and nationalist eras, and right through apartheid and democracy.

The first serious slum conditions were found where the poor Afrikaners had drifted into Johannesburg from the countryside: the industrial area of Brickfields. People called the area Poverty Point, and the families who lived there 'people to whom life has been a mistake'.[118] As Brickfields was not designed to be a residential area, the government provided no refuse services there. This had predictable consequences. The inhabitants, who were of various skin colours, dumped their refuse in the large holes that resulted from the brick-making. Among tin shacks and tents, children, stray dogs and white families were large, stinking holes spreading disease among the poor. By the late 1890s, there was no more work for the small brick-maker. Capitalism and consolidation meant that the industry was dominated by large firms, and the white poor had to look elsewhere for work. Some of those who lived in Brickfields moved to the newly established neighbourhoods set aside for them – Vrededorp and Burgersdorp – and the grinding poverty of the neighbourhood continued. In 1908, Johannesburg's newspapers were reporting that some of Vrededorp's Afrikaners were living on 'mealie-pap and water, the mealie meal often begged from kaffirs'.[119]

Adjoining Brickfields, towards the city centre, were wealthier areas whose inhabitants complained about the effect the nearby slums were having on the area, the unhealthy conditions and the racial mixing. Colonial soldiers and businessmen glared at the slums from high windows in rented rooms. 'Although this was appropriate accommodation at the right price, the unhealthy conditions and the multiracial component of the area made it thoroughly undesirable for the British workers who had to live there "and live in a manner that is repugnant to those who have been used to associate with their equals".'[120] In 1902 the government came up with the legislation it needed to act. The refuse holes and slum conditions led the government to declare Brickfields and parts of the surrounding neighbourhood an insanitary area, despite the refusal of some of the families to move from the slum. Two years later, disease broke out in the old so-called Indian Location and the government acted quickly. The city fire brigade was called and Brickfields was burnt to the ground. Watching from their high windows, the onlookers saw abandoned shacks, stores, signs, refuse holes and brick-making equipment disappear before them, the blaze throwing tall shadows on the surrounding buildings. Later, when the fire was extinguished and the wreckage cleared, the working-class suburb of Newtown[121] was built on the ashes.

The poor of the slums were a mix of whites, blacks, Indians and Asians, along with members of the white working class who 'lived at a very low standard'.[122] This multiracial composition characteristically seemed to upset the colonials as much as the cramped, unsanitary conditions: 'Narrow passages, or so called yards, exist into which open the doors of single rooms which are often let at 20 s. a month or more; and in these dwell whites, Chinese, Indians, natives and others on terms of equality, whilst latrines are provided for the common use of all.'[123]

Various nationalities operated businesses in the poor areas. In 1906 there were 44 Asian traders in Vrededorp. These stores were seen as a threat to legitimate white businesses. A witness before the Vrededorp Stands Commission of 1906 railed against how 'at every corner there is a Chinaman or an Indian, which prevents any white trader from trading here'.[124] The colonials and the nationalists were both particularly suspicious of Chinese- or Indian-operated laundries, which often employed poor Afrikaner women, bringing them into close contact with non-whites. The location of Fordsburg, Vrededorp and Burgersdorp meant that such contact was virtually inevitable. In 1902, for example, only a narrow road separated Burgersdorp from the Indian Location. This led to the settlement of whites and blacks in the Indian area, while Indians lived among whites in Burgersdorp. The proximity of neighbouring Fordsburg to the mines created a flourishing trade for 'kaffir-eatinghouses',[125] a form of bar, store and restaurant in one, which were frequented by black mineworkers, although whites were certainly present and the eating houses were often owned and run by recent Jewish immigrants. In fact, this mixing of races would occur not only in the slum in general, but also within a single building – a moral micro-geography that indicated the tensions caused by the lack of segregation in dwellings and shops. As one observer noted, 'in the back [room or yard] you have Hottentots and in the front the lowest class of whites who are living on liquor selling and prostitution'.[126]

The multiracial character of the area did not disappear as the years marched by. In 1930, *Die Kerkbode* complained that the area was still a slum for poor whites, noting that Vrededorp 'was meant to provide housing for people who streamed in from the countryside. Consequently the Afrikaners are all clustered together in a few streets, denser than in any other part of the city.' But the church publication seemed even more horrified that the racially mixed composition of Vrededorp – the Indians living among the blacks living among the whites – had not changed even as Afrikaner nationalism had risen: 'Most tragic of all is that one half of the town is given over to coloureds and Asians, and that the homes in that part will have to be broken down to the ground before they are fit for white habitation.'[127]

Johannesburg was certainly not alone in dealing with the existence of slums, or in the viciously racist way it viewed slum residents. In Cape Town, the dominant class 'discovered' poverty when the smallpox outbreak of 1882 forced them to examine the living conditions of the poor. The first suspected case of smallpox was in a house in the racially mixed, working-class area of District Six. The house was inhabited by 17 men, women and children. The city council investigated the area and reported that 'the streets were not made up, they had no guttering, there were pools of black filth "in every direction" and no dirt carts (to collect stercus) came that way. In respect of the actual house of the suspected victim, there was no lavatory, inside or out, and the resulting filth was piled up in the street against the walls of the house.'[128]

Newspaper investigations soon followed, reporting on the 'burrows' and 'warrens' of the poor. Labourers working at the docks lived 'here ten in a room, here a dozen, here perhaps fifteen'.[129]

The racially mixed composition of the slums and working-class areas meant the poor whites in Cape Town were also 'sinking, sinking, sinking into the social conditions of the snuff-and-butter coloured population'. These were people such as respectable white artisans, who were 'compelled' to live in the slums and were 'degenerating by reason of their surroundings'.[130] In 1895, a Grahamstown journalist told the *Cape Argus* that 'a fusion of races is going on here from which every other community in South Africa would shrink'. In the mission schools for the poor, 'the child of pure English blood sits side by side with the Kaffir as black as your hand, or the Malay of yellow-brown complexion and almond eyes'.[131]

The white slum was a standing and evident affront to the colonial racial order. The promiscuous mixing of the poor was seen as a barrier to white improvement and enterprise, and as contaminating and corrupting the inherent virtues of the white population. But the slum did not only corrupt, it was also dangerous for the continued survival of white civilisation in Africa and a threat to white authority in general. In 1920 the report of the Housing Committee made crystal clear the danger of slum conditions to white prestige:

> The poor whites as we have seen are living in the most degrading and undesirable conditions in many of the towns, and having regards to the

> preponderance of the black population and the importance, as all believe, of maintaining the prestige of the white race, this class of people cannot be permitted to remain where they are, but should be compelled to reinstate themselves in what must be their proper standing in the social scale.[132]

Understanding the urban poor

From the beginning, the commissions were concerned about the effect slums would have. Said the TIC:

> It is also of the greatest importance that the further creation of the squalid, unhealthy and the demoralising poor white settlements should be prevented. It is difficult, if not impossible, to hinder poor whites from drifting into the towns. But the tensions of the areas in which unsanitary or unhealthy conditions are likely to arise can be avoided by proper supervision of the poorer quarters. Adequate control in the early stages may render unnecessary the expropriation and clearing of whole sections of a town in order to protect the population from disease and to prevent the perpetuation of indigency and crime.[133]

By the time the government next investigated poverty, the efforts of various private and public institutions had created a resident pool of expert witnesses for commissioners to call on. These included members of the Rand Aid Association, the Salvation Army, Afrikaner women's organisations, charities, educational institutions, the police and state officials. In 1912 the Commission of Enquiry into Assaults on Women was chaired by M de Villiers, a criminal judge in the Orange Free State, who was an advocate at the time of the hearings. The members of the commission included the Afrikaner General Christiaan R de Wet and three women representing Afrikaner Christian women's associations. The next investigation, that of the Select Committee on European Unemployment and Labour Conditions, illustrates how the government relied on this pool of experts to give it knowledge of the poor. Both investigations shared the same concerns, namely miscegenation and protecting the virtue of white women, and both used the same language of eugenics. This is hardly surprising – Lange points out that not only did the select committee and the commission of enquiry call upon the same witnesses, but at least one of the members of the commission also gave evidence before the select committee.[134]

The overall conception of white poverty had not significantly changed from that put forward by the TIC in 1908. By 1913, the language of Social Darwinism was clearly observed in the Commission of Enquiry into Assaults on Women. If we accept that commissions were 'repositories of colonial anxieties', as Ann Stoler argues, then the Commission of Enquiry into Assaults on Women is dripping with colonial fear of miscegenation and the possibility of national decline. This commission used eugenic language to paint activities such as liquor selling and prostitution as indications of hereditary degeneration, rather than common survival strategies. The following year, the Report of the Economic Commission was published. It was intensely concerned about the effect of labour competition on poor whites, who would not be employed at the same low wages as black unskilled labour. The poor white could not compete with the native in unskilled labour, it said.

> Broadly speaking, the economies of South Africa are dominated by the fact that the population consists of two races in industrial partnership with nothing in common in their traditions and standards of living. They form a distinct social strata and there is a gap between them very imperfectly filled by whites who have abandoned white standards of living (known as poor whites).[135]

The commission did not bother to hide its intent: 'Put in the coldest and most prosaic terms, it is purely a question of securing for white people wages enough to live upon in order that the efficiency of white labour may not be undermined, slums may not be created and a standard of existence beneath what is recognised commonly decent for the white population may not be fostered.'[136] The commission advocated drastic intervention by the government to uplift the poor whites. In hushed, fearful tones the commission said that

> . . . the importance of the question in South Africa arises from the fact that the European minority occupying, as it does, in relation to the non-European majority, the position of dominant race, cannot allow a considerable number of its members to sink into apathetic indigency, and to fall below the level of the non-European worker. If they do, and if they manifest an indifference founded on the comfortable doctrine of letting things find their economical level, sooner or later, not withstanding all our material and intellectual advantages, our race is bound to perish in South Africa.[137]

Nearly a decade later, the Second Interim Report of the Unemployment Commission was also concerned specifically with poor whites. Although it also used the language of eugenics, the commission was much more concerned about the possibility of social unrest originating among the ever-increasing poor. Against the background of the Bolshevik Revolution of 1917, severe labour unrest in Johannesburg and World War I, the commissioners urged the government not to allow 'the poor whites to become the dupe of the extremist' and ominously warned that 'with the world movement of revolt against similar conditions . . . these people of ours too will not continue under such conditions in silence indefinitely'.[138]

The government gradually began to see the poor in a different light. Another investigation, the Unemployment Commission of 1922, accepted and framed poverty primarily as an urban problem. The concern with native competition had not abated, however. The commission's Interim Report definitively quoted Sir Robert Kotze, chairman of the earlier Low Grade Mines Commission:

> We have the policy [in South Africa] of dual labour, and the reason why we have white unemployment is due to the fact that we have native labour. The whole thing is tied up with the vast problem of the native question before us. I look upon the question in its widest aspect, and it seems to me, as far as the white races here are concerned, if you look five hundred years ahead there can only be one end to it, and we shall not be white in that time any more.[139]

It is clear that the commissions were ways of experimenting with racial theories. The state called upon experts to define the poor in ways that they wanted to hear. The Unemployment Commission asked Dr JT Dunston, the Commissioner in the Union for Mental Disorders, to testify before them. Dunston framed poor whites in explicitly detailed eugenic terms, noting their inherited lack of reasoning power, so that the commission eventually concluded that 'white poverty and unemployment may be due to various causes which are not fundamental, the primary cause is the inherent capacity, as the result of feeble-mindedness, to compete on equal terms with normal individuals'.[140]

These commissions are also notable for the musings of Professor Robert A Lehfeldt, a multidisciplinary academic attached to the University of South Africa. Also a member of the Royal Society and the South African correspondent for the Royal Economic Society, Lehfeldt regarded the poor white problem as 'perhaps the most serious that confronts the Union', but, crucially, argued that any attempt to solve the poor white problem inevitably raised questions as to the general policy of the country.[141] Lehfeldt's concerns are remarkable, in that they tie the 'poor white problem' directly to the racial policies of South Africa, including segregation and the later desire for a 'white South Africa'. Lehfeldt said:

> No policy that does not take into account the natives, who constitute three-quarters of the population, is even intelligible. In trying to put the large destitute class of whites on their feet and prevent the children now growing up from falling into the same conditions as their parents are in, do we expect them to live with the aid of native servants? Do we expect to segregate the white and coloured people, so that the poorer classes will have the same chance as in Canada or Australia? Do we expect the poor white to live side by side with the natives, and compete with them in the labour market? And how can we hope to carry out a settlement scheme on a large enough scale to deal with the whole country successfully if we cannot make up our minds on these questions?[142]

Thus the measures to uplift the poor whites could not be discussed without taking into account their influence on black South Africans. Lehfeldt sketched out two visions for the future, the first being 'real segregation of the black and white races – not mere segregation of land ownership. This would mean the reservation of some parts of the Union for development as a white man's country',[143] while other parts would be in native hands (although under the administration and supervision of whites). The second option would be 'complete equality of opportunity, competition and ultimately race mixture'. Somewhat presciently, he noted that 'any intermediate stage is probably destined to break down, and lead after much conflict to one or other of these stable conditions'.[144] Lehfeldt did not advocate either position, but he framed the poor white question in terms the government could understand – the question of land segregation.

In the final report of the Unemployment Commission, Lehfeldt argued that 'it is also possible to take the view that our South African problems are inevitably bound up with those of the great Bantu masses of Central Africa, that the whites can never be more than a handful in the midst of a black country'. He accurately sketched out the route the government would take, saying it was possible:

> . . . to maintain as closely as possible the present system; taking steps to keep as many as possible of the white population engaged in superior and supervising work; helping them to obtain land, and to improve their education, and importing unskilled labour whenever necessary. In this way considerable material prosperity may be attained, and the poor white class can probably be reduced in extent, but the latter effect is uncertain and it seems hardly possible that a radical cure of the 'poor white' evil should be effected, while native discontent could hardly fail to grow.[145]

Lehfeldt was more accurate in his theories than he could ever have surmised. His only mistake was in underestimating how determined and vicious the nationalists would be, when he said of segregation 'if there was a very sincere and widespread enthusiasm for a "White South Africa", it is just possible that the opposition of immediate pecuniary interests might be overborne but there is no sign of such enthusiasm'.[146] Less than two decades later he would be proven very, very wrong.

Deviance and degeneration

Just as the physical presence of whites in the unhealthy, dilapidated and overcrowded slums disturbed the colonials, so too did the vices, perceived or otherwise, of the residents threaten whiteness and white prestige. The colonials viewed the slums as the haunts not just of the poor, but of criminals, beggars and prostitutes – the lowest class of whites, who brought the race into disrepute. In short, the dregs of whiteness found their way into the slums, where they sat, brooding and degenerate, dragging their race downwards. Yet at the same time, the desperate conditions in the slums not only attracted criminals, it also created them, making thieves and prostitutes of the ordinary residents of the slums, whose only crime had thus far been poverty. The slums could produce and reproduce criminality, promiscuity, racial transgression and poor whiteism. Because the slums attracted and created liminal types, these areas became linked in the minds of the respectable classes with certain types of people – what scholars call the geographical imagination of the slums. In other words, if someone of the middle classes thought of a poor white family in the slums, they thought of a poor white family who thieved, begged, drank and sold their bodies. Perhaps of a father who could never find work and abused his wife; of their dirty children shouting loudly in the streets, stealing sweets and wallets. By the 1920s, as eugenics was running its course, the association of the poor whites with the dangerous class had been made.

When asked, for instance, by the Transvaal Indigency Commission whether there was crime to be found among the poor whites in the slums, the Commissioner of Police for the Witwatersrand replied: 'Yes, a great deal of immorality and crime – illicit liquor dealing, etc. They fall quickly into crime. It is a consequence of the dreadful conditions under which they live . . . A large number of them are forced into criminal life.'[147] Another witness, Johannesburg's Acting Commissioner of Police, Lieutenant Colonel O'Brian, stated authoritatively: 'By far the greater number of criminals is drawn from the indigent classes. The children of indigent parents get accustomed to thieving in small ways and are recruited into the junior ranks of the criminal classes.'[148] Because whites formed part of the criminal classes, these classes challenged white prestige. As a later commission noted: 'From his contact with, or observation of the white criminal classes and other experiences, the native's estimate of the European virtue has suffered, and from these experiences he probably forms an exaggerated and distorted idea of the vices of profligacy of the white man and especially of the frailty of the white woman.'[149] The colonials were concerned that blacks viewing whites as criminals and prostitutes would undermine the illusion of superiority on which colonialism rested, and in extreme cases lead even to miscegenation.

One of the major criminal occupations of the poor whites living in Vrededorp and surrounds was the unlicensed selling of liquor. In 1907 the police prosecuted 3 464 people under the liquor law, of which only 718 were black. The ruling classes became increasingly concerned over the illegal selling of liquor in the 1910s, when it was thought that unlawfully selling alcohol to the black population encouraged the assault of white women by black men. The link between poverty and unlicensed liquor selling had already been noted by the TIC, but the connection between the slums and liquor trafficking was made explicit by the Commission of Enquiry into Assaults on Women, which was partly set up to investigate reports of black men attacking white women. One witness testified that 'all women in Ferreira Town are running about all day buying bottles of liquor. If they get sixpence a bottle and buy a dozen in a day they have made six shillings. You see a woman going about with a perambulator containing a baby, buying bottles and hiding them under the baby.'[150]

In 1913 the same commission also noted that the selling of alcohol by poor whites was 'one of the causes of the natives losing respect for the white race, which is one of the strongest factors calculated to restrain him from even entertaining the idea of the possibility of having any sexual relations with a white woman'.[151]

Yet this was exactly the business of the poor whites who became prostitutes. The most serious crime a white person could commit was a common occurrence. The business had been present in Johannesburg nearly since the start, reaching its height in the 1890s. In those years, Johannesburg was a city of vice – the centre of the city was dominated not only by mining houses and banks, but also by brothels and bars, an area called Frenchfontein because of the European prostitutes. The city's most expensive districts were increasingly not in the hands of whites, but transformed into a strange country where whites and blacks drank together in bars, and got into drunken fights on darkened streets. It was a place where all colours visited loudly advertised brothels, where African, European and Afrikaner prostitutes plied their trade under the watchful eye of their equally international pimps. Despite the paper-thin condemnation of the richer classes, business was booming. In Frenchfontein a well-known brothel, such as Sylvio Villa, could entertain nearly a hundred clients on a good night in 1897.[152] Yet it did not last. Moral outrage and the panic over the virtues of whiteness and white women led to increasing government legislation and intensive policing of the district, and the end to overt prostitution early in the new century.

Frenchfontein did not disappear, however. It contracted, curled up tight and hid in the shadowy places of the city. The business of prostitution remained, constantly in evidence in the slums. It was a cause for concern to both the colonials and the Afrikaner nationalists who replaced them. For many poor it was a matter of survival. When times were bad, the girls would leave their houses and walk the road to a nameless building hulking anonymously in the slums. In 1939, shortly after the Great Depression, and four decades after the closing of Frenchfontein, the city council members for the poor neighbourhoods of Rosettenville and Fordsburg, FT Howarth and DJ Schoeman, conducted an investigation into prostitution in the city. They found 18 'boarding houses' run by black caretakers. When the poor white residents could not afford their rent, the caretakers simply sent men up to their rooms. Although the prostitutes in these houses were certainly not all poor Afrikaners, a significant number were, as demonstrated by the various investigations into prostitution undertaken by the Afrikaans church councils, as well as by fiery condemnation from the pulpit.[153]

Since prostitution inevitably allowed intimate contact between black and white, Johannesburg's brothels and boarding houses hummed with racial transgression, becoming moral blights for the ruling classes. It was not a simple matter, however. It was soft war fought in the bedrooms of the poor. CW de Kiewiet, the accomplished old historian, called the poor whites 'the frontier between the Europeans and the native. Through their weakness might pour a debasing stream of uncivilised blood.'[154] In a sense, prostitution was a battle lost on the ideological frontier of race. And it was far from the most serious of the battles. Poverty could foster prostitution, but it could also foster relationships across the colour line – relationships initiated through work and intimacy, a permanent surrendering of white prestige to the native or to the Asian. There was no greater sin, the colonials felt. No greater humiliation.

If the poor in the slums were guilty of more serious vices, such as prostitution and miscegenation, they were not spared from being stereotyped as lacking in character. Dr Gilchrist told the TIC that the Afrikaner poor were 'indolent, lazy and more or less incapable of sustained effort of any kind'.[155] Particularly annoying to the colonials was the Afrikaner habit of lounging about on the verandah, or stoep. These were places of socialisation, relaxation and, crucially, places where the poor were clearly visible. Stoeps were described by an early commentator as 'bearing about the same relation to the Afrikaner as his *café* does to the Frenchman'.[156] The Rev. D Theron told the TIC that 'many parents who are able-bodied, and can work, sit on verandahs and the children have to work for them'.[157] The stoep was not just a location, it was a practice, a habit, an icon. The stoeps were symbols of laziness and poverty, of a race of men and women rapidly decaying and even degenerating.

The poor whites were also viewed as being particularly prone to drunkenness. In 1926 *Die Kerkbode* reported that 'on the Witwatersrand, the terrible destruction caused by the scourge of drink makes a painful impression. There are households here in which heartrending scenes are played out week after week.' In 1939, Johannesburg churches reported that 60 per cent of the Afrikaner prisoners they had visited in the Johannesburg Fort were there due to alcohol.[158] Alcohol misuse and poverty led to broken families and dysfunctional households. In 1939 the charity *Randse Armsorgraad* observed that the first six months of that year had seen 400 cases of 'malicious abandonment' among the white poor in Johannesburg.[159] The charity reported between 6 000 and 7 000 broken marriages, which placed about 13 000 children in a precarious position.

Despite their poverty, perceived laziness and distaste for unskilled labour, the newly urbanised Afrikaners were not averse to employment. Poor whites were often to be found in the mines or serving in the police force and the army. They transported goods or drove trams, calling out the names of stops as they crawled through the new city. Most often they were found in 'employment by public bodies', building railways, dams and roads. They worked alongside the natives and this upset the ruling classes, who complained that 'in some factories white and coloured hands work side by side'.[160] Their lack of education, however, precluded them from skilled labour. According to the 1926 census, only 10 per cent of Afrikaners were found in the engineering trades, 20 per cent in woodwork and about 30 per cent in construction.[161] This made them more vulnerable to technological and industrial change. But the image of the Afrikaner lounging on his stoep is undeserved. 'It was only after the transport riders had been defeated by the railways, the cab drivers by the electric tramway, and the small brick-makers by the capitalist companies that chronic and extensive Afrikaner unemployment became a notable feature of urban areas.'[162]

The TIC decried the 'large class of professional beggars in Johannesburg, mainly amongst the women'. Miss Rogaly, secretary of the benevolent branch of the Loyal Women's Guild, told the commission that 'begging letter-writers and street beggars are frequently to be met with; unfortunately such a mode of life is undoubtedly on the increase'.[163] Colonel O'Brian agreed and stated that 'their numbers have been fostered in a measure by the extreme good nature and kindness of the community in general'.[164] In later years the sight of poor white women working as hawkers on the streets was 'conducive to a low estimate being formed by the natives of the standard of womankind amongst white races'.[165]

The effect of the slums on children, who had to work from a young age running messages or selling newspapers, was not neglected either. Their conditions were dire. The TIC was told that the 'children living in [Vrededorp and surrounds] have no sufficient clothing or wholesome food; the houses are wretched and the surroundings unwholesome'.[166] According to the experts, the disorder and unsanitary conditions in the slums were causing vices and reproducing poor whiteism in the children, like a disease carried from mother to child. Rev. Theron testified that the children:

> ... have grown up in a house where there is no order and they go into the streets and sell newspapers and so on. There are more children sinking into degradation in Johannesburg than we know of for that reason ... The difficulty is that they come here with a family. They have, perhaps, a few daughters and a few boys. The daughters immediately have to go into the laundry and the boys have to go and sell newspapers, and then the father, after going about from place to place, perhaps eventually goes off to the diggings at Christiana and comes back worse off than he was, and the poor children have to suffer for it.[167]

According to the TIC, many of these children had been abandoned because their parents could not afford to care for them. They grew up neglected, 'uneducated and weak'. The lack of access to caring relatives caused them to become 'poor whites and criminals'.[168] Said Rev. Theron: 'They go to the market and steal as much as they can get hold of there.'[169] The Chief Magistrate of the Witwatersrand complained about the perceived growth of 'child gangs' in the city, saying 'there is no question that in Johannesburg there is a marked increase of crime on the part of native youngsters ...

It is quite clear that the small native boys in the town are fraternising with European youngsters and looking upon themselves as youthful Dick Turpins, doing all sorts of horrible things.'[170]

Part of the reason for the concern over the criminal activities of poor white children was their unwillingness to attend school, and thereby pull themselves out of poverty. 'There is no need for us to explain how important it is to the future of the white race that as many of the rising generation of townsfolk as possible should become skilled workmen,' said the Transvaal Indigency Commission. The commissioners strongly recommended the government pass legislation to make school attendance compulsory. Mr Mills, the principal of the government school in Vrededorp, said that 'parents are, as a rule, anxious for their children to attend school but few recognise the need of continuity in a child's school life . . . In far too many cases school life means only two or three years' attendance of school, and these years are often not continuous.' He told the commission that many children did not attend school until they were eight or nine and did not pass grade 3 until they were ten or eleven. 'Few who leave school pass grade 7,' said Mills.[171]

The commission reported that in 1907, of the 470 scholars who attended school in Vrededorp, more than half were below grade 2; 74 (15.8 per cent) reached grade 6; and only five reached grades 8 and 9. The commission blamed this lack of education on the ease with which children could find employment as office boys and messengers. For this they could earn between £4 and £8 a month. This stopped them from progressing to training in skilled labour, where they did not earn more than £2 a month. There is no question that it was an economic necessity for the children of poor families to supplement household earnings. Yet the commission noted the same perceived distaste for work as their parents displayed, observing that boys in Johannesburg ' . . . often leave their employment after a few months because they are not paid higher wages, or are made to do "kaffirs'" work'.[172] 'The sooner the people recognised that all cannot be masters, the better,'[173] said Rev. JF Botha.

From the very beginning of the poor white problem, a clear connection was made between poor whites and the dangerous classes. The whites in towns lived in slums, where there was prostitution and crime, and so they were labelled on the whole as a lazy and criminal group. Except when they were found in the rural areas, where the poor whites were viewed as noble and innocent. The poor Dutch 'are unfit in every way for town life and so they sink into a very low scale of society and have taken to crime, illicit liquor selling being one of the easiest ways in which a man can get money,' Lt. Colonel O'Brian stated before the TIC.

By the 1920s, as the colonials were giving way to the nationalists, the poor were still viewed as criminals, although the ideology of eugenics had cast them as evolutionarily inferior as well. The poor whites 'lack foresight or reasoning,' said Dr JT Dunston. 'Unless they are supervised they gradually degenerate. They assume vices, they get married and they have large families, and they cannot support themselves because their earning power is small and they drop more and more and finally they become criminals.'[174]

When asked whether there was a direct link between poor whites and criminals, Dunston cautiously answered: 'It is an extraordinarily interesting thing that we expect to find these people, owing to their incapacity to compete, among the prostitutes and criminals and unemployed, and unemployables and weaklings. We expect to find them all there.'[175]

The moral geography of the poor white problem

Why did locating the slums and defining the people of the slums matter to government? Because once the 'moral geography' of a city is mapped, reconstruction and redemption are possible. Once the poor were known, the great project of the nationalist governments to rescue the poor could begin.

As Felix Driver has argued, mapping the poor areas provided a basis for social intervention: 'Through reconstruction of the urban environment, individual reformation would be achieved; model individuals from model environments.'[176] This mapping was problematic, however. The ideas used to define the poor were hampered by a contradiction between environmentalism, which conceived of the conditions of slums as creating social problems, and moralism, which conceived of the immorality of slum dwellers as giving rise to the character of slums.

This rift led to a dualism in how the urban poor whites were conceived of in places like South Africa. The inhabitants of Vrededorp in Johannesburg, and similar neighbourhoods, came to be characterised as vice-ridden, criminal and degenerate. At the same time they were also of precious rural Boer stock, unprepared for the corrupting influence of the city and desperate to escape the poor conditions in which they were trapped. The tensions between these views were never resolved, and are ultimately unresolvable: poor Afrikaners were essentially good, but also capable, under the weight of urban poverty, of descending the racial and moral scale. Kept away from the worst of the urban conditions, in the peri-urban fringes of cities like Johannesburg, poor whites had a chance of remaining more or less uncontaminated. But once they entered the city, they were lost. In the slums the poor could turn into the worst of colonial nightmares – men and women who turned their back on their racial privilege, betrayers of the *volk,* or *volksveraaiers*, who consorted with the lower races and descended into, at best, indolence and, at worst, vice, criminality and miscegenation. The poor Afrikaners were always defined by someone else, and they struggled to escape the paradox created for them. In the end, they could not – the Afrikaners needed the poor to find redemption.

The poor *volk*

Before he went to look for gold, Gideon Conradie collected human waste.

As the youngest of 12 children, he spent the evenings of the late nineteenth century with his older brothers gathering refuse that had been put out for collection. They called it 'riding the night wagon'. It was steady work, and his family needed the money.

When he grew older, Gideon Conradie decided to go and look for gold on the mines, walking the journey of more than 1 300 kilometres from his family in the poor area of Swellendam to the towers of Johannesburg.

Many years later, he liked to tell of his mother, a determined German woman, who said that even though the family was poor and sometimes went without food, they were not without manners. When he stopped for the night, perhaps begging a warm space to sleep among the cattle, Gideon Conradie's mother made him promise never to put his family to shame by being a glutton. If the farmer's wife should invite him in for *moerkoffie*,[177] said his mother, then he should be careful to take only a single piece of the food offered, no matter how much the farmer's wife insisted. He kept his promise, recalling in later years how hard it was to resist a plate of freshly baked *mosbolletjies*[178] on an empty stomach.

Gideon Conradie could not read or write, and when he reached Johannesburg, he struggled to find work among the hundreds of other equally eager poor whites. He was smart, however, and set himself up in business by buying bones from butchers and boiling them into a thin soup. His partner in the venture was a black man called Jonas. No one can remember his surname. When the miners returned from their dark worlds, hungry and blinking in the light, Gideon Conradie would stand by the roadside with a ladle, relying on the rumble of their bellies. Eventually he could afford a cow, and would offer the miners soup and milk.

Gideon Conradie made his fortune through soup bones. He used his money to buy a farm near Bloemfontein, where he worked until the end of his days.

The Afrikaners, as they are known today, did not exist at the turn of the century. In the flash of time between the Boer War and the present, an entire nation imagined itself into being, constructed heroes and villains, persecuted and was persecuted, ruled a country, shamed itself, fell from grace and was forgotten.

Although the struggle of the colonials to police their racial boundaries was a quiet war fought across the entire imperial world, it was amplified in South Africa. On the fringe of empire, this racial struggle became entangled with the 'invention' of the Afrikaner people and their destiny. To invent an entire culture, to collectively imagine a people, is no simple feat. It requires massive political intervention, will and social manipulation, and, in South Africa, it was spearheaded by the movement known as Afrikaner nationalism and crowned by the 1948 victory of the National Party, which ushered in the policy of apartheid.

'Afrikaners had no monolithic identity to begin with, no common historic purpose and no single unifying language,' argues social scientist Anne McClintock. 'They were a disunited, scattered people, speaking a medley of High Dutch and local dialects.'[179] Before there were Afrikaners, there were Boers fighting against the British fighting against the natives. After their defeat in their war against the empire, the Boers somehow had to pick themselves up, to clean the blood off their clothes and the smell of concentration camps off their women. The Boers were a defeated people, unable to look other Europeans in the eye. The solution was to create a new national identity where they could again be proud – to shape a European nation from the clay of Africa, smoothing ridges, removing a rib, creating form. A counterculture had to be created, which required, among others, the creation of a common vernacular, the establishment of a literary culture as well as a popular press.

It was obvious to any at the start of the twentieth century that in order to have power, you needed to be white. The new Boer culture – the Afrikaners – had to quell any whispers of racial mixing in their blood. The Afrikaners selectively defined themselves by highlighting their European heritage and downplaying the African and Asian influences. The geographer John Western argues that, far from being a race apart, Afrikaners are more accurately seen as a creole culture: 'Perhaps more so than many groups, Afrikaners have quite recently invented themselves. The appropriation of only the Dutch portion of their heritage serves to underline their purported whiteness.' Crucially, Western notes that racial intermingling since the seventeenth century has left very few pure 'white' Afrikaners. As such, 'there can be no objective borderline between persons classified as Cape Coloureds and those as white'.[180] There is no shortage of Afrikaner families in modern South Africa that can point to one branch of their family that brought the *volk* into 'shame' by crossing the racial line. The result is a *skaamfamilie*.[181] It is a culture in which the popular Afrikaner comedian Casper de Vries can easily trace his ancestry to Xhosa royalty. According to Teppo, 'several social scientists have presented estimations on the number of mixed marriages and the generality of mixed descent in the group classified as White during apartheid. These estimations vary from ten per cent to 40 per cent.'[182]

This 'imagining' of the Afrikaners is certainly not limited to these people alone. It is intrinsic to cultures across the world and throughout history. One could argue that it is to be found in the culture of the Cape Coloureds themselves, who have downplayed their Afrikaner heritage and emphasised the Malaysian contribution – a practice to which the first Afrikaners had no objection.

The invention of the Afrikaners started during the colonial period and carried with it the colonial concepts of racial superiority. In order to have any significant political power, then, the new nation would have to define itself first and foremost as white. Yet a significant obstacle stood in the way – a large underclass of poor whites, who were regarded by the colonials as morally and racially unstable. The Afrikaners could not be white, and could certainly not be white in British eyes, when so many of them were still lurking in the slums, among the blacks. It required, in short, the economic and moral upliftment of the poor whites and the solution to the *armblankevraagstuk*.[183] It required something nearly impossible – the eradication of poverty. And if poverty could not be completely removed, then the Afrikaners would rely on illusion – a national sleight of hand to remove the poverty from their past.

The moral rescue of the poor went hand in hand with the middle class's increasing identification with them, spurred on by churches, charities and newspapers. By viewing the poor not as a separate indefinable race of failures and thieves, but as 'our people', and by removing the taint of the slums from the poor and establishing them as a rural group corrupted and destroyed by the foreign towers of the city, the middle class could overcome their condescension towards the poor. The poor whites, in essence, had to be shepherded into the cultural space of the new Afrikaner *volk*.

The Afrikaner rescue of the poor began when the nation was divided – in the years of the Great War and the rebellion of Boer General De la Rey. It began with the churches, with the 1916 Cradock conference – a defining point in the ethnic co-option of poor whites. The congress was the idea of the then nationalist newspaper *De Burger* and held under the auspices of the Dutch Reformed Church. It was attended by various ministers, politicians and Afrikaner intelligentsia. The editor of *De Burger*, DF Malan, later prime minister and leader of the National Party, told the delegates that the poor white problem was the 'greatest, most urgent and most heartbreaking issue' facing the Afrikaner nation. Geo Hofmeyer, the secretary of education, told the delegates that unless something was done to solve the poor white problem, the entire Afrikaner nation was in danger of becoming poor whites. The Afrikaner people were like a ship, he said: 'When one end of it is sinking, it threatens the entire vessel.'[184]

The government at the time of the conference was the South African

Party (SAP) under the leadership of Louis Botha, and later Jan Smuts. The SAP was widely seen as sympathetic to British interests and unsympathetic to poor whites, understanding their poverty to be partly due to a lack of education – an impression given to them by the commissions. Despite the government's perceived indifference, it acted decisively to solve the problem, as it understood it, and in 1914 all education in secondary schools and institutions for the training of teachers was made free for whites. School attendance for children between seven and fifteen was also made compulsory. Yet the party was slow to perceive the increasing identification of middle-class Afrikaners with the white poor – driven by Smuts' later political rival DF Malan in his role as newspaper editor and clergyman. Smuts, especially, was viewed as having a distinct distaste for the group. In 1907 a crowd of Afrikaner and English unemployed had marched from Johannesburg, through the *veldt* and past the mines, to the Transvaal capital of Pretoria to petition Smuts, then colonial secretary, for work opportunities. The crowd was disgusted when Smuts told them that there was work to be found on the Pietersburg railway line for 3s. 4p. a day and a bag of maize meal.

Shortly afterwards, the editor of a Transvaal newspaper addressed a crowd of Afrikaner poor in Vrededorp, saying the offer 'was most insulting to the Afrikaner nation . . . The sting of the whole thing lay in the offer of maize meal. It was placing them on a level with Kaffirs.'[185] In 1923, even as the hysteria over white poverty mounted, Smuts told a Dutch Reformed Church delegation that the poor white problem was not as serious as depicted. The country was unprepared for the rapid industrialisation brought about by the mines, and the poor whites were but 'casualties on the battlefield'.[186] His perceived contempt would soon cost him his position.

The following year, the SAP and Smuts ran against a coalition of the

National Party and the South African Labour Party. 1922 had seen the Rand Rebellion bring virtual civil war to the streets of Johannesburg – an uprising swiftly and brutally ended when Smuts called in troops, artillery and tanks to beat back the dissatisfied miners. The 'Pact' coalition ran on a poor white ticket, promising to tackle the problem and highlighting the failures of the SAP to help the poor Afrikaners now streaming to the cities. In a climate of surging Afrikaner nationalism and increasing hysteria over the poor, it is perhaps not surprising that the SAP was defeated and the National Party – which would later institute apartheid – took over the government. The nationalist JBM Hertzog became prime minister of South Africa – a position he would hold for 15 years until the start of World War II and the end of the poor white problem.[187]

The Pact government of 1924, the first Afrikaner nationalist government, attacked the poor white problem with unprecedented resolve. Due to the prevailing racist colonial and nationalist attitudes, it had near unlimited powers to solve poverty, and with little chance of dissent. The Pact government made good on its election promises and increased state intervention massively in favour of poor whites – to the enormous detriment of black South Africans. In the same year that it won the election, the government established a Department of Labour in 1924, created, in its own words, because of 'a realisation of the existence of acute conditions in the economic and industrial life of the Union'.[188] In 1924 the government also instituted the notorious 'civilised labour' policy, whereby whites were paid more than blacks in order to foster a 'civilised' standard of living for whites. This was particularly focused on the railways – the home of the poor: 'The railways were the largest single employer of Afrikaners in the urban areas. In 1939, one in eleven of all adult male Afrikaners worked on the railways. In the period 1930–1935, this produced a fall in the number of Africans employed on the railways by over

25%.'[189] Poor whites were also taken up in the postal services, the police, the defence forces, prisons and local and provincial government.

The government proceeded in a methodical and utterly determined fashion to uplift the poor whites economically. Where before the state had been happy to import goods, it now created its own industries so that whites could find work. It quickly set up the Iron and Steel Corporation (Iscor, now Mittal Steel South Africa) and the National Electricity Corporation (Eskom). In later years it would create, among others, the fuel producer Sasol, the weapon manufacturer Krygkor and the Atoomkragkorporasie for nuclear energy. White jobs were overwhelmingly privileged in parastatals. A Wage Board allowed the state to enforce minimum wages for whites. Employers who had a whites-only hiring policy received preference for state contracts, and certain industries were informed that the customs on imports would be lowered if they employed a certain percentage of whites.

The state led by example, quickly adopting the policy of employing 'civilised' labour. Although it was not stated explicitly, in practice this meant employing whites – especially in the railways, local government, harbours and post offices. 'Between 1924 and 1933 unskilled white workers rose from 9.5% to 39.3% of the labour force, while unskilled blacks fell from 75% to 49%. By the early 1950s more than 100 000 mainly unskilled and semi-skilled whites worked for the railways, the biggest employer of white labour.'[190] Subsidies for temporary employment on public-works projects were increased and relief works, which provided employment for the poor, massively expanded, rising from 2.6 per cent of the budget in 1930 to 15.8 per cent in 1933.

In startling contrast to how the poor were viewed at the turn of the century – as beggars, thieves and hopeless failures – the poor whites were now lovingly embraced as part of the Afrikaner *volk*, as prodigal sons and daughters once lost but now found and given new robes. Throughout the Pact intervention, there was a conscious effort to view the poor whites as being part of the *volk*. At a 1934 congress on white poverty, DF Malan 'expressed the fear that the spiritual isolation of the poor white lay in being "no more a member of the *volk*, and the *volk* . . . no longer part of them". The poor white had to be regarded as "a human being and a partner of the nation (*volksgenoot*)". He had to be brought "once again to the stream of our *volk* life from which he had been lost".'[191]

The Pact victory had shown the other political parties that there was significant power to be achieved by courting the *armblankes*[192]and the working class. They competed fiercely, elbowing each other out of the way in their efforts to win working-class loyalty. This led to more extreme measures being implemented to win the approval of the waiting crowds, who had finally tasted power and were happy to trample on blacks to get it. The widespread fears of miscegenation, which had so haunted the colonials, contributed to the government's decision to outlaw marriages between blacks and whites in 1928. The law did not prevent marriages between whites and coloureds,[193] however, and it did not nullify existing mixed marriages. A later law to ban marriages between whites and coloureds was introduced in 1936 – by the NP member for Vrededorp, where the poor whites were to be found. Yet Hertzog's government was still accused of not doing enough to uplift the poor. Concern over mixed marriages became especially notable during the 1938 election, in which Hertzog's government was attacked for not being serious enough about preventing mixed marriages – an issue linked to the inadequate housing for poor whites and the desire for racial segregation.

In 1935 Hertzog's National Party formally joined with Smuts' South African Party to form the anti-isolationist Union Party. In protest, DF Malan broke away and formed the 'Purified' National Party, which he felt catered more for the interests of the Afrikaner *volk*. JG Strydom, the leader of the Purified National Party in the Transvaal, told the party's 1936 conference that 'the National Party has the task of keeping the white race white. It demands that a stop should be put to mixed marriages and that the races must live separately.'[194]

Care is needed when analysing the cultural and economic formation of the *volk*, however. In his remarkable study on the development of Afrikaner capital, *Volkskapitalisme*, economic historian Dan O'Meara is at pains to point out that the concept of Afrikaner nationalism should not be taken for granted as an all-encompassing notion of the Afrikaner nation during its imagining. The term '*volk*' is lazy shorthand, and has meant very different things at very different times – notwithstanding the fact that the *volk*, as such, did not exist until the late nineteenth century. Afrikaners would have outsiders believe that the *volk* spontaneously and divinely came into being. 'United by a sense of *eie*,[195] exhibiting an innate "race consciousness", inspired by a sombre Calvinism, and far removed from the eroding effects of industrialisation, this *volk* is presumed to have developed for itself an exclusive, but democratic and classless form of social organisation, again undermined by the encircling enemies of British greed and black competition,'[196] writes O'Meara. Equally important is that the *volk* gained its power not only from racial exclusivity and a grasping at white prestige, but also from '"the Hand which guides the fate of nations and men". Like the prophets of Israel, the ideologists have elevated Afrikanerdom to the special instrument in Africa of their Calvinist God. Divine Will explains Afrikaner history. Divine Will forged Afrikanerdom in a discrete organic unity and converted it into its special instrument.'[197]

In extreme contrast to how Afrikaners have viewed themselves is how certain British commentators have characterised the *volk* – especially those accounts written during the NP domination of South African politics. Some are openly disparaging in their view of Afrikaners, treating 'the Boer' as a backward, 'paranoid' simpleton 'out of touch with reality', suffering from an 'inferiority complex' and the 'gullible tool of manipulating leaders'. One study concluded that 'Afrikaners are "immature psychopaths" in a sociopathic culture'.[198] Yet both views – that of a united nation guided by a divine will, and that of a nation of backward racists – make the same mistake: of treating the *volk* as a single, easily defined concept, much as 'empire' was seen as an undifferentiated, unstoppable entity razing the developing world.

The *volk*, or Afrikanerdom, is not, and was not, what scholars would call 'a priori' – an always-existing concept that takes itself for granted. 'Embedded within the category "Afrikanerdom" are the questionable premises that all (white) Afrikaans-speakers are automatically integrated into the cross-class organic unity of the *volk*, instinctively share the presumably innate "Afrikaner" conservative values and are always available for ethnic mobilisation in terms of their common "Afrikaner" values,' argues O'Meara. It is obvious that at certain points in history large numbers of Afrikaners have unified themselves behind a particular racially exclusive political party or ideal. Says O'Meara:

> This is not in dispute. However, it is equally clear that at other junctures, Afrikaans-speaking whites of various classes have differentially resisted such 'ethnic mobilisation' and have been organised on other (and varying) bases. Moreover, the various Afrikaner nationalist movements in South African history were always constituted by a differentiated and shifting ensemble of social forces – each clearly articulating widely different conceptions and expectations of the 'volk' and what 'its' interests were.[199]

By accepting the *volk* – or equally generalised concepts, such as 'English', 'blacks' or 'whites' – we obscure the complexity of motivations, personalities and ideas behind an event – be it the capitalist development of twentieth-century South Africa, or the struggle for white prestige.

Separation and segregation

Apartheid – as the ultimate expression of racial separation – did not invent segregation. The practice of keeping different racial groups apart from each other dates back centuries in South Africa, and certainly centuries before that – for as long as one group has sought power over another by excluding them.[200] But the modern segregation of South Africa manifested by whites-only benches, drinking fountains and cricket teams, and native townships, began in the cities. The historian John Cell traces its development to Milner's South African Native Affairs Commission of 1903–1905.[201] The poor whites were crucial to the development of modern segregation, and it is through them that South Africa was eventually to experience the injustices of apartheid.

Twentieth-century South African lawmakers did not wake up one morning and decide at once upon the idea of racially separating the nation. The legislation needed to gradually seep through the national consciousness. Apartheid and segregation were made possible through many small deaths of conscience, and this began in South African cities[202] with the question of health. Turn-of-the-century colonials had, to put it mildly, a bit of an obsession with health and sanitation – what historians call a 'sanitation syndrome' – and this preoccupation was to interact in powerful ways with local racial attitudes to influence segregationist thinking.

It was health and sanitary legislation that provided the legal means to clear the slums and sites of crime and disorder in an effort to instil social discipline into wayward colonials.[203] The colonial concern with sanitation was not unwarranted: in the slums, filth was piled against walls and water was deadly to drink. The outbreak of plague in Brickfields in the early 1900s and the later influenza epidemic of 1918 illustrate that sanitation was a justified worry for residents and lawmakers. Yet in post-war Johannesburg, for instance, concerns over health hazards became entangled with calls for segregation. The tide of poor whites to the city and the lack of space for them to stay made slum conditions ever worse. And at the time, it was thought that racial mixing was actually physically unhealthy for all groups.

In 1919 Johannesburg fell under the control of the relatively small Labour Party – and not Smuts' SAP or Hertzog's National Party. Labour's victory in the municipal election is generally seen to be due to its promises of improved housing for whites. Within weeks of gaining control of the Johannesburg Council, the Labour Party threw its political weight behind a government project to build houses for the poor 'so that the mixing of poor whites and blacks could be remedied'.[204] This scheme had the advantage of reducing overcrowding in the slums and restricted the practice of rent racketeering, which allegedly affected the poor whites most acutely, and forced them to pay exorbitant amounts for inadequate accommodation – prices they could ill afford.[205]

Until this point the government did not have the legal right to evict on a large scale. A few years later, however, the Natives (Urban Areas) Act of 1923 made it possible for blacks to be forcibly removed from the cities so that poor whites could take their place. That year the Medical Officer of Health for Johannesburg, Dr Charles Porter, was tasked with conducting a survey of working-class housing in order to assess the need for the proposed white housing scheme. In his report Porter was disgusted by the 'close housing association of poor whites with Native and Coloured persons' and he 'unreservedly expressed the view that the necessity for assisted white housing was relatively negligible compared with the urgency for the segregation and decent housing of "Natives"'.[206] The need to implement the Natives (Urban Areas) Act eclipsed efforts to implement a white housing scheme, and the Johannesburg City Council concluded that instead of building houses for the white poor, their housing conditions in the inner city would be much improved by the removal of blacks from the area – forcibly. The black residents were duly relocated to townships outside the cities. This did not prevent racial mixing in the slums, however, as the government struggled to prevent the hundreds of blacks, whites, coloureds and Asians who clogged the roads into the cities in search of gold.

In the 1930s, as the poor white problem was at its worst and the slums of Johannesburg were home to a substantial poor white population, the call for suitable white housing became ever louder. The political climate, now thoroughly nationalist, was also particularly sensitive to the plight of the Afrikaner poor. The Johannesburg City Council was even criticised for constructing black accommodation (after their removal from the slums) at the expense of the whites in the slums. Susan Parnell argues that 'political imperatives of wooing poor whites, combined with elitist notions of the inherent superior potential of whites as opposed to blacks, made it essential that whites be provided with housing that would encourage their social upliftment'.[207]

In 1930 the state intervened and the Central Housing Board of Johannesburg was given state authority to provide loans for white housing schemes at very low interest rates (1.5 per cent). Similar white public housing schemes were soon approved in most major cities, and the poor whites were led from the slums to their new council housing estates. The

Slums Act of 1934 gave local authorities the legal right to seize whole sections of slum land for the building of these housing schemes, sending the black residents back to the townships put aside for them.

How things had changed in a decade. In the early 1920s, under the colonials, blacks were removed from inner city slums to discourage racial mixing and improve the housing conditions of the whites left in the slums. A decade later, the political climate had swung to the nationalists, but the poor were stubbornly refusing to segregate. The state directly intervened by agreeing to build massive white public housing schemes – grey towers where the white poor were hidden. This time it was the whites who were removed from the slums, and the blacks who remained. Burgeoning Afrikaner nationalism and political attention had pointed a spotlight onto the poor whites – or the poor Afrikaner *volk*, as they would now be termed. 'It was in order to deal with [poor whiteism],' said Hertzog, that blind and large-hearted nationalist, that he encouraged such expanded segregation.[208] If Afrikaners were going to be seen as upholding white prestige, and the prestige of the *volk*, then Afrikaners could not be living in the slums. And most certainly not among the blacks and coloureds and Asians. If the poor whites were to be white, they had to live in white spaces and in white housing. And if they could not be white, if they still refused to become respectable members of the *volk*, then they would be removed from view, kept in housing estates, away from the eyes of the British, and the blacks and the *volk*. Segregation was the terrible tool used to achieve that goal.

At the heart of segregation lay competition, argues Cell, competition 'at every conceivable level of relations – agricultural, industrial, commercial, political, and therefore social and even sexual'.[209] The poor whites were the weakest link in so many of those relations. As unskilled labourers, they could not compete with the blacks, who were willing to work for far lower wages. And although they developed significant political power, white supremacy could not tolerate their existence in any large numbers. And socially? Well, the poor whites were prone to the greatest sin of all – sleeping with the enemy. In a game of such high stakes, a weak link could not be tolerated:

> If segregation should fail. Then in their view the last hope of preserving white civilisation anywhere in Africa south of the Sahara must fail with it. Their beloved white man's country would inevitably degenerate into a mongrelised society like Brazil or Portuguese East Africa just next door. In the hostile African environment, degeneracy once in motion would surely be an irreversible, terminal cancer . . . At the last, 'little brown children,' as General Smuts used to say, 'would play in the ruins of Johannesburg'.[210]

Extreme nationalism and poor whites

An interesting case in the identification of Afrikaner nationalism with poor whites is that of the *Ossewabrandwag* (OB). Established in the wake of the 1938 centenary celebrations of the Great Trek, the OB consciously set itself up as a champion of the small man and the poor white. By 1941 the OB boasted between 300 000 and 400 000 members – about a third of the total Afrikaner population. This makes it one of the largest nationalist mass movements in recent history.[211] The OB is today chiefly remembered as a fascist Afrikaner paramilitary organisation with strong Nazi sympathies, yet, as historian Christopher Marx points out, the organisation was originally chiefly populist, with no broad aim beyond the promotion of Afrikaner unity.[212] Once its leadership began to define the aims of the organisation, which included sabotage and assassination, and gave it a fascist character, the OB's membership quickly declined – from as early as 1942.[213] It finally disbanded in 1954.

There is some debate about the impact of the OB on South African politics.[214] The rapid increase in its membership does show, however, that it initially struck a deep chord among Afrikaners with its emphasis on *volkseenheid* (*volk* unity). The OB's emphasis on the dangers of miscegenation and the loss of Afrikaner identity among the poor whites was taken to heart by a very great number of Afrikaners. The organisation was particularly concerned about the 'decadence' engendered in Afrikaners by their new life in the cities. At its peak, the OB had more than 60 000 members on the Rand – nearly half of its total Transvaal membership, and a significant amount of these were poor whites.[215] However, for the OB 'the city became the epitome of everything that constructed "tradition" contradicted . . . the challenge was to preserve and strengthen traditional values, and with them the survival of the *volk*, in a hostile modern world infested by temptations'.[216] Geoffrey Cronjé, a sociologist and prominent OB member, argued that the decadence engendered by cities was easily seen in the racial mixing in the slums and in the falling birth rate of Afrikaners. Cities were viewed as destroying the religious and moral fortitude of Afrikaners.

The organisation also viewed cities as being especially dangerous to women. In a similar manner to the colonials, Afrikaner women were portrayed as inviolate and virtuous. The OB noted that 'high esteem for its women has always been a feature of the Germanic race. In our *volk*, too, women are elevated to the most precious and inviolable ornament of our *volk*.'[217] Yet in the cities young, unmarried women found lodging in mixed boarding houses. They worked in factories or, if very poor, in laundries owned by Asians. The OB had assimilated some of the notions of eugenics, and came to regard the propagation of Afrikaners as intrinsic to the survival of the ethnic group. Yet the decadence found in the cities threatened that project: 'For under the *voortrekker kappie*[218] we often find the woman with red fingernails and a cigarette who doesn't want children.'[219] The OB's discourse on the cities was, therefore, infused with a sense of cultural loss. The cities alienated the Afrikaners from their *volk* and from their traditions – it left them decadent, or it made them poor. Their poverty was degrading to the *volk*, who were engaged in the process of nation-building. The cities were a challenge that the Afrikaner had to overcome, and in which the Afrikaner had to remain steadfast.

The OB's radical nationalist discourse had a mass appeal, and this is precisely why the organisation is useful as an object of analysis. The OB's members included students, university professors and, crucially, the poor whites. As a self-consciously ethnic organisation (an ethnic identity that hinged on being white), the OB's broad appeal epitomises the broader political and social climate, in which various factions were desperately trying to whiten the poor. The OB illustrates how, by the late 1930s, the process of Afrikaner imagination had come to include the poor whites.

Redeeming the poor

As the colonials tried to understand poverty through the commissions they set up to investigate the issue, the nationalists also had their own stories they wanted told. The most significant of the nationalist investigations, the Carnegie Commission of 1932, also stands as possibly the most important and thorough investigation into white poverty in South Africa. How then was the story told?

The Carnegie Commission differs from previous commissions of enquiry in significant ways. To begin with, it was financed by a company – the Carnegie Corporation of New York – which, in the government's mind, made its conclusions representative of broader society, and not the narrow halls of the Union Buildings. Secondly, although the white poverty problem had been brought to the attention of the Carnegie Corporation before, it was only after the express invitation of the Dutch Reformed Church that the corporation agreed to finance an investigation. From the outset, then, the commission was viewed as something outside government – as existing in the spheres of business and religion. This made the commission more legitimate. Its conclusions would be backed up, in a way, by third parties.

The five principal commissioners were drawn from the established pools of experts – the church, academia, health services and charities – but with a nationalist twist. The moral compass was provided by the Dutch Reformed Church, and its academics were drawn from the Afrikaans University of Stellenbosch, at the time often seen as the political and cultural heartland of Afrikanerdom. JFW Grosskopf, a playwright and journalist, was a Stellenbosch professor of economics, and RW Wilcocks was a psychologist at the university. The commission's moral expert was JR Albertyn, who wrote a volume on the sociology of the poor white problem. Albertyn, a Dutch Reformed minister, who brought the values and conservative outlook of the church to his study, was assisted by the remarkable Marie Rothmann, an author under the pen name MER, and at the time organising secretary of the Afrikaans Christian Women's Organisation. The commission's medical expert was AW Murray, the assistant Health Officer for the Union.

The commission was led by EG Malherbe, a prominent social scientist and director of the National Commission of Education. Malherbe was also a fierce believer in eugenist principles. In 1933, just after the publication of the commission's report, *The Star* published a speech by Malherbe under the alarmist headline 'Future of the White Race in Question'. In the speech Malherbe warned of the danger that biologically inferior poor whites held for the quality of the white race in Africa.[220]

Rothmann also displayed a strong belief in eugenics – an interesting view, given her own impoverished background. Writing of her poor white youth, Rothmann tells the story of her starving family unable to afford food and only rescued by a mysterious knock on the door. Her father had recently passed away and on the doormat lay a large parcel. Upon unwrapping it, the family discovered a large fish – enough to feed them for a few days. The parcel also contained an oily piece of paper bearing the words 'look in the mouth of the fish'. When the mouth of the fish was opened, 'two half-crowns lay in my mother's palm. And she cried softly, and the tears rolled down her cheeks.'[221] Many years later, Rothmann discovered that the package had been sent by Berria, a coloured servant of her grandfather who had made his fortune later in life and who had been very fond of Rothmann's father.

The commissioners of the Carnegie Commission framed their knowledge in a discourse that was pro-Afrikaner, with the morals of the Dutch Reformed Church and in the fashionably scientific language of eugenics. According to Marx, it is also significant that 'most of the contributors to the Carnegie report ... landed up in the nationalistic or ultra-right camp'. Marx presents the interesting argument that a preoccupation with poor whites, together with the decline of the *volk*, incited nationalism and defensive racism in observers.[222] The reactions of the Carnegie commissioners represented a microcosm of the Afrikaner nation, swept up in the task of imagining a nation and horrified by the lapses of whiteness and civilisation they now saw.

Unlike the investigations of the 1920s, which increasingly viewed white poverty as an urban problem, the Carnegie Commission looked closely at the countryside. The lingering drought of the 1920s and the Great Depression of the 1930s had brought rural poverty into sharp relief and intensified the flood of poor whites migrating to the cities. The commission was also particularly concerned with the perceived growth of class distinction among Afrikaners, which led to increased social intercourse between black and white people:

> The *bywoner* and farm labourer are in many cases no longer received as social equals by the land-owner and his family. They are very often allowed only in the kitchen of the house ... thus the poor white in time comes to associate with non-Europeans. The result is that the respect of the coloured man for the European fellow-worker disappears and from social intercourse to miscegenation is but a step.[223]

As might be expected of the period, the Carnegie Commission relied heavily on eugenics. Its commissioners were darkly amazed by the prevalence of poor whites with subnormal intelligence, and were particularly concerned about the propagation of the 'unfit'. Substandard parents, they feared, were breeding lazy and criminal poor whites, and their high fertility rates threatened the very survival of Europeans. One of the commissioners, EG Malherbe, who had brought the problem of white poverty to the attention of the Carnegie Corporation, remarked that 'poor families tend to be markedly larger than more prosperous ones, and the children of the former often show lack of intelligence ... This fact has bearings on the quality of our future European population.'[224]

Yet the discourse behind the Carnegie Commission is more complicated than these pessimistic racial emphases of Social Darwinism would suggest. Despite the eugenic reasoning of some of its commissioners, it ultimately settled on an environmental explanation for the poor white problem, referring to the traumatic urbanisation of poor whites and their painful entry into capitalism. The contradictions in the Carnegie Commission – its eventual dismissal of eugenic thinking despite relying heavily on it, and its emphasis on rural poverty despite Afrikaners being present in the Johannesburg slums for nearly 40 years – can be explained by the commission's endeavour to redeem the poor whites. If previous investigations had told stories of the poor as an uncontrollable cancer found in the hearts of cities, then the Carnegie Commission was trying to tell the story of the Afrikaner poor in much kinder terms. Through the Carnegie Commission, the nationalists were both trying to rid the poor of their slum trappings, and to actively foster Afrikaner consolidation. The poor whites were not in the end merely beggars or prostitutes, but honest, rural Afrikaners who had struggled in life and struggled in the cities. Their poverty was not inherent, or inherited, but ultimately due to economic and social factors beyond their control. General Jan Smuts, then justice minister, noted as much in a speech in 1936:

> What was feared was that a section of the European population, under African conditions, was degenerating but the Carnegie Commission has . . . entirely dispelled that delusion. There is a certain amount of degradation and degeneration, but in the vast bulk of cases there is no deterioration of the human stuff . . . The right stuff is there, and where you are going to work at the social problems of the country you have this assurance – you are not going to work in vain, you are not going to work on stuff that is intractable.[225]

Rescuing the *volk*

The Great Depression of the 1930s has hardened like amber in the world's consciousness, conjuring up images of broken families, their possessions piled high in broken-down trucks, making their slow way across the dull expanse of America, of stock market crashes and banker suicides, of begging, desperation and hard-lined sacrifice. The world's images are of America, but it was no better in South Africa, already burdened by the growing poor. As the barren winds howled across Oklahoma and the Transvaal, the political attention being paid to the poor whites went hand in hand with a growing ethnic mobilisation among the Afrikaners. The upliftment of the poor became a national Afrikaner project, and not just a political power play. Whereas before the state had taken the lead, it was now joined by charities, churches, newspapers, women's welfare organisations and secretive cultural societies.

In real terms the value of South Africa's output was £26.5 million lower in 1932 than in 1920. From 1930 to 1933 the income from private manufacturing declined by 20 per cent. The depression hit the farms and rural areas the hardest, sending the last of the nearly poor whites scrambling to the cities. Also in 1932 the value of agricultural commodities sold on the external market was 36 per cent of their value just four years earlier. The total value of maize – South Africa's major agricultural commodity – halved between 1929 and 1933. The average value of livestock products was also halved (wool fell in value by 70 per cent between 1929 and 1933). The secretary of agriculture described the period as 'the darkest and most difficult experienced for the last 30 years', and in the cities approximately 22 per cent of all white and coloured males were officially noted as unemployed.

In Johannesburg, the Afrikaners regarded established charities, such as the Rand Aid Association, the Social Services Association and the Children's Aid Society, with suspicion. These charities, it was thought, would more readily give money to the British than to the Afrikaners, and were no friend of the *volk*, nor could they understand their needs. Consequently, charities with the explicit aim of uplifting poor Afrikaners came into being. These were often established with the help of the Afrikaans churches and women's organisations. A good example of this ethnic cooperation is the *Randse Armsorgraad* (Rand Council for the Care of the Poor). The *Armsorgraad* was established by the Dutch Reformed Church in 1937 with the help of state subsidies, the Johannesburg Municipal Council and Christmas drives organised by *Die Transvaler* (under the editorship of later apartheid prime minister HF Verwoerd). In 1939 the Witwatersrand Association for the Welfare of the *Volk* was created, followed by, among others, the Association of Rand Mothers in 1941.[227] The *Helpmekaar* ('help each other') fund, which had been established in order to provide relief for those who had rebelled in 1914, was converted into a charity that concerned itself with Afrikaner poverty. The Federation of Afrikaans Cultural Organisations (FAK), established in 1929 for the promotion of Afrikaans language and culture, was also very involved and hosted the Institute for the Wellbeing of the *Volk* (*Volkswelsyn*), which was created to research the poor white problem.

The organisation that created the FAK started in 1918 as Young South Africa, but soon changed its name to the *Afrikaner Broederbond* – a name that still has an ominous, dark sound to it nearly a century after its creation. The Bond was a defining and driving force in the cultural and non-governmental response to poor whiteism and in Afrikaner culture in general. It should come as no surprise that the Bond was created during a time of economic depression and Afrikaner disunity, a time when the 'Afrikaner soul was sounding the depths of the abyss of despair'. The violent suppression of the 1914 Rebellion and the imprisonment of its leaders had created large divisions among Afrikaners: 'Agriculture was depressed and the influenza epidemic raged. The squeeze on land and the effects of the *Rebellie* drove increasing numbers of rural whites into the cities, accelerating the problem of "poor whiteism". All writings on the Bond stress the significance of this period when politically and economically the Afrikaner had been reduced to a slave in the land of his birth.'[228] The Bond functioned mainly as a secret semi-masonic organisation of (in the main) intellectuals until 1926, when Hertzog's government supported the Balfour Declaration, turning South Africa into a Dominion of the Empire, instead of a republic. This 'betrayal' prompted the Bond to expand its scope and systematically begin 'to infiltrate every arena of importance to the continued existence of the Afrikaner and to make [its] influence felt'.[229]

In 1929 the Bond unveiled its public face: 'The FAK was to be the most important and influential of the Bond's numerous public fronts. With token exceptions, the two bodies shared the same executives and officials who publicly implemented the FAK policies secretly decided upon in the Bond. By 1937 almost 300 cultural bodies were affiliated to the FAK.'[230] Through the FAK the Bond practised what it called *kultuurpolitiek* – cultural politics. The FAK busied itself with establishing Afrikaner alternatives to English institutions, such as the *Voortrekkers* for the Boy Scouts and the *Noodhulpliga* for the St John's Ambulance Brigade. Through such creations the Bond hoped to foster Afrikaner unity, creating a *volk* where there was none and inventing a united history, such as through traditional dances, or *volkspele*, where before there had been only individual stories. A few years earlier, the Bond had taken the decision to infiltrate members into key positions in leading institutions and recruit promising politicians, such as DF Malan. During the 1930s the Bond displayed a near obsession with class divisions among Afrikaners, doing its best to heal the rifts revealed by the poor whites and to mobilise the disparate groups into a single dubious organism known as Afrikaners. The Bond's position in the economic and cultural life of the Afrikaner enabled it to have an unprecedented influence in the formation of the new *volk*. To a very large extent, the culture of the Afrikaners today is the product of the Bond's policies, and it is in matters of culture and not economics, argues O'Meara, that the Bond's true power lay.

Before the 1930s the intellectual and capital power base of the Bond lay mainly in the Transvaal – in Johannesburg, Pretoria and the wide *platteland* surrounding them. In the Cape, among those richer, less wild Afrikaners, Afrikaner capital had begun consolidating in 1918 with the formation of the South African National Trust Company (Santam) and its life-assurance arm, Sanlam. The two institutions provided support to farmers and agricultural cooperatives in the Cape, and quickly began self-consciously appealing to the *volk* to attract more business. In 1921, the chairman's report read:

> Sanlam is an extensive institution of the Afrikaner *volk* in the wider sense of the word. As an Afrikaner, you will naturally give preference to an Afrikaner institution. I would just remind policy holders that we are busy furnishing employment to young Afrikaners, and training them in the assurance field. We hereby intend to provide a great service to South Africa. If we want to become economically self-reliant then we must support our own institutions. To that end, Sanlam offers you the opportunity.[231]

WA Hofmeyer, the founder of Santam, also established the Nasionale Pers (Naspers), a publishing company that was to produce *Die Burger*, the important nationalist newspaper under the first editorship of DF Malan.

The goal of the two financial institutions was to pool the money of their Afrikaner members and invest in production, yet Santam remained relatively small until the late 1930s. In the same decade the *Broederbond* created an Afrikaner bank, Volkskas, which marketed itself, with the help of the FAK, to rural Transvalers. Certain other small existing Afrikaner institutions in the Transvaal, such as the funeral group AVBOB (*Afrikaner Verbond Begrafnis Ondernemings Beperk*), were gradually smelted into the Bond.

In 1937, however, the two relatively weak Afrikaner groups, the Bond and Santam, agreed to a national alliance while the *Broederbond* was organising – what else? – a conference on poor whiteism. The two groups eventually organised the Economic Congress of the People (*Ekonomiese Volkskongres*) in 1939, which laid the groundwork for the economic expansion of Afrikaner nationalism. Significantly, the congress was carefully planned to occur soon after the centenary celebrations of the Great Trek, also known as the *Eeufees* or *Tweede Trek*.[232] Through the influence it had gained in Afrikaner cultural life over the previous two decades, and the persistent pressure of nationalism on the Afrikaners, the Bond was in a prime position to organise Afrikaner mass mobilisation along cultural lines. As O'Meara tells it:[233] 'By any standards the four-month event was great political and cultural theatre. Though initially there was little popular enthusiasm, by the time the *Tweede Trek* began, the Bond had prepared the ground for a massive cultural orgy.' The *Tweede Trek* was a masterclass in myth-making, in inventing history. 'Nine replicas of the oxwagons of the Voortrekkers, each named after a Voortrekker hero, travelled slowly from Cape Town to Pretoria, visiting as many towns as possible. All along the route ever larger crowds met the wagons with passionate enthusiasm.' Gone was the mention of Afrikaner division. Few mentioned that the Voortrekkers only represented a part of what became the Afrikaners, and were certainly not supported by all. But not now – now the Voortrekkers and their oxwagons became a symbol for the united Afrikaners, for a shared history:

> Men grew beards and women donned Voortrekker dress; street after street in hamlet after hamlet was renamed after one or other Trek hero; babies were baptised in the shade of the wagons – one was christened '*Eeufesia*' (best translated as 'Centennalia') – and young couples were married in full trekker regalia on the village green before the wagons. With tearful eyes old men and women climbed onto the wagons – 'Lord now lettest thy servant depart in peace,' said one old man – and the young ones jostled with one another in their efforts to rub grease from the wagon axles onto their handkerchief. Monuments were raised up and the wagons were pulled through freshly laid concrete so that the imprint of their tracks could be preserved forever. [233]

Few in modern South Africa would know where these immortal tracks now lie.

According to *Die Burger*, over 100 000 Afrikaners gathered at Monument Koppie in Pretoria on 16 December 1938 where three female descendants of the Voortrekker leaders Retief, Potgieter and Pretorius laid the foundation stone of the *Voortrekkermonument*, which still broods in the hills above Pretoria. The date for the ceremony was carefully chosen – it marked the anniversary of the Battle of Blood River, the Day of Dingaan, when the Afrikaners received a heavenly mandate to govern South Africa. The message now was clear. After years in the wilderness of poverty, God smiled once again on the Afrikaners and gave them his mandate to rule.

In the resultant fever of nationalism (a fever encouraged in part by the *Broederbond*) the *volk*, it was reasoned, would come together and be more receptive to the ideas proposed by the *Volkskongres*. During the celebrations, in which DF Malan told the Afrikaners their new Blood River was in the cities, the well-known pastor Kestell, who had ministered to the Boer commandos at the turn of the century, turned his gaze upon the disunited *volk* now coming together again amidst the creak of reconstructed oxwagons and asked of them a *reddingsdaad* – an act of salvation – by which the *volk* would rescue itself from poverty. His words, *"n volk red homself* (a people rescues or redeems itself), would become the slogan of Afrikaner economic expansion – its mantra and its comfort as it took the fight to the cities, blacks and British. His appeal for an act of salvation was taken literally by the *volk*, who set up the *reddingsdaadfonds* – a charity that collected money for the Afrikaner poor as the wagons made their way to Pretoria.

The *Volkskongres* resulted in the adoption of *volkskapitalisme*. As LJ du Plessis, chair of a committee investigating the creation of an Afrikaner finance company, put it:

> [In the past] we also accepted that the masses who were unable quickly and easily to adapt to capitalism would sink into poor whiteism. Sympathetically we belittled them and distanced ourselves from them, at best philanthropically offering them 'alms' or poor relief from the state. And meanwhile this process of adjustment was destroying our *volk* by denationalising its economic leaders . . . But, in the awakening of consciousness, the *volk* has perceived this too, and the new national economic movement sets for itself the goal of reversing this process; no longer to tolerate the destruction of the Afrikaner *volk* in an attempt to adapt to a foreign capitalist system, but to mobilise the *volk* to capture this foreign system and adapt it to our national character.[234]

In a later speech at the *Volkskongres*, on the subject of people's banks, JH van Vuuren said:

> So long as nearly 300 000 Afrikaans-speakers live below the breadline; so long as a large percentage of our fellow Afrikaners remain the hewers of wood and the drawers of water in their own country; so long as the Afrikaner is notable by his absence in our business life; and so long as a large section of the agrarian population are forced by circumstances to migrate to the cities in order to make a living, millions of pounds belonging to Afrikaners lie around unproductively.[235]

The end result of this congress was the adoption of the resolution to encourage Afrikaner investment and centralise their savings so the money could be used to further uplift the *volk*. Significantly, it tied the economic movement and the increasing nationalism of Afrikaners directly to the poor whites. Moreover, it linked poor whites directly to a desire for control of the state. Swept away on the tide of determined nationalism, future apartheid prime minister, HF Verwoerd, stated in his speech at the congress that the purpose of the economic movement was so that the Afrikaner could take his legitimate place in South African industry: 'What weapons can Afrikanerdom use in this great struggle?' he asked. 'There is that of state power. If we can take possession of it, public credit could be used, *inter alia*, for the founding of industrial banks, and firmly to establish Afrikaner undertakings, particularly industry.'[236]

The congress saw the formation of, among others, the Economic Institute of the FAK in order to create Afrikaner economic policies, the Afrikaans Commercial Institute (*Afrikaanse Handelsinstituut*, or AHI), which was an alliance of Afrikaner retailers, and the expansion of the role of the *Reddingsdaadsfonds* into a separate organisation, the *Reddingsdaadbond*[237]

(RDB), mandated to mobilise mass support for Afrikaner businesses and Afrikaans culture. The RDB was specifically concerned with healing the class divisions among Afrikaners and making the poor acceptable to the *volk* – 'the integration of the Afrikaner worker in the life of the *volk* as a whole, of which he forms an organic part, and from which we must not allow him to be sundered'.[238] As World War II raged, RDB membership rose from 45 890 in 282 branches to 67 131 in 343 branches in 1942. Despite a campaign for achieving 100 000 members, the RDB membership steadily declined after the war, and after the poor white problem had been solved, so that by 1952 it had virtually ceased to exist. During its height, however, the RDB had a significant influence on the business and cultural life of Afrikaners. It provided cheap life-assurance policies and burial schemes, set up trade schools, provided small loans and loans for study, and created an investment vehicle to trade in the shares of listed Afrikaner companies. And from a cultural perspective, 'each RDB branch had a department devoted to the regulation of every minute of the "free time" of its local constituents. These *vryetydsafdelings*[239] organised traditional dances, plays, concerts and art contests. They set up travelling libraries, handicraft schools, discussion groups, etc. A cultural mesh was woven around the local Afrikaner community in which all cultural activities were controlled by the RDB.'[240] The organisation even set up a film company that produced films with Afrikaner themes and developed Afrikaner boardgames, such as *Slagveld*, 'a variation of snakes and ladders, involving Boers and Kaffirs'.[241]

The Economic Congress of the People sketched the blueprint to rescue the poor whites and uplift the *volk*. The decisions made there would dominate Afrikaner life well into apartheid.

A white language

The thread tying Afrikaners across all classes was their language. Whereas Dutch had been born from the sea, one observer said that Afrikaans had been born from the *veldt* and the mountains.[242] Any effort to achieve Afrikaner unity had to take Afrikaans into account – a small, scrappy language that was by no means assured to achieve mass adoption. If the Afrikaners had to battle the 'greedy English' and native competition for their economic upliftment, their language would have to overcome not only English, with its significant advantages, but Dutch itself, which was preferred by the Afrikaner elite until the early twentieth century. And the new language, that 'mongrel patois',[243] was by no means regarded as a white language, and certainly not as a language of prosperity. In order to use Afrikaans as a weapon for white Afrikaner unity, the language itself had to be scrubbed clean of its poor and multicultural roots, and presented to the world as an authentic, new 'European' language.

By the middle of the nineteenth century, it seemed certain that English would triumph over both Dutch and Afrikaans as the language of the *volk*. In the Crown colony of the Cape, it was argued, it was self-evident that English should be the language of the government and the press. English was the language of business and English was the language of a vast body of literature and knowledge. English was already the language of schools, with scant attention paid to Dutch. In 1859, the Dutch Reformed Church in the Cape even began presenting some sermons in English, arguing that Dutch sermons were not widely understood by the congregation and that the church risked losing the Afrikaners to the English churches. If the Boers adopted English, it would foster national unity and social progress, enabling them to take their rightful place among the European nations in South Africa.[244]

Dutch, as it was spoken in Europe, was already nearly extinct in the Cape, argued the *Cape Argus* in 1857. The Boer elite clutched tightly to their modern Latin, but the Boers as a whole already preferred 'the miserable, bastard jargon' to which they had not yet given a name. This dialect, felt the *Cape Monitor* in 1857, did unimaginable damage to the Afrikaners. 'It cramps your thoughts. It impedes your energies. It brings the blush to every modest woman's cheeks, and makes the educated recoil with disgust too often. It corrupts the morals of your children, and befouls their innocent expressions . . . '[245] Those in support of Dutch as the language of the Afrikaners argued that it was the language of their religion, of the Bible and of their Dutch identity – their last link to that far European land they had left. 'Language, nationality and religion,' argued *De Zuid-Afrikaan* in 1857, 'are in every *volk* closely linked – to such an extent that if you remove one, you deprive the strength of the others.'[246] By the 1880s, increased agitation by the British to control South Africa, leading, among others, to the First Anglo-Boer War, resulted in significant anti-English sentiment, renewed calls for Afrikaner unity and the first '*taalbeweging*', or language movement for Afrikaans. The period saw the creation of the Cape *Afrikanerbond*, the *Broederbond*, the *Genootskap van Regte Afrikaners* (Fellowship of True Afrikaners, or GRA) and the proto-Afrikaans newspaper *Die Afrikaanse Patriot*. Campaigners for Afrikaans emphasised the unbreakable link between language and *volk*: 'Without language, no nation. Therefore, Afrikaanders, honour your country, your *volk* and your language!,' wrote SJ du Toit, the founder of the Afrikaner Bond party, in 1874. The following year, the GRA manifesto stated:

> The language in which we learnt to say 'mother' and 'father', the language of our first impressions, the language our dear mothers taught us the name of our Lord Jesus, the language in which our parents served their

> God, the language in which our father cautioned us on his deathbed, the language in which our mother, with her dying breath, said a prayer for us – this language is holy. We would not exchange it for any other and any attempt to take it away we regard as an insult to the memory of our forefathers, as oppression, and as injustice towards our children.[246]

Language and *volk* and God were intertwined and united against English oppression, against an English assault on their very identity.

Yet the English were not the only ones opposing Afrikaans. Dutch newspapers called Afrikaans 'a language without grammar, a Hottentot language, gibberish, a confusion of nonsense and idiocy, the language of shepherds and kitchens . . . it was in reaction to these and similar ideas that the campaigners for Afrikaans emphasised its Germanic character and denied the coloured contributions to its creation and spread.'[247] In August 1875, the front page of SJ du Toit's *Die Patriot* read, in screaming capital letters, 'OUR LANGUAGE IS A PURE GERMANIC LANGUAGE'.[248]

Despite these divisions, the campaigners did succeed in winning ground against the domination of the English language in the Cape. In 1882 members were allowed to speak Dutch in parliament and in the same year, schools were allowed to teach classes in Dutch. In 1895 magistrates had to have knowledge of Dutch to be permanently appointed. In the 1890s, leading theologians also began linking God, *volk* and language. Adriaan Moorrees wrote that every nation had a holy calling on this earth and that the Afrikaner *volk* was guided by the hand of God – so it was especially important for Afrikaners to hold onto their language, as 'what the *volk* is, is thanks to the language'. Another theologian, PJG de Vos, wrote in 1892 that God had a special task for the Afrikaner nation: 'That is why I place such emphasis on our nationality and the language of our church and our *volk*. They are woven together.'[249] In 1890 the *Zuid-Afrikaansche Taalbond* was founded in Cape Town, with De Vos as chairman, to promote the *volkstaal*, or language of the *volk*. Whether this would be Afrikaans or Dutch, it was decided, would be left to later generations.[250]

In the far north of the country, the Transvaal Republic under Paul Kruger had been established as a Dutch republic, with Dutch, and not Afrikaans, as the language of the government. The discovery of gold brought thousands upon thousands of immigrants to the Johannesburg goldfields, who relied on English as their common language, leading to fears among the Afrikaners that their language (or languages) would be overwhelmed by the imperial tongue. English was in fashion among young Afrikaners and 'by the time Boer children had learnt a dozen English words it was all they spoke and it soon became the language of their social and religious life. The danger [of losing Afrikaans] was greater as many of them were ashamed of Afrikaans and found English easier than Dutch.'[251] Before the Anglo-Boer War, this led to increased measures by the Transvaal Republic to enforce Dutch, and not Afrikaans, in schools and government. Afrikaner opponents of these measures felt that enforcing Dutch upon the *volk* was just as bad as enforcing English and that the government of Paul Kruger was discriminating against Afrikaners. It is significant that those in favour of Afrikaans in the Transvaal included Hertzog, Smuts and (later) DF Malan, as well the Boer generals Botha, De Wet and De la Rey.

The small advances made by the Dutch language in the Cape and the distractions of industrialisation in the north meant that the first language movement gradually died down. In the aftermath of the Anglo-Boer War, as the defeated, degraded and impoverished Afrikaners found themselves in a British South Africa, the battle for Afrikaans flared up again. In 1902, a banished Jan Smuts wrote to the theologian Abraham Fischer, predicting further setbacks for the Afrikaners, in part because they were 'plunged so deep, so wretchedly deep, into poverty and misery; and in part because the British were doing everything they could to anglicise the upcoming Afrikaner generation. It was the duty of Afrikaners to be on their guard.' Afrikaner poverty and the threats to the Afrikaans language were tied together, and they both needed to be solved if the Afrikaner was to be triumphant. The struggle against the *verengelsing*[252] of the *volk* was also led by the Dutch churches, which were again worried about losing their congregations to an English God, prompting Milner to exasperatedly wonder why 'the Church attaches so much importance to the thorough study of grammatical Dutch, about which the farmers left to themselves do not care a jot'.[253]

As the campaign for Afrikaans grew ever louder, the opposition from the English press intensified, once again emphasising the non-white origins of Afrikaans or its coloured contributions. In 1903 the *Transvaal Advertiser* wrote that Afrikaans had originated from the Low Dutch spoken by the sailors and craftsmen of the Dutch East India Company. In the Cape it was further modified by contributions from 'Malay, Hottentot and Kafir languages'. Why even bother to fight for such a language? mused the newspaper. In a sense, the newspaper was correct. The earliest printed examples of Afrikaans are written in Arabic, the script used to spell out Afrikaans words and phrases. The historian Achmat Davids points out that during the 1800s Muslim slaves in the Cape preferred Afrikaans as the white Afrikaners fought over Dutch and the new language.[254] The *Pretoria News* named Afrikaans an anachronism that was sure to die out in a generation. It was a '"mongrel patois", which without wishing to hurt anyone's feeling, must be pronounced absolutely impossible as a language'.[255] The novelist Olive Schreiner called it 'a linguistic wall which has grown up between the South African Dutch farmer and the outer world, thus cutting off the former from all the liberal movements of the last two centuries'.[256]

'Do you think the Boers will love and admire their conquerors for openly trying to Anglicise their children and for putting their language on the same footing practically as Zulu, Sesutu, or any other foreign language?' asked the Afrikaner leader General Louis Botha of the English. His letter, published in the *Times* of London in 1903, was an opening salvo in the renewed fight for Afrikaans, which was an easy shorthand for Afrikaner dignity. As Afrikaner nationalism increased, so did the struggle for Afrikaans, the holy language of the *volk*. Throughout, the emphasis was placed on Afrikaans as a white man's language. In 1905, the academic Gustav Preller called it 'the purest and youngest branch of the Germanic languages'. In 1914, under Smuts, Afrikaans, and not Dutch, became taught in schools and in the same year, the author CJ Langenhoven (who later wrote *Die Stem van Suid-Afrika*, which was adopted as the national anthem) argued that Afrikaans was 'the only white language which was created in South Africa and was not imported from over the sea, which carries the joy and sadness of everything that we and our forefathers lived through, struggled through and triumphed over; the one thread tying us together as a nation; the expression of our *volk*'s soul'.[257] In 1922, *De Burger* published its first edition in Afrikaans. DF Malan, then editor, argued in the front page article under the headline 'Our Own' that nations and languages were not the creation of governments and academics, but were created through the unknowable hand of God. 'Even today,' he wrote, 'we have thousands of people who have not realised that we are a separate *volk* with our own language and that both are the gift of our Creator. What his plan is, only time will tell. Our duty is to remain true to ourselves and our own.'[258] The triumph of the nationalists became the triumph of Afrikaans (and thereby proof of God's favour). In

1925, under Hertzog, Afrikaans became an officially recognised language and in 1933 the Bible was translated into its newest holy vessel.

In the 1930s, as Afrikaner nationalism was fired up by the threat of white poverty and fed by nationalist organisations, Afrikaans developed even more. In 1930, the Afrikaans Language and Cultural Association (ATKV) was formed by 12 members of the railway services – the old home of the poor whites. The *Broederbond* exerted a particularly powerful influence on Afrikaans via the FAK:

> Under Bond direction many local organisations were formed, many campaigns waged. Typical of these was the call by the Afrikaans National Students' Union: 'Never shop where you are not served in Afrikaans, and where Afrikaans is not accorded its rightful place on notices and signboards – and tell the trader why. Pay no accounts which have not been issued in Afrikaans, and patronise no firm which does not advertise in Afrikaans newspapers and magazines.'[259]

In 1936 Nicolaas Dierichs, Bond chairman and founder of the *Reddingsdaadbond*, emphasised the connection between the language and economic struggle in the Afrikaans National Students' Union journal *Wapenskou*: 'Consider further how you can contribute to the struggle. Act individually, act together with others, but ACT, ACT, ACT! We must seize the [economic] struggle and win through.'[260] By the end of the 1930s, Afrikaans had been made white – its coloured speakers and non-white origins ignored or belittled. As Afrikaner nationalism made way for apartheid, so too did the struggle for Afrikaans cease being one for respectability, but one of domination, culminating in the 1974 decree for Afrikaans to be the language of instruction (along with English) in black schools throughout South Africa. Two years later, on 16 June, the Soweto uprisings left

174 dead as an estimated 20 000 students marched in protest against this law.

The struggle for Afrikaans was not only waged in speeches and on podiums. To be a respectable language and to hold its own against the vast literary wealth of English, Afrikaans had to have a printed press. Afrikaans had to have literature. Organisations like the FAK and the ATKV enthusiastically sponsored writing competitions in a bid to encourage an Afrikaans canon. To a large degree they were successful. Afrikaans quickly developed books, poetry and short stories, and soon boasted an established crop of Afrikaans writers, such as CJ Langenhoven and later NP van Wyk Louw. In 1915 the Afrikaans publishing company De Nasionale Pers (Naspers) was established in the Cape to publish *De Burger*. The company was in part founded through money provided by JH Marais, a campaigner for Afrikaans who also established the initially Afrikaans-language University of Stellenbosch through a vast donation in his will. The following year Naspers published its first magazine, *De Huisgenoot*, to serve as 'the university of the *volk*'. In 1918 Naspers created the *Burger Boekhandel* to publish Afrikaans books. Other newspapers by other publishers, such as the *Transvaler* and *Volksblad*, soon followed as well as more academic journals, such as *Inspan* and *Koers*. *Koers* (or 'Direction'), which appeared in the 1930s, 'was effectively the theoretical journal of a major faction of the Bond'[261] and served as a platform for the spreading of Bond policies.

As the second, or post-Boer War, language struggle waged, Hertzog, in his role as advocate for Afrikaans, recommended that 'an organisation be established for the promotion of the Holland language and literature in South Africa'. During the language struggle, 'Holland' was used to refer to Afrikaans and 'The Netherlands' to refer to pure Dutch. In 1909 the South African Academy of Arts and Sciences was created (the *Zuid-*

Afrikaanse Akademie voor Taal, Letteren en Kunst). The academy's goal was 'maintaining and advancing Holland language and literature as well as South African history, antiquarian science and art'. The academy was careful to point out that by Holland language it meant 'both language variations used in South Africa'. The academy created the Hertzog Prize, still the most prestigious award for Afrikaans literature, and the Academy Award for the best translation into Afrikaans. Various other awards would soon follow for the promotion of Afrikaans literature, literary criticism, children's literature and literary science, such as the Louis Hiemstra Prize, the Eugène Marais Prize, the Gustav Preller Prize, the Scheepers Prize, the Tienie Holloway Prize and the CJ Langenhoven Prize. The academy established a Language Commission to unofficially regulate the Afrikaans language – similar to the French and Spanish academies. Its decisions are published on average every decade in the *Afrikaanse Woordelys & Spelreëls*, where it decides on correct Afrikaans usage.

As a natural consequence of the environment in which they were created, the first Afrikaans books displayed a preoccupation with many of the political concerns of the Afrikaner *volk*. Unlike English, which only offers idyllic pastoral novels, Afrikaans has an entire genre dedicated to the farm and farm life. These *plaasromans*, as the genre is called, initially sung the praises of country life but changed as times changed. As urbanisation became an increasing part of Afrikaner life, the farm novels took on the atmosphere of the end of an era. Literary historian Ampie Coetzee says that:

> . . . virtually every early farm novel featured elements of people leaving the farm . . . Some of them did return to the farm, although they were not heard from again; some continued struggling and vanished from the novel. Others went to the city and became 'Afrikaners in respectable

> positions'. But the majority went to the city and became part of the poor proletarian classes. The poor whites.[262]

In all of the canonised early farm novels (published between the 1910s and the 1950s), the farmers were threatened by outside forces that had the potential of ruining their way of life and forcing them into poor whiteism:

> Drought, phylloxera, hail, locusts, disease, medical bills, tobacco tax, sinking market prices and the farmer's ignorance of the markets. Wool which was sold at low prices, rising interest rates, depression, land which was bought when wool prices were high and could not be maintained, land mortgages. Farmers who did not store enough grain for the lean years. Human and natural causes contributed equally to the decline. But there would be no farm novel if not for the looming threat of the end of a way of life.'[263]

The city constantly figures as a symbol of destruction, of corruption and threat. In *Die Burgermeester van Slaplaagte*, Jochem van Bruggen writes (in 1954) that once the innocent Afrikaners from the countryside find themselves in the city, these 'children of the *veldt* . . . are lonely amidst the built masses and human activity. The mad rush and noise deadens their will and personality, making them only half the persons they were on the outside . . . A tremendous deadness reigns over the massive human constructions, etched by naked, narrow streets on which no living soul can be seen. A place where the day is born old.' Those who go to the city are too lazy, too unworthy to work on the farm and, once in the city, they drink and gamble and steal. And if not the dregs of humanity, then they were symbols of resigned sadness – an old farmer unable to find work and forced to join the ranks of the poor.[264]

Johannesburg figures largely as this modern Gomorrah. In *Donker Johannesburg*, written in 1910 during the time of Fordsburg, slums and brickmakers, J Lub's narrator walks through the city and sees drunks and prison cells. 'He hears of Asians which are legally allowed to smoke opium, sees shops selling stolen goods, men abusing their small children, drunk women. He experiences the misery of a mineworker descending into the earth "to dig for the gold he sees as a curse", which lowers him to work with Chinese and Kaffers and to take orders from people he would not receive in his own home. He hears a story of misery so great that he can't fully repeat it.'[265] The city brought poverty to the Afrikaners – not only economic, but also cultural. Van Bruggen often writes of the development of a class system dividing Afrikaners into rich and poor: 'Poor Afrikaners become servants, not only to foreigners, but to other Afrikaners.' The farmers who had lost their land and trekked to the city had lost their identity, their Afrikanerdom. 'To farm successfully meant keeping your land and ensuring the continuity of the generations on the farm. To farm badly meant losing your land and losing your roots. Farming successfully meant keeping your history and your identity. The result: poor whites had no identity and no history. No future.'[266]

As eugenic thinking about the inherent deficiency of poor whites took hold, so too did the portrayals of them change – from criminals to the simple-minded. In *Ampie. Die Natuurkind*, Van Bruggen writes tenderly of Ampie, a 'child of the Afrikaner', who lives a simple and tragic existence as a poor white with no potential to improve his lot in life. 'There is nothing to spark the desire for the comforts of a white man's life. The striving to stand higher than the kaffir who lives just as them, and often better, is dead.'[267] Coetzee notes that, for the characters and the narrator, the comparison with blacks, and black workers, denotes the most dire level of degradation.[268] As eugenics faded into Afrikaner nationalism, so too did poverty virtually disappear from Afrikaans literature. And as nationalism faded into disgrace, the theme of poverty in Afrikaner literature reappeared and culminated in *Triomf* (Triumph) by Marlene van Niekerk. The characters of *Triomf*, a poor white suburb in Johannesburg built over the remains of the vibrant black suburb Sophiatown, live their lives in the early 1990s, plagued by uncertainty over the outcome of the looming democratic elections in 1994. Van Niekerk treats her characters without sentiment. They are not simple-minded or thieves, but rather whites sunk into grotesque poverty – racist, cruel and inbred, disillusioned by the promises of the National Party. Although the nation had been uplifted and the poor white problem was no more, the characters of *Triomf* are left behind. The journey of the poor whites had ended, from the farms to the cities to poverty to political power and eventual disappearance into the middle class. Those left behind had nothing except their poverty, their invisibility and the promises of the party that had once championed them: 'There is a light at the end of the journey, they say. Not a gun at the end of the journey or a bread or a factory or a hawker's licence. No, always a damned light, a pillar of fire, a Spirit, a Higher Idea, an Ideal of bloody unity or something. And all of it because we all supposedly have the same culture. What damned thing is that?, I ask you with tears in my light-blue poor white eyes.'[269]

From poor whites to pure whites

The massive ethnic movement to uplift poor whites and their eventual disappearance were tied to two factors outside the state or Afrikaner control. Historian David Yudelman[270] argues that, if any date should be chosen as marking the turning point for the modern South African state, it should be 1933, when the gold price effectively doubled. This enabled massive state intervention to uplift the Afrikaners. In 1939, the Department of Labour reported that it could provide work for every man willing to do unskilled labour on relief works and projects aimed at alleviating poverty. This enabled the solution of the poor white problem through increased employment and a general multiplier effect. The other factor was the wartime economy of World War II, which took care of the rest: 'During the war years the demand for labour was so high that the government could stop supplying jobs specifically for unskilled whites.'[271] In 1939 'there had been in existence a total of 40 Afrikaner credit institutions, controlling funds to the value of £27 m. Ten years later, an AHI survey indicated that the number of Afrikaner credit undertakings had risen to 68, whilst funds under their control had grown to £74.4 m.'[272] Between 1936 and 1970, the number of Afrikaners working in the public sector grew from 97 000 to 268 000 – about 34.4 per cent of the total Afrikaner labour force. By 1977 there were 22 state-owned companies under Afrikaner management and employing mainly Afrikaners. In the 1970s unemployment was virtually unknown among Afrikaners.

In 1950 the FAK and RDB convened a second economic congress. LJ du Plessis once again gave the opening address, declaring that the great *reddingsdaad* had been completed: 'The poor white problem no longer exists and Afrikanerdom is now established in the most important strategic points in urban commerce.'[273] The previous year, Diedrichs, the Bond chairman, had even attacked 'Afrikaner apathy' after the steady decline of the RDB. Some new spectacular event, he said, was needed to re-ignite popular enthusiasm.[274] It was not to be. Without the threat of white poverty in front of them, without their worst fears of race suicide and the death of the *volk* constantly on display, the Afrikaners would not come together again in the same way.

Through the upliftment of the poor whites the *volk* was supposed to have been made whole, and Afrikaner prestige was on a much firmer footing. At the 1938 celebrations of the Great Trek, DF Malan made a key comment, remarkable for its admonitory as well as celebratory tenor: 'South Africa expects of its poor whites that they remain white and live white.'[275] That had largely been achieved. The poor whites had been made pure. The poor did not disappear, of course, but large-scale poverty did. The nationalist governments were now free to focus their full attention on the repression of blacks and the gathering of power, culminating in the institution of apartheid in 1948. Although apartheid has been described as an 'anti-poverty programme for whites',[276] it is also useful to view it as a system for, not only white dominance, but also one that sustained white prestige. Eliminating large-scale white poverty was crucial to establishing that prestige, but to maintain the prestige necessitated virtually writing poor whites out of South African cultural history. The re-imagining of Afrikaners as not having been poor was so successful that by 1968 the liberal politician Margaret Ballinger wrote in her memoirs that 'it is difficult now to remember or to appreciate the dark shadow which poor whiteism cast over this country in the 1920s and '30s of this century. Yet it was the formative force in standardising the relationship between black and white in this country.'[277]

The good whites

He was afraid of dying, the young man told the researcher. His arms were crossed with deep scars where he had tried to kill himself. He was often depressed and suffered from alcoholism.

He had no home, but rented a small garden shed of four square metres. The shed was in the backyard of a house owned by a coloured family – something that shamed him deeply.

He lived in this *'hokkie'* with his male partner of 15 years, but things weren't going well. His partner drank too much and often had unprotected sex with black African prostitutes who were happy to exchange sex for liquor.

He was afraid of dying because the prostitutes might have HIV/AIDS. This terrified him. He and his partner fought often. He lived in Ruyterwacht, where the poor whites had gone after they had been uplifted. It was where the poor whites were forgotten. They are still there.[278]

Every Tuesday and Thursday the routine is the same. On the long tree-lined road that cuts into Ruyterwacht, connecting it with the outside world, the old people trudge with their empty grocery bags.

At Rita's Tuck Shop (the 'T' naturally substituted with a poorly scrawled 'F') they turn right and walk towards the school. Rita's Coca-Cola sign advertises the necessities: cigarettes and toilet paper. The shop is run from a home – moderately sized, unassuming.

As the old people move on, singly or in groups, they pass open yards containing broken-down caravans and scrapped cars. Both serve as accommodation. Anticipating the muttered weekly march, a number of enterprising residents have also begun painting signs in sloppy white paint on their garden walls:

Tuck Shop. Cigarettes.

Somewhat oddly, one driveway contains a speedboat. Polished and gleaming.

Turning the corner again, the road runs past a school. The sounds of children come from inside the stately and somewhat run-down white building. Weeds grow between cement slabs. The netball court is cracked and dry. The voice of a teacher thunders loudly behind wooden shutters.

At the gate they are greeted by name and asked for their identification. One by one the old people root around in their handbags and pockets to produce a dirty white card.

Only in rare cases does the photo resemble the one presenting it. They had gone to great lengths to get their photo taken properly – hair made up, make-up or tie, a smile. Having your photo taken is an event and one must look respectable. They have no such concerns today.

The guard checks each card. It reads: Ruyterwacht Senior Centre. No one else is allowed in, the guard says. People steal food or belongings.

There are only so many donations to go around. 'You know how times are,' he shrugs.

Once through, they loudly greet friends and nod respectfully to the matron in charge. The school hall is filled with tables and talking and the smell of onions and perfume. They take their seats and wait for the sermon to begin.

A bell rings outside and the school children, mostly coloured, surge shouting onto the playground.

* * *

As the Afrikaner *volk* was imagined into being and its members climbed quickly into the middle class, the poor whites vanished from public discourse. Those who remained poor while the *volk* grew richer were seen as shameful and lazy. Not true members of the *volk* and not existing in sufficient numbers to pose a threat to the ruling classes and the new culture of Afrikanerdom. The *volk* was quick to wipe the traces of poverty from its mouth, focusing on the triumphs of the Afrikaner against the British and blacks. The story of the Afrikaner became one of victory, of triumph, and maintaining this prestige meant quickly forgetting the slums, the shacks, the brick-making pits and transport riders.

Where did those who stayed poor go? They stayed on in their enclaves of poverty – in the poor white suburbs, in the council estates. On the railways. Their neighbours grew richer and moved away, and the poor whites were forgotten. The system of social grants for the poor that had so uplifted the *volk* remained in place, keeping the remaining poor fed but not angry. The government had one last trick to play. In the 1930s, as the Depression crept across the country, a number of poor white suburbs were established with the express aim of uplifting the poor. The inhabitants were taught how to become 'good' whites and respectable members of the *volk*. Although those who lived there were poor, they were not expected to remain poor. They were taught how to be middle class.

The first of these suburbs was Jan Hofmeyer, established in 1936 in central Johannesburg. Two years later, Epping Garden Village was established on the Cape Flats. 'Eventually every South African town of substance had at least one poor white area,' notes social scientist Annika Teppo. In her remarkable dissertation, *The Making of a Good White*, Teppo argues that:

> . . . the end product of the rehabilitation conducted in the suburbs was supposed to be a successful and respectable citizen who moved out to live in a middle-class area. But while many of the poor whites of Epping Garden Village managed to leave the suburb, some never did . . . those who could not succeed became stigmatised. In the era of apartheid, the poor white suburbs became places where those who were unable to comply with the ideals of being a good white were placed, or into which they just drifted.[279]

Epping Garden Village serves as a model of these white spaces that sprouted in cities during the middle decades of the twentieth century. Today it is known as Ruyterwacht – a Cape Town area notorious for its white poverty.

A geographer with no knowledge of Ruyterwacht would be able to discern much from a map of the area. The suburb is capped by Goodwood to the north, where the streets are laid out in rows. Train tracks divide the two areas, and to the south, multiple train lines stab into the industrial area of Epping. The residents of the suburb clearly depend on the factories to provide work, and the trains to provide cheap transport. Owning a car would be rare. To the west the suburb is bordered (literally by Border Road) by the giant lit complex of the GrandWest casino and to the east a large open space separates it from the poor neighbourhood of Elsie's River. The area was clearly meant to be distinct from the surrounding neighbourhoods. Yet something is odd. Although the street patterns of the bordering suburbs indicate they were laid out in the late nineteenth and early twentieth centuries, Ruyterwacht's streets are laid out almost as a design to be read from the air.

The blocks are large and spacious – unusual for a poor or working-class area. The main street running into the suburb is Jan van Riebeek, the Dutch 'founder' of South Africa, which loops around a central circle (Vereniging or unity) before exiting Ruyterwacht as Livingstone Avenue – the significance of these street names perhaps denotes Afrikaner/British unity. On a map Ruyterwacht is a puzzle that can only explained by its history.

In 1926 the Dutch Reformed Church, the ACVV welfare organisation and prominent Cape business leaders formed the Citizen's Housing League (CHL), an Afrikaner housing company, to provide accommodation for the poor. The church had been involved in similar efforts since the discovery of the poor white problem in the 1880s, creating farming settlements such as the one at Kakamas for the upliftment of the poor. Says Teppo: 'There were also institutions for orphans and the disabled and teahouses for the aged. Between 1919 and 1932 the church had also built 160 boarding schools in the Cape "for the needy". In 1932 approximately 8 000 children lived in these boarding houses.'[280]

The CHL's first housing scheme for poor whites was the Good Hope Model Village in Cape Town and, in the late 1930s the company built Epping Garden Village. In 1938, in what used to be Epping Forest, the new suburb was opened with 700 'white' houses for the respectable and deserving poor. 'Everyone classified as white had to be situated in a space that would uplift this person. It was considered self-evident that whites needed more of everything: larger houses, more space in the yard, better services, and, in order to maintain all this, higher incomes.'[281] 'White' spaces produced proper whites.

In 1948 JH Albertyn, the moral expert for the Carnegie Commission, voiced his favour for these poor suburbs:

> There is a real need for model villages or residential areas near our cities. An example of this is the village of Epping Garden near Cape Town . . . Most of the houses are inhabited by less affluent Afrikaners . . . with a true Afrikaans spirit ruling in the village . . . in spite of all the men working in the city, the home atmosphere is Christian-Afrikaans. The new situation, created by the influx into town, necessitates the church to strive for the construction of similar villages or residential areas in the future. Not only in the countryside, as had been the case thus far, but particularly near the cities. In this way newly arrived congregation members can acquire healthy and affordable housing, and the church can maintain its influence over them.[282]

The idea behind the CHL's projects was to provide housing at very cheap rents to poor whites. This would take some of the financial pressure off them, allowing them to save, eat better, perform well at their jobs and eventually buy their own homes and move out of the suburb. But, as Smuts put it, you needed people with the right stuff. The CHL had a stringent selection process for allowing people to live in its houses. They wanted poor whites, but they wanted poor whites with the potential to improve. The CHL stipulated young white families who earned more than £10 per month, but less than £20. A resident of Ruyterwacht described this process to Teppo, which involved an initial application process and interview, as well as a visit by a social worker to the prospective family, 'who wanted to make sure they were who they had claimed to be: honourable, proper white people whom the CHL wanted as tenants'.[283] The CHL was also not too picky about race: 'Although the first residents were chosen very carefully, their racial purity was not as important as their ability to become good whites, the perceived potential for upliftment. A suitable tenant, who behaved and managed his finances correctly, who appeared neat and civilised, could be of darkish complexion, although too obvious blackness was frowned upon.' The company's more relaxed attitude towards race did not last, however. From the 1950s, as pass laws and identification documents came into effect, the company could not allow any candidates who weren't 'certified' as whites on their official papers. This also meant that the CHL was forced to change its strict requirements for entry as white Afrikaners moved out of poverty and into the middle classes. 'This led to a lack of suitable tenant candidates. The company saw no other choice but to accept those whites whom they would not have accommodated before.'

As well as cheap rents, Epping Garden Village offered the poor the 'white' standards they had not previously been able to afford. 'The houses were spacious, new and whitewashed. Every house stood on a big plot, where residents could cultivate vegetables and fruit to enhance their diet. Gardening and the work it entailed were seen as beneficial for the body and rehabilitation of the residents.'[284] The neighbourhood was a far cry from the slums the Afrikaner poor had come from. To ensure that they upheld white standards and practices of living, the inhabitants were monitored by social workers and priests, who would visit the families at home and question them about their progress. Naturally this partly stemmed from a genuine concern for the well-being of the residents, but any deviation from the expected norms – abuse, inbreeding, marital trouble, straying too close to the colour line – was quickly discovered and acted upon.

The very design of this model suburb was planned from the start to encourage Christian and Afrikaner values. Importantly, it was also designed so that the inhabitants would be protected and hidden from the outside world, but, at the same time, remain visible to the social workers monitoring them. Teppo notes that Epping Garden Village was planned as a neighbourhood unity – 'an area that was a self-sufficient social unit that would provide facilities for work and co-operation between a stable nucleus of residents'. The suburb was designed to be a world on its own – keeping the residents inside, and away from the eyes of the blacks and middle-class Afrikaners. 'The ideal was a peaceful and safe *gemeenskapseenheid*[285] . . . reflected in the way the planner Martin Adams used several smaller neighbourhood units in the layout. These units could, for example, consist of a central space surrounded by houses with a single entrance road circling the central space and exiting again via the entranceway.'[286]

These neighbourhood units were designed to reduce crime and restlessness: 'It was effortless to spot any deviant activities, since the houses were only surrounded by wire fencing, and each house faced several neighbours at once.' Initially only two roads connected the suburb with the surrounding area, making it easy to monitor who entered and who left:

> The original layout even included strategically dispersed homes for schoolteachers, *dominees* and police who would thus have a wide view of the suburb from their strategically placed houses on the street corners. The area was characterised by the openness of spaces, and the lack of *private* gardens [author's emphasis]. The yards only had low fences, if any. The only privacy was to be found within the houses, which were also carefully designed for the purposes of rehabilitation.[287]

The houses were designed to be large enough to accommodate white families. 'Overcrowding was perceived as a constant problem that had to be avoided through the several small bedrooms in the houses. Ideally, there would be enough space for everyone to have a bed in a bedroom and there were to be no more than three children per bedroom.' After the age of seven, male and female children had to sleep in different rooms; 'parents were also to have a separate bedroom. Ideally, bathrooms were to be separate.'[288]

Despite the eugenic connotations, inbreeding is the preferred explanation for much of the white poverty in modern Ruyterwacht. 'It's always been a very isolated, closed community,' says the matron after the sermon. 'There was a lot of inter-marriage and, well, it was a way of passing the time.' The centre also takes care of the mentally handicapped in the area.

When the last prayer is said, the organisers – mostly women and tough as nails – rise and take their positions. Voices are raised in a final, uneven hymn and then the hall falls silent. It is time for food and entertainment. The Senior Centre is run by the Dutch Reformed Church, which still concerns itself with the poverty of its congregation more than a hundred years after it first sounded the alarm. Church volunteers have set up a small orchestra on the unlit stage at the front of the dusty hall, and the sound of a trumpet rolls out from the shadows. Soon it is joined by a guitar and, as a jaunty tune makes its way through the crowd, the organisers start calling out the names of the tables at which the white elderly sit. They will be the first to receive donations of food.

The old people enthusiastically file past to queue in front of the matron. She notes down their names to make sure no one gets a double portion. Taking too much means someone else goes hungry. Large plastic containers are set to her side. The old people receive one bag of lettuce per family, a jug of carrots and onions, and, if it has been a good week for donations, a small amount of meat for stewing. Much of the food comes from nearby shops, which donate food that is close to, but not past, its sell-by date.

It is many decades since apartheid, and the Senior Centre now caters to all the elderly and mentally handicapped in the area. This being Ruyterwacht, however, many of the members are white. Or not quite. Even the most stringent apartheid official would have a hard time classifying the race of those queuing for food. Whites, but also many coloured people. One or two would be black. But after that it begins to break down. There are white features on coloured bodies – blue eyes and dark hair. It is hard to distinguish between a dark tan and a separate race. There are Afrikaners and British, and all the faces are equally enthusiastic for the food, glad to be in the company of friends. The eyes are all weary. But that woman over there . . . those eyes? Not Malaysian . . . perhaps Chinese?

Many are dressed simply. In tracksuits or T-shirts, often with a dirty cap on their heads. But a few view the social occasion as an opportunity to wear their finery. Dresses with bright floral patterns, earrings. Men fiddle with their ties and the sleeves of their suits. An old woman runs a comb through the last scraps of her hair.

An announcement blares out over the hall. Those interested can make their way to the stage where the orchestra will lead them in line dancing. A few of the old women smile shyly, and tease each other and eventually make their way to the front where they slowly turn and dance out of time to the music. Of those seated, a few turn to look briefly and then lose interest. Most are content to talk among themselves, or to fretfully adjust their ties and stare at nothing in particular.

Outside the hall, next to the netball courts, a number of large shipping containers are stacked. One is used as a small shop run by a smiling man who jokingly refers to himself as Gert Groente. The shop sells vegetables and toiletries. Every so often someone approaches Gert to buy the odd tomato and perhaps a little sachet of shampoo. No one considers buying the candy more common to such tuck shops, and none is on offer. The shipping containers are stacked against the side of the school, forming a small metal passage from which excited sounds emerge.

Behind Gert's store a table has been set up, overseen by one of the steely women organisers. On the table are stacked donations of clothes and blankets. The elderly flock around the table, pulling, examining, feeling, clutching.

The old women caw and hop about with bright eyes: 'Does anyone see a blanket for me?' 'This one looks warm.' 'That flower pattern is very pretty.'

Most of the members of the Senior Centre live off their state pensions, says the matron. Once a month they queue around the post office to receive the sum of R1 140. Of this about R900 is used to rent a room from CHL (now known as Communicare). For R400 they can rent a room without electricity. These are the lucky ones – those to whom life has been kind. They have a roof over their heads and a large room to call their own. No matter that the elderly pensioner often has to support their children, and sometimes grandchildren, who crowd into the same single room. Two people per room is the minimum. Three or four or five is more common. But at least they don't have to live in a shack, or an old car, or a caravan. Many of the cars outside seem well stocked with blankets.

The matron is frustrated with a family that refuses to move into a room she has found for them. They currently live in a small, filthy caravan in the backyard of someone's house. Here they are allowed to keep their dog, which they would have to give up if they were to move into the room. They refuse to abandon their dog – not even for a larger, cleaner and safer living space. 'That dog is their whole life,' the matron says and shakes her head.

Another announcement rings out. It is time for the hot food. The poor queue again – this time for a full plate of meat, rice and potatoes. Ceramic mugs are stacked in the kitchen, ready to be filled with coffee. The smell of dust and dishwashing liquid.

The same pension used for rent also has to support the family. The matron grunts in frustration. 'The children don't care. They just don't do any work and are happy to live off the pension.' A family often lives on just under R100 a week. 'It's a challenge,' the matron says blandly. Their survival is only made possible through the various charities in the area, such as the Senior Centre, which offer donations of food and run soup kitchens. According to the matron, there seems to be some rivalry between the charities, as the members of the Senior Centre are often not allowed into a rival soup kitchen run near the municipal swimming pool. 'It's ridiculous,' the matron huffs. 'There is no reason for it. Don't these people need all the help they can get?'

The food is served and the *dominee* makes his way onto the stage and calls for silence. 'Let us bow our heads to pray.' A hundred or more grey heads wilt like flowers. 'Lord, our God, thank you that we can come together this afternoon. Thank you for the opportunity you have given us to be here and thank you for the food you have made possible, that we can use it for our bodies. Would you bless those who prepared the food and bless those who serve it? Let it strengthen us all. Amen.'

Jane Jordaan and her husband, *Oom* Koos, are among those seated. A stout, smiling woman, Jane came to Ruyterwacht in 1976. 'Ag, something happened in my life – I was married, and then divorced and it became necessary to move here. I was terrified, though. People said it was an awful place to stay, that only low-class people stayed there. They said you couldn't leave your door open or your throat would be slit. In those days it was called Epping, but most people called it Konyntjiedorp.'[289] She laughs and looks at *Oom* Koos. He pats her hand and smiles, but never speaks. 'But I took a chance and moved here – I didn't have any other choice . . . And let me tell you, I've never regretted it. Not for a second. I've had some of the best years of my life here.' She looks around with a fierce pride. 'I've lived in the same house since I moved here and I've always said that even should I win the lottery, if I should win R50 million – not that I play the lottery – I wouldn't want to live anywhere else but here.'

Jane says she supposes she grew up poor. 'But it's not a shame to have been poor. Let me tell you, my father worked for seven shillings and a sixpence a week. I think it's about 75 cents now. And it was tough. I suppose it was.' Her father worked for the city, digging trenches and roads. '*Pik en graaf*',[290] as Jane says. 'He lost his job eventually. I think his nerves gave in or something. But eventually he got another job at the municipality as a truck driver.' He kept that job until he retired, after which he became a janitor at Ottery Primary School. Her mother was a housewife and often sickly. 'It was the poverty and the high blood pressure,' says Jane.

'I guess we grew up poor . . . we lived in a little shack in Ottery. There was no electricity and no piped water. We had water tanks. Eventually they gave us running water, but my mother died without knowing what electricity was.'

The first tin house they lived in consisted of a bedroom and a living room, in which the four children slept. As the family's situation improved they moved to another tin house – this one with two bedrooms. Her parents shared the one and her brothers the other. She and her sister slept in the living room on a couch that could be converted into a bed.

Her mother cooked food on a little coal stove, and, in the evenings, candles and a paraffin lamp provided light. 'There was never any danger of fire. Never. You know, I can't understand how these people in the townships . . . You're always hearing of a fire. And if the one catches alight then the others follow. You probably don't know this but those tin shacks? They're usually lined with wood on the inside . . . And there was never any danger of fire for us. I don't think the people in the townships properly extinguish their candles. My mother was very strict about that. We always had to use a candle holder or a bowl of water. We had to be very careful.' She beams at *Oom* Koos and he beams at her.

Would she call herself poor? 'Well, I didn't become rich but we certainly managed to get out of poverty. How? Through hard work, I think. Hard work and, well, circumstances changed. You grow up and you see how the people around you live and you want to improve your own circumstances.' Jane worked most of her life as a shop assistant, except for a short stint as a phone operator at the post office. Oom Koos was a foreman on the railways. 'But he's on pension now. Ag, and it's not much.'

'But I've never let life get me down,' she says fiercely. 'Like the *dominee* said this morning, you just need to laugh. And I met the most wonderful people here. The first two I met, they've both passed away now, were old *tannie* Meyer and old *tannie* Du Plessis. They were such wonderful people. Ag, and old *tannie* Doepie passed away only last year . . . But I've never had any problems with the people here. Okay, I must admit that in the last few years we've had a lot of coloured people move in, but I've never had any problems with them. I often see children playing soccer in the streets and when I drive past they expect me to yell at them, but I just tell them to keep playing and practising hard so that we can win the World Cup one day. And now they smile and greet me every time I go past. I think it's your attitude towards people. The other day a black girl ran in front of my car and I stopped and told her not to worry, that I was also young once. If I'd started shouting and throwing a tantrum then it wouldn't have helped anything. I think we can all live together in love and peace.'

She is, however, worried about a recent spate of burglaries at her home. 'I think they've broken in about three or four times now. The first time was quite bad because they damaged the bars on the windows and we had about R10 000 worth of damage. And we didn't have insurance on the house. Anyway, they've stolen things from the car parked in the yard a couple of times . . . But I can't say whether it's white people or coloured people.' For the first time her smile falters. 'I guess things have changed. Young people being robbed of their cellphones and things. And there's a problem with drugs – unfortunately mostly amongst the coloured people. But it happens everywhere. You get good people and bad people, and I'm not going to point a finger to Ruyterwacht. I've always come up for this town because, as I told you, I had my happiest years here.'

The air is filled with voices. Announcements, greetings, prayers. Someone has lost their bag of food and an organiser steps on stage, saying that any theft will not be tolerated. Eventually a shopping bag is slowly, hesitantly produced from the crowd. The guitar is still slowly, dreamily being strummed in the shadows of the hall. As the food is finished, the poor drift away, one by one, clutching their plastic bags filled with carrots and lettuce. In another few days there will be food again, and they will put on their fine clothes and comb their hair and walk the streets. But for now they wait outside the school, sitting on the pavement, smoking the cigarette they brought along for the event. One elderly white man jokingly admonishes his coloured friend that he 'is not a *meid* or a boy'.[291] They both laugh. A bored poodle watches from the window of an ancient yellow Datsun.

Those who have no one to pick them up begin the long walk back to their single rooms, past the cracked plaster of the school, the rusting backyards, the gleaming boat and Rita's Tuck Shop, their shoulders hunched against something that is not the cold.

Ruyterwacht, or rather Epping Garden Village, was initially successful. Those who were selected did improve their situation and move into the middle classes. Their houses were emptied, and new families selected to move in. As the years went by, however, fewer and fewer families decided to leave the suburb. Legislation such as the Urban Areas Act and the Population Registration Act made sure that the poor whites could not move into the black slums, where rent and living costs were cheaper. It also meant that suitable candidates (according to the CHL's criteria) were harder and harder to come by, as the company could no longer bend the racial lines. The name of the suburb was eventually changed to Ruyterwacht on the suggestion of the local headmaster, who believed the suburb to be on the site of an old Dutch watchtower built by governor Simon van der Stel. Like so much of Afrikaner history, this is fictitious. A tower called Ruijterwacht did exist, but it was nowhere near this suburb.

From the 1960s the suburb stagnated, the poor whites hidden, protected and taken care of. A world unto themselves, much like the many other pockets of poor whiteism in the country. Change came again in 1994, with the victory of the ANC in the country's first democratic elections. The new government removed the extensive state support for poor whites in favour of broadening support for all the impoverished in the country. The social workers left, and with them the last of the *volk*'s systems for uplifting itself. The poor whites were left to themselves, to rust and fade alone.

The CHL sold many of the houses it operated. Rents were raised, and young, upcoming coloured families moved into the previously all-white area. At first glance, Ruyterwacht seems neither as poor nor as white as expected. The members of the Senior Centre, the old Afrikaners, seem to have little problem with their new neighbours – at least certainly not in earshot of their coloured friends.

Now the suburb sleeps much as it always has. The poor whites here are the lucky ones, the ones who can afford rooms, and they have no desire to leave their friends and families behind. Ruyterwacht has always been, and always will be, their home. The cars and rented rooms, backyards and caravans: home.

But such concerns are far from their minds today. Their bellies are full and their shopping bags heavy. Perhaps they have come away with a donated blanket or jersey. Today, the old people hunch their backs against the afternoon sky and, when they have vanished from the roads and the sky moves into the bruised colours of evening, the casino begins to glow against the night.

The casino, like much of its kind, is a lavish construction with illuminated fountains, palm trees and golden trimmings. It was built on the buffer zone that keeps Ruyterwacht from the rest of the world. Initially this open area was used as festival grounds – for *volkspele* and farmer's markets. Later it was converted into a motor-racing track. On Sundays, as the people of Ruyterwacht slept, many would slip out to watch the cars roar past. The growling and revving of large engines filled the air and the crowd cheered in admiration. The bluegum trees would shake with the sound. Later, though, the air stilled and the racetrack was sold. The casino rose in its place, white and pristine.

The casino is a massive complex with a theatre that seats 5 000, a cabaret bar, conference facilities, two hotels and a presidential suite – the cost of one night's stay enough to sustain a Ruyterwacht family for a year. It has 2 500 slot machines, including Sun Pot, Hollywood Slots and Jackpot Deluxe. The denominations range from five cents to R100. In addition there are 78 gaming tables for blackjack, roulette and various types of poker. It has a cinema, an ice rink and a ten-pin bowling alley. There are bumper cars, go-kart races and a food court with various popular fast-food chains. The casino also boasts about 15 restaurants and bars.

There is a private club for the high-rollers with 24-hour service. Inside the casino is a dizzying barrage of impressions: opulence, the tiny ringing of the slot machines, the artificial sky painted on the ceiling; people milling about spending, gambling, laughing; crowds of families in the Spurs and Wimpys; beautiful women in long dresses gliding through the halls. Security officers guard a metal detector. The bells and sounds and shouts of the machines, where anonymous people feed coins into waiting mouths. R10 000 wagered on a roll of the dice. The lights whirling and whirling.

The casino complex is about a kilometre or so from Ruyterwacht, and the matron despises it. Not because her *mensies* gamble there. She is adamant that they would never be found there, and the other women agree. They could not afford it. Many of the younger people struggle with drugs, perhaps, or alcohol or prostitution, but the older poor have not the energy or money for such pursuits. No, the matron despises the casino because, despite the vast amount of money being spent there, it makes no contribution to the Senior Centre or charities in the area. The casino disagrees and says it has an extensive corporate social investment programme, which includes setting up a computer learning centre in Ruyterwacht, and educating people about the need for responsible gambling. It also invites the local children to partake in special-event days, and the casino says there is talk of refurbishing the school, where it has managed a feeding scheme for years. It has already planted a number of trees on the grounds. According to its social responsibility report, the casino has also had a positive effect on the property values of the area, raising them by as much as 10 per cent. Apart from Ruyterwacht, the casino also has charitable and environmental programmes in the other surrounding areas, such as Goodwood and Elsie's River.

The matron, however, is not impressed. The Senior Centre has received no money, donations or help from them, she says, and she wants to put food in front of the centre's members. Most of the money the centre does receive is from the Dutch Reformed Church, as part of its Badisa charitable programme, but it is never enough. Sometimes they also receive individual donations, but these are unreliable. But the Lord provides. The Lord always provides.

But who receives? The charities, casinos and churches give not to numbers, but to people. The old people walking, the long muttering march – each and every one of them a face, a story, a life lived, a white, a coloured, an Afrikaner, an Englishman, a John, a George, a Johannes, a Gert Groente and his little store run from a container. Elizabeth Pienaar, who worked all her life at Telkom, so proudly displaying the medals she won in the relay at the Golden Games. Jannie, who lost his leg, patiently waiting in line to receive food. Peggy Ulrich, who has lived here the longest of all, moving to Ruyterwacht as a girl of 15 soon after World War II. Now she sits alone at her table in the midst of all the talking and laughing around her, staring at nothing, tapping her fingers on the table, thinking of her husband, who was much older than her – gone now these 25 years – of her mother working at the shoe factory and the father she never knew, who worked on the mines in Kimberley, of the hostel she lived in until just recently. Peggy, who comes here for the company, she says, but won't turn down the hot meal in front of her, sitting alone at her table as the hall moves around her. She looks down at her hands, so different from when she first came here all those years ago. '*Ja*, I'm a widow now.'

The long line of people becoming lost, being forgotten, living the last edges of their lives as ghosts, haunting the weeds of the school, the scrapyards, Rita's Tuck Shop, and the long tree-lined lane that leads into Ruyterwacht. As night creeps on, a vast silence falls over Ruyterwacht and its spectres – dark now, sleeping, broken only by the lights of the casino burning against the sky.

The modern poor

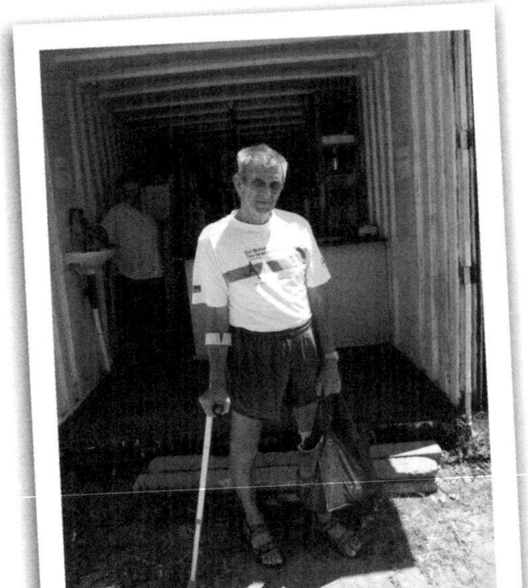

The autumn rains had come to Blikkiesdorp.

A short while earlier the sea-heavy air had hung dirty and lazy about the rows and rows of gleaming tin shacks. The metal roofs and walls baked in the filthy sunlight, sending up shimmering waves of heat-fed air. Small boys kicked a ball past open doorways where old fat women fanned themselves.

In the dunes beyond the township they had placed a number of burnt tyres to mark the edges of a football field. Men stood listlessly in the dust.

The rain had come over the many townships of the Cape Flats, with their incongruously Dutch names – Delft, Haarlem, the Hague. It eddied and swirled against the walls of Blikkiesdorp, where the police sat waiting in their brightly marked cars. A Nyala – an armoured vehicle used for riot control – stood dripping and the security guards who patrolled the suburb scurried for cover.

The dogs – strong, earth-coloured township mutts – barked excitedly and ran yipping and wet to their owners who brushed them off with annoyed grunts. Others sniffed the wet air then, nose to the ground, endlessly circled their little patch of nothing.

There were no tarred roads. The rain had turned the white dust of the Flats into thin mud. Row upon row of identical tin shacks braced themselves against the winds they knew were to come.

Canvas flapped in the breeze. A sheet shouting 'Africa's Greatest Gathering' marked some residential boundary. The tall poles that brought electricity to the shacks stood looming in the gathering grey.

The little houses were constructed simply and cheaply, two windows and a door. Toilets in narrow concrete boxes dotted the landscape. Tin sheeting was piled against the high fences that surround the township. Sometimes the shacks boasted shrubs or crawling ivy where the residents had tried to colour their surroundings. Near the entrance a shack had been converted into a nursery, spilling little brown pots into the street. A sign nailed to the wall read: 'Under New Management'.

The rain battered the tin shacks. A thousand raindrops hammered a thousand metal surfaces and a thunderous battering and clanging filled the air.

It is not officially called Blikkiesdorp, of course. It is the Delft Symphony Way Temporary Relocation Area, set up by the Western Cape provincial government to provide temporary housing for squatters. Half-built or empty brick houses in the areas surrounding Delft attest to some progress on the government's promises. But the suburb, if it can be called that, has become known for appalling violence and poverty. The roads are often blocked by burning tyres as the residents protest and the air fills with the smell of burning rubber.

It is here that some of the poor residents of Ruyterwacht were moved. They had been unable to afford the rents charged by the CHL and a white squatter camp soon sprang up between the suburb and the casino. In December 2011 they vanished, relocated by the city, and now white faces can be glimpsed in Blikkiesdorp among the poorest of the poor.

The police discourage anyone from entering the area, no matter how good their intentions and even the social workers have admitted to being too afraid to enter on certain days. The old women in Ruyterwacht are horrified at the suggestion of visiting the area. 'No one moves to Blikkiesdorp,' says the matron. 'You end up there.'

The sergeant behind the desk at the Delft Police Station laughs when asked if it is a good time to visit. 'It's always dangerous. Never stop your car for anything. But . . .,' he gestures at the half-empty police station, 'it doesn't seem too bad right now.'

Blikkiesdorp was built in 2008 to provide emergency housing for squatters. Officially, the settlement, which is situated in the east of Cape Town, on the no-man's land near the international airport, provides housing for more than 1 500 families – mostly coloured and black. Unofficially, more than 15 000 people are said to be living there. The sand gets into everything. Into food, into the toilets, into the thin beds, mattresses and cardboard boxes.

The residents often threaten to torch the entire settlement in protest against insufficient service delivery. The international press has branded Blikkiesdorp a modern concentration camp and accused the police stationed there of draconian policing tactics, such as beatings and illegal curfews.

Marinda Odendaal has lived in Blikkiesdorp only three months, but she says it's actually quite pleasant. She is one of the young Ruyterwacht squatters recently relocated by the city. 'Ag, it's not as bad as everyone says. I always say your circumstances depend on what you make of it. It's a matter of survival. If you can make the best of your circumstances then you'll survive.'

She regards the old women of Ruyterwacht with contempt. 'Those people are stagnating. They're so comfortable there. They have their food provided for them and they get taken care of. They don't know what it is to be independent. To look after yourself.'

She was born in the Eastern Cape but moved to Cape Town as a young girl. She studied nursing but dropped out and worked as a cleaner in various places. Until recently, just before she came to Blikkiesdorp, she had been a cleaner at the large Tyger Valley mall in northern Cape Town. Her sister had been living in Ruyterwacht and invited Marinda to join them with her two small children. She's doesn't say much about what happened to her partner. She lived in the boarding house among the other poor. As children were not allowed, she left her son and daughter in the care of her brother-in-law's aunt.

She could not afford the rent for long, however, and decided to start squatting among the other Afrikaners just outside Ruyterwacht. She hated it. 'It was wet and cold. The children suffered.' Whenever charities delivered food or clothing, the squatters would descend like crows and fighting often broke out as the residents pulled and pushed and punched to get a dry blanket or some tinned food.

'I objected when they told me I had to move to Blikkiesdorp, but my neighbour, old Mr Paxton, went to look around and he said it wasn't as bad as everybody made it out to be.' Nevertheless, she was unsure and put her two-year-old daughter into foster care to make sure she grew up well. The foster parents turned out to be kind and offered to 'sponsor' Marinda. This was a stroke of luck. An offer of sponsorship meant being provided food and clothing by a caring and, usually but not always, middle-class family. It meant stability and an escape from hunger. She gladly accepted and began her new life in Blikkiesdorp.

'It's nice and warm here. It's good to have a roof over your head,' she says. She doesn't think the area is particularly violent. 'Our local policeman is Mr Daniels and he doesn't let anyone cross him. But the police aren't hard – they're mostly worried about the drug addicts from Delft. Sometimes they get in here and cause trouble.'

Marinda still lives next to '*Oom*' Paxton, a thin, gruff man of 73. He has no job and cares for his three teenage sons on his meagre monthly pension of just over R1 100. None of them attend school and neither does Marinda's son, who dropped out of school at 14. 'They bullied him too much at school.' Besides, no one can afford the school fees. Most of Marinda's money goes towards electricity and taxi fare. That's the only downside of Blikkiesdorp, she says. The taxi fare is too expensive to go anywhere – certainly not to school. The boys spend their days watching television in *Oom* Paxton's little 6 x 3 metre shack. On sunny days they might play soccer with the coloured boys, when the sun slams down upon the tin and makes being inside unbearable.

Marinda doesn't know how long she will stay in Blikkiesdorp. 'Maybe six months, maybe ten years. It's okay here. People greet you when you walk down the street.' Her biggest concern is *Oom* Paxton. Her eyes grow suddenly pleading. 'Look – forget about me. I have my sponsor. I can survive. But *Oom* Paxton has no one looking after him. He's old and sick, and can't afford to eat or go to the doctor. He's the only one caring for those three boys.' She begs: 'Please – don't write about me. Write about *Oom* Paxton. Just get somebody to help him.'

Outside the rain swirls and howls, crashing down upon the shacks, signalling the start of autumn.

The new poor whites are spread out across South Africa, squatting on farms or ostensible missionary stations, buried in the townships, living under bridges. Unlike the old people of Ruyterwacht, they are not linked to the poor white problem of the 1930s. They have simply become poor or have always been poor and they are regarded with shame, suspicion, guilt and distaste by the middle classes.

This is perhaps not always undeserved, a social worker says. 'The minute a newspaper writes about the poor whites, all the bleeding hearts descend on the area and give them clothes, blankets and food. And then they just go out and sell the stuff to buy alcohol.'

She sighs in frustration. 'They just want handouts. They don't want to lift themselves up. I've secured them jobs before but they leave after a few days. It's easier just to live on handouts.'

One of the few large-scale organisations to concern itself with white poverty is *Helpende Hand* (Helping Hand) – the charitable arm of the South African trade union Solidarity. It was created in 1949 to cater for sick mineworkers, who formed the bulk of Solidarity's members. Solidarity itself was created in 1902 as the Mine Worker's Union. In the 1990s it merged with several smaller trade unions to create Solidarity – a decision not divorced from the union's desire to get away from its Afrikaner nationalist image, a problem with which Solidarity still struggles.

In a report presented to President Jacob Zuma,[292] *Helpende Hand* claimed that there are currently in the region of 600 000 Afrikaners who can be classified as poor and that nearly 131 000 white households do not have adequate housing. White poverty increased by 150 per cent between 1994 and 2005, the report says.

Much of this poverty is centred on the cities. Solidarity claims that there are 77 white squatter camps in Pretoria alone and more than 430 nationally. Nearly two-thirds of the Pretoria squatters are older than 60.

The organisation, which focuses mainly, but not exclusively, on poor whites, is particularly worried about the invisibility of these people. Whereas black squatter camps are within easy reach of satellite offices of the Department of Social Welfare, where the residents can register for subsidies on their electricity and water bills, and receive food stamps, no effort has been made to set up similar offices near the white squatter camps. *Helpende Hand* claims that poor whites are regularly excluded from government aid on the basis of their skin colour – because it is perceived as 'racist' to give aid to the white poor.

In the report, the organisation pleads for equal treatment of South Africa's poor:

> You will be shocked to learn that Heila Rothmaan, a sick and dying cancer sufferer, stood in a queue for days from six in the morning till five in the afternoon just to learn that her disability grant was refused for the fifth time. She died a week later. President Zuma – you said yourself that poverty knows no race. Why does it then seem as if the government looks at the poor white differently?

The report contains various photos of the township dwellers, the most affecting of which shows Sarie Rossouw, a former nurse who suffered from a stroke a decade ago. Sarie is lying on her back on a thin, filthy mattress. The walls of her home are peeling and cracked. The concrete floor offers little protection. A wheelchair is folded up and leans against the side of the iron bedrail. Sarie wears a T-shirt that is too small for her. Her arms are crossed helplessly over her chest. Grey hair is tucked carefully away from her eyes, which gaze fiercely at the camera. She wears a diaper and is horribly, inhumanly thin – the malnourishment has turned her legs and arms into twigs and given her a terrible and skeletal look. Her 70-year-old husband, Hennie Rossouw, feeds hers, bathes her and changes her diaper. She has been visited only once by a social worker, says the organisation. The report goes on to describe new-born white children abandoned on trash heaps because their parents could not afford to care for them and details suicide note after suicide note resulting from desperate living conditions.

The report ends by publishing a letter that *Helpende Hand* received from a certain Martie:[293]

> In Pretoria, just opposite the old HF Verwoerd Hospital, there are rooms. It's an old municipal building where there used to be electricity and a kitchen. The people would pay rent and be given food from the kitchen, but since the owner vanished with all the money, the municipality has refused to switch the lights back on.
>
> The people in these rooms live in desperate poverty. All ages. Children too. There is also an exceptional old woman – I'm ashamed to say that it's my mother because I cannot help her.
>
> Her circumstances are dire. At present my mother lives in a room with five other people. She sleeps on a mattress on the floor. My mother is 70 and receives only her state pension. She will never be able to afford a bed.
>
> She uses her pension to buy food for all five people, including a two-year-old child. They use basins to bath and wash their washing. It is terrible, especially for someone who is 70 and sick. I cannot even buy her a bed because I've been declared bankrupt. But I am not worried about myself. I am worried about her and the small child.

In a world and political climate so vastly different from the one in which they had first appeared, the poor whites have again begun to come back into view, spilling out from the holes they had been hidden in, forming white slums and discomforting the ruling classes. And as the urban white poor have begun to reappear, so have the *bywoners* emerged from their enclaves of poverty.

The outskirts of Cape Town are dotted with farms and vineyards that eventually lead into the countryside and the small farming towns of the Boland. Beyond the Afrikaner suburbs of Bellville, lies the suburb of

Kraaifontein – a shabby land of five-rand shops, carwashes, fences and anonymous lower-middle-class housing. To the side of the suburb a large Coca-Cola sign proclaims the Wallace Dean township, with its tin shacks spilling onto the bland concrete pavement. Mountains loom in the distance and the roads are filled with poor black and coloured residents walking to and from something. Next to the township, a narrow dirt track leads over an iron bridge to a group of white *bywoners* squatting on farmland.

'You won't find a *kaffir* on this farm,' says Tabbie Groenwald darkly. His eye is still purpled from a mugging a few evenings earlier. He and his son Andre had gone to the local petrol station to fill the tank of his small motorcycle with a few rands of petrol. A group of black men suddenly appeared and demanded their cellphones and wallets. Andre and Tabbie retaliated with fists flying and the fight was only broken up when a police vehicle appeared. Andre was taken, bloody, to the local police office. As the police van pulled away, the blacks grinned, says Tabbie, and came close once again.

He was lucky to escape with his life. 'That squatter camp across the road is full of blacks and *tikkoppe*.[294] Even the children are on drugs. You won't find them here, though.' He leans on the cheap brown fence and his lined face looks out over the yard where a number of ramshackle shacks have been constructed. His eyes are a sad, milky blue. A thin white dust covers rusting scrap metal and discarded plastic containers. The bluegum trees sway in the wind. In the distance the sounds of traffic, leaves and turtle doves. The air is thick and lazy, as if it has no particular place to be. A young coloured man walks past carrying a blaring radio. He is met by a girl, her head covered in large bright curlers, and they stroll aimlessly past the geese and chickens.

Three heads pop up next to Tabbie's tanned arms as his two younger sons and his wife, Elizabeth, join the conversation. Their two cats are stretched out in the sun in front of their three-roomed wooden shack. Elizabeth has sandy-blonde hair pulled back in a ponytail. She's much younger than her husband. The two younger sons – Andre is off looking for work – both have their blond hair shaved short. All of them have blue eyes.

Tabbie doesn't mind living among the coloureds. At least they all speak Afrikaans. 'They're like everybody. Some are crooked and some are straight. But you don't get a good *kaffir*.'

They have been squatting on the farm for two years along with about six or seven other white families. Tabbie used to work for Communicare in Ruyterwacht, but says a conspiracy forced him out. He gets wistful. 'Ja, I used to earn R10 500 a month. To go from that to *this* . . . ' He gestures at the dust and metal before him. 'It's tough.' He has no permanent employment now, existing on the irregular odd job or as a carpenter. Sometimes he gets a position building roads. Perhaps worried that his claims will not be believed, Tabbie vanishes into the little shack and reappears a short while later with a well-worn magazine, its cover scuffed and dirty from a hundred showings. It is the monthly newsletter of Communicare and he has circled an old photo of himself in orange marker. Tabbie stands smiling among the other employees – young and fat. It is a far cry from the thin, weathered man. 'Ah, well. It means that you finally went on a diet,' his wife jokes.

Elizabeth is a 'finals checker' – she makes sure that the little plastic taps on wine sacks are properly fitted. This is the only constant source of income for the family, about R3 000 a month. She has had to call in sick when she was unable to afford the train fare to work. 'When Tabbie lost his job the company pushed us out. Just put all our stuff on the sidewalk and told us to leave. It happens every day in Ruyterwacht.' She didn't want to live in the white squatter camp that had grown up around the suburb. The family heard about a farm where they didn't have to pay rent. The farmer didn't mind them squatting on a corner of his land. The family's little shack has chicken wire on the windows to prevent burglaries. There is no sanitation. When asked, Elizabeth points to the sandy pit next to the shack. 'We've got a bucket and when we're done we just cover it up with sand.'

Their neighbour is an eccentric old man called Swannie, who speaks in a rapid, maddening mumble. Swannie is restricted to a wheelchair ('calcification of the hips,' he shrugs) and the grey dust is patterned with his tyre treads. 'I've lived on this farm for 13 years now because I didn't have anywhere else to go, nowhere else to go. But I get by, I always say, I always say, these hands, who gave these hands? The Lord gave these hands.' He cackles, showing only a few remaining teeth between his wild grey beard. On his head is a cowboy hat and sunglasses.

Swannie was born in the Eastern Cape and, as a young man, started wandering along the coast. 'I picked apples with some coloureds, you know, and for a time, for a time I worked in a shoe factory for a Jew and then I went to the railways. You know, I always say people should write a book about me, you can write a book about all the things I've done, but no one ever believes me.' He laughs loud, clutching his chest and rocking back and forth in his wheelchair. He mumbles when asked if he has a job now. 'Um. Well, you know. No-o. No. Well, no. I, um, I sweep here and there. I sweep a little, yes. Sweep.'

Tabbie and Elizabeth seem to have no trouble understanding him and laugh easily at all his jokes, if they are jokes. The conversation is interrupted by an old coloured man dressed in funereal clothes. He wears his dark hat at a jaunty angle, and in it he has stuck a large, bright feather. He is swaying on his feet and desperately trying to make a point, but his mouth proves to slow to catch up with his thoughts. 'Sir, look, sir.' He pauses for effect. 'Jan van Riebeek landed here and, and . . . ' He stumbles and tries again. 'Jan van Riebeek landed here and when he landed here this all used to be what they called *hotnotland*.' The others laugh gently and shrug their shoulders – complaining about the blacks in the township is safe, but talking about the differences between coloureds and whites in a place like this is dangerous. 'And I don't know what race we are now – if we are coloureds or *hotnots* – we're all still deciding. But then, sir, then there was apartheid you know, and the whites were in charge. And now? Now the blacks are in charge. Now we have to live under the Bantu. I ask you, sir, is that fair?' Before he can continue he is rescued by a sympathetic friend.

Swannie watches him go. 'You know, that gets me to thinking. The government doesn't care about us, and the DA, that woman, that Zille woman, she lies, man. She talks rubbish – she doesn't care about us and now she wants us to vote for her. Do you know who I vote for? For Him. I always say I vote for Him. The blacks get everything in life, but I vote for Him.'

Swannie lives in a rusting bus that he has converted into a home. He bought the bus ten years ago for the princely sum of R8 000 and is extremely proud of it. Lately he has extended his house with a small caravan. His wife, an imperious woman of indeterminate race, watches him from the doorway, then comes over to scold him for speaking out about their conditions. Her hair is pulled back in a severe grey bun – 'No names, please. Not of me, my children or my grandchildren.' As she marches off, Swannie shrugs and dismisses her with a wave of his hand. 'Old dragon,' he says laughingly. His wife is right to be protective of him, however. Although the farm isn't dangerous, muggings are common, he says. 'The *kaffirs* ambush you at night. The other day I was near the squatter camp and they took my cellphone and my money and my watch – and I'm in a wheelchair!'

Muggings aren't the only danger. At weekends drunken fights are common. The residents have set up a small 'smuggling shop' where they can buy dubiously obtained goods otherwise difficult to buy affordably – cheap wine, tinned food, stolen cigarettes and methylated spirits, which is filtered through bread to make it drinkable. It is colloquially known as 'riding the Blue Train'.

The daily fare, the children say, is some chicken and breadrolls, or tinned spaghetti. Red meat is scarce, although Swannie is a staunch promoter of soya to supplement his diet. Like much of their possessions, including their clothes, the food is often donated. This has its own dangers: 'People pull up in a bakkie and it's like, it's like hyenas or buzzards around a kill, you know? They descend and five minutes later there's nothing left. You have to punch your way to the food.' The local church serves food on Sundays, but, according to Tabbie and Elizabeth, it refuses to serve the residents unless they have been in church. 'They tell you – if you haven't been to church, you're not getting any food,' says Elizabeth.

The donations rarely reach all the residents of the community and, when pressed, the family admits to 'some people' selling the clothes for alcohol. 'The people just take all the donations and put it in their home saying they've been sponsored,' says Elizabeth. 'No one cares for anyone around here.'

The families also live in constant fear of eviction. Elizabeth suspects the farm has new owners. 'But nobody tells you anything. We live in uncertainty'. Swannie chimes in: 'They come with, you know, lawyers and they come look around here, but there is that other lawyer who looks after us, the one in Stellenbosch, and she says to never sign anything, just never sign anything.' If they were evicted, the families would most likely be moved to Blikkiesdorp or leave to trudge the roads and find another unknown place to squat. 'Look, I've got nothing against Blikkiesdorp,' says Elizabeth. 'But I don't want my children growing up there. That place is full of tik and drugs. I don't want that for my children.' She smiles affectionately at the two blond boys next to her.

Tabbie is resigned to the matter. 'I'm used to paying rent in my life. We can pay rent.' He leans on the fence, looking at the ducks and chickens and the scrap of his world. 'Ja,' he sighs. 'I wonder what will happen to us.'

Beyond him the air fills with rain clouds. The air is sharp and smells of dust and damp and far-off things. As the evening descends, the clouds are lit brown and orange, yellow and grey – the colours of city rain. Soon the autumn rains will begin to fall on him and Elizabeth and Swannie, as it falls in Blikkiesdorp, where Marinda looks with concern at *Oom* Paxton while the children are bathed in the glare of the television, as it falls on the tin roofs of the black townships and the coloured townships, and drips down onto the earth where it is lapped by the half-wild dogs.

Conclusion

At the ragged end of the twentieth century, nearly a hundred years after the height of the colonial era, Italian journalist Ricardo Orizio makes his way to Sri Lanka in search of a lost white tribe – the remnants of Dutch colonialism in erstwhile Ceylon. In the capital, Colombo, he encounters the Burghers, descendants of the Dutch colonisers who had settled in Ceylon in the seventeenth century and stayed on through the British colonial era there in the 1800s. Living in poverty, among crumbling bungalows and dusty ballrooms, the Burghers are no longer recognised as white by the other cultures of Sri Lanka. Both physically and imaginatively, the Burghers have become native – the 'sad remnants of what used to be a vast and rich world'. Orizio finds the Burghers fiercely proud of their Dutch heritage, but sunk into melancholy over their degradation.

The old racial colonial attitudes have not altogether disappeared, even though the colour of the skin has darkened. One Sri Lankan tells Orizio: 'Although they're trash, they think they're better than we are.'[295] The Burghers remember, however, that another group of Dutch also set out in the great ships and settled in distant climes, far away from white civilisation. Unlike the Burghers, these other Dutch settlers had stood their ground against the British, conquered the natives (at unimaginable cost) and, above all, remained white. 'We weren't like the Dutch in South Africa, who held out,' a Burgher tells Orizio. 'The Boers – God bless 'em – are country people, tough and lots of them.'[296]

The fate of the Burghers in Sri Lanka represents the worst fears of both the colonials and nationalists. Their fears of swamping and racial extinction were, to a degree, not mere idle imaginings. They illustrated the fact that the 'colonials, or at least some of them, ended up defeated, too, despite or maybe because of the colour of their skin, just like the colonised'.[297] These tensions of whiteness were just as pressing in some of the British dominions, where the Europeans were surrounded on all sides by other cultures. There, whiteness had to be constantly upheld and its borders vigilantly policed. In South Africa, the poor whites certainly represented the greatest threat to whiteness that the state, both colonial and nationalist, faced. For the colonial project to succeed, the colonisers would have to remain white and maintain their perceived racial superiority. The existence of a large class of unskilled whites decisively challenged the aspirations of colonials and nationalists alike.

In order the solve the 'problem', the state needed to determine its nature and its extent. The state, in other words, had to discover the poor before it could rescue them and, in a colonial society in which black inferiority was taken for granted, this meant discovering and documenting only the white poor. Commissions were established, where government-approved experts testified to the nature of the indigent, in the process establishing the discourse – how the problem would be treated. The existence of slums, in particular, was troubling. Slums were characterised as liminal areas, places outside surveillance. Slum inhabitants were prone to crime and prostitution. And although often viciously racist themselves, the poor whites in the slums nonetheless consorted with lower races, even, in extreme cases, making themselves guilty in the state's eyes of the sin of miscegenation. The slums were another country altogether, and the whiteness of the inhabitants was in question – those 'anarchic, distant outposts of empire peopled by violent and primitive races',[298] as the slums in London had been called. But how much more important were these fears when they were realised in a colonial settler society, where the slums were not just the holes of the poor, but spaces in which the white poor took on another race entirely, where their skin became darkened and their eyes became angry? As concern over the poor whites grew, the state initially attempted to 'whiten' the slums by removing black Africans to townships outside the city. But the condition of the slums and poverty itself threatened white prestige and the state changed tack, demolishing the slums and relocating the poor whites.

The poor white problem was arguably at its worst during the height of the cultural and political awakening of the Afrikaners. The establishment of a unified white *volk* required all members of that group to be white. As such, poor whites became part of a sustained imagining of Afrikanerdom. They had to be racially re-inscribed, not only by raising their living standards, but also by raising the perception of the poor, still typified by the Victorian environmentalism and Social Darwinism that the commissions helped establish.

This is not to suggest that the problem of the large-scale poverty of its white citizens – afflicting at least a third of Afrikaners – was not an overwhelming concern of the state, but it is an attempt to re-examine colonial and nationalist motivations, to colour the picture of an era that has been depicted in terms too black and white.

The reimagination of poor whites as part of the white *volk* and, on a larger scale, the reimagination of the Afrikaners as not having been subject to a near crisis of impoverishment were, ultimately, so successful that modern commentators now pride themselves on 'discovering' poor Afrikaners in post-apartheid South Africa.

The modern white poor, living in shanty towns and under bridges, are treated ambivalently by white Afrikaans South Africans. In a sense, they are invisible in the broader poverty of the country, ignored and forgotten by the ruling classes. Yet their culture, or at least white working-class culture, has recently begun to be aped by white youth who ironically grow moustaches and wear threadbare clothes. It has been most successful, and most strange, in the international popularity of Afrikaans music groups such as Die Antwoord and Jack Parow, who consciously construct themselves as members of this poor culture.

The new white poor, and they are not historically new, deserve no special treatment, should not be singled out among the other poor of the country. They are neither more nor less poor than their black, coloured or Indian counterparts. It is only when they are ignored in favour of the other poor that a moral problem arises.

In telling the history of the poor whites, one must always keep in mind that black poverty was always much more serious and widespread. The actions taken by the colonial and nationalist governments to solve the poor white problem directly contributed to further impoverishment of black South Africans. Yet their story deserves to be told, as it has proved critical to the development of modern South Africa in its influence on Afrikaner nationalism and Afrikaner institutions. Without the 'poor white problem', the country today would have looked very different. South Africa is defined by that great magic trick – the pop and flash and smoke that caused an entire people to disappear from history. It is time that they returned.

Acknowledgements

This book could not have been written without the support of my father. It was his research, wisdom and unending enthusiasm that made this work possible. This is very much his book.

Phil Howell, my supervisor at Cambridge, gifted me with his patience and expertise. I have been and always shall be his friend.

Many friends, both in South Africa and abroad, were generous with their time and support. In particular, I would like to thank Milla van Zyl, Patrick MacKenzie, Michelle Viljoen, Rene Lotter, Christian Ponce, Julian Tuccillo and Emily Parton.

Credit must also go to my publisher, Gerhard Mulder, for his impossible deadlines and faith in my work. My editor Mark Ronan did a sterling job on making my academic language easier for the reader. My sister Nielen Bottomley took the fine photos in this book. More examples of her work can be found on Facebook.

I have benefited from coming into contact with many great geographers and historians during my research for this book, and the thesis on which it is based. My intellectual debt is heavy, and made clear in the references. South Africa can be proud of its world-class academics, among them Susan Parnell, Hermann Giliomee, Charles van Onselen, ELP Stals and Liz Lange.

I would like to thank the many people who allowed me to talk to them during the course of my research, and for allowing me to bring up the difficult subject of their poverty. They shared their lives with me and I hope I have not abused their trust. In particular I would like to thank Annette Bekker and all the good people at the Ruyterwacht Senior Centre for the crucial work they do and the goodwill they showed me.

This book was also made possible by a generous grant from Anfasa and the Norwegian government, which enabled me to take the time needed to write. My editors at *Sake24*, David van Rooyen and Riana de Lange, were consistently understanding during this period.

Lastly, I would like to thank my family, who have endured so much. Without them I am nothing.

Endnotes

1 Macdonald, K, 'Poverty, and Little Sympathy, in South Africa'. *The New York Times*, 25 June 2010.
2 Swarns, RL, 'South Africa's New Poor: White and Bewildered'. *The New York Times*, 12 September 2000.
3 Reuters News Service, 'Hardship Deepens for South Africa's Poor Whites', 26 March 2010.
4 Bloom, K, 'The Problem with Photographing "Poor Whites"'. *Daily Maverick*, 28 June 2010.
5 Bottomley, J, *Public Policy and White Rural Poverty in South Africa, 1881–1924* (PhD dissertation), 1990, p. 353.
6 Ibid.
7 Bottomley, *Public Policy and White Rural Poverty in South Africa*, p. 16.
8 Mandela, NR, *A Long Walk to Freedom* (London: Abacus, 1995), p. 260.
9 The broad strokes of the 'poor white' story necessitate glossing over the minutiae of political dealings. Unless specifically required, the governments of the period are not discussed beyond whether they were British colonial or Afrikaner nationalist governments. The dividing line between the two is 1924, and the coalition victory of the National Party.
10 This section is adapted from Bundy, C, 'Vagabond Hollanders and Runaway Englishmen: White Poverty in the Cape Before Poor Whiteism'. In Beinart W, Delius, P & Trapido, S (eds), *Putting a Plough to the Ground: Accumulation and Dispossession in Rural South Africa 1850–1930* (Johannesburg: Ravan Press, 1986), pp. 101–128.
11 Darwin, J, *The Empire Project* (Cambridge: Cambridge University Press, 2009), p. 3.
12 Said, EW, *Orientalism* (London: Routledge & Kegan Paul, 1978).
13 Stoler, AL, *Carnal Knowledge and Imperial Power* (Berkeley and Los Angeles: University of California Press, 2002).

14 Prakash, G, *Another Reason: Science and Imagination of Modern India* (Princeton: Princeton University Press, 1999), p. 13.

15 Belich, J, *Replenishing the Earth: The Settler Revolution and Rise of the Anglo-World, 1783–1939* (Oxford: Oxford University Press, 2009), pp. 15–16.

16 Belich distinguishes between settler societies, which reproduced a society through migration, and imperial expansion, which was the control of other peoples through conquest.

17 Darwin, *The Empire Project*, p. 217.

18 De Kiewiet, CW, *A History of South Africa* (Oxford: Oxford University Press, 1941), p. 114.

19 Van Onselen, C, *Studies in the Social and Economic History of the Witwatersrand 1186–1914, Vol. 1: New Babylon* (Harlow: Longman, 1982), p. xv.

20 Yudelman, D, *The Emergence of Modern South Africa: State, Capital and the Incorporation of Organized Labor on the South African Gold Fields, 1902 –1939* (Westport, CT: Greenwood Press, 1983), p. 9.

21 Swart, S, '"The Terrible Laughter of the Afrikaner": Towards a Social History of Humor', *Journal of Social History*, Summer 2009, pp. 889–917.

22 For an introduction to the colonial city model, see the pioneering study by King, AD, *Colonial Urban Development* (London: Routledge & Kegan, Paul, 1976). The development of urban planning and its use by colonial governments is discussed in Home R, *Of Planting and Planning* (London: Chapham & Hall, 1997).

23 Nuttal, S & Mbembe, A (eds), *Johannesburg: The Elusive Metropolis* (Durham, NC: Duke University Press, 2008), p. 38.

24 Parnell, S, 'Winning the Battles but Losing the War: Racial Segregation of Johannesburg Under the Natives (Urban Areas) Act of 1923', *Journal of Historical Geography*, 28 (2), p. 259.

25 Van Onselen, *New Babylon*, p. xv.

26 Murray, MJ, *Taming the Disorderly City* (Cape Town: UCT Press, 2008).

27 Naturally, there are exceptions, such as the excellent work of the historian Liz Lange, and the pioneering scholarship of the geographer Susan Parnell. Note that there is a sustained and lively scholarship on Johannesburg's black poor – a good example being Bonner, P, The Transvaal Native Congess 1917–1920: The Radicalisation of the Black Petty Bourgeoisie on the Rand. In Mark, S & Rathbone, R (eds), *Industrialisation and Social Change in South Africa* (London: Longman, 1987).

28 Stals, ELP, *Afrikaners in die Goudstad, Deel 2: 1924–1961* (Pretoria: HAUM, 1986b).

29 Ibid., p. 3. The Battle of Blood River, fought in 1838 between the Zulus and the proto-Afrikaners, was later interpreted by Afrikaner nationalists as a sign that the Afrikaners were a chosen people of God, destined to bring civilisation into Africa.

30 Grosskopf, JFW, *Rural Impoverishment and Rural Exodus: Report of the Carnegie Commission* (Stellenbosch: Pro Ecclesia, 1932), vol. 1, p. 19.

31 Giliomee, H, *The Afrikaners: Biography of a People* (Charottesville: University of Virgina Press, 2003), p. 322.

32 Malherbe, EG, *Education and the Poor White: Report of the Carnegie Commission* (Stellenbosch: Pro Ecclesia, 1932), vol. 3, p. 471.

33 Giliomee, *The Afrikaners*, p. 318.

34 Klausen, SM, *Race, Maternity, and the Politics of Birth Control in South Africa, 1910–1930* (Hampshire: Palgrave Macmillan, 2004), pp. 1–5.

35 Ibid. Merriman was arguing against the Natives Land Bill of 1912 and for greater co-operation with black South Africans.

36 UG 17-'22, 1922: 22.

37 Klausen, *Race, Maternity, and the Politics of Birth Control in South Africa*, p. 6.

38 Grosskopf, *Rural Impoverishment and Rural Exodus*, p. 18.

39 Bonnett, A. 'Geography, "Race" and Whiteness: Invisible Traditions and Current Challenges', *Area*, 29 (3), p. 197.

40 Teppo, A, *The Making of a Good White: A Historical Ethnography of the Rehabilitation of Poor Whites in a Suburb of Cape Town* (Helsinki: University of Helsinki, 2004), pp. 94–95.

41 Jackson, P, 'Constructions of "whiteness" in the geographical imagination", *Area*, 30 (2), p. 99.

42 Roediger, DR, *The Wages of Whiteness: Race and the making of the American Working Class* (New York: Verso, 1999).

43 Jacobson, MF, *Whiteness of a Different Colour: European Immigrants and the Alchemy of Race* (Cambridge: Harvard University Press, 1998).

44 Guess, TJ, 'The Social Construction of Whiteness: Racism by intent, racism by consequence', *Critical Sociology*, 32 (4), 257-275.

45 Stoler, AL, *Carnal Knowledge and Imperial Power* (Berkeley and Los Angeles, CA: University of California Press, 2002), p. 24.

46 Ibid, p. 43.

47 Lambert, D, 'Liminal figures: poor whites, freedmen, and racial reinscription in colonial Barbados', *Environment and Planning D*, 19, p. 335.

48 Giliomee, H, *The Afrikaners*, p. 315.

49 Stoler, AL 'Colonial Archives and the Arts of Governance', *Archival Science*, 2, 2002, p.104.

50 Giliomee, H, *The Afrikaners*, p. 315.

51 Lange, L, *White, Poor and Angry: White Working Class Families in Johannesburg* (Aldershot: Ashgate, 2003), p. 144.

52 TIC, 1908, p. 3.

53 Ibid., p. 4.

54 Ibid., p. 119.

55 Ibid., p.140.

56 Ibid., p. 5.

57 Ibid., p. 51.

58 Curtis wrote extensively on colonial affairs, especially on the Commonwealth of Nations. He would later become founder of the Royal Institute of International Affairs.

59 The Boer general, and later Prime Minister, Louis Botha was present at the preliminary hearings, but not for the drafting of the report.

60 TIC, 1908, p. 32.
61 Ibid., p. 15.
62 Ibid., p. 20.
63 Ibid., p. 24.
64 Ibid., p. 136.
65 Ibid., p. 27.
66 Ibid., p. 45.
67 Ibid., p. 147.
68 Ibid., p. 140.
69 Ibid., p. 111.
70 Ibid., p.111.
71 Ibid., p. 169.
72 Ibid., p. 59.
73 Grant, M, *The Passing of the Great Race or the Racial Basis of European History* (New York: Charles Scribner's Sons, 1936).
74 Ibid., p. 39.
75 Huntington, E, *Civilisation and Climate* (Honolulu: University Press of the Pacific, 2001), p. 33.
76 Osborn, WB, 'Preliminary Observations to Determine the Ultra-Violet Content of South African Sunlight', *South African Journal of Science*, xxvi, 1929, pp. 527–540.
77 Kennedy, D, 'Climatic Theories and Culture in Colonial Kenya and Rhodesia', *The Journal of Imperial and Commonwealth History* 10 (1), 1981, pp. 50–66. See also Crozier A, 'Sensationalising Africa: British Medical Impressions of Sub-Saharan Africa, 1890–1939', *The Journal of Imperial and Commonwealth History* 35 (3), 2007, pp. 393–415.
78 Dubow, S, *Scientific Racism in Modern South Africa* (Cambridge: Cambridge University Press, 1995), p.130.
79 Klausen, *Race, Maternity, and the Politics of Birth Control in South Africa*, pp. 42–43.
80 Dubow, S, *Scientific Racism in Modern South Africa*, p. 166.
81 Quoted in Klausen, *Race, Maternity, and the Politics of Birth Control in South Africa*, p. 19.
82 TIC, 1908, p. 198.
83 Stals, *Afrikaners in die Goudstad, Deel 2*, p. 30.
84 Driver, F, 'Moral Geographies: Social Science and the Urban Environment in Mid-Nineteenth Century England', *Transactions of the Institute of British Geographers*, New Series 13(3), 1988, p. 281.
85 Beckingham, D, *The Regulation of Drunkenness in Nineteenth-Century Liverpool* (PhD dissertation), 2008, pp. 164–165.
86 Scott, JC, *Seeing like a State: How Certain Schemes to Improve the Human Condition Have Failed* (New Haven and London: Yale University Press, 1998), pp. 2–3.
87 Joyce, P, *The Rule of Freedom: Liberalism and the Modern City* (London: Verso, 2003).
88 Poovey, M, *Making a Social Body: British Cultural Formation, 1830–1864* (Chicago: University of Chicago Press, 1995).
89 Foucault develops his concept of 'governmentality' in his series of lectures delivered

at the Collège de France. See Foucault, M, *The Birth of Biopolitics: Lectures at the Collège de France, 1978–1979* (New York: Palgrave Macmillan, 2008). The literature on colonial governmentality is rich. See, among others, Redfield, P, 'Foucault in the Tropics: Displacing the Panopticon'. In Inda, JX (ed.), *Anthropologies of Modernity* (Oxford: Blackwell Publishing, 2005); Duncan, JS, *In the Shadows of the Tropics: Climate, Race and Biopower in Nineteenth Century Ceylon* (London: Ashgate, 2007); Howell, P, *Geographies of Regulation: Policing Prostitution in Nineteenth-Century Britain and the Empire* (Cambridge: Cambridge University Press, 2009); and Legg, S, *Spaces of Colonialism: Delhi's Urban Governmentalities* (Oxford: Blackwell Publishing, 2007).

90 Report of the First Volksraad, 1897, p. 370. Author's translation from Dutch.

91 TIC, 1908: 18.

92 Ibid.

93 Ibid., p. 11.

94 For a good overview of the growth of Brickfields, see Van Onselen, C, *New Nineveh.*

95 Stals, ELP, *Afrikaners in die Goudstad, Deel 1: 1886–1924* (Pretoria: HAUM, 1986), p. 45.

96 Ibid., p. 48.

97 Stals, *Afrikaners in die Goudstad, Deel 2,* p. 23.

98 Stals, *Afrikaners in die Goudstad, Deel 2*, p. 22.

99 Grosskopf, *Rural Impoverishment and Rural Exodus*, p. 221.

100 TIC, 1908, p. 167.

101 Lange, *White, Poor and Angry*, p. 142.

102 Lange, *White, Poor and Angry*, p. 142.

103 TIC, 1908, p. 13.

104 Grosskopf, *Rural Impoverishment and Rural Exodus*, p. 221.

105 UG 30-'32, p. 17.

106 Lange, L, *White, Poor and Angry: White Working Class Families in Johannesburg* (Aldershot: Ashgate, 2003), p. 109.

107 Ibid., p.109.

108 Ibid., p. 109.

109 Stals, *Afrikaners in die Goudstad: Deel 1*, p. 54.

110 SC 170'34, 1934, p. 28.

111 TIC, 1908, p. 39.

112 UG 12-'14, 1914, p. 20.

113 TIC, 1908, p. 116.

114 Klausen, *Race, Maternity, and the Politics of Birth Control in South Africa*, p. 91.

115 Ibid., p. 93.

116 Albertyn, JR, *The Poor White and Society: Report of the Carnegie Commission* (Stellenbosch: Pro Ecclesia, 1932), vol. 5, p. 24.

117 Stals, *Afrikaners in die Goudstad: Deel 2*, p. 25.

118 Stals, *Afrikaners in die Goudstad: Deel 1*, p. 55.

119 Van Onselen, *New Babylon*, p. 169.

120 Lange, *White, Poor and Angry*, p. 57.

121 Note that by the 1940s even Newtown was displaying slum characteristics, the area described as unfit for whites to live in.

122 Parnell, S, 'Slums, Segregation and Poor Whites in Johannesburg, 1920–1934'. In Morrel, R (ed.), *White But Poor: Essays on the History of the Poor Whites in Southern Africa, 1880–1940* (Pretoria: University of South Africa, 1992).

123 UG 39-'13, 1913, p. 23.

124 Stals, *Afrikaners in die Goudstad: Deel 1*, p. 55.

125 Rogerson CM, '"Shisha nyama": The Rise and Fall of the Native Eating House Trade in Johannesburg', *Social Dynamics* 14(1), pp. 20–33. See also Sherman J, 'Serving the Natives: Whiteness as the Price of Hospitality in South African Yiddish Literature', *Journal of Southern African Studies* 26(3), pp. 505–521.

126 Lange, *White, Poor and Angry*, p. 82.

127 Stals, *Afrikaners in die Goudstad: Deel 2*, p. 23.

128 Bickford-Smith, V, *Ethnic Pride and Racial Prejudice in Victorian Cape Town* (Johannesburg: Witwatersrand University Press, 1995), pp. 100–101.

129 Ibid.

130 Ibid., p.119.

131 Ibid., pp. 199, 127.

132 UG 4- '20, 1920, p. 56.

133 TIC, 1908, p. 119.

134 Lange, *White, Poor and Angry*, pp. 150–151.

135 Ibid., p. 110.

136 Lange, *White, Poor and Angry*, p. 89.

137 Ibid., pp. 148–149.

138 UG 34-'21, p. 5.

139 UG 16-'21, p. 16.

140 UG 17-'22, p. 14.

141 UG 34-'21, p. 31.

142 Ibid., p. 33.

143 Ibid.

144 Ibid., p. 33.

145 UG 17-'22, p. 24.

146 Ibid., p. 27.

147 TIC, 1908: 117.

148 TIC, 1908: 137.

149 UG 39-'13, 1913, p. 210.

150 Lange, *White, Poor and Angry*, pp. 116–117.

151 UG 39-'13, 1913, p. 16.

152 Van Onselen, *New Babylon*, p. 124.

153 Stals, *Afrikaners in die Goudstad: Deel 2*, pp. 32–33.

154 De Kiewiet, *A History of South Africa*, p. 221.

155 TIC, 1908, p. 117.

156 Stals, *Afrikaners in die Goudstad: Deel 1*, p. 55.
157 TIC, 1908, p. 117.
158 Stals, *Afrikaners in die Goudstad: Deel 2*, p. 33.
159 Ibid., p. 34.
160 Grosskopf, *Rural Impoverishment and Rural Exodus*, pp. 194–198.
161 Ibid., p. 159.
162 Van Onselen, *New Babylon*, p. 159.
163 TIC, 1908, p. 136.
164 Ibid.
165 Lange, *White, Poor and Angry*, p. 150.
166 TIC, 1908, p. 119.
167 Ibid., pp. 116–119.
168 TIC, 1908, p. 185.
169 Ibid., p. 119.
170 Ibid., p. 135.
171 Ibid., p. 147.
172 Ibid., p. 154.
173 Ibid., p. 125.
174 Lange, *White, Poor and Angry*, pp. 116–117.
175 UG 17-'22, p. 15.
176 Driver, Moral Geographies, p. 282.
177 A type of filtered coffee.
178 Soft, sweet bread rolls.
179 McClintock, A, *Imperial Leather: Race, Gender and Sexuality in Colonial Contest* (New York: Routledge, 1995). McClintock's study, though perceptive, does suffer from oversimplification. She incorrectly assumes, for instance, that Afrikaner identity and apartheid are inseparable. Apartheid itself was certainly not a single monolithic national doctrine. See Giliomee, H, 'The Growth of Afrikaner Identity' in Beinart, W & Dubow, S (eds), *Segregation and Apartheid in Twentieth-Century South Africa* (New York, Routledge, 1995), pp. 189–205.
180 Western, J, 'Undoing the Colonial City?', *Geographical Review*, 75 (3), p. 350. See also Jordaan, K, 'The origins of the Afrikaners and their language, 1652–1720: A study in miscegenation and Creole' in *Race*, 15, 1974, pp. 461–495.
181 Literally, 'shamed family'.
182 Teppo, A, *The Making of a Good White: A Historical Ethnography of the Rehabilitation of Poor Whites in a Suburb of Cape Town* (Helsinki: University of Helsinki, 2004), p. 93.
183 Translates as poor white question or problem.
184 Bottomley, *Public Policy and White Rural Poverty in South Africa, 1881–1924*, pp. 320–322.
185 Van Onselen, *New Nineveh*, p. 147.
186 Stals, *Afrikaners in die Goudstad: Deel 2*, p. 36.
187 The industrial unrest (culminating in the 1922 Rand strikes) is often given as the reason for the SAP's loss. Although it certainly had a major role to play, I find this argument

unconvincing. See Bottomley, *Public Policy and White Rural Poverty*, p. 352 and Stals, *Afrikaners in die Goudstad: Deel 2*, p. 37.

188 Stals, *Afrikaners in die Goudstad: Deel 2*, p. 37.

189 O'Meara, D, *Volkskapitalisme: Class, Capital and Ideology in the Development of Afrikaner Nationalism, 1934–1948* (Johannesburg: Ravan Press, 1983), p. 90.

190 Giliomee, *The Afrikaners*, p. 342.

191 Hyslop, J, 'White Working-Class Women and the Invention of Apartheid: "Purified" Afrikaner Nationalist Agitation for Legislation against "Mixed" Marriages, 1934–1939', *The Journal of African History*, 36(1), p. 67.

192 'Poor whites'.

193 Note that this is an official term in South Africa, and in use today.

194 Hyslop J, *White Working-Class Women*, p. 67.

195 Meaning a sense of own identity.

196 O'Meara, D, *Volkskapitalisme: Class, Capital and Ideology in the Development of Afrikaner Nationalism 1934–1948* (Johannesburg: Ravan Press, 1983), pp. 6–7.

197 Ibid.

198 Ibid.

199 Ibid., p. 7.

200 For an introduction, see Keegan, T, *Colonial South Africa and the Origins of the Racial Order* (Cape Town: David Philip, 1996).

201 Cell, JW, *The Highest Stage of White Supremacy: The Origins of Segregation in South Africa and the American South* (Cambridge: Cambridge University Press, 1982), pp. 196–197.

202 Rich, PB, 'Ministering to the White Man's Needs: The Development of Urban Segregation in South Africa 1903–1923', *African Studies*, 37(2), 1978, pp. 177–191.

203 Swanson, MW, 'The Sanitation Syndrome: Bubonic Plague and Urban Native Policy in the Cape Colony, 1900–09'. In Beinart, W & Dubow, S (eds), *Segregation and Apartheid in Twentieth-Century South Africa* (New York: Routledge, 1995), pp. 25–42.

204 Parnell, 'Slums, Segregation and Poor Whites in Johannesburg', p. 118.

205 Parnell, S, 'Creating Racial Privilege: The Origins of South African Public Health and Town Planning Legislation', *Journal of Southern African Studies*, 19(3), 1993, p. 486.

206 Parnell, 'Slums, Segregation and Poor Whites in Johannesburg', p. 119.

207 Ibid., p. 129.

208 Quoted in Giliomee, *The Afrikaners*, p. 336.

209 Cell, *The Highest Stage of White Supremacy*, p. 194.

210 Ibid.

211 Marx, C, *Oxwagon Sentinel: Radical Afrikaner Nationalism and the History of the Ossewabrandwag* (Berlin: Lit Verlag, 2008), p. 4.

212 Marx, C, 'The Ossewabrandwag as a Mass Movement, 1939–1941', *Journal of Southern African Studies*, 20(2), 1994, pp. 195–219.

213 Van den Berghe, PL, 'Apartheid, Fascism and the Golden Age', *Cahiers d'Etudes Africaines*, 2(8), 1962, p. 599.

214 Giliomee in *The Afrikaners* (pp. 442–443) argues the OB's members never achieved

more than 100 000, and dismisses it. Gideon Shimoni, however, emphasises the organisation's 'broad appeal' to Afrikaners and argues that its ideas 'penetrated deeply' into mainstream Afrikaner nationalism. See Shimoni, G, *Jews and Zionism: The South African Experience, 1910–1967* (Cape Town: Oxford University Press, 1980), pp. 128–136.

215 Marx, 'The Ossewabrandwag as a Mass Movement, 1939– 1941', p. 209.

216 Marx, *Oxwagon Sentinel*, p. 228.

217 Ibid., pp. 228–231.

218 A bonnet worn by women during the Great Trek more than a century earlier, but adopted by the OB and various Afrikaner cultural organisations.

219 Marx, *Oxwagon Sentinel*, p. 231.

220 Klausen, *Race, Maternity, and the Politics of Birth Control in South Africa*, p. 42.

221 Rothmann, ME, *My Beskeie Deel: 'n Outobiografiese Vertelling* (Cape Town: Tafelberg, 1972), p. 23.

222 Marx, *Oxwagon Sentinel*, p. 125.

223 Albertyn, JR, *The Poor White and Society: Report of the Carnegie Commission* (Stellenbosch: Pro Ecclesia, 1932), vol. 5, p. 24.

224 *Report of the Carnegie Commission: Joint Findings and Recommendations* (Stellenbosch: Pro Ecclesia, 1932), pp. xxiv–xxv. Note that these recommendations are included in every volume of the report.

225 Quoted in Klausen, *Race, Maternity, and the Politics of Birth Control in South Africa 1910–1930*, p. 63.

226 This paragraph draws heavily from O'Meara, *Volkskapitalisme*, p. 76.

227 Translated from the Afrikaans Witwatersrandse Vereniging vir Volkswelsyn and Bond van Randse Moeders.

228 O'Meara, *Volkskapitalisme*, p. 59.

229 Ibid.

230 Ibid., p. 61.

231 Ibid., p. 98.

232 Centenary celebrations or Second Trek.

233 O'Meara, *Volkskapitalisme*, pp. 36–37.

234 O'Meara, *Volkskapitalisme*, p. 111.

235 Ibid.

236 Ibid., pp. 113–115.

237 League of the Act of Salvation.

238 O'Meara, *Volkskapitalisme*, p. 137.

239 Departments for free time.

240 O'Meara, *Volkskapitalisme*, p. 139.

241 Ibid., p. 139.

242 Zietsman, PH, *Die Taal is Gans Die Volk* (Pretoria: Unisa Press, 1992), p. 138.

243 Ibid., p. 6.

244 Ibid., p. 4.

245 Ibid., p. 6

246 Ibid., p. 6. Author's translation from Dutch.

247 Ibid., p. 9.

248 Ibid., p. 9.

249 Ibid., p. 11.

250 Ibid., p. 11.

251 Ibid., pp. 14–15.

252 'Anglicisation'.

253 Ibid., pp. 127, 136.

254 Davids, A, *The Afrikaans of the Cape Muslims* (Pretoria: Protea Book House, 2011).

255 Ibid., p. 106.

256 Ibid., p. 106.

257 Zietsman, *Die Taal is Gans Die Volk*, p. 196.

258 Zietsman, *Die Taal is Gans Die Volk*, p. 197.

259 O'Meara, *Volkskapitalisme*, p. 75.

260 Ibid., p. 103.

261 Ibid., p. 64.

262 Coetzee, A, *'n Hele Os Vir 'n Ou Broodmes* (Pretoria: Van Schaik, 2000), p. 90.

263 Ibid., p. 91.

264 Ibid., p. 94.

265 Ibid., p. 95.

266 Ibid., p. 96.

267 Ibid., p. 100.

268 Ibid., p. 100.

269 Van Niekerk, M, *Triomf* (Cape Town: Queillerie, 1994), quoted in Coetzee, *'n Hele Os Vir 'n Ou Broodmes*, pp. 103–104.

270 Yudelman, *The Emergence of Modern South Africa*, p. 42.

271 Giliomee, *The Afrikaners*, p. 353.

272 O'Meara, *Volkskapitalisme*, p. 205.

273 Ibid., p. 249.

274 Ibid., p. 139.

275 Giliomee, *The Afrikaners*, p. 349.

276 Wilson, F, *Carnegie Corporation Oral History Project*, 2006.

277 Bottomley, J, '"Almost Bled to Death": The Effects of the Anglo-Boer War on Social Transformation in the Orange River Colony', *Historia*, 44(1), p. 191.

278 Teppo, A, *The Making of a Good White: A Historical Ethnography of the Rehabilitation of Poor Whites in a Suburb of Cape Town* (Helsinki: University of Helsinki, 2004), p. 55.

279 Teppo, *The Making of a Good White*, p. 18.

280 Ibid., p. 41.

281 Ibid., p. 22.

282 Ibid., pp. 34–40.

283 Ibid., pp. 49–51.

284 Ibid., p. 48.

285 'Community unit'.

286 Ibid., pp. 116–177.

287 Ibid., p. 117.

288 Ibid., pp. 117–118.

289 'Rabbit Town'.

290 Pickaxe and shovel.

291 Derogatory terms for black women and men.

292 Helpende Hand, *Gesigte van Afrikanerarmoede*, 2010. Available at http://www.helpendehand.co.za/navorsing/armoede/#more-1138 (accessed on 20 March 2012).

293 Ibid., p. 16.

294 Meth-heads, people addicted to methamphetamine.

295 Orizio, R, *Lost White Tribes: Journeys Amongst the Forgotten* (London: Secker & Warburg, 2000), p. 2.

296 Ibid., p. 28.

297 Ibid., p. xi.

298 Beckingham, D, *The Regulation of Drunkenness in Nineteenth-Century Liverpool* (PhD Diss.), 2008, p. 165.

A Picture of Devon

TANTONS

A Picture of Devon

ROSEMARY LAUDER

Illustrated by
BILL WRIGHT

Robert Hale Limited
Clerkenwell House
Clerkenwell Green
London EC1R 0HT

British Library Cataloguing in Publication Data
Lauder, Rosemary Anne
A picture of Devon.
1. Devon
I. Title
942.3'50858

ISBN 0-7090-3823-2

Frontispiece: The ancient bridge at Bideford

Photoset in Baskerville by
Rowland Phototypesetting Limited, Bury St Edmunds, Suffolk
Printed in Great Britain by
St Edmundsbury Press Limited, Bury St Edmunds, Suffolk
and bound by WBC Limited, Bristol and Maesteg

See that ye hold fast the Heritage we leave you
Yea and teach your children the value that
never in the coming centuries their hearts
may fail them, or their hands grow weak.

Sir Francis Drake

Contents

Illustrations

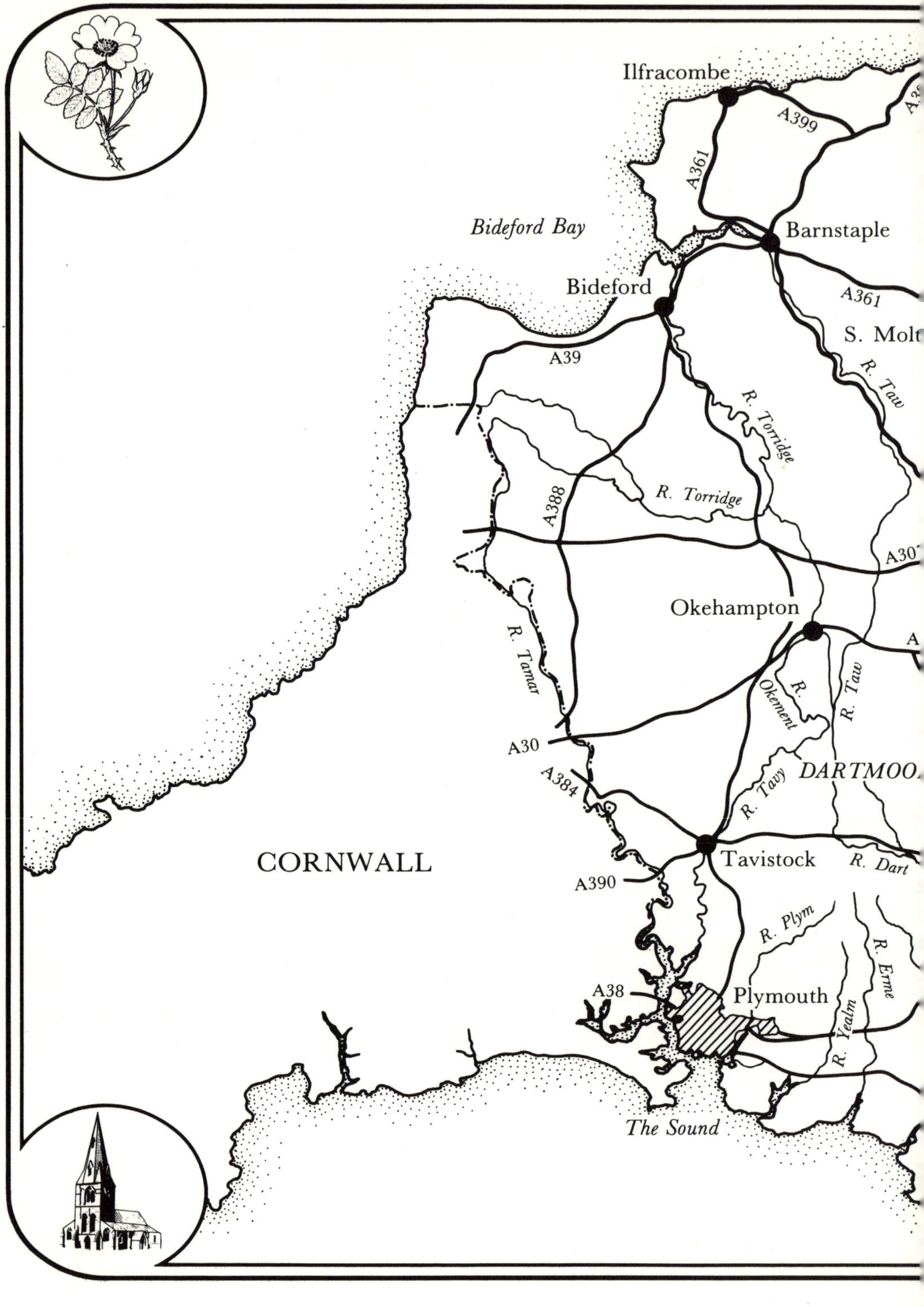

Ilfracombe
A399
A361
Barnstaple
Bideford Bay
Bideford
A361
A39
R. Taw
R. Torridge
A388
R. Torridge
Okehampton
R. Tamar
R. Okement
R. Taw
A30
A384
R. Tavy
Tavistock
R. Dart
CORNWALL
A390
R. Plym
R. Erme
A38
Plymouth
R. Yealm
The Sound

A PICTURE OF DEVON

Introduction

Devon is a giant of a county. In size it is surpassed only by Yorkshire and Lincolnshire. In richness and variety it is second to none – or so Devonians think.

No other county has so much to offer. Magnificent scenery wherever one goes; historic towns and pretty villages; an abundance of wildlife of all types, the estuaries being a paradise for bird-watchers and fishermen alike; the fields of daffodils and banks of primroses that are an annual star attraction; walking-country to tire the most energetic, and holiday centres offering every conceivable amusement. There are wide,

Thatched cottage, Appledore

open spaces and sheltered coombes, gaunt cliffs and sandy bays – for Devon is a county of contrasts: contrasts between north and south; between winter and summer; between natives and newcomers; between old ways and new ways; between crowds and quietness.

One contrast is between its two distinct coastlines, in which Devon is unique. Other counties with differing seaboards are usually peninsulas – Cornwall and Kent, and the Welsh and Scottish counties.

The English Channel south coast is picturesque. Its wooded creeks and estuaries penetrate deep inland, offering sheltered havens to wildlife and yachtsmen; quaint old fishing villages attract the tourists in their thousands, and the lush, often semi-tropical vegetation proclaims a mild, moist climate where snow and frost are almost unknown.

The majesty of the Atlantic Ocean and the fury of the wild west wind have formed a very different northern coast. Towering cliffs frown over contorted and tumbled rocks, heaped with ever-moving pebbles and washed by the ceaseless movement of this powerful ocean. For mile upon mile the cliffs appear deserted, uninhabited. All human dwellings are built well inland, protected from the gale-force winds. As the Atlantic gives way to the Bristol Channel, so the cliffs become more benign, but still there is an absence of human influence. The exceptions provide a stark and welcome contrast and are all well-known names – Clovelly, Ilfracombe, Lynmouth. It is in the sheltered waters of Bideford Bay and the estuary of the Taw and Torridge rivers that the largest settlements have grown up.

There is contrast, too, between east and west. Somerset and Dorset are both famed for their picturesque villages, their lush and comfortable scenery, and indistinguishably they merge into East Devon. Here the villages are larger and appear solidly settled. The countryside seems lush, prosperous – even self-satisfied. The rivers are calm and placid, ambling out to the smooth coastline of Lyme Bay.

Much 'typical Devon scenery' is to be found in the broad diagonal corridor running up from Exeter to Bideford Bay. Here are the steep coombes and rounded hills, the deep red soil and lush vegetation and a way of life that seems slow and murmurous.

Dartmoor, another contrast, is the dominating feature of West Devon, one that cannot be ignored or avoided. For centuries its great bulk has been a barrier between east and west and between north and south. Those who live within its confines know a harshness of climate and a way of life spartan beyond the belief of those who have never experienced such conditions. Dartmoor could be said to be the heart of Devon, an iron core surrounded by a softer countryside.

The western boundary of the county is formed almost entirely by the River Tamar, rising within four miles of the north coast. It is a valley of great beauty and much history, and once formed an important route from the coast into the hinterland.

For communications hold the key to Devon's past and to its development. In a country full of deep valleys, steep hills, wild moorland and windswept cliffs, development was possible only along the limited lines of the earliest tracks. Where the packhorse could travel, the countryside was developed and the settlements were formed. Devon is rich in small market towns, some still bustling on market days, others dwindled to overlarge villages. Almost all are on high ground, away from the damp, densely wooded river valleys, often flooded and formerly home to vagrants and robbers.

A bird's-eye view of the county would show the population heavily tilted towards the south. Plymouth is bursting at the seams; Torbay has sprawled, swallowing up the separate communities that were once little fishing villages or select Victorian resorts. Tourism is here to stay, and it has brought with it a growing number of holiday developments: caravans, chalets, amusement parks, huge and ever-insufficient car-parks. There is a growing battle between those who seek to develop tourism as the county's economic mainstay and those who seek to conserve Devon for future generations and not give in to a largely seasonal influx. There are fights over road routes, over reservoirs, over out-of-town shopping complexes, over almost any development anywhere.

The other influx that is currently causing problems is the growing number of elderly people who have chosen to take advantage of the county's mild climate and who, in some resorts, are threatening to take over from the holidaymaker.

The face of Devon is changing, albeit slowly, for she is still remote from central government, out on a limb known as 'the West Country' and bedevilled always by poor lines of communications; not for nothing was North Devon dubbed 'furthest from railways'. Only grudgingly was the M5 eventually extended below Bristol, and even now it stops short at Exeter. A controversial link road with Tiverton and North Devon should shortly be completed, and no one knows what effect this will have on a part of the country that is highly resistant to change. Politicians claim that it will bring new blood to the area, new industries to create employment, expansion because travelling-time will be cut. Sceptics say it will simply allow even bigger snarl-ups at new locations on summer Saturdays – the bottle-neck will have been moved a little further westwards. Perhaps it will not make any difference at all, apart from the destruction of acres of beautiful Devon countryside that have been sacrificed to the god of speed.

This book does not set out to write the history of the county of Devon

Statue at Brixham of William of Orange

– far more learned writers have already performed this fascinating and demanding task. Rather is it an attempt to portray Devon as she is today, Devon as her inhabitants see her, and Devon as the visitor sees her. It provides an insight into the nature of what, at times, is a very private county, and an insight into the nature of the elusive Devonians. Time does pass more slowly in the soft West Country, and life is unhurried, even leisurely. People remember simple pleasures, such as watching the sunset or stopping for tea, waiting patiently for a dog to move himself from the road or for a herd of cows to pass.

There are still remote areas where electricity is unknown, and water pumped from a well, where modern housewives would think themselves in a museum and be completely incapable of producing a meal. The old ways, now making a fashionable return elsewhere, have never disappeared, never been superseded by newfangled equipment or modern methods. Parts of rural Devon are very rural indeed.

Yet there are villages that come to life only in the summer, where the shutters go up with the last departing visitor and the village street is deserted, save for the forlorn debris that marks the end of another season. The 'summer visitors' have been with us for a long time; farmers' wives have been taking them in for fifty years or more, but never have they been such big business as they are today, when virtually the whole county has to be structured round them.

The beaches of the south are no place for the local or the lover of solitude once July is here. He must look inland, to a whole rich area, little-known and waiting to be explored. Once the main routes and centres are left behind, there are vast areas of Devon where one may spend a whole day in complete solitude, watching the dippers on the streams or the curlews on the moor, with only the passing sheep for company.

This is walkers' country, the country of naturalists, of artists (and even writers) and of the Devonians to whom it represents the true Devon, the abiding Devon that has always been and always will be.

1

The Devon Way of Life

Traditionally, Devon is an agricultural county. Farming has remained constant throughout its history and still has the biggest impact on its appearance and economy. The rich grazing-lands that first attracted the early settlers are still apparent today: the lush water-meadows where cattle peacefully browse, the flowery fields and the gentle slopes are more or less unchanged. Sheep still nibble the short turf of the moors and the exposed headlands, but the days when the county's wealth was founded on wool have long since gone, and it is upon the placid dairy herds that the economy of the farming community largely

Pondsworthy, near Ashburton

depends. Devon is one of the country's most important milk-producing counties, second only to Yorkshire.

The pattern of farming has changed only slightly over the centuries. In the old days country folk had a simple way of life with few wants, and the financial pressures on them were meagre. Farmers today find themselves increasingly hard-pressed, and farming is becoming less the way of life it always has been and more of a business. Small farms, traditional methods, father-to-son has been the pattern, but all this may well have to change. It will be a sad day when accountants take over and the Devon countryside goes the way of much of the rest of the country. It is our small fields, abundance of hedges, copses and boundary trees that make the Devon landscape so rich, so 'English', now that much of England looks like prairie-land.

Today the number of holdings has been reduced, and the size of the herds has greatly increased. In my childhood, farmers gave their cows names – 'Come up Bluebell, Buttercup, Daisy,' they would call at milking-time. Not any more. A number is stamped on the cow's flank, its only means of identification. Gone, too, are the traditional Devon breeds of cattle; the famous Devon Reds most notably have all but disappeared, pushed out of existence by the ubiquitous and boring black-and-white Friesian.

Farming policy, it seems, is dictated not by what is best grown in the county, or even by what the population most needs, but by what is considered economic by the Government and by Brussels, and which crops carry the greatest subsidy. In days gone by, the farmer got on with what he knew best – farming. Today he has to grapple with a mountain of paperwork; forms for this, subsidies for that; quotas which prevent his overproducing or force him to pour milk down the drain, and always there is the growing need for capital, for more expensive and up-to-date machinery. It is a miracle that so many family-run farms survive in Devon, yet they still make up the bulk of the holdings, though fewer in number and larger in size. Gone are the days when a farm was a small community with several farmhands treated as family and with large gatherings round the traditional long Devon farmhouse table at each meal. Farmers employ few people outside their own families, and usually only on a casual basis. One growing trend is to employ outside contractors at harvest time, and it is not unusual to see the huge modern combine harvesters working through the night. Somehow, the long rows of black plastic-wrapped bales lack the appeal of a traditional hayrick, a sight that has now vanished almost entirely from the landscape.

Old ways die hard in the country. When I moved down in the 1960s from the London area, the differences were most marked, perhaps more so then than now. Things that were beginning to be commonplace in the suburbs were unheard-of in rural Devon. Vacuum cleaners, fridges and central heating were rarities, and even electric lighting and indoor sanitation were by no means common. Most Devon farmhouses revolved around a traditional kitchen, large and cheery. The centrepiece was often a long table, capable of seating a dozen or even twenty at a time. There was always a kitchen stove, an Aga or Rayburn in the more-up-to-date kitchens, the old range still giving good service in many others.

Flagstone floors served in some farmhouses, but more often they were plain concrete or even earth. Few ordinary homes boasted carpet in any of the rooms; rag rugs made by the women of the house sufficed. The sink was in the back scullery, and most of the utensils and crockery were housed in a dresser, it was all a world away from today's luxury fitted kitchens. But farmhouse kitchens scored over today's bright and hygienic counterpart. They were always warm and welcoming; there was always time to sit and chat around that large table; there was usually one large chair by the range, and there was a kettle of huge proportions simmering on the stove. Many of these kettles were so large that it was almost impossible to lift them full; they were topped up from a jug and spent their entire life on the stove.

The kitchen was the most used room in the house, and it was here that everyone congregated. The front parlour, by comparison, was cheerless. Properly furnished with a horsehair sofa and family photographs, it was rarely used – and it was no mark of favour to be ushered into the parlour instead of the homely kitchen.

Bathrooms are a recent introduction in many farmhouses, and a jug and basin were standard bedroom articles. Today all these discarded items fetch high prices on the antique market. Who needed washstands and ewers once a bathroom had been installed? What was the point in keeping the old-fashioned oil lamps when the electric was connected? Out they went, and with them the long tables, the huge kettles and pans, the dresser and the wooden settles. They are now worth far more than their modern replacements.

In those not-so-far-off days, most of the smallholdings kept their own house cow, which was milked by hand and provided the household with rich, creamy milk from which butter and cream would be made. Some kept a pig, and nearly all farmers' wives kept chickens. The freshness and quality of food have definitely not improved in recent years. Today it is virtually impossible to buy good dairy produce from the farms. Gone are the numerous signs advertising 'clotted cream and milk' for sale. Years of harassment from officials have had their effect, and the final deathblow has been dealt by the EEC, who somehow consider that fresh milk is bad for you. A land flowing with milk and honey, indeed, but just try getting your hands on some of it! The taste of Devon these days has to be pasteurized, sterilized, regularized, and once all the traditional flavour and goodness have been removed, it can be neatly packaged and sold through approved outlets. What nonsense!

Most farmhouses and cottages have now been modernized with gusto as a new form of revenue has been discovered – the summer visitor. Taking in visitors is nothing new, but whereas old-fashioned homes were considered quaint, today's holidaymakers require everything to be the same as at home. Everywoman's dream kitchen has taken over from the traditional farmhouse kitchen – and the farmer's wife has far more time than she ever had before. But then she needs it, because she has to go out for her pleasures and company, and even her shopping, when before they were all around her.

But here and there the old ways prevail, or rather have never been superseded. What was good enough before is good enough now, and true old Devonians with accents you could cut with a knife still 'bide home by the fire, you'. A very few are still without electricity, and many are glad they have kept their own water supply. Just occasionally one of these homes from the past comes on the market, and it is with utter incredulity that modernized folk go and view, total disbelief written on their faces that people could still live in such conditions. Of course, those who have their own water and have kept the kitchen stove are hardly affected by power cuts and water shortages; a rare form of independence!

In a land where change comes slowly, there are many survivals not found elsewhere. The village shop has managed somehow to carry on into the twentieth century, often combined with the sub-post office, sometimes under a new shiny 'Mace' or 'Spar' banner, but the village shop still, where the shopkeeper listens with a sympathetic ear whilst weighing out the cheese, and the village news is exchanged whilst the customer is collecting the pension. It may cost a little more to shop in such places, but they provide an invaluable service and are an indispensable facet of village life.

The village blacksmith is another survival to be found in several Devon villages. Hunting plays a major part in rural life, and where there are horses, there must also be blacksmiths. Many of them have turned their hands to producing fancy wrought ironwork, such as weathervanes and fire grates, and now have showrooms to tempt the visitor, but there are still one or two unglamorous premises where farmers bring their machinery for repair, and welding has become a second skill.

Agricultural shows, too, remain an important strand in country life.

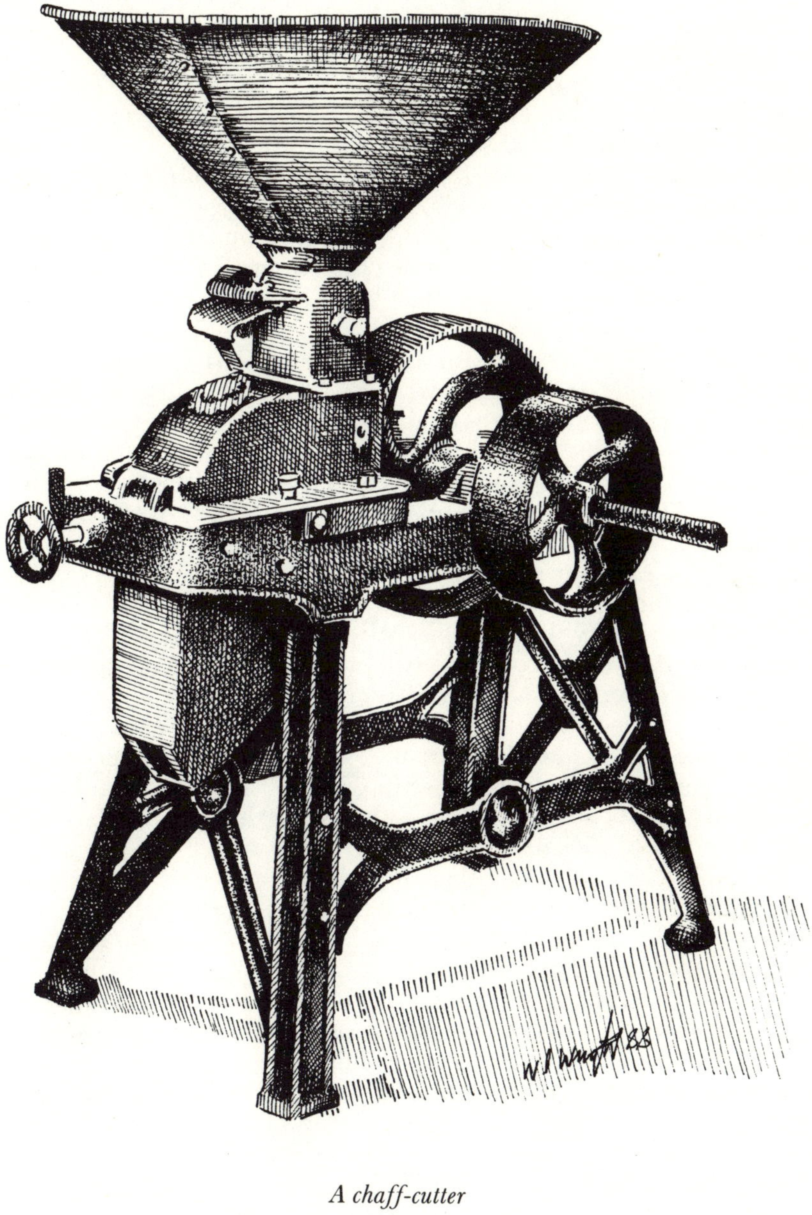

A chaff-cutter

Up and down the county there are innumerable small village shows, where marquees and tents mushroom for one day, and farmers bring their prize cows and bulls in the hope of going home the proud possessor of a rosette or two. There is a hierarchy with these shows. The winners at the smallest move on to the larger shows, such as the North Devon Show, and then to the Devon County Show the following May, and perhaps even to Smithfield. Another important aspect is show jumping. It is at such parochial shows that all international horseriders cut their teeth, make their first falls and collect their first rosettes. They are the first link in a chain that could lead to stardom, and every ponyclub member on his or her Thelwell-style pony dreams of reaching the Horse of the Year show, one day.

The Devon County Show takes place in May and for three days brings the traffic to a standstill around Exeter, where it has a permanent showground. In the next few years it is planned to move to a larger site which will become an exhibition centre for the Westcountry operating all the year. It remains the highlight of the year for many farmers and aspiring showjumpers and has become big business for the exhibitors. The car-salesmen and the double-glazing stands congregate around the periphery, and the agricultural machinery seems to get larger every year, but in essence the County Show is the same as the little village show from which it has evolved.

The village carnival is a special West Country delight. The amount of time and effort that people are still prepared to put into making these one-day celebrations a success is incredible. It is not unusual for a village procession to have as many as twenty or more floats, all designed and executed to a high standard, some artistic, some political, the majority comic. The carnival queen with her attendants, all properly decked out, heads the procession, followed by the village or town band, and the whole community turns out to cheer and throw money on the floats. Most carnivals take place in the summer, often in the pouring rain, which never deters either the participants or the spectators, who are determined not to let a little thing like the weather put them off.

Many of the fairs and carnivals have a special significance. Torrington's May Fair features the crowning of the May Queen, and the whole town celebrates for almost a week. At Ashburton they taste the ale, and Barnstaple's week-long September fair is proclaimed open with a gloved hand on a pole and pieces of dry toast and ale. Tavistock Goosey Fair is a major event in October, and they still turn the Devil's Stone at Shebbear, and send burning tar barrels down the streets to scare the Devil at Hatherleigh and Ottery St Mary. Regattas are still commonplace along the coast and rivers, and numerous small village fêtes enliven the summer and raise funds for the church or for local causes.

The agricultural show

The original purpose of many of these centuries-old fairs has been lost. Permission had to be sought to hold a fair, and these were often timed to coincide with a local saint's day. Dealers and farmers congregated to buy and to sell. Just as at today's agricultural shows, the hangers-on came too, the tinkers and the fortune-tellers, the sellers of quack medicines and the pedlars. The pickpockets and horse-thieves were an added hazard – nothing changes. As people congregated together so rarely in days before motorized transport, such markets and fairs became an excuse for a jolly good time, and it is chiefly the pleasure aspect that has survived. But they still serve as a meeting-place for people from outlying areas, giving them a reason to come into town and combine business with pleasure.

A great crowd-puller is the Traction Engine and Steam Rally, now a firm annual event, held at Umberleigh in mid Devon every August. The magic of these noisy monsters never fails, and many of the engines make the rounds of the agricultural shows and carnivals. In a spacious county the size of Devon, redundant machinery is often just pushed to one side waiting to be dealt with 'later'. Several decades 'later', what was once redundant becomes highly prized. Many of the engines have been lovingly restored at a cost of countless man-hours and much spit-and-polish. They range in size from the fairground and road-mending giants to almost miniature farm machines, and for anyone remotely interested in engines or engineering, they are fascinating – if somewhat deafening when viewed in close proximity.

Cob and thatch are almost as synonymous with the image of Devon as cream teas and cider, but they are by no means typical of Devon architecture. Churches there are in plenty; some excellent examples of farm buildings; a few manor houses, even fewer large houses and scarcely any castles, but there is a wealth of good, solid yeoman or cottage property throughout the county, and it differs widely from region to region.

Vernacular architecture is essentially that which belongs to a region and traditionally made use of locally available building-materials. Hence there are few timber-framed houses in the county because, although it is rich in oak woods, most are small scrub oaks incapable of providing large beams.

In the more exposed areas, something more solid than timber was considered necessary to keep the winds and weather at bay. Much of the delightful variety occurs because of the use made of local stone. Thus the quarries in the east provided the famous almost white Beer stone; greensand came from the Salcombe region; the well-known red from the quarries around Exeter and Crediton, and the blue/grey stone so prevalent in the west is the Devonian limestone found around Plymouth and Torbay. Much of Plymouth, including the breakwater, is built of this cold, cheerless stone. Quarried stone was in the main used for churches and the larger houses. Rough stone or slate was good enough for barns, walls and cottages, and around Dartmoor the loose granite collected from the moor was plentiful enough to satisfy most needs.

North Devon suffered from a lack of good local building-material and made use of whatever came to hand; there are numerous small craters in the woods or clifflands that yielded just enough stone for the local builder. And where there was no stone, cob was the answer.

Mud, of which there is usually plenty, is the basis of cob. Devon was not alone in using it for humble dwellings, but they seem to have survived in greater numbers here. It is said that as long as it has a dry foot and a dry head, cob will last for ever. The straightness of a cob wall depended entirely on the eye of the builder, and it was built up in layers, the mud having first been mixed with straw. Presumably it was also dependent upon the weather, a wet spell causing a complete cessation of work because the cob would never have set. The finished walling was then roughcast and nowadays is painted. A cob and thatched house is a remarkable structure, for it is cool in summer and takes little heating in winter. Maintenance is low, and even rethatching is not the expense some people think. No doubt the man of the house was quite accustomed to carrying out running repairs on his own roof – appearance not being the prime consideration it is today.

The exposed dwellings on the north coast and the high ground of the county were rarely thatched, but this form of roofing was common in the rest of Devon and recently has made something of a comeback. In the mid-1900s thatching was a dying art, and thatchers had to be booked several years ahead. A legacy of galvanized roofs was the result. But, along with other ancient crafts, thatching has been revived just in time, and many youngsters are now learning the art. Perhaps someone will take the plunge and try their hand at building a dwelling from cob.

Some farmhouses and cottages have been so ruthlessly modernized that it is hard to recognize them for what they are, or were. Harsh new windows may let in a lot more light, but they ruin the character, as do half-glazed front doors, concrete-tiled roofs and flat-roofed extensions. But here and there the traditional Devon longhouse survives, and at last they are becoming appreciated and properly preserved. Under one roof were combined living-accommodation for the family and shelter for the livestock. A central passage divided one from the other, and very often they were only one room deep. A massive external chimney breast, which in the earliest examples may well be a later addition, is

A thatcher at work

often an attractive feature, complete with cloam ovens. These were constructed of clay and were heated by means of burning faggots whose ashes were raked out, leaving a red-hot oven in which to bake bread and pies. The very earliest homes had no such luxury; the fire was lit on a central hearth, and smoke either found its own way out or escaped through a hole in the roof. Smoke-blackened rafters are evidence of this, not, as is often supposed, of a more serious fire. Upper storeys were not constructed until the sixteenth or seventeenth century – and a chimneystack then became essential.

Many Devon farmsteads boast a fine array of old buildings, barns and shippens for the livestock, granaries, stables, and linhays for the fodder. But vanishing fast are the semicircular threshing-floors once quite a common sight. A central post supported the roof of a low structure attached to one of the barns, and a horse or oxen was used to turn a thresher which separated the grain from the chaff. Once modern farming-techniques made these roundhouses redundant, they were of little use for any other purpose, being too low for storage, and most were allowed to fall into disrepair.

Other redundant farmbuildings are enjoying a vogue, and 'barn conversions' are all the rage. Any farmer who has spent years worrying about the upkeep of these traditional but now superfluous buildings has suddenly found himself in clover. Exorbitant prices are being paid for what are mere shells built only to agricultural standards and surrounded by working farmyards. In other cases the entire farmyard range has been converted into expensive holiday accommodation, and visitors from less rural areas seem only too pleased to spend their fortnight in 'The Piggery', 'The Shippen' or 'The Cow Byre'. Meanwhile the farmer erects huge, soulless structures of galvanized and concrete that somehow never seem to blend into the landscape in the way their predecessors did.

What an architectural disaster it was when concrete was first discovered – or invented! Gone are the rich varieties of local styles built up through long usage of local materials, and architecture suited to the area. Now all is of a uniform sameness and drabness. Precast, preformed, predesigned and utterly soulless. Each city centre resembling any other, each new housing estate duller and nastier and more compact than its predecessors. One might as well be in Lancashire or Cambridgeshire for all the difference it makes. Thank goodness for the old buildings that have survived and give our county its character.

Many of the inns are good examples of indigenous buildings, for, as they are still used for their original purpose, they have been less altered over the centuries. There are several worth a visit for the architecture alone, in particular the former 'church house inns'. Built originally as

Butcher's Row, Barnstaple

meeting-rooms or simply as a place in which churchgoers refreshed themselves before beginning the long journey back home on foot or horseback, they have adapted very well to the needs of twentieth-century travellers. It is sad to relate that this century has seen the destruction of many a fine interior; the breweries seem intent on doing to licensed premises what the Victorians did to churches. All too often a cosy, well-used, atmospheric inn has been ripped about, its internal walls removed, a shiny modern bar thrust through the centre, and bright modern lights and decorations added. Fitted seating replaces the old oak trestles and tables and, worst of all, a fruit-machine or jukebox stands in the cavernous fireplace where once a hospitable fire burned winter and summer alike. The extent of destruction of village inns has yet to be fully realized, by which time it will be too late.

There is a sorry story of destruction, too, in many of the old towns. Developers have demanded, and planners have given in. The heart and character have been ripped out to provide room for a new shopping precinct, a supermarket, a hotel complex, offices, flats, car-parks. And all in ubiquitous concrete, steel and plate glass. Street corners have vanished for road-widening; island blocks have been demolished to improve visibility and relieve congestion; yellow lines and one-way systems ensure that all character is lost, and pedestrian safety is sacrificed to the motor vehicle. What pleasure is there to be gained in wandering round any of the larger towns on foot? Even supposing you can find somewhere to park in the first place. Only in the smaller towns, such as Tavistock and Cullompton, has the atmosphere been preserved, and these are constantly under threat. An amazing amount of old Devon is vanishing under the bulldozer. Devonians will have to look sharp to preserve the character of their once unspoilt county.

Sir Francis Drake, Plymouth Hoe

2

Maritime Devon

The sea has played a vital part in the life of Devon. Many a famous sea-faring man was Devon born and bred, and many of her sons travelled to the far corners of the globe, leaving Devon names behind to mark their discoveries. It is the county of Drake, of Raleigh, Hawkins, Grenville, Frobisher and many more and is still home to the Royal Navy, at Dartmouth, where the officers train, and at Plymouth, where much of the Fleet has its home.

The county has also engaged in less publicized maritime activities. Ever since a government first thought of charging duty on certain goods, ingenious people have thought of ways of evading paying. Tax-dodging is as old as taxation itself; it is only the ways and means that change. Smuggling has acquired an aura of romance that is not entirely deserved.

The long and tortuous coastline of Devon, with its secretive coves and deep inlets, and the hinterland, with a network of sunken lanes leading to remote cottages and farmsteads, was almost impossible to patrol effectively. Smuggling in the eighteenth century became quite open, and bribing the excise men was the accepted method of achieving peaceful co-existence. The 'preventive officer' had a lonely and dangerous job. He was loathed wherever he went, and quite often openly attacked. Smugglers were a law unto themselves and were supported by the people as a whole. It was as rife on the north coast as on the south, with illicit cargoes coming from either Ireland or France.

Many are the tales told of smuggling deeds and of close-run battles both on land and at sea, and many are the characters who have acquired a gilded reputation for what were in reality often brutal and rough-and-ready methods of dealing with the law. One such who looms large in any West Country smuggling tale is Jack Rattenbury from Beer. His career started at a tender age, in the 1780s, and although he was caught and imprisoned many times, he always managed either to escape or to be released, and return to his illicit trade, until he had made sufficient to enable him to retire and die at last peacefully in his own bed.

The golden days of smuggling eventually came to an end with the opening up of the Continent, after the cessation of the Napoleonic wars, to more normal trading, so that it was no longer worthwhile running the risks. The customs officers were also becoming more efficient and better equipped. Today it is a very different kind of cargo they seek to prevent being run ashore along the unfrequented coasts of Devon.

From earliest times, fishing was a prominent industry, and almost every man, woman and child who lived in the small fishing villages around the coast was involved. The great herring shoals of the north coast have passed into history, and the pilchards of the south coast have gone the same way. Offshore deep-sea fishing grew in importance, and Brixham lays claim to being the inventor of trawling along the bottom, a development unknown before 1800. Professor Hoskins the Devon historian whose book *Devon* was first published in 1954 and is still the best source on the county, writes, 'The Brixham fishermen followed the fish up Channel, then through the Straits of Dover into the North Sea, and by the early nineteenth century some of them found it more convenient to settle in the east coast ports and carry on trawling from there, particularly Hull and Grimsby, which were poor places until the Devonshire men came and showed them how to fish.'

Salmon-netting

Brixham has always been linked with fishing; at one time it was the most important of the county's ports, with Plymouth and Bideford coming second and third. Plymouth surpassed it by the end of the nineteenth century and remains Devon's chief fishing port. Both towns still operate fish markets on the quayside, where the catches are sold and transported away to the markets and factories up country. For those who can make the effort to get up early enough, a visit to either fishmarket is a rewarding experience.

The wealth of Devon's fish lies in the great variety that exists in the coastal waters, not in the huge shoals that attract the factory ships. It is still possible to buy freshly caught fish from the trawlers; queues on the quayside at many of the small harbours announce the return of a local fisherman. His catch could well include turbot, a highly prized fish, Dover sole, plaice, skate, monkfish and dabs. Cod, ling, mullet, hass, pollock are all to be found on a good fishmonger's slab, most of them caught locally. But trout and salmon are becoming a rarity, pollution and overfishing taking a serious toll.

The industry is still important but has changed considerably. As with agriculture, the small man working on his own has been largely elbowed aside by more powerful vessels often in multiple ownership, and even these find it hard to survive against competition from Scottish and foreign vessels.

Official figures put Devon's fishing industry as twelfth in the country, and it is still reckoned to be a major employer in the coastal areas. The trade is nowadays centred mainly on Brixham, Plymouth, Beer, Seaton and Axmouth, and to a small extent on Appledore and Bideford. The South Hams are important for the shellfish trade, and mussels and oyster beds in the Exe, Salcombe and Teign estuaries have experienced recent growth, although there has been concern at pollution caused by, amongst other things, certain chemicals in marine paint.

Although fishing may have declined, other marine trades have experienced an upsurge. Sailing and yachting have become major leisure pursuits, and with this has come an increase in the need for marinas, for chandlers, for shipwrights and sailmakers, and for all the paraphernalia that attend those who put to sea in ships. Most of the former south-coast sailing villages now derive a considerable income from the yachting fraternity, even if many of them are 'weekend fairweather sailors'. Never mind. They spend money in the local shops, haunt the local pubs and eat in the local restaurants. They do no one any harm, and many people a great deal of good, while the presence of so many beautiful sailing-yachts of all sizes adds considerably to the picturesqueness of the estuaries and creeks. We may mourn the loss of 'the fishing fleets returning under full sail in the evenings' but in their place we have the stately ocean-going yachts and the brightly coloured sails of the local yacht club dinghies. At times we also have the magnificent sight of the tall-ships' race off Brixham to remind us of what things must have looked like in the days of sail.

Since the days of wooden ships, shipbuilding has ceased to be a major industry on the south coast. Only small yachtbuilders and the occasional specialist firm continue their trade in the creeks and coastal waters, with the exception of the naval dockyards at Devonport. On the north coast, on the Torridge estuary, shipbuilding has maintained its once important role, but even here the number of shipyards has dwindled to just two. Appledore was once home to numerous boat-builders and sailmakers; today they are concentrated in the enormous Appledore Shipyard and the smaller but equally famous family-owned yard of Hinks & Son.

The yard at Appledore was one of the first and largest covered docks in Europe – a huge hangar-like edifice dwarfing the riverbank but continuing the centuries-old tradition of shipbuilding on the estuary. It has had its ups and downs, faced bankruptcy more than once, been forced to close on several occasions, but it survives and hopefully will

An old boatyard, Appledore

continue to do so. Less eventful has been the history of Hinks & Son. They have carried on quietly for several generations making small vessels, wooden launches and yachts of high quality, but in the 1960s and early seventies they gained international recognition with their faithful and authentic reconstructions of two wooden sailing ships, the *Nonsuch* and the *Golden Hind*. There were still men in the area with the skills necessary to build those masterpieces of perfection, and the launching of these ships was a proud moment for all concerned.

An essential feature of Devon's long and often treacherous coastline is its lighthouses, and most of them are over a hundred years old. It is easy to forget their historic significance and regard them as functional symbols of navigation.

Trinity House, the governing body, has existed since the days of Elizabeth I. Ever since men first put to sea in ships, some means of marking the hazardous rocks of the Devon coast had been urgently sought by mariners and, with equal urgency, though for different reasons, by the wealthy shipowners.

Devon has a total of nine lighthouses, plus Trinity House guiding lights marking some of the estuaries. The two earliest lights are no longer in service, although the first, Old Light on Lundy, remains a magnificent monument. It is one of the most romantic buildings in the West Country, even though redundant. Old Light was built on the highest point of the island and first lit in 1820. This beautiful building proved useless as a lighthouse, being all too often surrounded by mist when the coast itself was clear. It was abandoned in 1897, and the two existing lights on the northern and southern extremities of the island were built in its place.

The lighthouse at Braunton dated from 1832 and was a strange structure with a wooden tower rising from the roof of the keeper's house.

The oldest lighthouse still functioning is at Start Point, built in 1836 on one of the most exposed headlands running into the English Channel. Designing lighthouses doesn't allow much scope for architectural imagination, but at Start Point a decidedly Gothic feel has been achieved, complete with battlements. The light used was the first of its kind and was a major improvement. With a candle-power of 800,000, it is one of the most powerful along the south coast. It was supplemented during fog by a strange device incorporating a bell operated by a weight which fell in a tube running down the cliff face. This was quickly replaced by the more conventional siren.

Next comes Hartland Point lighthouse, giving clear warning of this rocky and inhospitable promontory guarding the entrance to the Bristol Channel. It was built right on the very edge, its site inaccessible from

Old Light, Lundy

the land until Trinity House blasted the roadway out of the rock, and it had initially to be surveyed from the sea. The tower and adjacent keepers' cottages, all painted gleaming white, make an eye-catching group tucked in almost at the base of the cliffs, although there aren't many places from which they are easily visible.

The lighthouse has not been without problems: instability of the bedrock was a cause for concern, and areas of the cliff were dislodged in the hope that the fallen rock would form a protective barrier. This worked, but only temporarily, as the sea washed away the boulders, and in 1925 it became necessary to provide a more permanent protection in the form of a 130-foot-long sea wall, nineteen feet high and built of large rocks and concrete. At one time three keepers tended the Hartland Point light, but it is now fully automated and sends its powerful beam across the channel twenty-four hours a day. Often the fog siren continues to sound long after the mist has cleared and the sun has come out, the all-clear signal being somewhat delayed!

Bull Point on the north coast was originally built in 1879 but, owing to a landslip in 1972, when fifty feet of cliff crashed into the sea, the buildings had to be abandoned and a new lighthouse built. The most dramatically sited light is that on the Foreland, near Lynmouth. Here the whaleback cliffs fall steeply and a footpath curves round and down to the lighthouse, built in 1900. This lighthouse is the only one in Devon open to the public at certain times, on application, and visiting it necessitates a long walk. The power of the light, or optic, is still quaintly calculated in candle-power; that of the Foreland is rated at one million candles.

Berry Head, guarding Torbay and Brixham, was first lit in 1906. It must have been the most easily constructed of all Trinity House lights, and is the smallest in England. The optic is at a tall man's eye-level, set in a mini tower atop the cliff. There is no keeper's house but close by is a prominent coastguard lookout station.

A light also guards the entrance to Plymouth Sound. The mammoth breakwater was constructed to create a sheltered deep-water anchorage in the Sound. Work began in 1812 but was not completed until 1841. It was a major engineering feat and required some 4½ million tons of stone, much of it from local quarries. It also cost twenty men their lives. The workmen involved in the construction of the breakwater were mainly local and were rowed out to a sailing-hulk where they spent the week, returning at the weekend on payday. On 7 November 1838 one of the three pinnaces taking men back to the Cattewater was overturned by a combination of tides and groundswell, and its occupants drowned in sight of onlookers on the Hoe.

The most famous and historic lighthouse of all belongs to Devon. The Eddystone light was the first ever to be built on a small rock in the middle of the sea – thirteen miles south of Plymouth. It was first lit in 1698, when candle-power was just that!

The lighthouse was the work of Henry Winstanley, a wealthy shipowner, two of whose ships had been wrecked on the notorious Eddystone rocks. He designed an elaborate wooden structure and commenced work in 1696. So important was this work considered that the Admiralty provided him with a guardian warship – England and France were at war at that time. The story goes that on one occasion the warship failed to turn up, and the workmen were captured and kidnapped by a French vessel. Their release was instantly ordered by the French king, saying it was England he was at war with, not humanity!

The original design was found to be in need of modification after only one winter, and Winstanley went ahead with alterations and strengthening. But sadly it was not to have a long life. Winstanley had been heard to say he wished to experience a severe gale from the safety of his tower, and by chance or misfortune he arrived there in November 1703, when the greatest storm ever recorded blew up. When the seas eventually subsided, there was no trace of the lighthouse – or its occupants.

With the true tenacity of the maritime English, the Eddystone site was not abandoned, and to this day its lighthouse is considered one of the most important in the Channel. Winstanley's octagonal wooden tower was replaced with a smooth circular structure – but still built of wood. The lantern caught fire in 1755 and burned steadily downwards, forcing the keepers out onto the rock. One of them, in his attempts to douse the flames, swallowed a large lump of molten lead and died twelve days later. The third tower, Smeaton's, would be there still had not the rocks beneath it shown signs of weakness. It is that tower which now stands on Plymouth Hoe, a Grade I listed building. The final tower was built in 1882, by far the largest of the four structures, and it has been capped with a helipad. It is now fully automatic – no longer calling for men to spend long periods in solitary confinement, poised above an often wild and turbulent sea with only each other and the waves for company.

Lighthouse keepers are a rare and vanishing breed. Until recent technology made them redundant, keepers watched in shifts. Often they were the first to see a ship in distress and could raise the alarm. Where possible, their families lived close by. Where it was not possible, the keepers were relieved periodically. Lundy South Light and those at Foreland and Start Point are the only lighthouses still manned. All the others are now automated guardians, eerily silent and inhabited only by ghosts.

All Trinity House lights are immaculately maintained. The traditions and discipline are on a level with those of the Navy, and the standards are a credit to the men involved. Once there was a strict division between keepers and maintenance men; now it seems inevitable that keepers will diminish and electricians and engineers and painters take over this once proud tradition.

The towers themselves are monuments to Victorian craftsmen and solidarity. Everything gleams, everything shines, everything sparkles. 'If you can manage without using the handrail, I would be grateful,' was the plea from the keeper on Lundy. It was brass and had just been polished.

Vibrant spires of foxgloves

3

Natural Devon

Although Devon has suffered from the self-inflicted wounds of the twentieth century in the way of pollution, mechanization, building, road-construction, carelessness and sheer greed, it has perhaps suffered less than the rest of the country. The quiet, undisturbed backwaters remain rich in wildlife, undeclared nature reserves of a special kind.

Here the more domesticated species thrive – the owls and the hedgerow birds, the rabbits and foxes, mice and shrews, little voles and other tiny creatures that sophisticated man has all but forgotten. They still thrive in the untidy, unmodernized farmyards of rural Devon, where old barns and shippens, overgrown pigsties and henhouses provide them with a refuge. Here, too, are the unfrequented Devon lanes, topped with their exuberant hedges, home to a wide range of birds and mammals. Some of these hedges have been developing, or evolving, over hundreds of years. Most originated as banks of shale and earth and have been left to their own devices.

A Devon bank that has never been touched is a rich source of plant and animal life and a marvellous sight at any time of the year. From the earliest days of winter, primroses are to be found in sheltered spots, and as spring progresses, every bank seems to be ablaze. There are no primroses like the Devon primroses. Reluctantly they give way to an equal riot of bluebells before the stately ferns grow up, smothering everything until the autumn. Vibrant spires of foxgloves reach upwards in the more open areas, where the ragged robin and campion add their pinky red hue. Honeysuckle and dog roses scent the summer air, and for those who know where to look, there is the reward of the tiny wild strawberry. The froth of cow parsley lines the ditches, and always there is the green cover of dog's mercury, with here and there arum lilies and wild orchids.

Overhead are the arching branches of the trees – oak, holly, hazel, birch and sycamore – draped with strands of bryony, old man's beard and the ever-present bramble. The fauna that find shelter in a bank are less obvious but equally abundant.

It was a sad day that saw the introduction of the mechanical hedgetrimmer. In a few decades it has robbed so much of the country of its rich tapestry of hedgerows and reduced them all to a uniform neat green. Mechanization seems ultimately to lead to a dreary uniformity, killing off individual regional characteristics till all of England will look the same – large, boring fields surrounded by neat, boring hedges or fences, with trees restricted to forestry or the occasional block left for game-rearing. Or it would were it not for the work of the Nature Conservancy Council.

Devon has a wide variety of habitats, with a corresponding wealth of wildlife, and the Council has many interesting sites. These include the important sand dunes of Northam and Braunton Burrows on both sides of the Taw and Torridge estuary, the unique landslip areas on the East Devon coast, several woodland areas on Dartmoor, and the rare pebble beds of Woodbury and Aylesbeare Common to the east of Exeter. Dawlish Warren at the mouth of the Exe is an important staging-post for migrant birds, and the Berry Head country park on the south coast, the largest exposed area of Devonian limestone in the country, is a major breeding-site for large colonies of auks (the name embraces guillemots, kittiwakes and razorbills). Further to the west is Slapton Ley, where a ridge of shingle separates the sea from the two inland lakes or leys, surrounded by reedbeds which attract an enormous number of migrants and birds during the winter. The first Marine Nature Reserve has been declared around the island of Lundy in the Bristol Channel, and there are many voluntary reserves along the south coast.

Estuary life is particularly rich and draws many visitors. The mudflats left exposed by the receding tide attract a host of migrants and waders. The estuary of the River Exe is considered the most important wetland in the south-west, and on its sand and mud grow the weeds and eelgrass so essential to the birdlife, in particular to the Brent geese that arrive in large numbers every winter from Russia. Particularly associated with the Exe is the dainty avocet with its long legs and upturned bill. It is the symbol of the Royal Society for the Protection of Birds, which organizes rivertrips especially for avocet-watching. Fortunately the estuary of the Exe is generously provided with footpaths, and the western bank can be followed via the canal path along its entire length, ending at a pub that can be reached only on foot or by boat. The Turf Hotel occupies a splendid position between the river and the canal and was built originally as the lock house. It offers hospitality to wet and muddy walkers, for whom it makes a worthy objective.

There are many sights Devonians take for granted. Owls frequently perch on top of telegraph poles, most often the barn owl who hunts by day, although the tawny owl makes his silent swoop as dusk falls.

A heron stands motionless on the water's edge

Stately herons stand motionless on the water's edge with long neck outstretched; until disturbed, when their large wings lift them clumsily into the air, and the head shrinks back onto its chest. Buzzards, hawks and kestrels hover overhead on motionless wings before diving earthwards onto some hapless prey.

Patient, silent watchers are often rewarded by sight of the fox and the badger, and even the shy deer. The roe deer is to be found throughout the county wherever there is woodland to shelter it, but the red deer is confined to Exmoor; it disappeared from Dartmoor at the end of the eighteenth century. It is to be hoped that the red deer, the largest of British mammals, will survive on Exmoor despite the increasing pressures on this fragile area.

Both Dartmoor and Exmoor have their own particular breed of hardy ponies, most of which roam virtually wild, although, when it comes to selling them, someone will undoubtedly put in a claim. One of the hardest problems faced by both Park Authorities is how to prevent children feeding these lovable animals. Not unnaturally they want to proffer sticky buns and sandwiches, but the pony's ability to survive the harsh winters of the moor depends upon its being able to forage for itself – then there are no visitors to offer it food. Besides, a diet of sugary sweets and bread isn't good for anyone!

The problem over the years has been to preserve the purity of the moorland ponies. The introduction of aliens to produce larger or better-looking beasts has meant a loss of hardiness. Moves have recently been made on both Dartmoor and the island of Lundy, where the Lundy pony had all but disappeared, to revive the purebred native so that these distinctive breeds will survive.

Snakes, such as adders and slow-worms, occasionally scare the unwary walker on the moors or cliffs, but more usually they want to slip back into obscurity rather than turn and bite, as long as they are left undisturbed. Far more frequent, and far more of a problem, are the armies of fat black or brown slugs that luxuriate in the lush damp grass of the county, and there seems also to be a superabundance of snails.

It is sad that what was part of every child's heritage only a generation ago has now to be protected, cosseted and 'conserved'. Our parents and grandparents could roam at will, picking enormous bunches of wild flowers to take home, maybe to be made into wine. No one patrolled the daffodil banks then, and no stern notices warned 'Do not pick the wild flowers.' Currently Devon has bluebells and primroses to spare, and primroses still fill the churches at Easter, but elsewhere in Britain they have almost died out, and the great banks in Surrey and Sussex are a thing of the past. Hopefully this will never happen here, and God forbid that the day should ever come when the picking of blackberries is forbidden!

The wild harvest of Devon can be abundant for those who know what to look for, blackberries being the best-known and commonest of the free food. The damp climate encourages mushrooms – though no one will tell you where to look, and wild strawberries and watercress reward the observant walker. Sloes for gin-making, rosehips and elderberries – the hedgerows and uncultivated lands yield rich gleanings.

Devon is not renowned for great tracts of beautiful woodland, yet it is well blessed with trees of a wide variety of species. Oak is the natural tree found throughout the county, and the woodlands that clothe the valleys of the Lyn rivers close to the north coast are almost entirely of oak. The beech, with its greater height and shallow rooting system, is not suited to the wet and windy climate of most of Devon but it does grow in the sheltered valleys and estuaries of the south.

If most of Devon's surface was at one time densely forested, as it is assumed it was, the climate must have been markedly different. Few trees survive on the high moorland areas, and the cliffs and exposed hillsides are bare. The winds are too strong; they defeat even the

Primroses fill the churches at Easter

bravest sapling. But in the shelter of the valleys and along the banks of most of Devon's rivers are to be found some magnificent stands of trees. The parkland of the larger estates, too, contains some fine areas of woodland and also specimen trees, those at Bicton, now the county's College of Agriculture, and at Exeter University being particularly noteworthy. Most of the National Trust properties are well endowed, and the Trust is the largest single owner of woodland in the county, with over 2,000 acres, of which over one third is of special interest. Of the total acreage of woodland, roughly one quarter is reckoned to be ancient forest, either replanted or original, most of it concentrated in the deep river valleys of central and west Devon.

Wistman's Wood on Dartmoor is the most famous and with Black Tor Copse is considered of major national importance for wildlife conservation. It consists of small, stunted oak trees, of great age. Unlike the ground under beech trees, on which very little will grow, that beneath these Dartmoor oaks is rich in vegetation, and at one time the tangle was so great and the branches were so low that it was impossible to enter the copse. The trees have since grown a little higher, making exploration possible. Ferns, mosses and lichens cover the trees, and there is a profusion of bilberries, brambles and grasses. It is an intriguing place and one which is being managed with great care, not only to ensure its survival but to watch the wood's natural progression.

The Forestry Commission has a surprisingly large presence in the county – surprising because it is not immediately obvious in the way afforestation is on uplands and open moorland. Over eight per cent of the total surface of Devon is woodland, of which 31,000 acres are Forestry Commission. Some of their plantations are all too visible, favourite sites being around reservoirs and on the fringes of Dartmoor. And no one leaving Exeter on the Plymouth road could fail to notice the ranks of conifers in the Haldon Hill area. But in the quiet hinterlands of Devon, especially towards the north, there are some vast forests stretching away in endless silence, undisturbed and unfrequented, covering in all between eight and 9,000 acres, divided into three large areas.

Hartland Forest in the far north spreads inland of the A39, where there is a forest centre and trail, for a considerable distance. Another seemingly limitless forest stretches out around Halwill in the Holsworthy area. Here the Commission has its North Devon and Cornwall headquarters, and it is one of the youngest plantations. The average lifespan of the conifers is only around forty years – or for as long as the wind allows, as one forester put it. Wind-blow is a considerable problem, and once the trees start to topple, they go down like skittles. The third large area is at Eggesford, much of it on the former lands of the Portsmouth estate. From the valley of the River Taw, the ruins of Eggesford house, seat of the earls of Portsmouth, are still just visible above the encroaching firs. It is here that the first trees ever planted by the Forestry Commission still stand, giving Devon a claim to fame in the annals of forestry history.

The Forestry Commission was set up in 1919 to make good the woodlands devastated in the cause of the First World War. Following a meeting early in December, it was agreed that the time was ripe for the first Commission trees to be planted, and the chairman, Lord Lovat, left for Scotland with the intention of carrying out this planting on his arrival. But, so the story goes, his fellow commissioner Lord Clinton stole a march on him. He phoned one of his foresters from London with instructions to meet him at Eggesford station complete with spades and trees, and on 8 December 1919, on a site not all that far from the station, the first trees were duly planted. A telegram was despatched to greet Lord Lovat on his return home.

Another historic planting took place in May 1956, when Queen Elizabeth II planted a tree to mark the planting of one million acres.

Many of the Commission's woodlands have car-parks and well-marked forest trails, that over the Haldon Hills near Exeter having some particularly fine views across South Devon.

The Forestry Commission may be the largest single owner, but a larger proportion of forestry is privately owned, with the principal landowners having considerable plantations. The heavy soil and damp climate have proved excellent for the fast-growing conifer, and the acreage has been steadily increasing. Fortunately the proportion of deciduous woodland is also increasing and is roughly equal that of coniferous, although an accurate check is difficult, since permission is not needed to fell single trees or small areas.

There has been concern at the rapid disappearance of many small pockets of woodland, mostly on small farms. The old practice of coppicing has also disappeared, although many an overgrown copse bears evidence of this former usage, when fast-growing trees such as ash and sycamore were cut to the ground in rotation, allowing several stems to shoot up from one stool. These were harvested for many purposes about the house and farm, apart from providing timber for fuel, which in days gone by was in plentiful supply from other sources. The trees most commonly found throughout Devon are the pedunculate oak, ash, sycamore and birch, with pockets of beech, some rowans and chestnuts. The lesser trees include holly, hazel and alder with a plentiful supply of gorse throughout and a few large areas of rhododendron.

The landscape is characterized by the many hedgerows and small groups of trees, and it is particularly enriched by the large number of

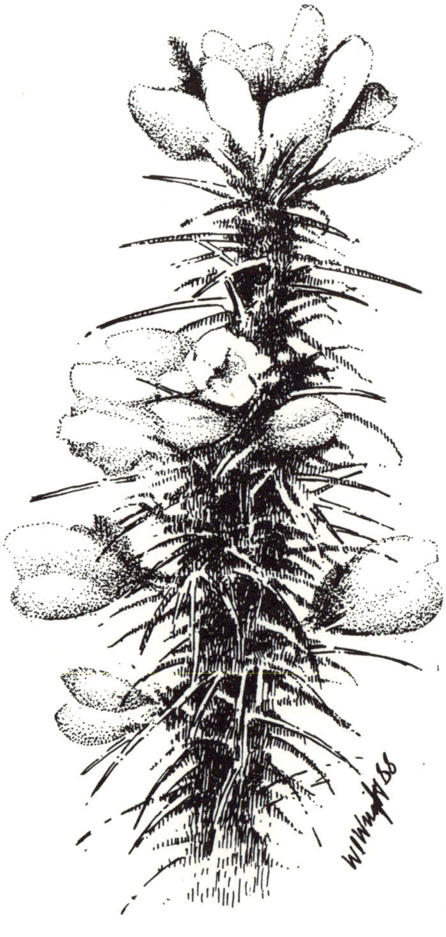

Gorse is found in many areas throughout Devon

single or isolated trees. A tree growing in woodland surrounded by other trees grows upwards but, allowed to grow without competition, it will develop a quite different outline, and some of Devon's specimen trees are magnificent. Many of them are to be found, as would be expected, in parkland, but there are not a few growing quietly in fields or on the roadside. Long may they survive, for elsewhere they all too often fall victim to road widening or the needs of enlarged agricultural machinery. Devon without its trees would be bare indeed.

It seems incredible that a county with such a high rainfall and such a wealth of streams and rivers could ever run short of water, but this has happened twice in recent history. Prolonged heatwaves and severe droughts are not the normal weather pattern in Britain, and certainly not in the south-west, but after the two scorching summers of 1976 and 1984 when the county's water-supply was all but exhausted, some kind of provision was called for. Standpipes with queues of bucket-carrying women are not something easily envisaged by the rest of the country, and they are out of place in the civilization of the twentieth century.

It is a fact that has to be faced that the seasonal influx of upwards of 500,000 holidaymakers brings problems as well as benefits. It is not the population of Devon that needs more and larger reservoirs. It is not the locals that need the new fast roads, the increasing car-parks and sewage-capacity. But it is the locals who suffer when the provision is inadequate. The holidaymakers stay only a week or two; the locals have to cope all the year round. The attitude of many of the visitors during that long hot summer of 1984, when water was rationed almost from the start of the season, was infuriating and selfish in the extreme – riots were almost caused when cars were washed on the caravan sites and frequent baths taken in the holiday lets – whilst the rest of us cherished every drop and saved every trickle. It was no fun, and it tipped the scales in favour of new reservoirs and extraction schemes.

What everyone had taken for granted before – water – had suddenly become of major importance, and the anti-lobbies found their case harder to fight. The Water Authority had already lost one battle for a new reservoir on Dartmoor at Swincombe and was having a hard time over its proposals for Roadford in mid Devon, not far from the Cornish border. It took them almost ten years to persuade the authorities that this was the right site and that, to prevent future hardship, work should begin as soon as possible. When completed, it will be the largest reservoir in the south-west, with a capacity of 8,120 million gallons – all from an insignificant little stream flowing through a little-known, steeply sided valley. Unfortunately several farms and cottages will have been drowned, some of architectural and archaeological importance, but the authority has co-operated in preserving as much as possible, and both the proposed visitors' centre and the museum in Okehampton will contain relics and reconstructions from the valley.

Many of the reservoirs have become popular as places of recreation, and visitors are encouraged by the Water Authority with car-parks, visitor centres, planned walks and areas for such sports as sailing, windsurfing and, of course, angling. Not so very long ago, reservoirs were virtually 'no-go' areas, hedged with barbed wire and 'Keep Out' notices. The change in attitude is welcome, though currently there is mounting concern for the future of our reservoirs and the large amount of land surrounding them, should privatization become a reality. It is ironic that, once the upheaval of construction and impounding for a new reservoir is over, the immediate environs become a haven for wildlife, safe from all future development – that is, at present. In the past Forestry Commission and Water Authorities have often combined; if both are freed from Government control and become subject to commercial pressures, the landscape of some of the most sensitive areas of the county could radically change.

The increasing importance of Devon as a prime holiday region has brought the related problem of sewage-disposal. What was acceptable fifty years ago is so no longer. The increased usage of the coastline for pleasure means that an already overloaded and outdated system of sewage-disposal creaks and groans under the additional burden, and a more environmentally and health-conscious generation vociferously protests. Sea outfalls, those encrusted pipes disappearing from most of the towns and villages around the coast to lose their unsavoury contents in the no-man's-land of the sea, are the cause of heated outbursts of anger and expressions of shock and horror. The Water Authority defends them on the grounds that all sewage treatment throughout the country ultimately ends up in the river system, and therefore the sea, and points out that a high proportion of their beaches are acceptable by EEC standards – forty-eight in Devon. The main problem seems to be that the outfall pipes are old and often too short. Plus a growing population means more sewage.

4

Travelling Past and Present

Devon has always lagged behind the rest of the country where transport is concerned. The sheer size of the county and its hilly nature present problems that even in today's mechanized age cause the engineers not a few headaches. It took almost twenty years for the railway to reach Devon, and long after trains were commonplace and widespread in the rest of the country, they were still considered a novelty and a wonder in the West Country.

Motorways had existed for a similar length of time 'up-country' before the system spread beyond Bristol, and the motorway as such stops at Exeter. It is big industry that calls the tune of motorway priority, and Devon and Cornwall are significantly short on this. All to the good, say many folk, who prefer to let the West Country slumber on, a peaceful backwater. Not so, say others; for too long we have been bypassed, and it is time Devon woke up and marched forward towards economic prosperity. Whether we shall like this promised land, when and if it materializes, remains to be seen and is a point that does not appear to have worried the progress lobby unduly. Suffice it to say that every county is unique; each has its own identity, its own character, and this should not be thoughtlessly sacrificed.

Devon has a huge network of lanes, the largest in proportion to its size of any county in England – around 7,000 miles – and these lanes form a major ingredient of its character. They are not to be rushed along, not to be treated with impatience, but rather to be savoured, to be enjoyed as part of Devon's rich history that has managed to survive so remarkably intact – and will hopefully survive for another century or so.

Most of the lanes are old, hundreds of years old in some cases, and a few so old no one knows whose feet first trod them. Many came into being as parish boundaries, which explains their zigzag course. All those sharp corners follow the outline of someone's fields. Others linked one small farming community with its neighbours and with the nearest market town.

The new bridge across the Torridge below Bideford

Those that lead to the sea often developed because of the need to transport sand from the beaches, or lime to and from the kilns. Lime was an important fertilizer on the heavy Devon clay, and it was landed in the small ports and even on beaches, where it was fired in kilns before being transported to the farms. A few of the lanes, a very few, were the romantic smugglers' paths, sheltered, as are most Devon lanes, between high banks or hedgerows. The oldest have 'sunk' through much usage over the passage of time, and as most lanes act as drainage channels, the action of the water has eroded the soil still further until in many cases bedrock is reached. The lanes are thus sheltered in winter from the worst of the gales and in summer become mysterious shady cloisters, havens of green stillness.

Many of the oldest lanes are no longer negotiable by motor car – if they ever were! But travellers on foot have time to appreciate the wealth of wildlife, the sheer luxuriance of the plants and trees. Away from the hustle and bustle of the resorts and the beaches, it is possible to experience a peace and tranquillity rare in the modern world. On a hot summer's day the delicious coolness is highlighted by the dappled sunshine piercing the high canopy of leaves, and in autumn those same leaves provide a russet carpet underfoot.

In Devon, as elsewhere, modern farming methods have sounded the death-knell of many miles of ancient hedgerows, but those bordering the lanes have largely been left, in many cases untouched for years. Some of these lanes once formed part of the network of packhorse routes that covered the county. Until the coming of much-improved roads in relatively recent times, the packhorse was the most effective means of transporting bulky goods across hilly country served only by narrow tracks that all too often deteriorated into a sea of mud. These small, stalwart animals were laden with panniers – a form of wicker basket – and driven across country. They travelled in strings of up to fifteen at high speeds and took up so much room that other travellers had quickly to get out of the way. In many parts of the county, particularly in mid Devon and the fringes of the moors, the narrow packhorse bridges survive, some even in use – just wide enough to take a motor vehicle.

Two very ancient routes, according to tradition, are the Abbots Way, across Dartmoor from Tavistock to Buckfastleigh, and the Mariners Way, which supposedly connected the north coast in the area of Bideford with Dartmouth on the south. Some historians have poured cold water on the origins of these romantic routes, but old traditions die hard, and certainly there is an unusually straight and direct interconnecting route from north to south, much of which has recently been widened and utilized to link Winkleigh with the improved A30 at North Tawton. The ghosts of ancient mariners would have to look smart to dodge the racing traffic that now speeds along its broad, smooth surface. South of the A30 the route reverts to quiet and peaceful trackways where it is possible to imagine their original usage.

Many of the high-level lanes and minor roads are surprisingly straight and direct. These are the original old roads linking one market town with another, always keeping well to the high ground, for in the early days of travel valley bottoms were to be avoided; not only were they liable to flooding but the dense woodland and undergrowth provided a refuge for robbers. There are many ridge routes which were once the main thoroughfares and still provide pleasant alternatives to the busy main roads, few of which were in existence before the coming of the turnpikes in the early days of the nineteenth century. And until the improvement in the roads, there were many parishes in the county where even the horse and cart was a rarity. How suddenly life must have changed, from a life where horizons were bounded by the distance a horse could plod or a man could walk, to one where the distant towns became a possibility – and even the next county!

An old Barnstaple – Lynton railway engine

In many instances the main river valleys provided a route for both the new roads and the railways. No form of transport has ever evoked so much nostalgia as the steam train. Perhaps to the West Country its coming had greater significance; no equivalent of the Great North Road had penetrated Devon and Cornwall, and the iron road took its time. When it did reach Exeter from Paddington in 1844, it was heralded as the beginning of a new age. At last Devon was rescued from isolation and had a fast connection with the prosperous markets of southern England. The Great Western was a legend in its own time and still brings tears to the eyes of those who remember the Age of Steam, and those who worked with the cream-and-brown leviathans. Brunel was a great engineer in many spheres, but to Devonians of the railway era his claim to fame was the creation of the Great Western and of the Saltash Bridge that ultimately continued the line on into Cornwall. He was not to have it all his own way, however, for the Southern Region brought a line from Waterloo and then ultimately took it north of Dartmoor. The very nature of the county meant that the construction of railways was difficult and expensive, and many were considered and planned only to be discarded on grounds of costs, but by the end of the century a fair network covered Devon, although many of the branch lines were to be short-lived.

One of the last to be built was also one of the first to go. The little line from Bideford to Westward Ho! was opened in 1901, extended to Appledore in 1908 and dismantled to provide engines for the First World War. The line from Barnstaple to Exeter, opened in 1854, still carries its quota of trains to connect with the inter-city expresses, and British Rail still runs to Paignton, where the steam train to Dartmouth connects. The branch line from Plymouth to Gunnislake carries daily commuters. But the rest of Devon is a blank as far as railways are concerned.

Halwill Junction, once a busy intersection of railway lines complete with a revolving table, sidings, junctions etc, is now a deserted, grassy wilderness but very atmospheric. The old station is haunted still, and it is not so long ago that carriages crowded with expectant holiday-makers, children leaning from the windows, paused on their way to Bude or Bideford.

The coming of the railways was heralded as an era of expansion of prosperity and development. History proved that, although it did indeed enable the fresh produce of Devon to reach London markets within hours, thus bringing cream and milk, strawberries and fish to an urban population, it also caused the decay of many a small market town and the death of many a small business. Time will tell whether history repeats itself or not. The railways have had their day, and only the main

The old railway station, Barnstaple

lines survive. Branch routes are largely only overgrown tracks, some not even that. But still they conjure up a nostalgic affection – how many will mourn the passing of the motorways, the cloverleaf junctions and the spur roads when they, too, have passed into oblivion?

No one has ever counted the number of bridges in Devon, but it must run into thousands. There could be little movement in a countryside of steep valleys and many rivers without bridges. Often they replaced hazardous river-crossings and fords passable only at low water. Across the wider estuaries, ferries often provided a safer mode of crossing, and in some places these still operate. Across the estuaries of the Dart, the Exe, the Avon at Salcombe, the Torridge at Instow, and even at Plymouth, passengers still follow the ancient routes.

Many of the bridges are insignificant, little more than stone arches where the streams are crossed and recrossed. Often the oldest were built at the instigation of the Church, seeking safe passage for its emissaries as they travelled – collecting tithes as much as ensuring the spread of Christianity. It is a tribute to the builders of these grey-stone structures that they have withstood the use of centuries and today carry traffic that their builders could never have envisaged, even in their wildest flights of fancy.

North Devon boasts two ancient, beautiful, long bridges, at Bideford and at Barnstaple. Around these important crossings grew up the two ports and market towns. South Devon has many smaller, ancient structures, the oldest of which are those at Clyst St Mary, Exeter, Totnes and Teignmouth, although in some cases much rebuilding has obliterated the original structure.

There have been two major new bridges built this century. One is the Tamar Bridge at Plymouth, still toll-paying after over twenty-five years, which replaced the Saltash ferry and saved a long detour inland. The most recent is the high-level bridge over the Torridge, opened in 1987, providing a crossing downstream from Bideford and forming a crucial link in the bypass and new link road that will connect remote North Devon with the motorway system. The construction of this important bridge was a major engineering feat. Built of huge concrete sections moulded on site, it is nearly half a mile long, with eight spans clearing the waters of the river by a tremendous 78 feet – to enable the port of Bideford to continue to function. The total cost of the bridge and its approach roads was estimated at around £15 million.

Water has played an important part in the county's transport system. Between all the small ports along both coasts considerable traffic plied, carrying all kinds of bulky and heavy cargoes. Given the nature of the coastline, with its deep indentations, transport by sea was the obvious solution, and many people also preferred to travel this way. Bristol was easily accessible as a major port, and London and the other south-coast harbours were within reach. Nowadays very little comes by sea; the fishing fleets are much reduced, and coastal traffic is confined largely to sand and gravel dredgers, with the occasional large vessel to justify the title of port. Most of the south coast harbours are given over to pleasure craft and yacht marinas – and the character of the quaysides has changed to match.

Devon had one other form of transport, now almost entirely sunk into oblivion, doomed from the word go. Canals would never have been seriously contemplated had it not been for the 'canal mania' that insisted the county must have its share. Of the many planned, only a handful were built, and these were short-lived, their shallow waters quickly becoming stagnant and weed-infested. Two in the north have virtually disappeared altogether – the Bude to Holsworthy canal and the Landcross to Torrington, whose ambitious course ran alongside the River Torridge. A short length of the Tiverton canal that was to link Devon with the rest of the country's canal system has recently been rescued, and the horsedrawn barges that travel leisurely along it from

Barge on the Tiverton canal

the Tiverton canal basin are proving a popular attraction. From Tavistock a waterway was built to link the town with Morwellham on the River Tamar, its navigational limit and the scene of great mining activity. The canal banks offer a pleasant stroll for some of its length.

But it is the oldest canal that has survived the longest, still in use today. Running alongside the River Exe from Topsham to Exeter is the ship canal, begun in 1564, one of the earliest in the country. It was necessitated by the building of weirs across the river itself forcing shipping to make use of Topsham as the port, to the detriment of Exeter but to the great advantage of the Countess of Devon, whereupon the city fathers took retaliatory action and dug the canal. A walk along the canal bank that separates it from the river is a marvellous way to view the broad expanse of the estuary with its rich bird life and lovely scenery.

One other canal was also built by private enterprise to facilitate industrial activity. For a short time granite from Haytor on Dartmoor was transported down off the moor by means of a horsedrawn tramway, and then by canal to the sea at Teignmouth. Both were the work of the Templer family, who were also responsible for the New Quay at Teignmouth. The Stover canal was built in 1790, to carry ball clay from the Bovey Tracey valley. The Templers also owned quarries at Haytor, and when the demand for building-material grew in the nineteenth century, they built the tramway. Made of granite to carry granite (the granite rails can still be seen), it was opened in 1820, but by the end of the 1850s the boom was over, and quarrying operations ceased. The railway branch line from Newton Abbot took over some of the canal and tramway route, but the lower section to Teignmouth continued in use until the 1940s, still serving its original purpose of carrying ball clay. The whole route is currently being turned into a long-distance footpath, named the Templer Way, and it will take walkers not only through some lovely countryside, beginning on the heights of Dartmoor and ending on the Teign estuary, but also along a route full of historic interest.

Most counties have now recognized the value of their former transport systems and wherever possible salvaged what they can. Steam trains are an asset, and Devon has two still operating. The Dart Valley Railway, running from Totnes to Buckfastleigh, is very popular; the Torbay & Dartmouth Railway is functional as well as decorative, for it connects with British Rail. This line never closed – a rarity in branch-line history – and has run continuously since 1864. It is in great demand with film companies.

Devon is able to offer an enormous range of bygone transport: horsedrawn barges on the Tiverton canal, trams at Seaton, a cliff railway at Lynton, horsedrawn carriages at Arlington, ferries, paddle-steamers annually on the north coast – almost every form of transport you can think of, bar a stage-coach and four.

Devon is justly famous for its cream teas

5

Devon Food

Food, glorious food! Clotted cream and Devon scones; pasties and pies; rich, golden milk and home-made cheeses; fish fresh from the sea or river; cider made with apples from the orchard. Devon has always excelled in mouth-watering home-produced food. And today, as more and more people turn from mass-produced, tasteless, pre-wrapped supermarket 'food', the county finds its goodies in greater demand than ever before.

As good food has never disappeared here, it doesn't need reviving. The county is not renowned for sylphlike women or athletic men, just amiable, well-fed bodies with that contented look that stems from a replete stomach. 'Cholesterol' is a word that few Devonians understand. They eat the same food their fathers and grandfathers ate, and expect to grow old on it in just the same manner.

Clotted cream can still be purchased in some of the local markets, but it is so hedged around with restrictions and regulations that not many farmers' wives can be bothered to make it. Properly produced, it is one of the gastronomic delights of this county and has a taste like no other. Production is simple but requires two things once commonplace in farmhouses – a cool surface for the start and finish of the process, and a gently warm surface for the middle. Milk straight from the cow was poured into wide, shallow pans and set on marble or slate slabs in the dairy, where it stood overnight. The cream rose to the surface, defying gravity as it is heavier than the milk! The pans were transferred, very gently so as not to disturb the creamy surface, to the coolest part of the stove and left until the cream formed a crust. Never was it allowed to become any hotter than blood-temperature. Again very gently, it was transferred back to the dairy to cool and to 'set', after which the cream could be lifted off. The skimmed milk was either used for cooking or fed to the pigs. And the cream went on everything: on the home-baked apple pie, on the scones, or cut-rounds as they are called, or simply on pieces of bread. (Cut-rounds are lighter than a scone, being baked with yeast, and are traditional to the county.)

The pasty is another famous ingredient of the Devonshire table. Meat and potatoes contained in a pastry crust were a suitable lunch for a man in the fields. In rural Devon, farmworkers did not eat breakfast as such. After two or three hours work, the menfolk either came in for their 'lunch' or ate where they were. The main meal, dinner, was in the middle of the day, and high tea was always ready at the end of the working day, when a rich variety of home-baked pies and pasties, including 'tiddy pasty' (potato pie), pickled pork, chutneys and cheese, was laid out on the table. Pasties today have become more of a tourist attraction, and they vary enormously. The very best are mouth-watering, made from the best-quality beef with onion, swede, potato and gravy in a rich crust. The worst are disgusting: pappy, soggy pastry filled with grey, gristly mince, far too much potato and highly spiced to disguise the taste. They make good food for the gulls, and that is about all.

Another standby is the ploughman's lunch. This used to be a West Country speciality and was unknown in the north, but today it has become synonymous with pub food far and wide. The name is said to have been a clever piece of marketing thought up by the Milk Marketing Board to promote the sale of English cheese. The thing itself is very traditional and was another staple food of men working far away from the farmhouse. In its original and simplest form, a ploughman's lunch consisted of a hunk of bread or cut-rounds, a large chunk of cheese and maybe a pickled onion, all wrapped up in a cloth. The complicated cheese salad so often served in pubs and cafés is not a true ploughman's lunch, and the variations using ham, pâté, fish etc are pure invention.

Devon is quite rightly proud of its fine tradition of food. The county has a large number of first-class restaurants, some of national and international acclaim. It also has a high number of very small establishments serving good-quality home-made food prepared by the proprietors. The tradition of home baking has never been lost, and all towns and most of the larger villages still have a local baker producing that mouth-watering, unmistakable aroma of freshly baked bread. Butchers, too, survive, many of them old family firms who until recently slaughtered and even raised their own meat. These traditions have lingered on, and now they are enjoying an upsurge in popularity as a more discerning population demands once again food that tastes as it should and that is free from additives and other undesirables. There are at least two farms in Devon specializing in producing 'pure meat' that is free from all taint and meets the standards of the Guild of Conservation. One has a collection of rare breeds of pig, allowed free pasturage, from which a range of sausages, pâtés and cooked meats is produced.

Starting in a small way, such ventures have been surprised at their rapid success.

Cheese-making was another farmhouse skill that all but died out – but not quite, and now there are a surprising, and growing, number of Devon cheeses in production. Most are of the Cheddar type but there are variations. At least two cheese-manufacturers have become successful in a big way. Hawkridge cheese is sold all over the country, though when you buy it from one high-class supermarket chain, it does not say it came from this small farm near Winkleigh. The Beer family have been making cheese for twenty-five years and produce about three tons per day, all of it Cheddar and using milk either from their own dairy herd or from neighbours. It all began by accident, when Mrs Beer became interested in a cheese vat she had purchased, and decided to try her hand.

There have been Quickes at Newton St Cyres since the days of Henry VIII, when one of them married a local heiress. They are there still, farming their considerable acreage as they always have, but with one noticeable and hugely successful addition – cheese. Back in the 1970s, Sir John Quicke thought it would be advisable to find an alternative to straightforward production of raw materials and looked for a high-class product that would both appeal to the public and buffer the family from future agricultural policies or depressions. His solution was to produce a natural Cheddar of extremely good quality, using milk from his own dairy herds. Production began in 1973, and today Quicke's cheese is well known throughout the county and is sold nationally as well.

The process of cheesemaking by traditional methods requires skill, patience and strength. A vat full of solidifying milk takes a lot of stirring. The whole process is carefully controlled, and hygiene is of the first importance – cheesemaking could never become a major tourist attraction because all visitors must wear overalls and hats. Apparently cheese in the making is very easily upset.

Quicke's still produce the traditional round cheese, around 20,000 of them a year. They are wrapped in cheesecloth, to encourage the development of the all-important rind, and are stored for about eight months; real cheese buffs go for one that has been maturing for over eighteen months. The ice-cream for which Quicke's are also well known began as a by-product from cheesemaking, using egg yolks, cream and whey in a traditional family recipe.

A new by-product from the dairying industry is yoghurt. Peter Duncan of Stapleton's Farm, near Torrington, also wanted an end-product that was free of Government price restrictions, and the price of milk has always been regulated. When, in 1975, the Duncans went into the yoghurt-making business, they were among only a very few independent yoghurt producers, selling locally from the back of their van; now Stapleton yoghurt sells as far afield as Birmingham and Reading.

Cream is the by-product here, and whereas this used to be made into double or clotted cream, eating-fashions have changed and the 'waste' milk is turned into another traditional Devon delicacy – ice-cream. Connoisseurs will be in their seventh heaven in Devon. As a child, one of my highlights was having a daily cone full of richly delicious ice-cream. It is still made – and still a treat. Properly produced ice-cream and mass-produced shaving-cream are as different as chalk from cheese, and it is encouraging to see the growth of this 'industry' from small back-kitchen concerns to major producers, with a wide range of flavours.

To keep pace with all this locally made produce, the number of small, good food shops is on the increase. Another source of local produce is the markets still held in several of the towns and larger villages. A visit to the pannier market is a rewarding and enjoyable experience, and it is here that many of the farmers' wives still go on market day, selling their butter and cream, fruit and home-made jams whilst their husbands buy and sell at the cattle market. These markets all but died out, and when the professional marketeers started to take over, with stalls selling cheap factory 'seconds', they lost their atmosphere. Here, too, interest has been revived, and it is to be hoped that the long tradition of market day will be maintained.

Once reserved for the tables of the wealthy landowner, venison has grown in popularity in recent years. Deer parks are nothing new, and the herds that graced many a large estate were an essential feature, providing meat at a time when there was little else. Deer farms are a relatively new introduction, and it is claimed that the venison produced is less variable and more tender than venison shot in the wild. Around the fringes of Exmoor and in East Devon deer farming has become established, and venison pâté, sausages, steaks etc are appearing in the shops.

The large herds of deer roaming the Powderham estate in South Devon are not just there for ornament. Since the 1700s, deer have been providing food for the estate on a domestic basis, but today they are also an important commercial aspect. Currently there is insufficient venison to meet the growing demand, according to the head gamekeeper. Deer are relatively easy to manage, providing there is sufficient acreage of pasture and woodlands, and at Powderham they are shot in the wild, so that, apart from being contained, they lead a free and natural life. The export of live deer to start new herds all over the world is another side of the business, and sadly poaching is an ever-present attendant menace.

Well within living memory several famous family breweries were still satisfying local thirsts. One by one they have disappeared, bought up by the giants, who keep the breweries going for a few years, then 'streamline' their operations and close down the local plants. The black horse of Starkey, Knight & Ford was a well-known symbol on north and mid Devon pubs, the last one being painted out within the last decade, and there were many similar breweries. The tradition has not quite died, and recently one or two small concerns have started up, so that hopefully Devon pubs will once again sell Devon beer.

Devon wine is on the increase, surprisingly in such a damp county. Viticulture is a particularly satisfying hobby, and the steep slopes of many Devon hillsides are well suited, with a comparative lack of frost. There are several small amateur vineyards throughout the county, some producing commercially, some just for the owner's satisfaction, but there are also one or two larger concerns, the most notable being outside Tiverton, where visitors are welcomed to Yearlstone vineyard to find out how wine is produced.

There is one drink above all others that belongs to the West Country, and that is cider. There is nothing special or mystical about it: basically it is fermented apple juice. Just as all farmers' wives once made their own cheese and butter, so the farm produced its own cider. It varied tremendously in quality. Each farmer had his own secret method, but by and large the variation was caused by the apples used.

Orchards are no longer a common sight, but they are still to be found in the sheltered locations of the county, and in particular around the Crediton area. Most of the apples harvested there go to Inch's Cider Company at Winkleigh, where good cider has been produced since 1916. Sam Inch began as a boy, when he was paid for his labours in apples – and the best way to make money from them was to brew cider. Old Sam never advertised; the fame of his cider spread by word of mouth – or taste. Today his son carries on in large new sheds with a fleet of lorries delivering Inch's cider all over the country. The variations include sweet, dry and medium farmhouse or ordinary cider, both still and sparkling, and scrumpy in sweet and dry – and a rather special vintage.

It is a particularly pure drink in that nothing is added – no water, no chemicals, only yeast where necessary. The flavour is achieved by skilful blending of the apples. According to Derek Inch, Sam's son, cider is one of the oldest drinks known to man, with a history going back to 55 BC. It is still made in much the same way, although mechanization has crept into the pulping-process and the bottling. But there is still a marvellous atmosphere, not to mention aroma, in the huge sheds where the towering wooden vats stand in rows, their contents fermenting silently for many months, and it is still a popular drink with the farmers and their workers, who at one time were paid part of their wages in pints of cider. They reckon it kills you in the end – but usually not until the drinker is over eighty!

6

Exmoor

Although the greater part of Exmoor lies in Somerset, Devon is blessed with many of the famous beauty spots. The outlying southern ridges, from which there are such magnificent views, are in Devon, as are the heights of Brendon Common, typical moorland, stretching treeless and featureless for miles. From here several small streams and rivers flow through delightful valleys, such as Farley Water and Hoaroak Water. The coastal scenery and the hinterland of Lynton and Lynmouth are Exmoor jewels firmly in Devon's crown, and of course she lays claim to that famous valley, the last in Devon, the valley of the Doones. This particular valley is no more and no less beautiful than many another Exmoor valley; its claim to fame lies entirely in R. D. Blackmore's novel *Lorna Doone* – and only he knew just how much was fact and how much he invented. But at least it ensures that many visitors see something of the Moor, because they are prepared to walk just a short distance to say they have been in Doone country.

At its meeting with the Oare Water is the small hamlet of Malmsmead, which has good reason to be grateful to Blackmore. It does very well out of the legend, and the whole setting, with cottages and ancient humpbacked bridge alongside the ford, is very picturesque.

Autumn is a magical time on Exmoor. The bracken, so tiresome in the summer, has died and withered. The skies are often clear and the trees are turning. The valleys of the Lyn rivers are glorious. Underfoot is a carpet of burnished gold, copper and rich bronze. Overhead is a canopy of russets and tans – a blending of every conceivable hue and tint of orange and yellow to make a tapestry of unbelievable beauty. No firework display ever rivalled the glory of these woodlands as they end their year in a final blaze of glory. Lovely at any time of year, the steep gorges of the Exmoor rivers are at their spectacular best as the oak woodlands that clothe the valley sides turn colour, illumined by the late sunshine.

A noted beauty spot is at Watersmeet, where the Hoaroak and Farley Waters join the East Lyn. Much of the area is owned by the National

Trust, and along the riverbanks and through the woodland are many footpaths along the water's edge or climbing to the airy heights above, where, clear of the woodland, the steep gorges lie displayed beneath. Motorists are fortunate in that they can travel much of the length of the valley along the road, but the true beauty of it is appreciated only from the many viewpoints above the cleaves and by walking over that carpet of gold and bronze – giants' cornflakes waiting for the cream and sugar sprinkling of the first frosts.

A complete contrast, a few miles inland, is one of the bleakest and most inhospitable areas of the moor. The Chains are notorious for their high rainfall, shifting and supposedly bottomless bogs and the pathless wilderness where, less than five miles from civilization on either side, it is possible to become thoroughly lost, confused and somewhat frightened up on these eerie, deserted wastes. It is the least-known, least-visited and least-loved area of Exmoor. Perhaps early man found it a little less daunting, for several relics and a castle on the Chains are believed to be of Bronze Age origin. The Chapman Barrows form a large group of tumuli, some of them quite extensive, and on the outlying ridge is Shoulsbarrow Castle, occupying a commanding position overlooking the lowlands of North Devon. The Chains themselves are one of the highest areas of Exmoor, and Shoulsbarrow Castle is 1,528 feet above sea-level.

Exmoor is the second smallest of the National Parks, only 265 square miles. It faces continual pressures and has been in danger of disappearing altogether. Only the heroic and concerted efforts of such bodies as the Exmoor Society founded in 1959, the Council for the Preservation of Rural England and the National Park authority itself prevented ploughing on such a massive scale as would have rendered the remnant meaningless. Today the buzzard hovers above acres of moorland upland over which battle raged in the 1960s between landowner, farmer and conservationist, and the red deer can still find solitude and sanctuary in the undisturbed woodlands.

Once again two different Government departments found themselves at loggerheads, with bitter battle-lines drawn between them. The Ministry of Agriculture was offering grants to farmers to plough hitherto 'waste', or uncultivated, land. Planning-permission was not required, no notification had to be given to the Park Authority, and only the timely intervention of the Exmoor Society drew attention to the rapid and serious loss of open moorland. Of course, compensation had to be agreed to stop the ploughing. At such times it really does seem a case of the right hand not knowing what the left is doing, of robbing Peter to pay Paul. Nowadays there is talk of grants (yet more) being paid to return ploughed fields to moorland.

7

Journey along the North Coast

Sand and rock, soaring cliffs and low-lying marshes, banks of pebbles and hummocky dunes: the North Devon coast has them all. The mudflats of the narrowing Bristol Channel have been left behind in Somerset, and the cliffs become ever bolder the further west one travels.

The coastal scenery of North Devon is magnificent, its great variety adding to the attractions. And it is relatively unspoilt, thanks to the National Trust and the few landowning families who between them own most of this coast. In all but a few places development has been kept out of sight, and the only intrusive elements occur where small

Lundy

pockets of coast have changed hands and are regarded as commercial entities rather than as a small part of a precious whole, or where municipal authorities have given way to the need for car-parks etc. It is only when travelling along other coasts of Britain and seeing the unsightly acres of caravans, the scars of development – marinas, yachting complexes, permanent car-parks and the hideousness of amusement arcades, that you realize just how lucky North Devon has been to escape these horrors. Such eyesores as we have tend to be concentrated in one or two areas, the meccas of tourists – deserted and dead for two-thirds of the year.

County Gate on the border with Somerset is a popular spot with motorists. Here Exmoor reaches the sea – still within the boundary of Exmoor National Park, which has an information centre and car-park with spectacular views along the coast and across the Channel to Wales.

The first valley beyond the border is a most unDevonian mixture of larch and birch, with the more typical beech and oak, and a riot of rhododendrons threatening to take over. Perhaps the Reverend Halliday, who built Glenthorne house down at the bottom of his 'glen', hankered after Scottish scenery. A network of tracks and paths allows walkers to explore the delights of this area, recently opened up when the estate changed hands and the National Trust were able to purchase some of the land.

The lush vegetation dies out as the Foreland is approached, the most northerly point of the coastline, its lighthouse a prominent and welcome sight to shipping. The cliffs here are steeply plunging scree slopes, unattractive and unassailable to the average mortal.

Fishing villages and tiny ports were the only coastal settlements to be found along this coast until the Napoleonic wars made holidaying at home a necessity. Suddenly the wealthy travellers began to see merit on their own doorstep, and the praises were sung, often in poetry, of such a remote and unknown place as Lynmouth. It comprised a cluster of fishermen's cottages built around the River Lyn and the rocky foreshore with its small pier, the herring catch being virtually the sole means of support for the inhabitants until the early nineteenth century. Thereafter the tourists came in increasing numbers, and with them hotels and tea-houses, improved roads and coaching establishments. Little by little the coast was opened up, and the local inhabitants found themselves the object of curiosity to ladies and gentlemen from 'up country' – an attitude which has not altogether changed with the years and which is resented just as much today as it was a hundred years ago.

Lynton, up on the hillside above the much more picturesque Lynmouth, owes its existence almost entirely to the influx of Victorian

Rhenish Tower, Lynmouth

visitors. Large hotels, parades of shops, level walks and viewpoints – all were constructed to attract and keep happy the summer visitors. It also attracted one very wealthy Victorian magnate who will be remembered as long as the cliff railway linking Lynton with Lynmouth continues to function. Sir George Newnes, a successful publisher, became the local benefactor in a big way. The cliff railway was opened in 1890 and remains to this day a rare but singularly efficient method of transportation. Sir George was also responsible for the town hall, the small-gauge Lynton to Barnstaple railway and an imposing mansion overlooking the town – only the first survives.

The beautiful scenery of the river gorges of the East and West Lyn is one of the area's principal attractions. The rush of the two rivers is short but spectacular. Rising on Exmoor, they have cut for themselves deep 'cleaves with densely wooded scrub oak, lovely in the spring with young foliage and providing a rich and vibrant finale to the year with a display of autumn colours rare in windswept North Devon. In the valley bottoms the waters romp over a million rocks and boulders, home to trout and a great variety of birds and other wildlife, and a delight to those who walk along the many footpaths. Watersmeet, where the East Lyn and Hoaroak Water meet, is a popular haunt. This Victorian fishing lodge is now a National Trust shop and café, and much of the cliffs and glorious hinterland are also in their ownership.

Lynmouth needs no claim to fame other than its own charms and beautiful setting. Too many writers and guidebooks have laboured the tragic events of a summer night in 1952 when the waters rose to unprecedented heights. The loss of life and of property was catastrophic and for a while overwhelmed the village community, torn apart by the muddy floodwaters. But they have risen above their tragedy and built anew. They have their memories, as the small museum records, but prefer to look on the brighter, sunnier side of life rather than be reminded of a tragedy with few parallels in Britain's history.

The Valley of the Rocks is one of those scenic anomalies that the Victorians loved to find 'Awesome'; they read great mysteries and exaggerations into the rock shapes. Certainly it is unusual, with its high rocky promontories overlooking the sea, but it takes a good imagination to see some of the fantasies claimed for the rock shapes – the wild goats that live among the rocks are much easier to spot.

A narrow road winds through the valley, past an idyllically sited cricket pitch. The roundabout is necessary, as many motorists come only to have a quick look at this famed beauty spot – a drive up and down will suffice – and they may well be disappointed, for its name is more impressive than the scenery merits. It is also necessary because the only exit at the far end is via a privately owned toll road. Free travel

Lynton – Lynmouth cliff railway

and access are taken so much for granted that folk seem to resent being asked to part with a few coins to travel through someone else's land, and in this case those who turn back will have missed some very lovely scenery and a gem of a small bay.

Lee Abbey is run as a Christian community, offering a haven of peace for those who feel in need of space apart from the bustle of modern life. It has few permanent inmates but exists to 'recharge the batteries' and provide a welcome alternative to the more normal holiday venues. It was founded in 1945 specifically as a place where the horrors of the Second World War could be forgotten and where people could once again discover the true meaning of Christianity. The cliffs are private, but not the small sandy bay, which has a plenitude of ledges for sunbathing and rocky outcrops for diving from, or swimming to. Endless miles of sand have their fascination, but for swimmers they can prove boring.

The steeply wooded cliffs of Woody Bay are now in the ownership of the National Trust but were once the scene of much activity and controversy. Old guidebooks and the National Trust guide mention the Woody Bay pier but only the sharp-sighted who know where to look will discover evidence of this ambitious structure.

At the end of the nineteenth century tourism was a new and growing thing. Paddle-steamers were popular, with excursions from all the Bristol Channel ports and Bristol itself. They criss-crossed from the Welsh coast, hopping from one port of call to the next. And why not include Woody Bay? This was the thinking of one resident, and to this end he constructed a pier. To cope with the considerable rise and fall in tides along this coast, the pier had to be tall rather than long. Constructed of timber on a concrete base, it became a reality in 1897, when the first boat called. Woody Bay was all set to become another tourist attraction, and no doubt it was hoped that the cafés and hotels would soon follow. But the North Devon coast is not kind to fragile structures so optimistically constructed, and the winter storms put paid to Woody Bay pier. By 1902 it had been dismantled, and so ended another dream. The steep approach road remains, ending at the stonebuilt buttress, and parts of the concrete foundations are visible at low tide. Had a sheltering stone jetty been constructed instead of the more ambitious pier, Woody Bay might today have an attractive small harbour, popular with yachts and motorcruisers, but fishermen were poor fry then compared with the paddle-steamers, and such a development would not nowadays be permitted. Woody Bay remains quiet and unspoilt, with a pleasant car-park above the woodland and unfrequented walks through the woods, one of which leads round the headland to Heddon's Mouth.

Once out of the shelter of the bay, the cliffs again become bare and wind-swept. High above the sea is a circular earthwork known as the Beacon and once a Roman signal station. Its prominent position was not overlooked by later generations either.

The twin parishes of Martinhoe and Trentishoe overlook the steep valley of the River Heddon. The two little churches serve scattered populations, and both have been over-restored. Trentishoe's tiny church is reached with difficulty at the end of a narrow lane, beyond which the road down to Heddon's Mouth deteriorates into a track. Although inland all is lush farmland and woodland, Heddon's Mouth itself is a bare and fearsome place. Steep scree slopes, rare in Devon, and unclimbable except by the most determinedly foolhardy individuals, plunge down to the river, running in its narrow gorge out to a stony beach. A well-used track, originally serving the lime-kiln on the beach, now provides a level walk from the Hunter's Inn half a mile inland.

The Great Hangman is an evocative name – but it has nothing to do with the gallows and the noose. The name derives from the Celtic for boundary stone. The Hangman Hills are an outlying bastion of Exmoor, heathery moorland over a thousand feet high. Most of this beautiful area is now owned by the National Trust, much of it left to them through bequests.

Combe Martin's straggling village street is said to be the longest in England. Over two miles of cottages, shops, cafés and pubs line the main and only true street, squashed together by the steep valley sides. It seems that little happens in Combe Martin except in the summertime, when the unending streams of visitors pass from one end to the other, but the village has an interesting past. From earliest days the area was important for its silver mines, which were once so prosperous that miners had to be 'imported' from the north. Mining continued intermittently until the end of the nineteenth century and ceased only because it became uneconomic. A few traces still remain in the form of spoil heaps and old engine houses.

The harbour also brought trade. Small coasters called and were offloaded onto horsedrawn carts. All along the coast small vessels put in wherever it was humanly possible, with bulky cargoes of fertilizers, coal and building materials. In the days of deeply rutted, muddy Devon lanes, the sea provided by far the easiest means of transport.

More recently Combe Martin was renowned as a market gardening centre. Those steep valley sides proved ideal for early crops, in particular strawberries, which were exported all over the country. Only a few stalwarts till the ground today, but evidence of the former cultivations can be seen, and Combe Martin strawberries are still the earliest to ripen. There are two buildings of note in the village. At the inland end is the fine church of St Peter ad Vincula, with its tall tower and fine old interior with wooden barrel ceiling and carved rood screen, a monument to Combe Martin's former prosperity. The other is purely secular and has become a tourist attraction of greater fame. The Pack of Cards Inn was built as a private house in the early 1700s by an avid gambler to celebrate a spectacular win. Hence the building had fifty-two windows and four floors, with thirteen doors on each floor. It also contains a rare and curious piece of furniture – a big oak table with a cavity large enough to conceal three desperate men, and they would be desperate if they were seeking to avoid the press gang! The fishermen of seafaring communities such as Combe Martin were a prime target for the dreaded press gangs of the Navy, from whom no able-bodied man was safe, especially in time of war. It is hard to imagine that, in a free and enlightened country that had condemned slavery, a man could not venture forth in his own village or town without forever glancing over his shoulder, and that if he was unlucky he would be dragged off without warning for an unspecified time and might never see his family or home again. No wonder so many inns had hidden chambers and as many exits as possible.

Many of those same fishermen would also have been smugglers. The coast abounds in hidden coves, with landing-places known only to the few who could skilfully manœuvre their vessels under the cliffs. There are several such coves around Combe Martin, and many local tales of smugglers and their exploits. One such cove was the deep inlet of Watermouth Harbour, one of the few privately owned along the north coast. Sheltered from the sea by a high promontory, today the area is popular as a yachting centre and camping and caravan site. It was once, so the stories go, a tailor-made haven for smugglers, with its own direct tunnel leading to the cellars below Watermouth Castle. The tunnel has never been found, but the cellars exist and are filled with ghostly apparitions and 'haunted horrors'. The nineteenth-century castle has become a popular tourist attraction. Externally it maintains its sombre castellated appearance, but inside all has been transformed to provide fun for all the family. There is a model railway, rooms full of the memorabilia of former ages, mechanical music machines, slot machines, puppet shows, talking parrots etc. Has it come down in the world – or is it giving more pleasure to more people than ever it did as a private house?

And Ilfracombe? This once great Victorian holiday resort is built in a most beautiful spot. It has a fine natural harbour, and the town has grown up in the sheltered valley behind it, surrounded on all sides by hills and headlands, owned largely by the National Trust. The original fishing port has been completely submerged by the subsequent growth that occurred when Ilfracombe was at its zenith. The population doubled in the last half of the nineteenth century, and most of the town's large buildings and long terraces date from this period. But the former attractions no longer hold the same appeal, and the once smart town has visibly decayed. The large hotels, the bandstands and the pleasure grounds, even the famous glass pavilion, a smaller version of the Crystal Palace, have all fallen victim to the passage of time.

The harbour is still busy, but the days when the pleasure steamers were moored three or four deep, with thousands of day-trippers pouring into the town, are but a memory. A lone reminder of those halcyon days is the paddle-steamer *Waverley* which once a year steams down from her native Clyde to spend a few weeks sailing around the North Devon coast, delighting all who sail in her and the many who cheer her on her way. For Ilfracombe, the future is uncertain. Many schemes are proposed, some for ambitious marinas, some for ever more self-catering accommodation and amusement centres, some even for a Victorian revival. Ilfracombe has much to offer – it deserves a better fate than its current slow decay.

The heights to the west, known as the Torrs, begin an almost unbroken stretch of National Trust-owned coastal magnificence that extends right round to Braunton Burrows. The Torrs are seven hummocky headlands, upon the highest of which a tea-house once provided welcome refreshment and around which several well-made paths zigzag from base to summit.

The first of North Devon's famous long sandy beaches is Woolacombe, held between the twin outcrops of Mortehoe and Baggy Point. These sheltering arms concentrate the breakers, and here, and at Croyde the other side of Baggy, the unbroken rollers attract large numbers of surfers. At both places there are pockets of coast in private ownership, at Woolacombe deriving an income from car-parking and ice-cream, at Croyde from caravans and chalets.

Much of Woolacombe is relatively modern, but Croyde is one of the prettier old villages, with several cob and thatched cottages and a stream running alongside the main street. Its narrow lanes have difficulty coping with the summer traffic – or perhaps it is the summer traffic that cannot cope with narrow lanes.

Underneath Saunton Down the main road runs close to the cliff edge, giving spectacular views across the wide estuary of the Taw and Torridge and the expanse of Bideford or Barnstaple Bay. Is there any other place on the map of the British Isles so honoured? Both ancient towns lay claim to the bay formed by the two rivers, and diplomatic

Barnstaple

An otter

mapmakers have refused to take sides: it remains on the OS map with a choice of title, take your pick.

Estuaries are romantic places. Punctuation marks along a stretch of coastline; areas of transition where the waters of a river merge imperceptibly with the sea – a beginning and an ending. Most estuaries have their own history. Mariners of old set sail with great hopes to make voyages of exploration; merchantmen began their often perilous and lengthy passages to foreign ports; warships of all ages have sailed forth to defend the nation, and for many, leaving the safety of the estuary was the last sight of a dear and familiar land as they embarked on the first stage of a new life. But the guiding lights are a welcome sight to all returning seafarers – home and safety at last.

North Devon has only one estuary, but that is a grand one marking the end of the two principal rivers, the Taw and the Torridge. The Taw flows straightforwardly across Devon from Dartmoor, but the Torridge begins its 60-mile journey close to the Cornish border, only four miles or so from the north coast, and meanders its way in a series of large loops through North Devon to within sight of Dartmoor, and back again to the coast. It is a beautiful river, flowing for much of its course between steep, wooded banks, secretive and little known. In recent years it has become the subject of heated battles with the water authority and farming communities, as this once vibrant and sparkling river has succumbed to years of abuse and neglect. Today the level of life in its waters is virtually nil, and some have already declared the Torridge a dead river. Sewage is never a nice subject, but it does seem that in years past various local authorities all too often took the easy way out, and where there was a handy stretch of coastline or river, that is where the sewage ended up. At last it appears that some have seen the error of their ways or bowed to the weight of public opinion, and the Torridge should benefit in future from a proper treatment works to serve the area.

In former centuries the estuary was much busier than it is today. Both Barnstaple on the Taw and Bideford on the Torridge were ports of some considerable note, and both lay claim to having sent ships to fight the Armada. Silting in the Taw eventually brought Barnstaple's maritime life to a halt, but Bideford maintains its role, and ships of considerable size continue to sail up river on the tide, under the new high-level bridge specifically designed to allow their passage and discharge their cargoes at the centuries-old quayside. Sand-dredgers work away in the estuary, some say to the considerable detriment of the

Almshouses, Barnstaple

river banks and even the dunes themselves, and the occasional coaster calls.

At weekends on a summer evening at high tide the water is gay with the bright sails of the competing yachts from the Instow Yacht Club, and at other times windsurfers and waterskiers enliven the scene. But the estuary can be a dangerous place. Its entrance is guarded by the Bideford Bar, a broad sandbank on which the seas continually throw up a line of white surf. At low tide the two mighty rivers are reduced to a narrow trickle winding across the mudflats, over which at times it is possible to walk, and it is only close to high tide that vessels may pass with safety across the Bar and up channel, following a carefully marked course from bank to bank. Visiting ships of any size require a pilot, such are the hazards of the estuary.

Just as there are two rivers, with two ancient ports, so is the estuary flanked by two expanses of sand dunes, both of considerable interest to naturalists and scientists, and both serving a multiplicity of uses that occasionally leads to problems. Braunton Burrows on the eastern bank is the larger and is part of the Christie estate, owners also of Tapeley Court at Instow, and Glyndebourne in Sussex. The vast acres of tall sandhills and grassy valleys seem to stretch endlessly, and it is quite possible to lose all sense of direction and become completely lost. Visions of dying men staggering towards a mirage of water, only to fall exhausted on some sandy slope, their bones left to bleach in the strong sunlight, come unbidden to your mind as commonsense exhorts you to climb a hill and get your bearings. Such things happen only in films – for which the Burrows have been used on many occasions.

Northam Burrows to the west are not so vast, being a low-lying area of sand ringed by dunes on the estuary side and protected from the sea by the Pebble Ridge. This natural barrier is all that stops the sea reclaiming what was once its own territory, and it has in times past been breeched when high tides coincide with gale-force winds and mountainous seas. Maintaining the Pebble Ridge is a matter of some importance – though naturally no one agrees as to the best method of achieving its stability.

Both Braunton and Northam Burrows are home to important golf courses. The Royal North Devon at Northam is the older but has to share its turf with sheep, ponies and a constant stream of cars crossing to park behind the Pebble Ridge. Across the estuary, Braunton Burrows are shared by the Ministry of Defence, the golf club and the Nature Conservancy, with the golden sands of Saunton another attraction.

The famed three-mile beach of Westward Ho! has one great advantage – there is no shortage of car-parking space right the way along its length. On a hot summer's day, unbroken lines of shiny metal and flashing windscreens reflect its popularity. Some folk never make it to the sea: they are content to sit beside their parked vehicle as if afraid to leave its protection, perhaps too insecure to venture forth under their own steam, moving only when the ice-cream van cruises slowly past. Others troop over the pebbles to pitch upon the sand, following the same pursuits that have occupied people on beaches ever since children first built sandcastles and Dad set up his impromptu cricket stumps.

The chances are that Westward Ho! would sooner or later have been developed, but had Charles Kingsley not written his famous novel, it might well have been called something else. Before a group of local landowners and speculators seized on the opportunity, the area now known as Westward Ho! consisted of two or three farmhouses and nothing else. Suddenly it became a gold mine, the resort to attract the aristocracy and the wealthy – or so its promoters hoped. In the space of a few years the land had been bought and apportioned – here a large hotel, there a villa, here a row of select boarding houses and there a few shops. The golf club was an integral part of the scheme, and although some of the ideas never reached fruition, the huge, high terraces, the broad streets, the church, the swimming-pool, tennis courts and cricket pitch are all relics. There was even a pier that went the way of all such on this coast, leaving a few twisted metal reminders uncovered at low water.

Westward Ho! is the last outpost of 'touristy resort' North Devon. From here onwards the coast is as nature formed it, with few habitations, few villages and few roads. It is the country of walkers, of naturalists and birdwatchers and of those who seek quiet and solitude. Mile after mile of empty heady cliffland, broken by few deep valleys, this was once unfrequented country. Only the farmer, the occasional gatherer of blackberries or sloes, and the very occasional walker were to be seen. But with the advent of long-distance walking as a popular leisure pursuit and with the setting-up of the South West Way, earnest walkers, staggering under heavy backpacks, weighed down with fell-boots and intent on completing their self-imposed stretch before teatime, are to be met in increasing numbers.

It is rightly said that this very long-distance path, stretching from Minehead around the south-west peninsula to Poole in Dorset, some 550 miles, takes the walker through a great variety of lovely scenery. It seems a shame that so many of them have little time to stop and admire it! The South West Way was a long time coming. It was enacted in the National Park Act of 1949, yet is still not quite complete. Most people walk only a section at a time, and walkers vary from students and youngsters undertaking special projects, youth hostellers and school

Walking the coastal footpath

groups, to the solitary hiker walking for pleasure and the locals and holidaymakers enjoying just a mile or so.

Coastal walking requires great energy and stamina, for there are many steep ups and downs to be traversed, and long sections without any habitation, never mind hospitality. But the coastal scenery is said to be amongst the best in the country. The South West Way is subdivided and on the north coast is known as the Somerset and North Devon coastal footpath, and on the south as the South Devon and Dorset. The paths are waymarked throughout, and a South West Way Association exists to promote the enjoyment and use of this amazing path. One of its effects has been to open up areas of the coast that were hitherto relatively unknown. Many a quiet, undisturbed cove has had its privacy invaded by bands of energetic hikers, and the occupants relaxing in what they had thought was blissful privacy have hastily to retrieve discarded items of clothing. The coast of Devon has few official naturist beaches, but many unofficial ones!

The cliffs immediately beyond Westward Ho!, known as Kipling Tors, are National Trust property, and from the former coastguard and wartime lookout the whole sweep of Bideford Bay from Baggy Point to Hartland Point is laid out before you. Below is the level track that was once the Bideford to Westward Ho! railway, a brave little line that had more obstacles in its short course than is fair and whose tracks were removed during the First World War and never relaid.

Across the bay two white slashes mark the cliffs. The larger is Clovelly, but before that is the former fishing village of Bucks Mills. Hereabouts was all part of the Pine-Coffin estate, one of North Devon's oldest families, said to have come over with the Conqueror. In recent years most of the village has been sold off, and some of the coastal land has been purchased by the National Trust.

Local stories tell of a Spanish vessel wrecked off Bucks and attributed to its sailors the swarthy looks of the Braunds, who were the bulk of the inhabitants and who controlled this stretch of coast. They had a reputation for toughness and for maritime pursuits that were not altogether legal. It would take a brave preventive officer to run the gauntlet of the Braunds in their stronghold, and the chief of the clan was known as 'the King of Bucks'. Beneath his cottage, the last in the village, is a superb lime-kiln, often mistaken for a ruined castle, so vast are its proportions.

Beyond Bucks the cliffs rise again, wooded for the most part, to Clovelly. No picture of Devon would be complete without a mention of Clovelly. It is difficult to reach a fair assessment of this unusual village, for so much has already been written about it. It appears on countless calendars, in pretty picture-books, on postcards and souvenirs; to many tourists Clovelly is the only place in North Devon of which they have heard. It follows that those who loathe 'tourist attractions' are adversely affected by the publicity and either give Clovelly a miss altogether or go prepared to find fault, which is a shame, for Clovelly has many charms.

Although the fishing fleet is much reduced and the herring shoals no longer visit these shores, bringing a flurry of activity and some prosperity, Clovelly has always been a fishing village with a fine tradition of seamanship. The harbour is believed to date from the end of the fourteenth century, and around it grew up the cottages and storesheds, the boathouses and lime-kilns. Once the level land around the Quay Pool was built over, the only place to go was up, so up the hillside the village grew, straddling the stream that once ran down the main street and today is confined to drainage tunnels. The hill being too steep to permit the passage of wheeled vehicles, the original cobbles have never been covered over as has happened elsewhere, and they provide a rough, uncomfortable surface for the passage of the countless pairs of feet, many unsuitably shod, that slip and slither downwards every

Clovelly

summer. Many take the easy way up, travelling by landrover on the parish road that ends at the Red Lion at the bottom.

Exploring Clovelly once the coachloads have begun arriving is useless; by far and away the best time is early evening, when most folk have gone back for dinner and the sun is beginning to set across the bay, lighting up the cottages and reflecting off the panes of glass. Each cottage is individual, many with unusual carving and nearly all with cheerful floral displays. Up the little alleyways and sidewalks are glimpses of lush gardens, for Clovelly enjoys a mild climate, sheltered from the worst gales, with frost and snow rare visitors.

The village is entirely owned by the Clovelly Estate, the local landowners who have held sway for well over 200 years. No development is permitted within the village, and no cottages are sold or used as holiday lets. Whilst some might call their policies feudal, this has meant a rare continuity in village life. Many become ghost towns in the winter, with few remaining permanent residents to support the local shops, so they in turn become seasonal and the downward spiral continues. Not so Clovelly. Almost the reverse. Life flows back again in the autumn when the villagers have time to do other things than cater for the needs of the visitors.

The Clovelly Estates are entirely responsible for the upkeep of the village and its amenities – a fact it is well to remember when confronted with what many consider the extortionate entry fee. A bonus for those approaching from the Bideford direction is to travel along the Hobby Drive. Beyond Bucks Cross a lodge gate marks the entrance to this delightful drive that winds through woodlands, a picture in spring when bluebells carpet the ground, and with glimpses of the sea and Clovelly far below. The drive ends at the top of the village, although walkers may discover the other half that continues westward from the parish road. This leads through the parkland of Clovelly Court, past a delightful summerhouse, an unusual seat canopied with angels' wings, and on over the cliffs. The Hobby Drive and network of carriage drives were laid out in the nineteenth century as a means of providing employment at a time of great hardship.

With only two exceptions, the shore is inaccessible between Clovelly and Hartland Point. Mouth Mill was once used by the Estate as a landing beach. The old stone wall protects the former mill and ruined lime-kiln, and it is amazing that sailing-vessels once discharged a cargo on the unwelcoming pebbly beach.

At the Iron Age fort of Windbury the woodlands come to on end and the bold, windswept cliffs characteristic of the Hartland promontory begin. Inland are ancient woods and steep valleys, the occasional farmstead and placid meadows – but within a few miles of the sea that searing, unrelenting wind ensures little grows, and no one would choose to live so close. Walkers who stride out with pleasure admiring the uninterrupted views and lack of habitation would find it a different world in winter, when at times it is impossible to stand against the fury of the westerlies.

Shipload Bay, just short of the point, is reached by a steep flight of many steps. Owned by the National Trust, it is more akin to a Cornish cove. Always sandy and usually sheltered, it has its devotees who throng the small car-park provided by the National Trust, whose ownership extends back to Mouth Mill.

Hartland Point could be said to mark the end of the Bristol Channel coast and the beginning of the Atlantic. Here the cliffs bend to the south, presenting a scarred and battered face to the westerlies and the huge breakers that pound against them. There is nothing between these cliffs and the coasts of Newfoundland but mile after mile of Atlantic Ocean. The point itself is something of a mixture. The RAF have a radar tracking station here; the coastguards at present maintain a lookout; at one time it was the helicopter port for flights to Lundy, and there is a lighthouse.

Were it not for the fact that Hartland Point is reached only via a long network of narrow lanes, it would be much more popular, for it must have one of the most scenic car-parks on offer, with a wide-ranging panoramic view.

Hartland Quay, a few miles down the coast, is historically and scenically one of the most interesting places along the whole North Devon coastline. Incredible though it may seem, there was indeed once a quay – a long, snaking stone jetty built to provide the only safe anchorage on this treacherous coast. The buildings that now house the hotel, shop and museum were once fishermen's cottages and stores, a coastguard's cottage, a malthouse and inn, and even a bank printing its own £5 notes. Remnants of the lime-kiln are visible as is some of the quay for those who know where to look. It was first breached in 1887 and gradually decayed until the greater part was washed away in a severe gale in 1896.

The museum houses an interesting display based largely on the numerous shipwrecks, the structure of the cliffs, and the history of the quay. The quay and most of the adjoining cliffs and farmland form part of the Hartland Abbey estate, owned by the Stucleys. Since their first acquiring the abbey at the time of the dissolution, the estate has never been sold, and it is this continuity of ownership here – and at Clovelly and the Pine-Coffin estates – that has preserved much of the character of the North Devon coast.

Stoke church, a few miles inland from the quay, has been named 'the cathedral of North Devon', and with justification, for it has few, if any, rivals. It is fitting that the largest parish in Devon should have a church to match with a tower soaring 130 feet into the sky. Its position several miles from the community it now serves is explained by the former presence of the abbey.

Hartland Town, as it is called locally, was once dubbed 'farthest from railways'; nowadays it could equally well claim to be farthest from motorways, and there are few who would wish to alter that.

Geologists are frequent visitors to the cliffs of Hartland. All kinds of interesting features abound. There are two good examples of truncated river valleys, the stream having been captured by the sea at an earlier point. One of these is just south of Hartland Quay and has left a conical cliff known as St Catherine's Tor, of which only half remains. Supposedly there was a small chapel atop, but no proof has ever been found of its existence.

To the south is the magnificent fifty-four-foot waterfall at Speke's Mill Mouth, the best example of many pretty falls that occur along this length of coast. Several short, swift streams drain the high land of Hartland parish, flowing through wooded valleys. Many of them once had watermills, as at Blackpool to the north of Hartland Quay and inland at Speke's Mill. The waterfall at Speke's Mouth is a superb fifty-four feet and after heavy rain it throws spray high into the air. On very rare occasions it has frozen over.

The structure of the cliffs themselves, their strange contortions and twisted rock strata, are also a source of great geological interest, though they provide few homes for sea-birds and are highly dangerous to climb. From Speke's Mouth the cliffs rise up in unbroken line to fall again at Welcombe Mouth, the last small bay before the Cornish border.

Sometimes the island of Lundy seems so close that only a giant step is required to land on that flat, windswept granite surface. At others, it fades into the distance, a remote, indistinct blur, and for weeks on end the island disappears altogether beyond the horizon, yet it is only some twelve miles from the North Devon coast across Bideford Bay. Three miles in length and half a mile or so wide, Lundy makes up what it lacks in size by its strength of character. The island is a freak upthrust of granite rising sheer out of the sea, its high cliffs barring access in all but a few places, and even here it is by no means easy. Most visitors reach the island plateau via the main track from the landing-beach – wide enough for a tractor, it needs constant maintenance, but without it life on Lundy would be difficult indeed.

Lundy has long had a reputation amongst naturalists for the variety of bird life and for its breeding-colonies of sea birds, including puffins. The numbers have declined sharply, but there are still sufficient to attract almost equal numbers of binocular-hung ornithologists.

The marine life in the waters surrounding Lundy is so rich and unique that the status of a marine reserve has now been conferred, the first in the country. More easily sighted are the colonies of seals, the wild goats and Soay sheep, and the shy deer. Rock-climbers find endless challenges in the sheer cliffs, and others are attracted by the archaeological remains. But for many it is the peace and tranquillity that Lundy offers, an island within view of the mainland, yet remote and often inaccessible, a world unto itself.

Situated in the middle of a busy shipping lane, subject to gale-force winds, mountainous seas and fogs, Lundy has featured prominently in the maritime history of the Bristol Channel. At one time it was the base of pilots who would row out to incoming shipping to navigate them safely up channel or were dropped off by outward-bound vessels. The island itself was a considerable hazard to shipping, and the first lighthouse was begun in 1819. The Old Light is a magnificent and eye-catching building on the highest point of the island. Built of granite with a gilded weathervane, it flashes and glints in the sunlight. Despite

North Light, Lundy

the beauty of its architecture, however, it was visible only in clear weather, and in 1896 work commenced on the two replacement lights, one at either end of the island. North Light is no longer manned, being controlled from South Light, which at present remains one of the dwindling number of occupied stations with a crew regularly relieved by a Trinity House helicopter.

The island was acquired in 1969 by the National Trust and is administered by the Landmark Trust, who carried out major renovation and building work. A new jetty and access road are planned to enable passengers from the MV *Oldenburg*, Lundy's supply vessel, to disembark more easily, as many as 200 of them at a time. Farming operations, too, are more intense, and inevitably something of the peace and freedom of Lundy have been lost; it may be that its status as a special offshore nature reserve will be difficult to combine with its role as a tourist attraction.

Beardown Man, Dartmoor

8

Dartmoor

Vast acres of wilderness; vast expanses of sky, of rolling clouds moving from one limitless horizon to another across the dome of Devon. An unyielding granite mass, alien and barren, foe to those who deny it its due reverence, yet friend also to those who know and love their Dartmoor and have learnt to treat it with respect, and playground for the thousands who come in cars to the popular areas for just a few hours in the countryside.

Within the confines of the National Park of Dartmoor are fifty-nine miles of some of the highest and most desolate land in England, and some of the most famous of beauty spots, a notorious prison and a village that gave rise to a well-known song immortalizing a certain old grey mare.

Battles have raged over its usage. Such open, undeveloped land has attracted the Ministry of Defence, the water authority and the road-builders, all of whom have got their own way, as well as private developers, most of whom have not. There are those who see open space only as possible development land, who cannot envisage its having any use or value left alone. All too often it is a department of the Government, or officially backed enterprises, whose fingers itch, and all too often they receive support from the very people who should be preserving our heritage.

Feelings still run high on Dartmoor over the siting of the A30 Okehampton bypass. No one who has witnessed, or sat in, the monumental traffic jams of summer Saturdays that built up around Okehampton would deny the need for some kind of relief road. What was so hotly contested was its route. Devotees of Dartmoor, championed by the redoubtable Lady Sayer and the National Park Authority, were vigorously opposed to the route that would cut across the northern fringes of the moor, ruining some of the most attractive woodland areas that have provided a recreational facility for the town. The farming organizations were just as strongly opposed to the alternative route to the north that would have caused disruption to several

Okehampton's busy main street

farms. Many folk didn't care too much where it went, just so long as it was built, and built quickly. At the end of the day, when the battle seemed conclusively won by the conservationists and anti-southern route, the Government overruled the appeal judgment and decided in favour of the divisive southern route. The National Park Authority put on a brave face but in its heart bitterly resented the decision. 'They changed the rules at the last moment to suit themselves,' was one comment. The whole concept of a National Park should surely guard against such development within its boundaries, and for one Government-sponsored body to fight for its life against its own creator seemed, and still seems, criminal. The final adjudicator on behalf of the Government was Nicholas Ridley, who was later promoted to Secretary of State for the Environment – 'Like putting King Herod in charge of the maternity unit,' was the wry verdict of one National Park member.

Hopefully the scars will heal in time, and the new road, finally opened in 1988, become an accepted facet of the Okehampton landscape, although the noise created by such roads cannot but be intrusive in the environment of the moor. Just one more of man's indentations on this upland wilderness, it ranks with the blows dealt by the reservoirs at Meldon, Burrator and Fernworthy, the quarrying at Meldon, which at one time supplied most of the trackbed material required by the railways, and the clay works at Lee Moor.

Man has left his mark on Dartmoor since earliest times, but until the twentieth century his efforts were like those of a child with a toy hammer – a little surface dent and nothing more. But the advent of the age of mechanization, with the development of enormous earth-moving equipment, has meant that nothing is sacred, nothing inviolate and nothing impossible. In a few short hours a landscape that has taken thousands of years to form can be destroyed forever.

Although within the confines of Dartmoor National Park, which was set up in 1951, the land itself is owned by many different people and organizations. The Authority owns 3,500 acres, the National Trust another 3,551 acres, and the Nature Conservancy Council 17,371 acres. Other owners with differing aims and interests in the moorland are the Forestry Commission (1,752 acres), the Ministry of Defence (13,332 acres) and South West Water (3,602 acres). Much of northern Dartmoor is owned by the Duchy of Cornwall (over 50,000 acres in total), and the remainder is divided amongst individual farmers and one or two larger estates, with even the Dartmoor Preservation Association owning small pockets around Swincombe, Sharpitor and Harford.

Dartmoor survived as open moor because it was a Royal Forest, created in Norman times as an enormous hunting-ground over which the repressive forest laws operated. Later it was the revenue from tin mining that made it a valuable possession of the Crown. It was vested in the Duchy of Cornwall by Edward III and has remained part of the Duchy lands ever since.

'Enclosure' is a commonplace word today, but in the eighteenth century it brought ruin to thousands of peasants and irrevocably altered the face of the countryside. Until then a system of communal fields and common land had supported the villagers and small farmers. Enclosure meant that the common land became fields, usually annexed by the larger landowners, and the people lost their rights. On Dartmoor the effect could be said to be temporary – the nature of the soil and the climate prevented its being good agricultural land, and many of the 'newtake' walls built in the 1780s are now low mounds of stone. Enclosure was stopped in 1820 on Duchy land after some 15,000 acres had been affected.

The rights of commoners are at the heart of Dartmoor and include the right of turf-cutting and of pasturage. Each commoner has the right to turn a certain number of sheep, cattle and horses out onto the moor to roam free over the summer months. Every autumn, the stray stock are rounded up and those not claimed, impounded. Many are sold, but a large number return to the moor.

More than forty per cent of the moor, around 90,000 acres, remains common land – open moorland, the heartland of Dartmoor over which the public have right of access. It is this land which the National Park Rangers consider to be Dartmoor pure and simple. 'The fleshpots round the fringes are fine and provide many people with a pleasant day out, but it is the wild and desolate moor that is what it is all about,' was how one Ranger summed up Dartmoor. There are nine Rangers whose job it is to patrol the moor, help the visitor, maintain the footpaths and signposts, clear the litter and protect the moor from the damage caused by too many people, or too many horses, all wanting to use the same small areas.

Half of the Authority's total budget goes on conservation measures. 'If there were no National Parks, by the end of the twentieth century it is more than likely that there would not be any areas left worthy of being called a national park,' is how one of the Rangers put it. You only have to look out from Dartmoor's rugged heights at what has happened to the rest of Devon to see exactly what he means. High up on the plus side of their job is showing people how to enjoy the moor. Parties of schoolchildren are taken on outings, encouraged to plant trees, to study the wildlife and the history of the moor. Youngsters aiming for the Duke of Edinburgh Award are given a helping hand, and the countless questions of the energetic walker or climber or the car-bound tourist are answered.

Once a year, on a weekend in the middle of May, upwards of 2,000 youngsters converge on Dartmoor to take part in the Ten Tors Walk. The event first took place over twenty-five years ago, and the numbers participating have been steadily growing and have reached invasion proportions. It is organized and run by the Army, who decide who may enter and thus control the numbers. The Rangers' only responsibility is to ensure that local life is disrupted as little as possible and that private property is respected. For many the walk proves a severe endurance test, and the drop-out numbers, especially in bad weather, can be as high as ninety per cent.

Far more of a problem are the 'letterboxes'. Believed unique to Dartmoor, they began in the 1870s with that at Cranmere Pool, then one of the most inaccessible spots on the moor. The idea was that the visitor posted a card of his own whilst collecting the one previously deposited in the box, to prove his visit. Unfortunately this has now become such a craze that there are well over a thousand boxes dotted all over the moor, and considerable damage is caused by those hunting for them.

As long ago as 1883 a need was seen to protect the wilderness of Dartmoor. If it was to survive at all, unsympathetic development had to be guarded against. The Dartmoor Preservation Association was founded, and today it is the granddaughter of the founder who is its patron and leading light. To many, Lady Sylvia Sayer is a nuisance, a domineering elderly lady who wants Dartmoor kept just as she remembers it when she was a child, who ought by now (she is eighty-four) to be a retired grandmother. What must be acknowledged is that, without her and her fellow members, Dartmoor would have suffered incalculable losses and be a place very different from that which we know today. A thorn in the flesh of many she may be, but would there were more Lady Sayers to defend so capably, at her own expense and in her own time, what so many of us enjoy and want our children to enjoy.

Without the work of the DPA, she says, there would be far more developments, there would be more pylons marching across the moor, there would be another reservoir, there would be vast acres of forestry, and there might be even more of a military presence. The DPA and Lady Sayer have fought countless battles and defended the moor at countless public inquiries, most of which have been lost, but there have been some successes, of which the defeat of the Swincombe Reservoir plan was one, and the removal of the MoD buildings on Sharpitor another. The BBC mast on Hessary Tor was a major defeat, as were the Okehampton bypass and the continued military presence on the northern half of the moor. The moor, Lady Sayer feels, is a unique and precious wilderness area and is irreplaceable. There are plenty of alternative sites without infringing on the moor simply because it is there and it is empty. Lady Sayer refers to all those who cast greedy eyes on Dartmoor as predators, often wolves in sheep's clothing, but she has won the respect of most of those with whom she has crossed swords.

Forestry and enclosure were two of the earliest threats, fought by her father and grandfather. Enclosure had all but stopped by the end of the century, but large areas of Dartmoor have disappeared under blanket coverage of conifers, interrupting the moorland sweep and robbing the commoners of their right of pasturage – and the public of their right of access. This threat, too, seems now to be contained, and Lady Sayer takes heart from the new attitude of the Duchy of Cornwall, whose administrators seem more interested in preservation and conservation than in times past. Her next battle is designed to rid the Okehampton and Lydford areas of the military and their live firing-ranges, and she is particularly concerned that the military road from Okehampton far into the heart of Dartmoor should be either blocked or allowed to fall into a 'state of benign neglect'. This particularly desolate area of Dartmoor has become too easily accessible for motor vehicles, and she considers it should be left to nature. Her sympathies are with the National Park Authority, which largely consists of members of Devon

Iron Age settlement, Dartmoor

County Council who thus wear two hats and find themselves increasingly at odds with their masters, the Government, and without adequate funding either to fight them or to achieve their own objectives. But at least, between them, the NPA and the DPA make a noise that has to be listened to.

Another subject of some controversy is the clay workings at Lee Moor, amongst the world's largest, on the south-west edge of Dartmoor. China clay is a rare commodity, and only in China are there deposits larger than those found in Devon and Cornwall. For centuries Chinese porcelain was highly valued, yet despite much experiment the Western world failed to discover the secret of its manufacture. Then, in the eighteenth century, a Plymouth chemist, William Cookworthy, discovered that its principal ingredient was kaolin, and fine English china has been produced ever since. Unfortunately, the production of one ton of kaolin leaves eight tons of waste mica, and it is this that is responsible for the huge white spoil heaps that so disfigure a large area of the moor. Experiments are being carried out to find some way of making them more acceptable, but there is little that will grow on such poor stuff.

Evidence of man's former activities holds fascinating clues to the history of the moor and, because his efforts are so puny compared with the sheer scale of the moor, have become imbued with a certain romance. Dartmoor is littered with stone circles and stone rows whose meaning is not entirely clear, remnants of early hut settlements and enclosures, and still there is the occasional find of an early flint arrowhead or knife. There are several deserted and ruined longhouses, where once a community farmed in contentment if not great wealth. Some such houses were occupied within living memory and have been vacated only because of the lure of 'better living' off the moor and the cost of bringing modern amenities was too high – amenities such communities had previously managed very well without. But most are far older, remnants of medieval settlements now long forgotten.

Somewhat younger is Drake's leat, running over many miles of moorland to bring water to the people of Plymouth, an early attempt to harness the abundant natural resources, and one that was entirely successful. Begun in 1590, it took thirty-five men just five months to complete. Old mineworkings and tinners' shafts seem part of the scenery; former railways provide pleasant footpaths, and even the Army, to its amazement, has learnt that some of its earlier firing-ranges should not be removed because they, too, are now considered part of the archaeological history of the moor!

Although containing the highest land in southern England (High Willhays rises to 2,039 feet), Dartmoor is not a range of mountains; it is

Tors on Dartmoor

high upland with smooth flanks and long ridges, punctuated by rocky summits. These are known as 'tors', and the plentiful granite rock scattered all over the moor is called 'clitter'. The mass of high land contains some notorious boggy basins where the water settles, seeping slowly through the peat to feed the myriad streams and provide the all-important grass that survives even in the hottest and dryest of summers. At one time the moor had a reputation for providing the greatest number of fat and healthy sheep anywhere in the country, and at the end of the nineteenth century it was not unknown for cattle to be sent to Dartmoor from far afield during times of drought.

These damp and rainsodden uplands are also the birthplace of most of Devon's rivers. The Okement and the Taw drain to the north, the Tavy feeds the Tamar river, and innumerable streams and rivers run swiftly to the south coast, the Dart and the Teign being the longest and most spectacular. From infant streams, full of gurgles and splashings, the clear, sparkling water rushes from the moor into valleys, at first little more than gentle folds that quickly become steep-sided and wooded with tall, stately trees. Reflections are rare in Dartmoor rivers, for the waters are too turbulent, too fast-flowing, but occasionally a still, deep pool provides a calm sheet of water, broken by trout rings.

In some instances the early bridges that first spanned these streams and rivers are still in use today. Sturdy stone structures designed for

Stone bridge over a Dartmoor stream

horse-drawn vehicles or packhorse trains, they somehow cope with today's motor traffic, although their width causes major hold-ups as coaches ease their bloated bodies across. Two of the oldest are at Holne across the Dart. One is a true packhorse bridge, the other a replacement of an even earlier bridge, but still dating from 1413. At Two Bridges and Merrivale, the old stone bridges stand in retirement alongside modern counterparts.

It is a sunny Sunday in the summer. Cars and coaches in their thousands are heading for Dartmoor. Some belong to holidaymakers, many to local people for whom the moor is their playground. All of them will be looking for a day 'away from it all', an outing to remember with pleasure, but how they achieve their objective will vary considerably.

A large number will head straight for the well-known beauty spots around the fringes of the moor – Holne, Lydford, Haytor, Dartmeet, Fingle Bridge. A short stroll from the car, an ice-cream or cup of tea and a pleasant sit down by the side of one of Dartmoor's many sparkling streams, and they will be well content. Almost as many will make for one of the scenically sited car-parks just off the main roads with views over miles of moorland – and some may never even leave their cars. Places such as Princetown, Widecombe, Chagford and Yelverton appeal to those who like rather less moor and rather more in the way of shops and cafés. And many will head for the reservoirs, good starting-points for expeditions onto the moor proper. The relatively few roads, many of them very narrow, cause congestion and parking problems, and for the Rangers a sunny Sunday is the busiest day of the week. But somehow the moor absorbs them all, and nearly everyone will find his own ideal.

For walkers Dartmoor offers vast areas crossed by many paths, and it is a simple matter to leave behind the noisy clutter of tourism. Everyone has their own particular spot, their sanctuary for a day out.

There are many delightful villages around the moor, some well known, some rarely visited. Some remain as they have always been, small settlements of a farming community. Others have had to accept an influx of modern building, usually of retirement bungalows or the homes of wealthy commuters. One or two have succumbed entirely and become tourist traps, but most retain their essential moorland character.

Widecombe is a name known to all tourists, even to visitors from abroad, for ever associated with the song about Widecombe Fair. Uncle Tom Cobley borrowed the poor old grey mare to visit the fair with his companions, and it was on the return journey, when they were somewhat the worse for drink, that she gave up and died. The original fair was for the sale of cattle, sheep and ponies, when great numbers were rounded up and brought down off the moor. This was its chief purpose, but such gatherings were also an occasion for much celebration and jollification. Fairs were also held at Lydford and Tavistock and other towns around the edges of Dartmoor. Some survive more as 'pleasure' fairs and tourist attractions, which is what Widecombe's fair has become. Uncle Tom and his grey mare still play a prominent part.

The village lies in a hollow surrounded by high moorland, with its church dominating the valley. Often referred to as 'the cathedral of the moor', it has a fine granite tower which is a notable landmark. In 1638 the church was struck by lightning, killing some of the worshippers and injuring many more. A fine church house alongside the church is now a National Trust shop. Widecombe would be a pleasant enough village were it not for the profusion of gift shops and cafés and a constant stream of coaches and cars.

Much less frequented but equally attractive is Buckland-in-the-Moor. It is not nearly so easy to find, being buried down a network of singletrack lanes. Most unusually for Dartmoor, nearly all the cottages are thatched, and surprised motorists stopping to take photographs are an added hazard. An interesting complex of former agricultural buildings has been turned into a craft centre and restaurant, but that is the only 'commercial' presence. The church is delightful, on a small and intimate scale. It has several features of interest, one being the rood screen which still retains its original paintings. Those on the west side facing the church depict the predictable religious figures and events. Those on the inner, east side adjacent to the choir stalls are curious in the extreme. The figures appear to have no Christian significance and are almost medieval cartoons or caricatures.

Around the periphery of the moor are the larger settlements, the market towns and those that have now declined to become large villages. Such places as Moretonhampstead, Bovey Tracey and Ashburton thrive amidst encircling residential development. Those along the southern limits of the moor have all but lost their identity as dormitories of Plymouth linked by the new, fast road and submerged beneath industrial sites, out-of-town shopping centres and more and more housing. To the west and north the towns and villages have fared better, keeping their intrinsic Devon flavour and making only modest allowances for visitors. Perhaps the wetter side is less attractive!

Both Lydford and Chagford are still delightful small towns, both former stannary towns in the days when tin mining was of vital importance to Dartmoor and the tinners had to bring their ingots down to be stamped and sold. Ashburton, Plympton and Tavistock were the

The Market House, Chagford

other stannary towns, with Lydford the seat of stannary justice. Its grim castle dungeons played host to many a reluctant tinner who fell foul of the rough tinners' laws. Today the old keep on its grass mound seems rather benign, situated between the far more pleasantly hospitable Castle Inn and the church.

The town has a long history, being one of the county's four original Saxon burgh settlements, with its own mint, and traces of the Saxon streets and the original protective rampart can still be seen. Most visitors are more interested in Lydford Gorge, lying below the village, owned by the National Trust. The White Lady waterfall is one of the highest in the West Country and after heavy rainfall is magnificent, as is the whole of the gorge. Unfortunately the best part is viewed from a one-way-only narrow and slippery path, which is perhaps why the National Trust close the gorge during the winter months, when it could reasonably be expected to be at its best.

Chagford has something of an 'up-market' image, being surrounded by high-quality hotels and containing some first-class shops, centred around an attractive market square where the six-sided former market building still stands. There are several good inns to choose from and it was one of the first towns in Devon to have electricity, powered by a hydro-electric plant built in 1891.

Close by is a particularly notable stretch of the River Teign where abundant wild daffodils crowd the banks in the early spring. Wardens now protect them, as some people seem incapable of looking without picking.

High above the river a modern castle stands sentinel. Castle Drogo was begun in 1910 and took twenty years to complete. Built almost entirely of granite, even down to the bath, it was the last castle to be built in England – if 'castle' is the correct term for what is a private residence with castellations. The architect was Sir Edwin Lutyens, and its builder was Julius Drewe, founder of the Home & Colonial grocery store. It is now owned by the National Trust.

Below the castle is the scenically magnificent gorge through which the river flows, and a footpath leads down to Fingle Bridge. The bridge itself is quite modern by Dartmoor standards, dating only from the sixteenth century, but it has become much visited, with provision for coaches and a large café and inn by the water's edge. Originally it was known only to fishermen and walkers, for the bridge is for foot traffic only, so at least the environs of the river are spared the noise of passing cars.

The inn and café have an interesting history. Jessie Ashplant from Drewsteignton first began serving teas to fishermen in 1897. Ten years later the first crude shelter was erected, nothing more than a three sided tin shack with a roof. But Jessie continued, and such was her popularity that in 1957 she and her family ultimately built the Anglers Rest. It is still run by Jessie's descendants, who have just celebrated ninety years of catering at Fingle Bridge.

The strangest settlement on the moor is Princetown, centred around the grim bastions of Dartmoor Prison. It is totally manmade, and even the name seems alien in the wild landscape, conjuring up images of a Brighton-type development. It was planned originally as an agricultural settlement by a visionary who thought he could beat the moor, one Thomas Tyrwhitt, a friend of the Prince Regent – hence the name. Work began in the 1780s, though the choice of a site some 1,400 feet above sea-level with one of the highest records of rainfall in the country, sometimes as much as one hundred inches a year, seems strange. Had Tyrwhitt's original intention been to build a prison, a more inhospitable place would be hard to find. The small settlement was soon in difficulties, and he came up with the proposal to build a prison to house the Napoleonic and American prisoners of war, at that time kept in appalling conditions usually in former wooden sailing-ships known as prison hulks. He was given permission, and work began in 1806 on those great granite blocks that seem to epitomize the word 'prison'. At one time over 7,000 prisoners were crammed inside, but the fortunes of Princetown were secured. The prisoners had to provide most of their own food and clothing, and prized possessions these days are the small models, usually of ships, carved out of bone by the prisoners and used for barter. After the prisoners thankfully returned home, presumably fervently hoping never again to come anywhere near Dartmoor, the prison closed and Princetown went into a decline until it was reopened as part of the country's penal system in 1850.

Tavistock has been described as the most delightful town in West Devon. It is a marvellous example to all modern town planners, who should be transported willynilly to spend a day wandering around the town to learn at first hand just what makes it both appealing and successful as a place in which to live and work. It is not a new town: the Tavistock that is so evident today was largely built in the mid-1800s by one family, the Russells, and one man in particular, the seventh Duke of Bedford.

Until 1910 Tavistock was a town in private, rather than municipal, ownership. It grew originally around its dominating abbey, founded in 974. At the time of the dissolution it was the second richest monastic establishment in the county. The abbey and all its vast lands were acquired by the Russells, earls and later dukes of Bedford and marquesses of Tavistock. A student of history would find much of interest here: it was one of the four original stannary towns; the monastery contained one of the earliest printing presses; the woollen industry was important, but by far and away the largest source of its prosperity was mining in the nineteenth century.

Tavistock is rich in industrial archaeology, surrounded by derelict mines and workings. All contributed to the wealth of the landowners, but it was the discovery of copper, and later of arsenic, in the countryside around Morwellham on the banks of the Tamar that led to the amazing growth and development of Tavistock – and lined the coffers of the Russells for generations to come. The great mining boom lasted from the 1790s for over one hundred years, reaching a peak in the 1860s, when it was claimed that the famous Devon Great Consols mine was the richest copper mine in the world. It eventually closed down in 1901, but even today it is said that the old dumps, now mostly tree-covered, still contain around £5 million worth of ore. A canal was constructed from Tavistock, via the mine, to reach the Tamar at Morwellham so that the ore could be exported by ship, and much of this can still be followed, starting from the town's park. It necessitated a tunnel 1¼ miles long, and the whole thing took fourteen years to build, opening in 1817.

For the Russells the royalties were enormous, but they were not uncaring landlords, and with this wealth the seventh Duke planned and built the rows of neat miners' houses on the Plymouth road, which he also built, and remodelled the town centre, erecting in 1848 the fine

The Bedford Hotel, Tavistock

guildhall and library buildings around the market, over which his statue presides. Together with the old church built on the former abbey lands, and the Bedford Hotel built largely of abbey stones, it makes as pleasing a town centre as it would be possible to find anywhere. Inside that same town hall is an information centre giving a graphic display of the development of the town and, perhaps somewhat churlishly, suggesting that the dukes of Bedford got rich on the backs of poor struggling miners paid a pittance to work themselves to death on their behalf. Each generation must be judged by its own standards, not by those of succeeding generations. By the light of their times, the Russells must have spent a very great deal on improving the lot of the working people by, at the very least, providing decent housing that is still occupied, and laying out a town in a way which has not materially altered – money better spent than gambling it away at cards or on new finery.

Fragments of the former abbey remain around the town, but most of it was robbed for its stone shortly after its dissolution. The old abbey gatehouse is incorporated in the guildhall, part survives in the Bedford Hotel, and areas of walling and the former stillhouse are to be seen around the car-park and river bank.

The covered market operates once a week on a Friday, when the town is crowded, for it forms an important centre for northern Dartmoor and the western area of Devon. Among its less appreciated monuments are the great railway viaduct high above the town, the canal itself, the quiet Quaker burial ground with its beautiful trees on the river bank from where there is an unusual view of the roofs and turrets of the guildhall and church, and the statue of Sir Francis Drake in the middle of the roundabout on the Plymouth road. This is the original; that on Plymouth Hoe is a copy. Sir Francis' birthplace, Hayes Barton, lies just outside the town, not far from the canal.

Okehampton is the most northerly of the moorland market towns, but it has been so beset with traffic problems that much of its former ancient character has been lost. The castle still occupies its mound, and a cattle market is held here, but much of the centre of the town has either been demolished to make way for the summer traffic that clogs the A30 or rebuilt and modernized. It remains to be seen whether the new bypass will materially alter the town or leave it a deserted, broad thoroughfare.

9

South of Dartmoor

Between Dartmoor and the sea is a fertile, densely populated area known as the South Hams. It is still largely a rural area, fighting off threats from Plymouth on one side and Torbay on the other.

Backed by the heights of Dartmoor, the South Hams have much to offer. In the space of an afternoon it is possible to leave behind the largest city in the West Country, stop beside a moorland stream in tranquil surroundings, explore a quiet market town, stroll along a beautiful estuary, swim from a sandy beach or admire the view from a breezy headland. The whole area is a maze of lanes, many leading only to farms or small forgotten villages. It is not a place to visit if you are in a hurry, for there isn't a straight road anywhere.

Kingsbridge is the undoubted centre; all the signposts point to Kingsbridge. The town itself is bypassed but, like most of the South Hams towns, it is worth exploring on foot.

The main A38 between Exeter and Plymouth runs a ring around the southern edge of Dartmoor, and the places on its route have suffered first from the increase in traffic and latterly from an explosion of development. Such towns as South Brent and Ivybridge are in danger of losing their identity altogether and of being swallowed up by Plymouth.

Several short and lively streams drain off Dartmoor, the clear, brown-tinted water sparkling over rocky beds in an energetic dash to the sea. Many of them end in deep, tidal creeks – the Erme, the Yealm, the Avon and the Dart – and it is these wooded inlets that give the coast of the South Hams its special character. Continuous exploration is impossible, and walkers find themselves making long detours inland or using the age-old ferries in the summertime. Exploring by road means a series of zigzags out to the sea, back in round the estuary.

South Devon as a whole is far more densely populated and developed than the north. Urban sprawl affects many of the former villages, and small towns have grown at an amazing rate, attracting large numbers of the new class of wealthy retired. In places bungalows reach almost to

Dartmouth

the cliff edge; caravan parks and kiosks sit right on the beaches. Commercialism is much more apparent all around.

Fortunately the National Trust realized the threat and have managed to acquire some thirty-five miles of the South Devon coastline. Enterprise Neptune, the name given to the special fund-raising project to safeguard the coast, had its beginnings in Devon, activated by the threat to the Dart Estuary. In 1969 the fund made its first purchase around Little Dartmouth, and since then it has pursued a policy of 'anything and everything around the Dart at whatever price', with the result that it now owns most of the cliffs to the west of Dartmouth and almost everything between Dartmouth and Brixham.

Their coastal ownership begins at Wembury, now almost part of Plymouth. A popular sandy beach is provided with a car-park, and the former mill, which is at least Elizabethan, is a Trust gift shop and café. Above is the sturdy church of St Werburgh, built in a prominent position to serve as a landmark to sailors – a form of early lighthouse.

Offshore is the Great Mewstone rock. It has nothing to do with cats: 'seamew' is an old name for gulls and describes their distinctive cry. It is hardly large enough to be called an island, yet the Mewstone has been inhabited at least twice. In 1744 a local man and his family were sentenced to exile on the rock, presumably preferable to imprisonment, for a term of seven years. When the time came to leave, one of the daughters decided to stay on, in time acquiring a husband and three children, all of whom lived on the Mewstone. The last inhabitant was a colourful character called Sam Wakeham. He enlarged the house, whose ruins can still be seen, and made it habitable for his new wife, created a garden and cut steps and a landing-stage. Boatmen from Plymouth regularly called, and Sam himself offered to row out sightseers from Wembury for two pence each – and the hope of a little snuff. His term of tenure came to an end when he was caught smuggling.

The further side of the Yealm estuary was formerly part of Lord Revelstoke's estate. Around the cliffs he constructed a carriage drive beginning and ending at his home at Membland. Much of this still exists and follows the cliffs from Noss Mayo round Gara Point to Stoke Point and the forlorn church of St Peter at Revelstoke, now surrounded by caravans.

The cliffs here are low, dipping almost to sea-level. Beaches as such are few and far between, with long areas of low rocks and seaweed-filled channels.

Around Bigbury-on-Sea the headlands have become disfigured with bungalow development and typical seaside paraphernalia. Offshore is Burgh Island, reached at low tide across a causeway and also by a strange contraption known as the sea-tractor that cautiously edges its way above the seawater when visitors have left it too late to cross dryshod.

The twenty-six acre island has two claims to fame. One is its extraordinary hotel built in the Art Deco style, complete with Palm Court interior, and the other is Agatha Christie. She wrote two of her murder mysteries whilst staying at the hotel, and one of them uses the island, loosely disguised, as the setting for what used to be entitled *Ten Little Niggers* but is now known as *And Then There Were None*. The hotel has recently been restored to its former glory and is once again the popular haunt of the famous and the wealthy. The whole place is atmospheric in the extreme.

Hope Cove was once a fishing community and the centre of great smuggling activities. Now it is the centre of much commercialism. The attractive small harbour and sandy foreshore shelter under the lee of Bolt Tail. Here the nature of the cliffs changes and the scenery becomes one of grandeur, with a high, unbroken plateau falling dramatically to the shoreline, for the most part inaccessible. Sandy coves to attract the developers and the crowds are lacking – just six miles of glorious scenery – all safe in the ownership of the National Trust.

Footpath erosion around Bolt Tail has caused problems, for it makes a convenient circular walk from Hope Cove. Many of the walkers, who no doubt will have ignored the information boards, will be unaware that they are strolling around an Iron Age fort at least 2,000 years old, and that the massive bank is not a field boundary at all but an amazing survival from the fort.

Tall radio masts of the Decca Navigation Station distinguish Bolberry Down. On the cliff top is a large area where parking is permitted, with outstanding views for the car-bound, and level walking for several miles in either direction. So often on the south coast a seemingly insignificant lane leads to a well-sited car-park; usually there is no indication, no signpost. Such delights are for the informed or the adventurous and optimistic – often they are not even marked on the Ordnance Survey maps, and this is true of both Bolberry Down and Soar Mill Cove.

This stretch of coastline has seen its fair share of shipwrecks, one of the most recent being in 1936 when the Finnish barque *Herzogin Cecilie* struck the Ham Stone off Soar Mill Cove. She was towed off, but disaster struck again at Starehole Bay, where she was abandoned to her fate and where her outline can occasionally be seen. One of the most tragic losses was the *Ramillies*, a seventy-four-gun naval ship with a crew of 700. In February 1760 she met her doom on the rocks below Bolt Tail, where an inlet commemorates her ending – and the graveyard of all but twenty-six on board.

A World War II lookout survives on Bolt Head. These ugly structures that disfigure the coast have acquired an historic aura over the years, and although their removal at one time seemed desirable, they are part of our history, and a link in the chain that begins with the Iron Age fort on the twin headland of Bolt Tail. A steep climb down leads to Starehole Bay, once a beautyspot known only to the energetic, whose privacy has been invaded by the creation of the coastal footpath. There is something unnerving about being stared down upon from a great height.

The land rises steeply to Sharp Tor, and here Salcombe and the Kingsbridge estuary open out. From this exceptional viewpoint, which is higher than Bolt Head, Eddystone Lighthouse, over twenty miles away, is often visible, although it can only be optimism that includes Cherbourg and Ushant on the view indicator! The walk to Sharp Tor from the unattractively named Stink Cove was laid out by the Courtenay family, one-time owners of the land (still National Trust).

Civilization begins again with tarmacked roads and houses at Overbecks, named after its eccentric builder – Otto Overbeck, who was a collector of most unusual artefacts, the house's principal attraction.

Salcombe has seen a complete upturn in its fortunes, from decaying fishing village to resort of the wealthy. Most of the former fishermen's cottages have been altered out of all recognition into very upmarket residences, with plate-glass windows, balconies, windowboxes and roof gardens. There is nothing very fishy about Salcombe anymore. Its 'gentrification' began in the late eighteenth century, when the mild climate and sheltered position proved attractive and several villa-type residences were built. Had the proposed railway from Kingsbridge via Snapes Point ever been built, Salcombe might have developed even further, but nothing came of this ambitious plan, which is largely forgotten, marked only by a landing-stage on Snapes Point and gate pillars built optimistically to mark the proposed villa entrances. A ferry crosses to the Portlemouth side, where the ruins of former defensive forts guard the harbour entrance.

Geologists find much to interest them along Devon's long coastline, and in the vicinity of Prawle Point they have an area to get their teeth – or hammers – into. Ice Age fluctuations have left behind three distinct sea-levels, giving three different sets of cliffs for them to explore. To the uninitiated, the spiny, upthrusting rocks and sudden dips and outcrops may be interesting to look at, but they are not always easy to traverse.

Prawle Point was the site of a medieval chapel, now disappeared and superseded by a Lloyd's signal station and lookout.

The rocky promontory that comprises Bolt Tail, Bolt Head, Prawle Point and Start Point is the most southerly area of mainland coastline, and beyond the land falls back to Berry Head. The cliffs are gone. Start Point marks their end, and from this last upthrust they fall gently down to the shingle beaches of Start Bay.

Huddled under the cliffs perched on rocky platforms are some pathetic remnants – all that is left of the lost village of Hallsands. It came to a sudden end on a wild night in January 1917, when villagers fled for their lives, trapped between the sea and the cliffs, their homes crumbling beneath the deluge of sea water as it rose over the sea wall in front of them and crashed again on the cliffs behind. Water in front, water behind, water through them and over them. Just two of the cottages remained habitable; the rest of Hallsands was turned into a 'jagged spectre on the coastal landscape, a debris of fallen tiles and broken walls, the only monument to generations of courageous fishermen', as one former inhabitant described the scene.

The disaster had been forecast: dredging of the shingle since 1898 had slowly but surely destroyed the stability of Hallsands. It had been a typical fishing village, inhabited by proud and resourceful people to whom poverty was an ever-present companion. Villagers then were close-knit and helped each other in times of trouble. But everyone was in trouble in 1917 – and it seemed no one wanted to take on the responsibility for the disaster. Eventually new cottages were built inland – by a fishermen's trust, not by the local council and without government help. The most resourceful family of Hallsanders remained, building a hotel on the cliff top. The Trout family was remarkable by any standards. A widow and four daughters, they earned their living by fishing alongside the menfolk; except that the girls were more venturesome.

The south-west has its own Grace Darling: Ella Trout was awarded the OBE for rescuing a man from a sinking ship off Start Point. She was only twenty years old at the time, and photographs of the Trout sisters show laughing, weather-beaten faces, indistinguishable from their male companions. The Trout women weren't going to be beaten by the sea. Making the concrete blocks by hand and working often late into the night, they built the Trout Hotel and restaurant up on the headland. The last surviving sister lived until quite recently all alone in the hotel, which she kept prepared for guests and customers but never opened, running off when anyone approached. The hotel is now holiday flats.

A row of cottages perches somewhat precariously next to the hotel on the headland, and below them are a car-park and the new village that is so very different from the old.

Beesands huddles behind the protection of a sea wall, the level of the shingle beach seemingly above that of the roadway behind. It suffered from a stray bomb in 1943, when several people were killed. Here there is ample free parking and a beach that stretches for miles, broken only by the rocky headland of Torcross. It was from here that the butcher set out at low tide with his horse and cart to his customers at Beesands and Hallsands.

Torcross today is a busy holiday resort, catering for the many travellers who idle down the coast road from Dartmouth, stopping to look over the nature reserve of Slapton Ley and to read the memorial on Slapton Sands to the American Forces who used this area for training purposes in the last war and took over many of the neighbouring villages. No doubt they were familiar with Stokenham, just inland of Torcross and noted for its church, Church House Inn and thatched cottages.

Slapton Sands is a spit of sand and shingle that keeps the sea from flooding the two leys or lakes, which are administered by the Field Trust.

Stoke Fleming church is another that is prominently sited as a landmark to sailors, and from it there are fine views over Leonard's Cove towards the Dancing Beggars' rocks that mark the beginning of the Dart Estuary.

Nowadays the valley of the River Dart is a bustle of tourist activity for much of its length. One of the major attractions is Buckfast Abbey, providing an unusual opportunity to visit a monastic settlement.

An abbey and its foundation stood on the site from pre-Conquest times until the Reformation, after which the buildings gradually fell into disrepair and were finally demolished in the early 1800s, a house and woollen mill taking their place. But in 1882 the site attracted a community of French Benedictines who undertook the immense labour of once again raising an abbey and its attendant buildings. The abbey church was not consecrated until 1932 and was largely the work of just four of the brothers – a labour of love indeed. The history of its building and of monastic life at Buckfast is recounted at an audio-visual centre.

The abbey church is open to the public and has become big business, with around half a million visitors a year, God and Mammon mixed on a large scale. Why does the abbey attract such vast numbers, most of whom are neither Catholic nor particularly religious? With them have come the attendant problems of adequate facilities, but the tranquil atmosphere of a House of God is somewhat lacking. Visitors who come expecting to see columns of robed monks going about their devotions in solemn and devout silence will be disappointed.

It is sad to relate but the British seem unable to spend a holiday happily unless they are provided with an ample supply of shops. We may once have been a nation of shopkeepers, but today we seem to have become a nation of shoppers. Around Buckfast Abbey there are several

Buckfast Abbey

shops, only two of which have any direct connection with it. But for all its possibly unsought tourist trappings, it is still a religious foundation and is respected as such.

From the lower side of the A30 – indeed, from almost underneath it – is the terminus of the Dart Valley Railway. Steam-train enthusiasts have long flocked to travel on the seven-mile line that runs along the Dart to Totnes. First opened in 1872, it fell victim to the Beeching Axe in 1962 and was reopened by the Dart Valley Light Railway Company – ironically by Dr Beeching – seven years later. It has never looked back and must have given the hatchet-happy Doctor much food for thought. The same company operates the branch line between Torbay and Kingswear.

Close to the ancient town of Totnes is the veritable mecca of the Dartington centre at Shinner's Bridge. Here are gathered together a collection of shops, showrooms and eating-places carrying on a roaring trade in articles produced largely by rural craftsmen or Devon industries. Few of the visitors realize its significance, and even fewer have ever heard of the Dartington Hall Trust.

A small signpost on the main road by the Victorian church points to Dartington Hall and the Devon Centre, headquarters of the Trust. Here, past enormous car-parks and ranges of low, modern scholastic buildings, is to be found another unique Devon foundation, another blend of high moral aims and commercialism. The Trust had its origins in an experiment in rural life begun in 1925 by Leonard and Dorothy Elmhirst. He was interested in farming and forestry methods, she in the promotion of arts as a means of personal development. Using their considerable wealth, they purchased Dartington Hall and set about realizing their aims: the encouragement of living-patterns which draw strength from a rural environment, are economically viable, meet the emerging needs of society and offer the individual a fulfilling, well-balanced life.

Today the project has become a serious education centre, with degree courses in various aspects of the arts; it encourages young musicians and actors as well as artists and craftsmen, sponsors many artistic ventures, such as concerts and exhibitions, and runs a successful touring theatre company and an arts centre in mid Devon. Seemingly by complete contrast, it also runs the goldmine of Shinners Bridge, a woollen shop, a carpentry business, a cattle-breeding centre, a book shop, the highly successful Dartington Glass factory in North Devon, now a major tourist attraction in its own right, and the goliath of Morwellham Quay on the Tamar. Here the derelict mines, wharves and associated buildings were rescued and turned into a living museum – one of Devon's most popular attractions.

Waterwheel, Morwellham Quay

A visit to Dartington Hall restores the balance. Here a university atmosphere pervades, helped by the ancient stone buildings and the soft green lawns.

When the Elmhirsts purchased Dartington, once the largest medieval house in the West of England, it was semi-derelict. The Great Hall was roofless, the outbuildings were in a state of collapse, and many of the original buildings had been demolished. Built by the half-brother of Richard II, Dartington once housed an enormous community of nobility, their families and retainers. The huge hall was one of the earliest of its kind, complete with a marvellous hammerbeam roof.

Unfortunately the original has not survived, but the reconstruction has been faithful, and visitors are welcome to admire it, providing the hall is not in use.

Totnes, just a little lower down the Dart, is one of Devon's oldest and most interesting small towns, though its steep and narrow main street can be a nightmare to motorists. Park on the outskirts and explore on foot is the best policy. It was originally a defensive town built in Saxon days in a commanding position overlooking the river valley, and there is much evidence of its past history, including the castle and town walls. Many of the houses that crowd the streets are also very old. The church dates from the fifteenth century, but the original priory has disappeared to give place to the sixteenth-century Guildhall built close by.

Totnes was and still is a river port. Nowadays few trading-vessels use the quay area down at the foot of the town, but many pleasure trips are run from Dartmouth to Totnes, and there is even a circular tour using steam train, river trip and interconnecting coach.

The whole of the Dart estuary is outstandingly beautiful. The tidal waters ebb and flow between treelined banks, with innumerable little creeks and inlets, many with ruined boathouses, decaying landing-stages, rotting boats and even evidence of former boatyards. But the estuary is far from finished, although the emphasis may have changed from working boats to pleasure craft. There is still one boatyard on Galmpton Creek, which was also the scene of former quarrying. It is barely a mile from here across the isthmus to Torbay.

Stoke Gabriel is a delightful village – but full of hazards for the motorist unused to coping with steep gradients and blind corners. It has an interesting church, several ancient hostelries, as would be expected in a fishing village, and a most attractive quay area where there is ample parking on the water's edge. On the opposite bank is Dittisham, with its fine church, and from here a ferry crosses to Greenway, where, as no doubt the boatmen will tell you, Agatha Christie lived in the large house overlooking the estuary. Many of her mysteries are set in the Devon countryside, but she never used the beauty of her own surroundings for death and murder. Perhaps the atmosphere of the Dart was too peaceful, too precious, to be connected with sudden death.

Further down the Dart valley, almost in Dartmouth itself, is the imposing building of the Britannia Royal Naval College. It is here on this quiet Devon estuary that every naval officer receives his initial training. 'We cannot guarantee that you will enjoy every minute of your time as a Midshipman at Dartmouth – though some do. We do hope, however, that when you reach senior rank you will retain some fond memories of the place where you began to learn what was involved in

Totnes

Royal Naval College, Dartmouth

becoming the blend of leader, manager, administrator, teacher, counsellor and technologist that goes to make up an officer in the Royal Navy': so ends the Navy's prospectus.

The naval college arrived in Dartmouth almost by accident. Early training for cadets was at Portsmouth, when the usual age of entrants was just thirteen. The original college proved unsatisfactory and after a lapse of some years was replaced with a training-ship, also at Portsmouth, which opened in 1857. *Britannia* was the second ship used for this purpose, and she was moved away from Portsmouth to Portland and ultimately, in 1863, to Dartmouth. The influence of the naval town and dockyard was considered unsuitable for such impressionable young men, who continued to be trained in redundant wooden vessels until the opening of the permanent college in 1905. The last *Britannia* remained in the estuary until 1916.

Dartmouth is one of those places that you never tire of visiting. It is a busy little town, always something going on, always something moving on the river. Every so often the steam train pulls in at Kingswear on the opposite bank; occasionally some large vessel moves majestically upstream. The ferry plies patiently across, and in the summer season the passenger boats jostle with one another for custom. Wooded heights guard the estuary, creating a narrow entrance defended by ancient forts and a more modern castle.

The sea is not visible from either Dartmouth or Kingswear, making it a sheltered and protected anchorage much appreciated by the many yachtsmen who moor here. From almost anywhere the views are of the first calibre, and it is just such a place as Dartmouth that inspires feelings of patriotism – *this* is what England is all about, *this* is worth going out and fighting for. And from its safe anchorage in former days men did go out and fight, for Dartmouth was an early home of the Navy and raised many notable seafaring men who were voyagers and explorers.

Both sides of the estuary are National Trust property acquired over a period of years. Some they bought outright, some was purchased with funds left to them for that purpose, and some was given – one area, which includes Dartmouth's ancient Rope Walk, by the South Hams council. Their latest acquisition has opened up an area previously jealously guarded against intruders. From the Dart round to Sharkham Point, the land was privately owned, and the coastal footpath went inland until the purchase of the Coleton Fishacre estate, so that now the Trust have at last made available a most beautiful stretch of coastline.

Visible from most of the surrounding coast is the tall tower built as a daymark to the Dart Estuary by the Dart Harbour Commissioners in 1864. It is an extraordinary structure, more like a mining chimney than a navigational aid, and many a walker must be startled by the unearthly noises emanating from the tower as the wind moans through the open arches and up its eighty feet to the top.

Pine trees, unusual along the coast, crown the headland above Inner Froward Point, and it is here that the 'Military Road' leads to a Second World War gun battery perched above Froward Cove. It has survived almost intact and no doubt will shortly be awarded some kind of listed status. Much of the cliff area has been designated a nature reserve and is managed by the Devon Trust for Nature Conservation. It is also an important area for ornithologists, the offshore rocks around the Mew Stone being popular breeding-sites.

In all this long stretch of coastline, the former coastguard cottages down on the beach at Man Sands are the only form of habitation, a sharp contrast to the development elsewhere along the south coast.

At Sharkham Point the slate and grit rock formations come to an end, to be replaced by the Devonian limestone. The headland is a nature reserve with a large secluded car-park, footpaths and nature trails. The only problem is finding it in the first place, since the whole hinterland is now part of Brixham, with a sprawl of caravans and campsites, and Sharkham Point can be found only by instinct and a network of built-up roads. It is worth the search, though the cliff walk around St Mary's Bay to Berry Head is now backed by netting and hedges, the perimeter of camp sites.

Berry Head, occupying a position of strategic importance guarding Torbay, is over-burdened with titles. It has been created a country park, a nature reserve, a Site of Special Scientific Interest, an Area of Special Protection and an Ancient Monument; it also has a lighthouse and coastguard lookout. It was fortified during the Iron Age, the Roman occupation, the Napoleonic Wars and the Second World War. Unfortunately each developer destroyed much of the foregoing work, so that little now remains of the earliest. Records talk of an eighteen-foot-high rampart across the narrowest neck constructed of stone, inside which Roman coins have been found, and it would have been contemporary with the fort on Bolt Tail.

The forts themselves are remarkable. The first wooden huts on this exposed site were built in 1795, condemned as unfit in 1798 but kept in use until the new forts were completed in 1803. According to contemporary accounts, living-conditions were never anything but appalling, and the length of duty was kept purposely short. Nowadays, with the sun shining on the short turf, the sea sparkling all around and visitors enjoying tea in the former guardhouse, it seems a pleasant enough spot. A visitors' centre gives the full history of the forts, which were abandoned only twenty years after their completion, and information on the local wildlife, in particular the sea birds, for the cliffs and rocks off Berry Head are an important breeding-site. Quarrying-operations were carried out on the cliffs below the fort until quite recent times and only ceased completely when the headland passed into the ownership of the Borough Council.

It isn't possible to see Brixham from Berry Head, for it lies back, tucked under the cliffs. Here rural Devon ends and the urban coastline (which continues to the Exe estuary and beyond) begins.

Brixham struggles to retain its identity as a working port, but tourism threatens to overwhelm everything. It is still a fishing-port, maintaining its role as home to a large fishing-fleet, and the quayside is still an important fish market. The working port is strictly segregated from the tourist end of the harbour, where there is an interesting museum of the history of fishing. The great days of the fishing-fleet, when the town boasted some 270 vessels employing about 1,600 seamen, collapsed suddenly at the end of the First World War, but the town survived and gradually the fishermen adapted to new methods and new ships, so that most people still think of fish when they think of Brixham.

'Torbay' is the collective name now given to Goodrington, Paignton, Torquay, Cockington and all the other villages that have been swallowed up by the largest conglomeration of seaside and urban sprawl to be found in Devon, if not the West Country. Retirement is responsible for much of the recent growth, the mild climate being one of the bay's attractions, and at least the elderly bring year-round business, unlike the summer visitors, who disappear at the end of August.

'New' Paignton grew up along the seafront. The railway brought prosperity, and the former fishing village was turned into a south-coast starlet. The working harbour survives, hidden amongst a welter of boarding houses and seaside terraces.

The main fault of all such seaside towns is that, once the visitors have left and the floral displays have been grubbed up, the hanging baskets taken down and the tinsel and glitter of the seafront packed away for another season, there is little left but a deserted promenade and rows of shuttered shops and amusement arcades, looking tawdry with a morning-after-the-night-before air.

The oldest and most interesting areas of Paignton are around the parish church, usually the centre of a village and in this case built of distinctive red sandstone and containing much of the original twelfth- and fifteenth-century building, and a ceiling noted for its 'fragile beauty'.

Paignton also possesses a very fine zoo and botanical gardens. The promenade and pier could have been transported straight from the

Sussex coast but, somewhat surprisingly, Paignton's pier is the only one in Devon.

Somehow sea fronts seem to attract the worst kind of development, the brashest shopfronts, the continual noise and flashing lights. All planning restrictions seem to vanish, and any form of good taste or self-restraint appears to have been flung to the sea winds: if it's on the sea-front, anything goes! Unfortunately, Torquay is no exception. If all the clutter were cleared away, the harbour area would be pleasant, for it is shaded with trees and well laid out. Away from the sea, Torquay is a well-planned Victorian town, with broad, tree-lined streets, imposing villas and some excellent town architecture in the form of crescents, shops, hotels etc. It was designed specifically to attract the wealthy; the common people were not wanted, and Torquay turned its nose up at anything as vulgar as trade. Perhaps that is why there is no pleasure pier in the one place along the whole of the Devon coast where you could reasonably expect to find one.

The original fishing village of Torquay consisted of little except the ancient remains of Torre Abbey and its small quay, until the mid seventeenth century, when the Continental wars brought the Navy, looking for a safe anchorage. The sheltered waters of Torbay proved admirable, and as the wars dragged on, wives and families were found lodgings. The fleet left, but the mild climate was found to be beneficial for delicate constitutions and so the area continued to develop. So important was its role as a health resort that the beach was actually bought in 1869 by the Board of Health, from the Duchy of Cornwall. By the mid 1850s Torquay was firmly established and was known as 'the Queen of Watering Places'. Until then it had grown haphazardly, but over the next few decades the town layout as we see it today was planned, and Torquay has been very little altered since. On the heights that lead to the viewpoint of Hope's Nose, the atmosphere of a vanished age of elegance still pervades the avenues and drives. Gentlemen doffing their top hats to ladies with parasols would seem more in keeping than the jeans and sweatshirts of today. Unfortunately a modern monstrosity many storeys high quite ruins the next bay.

There seems to be very little accessible coast between Torbay and the Exe estuary. The road winds its way along to Shaldon, passing Maidencombe, where a narrow lane leads down to a few houses and the beach, and then nothing until Labrador Bay. There are good views from the road, which makes a detour seawards at this point, and a car-park is provided for the popular beach, which is privately owned. The National Trust have made no inroads here, and access is not encouraged over the farmland between the main road and the cliffs.

The seafront at Torquay

The Teign estuary is shorter than that of the Dart and lacks its tree-lined charm, but the waterfront at Shaldon is a good place from which to view the sun setting over the broad waters and mudflats of this Dartmoor river. Shaldon is not large, but it has some good Georgian architecture, rare along the south coast! Both Shaldon and its larger neighbour across the water, Teignmouth, have remained compact, contained between the heights behind and the water in front. There is a pleasant, friendly air about both places, and as the main road misses the centres, they remain relatively peaceful.

Teignmouth has two water-fronts: the working riverside harbour and the spacious, genteel sea-front. The little town was a notable fishing harbour long before it became fashionable as a resort, which happened very early on, making it one of the earliest in Devon. There are thus two sides to Teignmouth: the narrow, winding streets that lead down to the estuary and the quayside, and the broad streets and terraces built in the early nineteenth century for the summer residents. It even boasted that essential of all Georgian watering-places, an assembly room. The port has seen much trade; at one time granite from Haytor was exported, and for centuries it has shipped the ball clay mined in the Teign valley. It is still a working port, part of the Association of British Ports, which owns the quayside.

Between Teignmouth and Dawlish the coast is a busy place. The main road is never far away, but running along the water's edge is the main-line railway. Great Western carriages used to display pictures of the Dawlish section of the line, with trains disappearing under billows of spray. It is a marvellous piece of railway engineering, alternating between built-up sea walls and tunnels piercing the red sandstone cliffs, and the impact must have been considerable on children who had never before seen the sea. Today's high-speed trains pass too quickly to do the scenery justice.

A few miles further on, the railway turns inland, following the Exe estuary, and all but cuts off the area of sand dunes, marsh and shingle known as Dawlish Warren. The near end, owned by the council, is wholly given over to beach-lovers and their needs, including the ever-present amusement arcades, but beyond the first car-park the atmosphere changes. Dawlish Warren proper can be explored only on foot, and that is asking just too much of some people. The area is designated as a nature reserve, and an information centre gives details of the rich wildlife to be found here. The rare sand crocus and the evening primrose are two of the many dune-loving plants. But it is the birdwatchers who flock to Dawlish Warren, for it marks the beginning of the Exe estuary and as such it is an important staging-post for migrant birds and for river birds of all types. They seem not to be

A kingfisher

disturbed by the roar of the express trains, although across the still evening air the noise is alarming.

Evening on the estuary at the end of a long day when all around is peace. The coloured lights strung out along Exmouth's front across the water belong to another world as the sky darkens and the hues of sunset fade. The sounds are all around, the little waves of the estuary as the tide begins to flow, the soft call of the birds, the occasional boat out on the water, and above, the skeins of birds flying in formation as they home in on the mudflats and marshes.

Back along the shore with the rhythmic sound of the sea, the lights of Dawlish beckon.

Main gateway to the royal citadel, Plymouth

10

Plymouth

Plymouth is a city, a huge urban area, somewhat alien in character to the rest of the county. It bustles and hums. Its people rush and its streets are constantly full of traffic. It spreads and sprawls and is full of new development, new initiative, new growth.

The city is far older than its present appearance indicates. Originally it consisted of three separate villages, and Plymouth as such was not created until 1914. By then Devonport, Stonehouse and Sutton had grown to such an extent that the boundaries between them had long ceased to have any meaning, except as political and civic divisions.

The priors of Plympton founded the fortunes of the city by developing a small port and borough alongside the deep waters of the Sound at Sutton Pool, which quickly grew in importance. But it shot to prominence in the heady days of Queen Elizabeth I. Many a famous sea-faring name belongs to Devon, and most of them were familiar with the former fishing village and the deep waters of the Pool and Plymouth Sound. Several historic voyages began from the old quay: the Pilgrim Fathers sailed from there, the Elizabethan adventurers and merchantmen, and that indomitable twentieth-century explorer Sir Francis Chichester began his round-the-world lone voyage.

The Barbican area behind the quay is judged to be by far the most interesting area of Plymouth. Certainly it is the only truly old part of the city to survive intact. Here the merchants congregated, many of them building townhouses specifically to look after their maritime interests. Tall warehouses stored their merchandize, and all around grew up the inns and taverns, the chandlers and sail lofts that are part of any thriving port. A few survive, but most have now become tourist-type shops full of knick-knacks and arts and crafts, or the endless cafés and restaurants that seem to have become an essential part of the tourist scene.

The fishing-fleet is still very much in evidence, and the busy fishwharves down on the quay are interesting, especially in the early morning when the trawlers return and the catch is auctioned off. Most

The Barbican, Plymouth

of the Barbican these days seems to be purely superficial. Not so the fish market: that is for real.

The Hoe is the best-known area of Plymouth and is also one of the oldest. Few of the many thousands who daily drive along the front or stroll above on the promenade realize that the wall of white limestone built off the rocks was part of the original defensive sea wall sheltering the old village. High above is the Citadel, the fortress built in the days of Charles II to defend Plymouth and still in use, although its guns have never been fired in anger.

But it is the broad green sward of the Hoe that draws people like a magnet. As a viewpoint it is magnificent, commanding the whole of Plymouth Sound and the sheltering arms of Mount Batten and Mount Edgecumbe. And whatever else schoolchildren forget, Drake's famous game of bowls on Plymouth Hoe seems indelibly ingrained.

It was the Spanish Armada of 1588 that finally sealed Plymouth's future as a great naval base. Here the great English fleet assembled and set sail in pursuit of the Spanish galleons, proving the strategic importance of Plymouth at the entrance to the English Channel. Naval use of the Cattewater at the mouth of the River Plym continued until the development of the Hamoaze, the oddly named mouth of the River Tamar, in the eighteenth century. This planned adoption of Plymouth by the Navy marked the second great phase in the city's expansion. During the 1760s and 1780s the dockyard area grew and grew, and with it the surrounding area, until within a very short space of time Dock, as it was known, was the second largest town in Devon.

The impressive naval buildings stand out from the maze of later developments and housing, still dignified, still upholding their proud tradition, solid stone buildings, well designed and good for a few centuries yet.

The Royal William Victualling Yard covers over fourteen acres, some of it reclaimed from the sea and the foundation stone was laid from a diving-bell on the seabed. It is a massive complex, the work of Sir John Rennie, and was designed to look after the complete needs of the Navy. The yard survived the Blitz, but its future is in some doubt, and recently plans have been put forward to develop this unique but now redundant historic area, as housing and piazza-style shops – to create in essence a self-contained village.

With the building of the breakwater across the Sound in 1841, the creation of a safe, deepwater harbour was complete. But being the foremost naval base in the country is not without its drawbacks. Plymouth suffered horribly in the Second World War, being ruthlessly and mercilessly bombed. When peace finally came, the devastation could be counted: 1,172 dead and over 3,000 injured – not including service personnel; 3,754 houses totally destroyed and over 68,000 damaged. Virtually the whole heart of the historic city had been flattened, and over forty churches and twenty schools had gone.

On the worst nights, the flames of burning Plymouth could be seen all over the county – and the hearts of every Devonian went out to those who suffered.

Life goes on. Plymouth has been rebuilt. It is hard to imagine the scenes of dereliction that must have existed where now the broad new streets and proud civic buildings stand. Old photographs show the mounds of rubble and the ruined walls – but to a generation used only to the tidy demolition of the building-site, it is inconceivable.

Plymouth is an early example of town planning: the city fathers rightly decided that, as so much had gone, an overall plan should be drawn up for the whole city, with broad streets and shopping arcades and a new guildhall – a city Devon could be proud of.

Plymouth has grown at a tremendous rate. Travelling outwards from the city centre, first there are the narrow streets and terraces of the late nineteenth and early twentieth centuries, row upon row of seemingly mean housing with tiny backyards, no garages and no trees because no land was left on which to plant them. They march, with no regard for contours, in straight lines up hillsides and across the skyline. Then comes the development of a so-called more enlightened age: terraces of quick-build housing surrounded by sterile open grass which no one ever uses but on which nothing is allowed to be planted. The newest ring of housing, all architect-designed, all executive-style, with at least one garage and open-plan front gardens so that no one has any privacy, occurs on the outer edge of the city, close to the open countryside. Little boxes all squashed up on what were once open fields. Where do all the people come from?

Modern Plymouth has come a long way from those three small fishing villages. It has all the hallmarks of the twentieth century, with an airport, a cross-Channel ferry and a busy and ever-expanding network of roads. The television units for the south-west are based here, and a huge hospital complex has recently been completed on the outskirts. New marina developments are creating a luxury air along the water-front, and there seems to be an insatiable need for multi-storey car-parks and hotel blocks.

There is tremendous pressure on the City Council to develop, and these days it finds itself increasingly at odds with its neighbours. The City says it has run out of land and must have more and yet more for housing estates and industrial development, and shopping centres, for everyone wants to be 'out of town' these days. The South Hams and moorland parishes say, not so, find room within your own borders and don't come pushing your nasty urban sprawl into our green acres, carefully preserved for people's enjoyment, not for greedy, land-grabbing fingers.

11

Tamar Country

The western border with Cornwall follows for the most part an obvious divide – the River Tamar. The beauty of this magnificent river is very little praised, perhaps because one bank is in Cornwall and the other in Devon, so neither county feels it is wholly theirs to boast about.

Through many miles of the most beautiful scenery, full of historic reminders and attractive villages, the Tamar winds its way to the south coast of Devon and ends its long journey in the still deep waters of the Hamoaze. For its last few miles it is joined by the waters of the River Tavy, both tidal for a considerable distance inland. Between the two rivers is a narrow peninsula, never more than a few miles in width and difficult to reach by road, so that it is bypassed by many, totally unaware of its quiet beauty. Fortunately Dr Beeching has left us a splendid way of discovering this area and the lower reaches of the Tamar, in the form of the branch line from Plymouth to Gunnislake which, if it was in private ownership, would undoubtedly have become a major tourist attraction. 'View the glories of the Tamar Valley,' the posters would say. 'Travel on the Strawberry Line.'

Once the dockland of Plymouth is left behind, with its ranks of grey roofs and dreary little halts, the main line continues on into Cornwall, and the two-carriage Gunnislake train slips away up the river bank. It sneaks beneath the arches of Brunel's great suspension bridge across the Tamar, supported by its mammoth curving tubes – a dramatic drawbridge out of Devon over which the giants of the Great Western once thundered. 'I K Brunel, 1859', the bridge proudly announces and, not to be outdone, the neighbouring road bridge, a more conventional suspension bridge with supporting pillars, states it was completed in 1961. Downstream the river becomes the Hamoaze.

The branch line has its own bridge crossing an inlet running up to Tamerton Foliot, once a riverside village, now a dormitory of Plymouth, and then a further grander structure across the broad waters of the River Tavy. The tidal flow is restricted a few miles upstream by the Lopwell dam, above which is a broad expanse of water, fringed by

Rotting hulks on the river bank

woodland. The adventurous drive across at low tide below the dam, but most people are content to sit and enjoy the peaceful scene and watch the birds.

The first station is Bere Ferrers, a little distance from the village. Bere Ferrers belongs to the Tavy. Its small quay is deserted now but once served the river traffic bringing lime and coal, building-materials and other bulky goods. Both rivers were important highways, providing easy transport downstream to Plymouth and the sea. Much of the early mineral wealth of the Tamar valley was conveyed in barges or sea-going vessels, and there are numerous old quays on both rivers.

The village is quiet these days, just a few cottages and an inn grouped around the church, all built almost at river-level. The church is worth a visit. Rebuilt in the fourteenth century, it has an older tower and Norman font. It also contains interesting bench ends, medieval tombs and the only fourteenth-century stained glass in the county outside Exeter Cathedral.

Bere Alston has grown to become much the larger village, the centre of the market gardening that occurs all over this peninsula. From the train, glass tunnels and greenhouses are a frequent sight, as are the 'Pick your own' signs on the road.

Down on the Tamar bank is Weir Quay, which once served the village but now is home to a yacht club and some very desirable houses. From the road that runs along the river bank it is possible to sit and watch the water of the Tamar ebb and flow, the waders feeding on the mudflats exposed at low tide and the occasional passing pleasure boat at high tide, all the while listening to that most evocative of river sounds to anyone with seablood in their veins, the slapping of rigging and pennants in the wind. A most delectable place. But it is not visible from the train, which carries on across the heights to Bere Alston station, which it enters and leaves on the same rails, the driver changing ends.

The line used to continue on to Tavistock, a victim of the railway cuts. It is a sad reflection on British Rail that they should care so little for their few remaining branch lines. The trains are scruffy, the stations sad left-overs, unmanned, untended, looking as if they know it is only a question of time before they, too, become just a memory, another piece of railway history. Along the entire line there is just one station that can justifiably claim the title. At Bere Ferrers there are flowers on the platform. The wrought ironwork is freshly painted. The signs are clear, and there are some interesting posters, although the one informing passengers of the positions of first- and second-class carriages on the 125 inter-city trains is surely a little out of place? One door is optimistically marked 'Porters', and above it is a sign that says 'Ladies'; the signal box at the end of the platform is marked 'Pinhoe': the station is now the home of a railway enthusiast. But for one moment it seemed that the spirit of the railways lived on, officially.

From the high ground, the views stretch away over Cornwall to Bodmin Moor; Dartmoor forms the horizon in the other direction, with glimpses on both sides over the steep river valleys and their wooded banks. Everywhere is evidence of former industrial activity. Ruined lime-kilns mark the western bank of the river, and derelict chimneys rise above the trees, as numerous as foxgloves in a hedgerow.

At Calstock there isn't even a station any more, and hardly a platform, but there is a memorable railway viaduct high above the Tamar. Cotehele House, a National Trust property, peeps out of the trees downstream, and far below, on the Cornish bank, are cottages and jetties with a sprinkling of river craft. Pleasure boats frequently come as far as Calstock and occasionally, if the tide is right, carry on as far as Morwellham, with its thriving quayside museum which can only just be glimpsed through the trees. As the train approaches Gunnislake, the steep woodlands of the far bank of the Tamar are clearly visible, with the bleak heights of Dartmoor a contrast beyond.

Newbridge at Gunnislake is anything but, having been built in the early 1500s. It is the first of three historic and lovely arched stone structures crossing the Tamar, all unaltered, none of them much more than twelve feet in width and negotiated only with difficulty by today's traffic. But, thankfully, it is the traffic that has to suffer, not the bridges. A new road bridge is in course of construction at Gunnislake, which may improve the traffic flow, but not the scenery.

Even older is Horsebridge, so named because it was '*haut*' – high, which indeed it is, with its cutwaters projecting into the river, enabling pedestrians to escape the horse-drawn traffic or trains of packhorses. Several miles and many loops further upstream is the Greystone Bridge, marking a prehistoric crossing of the river. The tall, arched structure is of age and design similar to the Horsebridge's, and both are known to have been in existence by the 1430s, when they are mentioned in the Exeter episcopal records. Greystone Bridge carried the road from Tavistock to Launceston and Cornwall and would have been important to the clergy, who were indefatigable travellers. The see of Exeter extended into Cornwall, and there were tithes to be collected and livings to be bestowed – and indulgences to be received. These last were a way of raising money, and many a Devon bridge was founded on man's hope of buying his way out of Purgatory, if not into Heaven.

Close to the road, but in splendid isolation from any dwellings, stands the church of Dunterton, perhaps strategically placed, as it dates from around the same time as the Greystone Bridge.

A few miles across the fields, high up and overlooking a broad loop of the Tamar, is a property of rare distinction. Endsleigh was built in 1810, in the *cottage orné* style, by the Duke of Bedford. Although the Russells derived much wealth from the Tavistock lands which had been in their possession for several centuries, they had no personal property in the county. But their enjoyment of their 'fishing lodge' was short-lived, for the eighth Duke met his death whilst out shooting in the woods in 1953, and the family ceased to visit Endsleigh. It is now a select hotel, with fishing rights for its guests along the Tamar. The building was designed by Jeffery Wyatville, who later remodelled Windsor Castle, and its Gothic interiors remain intact. The beautifully situated grounds were the work of Sir Humphrey Repton and have been described as the finest in the West Country.

Between Gunnislake and Launceston the Tamar winds and loops between steep banks, tree-lined for the most part. For long lengths it flows through private land with no right of access, and although footpaths exist along either bank, they are not public rights of way. Yet what a superb long-distance footpath the Tamar valley would make, having some of the most beautiful scenery either county has to offer, and a nature trail unparalleled elsewhere. To preserve the rights of fishermen, walkers no doubt would be banned during the salmon season, but for the rest of the year the banks of the Tamar are little known, unfrequented and a secret world awaiting quiet exploration.

There is a distinctly Cornish feel to the far-western areas of Devon. Granite becomes the predominant building-material; cob and thatch have all but disappeared. The villages have that plain, no-nonsense air with little time for ornament or superfluous decoration.

Around Launceston the Tamar is fed by numerous tributaries. The rivers Ottery, Carey, Wolf, Threshel and Lyd all add their waters to the Tamar to turn it from an immature young stream into a majestic river. Few counties can have a more lovely boundary than the Tamar. From Launceston to its source it flows quietly and undisturbed through rural Devon. As with the Torridge, its early life is secretive, known only to a few fishermen and naturalists and the farmers who own the lush water-meadows. It is amazing how quickly the relative bustle of south Devon is left behind. Leave the A30 and you enter another world. Here life goes on unchanging, the patchwork of fields much as it has always been, the small hamlets sleepy and unconcerned. Here you can travel for mile after mile upon empty roads through empty villages and wonder if it is a sleeping-beauty landscape or if people do inhabit the cottages and work on the land. Few visitors ever find this part of Devon, and there is little enough for them if they do venture off the beaten track – except the scenery.

At Luffincott is another isolated church, perched above the river

Holsworthy

valley with only a farm for company, and reached through the farmyard.

Tetcott is the next small hamlet, with just a few cottages, a church and a gem of a manor house. Here, too, the church is difficult to find, built in the midst of a collection of picturesque farm buildings, including a rare raised granary, and adjoining the low, rambling manor house. The villagers may have had to travel to church, but not so the squire. A lane crosses the parkland to reach the well-kept churchyard, and you seem almost to be trespassing to pass through the gates and enter the church itself. It is in such places that the centuries roll back, for there is little evidence at Tetcott of the twentieth century.

One of the oldest recorded bridges crosses the Tamar at Bridgerule, and some of the village is in Cornwall and some in Devon, including the church, built a little way off on high ground. It is a good example of a granite church with a fine interior.

The Tamar is lost to view above Bridgerule, a much-reduced stream wiggling and squiggling through a rural countryside, hidden beneath treelined banks and scrubby undergrowth. A few more bridges, a few minor tributaries and its tale is almost told. But not quite, for in the early years of the nineteenth century its waters were harnessed to provide a controlled flow for the Bude to Holsworthy Canal in the form of a small lake. Later, in 1967, a second lake was constructed to act as a reservoir. The Tamar Lakes have become a popular haunt, the upper lake used for sailing and the lower, with its reed-fringed banks, a nature reserve. A small shop provides home-baked food and gifts, and it is a popular run-out for locals escaping from the crowds who congregate on the coast.

The Tamar ends its long journey some four miles short of the north coast. The A39 trunk road follows the principal watershed from which several small streams rush the short distance to the Atlantic, but to the south-east all the water drains into two major rivers, both of which begin their long journeys just over the border, in Cornwall. The Torridge rises ignominiously in a bog, the start of a sixty-mile course that ends at Bideford Bay. Some romantics have claimed that the Tamar starts on the other side of the same clump of reeds, but as all this area is soggy, marshy country, it is not easy to be precise as to which particular clump of reeds claims to have this distinction!

12

Open to the Public

Paying to walk round someone else's house or garden seems to have become a major growth area. Although Devon has always been too far from the centre of things to attract the powerful and wealthy, it has a number of attractive minor 'stately homes' dating from medieval times to the twentieth century. Most are regularly open, and some are becoming tourist attractions with a wide variety of facilities apart from the house, and often the garden and grounds attract just as many, if not more, visitors.

Not surprisingly for a county blessed with a mild climate, there are some very beautiful and famous gardens. Although the damp is not to everyone's liking, it does encourage prolific growth, of almost tropical

Ford House, Newton Abbot

proportions along the south coast. Winters are not normally severe, with only a sprinkling of snow on the high ground, and frosts are more of a decorative than a damaging nature. Because severe weather is not the norm, when it does strike the results can be catastrophic, taking many years before the damage is made good.

It is in the springtime that Devon is at her glorious best. The primroses and abundant spring bulbs that never seem to fail, the fresh foliage and flowering trees, the rhododendrons and magnolias bring visitors back year after year. Summer gardens are not so spectacular, because the pure, humid air of Devon requires constant battles against blackspot and mould on the roses, and all too often the autumn leaves are stripped from the trees just as they are beginning to colour, turning the fall of the year into a sorry, tatty mess of decaying foliage underfoot.

The county's best-known gardens are all sited in protected valleys or on south-facing slopes. Several of the largest are now in the ownership of the National Trust, providing fitting settings for the historic houses they surround.

At Killerton, to the east of Exeter, the former home of the Acland family is surrounded by over fifteen acres of woodland. The property, given in 1944, is of particular note because of the maturity of many of the species. The garden was first laid out at the end of the Napoleonic Wars, well over 170 years ago. Sir Thomas Acland was helped in his mammoth project by Robert Veitch, founder of the Exeter branch of the famous Veitch nursery which played such a large part in sponsoring the enormously successful plant-hunting expeditions all over the world. Many species now commonplace in our gardens began life as seeds in Veitch's nurseries, which still exist on the outskirts of Exeter.

Many of the new discoveries found a home in the grounds of Killerton. In particular, it is thought that the magnificent specimen of the giant Wellingtonia, *Sequoiadendron giganteum*, was raised from the original seed sent back from California about 1853; it is now around 120 feet high. Quite apart from their obvious visual appeal, the gardens at Killerton are an important living museum, even a memorial, to those daring and intrepid men who spent long years in arduous conditions, risking injury and even death in the search for botanical rarities. Walking amongst the towering banks of rhododendrons and admiring the many fine conifers or unusual deciduous trees, it is well to remember them.

Equally magnificent is the garden surrounding Knightshayes Court, near Tiverton. It is more recent, having been begun after the Second World War. Knightshayes was the home of the Heathcoat-Amory family. The large Victorian edifice overlooks the town of Tiverton, whose prosperity was very much linked with the Heathcoats, who were the owners of the lace and textile mill. The continuity and preservation of their garden was of concern to Sir John and Lady Heathcoat Amory from the very first, and in the mid 1950s they created an educational trust and some ten years later began discussions with the National Trust over the future of Knightshayes, which were successfully concluded.

The gardens are magnificent, especially in the springtime, when the camellias flower abundantly in the sheltered woodlands, giving way to banks of rhododendrons and azaleas, huge magnolias and tall flowering cherry trees – and bulbs everywhere. A much-photographed tree is the shrimp-coloured *Acer brilliantissimum* growing in solitude by the lily-pond, itself set in a perfect lawn surrounded by clipped yew hedges, a dramatic yet peaceful scene. The terrace in front of the house is noted for its *Clematis montana* used in a most unusual manner, cascading down the terrace steps. The house walls provide shelter for some splendid semi-tender shrubs, such as *Magnolia grandiflora*, *ceanothus* and many roses and other climbers. The topiary of the yew hedges is interesting, and there is a delightful small rock garden with herbs and alpines. For many, Knightshayes is Devon's most beautiful garden.

The Garden House at Buckland Monachorum, near Yelverton, was home to Mr Lionel Fortescue, and the garden was his life's work. He was one of the first to set up an educational trust to ensure its continuance after his own lifetime and, although not large, it is a charming, intimate garden full of herbaceous plants, shrubs and herbs. It is now in the hands of the National Trust, as are the recently acquired gardens of Coleton Fishacre, once the home of the D'Oyly Cartes of Gilbert and Sullivan fame; Sharpitor, overlooking the estuary at Salcombe and renowned for a fine specimen of *Magnolia campbelli*, and Saltram, near Plymouth.

Saltram is the most important of the National Trust's Devon properties and came to them from the Treasury in 1957, since when it has been regularly opened to visitors. Apparently in those early days it was severely under-capitalized, as it was accepted without the endowment required nowadays by the Trust. The task of repair and restoration was formidable, on top of which provision had to be made for the great influx of visitors, who in themselves create problems of which most of them are totally unaware. There is a limit to the number of people who can be allowed through a historic house at any one time, owing to the size of the rooms, doorways, one-way routes, fire risk etc, and all of them cause considerable wear and tear and have to be provided with car-parks and toilets. Even today the entrance money in no way comes anywhere near meeting the annual expenditure for the upkeep of a house the size of Saltram.

This pleasant property is set in beautiful parkland close to Plymouth. In recent times the Trust fought an important test-case as to whether their land was inviolate or whether some of it could be compulsorily purchased for a new road, a battle they lost. The interior of the house is splendid and contains many fine plaster ceilings, portraits by Sir Joshua Reynolds and a superb collection of Wedgwood vases and urns. But its most impressive feature is the double cube room known as the Great Room or saloon, arguably the grandest room in the west of England, and one writer estimated its cost at £10,000 when it was created in 1768. It was magnificently decorated by Robert Adam, with painted ceilings by Zucchi, and retains an Axminster carpet especially woven for it. Adam's master touch is also apparent in the library, which has been somewhat altered since his original designs. The Adam plans for the rebuilding of Saltram were never carried out, although his influence can be seen in many areas of the house.

Very different from Saltram but also the work of Adam is Ugbrooke Park at Chudleigh, not far from Newton Abbot. The Cliffords have been at Chudleigh since the late sixteenth century, but the present house was built in the 1760s. The then Lord Clifford had risen to eminence as Lord Treasurer to Charles II, but his conversion to Catholicism meant resignation and retirement from public life. The family remains one of the great Catholic families of this country, and one of the most important features of the house is the chapel. Ugbrooke was the first attempt by Robert Adam to design a castle, and it remains an important architectural example of his work, although the façade was much altered by the addition in the nineteenth century of the strange tubular-style mouldings around the doors and windows. The interior is well furnished, with the library carried out to Adam's design. 'Capability' Brown was called in to reshape the parkland, but although several of the small buildings considered *de rigueur* at the time were designed, they were never built. The Cliffords still live in their ancestral home, although it almost went the way of so many other large houses, requisitioned during the war, then used for grain storage in the years following but then rescued by the family.

Three other notable properties still inhabited by the families that built them are Powderham Castle on the banks of the River Exe, Castle Hill on the southern fringes of Exmoor, and Fursdon House, near Tiverton.

The Courtenays, earls of Devon, crossed the Channel in 1152 with Eleanor of Aquitaine, wife of the future King Henry II, and as such can claim to be one of the longest-established families in the country, and certainly in the county. The family has had its ups and downs: the fifth Earl was beheaded in 1461 for supporting the wrong side – a dangerous

Powderham Castle

habit in medieval times – and his brother went the same way five years later; another brother was killed at the battle of Tewkesbury. The eighth Earl narrowly escaped execution; the ninth Earl did not, and his son died in Italy in 1556, some said of poison, after spending fifteen years in the Tower of London.

It was a lesser branch of the family who inhabited Powderham Castle, preferring a more peaceful and certain life out of the dangerous mainstream of politics and royal favours. They were rewarded with the viscountcy of Devon in 1762 and successfully claimed the earldom in 1831.

The original castle dates from the end of the fourteenth century, although succeeding generations have extended and altered it through the centuries. It is not a particularly grand house but it does contain some notable pieces of furniture and portraits and gives the impression of being very much a family home, a little worn around the edges, a little inconvenient in its layout.

The setting is most attractive. From the sunny terraced gardens, the castle looks out across the deer park to the waters of the Exe estuary that at one time came right up to the terrace walls. Large herds of deer roam at will throughout the grounds, and the parkland is open to visitors without charge, many of whom come simply to picnic in this delightful setting.

A property with a similar background but of more modest proportions is Fursdon, situated in a sheltered fold of the hills between Tiverton and Exeter. Unlike the Courtenays, the Fursdons have inherited in unbroken male line since they first came to their peaceful Devon backwater in the days of Henry III, despite their menfolk's departing to fight in various wars throughout the ages. Opening the house to the public is a recent venture, and personal touches make it all the more interesting: the toys of the latest generation of Fursdon children (three boys) are frequently left around. The rooms are still very much in use, and one has become a family museum. Here, too, the parkland and gardens can be wandered round at will – and in the stables one of the best cream teas in the county is available.

Castle Hill in North Devon is one of the county's more imposing mansions and has been the home of the Fortescues since the mid fifteenth century. The house was built in the 1720s by Hugh Fortescue and his half-brother, who were also responsible for the laying-out of the grounds in the formal manner of the time.

It is most impressively sited. The long façade, flanked by stable and office blocks, all painted a creamy-gold, stand out against the backdrop of woodland. The true gold of the cupola surmounting the house, a later edition, shines above the main house. This is a replica of the original building which was destroyed in a fire in 1934, when many of its treasures were also lost.

Behind the house, and open annually to the public, is a fine spring garden filled with banks of rhododendrons and many mature trees. Although very lovely and well worth a visit, it is not the garden that is exceptional. The parkland surrounding Castle Hill is an important eighteenth-century landscape, unrivalled in Devon or anywhere else in the West Country, and is a rare survival. The original plans were drawn in the 1730s for a garden on a par with its contemporary, Stowe in Buckinghamshire. Long avenues of trees radiated from the house, punctuated with small buildings or follies. Canals and lakes were planned, though these did not materialize, or if they did, they did not survive, and the church had to be moved from its position close to the house and rebuilt alongside the main road.

Castle Hill's grounds survived numerous changes in fashions, when many such formal schemes were swept away in favour of more natural parkland, and even today they are far from safe. A twentieth-century threat in the form of a proposed major road straight across the parkland would have cut in two the carefully planned vistas from the house. The road itself, part of the North Devon link with the M5 at Tiverton, was not defeated, merely resited to the north of the house in the valley once occupied by the railway.

Two other gardens of architectural as well as horticultural appeal comprise the great terraces and tiltyard at Dartington Hall, and the Italian gardens at Tapeley Park on the Torridge estuary, where there are also some fine herbaceous terraces and woodland gardens. The house, home of the Christie family, is open at certain times.

One of the few houses open to the public in the north of the county is Arlington Court, another National Trust possession, which it acquired in 1949 following the death of Miss Rosalie Chichester. The 3,470-acre park had been laid out as an early form of nature reserve. Miss Chichester was an ardent supporter of 'nature' but, more importantly, believed in sharing and annually opened the grounds and held natural history classes for the local children. Her exquisite water-colours of wild flowers are well known to visitors to the house. The herds of Jacobs sheep and the Shetland ponies with which she stocked the park still delight the children who come to Arlington, although not everyone takes advantage of the many walks laid out around the estate, most of which gravitate to the lake, a centre of wildlife. The Chichester emblem was a heron with a wriggling eel in its bill and it is fitting that the beechwoods house one of the largest heronries in the West Country. The lake forms an important fishing-ground for these large, unwieldy birds. It is one of the few places where it is possible to watch them in the springtime from comparative comfort, as most heronries are far less accessible than that at Arlington. The lake attracts many visiting birds, even some rarities, though it is the ducks and the moorhens that delight the younger visitors. There is even an observation hide from which to view the wildlife.

The house itself is of no great antiquity, dating only from 1820, and is somewhat severe in appearance. Miss Chichester was a notable collector of, among other things, shells, model ships and butterflies, and the stables contain a fine collection of horse-drawn vehicles, one of which takes visitors around the grounds.

The only other property in North Devon open regularly is Chambercombe Manor near Ilfracombe. Hartland Abbey in the far west is open on certain days, when visitors can explore both house and grounds.

Two very fine twentieth-century gardens are located in North Devon, each created by the energy of their owners and each set to become established gardens of great national importance.

Rosemoor, near Torrington, is the home of Lady Anne Palmer. In 1973 she formed a charitable trust to administer the garden, and in

Carriage driving, Arlington Court, near Barnstaple

1987 she gave the entire property to the Royal Horticultural Society, who willingly accepted it. It is their first important acquisition to date and will in future years become as much a magnet to keen horticulturalists as is their main garden at Wisley in Surrey. In the same year Lady Anne was awarded the Society's Victoria Medal, their highest accolade, for her services to horticulture. The garden is not large, but it is well sited in the Torridge valley.

The garden at Marwood Hill is also something of a plantsman's paradise. Its creator, Dr Jimmy Smart, is a much-travelled man with a liking for Australasian plants. His original garden contained many fine specimens, and one large greenhouse is entirely devoted to the more tender species, such as acacias; another houses his enormous collection of camellias which he has hybridized, raising many new varieties. More camellias fill the older part of the garden, which has grown beyond all recognition since he started in the 1960s. No sooner is one area completed than the Doctor begins work on another, so that Marwood Hill garden now spreads down the valley and along both sides. The original lake has grown to three, and the original plantings are now mature, established gardens. It is a most useful place to visit for anyone wanting to see what a particular tree or shrub looks like, as everything is meticulously labelled.

In the early days, Dr Smart was helped by just one gardener, and the plants for sale were left out on a help-yourself, money-in-the-box basis. Nowadays Marwood Hill is so well known that there are several gardeners, the thriving nursery is properly controlled and open only at certain times, and Dr Smart has had to provide such basic necessities as lavatories. The garden is most generously open every day of the year from dawn to dusk, with the exception of Christmas Day. A good garden is always interesting and always worth visiting whatever the time of year.

A large number of small gardens open on specified days throughout the year mainly under the National Gardens Scheme. In recent years the number has risen to over one hundred. The smallest is a backyard in Plymouth; the largest is Marwood Hill. Inevitably the majority are open in the springtime, when the flowering bulbs and cherry trees are at their best, but there is a smattering throughout the year and throughout the county. Many of the owners provide teas for their visitors, and others have well-stocked plant stalls. Nearly all of them are happy to stop and talk gardens, and it is encouraging that so many people are prepared to share their garden with strangers.

Ruins are not common in Devon – stone was too valuable a source of building-material to be left alone for long. But at Okehampton, Lydford and Totnes the castle ruins have survived; the ivyclad walls of

Berry Pomeroy Castle are said to be haunted, and all sorts of grisly stories abound. Parts of the original Bickleigh Castle remain, but it was largely rebuilt in the fifteenth and seventeenth centuries. It was once a Courtenay possession, as was Tiverton Castle, another de-fortified and privately owned home. Castle Drogo, overlooking the River Teign, is entirely modern, having been built in the early years of this century to the designs of Sir Edwin Lutyens; it was given to the National Trust by the Drewe Family in 1974. Compton Castle is more of a fortified manor house, associated with the Gilbert family for seven generations. The Gilberts were one of Devon's famous seafaring families, and from Compton Castle Gilberts set sail to found colonies in Newfoundland, Maine and Virginia. The estate was sold in 1785 and gradually declined, until a naval cadet, aged only fifteen and beginning his career at Dartmouth, visited his former family seat and vowed one day to buy it back. This he did in 1931, 146 years after the Gilberts left, and twenty years later he gave it to the National Trust on the condition that Gilberts should continue to live in their ancestral home.

Another property with Elizabethan naval associations is Buckland Abbey, owned by the National Trust but now administered by the City of Plymouth. This was the home of the greatest sea-dog of them all – Sir

Buckland Abbey

Francis Drake. It was originally a Cistercian monastery and was bought at the dissolution by another famous Devonian, Sir Richard Grenville. The Grenvilles converted the old abbey and its buildings into a home, and the last Grenville to live there was the Sir Richard Grenville of the *Revenge*. Sir Francis Drake bought the property around 1582, when he was Mayor of Plymouth, and after his death in 1596 it passed through a succession of Drake heirs, but rarely from father to son, until it was sold in 1946. The new owner gave the property to the National Trust.

Buckland Abbey has recently undergone extensive renovations and restorations, and the interior now houses an interesting exhibition and display on Drake and the Armada. The former tithe barn is one of the largest in the country. Built around 1300 to house the 'tythes' given to the abbey by their tenants, it is 159 feet long and thirty feet wide and extends sixty feet up to the ridge. The massive oak beams are pegged together, and discreet lighting enables the visitor to see the interior of this vast, dark cavern.

In recent years the lack of major stately homes in Devon has been more than compensated for by the appearance of a large number of wide-ranging 'museums' all over the county. The diversity is amazing, and it seems that Devon can offer something to interest everyone, from butterfly farms to aircraft museums.

Gone are the days of hushed and dusty halls full of old coins and stuffed birds, with frowning attendants, looking more like gaolers, waiting to pounce on any child so much as daring to reach out a finger. Today's museums seem rather to encourage participation, and most have well-presented, lively displays, often with audio-visual shows to provide everyone with a welcome chance to sit down. Such places have become the answer to wet days on holiday – but this is to undervalue them, for many are worth a visit even in a heatwave.

Most of the larger towns have a museum, usually based on the area's past history, and many of the smaller villages or towns also have a specialized display. Thus Lynmouth has a room devoted to the flood disaster of 1952; at Hartland Quay there is a museum of wrecks, smuggling and coastal activities, and Clovelly's visitors' centre has a display dealing with the village's history. At Starcross, on the Exe estuary, the pumping station of Brunel's atmospheric railway is now a museum, all that remains of this novel idea, and Brixham houses the British Fisheries Museum in the former Market House on the quayside. There are railway museums and combat vehicles, miniature villages and a motor museum, carriages and motorcycles, collections of shells and aircraft – it seems Devon has them all.

Morwellham Quay is a marvellous example of what can be achieved with imagination and a 'thinking' outlook. Industrial relics always exercise a certain fascination, but here on the banks of the River Tamar this fascination has been harnessed to the full. For many years the vast area covered by the former mine workings and the quay from which copper and arsenic were exported languished like some sleeping beauty. Once a hive of activity and a begetter of great wealth, the mines had sunk into decline by the end of the nineteenth century. The mineral railway, the inclined plane connecting it with the canal, the mineshafts, furnaces and docklands had all been abandoned, along with the cottages, inn and offices. It was the action of Dartington Trust that halted the decay before it was irretrievable and who were largely responsible for the drive and energy that have turned Morwellham into one of the country's most interesting 'museums'. Where possible, everything has been restored to working order, so that visitors can actually ride into the tunnels on miner's trucks and see the various pieces of machinery at work. They can also enjoy the beautiful scenery of the Tamar and the quayside which began life long centuries ago as a medieval port for the monks of Tavistock Abbey.

Another unusual working museum is to be found at Sticklepath, near Okehampton, where the Finch foundry makes use of water-power from the infant Taw as it rushes off Dartmoor. The water travels in a raised leat or launder along the backs of the houses to discharge over the wheels that power the various bellows and machines inside the foundry. Today it still turns out agricultural handtools such as scythes and shovels, and will repair and sharpen existing tools. It was rescued from decay by members of the Finch family, who have owned the foundry since 1814 and now run a charitable trust. It is a rare opportunity to see what can be achieved by a small amount of water and a large wheel.

The City of Exeter has several interesting museums, including the original Royal Albert Memorial Museum, the restored guest-room in the St Nicholas Priory, the Guildhall itself and the museum of costume and lace elegantly displayed in the Regency Rougemont House overlooking the castle.

The most ambitious of the city's museums is the maritime collection housed down on the historic waterfront. Opened in 1969, it was the idea of one man, Major David Goddard, and achieved with the co-operation of the City Council and a large number of hardworking individuals and organizations. There is nothing quite like it anywhere else in the country. The site is perfect, making use of former warehouses and associated buildings around the canal basin and on the river frontage. Addicts of the 1970s television series *The Onedin Line* will recognize it instantly. A collection of vessels from all over the world are on display, from Arabian dhows to the extraordinary swan built for Captain Peacock of Starcross. He used this floating eccentricity for ferrying his

Exeter Maritime Museum

Replica of the Golden Hind *at Richmond Dock, Appledore*

guests out to a far larger swan moored in the estuary, where he could entertain sixteen to dinner; unfortunately this was destroyed by fire just three years before the formation of the Maritime Museum. Most of the craft can be properly inspected; many are afloat and even take visitors on river trips. This is definitely not one of those 'don't touch' museums.

Neither is the equally fascinating Maritime Museum at Appledore on the north coast. Although it lacks the attraction of actual boats, the old house at the top of the town is full of memorabilia of the days of sail, when Appledore was bustling with fishermen, sea-going vessels, shipbuilders and repair yards. It also contains rooms devoted to wrecks and smuggling, re-creations of the conditions endured by emigrants to the New World, and reconstructions of a nineteenth-century home.

Completely different is Watermouth Castle on the outskirts of Ilfracombe, filled with mechanical musical and fairground instruments, railway memorabilia and household bygones. Agricultural bygones are housed at the Milky Way close to Clovelly, where there is an interesting collection of farm and farmhouse implements, many of which were in daily use until recent years – elderly tractors, butter-churning equipment, the precursor of the combine harvester and many smaller items. The Milky Way itself is a new idea in holiday attractions, now catching on elsewhere. Town children these days often think milk miraculously appears in a bottle – a visit to the dairy farm will disabuse them of this idea, for they can watch the cows being milked, and at the right time of year they can get close to calves and lambs and even try their hand at milking.

Animals and other live attractions are proving more and more popular. The marvellous heavy shire horses never fail to fascinate children, and they can be seen at a South Devon centre as well as at annual ploughing displays throughout the county. Wildlife parks, rare breed collections, aquariums, an otter park, sheep and lambs, trout farms and butterfly collections have all sprung up in the last decade. There is even a gnome reserve, buried deep in the North Devon countryside at West Putford, although sighting of a genuine gnome cannot be guaranteed!

The Quince Honey Farm at South Molton is a genuine honey-

Coldharbour Mill, near Tiverton

Branham Pottery, Barnstaple

producing unit. Here visitors can watch the bees at work, and see the fascinating process of creating the honeycombe and the interior of a hive (all safely behind glass). They can also buy a range of products all made from beeswax or honey.

In East Devon there is a first-class town museum at Tiverton which houses not only a good collection of local history but a genuine steam-engine over which children can climb, and also the history of the town's association with lace and the textile industry.

It seems that what is no longer viable commercially often takes out a second lease on life by becoming a working museum. Much of the county's history that would otherwise be lost is being preserved in this way, and some worthwhile buildings are kept alive. At Uffculme a traditional woollen mill has been restored to full working condition, after many years in the doldrums. At Otterton visitors can watch the millstones grinding corn in the traditional manner, as they have been doing for over 300 years. Stoneground flour is once again in demand, so that such mills, and there are several in Devon, are more than just a tourist attraction.

Several small complexes house traditional craftsmen operating in a small and highly individualistic way. The Devon Guild of Craftsmen has gathered many of them together under one roof at Bovey Tracey, and organizes permanent exhibitions. It is the county's proud boast that some of the best and most skilled artists and craftsmen are attracted to Devon, but they need a showplace, a shop window where prospective purchasers can easily admire their work. The centre at Bovey Tracey provides such a place.

The pace of life in Devon seems to encourage artistic talent. Every town seems to have its art gallery, and each of them displays a remarkably high standard, not just by professional artists. There are several summer art shows, where the red 'sold' stickers appear with rapidity. Many an unknown artist has found encouragement in the West Country – and it cannot just be because of the lovely scenery.

St Andrew's Church, Plymouth

13

Churches

Wherever you go in Devon, you are never far from a church. The landscape is punctuated by the towers and occasional spires of ancient parish churches.

The county is a church visitor's paradise. Most of the buildings are very old, dating from the twelfth century in a few cases, with many from the fourteenth and fifteenth centuries. Some are outstanding, some are huge, and some are very small. Many suffered at the hands of the Victorians, though it is only fair to say that the deterioration was such that some would have fallen down if they had not been rescued and 'restored'. An ancient church built of mellow stone is an essential ingredient of any English village, but some of Devon's churches are tucked away down grassy lanes, some are isolated in the middle of fields – they pop up in the most surprising places.

It was the Celtic saints who first brought religion to the West Country. From Ireland, from Wales and from France, they came across the stormy seas to preach Christianity to a superstitious and pagan people – and many of them were most unkindly received. More than one saint is reported to have been murdered by those he or she sought to convert, and the prolific foxgloves that so brighten the North Devon lanes are said to be drops of St Nectan's blood. His miraculous powers enabled him to walk about for some time with his head tucked under his arm. If the foxgloves are any indication, he covered quite a few miles! Many churches, especially those around the coast and estuaries, bear Celtic dedications, and there is much evidence of links with both Welsh and Irish communities.

By the time of the Norman Conquest, the Church had become a powerful force in the county. The diocese of Exeter included most of Somerset and all of Cornwall, and the bishop was recorded at the time of Domesday as being the third largest landowner in Devon, only the King and Baldwin the sheriff excelling him. The next century saw a great number of parish churches built, and several monastic foundations came into being. Most of the churches survive but the monasteries disappeared at the Reformation. Also lost are the great number of private chapels and oratories built in the remoter parts of the county, enabling the local inhabitants to worship close to their homes.

There are five churches in the county in the hands of the Redundant Churches Fund. St Peter the Poor Fisherman at Revelstoke was formerly the parish church of Noss Mayo but now hides amongst the trees on the cliff edge above a caravan site. Abandoned in the 1870s, it has now been tidied up and is a romantic, unroofed ruin still surrounded by a well-kept graveyard. The old church at Parracombe in North Devon, although recently reroofed, is an architectural gem. Abandoned when a new church was built in the village, it was threatened with demolition. But St Petrock's survived with a virtually intact eighteenth-century interior complete with box pews, three-decker pulpit, screen and musicians' gallery, and a row of pegs for hats and cloaks. (A similar Georgian interior is to be found in the Exmoor church of Molland, and St George's in Tiverton is the only church in Devon built in the Georgian era.) The isolated church above the Tamar at Luffincott, the churches at Torbryan and at West Ogwell near Newton Abbot are also now cared for by the Redundant Churches Fund.

Several other churches in the diocese have ceased to serve their original function, and a variety of uses has been found for them, ranging from houses to sports halls, a theatre and Greek Orthodoxy. The ruined church of South Huish near Hope Cove is cared for by the Friends of Friendless Churches.

Honeychurch is not redundant but is one of many small parish churches now under the protective wing of the Devon Historic Churches fund. Time seems almost to have stood still since the twelfth century, when the little church was built, making it a rare Norman survival. Professor Hoskins, the Devon historian, says in his book *Devon* that just to see the church on a fine morning puts him in a good humour for the rest of the day. It has, he says, one of the simplest and most appealing interiors of all English country churches and lives up to its name.

Honeychurch now belongs to the parish of Sampford Courtenay. This mid-Devon parish earned a place in ecclesiastical history for it is where the Prayerbook Rebellion of 1549 began. It seems strange that the introduction of the prayerbook and the church services in English instead of Latin, should have caused such a heated and violent outburst, but so it was. Perhaps it was the ingrained Devonian antagonism to change that sparked things off. The congregation of Sampford Courtenay rejected the new service as soon as it appeared. Local justices came to try to calm things down and persuade the people of the village to accept the new rites, but they only made things worse, and feelings ran so high that one of the gentry was struck to the ground and set upon and '. . . notwithstanding his pitiful requests and lamentations, a number of the rest fell upon him and slew him and cut him in small pieces.' Standing in the middle of peaceful Sampford Courtenay beside the churchhouse steps where this gruesome scene took place, it is hard to imagine that such a thing could happen.

The ensuing rebellion lasted just ten weeks, but in that time the gallant band of Devon and Cornish men laid siege to Exeter so successfully that for 200 years or more afterwards the city's deliverance was still celebrated. It was a hopeless and futile rebellion, and the end came at Fenny Bridges outside Honiton, where an army of mercenaries inflicted a crushing defeat. One last, sad stand was made where it had all begun, back in peaceful little Sampford Courtenay.

Once the excitement of the rebellion was over and forgotten, Devon quickly turned to the Protestant faith and became firmly anti-Catholic. It went further, embracing Puritanism during the days of the Commonwealth, and it was at this time that so many of the church monuments and carvings were disfigured.

The Act of Uniformity, 1662, from which the modern prayerbook and structure of the Anglican Church date, saw also the beginning of Nonconformity. During the religious reversals, parish priests came and went, depending on their leanings. Many of the Puritan clergy remained by agreeing to fall in line, but several did not and instead founded chapels for the Dissenters. Throughout the county there are many fine meeting-houses or chapels that date from this period but it is churches that people visit, largely ignoring these interesting and historic buildings, many of which survive a good deal less altered than the parish churches. Notable examples are the 1664 Congregational chapel at Ottery St Mary, Loughwood meeting-house at Dalwood, near Axminster, which is important enough to be in the hands of the National Trust, and a Baptist chapel at Prescott near Uffculme built in 1715, still with its original galleries.

At Spiceland in the same parish of Culmstock is one of the earliest Friends' meeting-houses, built originally in 1670, although the existing building dates from 1815. Quakers are quiet people, not prone to boasting about their religion, but they have existed in the county since the beginning of the movement. There are not many Quaker burial grounds, but in Devon there are two worth visiting, one secluded, one more prominent and not usually recognized for what it is. This is at Tavistock, bordering the Princetown road and sandwiched between the hillside and the road. It is beautifully laid out, with many fine trees and shrubs. Tucked away out of sight at Sticklepath is the second burial ground. Because at one time the Quaker faith was unpopular and they suffered from mild persecution, particularly in the rural areas, burial grounds were sometimes 'hidden', but nowadays it can be boldly entered via the gardens and car-parks to the rear of the Finch Foundry, many of whose employees were Quakers. The original entrance was down a narrow path concealed between high walls and hedges, through a very narrow gate. This path continues to the river, where there is evidence of a ford; Quakers and their dead from further afield would have come this way. The little cemetery is surrounded by walls and trees, a pleasant, tranquil spot.

The missionary zeal of John Wesley fell on largely deaf ears in Devon. He recorded that he met with 'such stupid rudeness as I have not seen for a long time in any part of England'. He did have to compete with a huntsman and pack of hounds at one of his meetings, so perhaps it is not surprising he thought little of the Devonians.

Travelling around the countryside today, one still sees many of the numerous wayside chapels. Some date from the early years of the nineteenth century, when the recognized Church had fallen into slack and uncaring ways, with parsons absent for long periods and services infrequent and sketchy in ill-cared-for churches. The truly devout turned from the image of the drinking-hunting parson to the plainer faith of Methodism. Country folk liked to look up to their church; they needed a firm creed and code of conduct by which to live their lives; but at that time the Church of England in rural Devon failed to provide this. Methodism is still strong in both town and countryside but, just as the number of churches required for a dwindling religiously minded population has fallen, so too has the need for the great number of chapels that served the scattered populations. Many of these have been converted to homes; in the towns they have found a variety of new uses, from factories and warehouses to restaurants, art galleries and shops.

In total, Devon has 636 churches, one cathedral and several small chapels. They are all within the enormous diocese of Exeter, still one of the largest in the country and run from the quiet seclusion of the Cathedral Yard.

The contrast between those churches that have been restored, and those that escaped the heavy hand of Victorianism is most marked and highlights just how much was swept away and destroyed. One enters a church in a mood of expectancy, pushing open the heavy door almost nervously; so often in Devon one is doomed to disappointment. Perhaps the passage of years will soften the dull, heavy work and lend its own atmosphere. But how great the reward when one stumbles on an original interior – or one that has been sympathetically maintained.

Travelling with a guidebook in a prepared state of mind robs one of this pleasurable experience, although it saves many a wasted journey.

I stumbled upon the original Parracombe church simply because I saw a second church tower above the village and went in search. What a rich reward! At Honeychurch I followed the name – it sounded so attractive. Indeed, you never know what you are going to find down a Devon lane.

One such reward is Abbots Bickington church, one of the smallest and least known in Devon. Lying in farming country not far from the infant Torridge, here is an example of a survival from the days of small chapels serving their immediate communities, in this case the fine old Court Barton; both were part of the Hartland Abbey endowment. Dating from the thirteenth century, it has a small spire – which in itself is unusual. Repair and restoration were necessary in the mid 1800s but it remains a charming, simple and intimate little church, set in a delightful churchyard, not least of its charms being the skill needed to find it!

Most Devon churches were originally rich in wood. The ceilings, particularly when barrel or wagon-roofed, are often richly carved with bosses and beams, and many still have fine bench, or pew, ends. The rood screen, too, formed an important feature, but these have disappeared in church after church. Here and there they do survive, especially in the north of the county, the oldest being at Welcombe, and a fine example still divides nave from chancel in neighbouring Stoke. But at Atherington is the sole surviving example of a screen complete with its rood loft, from which the visitor can look out over the church below. In Cullompton's fine church the screen has managed to retain its original colouring. Another universal loss is medieval stained glass. Only fragments survive in the parish churches, providing a quiet, muted contrast with the bright and garish glass of later generations. Plain glass is all too often to be preferred.

For over 800 years a Saxon crypt existed underneath the church of St Giles at Sidbury inland from Sidmouth, but it was forgotten, its entrance covered over, and no records gave a clue to its existence until it was uncovered during restoration work in 1898. It is the only Saxon crypt in Devon, and one of only half a dozen or so in the entire country, yet it remains comparatively unknown.

Few churches anywhere occupy a more spectacular site than that on Brentor. The solitary granite outcrop is a feature of the landscape from most of Devon, and from the neighbouring heights of Dartmoor it stands out clear and intriguing, almost an afterthought that doesn't belong out there on the plain. It is easy to imagine it as an offshore island and the intervening lowlands covered by the sea, as presumably they once were. Imaginative people see in Brentor some psychic significance and relate it to 'ley lines' and the lost land of Lyonesse that is supposed to have existed off Land's End. These mystic lines connect with such places as Glastonbury and its lonely tor, Burrow Mump, closer in Somerset, and even Brent Knoll, familiar to all travellers along the M5 and at whose foot now nestles a twentieth-century place of worship – a motorway service station. The more mundane of us who are not so susceptible to atmosphere still find the church and the rocky hill an interesting and fascinating place. A small car-park is provided, though Brentor has, fortunately, so far avoided exploitation as a tourist attraction. Perhaps the stiff climb up the hill, over 1,100 feet above sea-level, is one reason?

Not surprisingly, the church is low, squat even, and sturdily built from stone quarried from the hillside itself. The original church was built in 1140 by Robert Giffard at his own cost, and one story relates that it was in gratitude for deliverance from shipwreck. As is to be expected of a church so unusually sited, another story connects it with the Devil, relating that, however hard the builders worked at the foot of the tor, the Devil moved the stones to the summit overnight, so that in the end this is where the church was built. Quite why the Devil should wish to move the church 1,100 feet nearer Heaven has never been explained, but that is where the church has remained. It is much more likely that Robert Giffard wanted to build his church in the most prominent spot he could find – and he certainly succeeded.

The little church (it measures thirty-seven feet by fourteen) is full of simple atmosphere. It is dim, because of the small windows, and plain. In such churches the centuries of worship seem to pervade the interior and make a far greater impression than in the larger, wealthier churches of the county. It is possible to sit quietly and commune in one's own heart in Brentor church.

14

Exeter

'Before the Germans wrecked it, Exeter was one of the most beautiful and appealing cities in England, full of colour, light and movement. Even now, for all its ruins, it has an appeal unlike that of any other town in Western England. Exeter is the mother city and the tribal capital still.'

Professor Hoskins was writing in 1954, but every word in his book *Devon* rings true even today. The bomb scars have disappeared; those who never knew the pre-war city are unaware of their loss. Post-war Exeter has its rash of new buildings, one-way systems, pedestrian precincts and those most ugly of monuments to our age, the multi-storey car-parks, but somehow in Exeter they never look as bad as they do elsewhere. The city has kept its identity, its air of elegance and of agelessness, come what may.

Within the confines of the city are gathered together so much history, so much diversity, so much beauty, that it is difficult to do it justice. It has an ancient and superb cathedral with an attached choir school; it has a bishop and his palace; it has several ancient churches and the evidence of equally ancient institutions in the form of the Guildhall and Tuckers Hall; it has a university – and a prison. The magnificent Brunel-designed station was the pride of the Great Western Railway when it first thundered through from Paddington on its comfortable broad-gauge lines. The waters of the River Exe curve round the city, and on the historic quayside of the former port is the internationally acclaimed maritime museum. A large proportion of the city walls survive, and some of the castle, and beneath the modern buildings are many foundations of ancient Exeter. It remains the seat of county administration run from architecturally pleasing buildings in equally pleasing grounds. With a history that stretches back to pre-Roman times, it has almost everything that any city deserves to have, and in some kind of special way, Exeter has merged itself into the twentieth century without ruining the foregoing chapters of its history.

Visitors will perhaps be aware of what so many Devonians take for

Detail from Martyrs' Pulpit, Exeter Cathedral

granted, that Exeter is a garden city in the true sense of the word. Everywhere carefully planned and meticulously maintained floral displays, designed to grow to a beautiful maturity, enhance the city. Houses built along the approach roads have been carefully screened by banks of trees and shrubs, so that their privacy is now ensured. Small areas in the city centre have been allotted tough but attractive plants that will provide a permanent cover. The old squares are tree-shaded, reminiscent of the more fortunate of London squares, and bright with bedding plants in spring and summer. There is always an oasis of green somewhere close at hand.

Exeter is not only a visually beautiful city; it is also an intimate city, full of little corners, narrow streets and friendly doorways. People live in Exeter; they don't just commute leaving a sterile, empty town behind when shops and offices close for the day. Most visitors come only for the shops. This is a shame, for although they are good, offering a range from the usual multiples found in every city to the localized crafts, secondhand books, rare prints etc, the city has so much more to offer. The only way to truly explore is on foot, and a whole day would not be wasted, nor would it be long enough if every church, every interesting building, were properly studied.

Those who do forsake their motor car and take to their legs will discover one fact that motorists tend to forget – Exeter is very hilly. In every direction except the north-west there are steep slopes, disguised by buildings, but particularly noticeable as the land falls to the river. Looking up from St David's railway station, Exeter rises high above you, and it was its defensive role that was responsible for its growth. The Romans saw this and developed the town: Isca Dumnoniorum they called it, and their work can still be seen in the city walls. The Saxons held out long against the Conqueror, who in turn decided to build a castle on the high ground to ensure his continued sovereignty. The main gateway, one tower and other fragments survive of Rougemont Castle, built of the distinctive local red stone and now surrounded by peaceful gardens. Many visitors never discover the castle at all, nor the protective city walls. Close by are the law courts, and the nineteenth-century Rougemont House, which now houses a costume and lace museum. The gardens lead on to Northernhay, possibly the first public park in England and still complete with bandstand and broad promenade.

Throughout the city discreet boards describe the most interesting features and point the visitor in the right direction, but these information boards are unobtrusive, and nowhere does the city boast about its past or ram it down the visitor's throat. It is all there waiting to be discovered, if you are interested.

Statue of Hooker in the Cathedral Close, Exeter

The jewel in the crown, the most obvious and most magnificent of Exeter's buildings, is the cathedral of St Peter. It has been claimed that it is the most lovely of all English cathedrals, but no doubt this would be disputed. It is surrounded on all sides but one by the cathedral green, so that the visitor has time to appreciate this gem of ecclesiastical architecture. It is not large, and the main structure presents a near perfect example of early fourteenth-century building. Of the original pre-Norman church nothing remains, and of its Norman replacement there is very little, except the two transeptal towers, which are unique and which give the cathedral so much of its character. Other cathedrals soar upwards, but Exeter presents a squat outline; like the city, it is unobtrusive but full of worth.

The other great external feature is the west front. Three rows of beautifully sculpted figures look out across the precinct, under which extensive Roman remains have recently been discovered. Built of the pale local Beer stone, as is most of the cathedral, these figures have suffered with age, so that in many all but the outline has been lost. Attempts have been made at repair, and even replacement, but these in no way compare with the originals.

The interior is more welcoming than that of many cathedrals. It is full of treasures, from the 300-foot span of vaulted roof high overhead to the beautifully worked kneelers at your feet. The ceiling bosses, the tracery of the windows and their delicate stained glass, and the numerous side chapels are all part of its splendour.

An ancient astronomical clock in the north tower is believed to be one of the earliest surviving clocks in the country; although its exact age is uncertain, parts may well be fourteenth-century. It lacks the fascination of moving figures striking the hours; these are softly chimed on the hidden bell of Great Peter hanging above in the tower. At over six tons, it is one of Britain's largest bells.

The bishop's throne has twice been removed for safety: on the first occasion it was Cromwellian soldiers who posed a threat, on the second indiscriminate German bombs. This beautifully carved oak structure rising almost to the vaulting was constructed without a single nail. The list of treasures seems endless, and some of the most priceless are not on view. The Chapter Library contains many ancient manuscripts, amongst them the Exon Domesday and the 'Exeter Book' containing Anglo-Saxon poetry. Although the glorious west front escaped the war, its window covered with a protective screen against bomb blast, the east end and one of the chapels were damaged.

Much of Exeter was blitzed. One of the most tragic losses was that of Bedford Circus. Two perfect curved terraces, one of fourteen houses, the other of similar size but divided by a small chapel, were considered

Exeter Cathedral

Tudor House, Exeter. A survivor of the blitz

to be among the best examples of Georgian town architecture anywhere in the country. Many other fine features disappeared, leaving gaping holes and piles of rubble, but the devastation was not so great that wholesale rebuilding was necessary, as at Plymouth. Redevelopment has generally been as inconspicuous as possible, though inevitably the broad thoroughfares and modern shopfronts seem at variance with Exeter's traditional character. At least the worst of the modern intrusions are well away from the centre and, apart from possibly having to leave one's car in one of them, can be ignored by the visitor.

The music of the cathedral is of major importance. It breathes life into the ancient stonework, re-creating the spirit and atmosphere known to worshippers centuries ago, when the services were sung, or chanted. To say the cathedral seems dead without music is not necessarily an overstatement, but to those who have attended the concerts or festivals, or been lucky enough to be visiting when someone is playing the organ, the difference is most marked. Many musical events are held throughout the year, and the sung services celebrated daily during term time. Above all, it is the voices of the choristers that underline the close link between religion and the beauty of music and the human voice uplifted to the glory of God.

A most memorable experience was one early summer evening, the cathedral filled to capacity, lit only by candles, the flickering light softening the lines of the old building so that the roof, soaring high above, could be only dimly discerned and the nave and side aisles vanished in the twilight. The voices of the choristers were all that mattered. With no accompaniment, they kept their audience spellbound.

Not all cathedrals have choir schools. That at Exeter is one of the oldest, established in the thirteenth century, and is one of only thirty-seven in England and Wales. Until the 1950s, Exeter Cathedral School was purely for choristers, but then the decision was taken to admit non-choristers, so that today it is a fee-paying prep school attached to the cathedral.

Of the 166 boys, twenty-five are choristers, and many of these have been awarded 'assisted places'. Both the boys and their families need to be dedicated: not only are the boys expected to fit the choristers' duties around normal school requirements, they also have to give up a fair amount of free time. At Easter and Christmas, and of course on Sundays, when other boys are free of school, a chorister is very much on duty. The rewards are a far more varied school life, the highlights of foreign tours to sing in other cathedrals and concert halls, visits to other choir schools in Britain, concerts and recordings, and distinguished visitors – in the case of Exeter, the Prince of Wales. Recently the

Cathedral School decided to raise money to ensure the continuation of the choir school and the important tradition of being able to offer places to choristers purely on their ability to sing and not on their ability to pay. Various large organizations contributed, and there is now one Duke of Cornwall sponsored place.

Any boy who attends the cathedral school will not only receive an education rich in music and musical opportunities but will start his school life in the special atmosphere of the cathedral precinct in a range of buildings overlooking the Bishop's Palace and the cathedral green, one a hallowed haven of peace, the other a sort of Hyde Park Corner of Exeter where anything and everything goes on. There has never been a shortage of boys coming forward for voice trials, so that it seems the great tradition of music at Exeter Cathedral is safe for the foreseeable future.

15

East of the Exe

If county boundaries followed geological features rather than parish boundaries or administrative quirks, Devon would end at the River Exe, and East Devon would be part of Dorset. But the country east of the Exe is an attractive addition by which the county gains a further dimension and which adds yet greater variety to its already varied character. There is a softer, gentler feel, with larger, more attractive villages. The houses seem less defensive than elsewhere, especially in the north and on high ground and there are a greater number of mellow, ancient farmsteads.

The M5 from Taunton to Exeter has created an artificial barrier. Old roads connected; new roads divide. The former main highways led from one town to the next with a network of minor roads and lanes linking the villages and hamlets. People travelled on roads; only vehicles use motorways. Coaching inns and settlements grew up along the old roads; only service stations are permitted on the motorway's sacred territory, and what featureless places they are. No vernacular architecture there to give the traveller a clue as to which county he may be in. The M5 has disrupted a centuries-old network of communications, with lanes ending abruptly or re-routed to avoid the twentieth century's answer to traffic congestion. Yet it seems that motorways are built least to serve the local population whose lives and landscape they have disrupted, for there are few points of access along their route.

Tiverton has always been strategically placed at the meeting of the main north/south and east/west routes. The main railway passes close by, and it has become an important junction on the M5, the connecting-point for the North Devon Link Road.

The town grew originally around the castle, but its prosperity, in common with that of most of East Devon, was founded on wool. It is rich in history, with a wealth of fine old buildings, not least being the large fifteenth-century parish church with its finely carved exterior. Close by is the castle, built of soft red sandstone, converted to a dwelling-house many centuries ago and now open to the public. The

Tiverton Town Hall

church of St George, close to the Victorian town hall, is the only Georgian church in Devon. Tiverton is well known as the home of Blundell's public school for boys, founded in 1599 in a building that still stands down by the ancient ford across the River Lowman. The school moved to much larger premises on the outskirts of the town in 1880.

Tiverton was saved from complete economic decline by a Midlands industrialist whose net-lace factory had been destroyed in the Luddite riots of 1815–16. John Heathcoat came to Tiverton and restarted his business in a disused cotton mill. The name of Heathcoat has been linked with the town ever since.

John Heathcoat was a philanthropist. He built decent houses for his workers and the first factory school for their children; he organized works outings to the seaside, and his successors later funded the first pension scheme in the country. The original mill was burnt down but the rebuilt factory still stands, now part of the Coates Paton Group. The Heathcoat Amory family retain an interest in a smaller textile company in the town, and family trusts set up in 1940 benefit many individuals and charities in the area.

East Devon is an area of deep valleys and steep hills. The lanes twist and turn, leading to little-known villages. The signposting is haphazard, with a resultant loss of all sense of direction, all sense of time and all desire to hurry. You'll get there – somewhere – in the end, though it may not be quite where you had planned.

But no one should miss Holcombe Rogus. This attractive village possesses one of the finest Tudor manor houses in the county, an ancient and interesting church and a priest's house. The unusual name comes from the Norman knight Rogo Fitz-Nigel who was granted the manor of Holcombe and whose descendants stayed in possession until 1858, when the estate was sold to pay off gambling debts.

And now the race is swept away
All to their dusty beds,
Still shall the mellow evening ray
Shine gaily on their heads,
While other faces fresh and new
Shall occupy the Squire's Pew.

(This epitaph on 800 years of continuous ownership was written by a Mrs Laura Jordan in 1909.)

Tantalizing glimpses of Holcombe Court are gained from the gateway – a lovely greystone building with three-storey tower porch and tall, mullioned windows. A fourteenth-century dovecote, a rare survival in Devon, is just visible. Adjacent to the Court is the church, which contains many monuments to the lords of the manor, and a court pew. The north aisle has a fine roof with carved bosses and supporting angels.

The village has shrunk in size from the days when it boasted a thriving chair industry, which continued until the 1900s. Originally most of the cottages were thatched, but disastrous fires and rebuilding have reduced the numbers, so that today just one house retains its original cover. It is interesting to note that mains water did not reach Holcombe Rogus until 1950.

For the next few miles the peace of East Devon is shattered by a succession of large lorries. Limestone outcrops throughout the area have long been quarried for building and agricultural purposes, but in a small, localized way. The need for roadstone has led to the more profitable quarries being enlarged and mechanized in a big way, and this has caused a transformation of the landscape. Large chunks of it have actually disappeared – 'Little of the pleasant wooded ridge with its cottages that used to mark the parish boundary now remains,' says the guide to Holcombe Rogus. A thick white film of dust covers everything, and a journey over narrow country lanes to Burlescombe becomes a constant battle against a tidal flow of lorries. Burlescombe itself suffers from constant thunderous through-traffic.

The valley of the River Culm was once the centre of a prosperous woollen industry, and along its length are several industrial relics.

Cullompton was one of the main centres of the Devon wool trade and has a magnificent church built by wealthy merchants, either as a mark of gratitude or perhaps as a form of insurance policy? Built of red sandstone and replacing a much earlier collegiate church, it is mainly fifteenth century, with a stately tower dominating the town. Its great glory is the rood screen, one of the longest in the county and still retaining the original decoration in places. Fortunately no attempt has been made to 'restore' the paintwork, for modern man is quite incapable of matching the colours produced all those centuries ago, just as he is incapable of reproducing the soft stained glass or gentle carving of medieval craftsmen.

The town was devastated in the Great Fire of 1839, when 264 houses were destroyed. Some early buildings do survive, and though Cullompton is no longer a prosperous centre of anything in particular, it is a fine example of a Devon market town.

At Uffculme, also a former woollen centre on the River Culm, one of the mill buildings has been revitalized as a working museum, once again producing the woollen cloth for which the area was once renowned. Higher up the Culm another fine eighteenth-century mill building has been rescued from dereliction and successfully converted into homes.

The Blackdown Hills, which rise to over 900 feet in places, form the boundary with Somerset, and from them the panorama includes Exmoor, the Quantock Hills and the Mendips, and the plain of Somerset between. Along the ridge is Culmstock Beacon, where a stone building provides shelter, but the views over the valley of the Culm and much of East Devon can be appreciated only from outside, as it has no windows!

A lane leads down through Culm Davey, where the lovingly maintained ancient chapel is one of many restored by the Devon Historic Churches Fund. In the centre of Hemyock village is a strange ornate pillar commemorating the end of the South African War and garlanded with a lavish floral display. The remains of a small castle can still be viewed, although it has long been a dwelling-house.

There is even less to see of the once great abbey at Dunkeswell. The Cistercian order chose a peaceful place in a hidden river valley, but much imagination is needed to picture the vast abbey buildings, for there are only a few foundations and fragments of walls. The gatehouse is all that survives reasonably intact.

The ancient Iron Age hilltop fort of Luppit, on the edge of the Blackdown plateau, overlooks the valley of the River Otter, which rises on the Blackdown Hills and flows south through Honiton and Ottery St Mary to reach the sea at Budleigh Salterton. The upper valley is shared with the A30, now very much quieter than it used to be. This is hilly, domesticated Devon, land that has been cultivated for hundreds of years. It all looks pleasantly secure and undisturbed.

The A30 and Honiton used to be infamously linked with traffic jams on summer Saturdays, when long queues in both directions were the norm. Now that the M5 takes most of the traffic, and a much-needed bypass has been constructed, the broad main street of Honiton has assumed a less harassed air, and visitors can appreciate the town for what it is, not just as a blockage on the main arterial route.

The town is more attractively linked with lace – Honiton lace being the finest in the country. But the exquisite workmanship which can be admired in the town's museum was not achieved without great human suffering. Women and children worked long hours in poorly lit and poorly ventilated rooms, ruining both their eyesight and their health. It was said you could always tell the children of a lacemaker by their pale and wizened faces and hunched-up shoulders. Lace is still made today but it does not compare with the priceless work of a century ago.

Honiton is much older than its appearance would suggest. East Devon towns were particularly susceptible to fire, containing far more

Village stocks at Ottery St Mary

thatch than other areas of the county, and Honiton was devastated several times, so that many of the original dwellings were destroyed.

Ottery St Mary also suffered in this way, the last great fire being as late as 1866. But much of the attractive old town survives, and it has never suffered the damaging intrusion of heavy traffic. It grew up on a crossing of the River Otter, and on its banks were the mills that manufactured woollen serges. A tumbling circular weir, believed unique, can still be seen. Nearby is Cadhay House, a Tudor mansion on the outskirts of the town and occasionally open to the public.

The town's most important possession is its church. Far larger and grander than a parish church, it was built originally as part of a college for secular priests, suppressed by Henry VIII. In common with Exeter Cathedral, it has two transeptal towers, unusual enough for a cathedral, unknown elsewhere for a parish church. The interior is magnificent, with much fine stone fan vaulting and many priceless treasures. Restoration was necessary in the 1840s, and this was carried out by William Butterfield, who was responsible for the ornate font – not to everyone's liking. During the restoration the reredos behind the altar was uncovered, and although it had lost most of its figures, these were replaced, recalling some of the former glory of this beautiful church.

South of the A30 much of the land is owned by the Clinton Devon Estates, one of the largest single private landowners in the county. Although much has been sold off, they still have 2,500 acres of woodland in North Devon and another 2,000 acres in the Bicton area, 25,000 acres of farmland and Woodbury Common, which is of great value in amenity and conservation terms. It is composed of pebbly, sandy soil covered largely in heath and moorland species. In 1927 the Estate dedicated an area of 3,000 acres to the public, but they are still responsible for its maintenance and provide a warden to patrol it. The herds of deer that roam Woodbury Common have flourished so successfully that a certain amount of culling is necessary. Deer and forestry, of which there is a fair amount, do not mix, and the pine trees that occur naturally would soon disappear if the numbers of deer were not controlled.

Bicton was the ancestral home of the Rolles, forebears of Lord Clinton, who now lives at Merton in mid Devon, and the house is leased to the County Council, who use it as an agricultural college. The beautiful gardens and grounds, quite separate, are a major tourist attraction. All around this area are reminders of its noble associations in the form of gates and lodges, palings and parklands, and a brick column at the road junction that leads to Otterton, one of Devon's prettier villages with unspoilt cob and thatched cottages lining the main street. The same cannot be said of the church and former monastic buildings beside it.

Much of the coast immediately east of the Exe is also in the ownership of the Clinton Devon Estates, including large chunks of both Exmouth and Budleigh Salterton, where the seafront is let on a long lease to the East Devon District Council. It is this single historic ownership, and tradition of preservation rather than exploitation, that has kept the coastal belt relatively unspoilt and undeveloped, for the Clinton lands stretch as far as Sidmouth, with one break at Ladram Bay. There are caravans at Ladram Bay.

Exmouth was one of South Devon's earliest holiday resorts and has been popular with the townsfolk of Exeter for centuries. It has the only sandy beach east of the Exe and makes the most of it. Rapid growth in recent years has almost overwhelmed the original town centre, and the new shopping centres and ringroads have taken away much of its character. On the estuary side is a thriving dock area, but beyond that the atmosphere of a seaside town takes over, with a promenade, coloured lights and flowerbeds, elegant terraces and hotels. The sand stretches for miles, and at the far end of the town are endless rows of beach huts. Exmouth once bemoaned the lack of a railway, but perhaps, if it casts its eyes across the estuary at the fate that has overtaken Dawlish, it may think again.

Beyond the sand dunes the red cliffs rise above the long shingle beach that runs all along the remainder of the coast. Around the headland, and hidden from Exmouth, is Sandy Bay, owned by one of the large holiday organizations. What can only be described as a small town of caravans has been developed, along with all the attendant facilities of club houses, shops, swimming-pool and even a museum of country life – a gentle touch of irony perhaps?

Budleigh Salterton occupies a dip in the cliffs and was a select watering-place developed in the nineteenth century. The pebble beaches of East Devon are not popular with children, so it is mainly the elderly who are drawn to exercise along the sea-front, enjoying the bracing breezes or relaxing in deckchairs. The main street runs away from the sea, and Budleigh itself is largely sheltered by the cliffs, enjoying a mild climate. It grew up at the mouth of the River Otter which winds across the valley to cut for itself a deep cleft between the high shingle bank and the outcrop of red sandstone cliff that forms an impenetrable barrier. Walkers find themselves making a long detour inland before regaining the coast.

Many guidebooks describe Sidmouth as a mini-Brighton, but whereas Brighton has bowed to modern-day pressures, Sidmouth has been bypassed and remains very largely an unspoilt Regency seaside town. Its roots go back to Celtic times, and the Romans developed Sidmouth as a port. Then came long centuries as a humble fishing village before it was discovered as a watering-place of gentle climate to attract the aristocracy and the wealthy. The old fishing village survives, its narrow streets falling below the level of the esplanade and twisting and turning to break the force of the salt winds. Its sea-front was protected by a rocky spit, but this and the quays developed to cope with the Newfoundland fishing-trade were all swept away at various times during the winter gales. It is a curious fact that the sea is not visible from the old village. Apparently the seafaring population was not in the least

A corner of Sidmouth

bothered about 'sea views', not wishing to be reminded of the hazards of their livelihood once ashore and seeking shelter from the salt winds. It was the newcomers who built their houses fronting the sea.

The architecture is delightful. Sidmouth is not large, and the seafront, constructed in the 1830s, is only a short stroll, but along it and surrounding the core of the old village are some fine Regency terraces. The town does not seem to have been developed to any overall plan, so that it lacks the symmetry of Bath or the imposing terraces of Brighton, but because of its small scale and haphazardness it is all the more charming. Many of the terraces were only half built, and no two are quite alike or indeed link up with any of the others, so that a stroll around the town is full of interest, with all kinds of unexpected surprises down little alleys including the cottage where a certain Miss Cash once embroidered names on linen tapes – a name known to every school child, or its mother. And right on the water's edge are a group of thatched cottages seemingly impervious to their exposed position.

Beyond Sidmouth begin many miles of National Trust headlands, including the cliffs of Branscombe. Here there is a long, shelving shingle beach with car-park, shop and tea-rooms. The long, winding valley that is Branscombe stretches inland, with farms and cottages scattered along its length. The church is much visited, for it is unusual and full of antiquities, with a central tower surmounting a cruciform structure, rare in parish churches. Much of it is Norman, with some later additions and alterations, but it escaped wholesale restoration and has kept its Elizabethan gallery, seventeenth-century three-decker pulpit and altar rails.

The cliffs rise steeply again beyond Branscombe, and the chalk is inescapable. Below is an area of ancient landslip, dating from 1790 when ten acres dropped over 200 feet. Wandering through this strange area of almost jungle-like growth, caverns and chalky white outcrops, one has the feeling of being in a forgotten land where unheard-of beasts still roam and where Tarzan-like figures might suddenly appear swinging on the creepers that festoon the trees and cliffs. Both landslip and shingle beach end abruptly at Beer Head, and the only way eastward is over the top.

Between Branscombe and Beer the cliffs rise to over 400 feet, but on a good day the views make the climb worthwhile. There is a ghostly, chill atmosphere when the sea mists swirl around the white cliffs, but when the sun shines they make a sparkling contrast with the blue sea below. These cliffs have an alien feel to many Devonians, who rarely stray this far east. White cliffs belong to Dover, not to craggy old Devon.

A long village street leads down to the small harbour of Beer. This former fishing village now gains more from the tourist than it does from the sea, but enough fishing is carried on to give it an authentic air. Crabs and local fish are sold direct from the trawlers and small fishing-smacks, and another profitable catch for the fishermen is 'Trips around the Bay' to view Beer Head and the landslip. The bay is completely enclosed by the tall white cliffs in whose shelter are rows of beach huts. These simple wooden huts, once taken for granted, are becoming a rarity and despite much loving care must inevitably decay; perhaps the last few will become protected buildings – a Grade I listed beach hut?

Beer village has a broad main street, accompanied by a swift-running stream and crossed by paving slabs. It is full of gift shops and tea-rooms, gay with summer bunting overhead to welcome the annual influx of money-spending visitors.

Inland from Beer is a good example of a former hive of industry, long redundant, being given a new lease of life. Beer quarries, now an important tourist attraction, have a very long history. The Romans first worked the soft white stone, and quarrying continued until the early years of this century. The quarries are entirely underground and were worked without machinery. The resulting caverns and chambers leading deeper and deeper underground open like vaults, or a cathedral crypt, and much Beer stone went in the building of cathedrals, including Winchester, St Paul's, Westminster Abbey – and Exeter. Most of the neighbouring parish churches and many of the better-quality houses were built of Beer stone. For many years after closure the quarries remained shut up and deserted, a dangerous place to explore without a guide. But they have reopened as a museum and are a memorial to generations of skilful workmen and masons, a fascinating example of industrial archaeology.

Seaton is separated from Beer by a headland. At one time it had its own branch line from the Southern Region, but the town never quite made it as a popular seaside resort. It retains one distinct feature, again recently resurrected as a tourist attraction – the Seaton Tramline. Tramways are usually associated with town streets, not with open countryside, but Seaton's tramway follows the valley of the River Axe as far as Colyton, and its open-top cars make an ideal viewing-platform.

Colyton is an ancient settlement on a tributary of the Axe close to its confluence. Once an important town, it has now shrunk considerably but contains many fine buildings, grouped around the handsome church. Inside there are some good monuments and a Jacobean screen, but it is the unusual tower and octagon lantern, surmounted by a magnificent weathervane that glitters in the sunshine, that take the eye.

Across the estuary is the far older settlement of Axmouth. The Romans knew Axmouth, for them the southern terminus of the Fosse

The Seaton Tramline

Way, and a port even then. It has grown and declined over the centuries, and its houses seem to date from every period. Built on the estuary, not on the coast, the harbour flourished until the long battle against silt was finally lost in the seventeenth century. Land-reclamation has further narrowed the channel. The estuary of the Axe is a noted wildlife habitat with a variety of species attracted to the salt marshes and mudflats. When one is seated on the riverbank listening to the cry of the curlew, life seems to slow down and adopt a much more leisured pace.

Naturalists and geologists flock to this last stretch of coastline. It is the most extensive and spectacular area of landslip in England and occurred in 1839, with minor slips since. The sticky white chalk became saturated with water, its underlying rocks could not support it, and the whole mass slipped seawards, but not into the sea or even onto the beach. A wide chasm opened up, leaving one stranded area with a further distorted area of chalk beyond, over five miles in length. All this has been left largely undisturbed and over a century and a half has become a haven for wildlife; the enormous tangle of vegetation provides cover for roe deer and badgers as well as many other, more common species. A wide variety of birds are attracted to the area, and the rocks are rich in fossils.

Despite the landslip area's special status, the approaches to it are not well signposted and there are no official car-parks. A footpath traverses it from end to end but, as the Nature Conservancy Council point out, it is a long way – over six miles – with no short cuts leading back to the road or down onto the beach. It is the whole landslip or nothing. From the point of view of the geologist and naturalist, it is fascinating; walkers who are following the coastal path, of which this is a most unusual section, may not be so keen. The path is narrow, twisty, slippy and out of sight of the sea.

The coastline of Devon ends just short of the delightful Dorset resort of Lyme Regis. A low cliff, Devon Head, juts out into the sea overlooking the famous Cobb and little harbour. Without any fuss, without even any indication of a county boundary, Devon ends. An ignominious concrete post can be presumed to mark the spot.

Index

Junior ATLAS

The World in Maps

SB
Silverdale Books

Published by SILVERDALE BOOKS
An imprint of Bookmart Ltd
Registered number 2372865
Trading as Bookmart Ltd
Blaby Road
Wigston
Leicester LE18 4SE

Graham Beehag Books
Christchurch
Dorset

This edition printed 2007

ISBN 978-1-845094-36-2

The material in this book is revised and previously appeared in the series The World in Maps

Printed in Singapore

1 3 5 7 9 10 8 6 4 2

Rio de Janeiro, Brazil

CONTENTS

North America

North America is the third-largest continent after Asia and Africa. North America stretches 3,300 miles west to east from the Pacific coast of Washington State to St. John's in Newfoundland (Canada). The continent extends 3,500 miles north to south from the icy shores of the Arctic Ocean to the warm blue waters of the Gulf of Mexico. North America's total land area is more than 9.3 million square miles.

The continent is a land of contrasts, with every imaginable kind of scenery and habitat. Frozen tundra (permanently frozen ground) and dark pine forests in the far north give way to the colourful deciduous woodlands of New England and the Appalachian Mountains and then to the vast Great Plains of the American heartland. The Coast Ranges, the Rocky Mountains, and the Mexican Highlands dominate the western one-third of the continent. The southwestern states and Mexico contain some of the world's most spectacular desert scenery. The subtropical forests and swamps of the deep south and Florida and the long chain of Caribbean islands complete this kaleidoscope of landforms.

More than 400 million people live in North America. There are 298 million in the United States, 106 million in Mexico, and 32 million in Canada. More than 30 million additional people make their homes on the thousand or more islands and cays (keys) of the Caribbean.

North America is a land of stunning contrasts. People come from all over the world to see the spectacular scenery of the Grand Canyon (*below*).

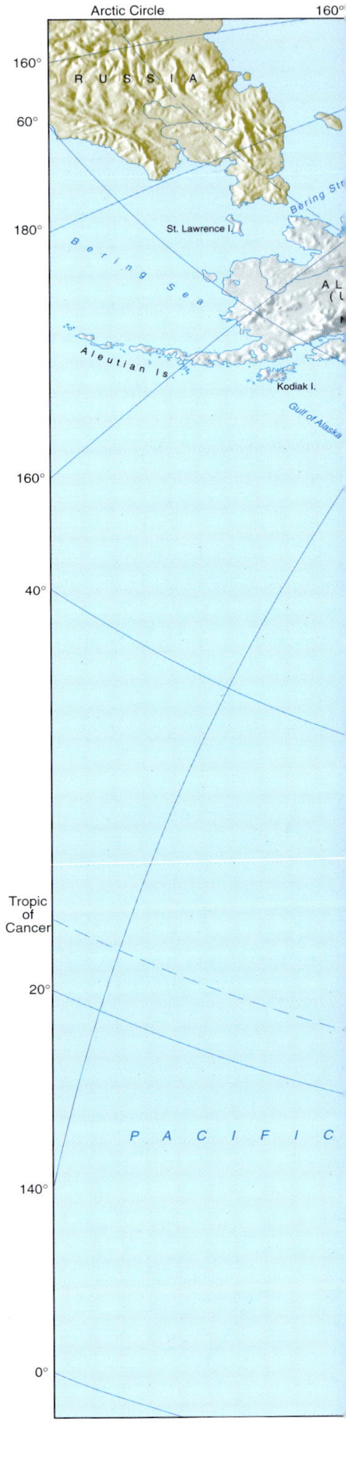

80°
80°
0°
Arctic Circle
0
500
1000
1500
2000 Miles
0
500
1000
1500
2000
2500
3000 Kms
A R C T I C
O C E A N
G R E E N L A N D
ICELAND
Ellesmere I.
Pt. Barrow
Beaufort Sea
Baffin Bay
Baffin Island
Victoria I.
Porcupine
Mackenzie
Great Bear Lake
C. Dyer
C. Farval
MACKENZIE MOUNTAINS
YUKON TERRITORY
NORTHWEST TERRITORIES
NUNAVUT
C. Chidley
Labrador Sea
Great Slave Lake
Coast Mountains
BRITISH COLUMBIA
Hudson Bay
NEWFOUNDLAND & LABRADOR
C. Bauld
Peace
ALBERTA
Athabasca
MANITOBA
Belcher Is.
Newfoundland
C. Race
R O C K Y
C A N A D A
N. Saskatchewan
SASKATCHEWAN
Q U E B E C
St. Lawrence
Prince Edward Is.
O N T A R I O
NEW BRUNSWICK
NOVA SCOTIA
S. Saskatchewan
C. Flattery
WASHINGTON
Mt. Rainier
MAINE
C. Sable
L. Superior
Missouri
NORTH DAKOTA
MINNESOTA
VERMONT
NEW HAMPSHIRE
MONTANA
MASSACHUSETTS
C. Cod
Cascade Range
OREGON
MICHIGAN
NEW YORK
RHODE ISLAND
CONNECTICUT
IDAHO
SOUTH DAKOTA
WISCONSIN
L. Ontario
WYOMING
L. Michigan
L. Erie
PENNSYLVANIA
NEW JERSEY
Sierra Nevada
NEBRASKA
IOWA
Mississippi
Platte
DELAWARE
Great Salt Lake
OHIO
WASHINGTON D.C.
C A L I F O R N I A
UNITED STATES OF AMERICA
INDIANA
WEST VIRGINIA
Coast Ranges
NEVADA
UTAH
ILLINOIS
MARYLAND
Mt. Whitney
Colorado
COLORADO
KANSAS
VIRGINIA
Arkansas
KENTUCKY
C. Hatteras
Bermuda
MISSOURI
NORTH CAROLINA
Pt. Arguello
ARIZONA
Canadian
OKLAHOMA
TENNESSEE
C. Fear
ARKANSAS
SOUTH CAROLINA
NEW MEXICO
Red
MISSISSIPPI
ALABAMA
GEORGIA
Alabama
A T L A N T I C   O C E A N
Tropic of Cancer
LOUISIANA
T E X A S
Colorado
FLORIDA
Mississippi Delta
Baja California
Pa. Falso
GULF OF CALIFORNIA
Rio Grande
M E X I C O
Eastern Sierra Madre
Western Sierra Madre
20°
BAHAMAS
Turks & Caicos Is.
Gulf of Mexico
Leeward Is.
DOMINICAN REP.
PUERTO RICO
C. San Lucas
CUBA
Caymen Is.
HAITI
Windward I.
JAMAICA
Barbados
C. Corrientes
Yucatán Peninsula
Caribbean Sea
Neth. Antilles
Trinidad & Tobago
BELIZE
Aruba
HONDURAS
GUATEMALA
EL SALVADOR
NICARAGUA
Orinoco
COSTA RICA
VENEZUELA
Apure
PANAMA
Meta
COLOMBIA
Guaviare
BRAZIL
100°
80°
60°
20°
40°
40°
20°
60°
0°
0°

The Arctic Regions

The Arctic regions consist of the Arctic Ocean and the land that nearly encircles it. The northernmost edges of Alaska, Canada, Norway, Sweden, Finland, and Russia form this land ring. Hundreds of islands and island groups called archipelagoes dot the Arctic Ocean. The largest island group, known as the Canadian Archipelago, lies off Canada's northern coast. The biggest single island is Greenland. Fewer islands—most notably Spitzbergen (part of Norway) and the three Russian island groups, Franz Josef Land, Novaya Zemlya, and the New Siberian Islands—exist on the European and Asian side of the Arctic Ocean.

Abyssal plains (very deep regions) separated by underwater mountain ranges cover much of the Arctic Ocean's floor. The deepest area is the Pole Abyssal Plain, which plunges near the North Pole to more than 15,000 feet below sea level. The Lomonosov Ridge rises to 10,000 feet and bounds the plain on one side. On the other side of the plain is the Arctic Mid-Ocean Ridge, a volcanic mountain range of molten rock rising through cracks in the seafloor. Shallow continental shelves, up to 1,000 miles wide, skirt the ocean's edge. Thick ice covers the Arctic Ocean in winter, but in summer much of the ice melts over the continental shelves, allowing boaters to reach some of the world's richest fishing grounds.

Most of the Arctic landscape is tundra—low plains covered in deep snow in winter and frozen solid for many hundreds of feet down. In summer the snow and the top layer of soil melt, turning the ground into a patchwork of muskeg and drier ground clothed in mosses, lichens, grasses, wildflowers, and small shrubs. Native peoples in the Arctic include the Inuit of North America—historically hunters of seals, whales, and walruses—and the Sami (Lapps) of Scandinavia and the Chukchi and Samoyed of northern Russia, who traditionally herd reindeer.

Selected Arctic Facts

- Nearly 1,700 different plant species grow in the Arctic. Almost 1,000 are flowering plants.
- There are about 830,000 native peoples spread across the icy lands of the Arctic regions.
- The highest spot in the Canadian Arctic is Barbeau Peak (8,544 feet) on Ellesmere Island.
- Robert Peary, Matthew Henson, and four Inuit companions are credited with being the first people to reach the North Pole, on April 6, 1909.
- In Siberia, the average temperature in January is –40°F.
- In Russia, the permafrost can extend down to 5,000 feet.
- At 5.4 million square miles, the Arctic is the smallest of the oceans. Its average depth is 4,360 feet.

About 120,000 Inuit (Eskimo) live in the Arctic regions of Canada, Alaska, Greenland, and northern Russia. Most of them live in towns and small settlements and work in the fishing, mining, oil, and construction industries. Many incorporate the old way of life—fishing, hunting seal and caribou, and travelling by dogsled.

0
1000
2000 Miles
0
1000
2000
3000 Km
PACIFIC
OCEAN
Gulf of Alaska
Bering Sea
Sea of Okhotsk
Bering Strait
ALASKA (U.S.)
CANADA
Chukchi Sea
Wrangel I.
Pt. Barrow
East Siberian Sea
Siberia
Great Bear Lake
Great Slave Lake
Beaufort Sea
New Siberian Is.
ARCTIC
OCEAN
Banks I.
McClure Strait
Victoria I.
Laptev Sea
Arctic Mid-Ocean Ridge
North Magnetic Pole
Queen Elizabeth Is.
Cape Chelyuskin
Severnaya Zemlya
North Pole
Ellesmere I.
Average permanent extent of sea ice
Foxe Basin
Lincoln Sea
Franz Josef Land
Baffin I.
Baffin Bay
Kara Sea
Novaya Zemlya
Spitsbergen
Davis Strait
GREENLAND
Greenland Sea
Barents Sea
North Cape
NORWAY
Denmark Strait
Norwegian Sea
ICELAND
FINLAND
SWEDEN
ATLANTIC OCEAN

Greenland, the Faeroe Islands, Iceland

Greenland (Kalaallit Nunaat)

Status:	Province of Denmark
Area:	840,000 square miles
Population:	58,000
Capital:	Nuuk (Godthåb)
Languages:	Greenlandic, Danish
Currency:	Danish krone (100 øre)

Greenland—in the local Greenlandic language, Kalaallit Nunaat—is the world's largest island. It is 1,650 miles long and 750 miles wide and lies to Canada's northeast. Only 16 miles from the coast of Ellesmere Island, Greenland is a self-governing province of Denmark, which is located 1,300 miles away. Many Greenlanders have both European (mainly Danish) and Inuit ancestors and most speak Greenlandic. Greenlandic place names are replacing most of the island's Danish titles.

A huge ice cap, 5,000 feet thick, covers nearly 85 percent of the island. The only permanently ice-free areas are in fjords and bays—mainly along the south-western coast, where the natural vegetation consists of grasses and clumps of birch, alder, and willow trees. The island has very little farming, but Greenlanders plant a few vegetables and grow hay to feed their cows and sheep.

Greenland's primary industries are fishing and canning of halibut, cod, shrimp, and salmon; hunting for fox, polar bear, and seals; and mining cryolite—a mineral used to make aluminium. The island also has deposits of lead, zinc, uranium, and gold.

The Faeroes are a cluster of 18 small islands between Iceland and Scotland. They, too, are a self-governing province of Denmark. The islanders make a living by fishing, raising sheep, and selling seabird eggs and feathers.

Iceland

Status:	Republic
Area:	38,707 square miles
Population:	294,000
Capital:	Reykjavík
Language:	Icelandic
Currency:	Icelandic króna (100 aurar)

Iceland lies 160 miles southeast of Greenland and 500 miles northwest of Scotland. Volcanic eruptions on the Mid-Atlantic Ridge created the island. At least 200 eruptions have occurred since the island was first inhabited 1,000 years ago. In 1963 an eruption on the seafloor near Iceland created a new island named Surtsey. Ten years later, volcanic activity destroyed part of the town of Vestmannaeyjar on nearby Heimaey Island.

Ice covers much of Iceland, but about one-fifth is rough grassland where the islanders graze cattle and sheep. Islanders produce all the meat and dairy goods needed and export wool and sheepskins. Iceland's primary industry is fishing, mainly for Atlantic cod, and 70 percent of Iceland's exports consist of fish and fish products such as fish oil and fish meal.

The island's volcanic activity creates an endless supply of geothermal energy. Steam is piped from deep underground directly to heating and electrical systems in homes and offices in the capital city of Reykjavík. This cheap energy source powers the island's main manufacturing industries—cement making and aluminium smelting (using imported bauxite, the main aluminium ore). Icelanders use geothermal energy to heat greenhouses for year-round food production.

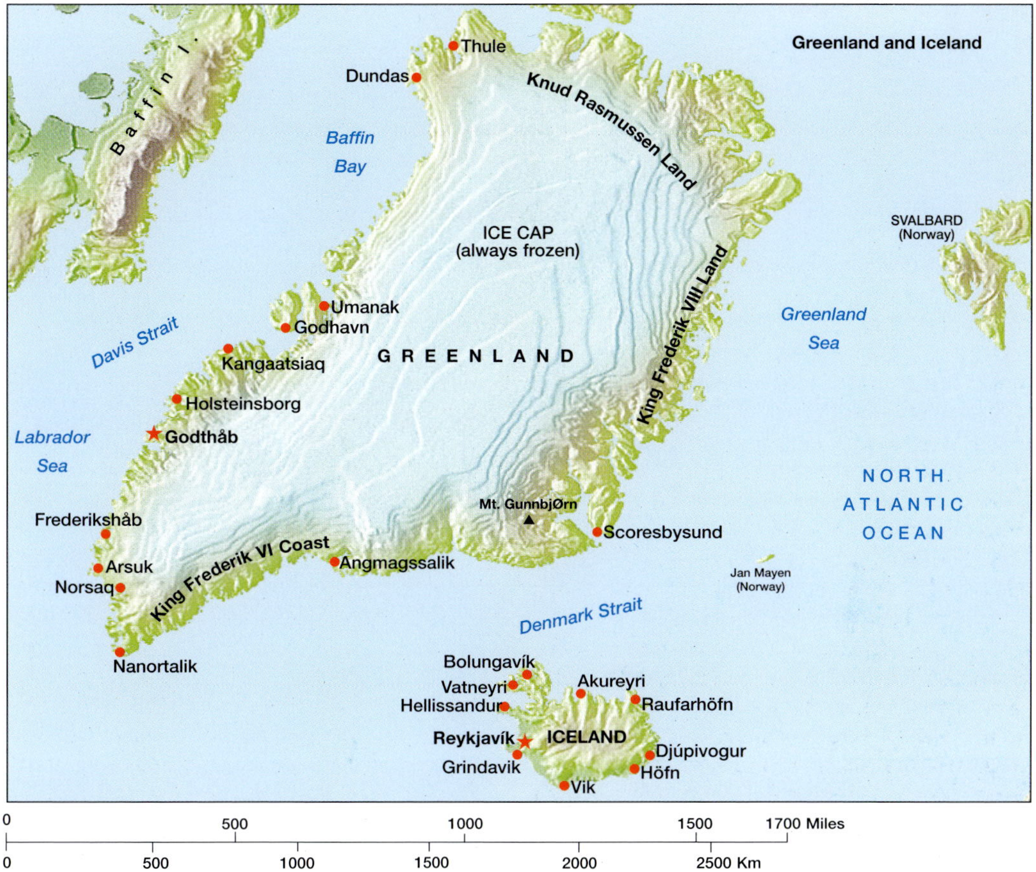

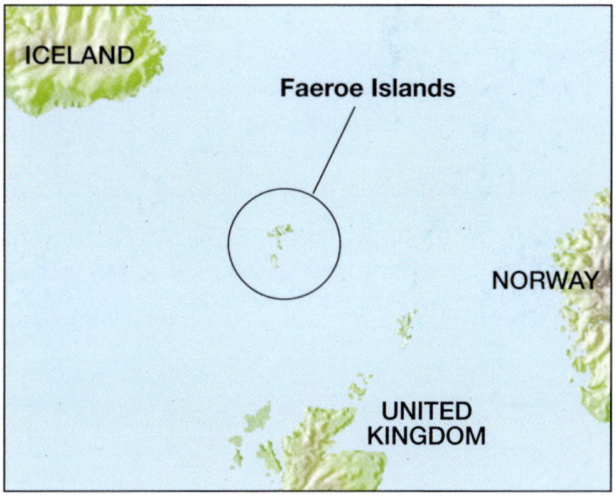

Left: The Icelandic Parliament building in Reykjavík is home to the world's oldest parliament. Called the Althing, it dates back to A.D. 930.

Canada

Canada is the world's second-largest country after Russia. This vast expanse covers more than half of North America, from Canada's shared border with the United States to the Arctic Ocean and from the Pacific Ocean (excluding Alaska) to the Atlantic shore.

Canada's far north consists of the Arctic islands and tundra of the Northwest Territories. South of the tundra lies a broad belt of dense coniferous forest dotted with lakes and crossed by the country's major rivers, such as the Fraser, the Mackenzie, the Saskatchewan, and the St. Lawrence. Continuing south the forests open to the flat open grasslands of the central prairies.

Canada's west contains some of North America's most dramatic mountain scenery. The Rocky Mountains rise to more than 13,000 feet. Beyond them are the Pacific Coast Mountains and the spectacular fjord coast of British Columbia. Low mountain ranges snake along the eastern half of the country, and gently rolling hills drop to the Great Lakes lowlands, the St. Lawrence River, Québec, and the Maritime Provinces of Newfoundland and Labrador, Nova Scotia, New Brunswick, and Prince Edward Island. The eastern region, claiming some of the most fertile farmland in Canada, is home to most of Canada's people.

An arctic climate embraces Canada's far north. Winters are long and bitterly cold. In the brief cool summer, the average temperature doesn't rise much above 50°F. On Canada's western coast, the Pacific Ocean creates a gentler, wetter climate. Winter temperatures are around 35°F, rising to 65°F in summer. The western region also receives the most rain. Winters in the eastern lowlands are long and cold with temperatures around 14°F, but the summers are much warmer, with average temperatures of 68°F.

Status:	Constitutional Monarchy and Parliamentary Democracy
Area:	3.55 million square miles
Population:	32.8 million
Capital:	Ottawa
Languages:	English and French
Currency:	Canadian dollar (100 cents)

0
500
1000
1500 Miles
0
500
1000
1500
2000 Km
Lincoln Sea
Ellesmere I.
GREENLAND
Denmark Strait
ICELAND
Devon I.
Baffin Bay
Baffin Island
Davis Strait
Cumberland Sound
Foxe Basin
Amadjuak Lake
Frobisher Bay
Southampton I.
Baker Lake
Hudson Strait
Labrador Sea
Coats I.
Mansel I.
Nain
Feuilles
Hudson Bay
Churchill
Smallwood Reservoir
Happy Valley-Goose Bay
Churchill
Nelson
Belcher Is.
La Grande
Gander
St. John's
Severn
James's Bay
Fort George
Monts Otish
Laurentien Plateau
Akimiski I.
Péribonca
Anticosti I.
Gulf of St. Lawrence
Fort Albany
St. Lawrence
Albany
Lake Winnipeg
Lake Manitoba
Lake Nipigon
Charlottetown
Québec
Fredericton
Winnipeg
St John
Halifax
Thunder Bay
Lake Superior
Montreal
Ottawa
Georgian Bay
OF AMERICA
Lake Huron
Lake Michigan
Toronto
Lake Ontario
ATLANTIC OCEAN
Lake Erie
Mississippi

Canada

Most Canadians are descended from European immigrants. First arrivals to the region were French settlers, who came in the 1760s, followed quickly by the Scots and later by the English and Irish in the 1800s. Europeans immigrated to Canada in great numbers following World War II, resulting in a population tracing its roots to Germany, Italy, Greece, Hungary, Ukraine, Poland, Norway, Sweden, and the Netherlands. Since then the bulk of immigrants has been from Southeast Asia. The largest non-English-speaking group is the French Canadians, who account for about 28 percent of the population. Nearly five million French Canadians live in French-speaking Québec. Another four million reside in the eastern half of the country. Some members of the separatist movement want an independent French-speaking Québec republic. Others simply want to preserve their French culture while remaining part of Canada. Native peoples of Canada account for about 2 percent of the population. Inuit claims to be properly recognized resulted in the new territory of Nunavut being formed in 1997.

Canada's mines produce a wide range of mineral ores, including iron, nickel, copper, zinc, molybdenum, uranium, gold, and platinum. The country also claims rich deposits of sulphur, asbestos, potash, and gypsum. These resources make Canada one of the world's largest mineral exporters.

Much of Canada is forested, and the country is a major exporter of lumber, plywood, wood pulp, paper, and cardboard. The rich prairie soils of Alberta, Saskatchewan, and Manitoba produce most of Canada's wheat, oats, barley, and rye and feed crops for large herds of beef cattle. The eastern lowlands, with their milder climate, produce corn, vegetables, fruit, tobacco, and poultry and dairy products.

0
500
1000
1500 Miles
0
500
1000
1500
2000 Km
Lincoln Sea
Ellesmere I.
Greenland Sea
GREENLAND
Denmark Strait
ICELAND
Devon I.
Baffin Bay
Baffin Island
NUNAVUT
Auyuittuq N.P.
Davis Strait
Foxe Basin
Southampton I.
Baker Lake
Hudson Strait
Coats I.
Mansel I.
Nain
NEWFOUNDLAND AND LABRADOR
Happy Valley-Goose Bay
Smallwood Reservoir
Feuilles
Hudson Bay
Churchill
Belcher Is.
La Grande
Gander
St John's
NEWFOUNDLAND AND LABRADOR
Nelson
MANITOBA
Severn
James Bay
Fort George
QUÉBEC
Anticosti I.
Akimiski I.
ONTARIO
Fort Albany
Péribonca
St. Lawrence
Gulf of St. Lawrence
Lake Winnipeg
Albany
PRINCE EDWARD I.
NEW BRUNSWICK
Charlottetown
NOVA SCOTIA
Lake Nipigon
Québec
Fredericton
St John
Halifax
Pukaskwa N.P.
Thunder Bay
Montréal
Ottawa
Lake Superior
Georgian Bay
ATLANTIC OCEAN
OF AMERICA
Lake Michigan
Lake Huron
Toronto
Lake Ontario
Lake Erie

United States of America

Status:	Federal Republic
Area:	3.53 million sq. mi.
Population:	298 million
Capital:	Washington D.C.
Language:	English
Currency:	U.S. dollar (100 cents)

The United States forms the world's third-largest country by population and the fourth-largest by size. Only China and India have more people, and only Canada, China, and Russia have greater land areas. The United States occupies the entire central section of the North American continent, as well as Alaska in the far northwest and the Hawaiian Islands in the middle of the Pacific Ocean. A 5,500-mile border separates the United States from Canada, which is America's most important trading partner. In the south, Mexico and the United States share a 1,930-mile boundary. The U.S. Pacific coastline is 1,300 miles long. The East Coast runs for nearly 3,700 miles along the Atlantic Ocean and around the Gulf of Mexico.

The country's varied climate, fertile farmlands, and vast resources of timber minerals, fossil fuels, and water power make it one of the world's richest nations. In fact, some of its 50 states are like small countries in terms of their size, their population, and the amount of food and industrial goods they produce. The United States is a federal republic, comprised of 50 states and the District of Columbia (D.C.)—where the country's government meets. In the federal system, the federal government makes decisions regarding foreign policy, defense, the justice system, health services, agricultural

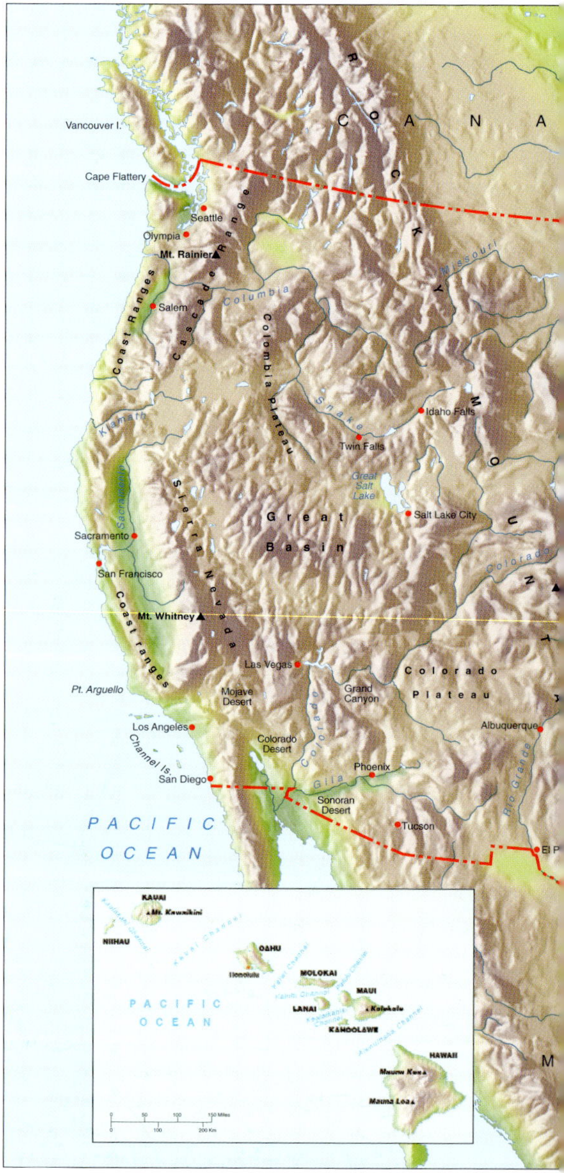

and industrial policy, and many aspects of taxation. These laws apply to the entire country. State and local governments discuss and regulate other issues such as education, public health, crime control, and local taxation.

Throughout its history, the United States has attracted immigrants from all over the world. The U.S. population mix is roughly 73 percent white—mainly of European origin—12 percent African American, 11 percent Hispanic, 3 percent Asian, and about 1 percent Native American. Nearly three-quarters of the population live in cities and towns.

United States of America

Geology and climate have created a variety of natural resources. The West Coast—a region of forested mountains and fertile valleys—has a mild climate that is wet in the north and much drier in the south. Inland from the coast lie broad valleys and basins, rising to the rugged peaks of the Rocky Mountains. This basin and range area has few people but contains valuable minerals and is a vital mining and manufacturing area. Cattle graze in the north. To the south lie the deserts of Utah, Nevada, and California.

The Great Plains east of the Rockies have relatively little rainfall, but the rain they do receive falls mainly in summer, allowing these fertile plains to produce huge quantities of grain, meat, and dairy products. New England and the Atlantic states along the East Coast are famous for their historic sites and scenery but also have rich farmland and industrial centres such as Philadelphia, Buffalo, and Pittsburgh. The southern lowlands traditionally produce cotton, tobacco, and other warm climate crops. The oil industry, manufacturing, and tourism are also essential to the economy of the south.

Opposite Left: Los Angeles, California. The city is a major seaport, the home of the movie industry, and a centre for the aviation and petroleum industries.

Opposite Right: Alaska is the largest state in area, and the smallest in number of people. Its population of 552,000 includes 85,000 Eskimo, Native Americans, and Aleuts. The main industries are tourism, forestry, fishing, mining, and oil and gas.

C A N A D A
MAINE
Bangor
Augusta
Portland
VERMONT
Burlington
Montpelier
NEW HAMPSHIRE
Concord
MASSACHUSETTS
Boston
Providence
RHODE ISLAND
Hartford
CONNECTICUT
NEW YORK
Albany
Syracuse
Rochester
Buffalo
New York
NEW JERSEY
Trenton
PENNSYLVANIA
Scranton
Harrisburg
Philadelphia
Pittsburgh
Erie
Wilmington
Dover
DELAWARE
Baltimore
Washington D.C.
Annapolis
MARYLAND
WEST VIRGINIA
Charleston
VIRGINIA
Richmond
Norfolk
Roanoke
NORTH CAROLINA
Raleigh
Greensboro
Winston-Salem
Charlotte
Wilmington
SOUTH CAROLINA
Columbia
Greenville
Charleston
GEORGIA
Atlanta
Augusta
Macon
Columbus
Albany
Savannah
FLORIDA
Tallahassee
Jacksonville
St. Augustine
Daytona Beach
Orlando
Tampa
St. Petersburg
Fort Myers
West Palm Beach
Miami
Everglades N.P.
Key West
Florida Keys
Straits of Florida
Bahamas
ATLANTIC OCEAN
Gulf of Mexico
Mississippi Delta
ALABAMA
Birmingham
Montgomery
Mobile
Pensacola
MISSISSIPPI
Jackson
Meridian
Greenville
Biloxi
LOUISIANA
Baton Rouge
New Orleans
Shreveport
Alexandria
TENNESSEE
Nashville
Knoxville
Chattanooga
Memphis
Great Smoky Mountains N.P.
Tennessee
KENTUCKY
Frankfort
Lexington
Louisville
Paducah
Evansville
OHIO
Columbus
Cleveland
Toledo
Dayton
Cincinnati
Ohio
INDIANA
Indianapolis
Gary
MICHIGAN
Lansing
Detroit
Grand Rapids
Marquette
ILLINOIS
Springfield
Chicago
Rockford
Peoria
WISCONSIN
Madison
Milwaukee
Green Bay
Eau Claire
La Crosse
MINNESOTA
St. Paul
Minneapolis
Duluth
St. Cloud
Voyageurs N.P.
IOWA
Des Moines
Cedar Rapids
Davenport
Sioux City
MISSOURI
Jefferson City
St. Louis
Kansas City
Springfield
ARKANSAS
Little Rock
Fort Smith
OKLAHOMA
Oklahoma City
Tulsa
Topeka
Salina
Wichita
Lincoln
Omaha
Grand Island
Norfolk
Sioux Falls
Aberdeen
Grand Forks
Fargo
Jamestown
TEXAS
Austin
Dallas
Fort Worth
Waco
Houston
San Antonio
Beaumont
Port Arthur
Galveston
Laredo
Corpus Christi
Brownsville
Wichita Falls
Texarkana
Lake Superior
Lake Michigan
Lake Huron
Lake Erie
Lake Ontario
Mississippi
Missouri
Red
James
Alabama

Mexico

Status:	Federal Republic
Area:	736,946 square miles
Population:	106.4 million
Capital:	Mexico City
Language:	Spanish
Currency:	Mexican Peso (100 centavos)

Mexico has a variety of topographical features. North of the capital, Mexico City, the land is dominated by two north-south mountain ranges. The western Sierra Madre has peaks rising to 11,000 feet, and the eastern Sierra Madre reaches heights of more than 13,000 feet. Between the two ranges lies the Mexican Plateau. The northern part of the plateau is dry. It merges into the desert regions that stretch north and west to the U.S. border and the 760-mile-long desert peninsula of Baja (Lower) California. The plateau's southern section hosts a milder climate with more rain, and its rich volcanic soils support much of Mexico's fertile farmland.

A narrow coastal plain runs along the Pacific Coast. A wider plain, which snakes along the Gulf Coast and goes north of the seaport of Tampico, is covered with thorn bush and scrub. South of the city, the climate is more moist, and the vegetation becomes richer as it becomes part of the tropical rain forests of southeastern Mexico. The Yucatán Peninsula, a low lime-stone region, juts into the Gulf of Mexico. Dry scrubland covers the northern peninsula, but the southern end merges with the tropical forest claiming most of the narrow Isthmus of Tehuantepec.

More highlands dominate southern Mexico. To the south of Mexico City, a range of volcanic mountains cuts across the country. This range contains Mexico's highest peak—the 18,410 foot Pico de Orizaba—and many active volcanoes, including Iztaccíhuatl and Popocatepétl, both more than 17,000 feet above sea level. The Chiapas Highlands line the Pacific Coast in the far south, stretching into the Central American nations of Guatemala and El Salvador.

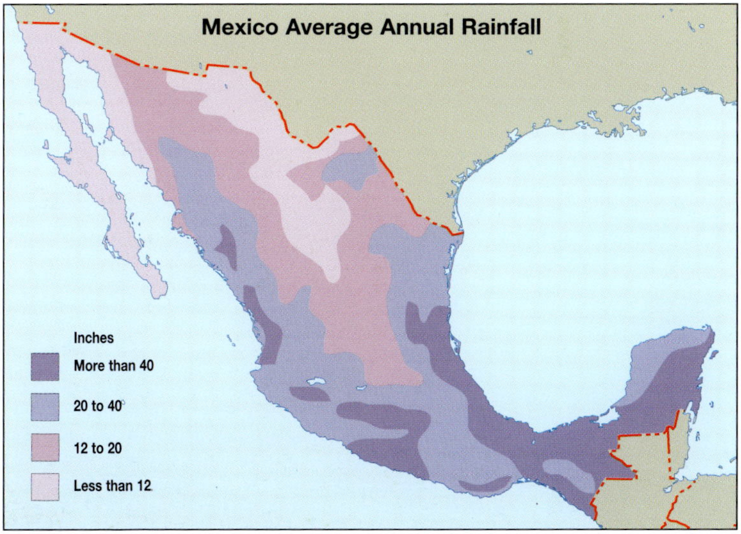

Opposite: Roughly one quarter of the Mexican people are farmers, and most of them work small farms in the highlands. Most of the country's wealth comes from its vast oil reserves and from minerals, textiles, forestry, and tourism.

Above: Mexico has hundreds of ancient monuments, such as this Mayan pyramid, and many colourful local traditions.

Mexico has a long history. By 2000 B.C., large farming villages were dotting the southern highlands. Around 1000 B.C., Mexico had sizable towns, with elaborate temples and stone carvings. And by 400 B.C., the Olmec Indians had invented the calendar and systems for writing and counting. The great empires of the Mayan, Olmec, Mixtec, Toltec, and Aztec peoples flourished for centuries. In a.d.1521, Spanish soldiers conquered the Aztecs. For the next 300 years, Spain ruled the country as one of its colonies. In fact, most modern Mexicans are mestizos—people who have both Indian and European ancestors.

Mexico gained its independence from Spain in 1821, but a century of wars and unrest followed. Successive governments have introduced land reforms and have encouraged industry, but the country still struggles with a weak economy, high unemployment, and a growing population. The birthrate is very high, and more than half the people are less than 20 years old. Poverty troubles both rural and urban areas. Mexico City has a population of more than 15 million, and five other cities have more than a million people.

Roughly one-quarter of Mexico's people make their living from farming, mainly in the southern part of the plateau and in the valleys of the south. The northern regions are so dry that farmers must irrigate their crops. The primary agricultural products are corn, wheat, coffee, cotton, and a wide variety of fruits and vegetables. Beef cattle, sheep, and goats graze in the north. Dairy cows thrive mostly in the south where the pasture is better. The eastern Sierra Madre contains rich deposits of coal and iron ore, and Monterrey is home to the iron and steel industry. Other manufacturing centres include Mexico City, Guadalajara,

Right: Veracruz, on the Gulf of Mexico, is the country's main port. It was founded in 1519 by Hernán Cortés.

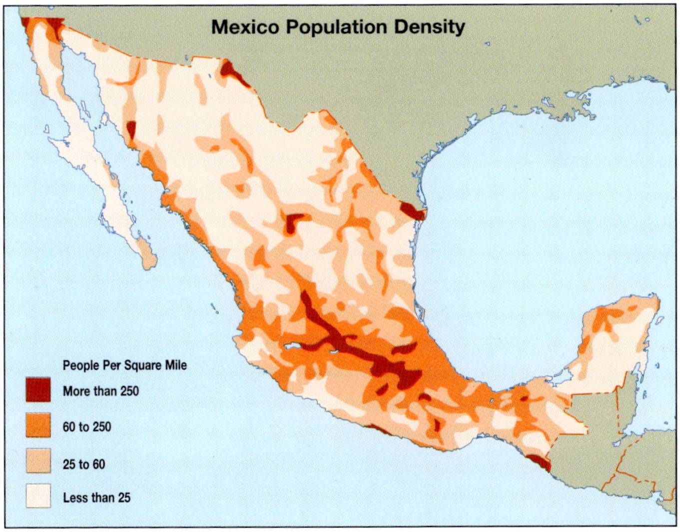

Despite improvements in fuel quality and vehicle emission standards, Mexico City's three million automobiles and thousands of trucks and buses make it still one of the world's most polluted cities.

Chihuahua, Mexicali, Puebla, Tijuana, and Veracruz. Workers produce cars, foods, beverages, chemicals, petroleum products, cement, and fertilizers. New factories built near the U.S. border manufacture car components and electrical goods for the United States. The oil industry operates from platforms in the Gulf.

Bermuda, Bahamas, Turks and Caicos Islands

Bermuda

Status:	Self-governing British Crown Colony
Area:	21 square miles
Population:	65,000
Capital:	Hamilton
Language:	English
Currency:	Bermudan dollar (100 cents)

Bermuda is a cluster of more than 300 small islands, 580 miles off Cape Hatteras, North Carolina. Most of the islands are tiny. Only 20 of them are inhabited, and the largest, Great Bermuda, is linked by bridges and causeways to the five other main islands. The islands are made of limestone—the remains of ancient coral reefs—and they are still surrounded by living reefs. The warm, mild climate, sandy beaches, pastel-coloured buildings, and profusion of wildflowers attract more than 500,000 visitors each year. Tourism is the main industry, along with banking and insurance. The islands have no rivers or lakes, so rainwater is collected from roofs and stored in underground tanks. There are a few small farms, but most of the islands' food supplies are imported.

Hamilton is the capital and chief port of Bermuda. It is a popular tourist resort, and cruise ships can tie up right alongside the city's main street, Front Street.

Turks and Caicos Islands

Status:	British Dependency
Area:	166 square miles
Population:	13,000
Capital:	Cockburn Town
Language:	English
Currency:	U.S. dollar (100 cents)

The Turks and Caicos group contains about 30 small islands located at the southeastern edge of the Grand Bahama Bank. Eight of the islands are inhabited, and the people earn their living from tourism and banking. Grand Turk, the largest island, houses an important U.S. missile tracking station.

Bahamas

Status:	Independent Nation
Area:	5,365 sq. miles
Population:	321,000
Capital:	Nassau
Languages:	English, Creole
Currency:	Bahamian dollar (100 cents)

The Bahamas consist of 27 inhabited islands and nearly 3,000 uninhabited small islands and cays. These small landforms are scattered across 90,000 square miles of limestone and coral reefs known as the Grand Bahama Bank in the western Atlantic. The islands nearest the U.S. mainland lie 60 miles off the Florida coast, while the southernmost islands in the archipelago are just 50 miles from the Caribbean island of Cuba. The Bahamas enjoy a subtropical climate, and the economy is based on tourism, sport fishing, gambling, and banking. Many historians believe that Columbus's first landfall in 1492 was on the Bahamian island of San Salvador.

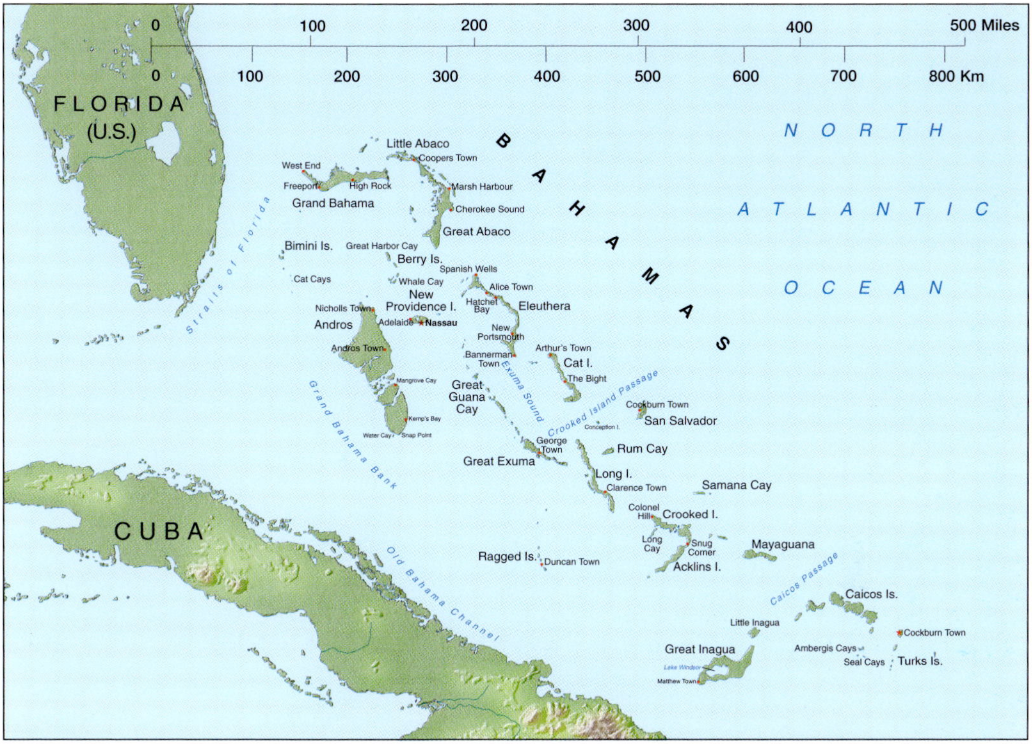

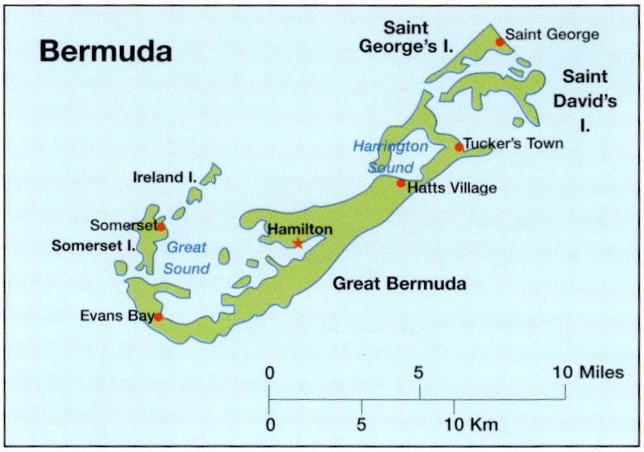

Golden beaches and subtropical vegetation make the Bahamas a vacationers' paradise.

Cuba

Status:	Socialist Republic
Area:	42,402 square miles
Population:	11.3 million
Capital:	Havana
Language:	Spanish
Currency:	Cuban peso (100 centavos)

Cuba lies 90 miles south of the tip of Florida. The largest of the Caribbean islands, Cuba is 120 miles wide and more than 750 miles long. The landscape is varied with high mountains to the west, middle, and east. Nearly three-quarters of the land consist of low rolling hills, fertile valleys, and broad plains. Cuba's climate is subtropical, with a warm dry season lasting from November to April and a mild rainy season occurring from May to October. Hurricanes frequently hit the island in the second half of the rainy season, often causing great damage to crops and buildings.

Spain ruled Cuba for nearly 400 years, but the island gained its independence in 1898. Decades of political troubles followed. For 12 years, the country had a democratic government that Fulgencio Batista overthrew in 1952. He, in turn, was ousted by Fidel Castro in 1959. President Castro's Communist government took control of the island's industries and most of the farmland. Under the Communist regime, education and health improved. Roughly 94 percent of the population can read and write, and life expectancy is 75 years.

Tobacco and coffee are grown on the higher ground, along with Cuba's main crop, sugarcane, which dominates more than half of all the cultivated land and accounts for nearly 80 percent of the island's exports. Bananas, citrus fruits, rice, tomatoes, and a wide variety of vegetables thrive on the fertile lower ground, and beef and dairy cattle graze on the rich grasslands. Fishing is another state-run industry. In addition to chromium, iron, manganese, copper, and silver, Cuba has one of the world's largest deposits of nickel. The country exports these minerals in great quantities and manufactures cement and fertilizers for export. Cuba's factories produce farm tools, paper, rum, textiles, and cigars.

Above right: Royal palms dot the sugarcane fields of the "Valley of the Sugarmills" near the old town of Trinidad on the island of Cuba.

Right: Small farms on Cuba grow tobacco, sugarcane, and fruit and sell all their produce to the government.

FLORIDA (U.S.)
NORTH ATLANTIC OCEAN
BAHAMAS
Little Abaco
Coopers Town
West End
Freeport
High Rock
Marsh Harbour
Grand Bahama
Cherokee Sound
Great Abaco
Straits of Florida
Bimini Is.
Great Harbor Cay
Berry Is.
Spanish Wells
Cat Cays
Whale Cay
Alice Town
New Providence I.
Hatchet Bay
Eleuthera
Nicholls Town
Adelaide
Nassau
Andros
New Portsmouth
Andros Town
Arthur's Town
Bannerman Town
Cat I.
Exuma Sound
The Bight
Great Guana Cay
Crooked Island Passage
Cockburn Town
San Salvador
Grand Bahama Bank
George Town
Rum Cay
Great Exuma
Long I.
Clarence Town
Samana Cay
Colonel Hill
Crooked I.
CUBA
Old Bahama Channel
Long Cay
Snug Corner
Mayaguana
Ragged Is.
Duncan Town
Acklins I.
Caicos Passage
Caicos Is.
Little Inagua
Cockburn Town
Great Inagua
Ambergris Cays
Seal Cays
Turks Is.
Little Cayman
Cayman Brac
CAYMAN ISLANDS
Grand Cayman
HISPANIOLA
HAITI
DOMINICAN REPUBLIC
Montego Bay
JAMAICA
Spanish Town
Port Antonio
Kingston
Port-au-Prince
Les Cayes
Jacmel
Bani
Barahona
0 100 200 300 400 500 Miles
0 100 200 300 400 500 600 700 Km

Havana
Matanzas
Marianao
Artemisa
Cárdenas
Sagua la Grande
Colón
Pinar del Río
Santa Clara
Guane
Aguada de Pasajeros
Caibarién
Nueva Gerona
Cienfuegos
Sancti-Spíritus
Santa Fé
Trinidad
Isla de la Juventud
Yucatan Channel
Florida
Camagüey
Jardines de la Reina
CUBA
Banes
Holguín
Manzanillo
Baracoa
Guantánamo
Santiago de Cuba
Cayman Islands
0 100 200 300 miles
0 100 200 300 400 Km

Jamaica and the Cayman Islands

Jamaica

Status:	Constitutional Monarchy
Area:	4,181 square miles
Population:	2.7 million
Capital:	Kingston
Languages:	English, Creole, Hindi, Spanish, Chinese
Currency:	Jamaican dollar (100 cents)

The third-largest of the Caribbean islands (after Cuba and Hispaniola), Jamaica is located about 100 miles south of the eastern end of Cuba. The 145-mile-long, 50-mile-wide island is mountainous, with Blue Mountain Peak rising to 7,400 feet above sea level near its eastern end. Moisture-bearing winds blowing from the west carry up to 200 inches of rain a year to the highlands, most of it falling between May and October. Jamaica's lowlands are drier, with an average of 80 inches a year.

Jamaicans are an interesting mix of people. Most are of African descent, but others are descended from British, Portuguese, Spanish, German, Indian, and Chinese immigrants. Claimed by Christopher Columbus in 1494, Jamaica was ruled by Spain until 1655, when Britain took control.

Thin soils on top of limestone make farming difficult, but sugar-cane, fruits, coffee, cacao beans, and spices do well in the fertile valleys and coastal plains. Jamaica exports much of its produce, mainly from the cities of Kingston and Montego Bay. Most of the island's income derives from tourism and from mining and exporting bauxite—the principal ore of aluminium and of alumina.

Cayman Islands

Status:	British Dependency
Area:	100 square miles
Population:	29,000
Capital:	Georgetown
Language:	English
Currency:	Cayman dollar (100 cents)

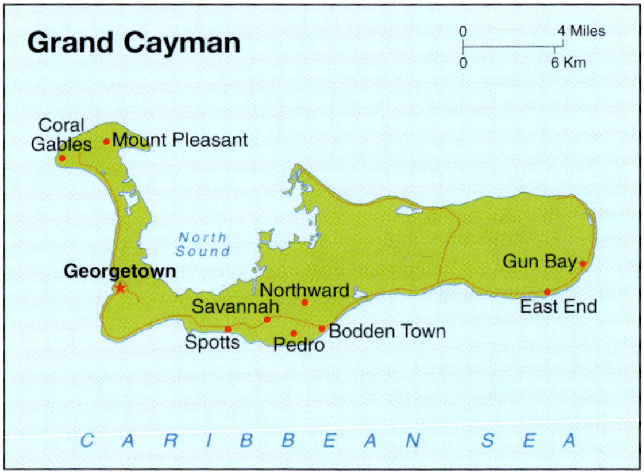

Columbus claimed the three tiny Cayman Islands for Spain in 1503, but they have been governed by Britain since 1670. About 75 percent of the people are of African descent. The rest are mainly British and American. The islands are made of limestone and are fringed by coral reefs. Temperatures range from 55°F to 95°F, and rainfall is low at around 56 inches annually. The islands support a small fishing industry, and farmers raise tomatoes, bananas, pigs, cows, and poultry. The Cayman Islands' principal businesses are finance and tourism. Very liberal tax laws have attracted the headquarters of nearly 18,000 companies and more than 400 banks. Luxury tourism and the world's most expensive beachfront real estate provide 70 percent of the islands' total income.

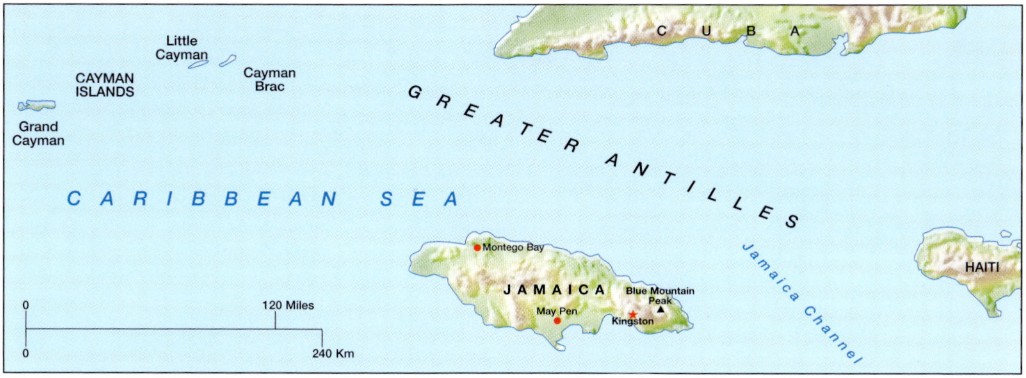

Below Left: Sugarcane is the main ingredient of rum, one of Jamaica's famous exports.

Below: Some stretches of the coast are a tourist's paradise, while others provide loading points for the bauxite carriers.

Haiti and the Dominican Republic

Haiti

Status:	Republic
Area:	10,641 square miles
Population:	8.5 million
Capital:	Port-au-Prince
Languages:	French, Creole
Currency:	Gourde (100 centimes)

Haiti makes up the westernmost one-third of the island of Hispaniola, the second-largest island in the Caribbean. Haiti is a mountainous nation, with very little farmland and few natural resources. It is also heavily populated and, as a result, is one of the poorest countries in the world. Almost two-thirds of the people just manage to make a living on small farms in the valleys and on steep hillsides or by fishing along the coast.

From 1697 until 1804, France ruled Haiti. The country gained its independence after a slave revolt, giving Haiti the distinction of being the world's oldest black republic. Nearly 200 years of turmoil followed. Among the worst periods was the brutal father-son regime of François and Jean-Claude Duvalier. It lasted from 1957 to 1986. In 1990 the first democratically elected president, Jean-Bertrand Aristide, took office but seven months later was forced into exile by supporters of the old regime. In 1994 the United States sent troops to restore democracy and to return Aristide to power. Haiti's later governments have continued to struggle for stability.

Dominican Republic

Status:	Republic
Area:	18,680 square miles
Population:	9 million
Capital:	Santo Domingo
Language:	Spanish
Currency:	Dominican Peso (100 centavos)

The Dominican Republic has fared much better than its neighbour on Hispaniola. The land is dominated by mountains, including the highest peak in the Caribbean, the 10,414 foot Duarte Peak. But the country also has fertile valleys, lowlands, and coastal plains. The climate is tropical, with average temperatures around 77°F, and ample rainfall, especially in the summer.

The Dominican Republic produces sugarcane, coffee, rice, and tobacco, as well as cacao beans, fruits, and vegetables. In rural areas, most people farm small holdings, producing enough for their families and a small surplus to sell in the local markets. In the lowland areas, privately owned estates employ large numbers of workers in the sugarcane fields and coffee and cacao plantations. Mineral exports include bauxite, nickel, silver, and gold. The Dominican Republic is also developing its tourist industry by building resorts along the northern coast. Visitors increased from 5,000 to 65,000 between 1987 and 1990, and numbers continue to rise. Most of the tourists are from Canada, the United States, and Europe.

Big hydroelectric projects can sometimes be environmental disasters. When this dam was built at Pelgré in Haiti, the surrounding forests were cut down. With no trees to protect them, the hillside soils were soon washed away by the heavy rains, and the reservoir was clogged with silt.

Troops patrol the streets in Haiti after a disturbance. Political unrest is common in countries where a few people hold most of the wealth, while the rest struggle to survive in poor housing, with not enough food or adequate medical services.

Puerto Rico

Status:	Self-governing U.S. Commonwealth
Area:	3,421 square miles
Population:	3.9 million
Capital:	San Juan
Languages:	Spanish, English
Currency:	U.S. dollar (100 cents)

Puerto Rico is about 100 miles long and 35 miles wide. It is mountainous, with a narrow coastal plain, so agricultural land is scarce. The best land is used for growing sugarcane, coffee, bananas, tobacco, tropical fruits, and spices. The climate is tropical, creating good growing conditions on the moist northeastern side of the island, but the island lies in the track of Atlantic hurricanes and often suffers devastating storms.

Since a referendum (a public vote) in 1952, Puerto Rico has been a self-governing commonwealth of the United States. The island creates its own laws, as long as they don't conflict with those of the United States, and its people can travel freely to the mainland. Puerto Ricans can vote in U.S. presidential primaries but not in the actual elections. The government of Puerto Rico is based on that of the United States, with a Senate, a House of Representatives, and a president who is elected every four years. Health and education have improved faster than anywhere else in the Caribbean. Free medical and dental care is available to everyone, life expectancy has increased from 46 years to 74, and 90 percent of the population can read and write.

Compared to most other Caribbean islands, Puerto Rico is heavily industrialized, and a large proportion of the people make their homes in urban areas. Nearly half the population lives in or around the capital, San Juan, working in factories that produce textiles, clothing, electrical goods, leather goods, and processed foods. More than 85 percent of the country's exports and 65 percent of its imports are with the United States. Other major employers are the huge petroleum refinery and chemical works on the southwestern coast; the mining and smelting of copper; and the growing tourist industry.

Opposite: An aerial view shows one of the large rum distilleries in San Juan, Puerto Rico. Rum—made from sugarcane—is one of the traditional exports of the Caribbean.

Right: Puerto Rico's lowlands are mainly farmed, but the inland areas still contain large tracts of untouched tropical rain forest.

Below: Puerto Rico has one of the fastest-growing economies in the Caribbean. The country's success is shown by the modern buildings in Hato Rey—San Juan's financial district.

Leeward Islands

The Leeward Islands form the northern section of the long island arc known as the Lesser Antilles, which stretches from just east of Puerto Rico to the coast of South America. The Leeward Islands extend from the Virgin Islands to Guadeloupe, while the Windward Islands continue the island chain almost to the coast of Venezuela. The Leeward and Windward Islands are the tops of a chain of submarine volcanoes that mark the line on the seabed where two sections of the earth's rocky crust meet. They form a natural breakwater of islands and coral reefs separating the Caribbean Sea from the Atlantic Ocean.

The Leeward group contains about 15 main islands and hundreds of small islets. It totals roughly 1,500 square miles and is home to about 700,000 people. The Leeward Islands contain two independent countries, as well as several dependencies of the United States, Britain, France, and the Netherlands.

The islands have warm, dry, tropical climates, with temperatures around 80°F for most of the year and total annual rainfall of 30 to 40 inches. Local farmers grow tobacco, cotton, sugarcane, and a wide variety of fruits and vegetables. Tourism is essential to most of the islands' economies.

0
500
1000 Miles
0
500
1000
1500 Km
ATLANTIC
OCEAN
BAHAMAS
Andros I.
Turks & Caicos Is.
Great Inagua I.
CUBA
HAITI
DOMINICAN REPUBLIC
PUERTO RICO
LEEWARD ISLANDS
VIRGIN IS.
Anguilla
Barbuda
Saint Kitts & Nevis
Antigua
Montserrat
Guadeloupe
Marie Galante
Dominica
Martinique
Saint Lucia
BARBADOS
Saint Vincent
WINDWARD ISLANDS
Grenada
TOBAGO
TRINIDAD
GREATER ANTILLES
JAMAICA
CARIBBEAN SEA
LESSER ANTILLES
Netherlands Antilles
VENEZUELA
COLOMBIA
Gulf of Panama
BRAZIL

Leeward Islands

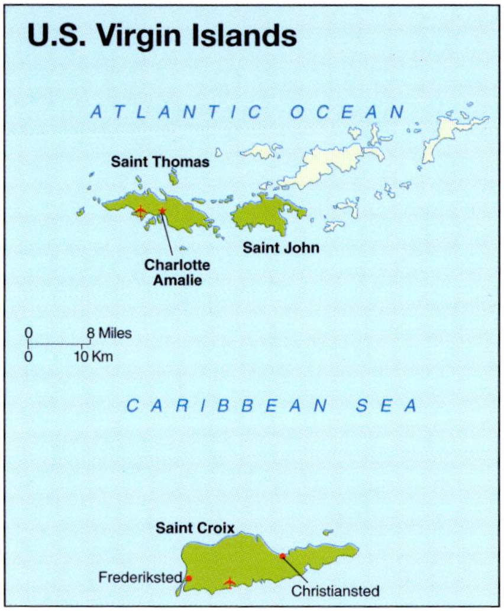

U.S. Virgin Islands

Status:	Self-governing U.S. Territory
Area:	130 square miles
Population:	102,000
Capital:	Charlotte Amalie (on Saint Thomas)
Language:	English
Currency:	U.S. dollar (100 cents)

U.S. Virgin Islands

Most of the population of this island group lives on the largest islands—Saint Thomas, Saint Croix, and Saint John—but the territory also covers 65 smaller islands. Residents are U.S. citizens. Tourism is the primary industry, but Saint Croix also has oil refineries and bauxite processing plants.

Antigua and Barbuda

Status:	Constitutional Monarchy
Area:	170 square miles
Population:	68,000
Capital:	Saint John's (on Antigua)
Language:	English
Currency:	Eastern Caribbean dollar (100 cents)

British Virgin Islands

Status:	British Dependency
Area:	59 square miles
Population:	18,000
Capital:	Road Town (on Tortola)
Language:	English
Currency:	U.S. dollar (100 cents)

British Virgin Islands

This British island group contains 4 main islands and 36 smaller ones. About 75 percent of the people live on the largest island, Tortola. The islands receive more than 325,000 visitors each year and are a popular tax haven. Rum is the main export.

Antigua and Barbuda

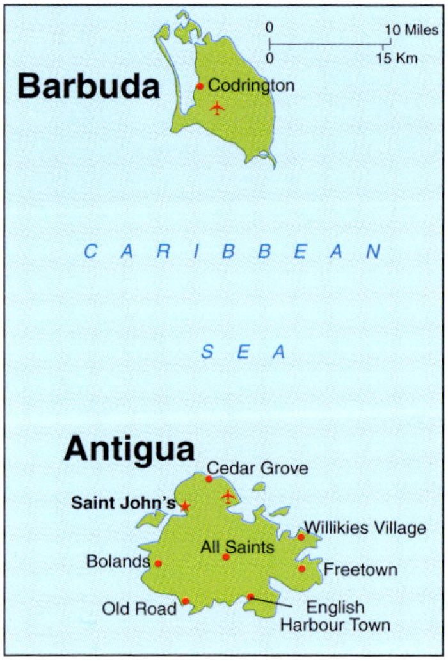

Antigua is hilly and rugged, made of volcanic rocks that create good soils in the valleys and lowlands. Barbuda is a low, mainly wooded coral island. Tourism is important, in addition to fishing (especially for lobster), market gardening, and Sea Island cotton production.

Saint Kitts and Nevis

These twin volcanic islands feature peaks of more than 3,000 feet above sea level that are covered with lush tropical rain forests. The lowlands are fertile and are used mainly for growing sugarcane, cotton, and tropical fruits. Tourism is the biggest industry, but the islands also produce textiles, leather, and electronic goods.

Montserrat

Rugged and hilly with dense forests, Montserrat is famous for its volcanic eruptions. Volcanic rocks provide fertile soils and dark-coloured sandy beaches. Tourism supplies one-quarter of the island's income, but Montserrat also exports Sea Island cotton, tropical fruits and vegetables, and manufactured electrical goods.

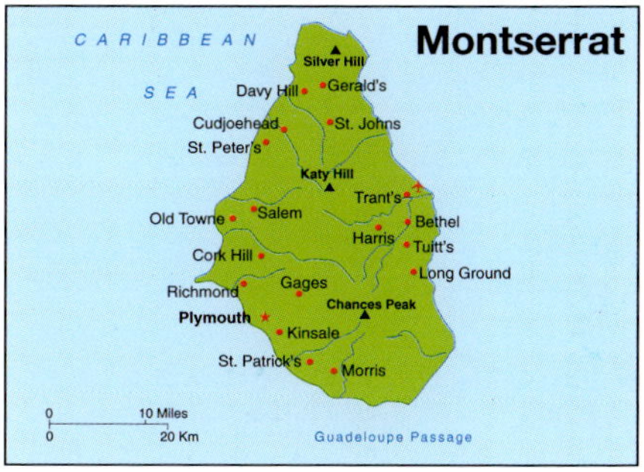

Anguilla

This long, thin coral island is very flat—rising only to 200 feet above sea level. Low rainfall and poor soil hamper farming. The main crops are peas, beans, corn, and sweet potatoes. Anguilla's economy relies mostly on tourism and on exporting lobsters. Many of the island's most beautiful reefs have been damaged by removing coral to sell as tourist souvenirs.

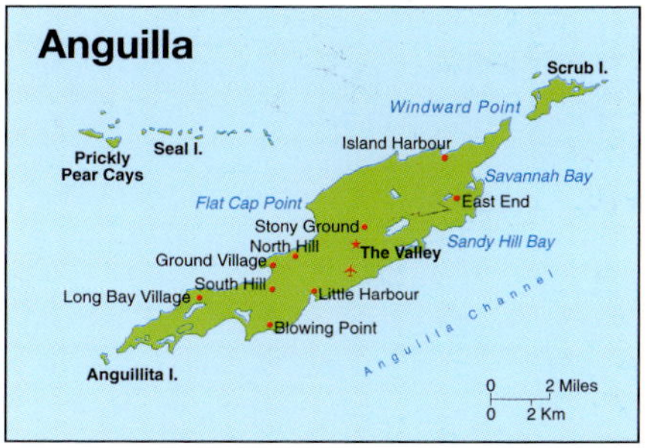

Guadeloupe

Guadeloupe is a group of eight islands, the two largest being mountainous and volcanic Basse-Terre and lower Grand-Terre. The islands export sugar, bananas, and rum but depend heavily on aid from France.

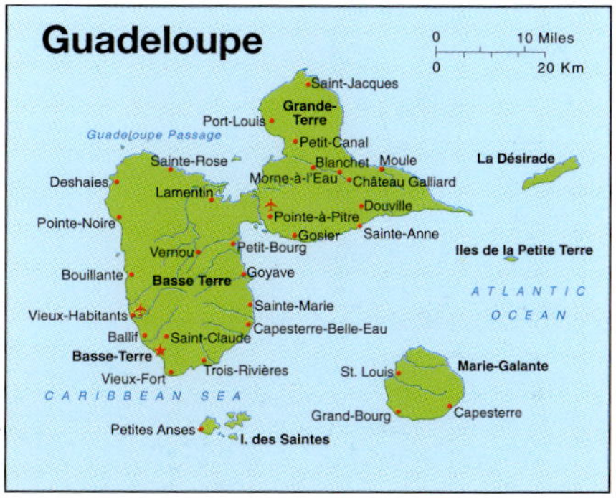

35

Windward Islands and Barbados

From north to south, Dominica, Martinique, Saint Lucia, Saint Vincent and the Grenadines, and Grenada make up the Windward Island group. Barbados, lying about 40 miles to the east, is considered a separate island because it is not geologically connected to the Windward Island chain. Total land area of the Windward Islands is approximately 1,000 square miles, and the population numbers roughly 720,000.

Like the Leeward Islands to the north, Arawak Indians originally inhabited the Windward group, which Europeans (mainly British and French) settled on in the early 1600s. Martinique has remained a French possession, while the other territories became British colonies and later gained their independence. Years of migration has resulted in a population of mainly African descent, with small numbers of immigrants from Europe and North and South America.

Some of the smaller islands are composed of limestone and coral and therefore have very thin and infertile soils. These islands rely mainly on tourism. The larger islands are volcanic, and their mountainous interiors are covered in dense forests. The volcanic rocks produce rich soils that collect in the valleys and coastal plains, providing good farmland. Primary agricultural products are bananas, cacao beans, sugarcane, arrowroot, nutmeg, and mace. Tourism is generally the most important source of income.

0
500
1000 Miles
0
500
1000
1500 Km
A T L A N T I C
O C E A N
BAHAMAS
Andros I.
Turks & Caicos Is.
Great Inagua I.
CUBA
HAITI
DOMINICAN REPUBLIC
PUERTO RICO
VIRGIN IS.
LEEWARD ISLANDS
Anguilla
Barbuda
Saint Kitts & Nevis
Antigua
Montserrat
Guadeloupe
Marie Galante
Domínica
Martinique
Saint Lucia
BARBADOS
Saint Vincent
Grenada
WINDWARD ISLANDS
TOBAGO
TRINIDAD
GREATER ANTILLES
JAMAICA
LESSER ANTILLES
CARIBBEAN SEA
Netherlands Antilles
VENEZUELA
COLOMBIA
BRAZIL
Gulf of Panama

Windward Islands, Barbados

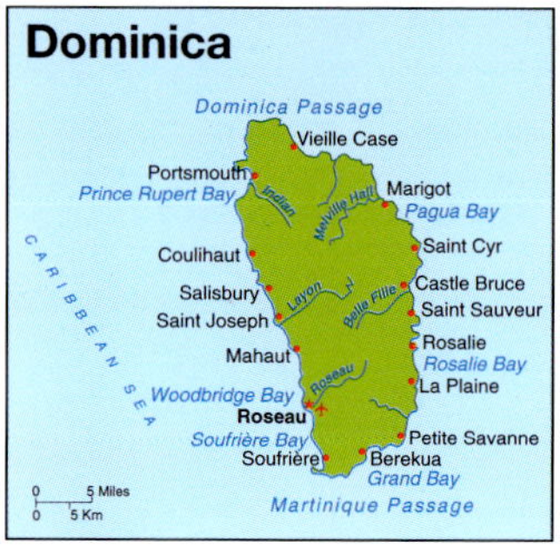

Status:	Republic
Area:	290 sq. mi.
Population:	71,000
Capital:	Roseau
Languages:	English, French patois
Currency:	Eastern Caribbean dollar (100 cents)

Status:	Overseas Department of France
Area:	409 sq. mi.
Population:	400,000
Capital:	Fort-de-France
Languages:	French, Creole
Currency:	French franc (100 centimes)

Status:	Constitutional Monarchy
Area:	236 sq. mi.
Population:	152,000
Capital:	Castries
Languages:	English, French patois
Currency:	Eastern Caribbean dollar (100 cents)

Dominica

The island is mountainous, volcanic, and densely forested. Its climate is hot, averaging 80°F, and wet, with 70 inches of rain falling annually on the coast and well over 200 inches blanketing the hills. A small tourist industry exists, but the islanders primarily support themselves by exporting bananas, coconuts, oranges, and grapefruits—mainly to the United States and Britain.

Martinique

Martinique's highest peak is the volcano Mont Pelée (4,583 feet above sea level), which erupted in 1902, engulfing the town of Saint-Pierre and killing 30,000 people. Farmers grow tropical fruits for export and vegetables for local use. Other islanders work in tourism and in the oil refineries, rum distilleries, and sugar-processing factories.

Saint Lucia

Saint Lucia is mountainous, with dense forests and deep, fertile valleys. About one-third of its people work in agriculture—producing bananas, cacao beans, and copra for export. Light industries operate in the free-trade zone at Vieux Fort, a deepwater port for transferring oil between tankers. Cruise ships dock at the modern harbour of the city of Castries.

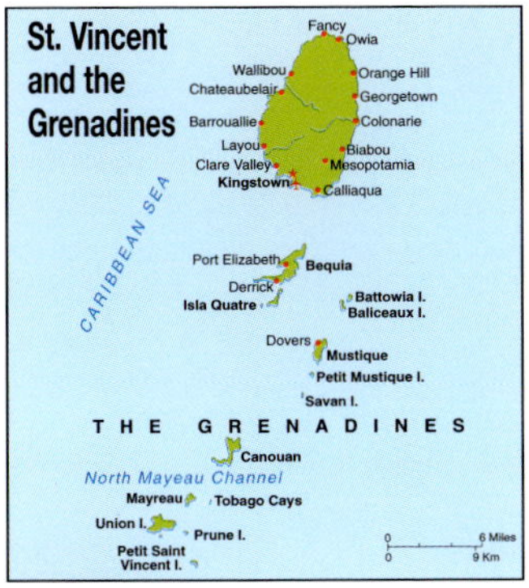

Status

Status:	Commonwealth Nation
Area:	151 sq. mi.
Population:	121,000
Capital:	Kingstown
Languages:	English, French patois
Currency:	Eastern Caribbean dollar (100 cents)

Saint Vincent and the Grenadines

This small country consists of the island of St. Vincent and the northern-most islands of the Grenadines group, including Union and Bequia. Bananas and arrowroot are the primary export crops. Tourism is essential to the economy, and some of the smaller islands are the lavish hideaways of the world's wealthy.

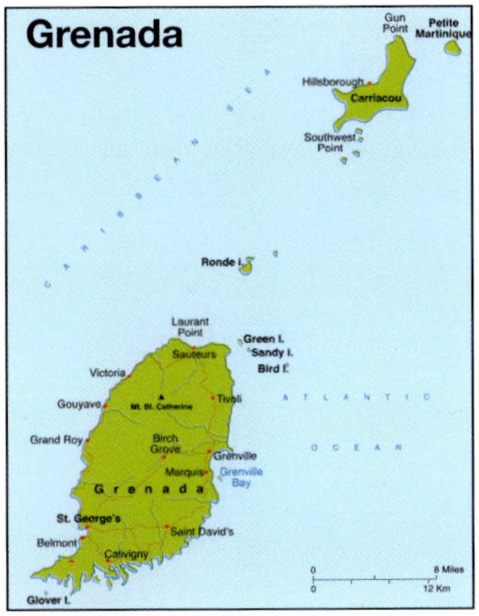

Status:	Commonwealth Nation
Area:	131 sq. mi.
Population:	103,000
Capital:	St. George's
Languages:	English, French patois
Currency:	Eastern Caribbean dollar (100 cents)

Grenada

An independent nation since 1974, this island country includes the island of Grenada and the southern islands of the Grenadines, the largest of which is Carriacou. Grenada is the world's foremost producer of nutmeg and mace. Other exports include bananas, citrus fruits, and cacao beans.

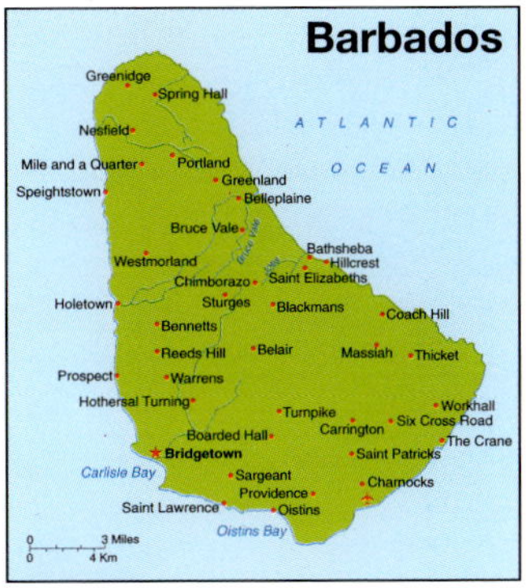

Status:	Commonwealth Nation
Area:	166 sq. mi.
Population:	272,000
Capital:	Bridgetown
Languages:	English
Currency:	Barbados dollar (100 cents)

Barbados

Barbados has a warm, pleasant climate that supports a growing tourist industry. Nearly 500,000 visitors a year come mainly from the United States and Britain. Sugar, and sugar products such as molasses and rum, are important agricultural exports, but the island is also developing new industries such as banking and data processing. Barbados is one of the most densely populated countries in the world but has good health and educational systems.

The Netherlands Antilles, Aruba, Trinidad and Tobago

The Netherlands Antilles consists of two groups of islands 500 miles apart. The two largest islands, Curaçao and Bonaire, lie about 50 miles off the coast of the South American nation of Venezuela. The other territory lies at the northern end of the Leeward Islands, about 160 miles east of Puerto Rico. Comprised of the southern part of Saint Martin Island and the islands of Saba and Saint Eustatius, the Netherlands Antilles is a self-governing entity of the Kingdom of the Netherlands.

Trinidad and its tiny companion Tobago lie a few miles off the coast of Venezuela. The islands have high mountains in the north and lower ranges of hills across the central and southern regions. Between these highlands sit broad plains and swamps. Nearly half the island nation is forest. Islanders grow sugarcane, coffee, cacao beans, rubber, and tropical fruits for export, but the islands' main wealth comes from oil and natural gas and from the petrochemical industries based on those resources. Trinidad is also the world's largest source of asphalt—a thick, tarry substance used internationally for paving roads. Food processing, cement making, and textiles are other major employers.

Aruba sits 48 miles west of Curaçao and until 1986 was also part of the Netherlands Antilles. The island was scheduled to achieve full independence in 1996, but the people chose instead to remain a self-governing part of the Kingdom of the Netherlands. Many Arubans and citizens of the Netherlands Antilles work in tourism, banking, and other financial services, all of which are essential island industries. The islands have no mineral resources and no industries apart from local crafts. Local businessowners operate refineries that process Venezuelan oil for export, mainly to the Netherlands. Other mineral exports include phosphates from Curaçao and salt from Bonaire. The islands are not very fertile, growing only sorghum, groundnuts, aloes, and tropical fruits.

Status:	Self-governing Region of the Kingdom of the Netherlands
Area:	309 sq.miles
Population:	200,000
Capital:	Willemstad
Languages:	Dutch, English, Spanish, and Papiamento
Currency:	Guilder (100 cents)

Netherlands Antilles

Nearly 80 percent of the population lives on the largest island, Curaçao. The standard of living is high, with efficient health services and schools and almost 100-percent literacy. The soils are too poor for large-scale farming, but tourism, banking, and industries ensure a high rate of employment.

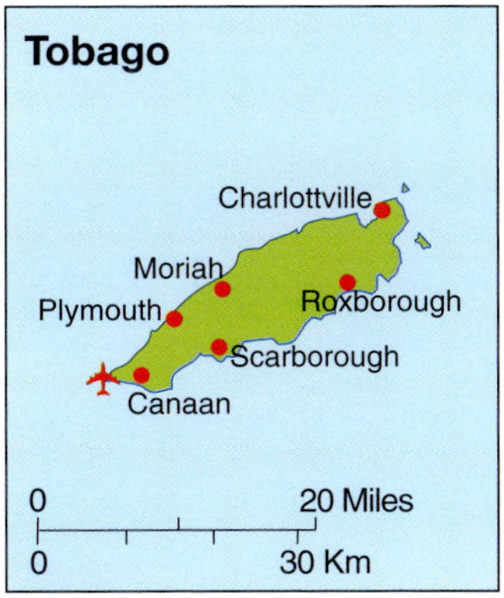

Trinidad and Tobago

Trinidad's population is 43 percent Afro-Caribbean, 40 percent East Indian, and 16 percent mixed background. Settlers from Europe, China, the Middle East, and elsewhere comprise the other 1 percent. This blend reflects the island's colonial past, when huge plantations produced sugarcane for Spanish, French, and British owners. The economy combines agriculture, tourism, financial services, and petrochemical industries.

Aruba

Almost half the people of Aruba are descended from the Arawak Indians, the island's original inhabitants. On most Caribbean islands, the Indians were wiped out by European settlers or by the diseases they brought to the islands. The modern Aruban economy depends on oil refining, fertilizer production, food exports, and tourism.

Central and South America

Seven countries—Belize, Guatemala, Honduras, El Salvador, Nicaragua, Costa Rica, and Panama—occupy the isthmus of Central America, a narrow strip of land joining North and South America. A total land area of 201,000 square miles supports about 35 million people. A volcanic mountain chain stretches 800 miles along the west side of the isthmus from Mexico to Panama, with peaks rising to 12,000 feet. Lowland plains of dense rain forest cover the eastern coast, which is frequently struck by hurricanes that sweep in from the Caribbean Sea.

The Mayan civilization, which had developed great cultural and economic advances, occupied part of Mexico and Central America for 1,500 years. Spanish invaders conquered this remarkable people in the 1520s and ruled Central America for 300 years. In 1823 five of the countries merged into a federation but disbanded in 1838. In the intervening years, Central America has suffered bitter conflicts between rich and poor and a succession of military dictatorships, revolutions, and wars.

The continent of South America stretches 4,600 miles from north to south and 3,200 miles from west to east. It covers an area of 6,898,579 square miles and has a population of more than 339 million. The Andes—the world's longest mountain chain—and the world's mightiest river, the Amazon, dominate the landscape. South America's climate and vegetation zones range from the rain forests of Brazil, through savanna and scrub in Paraguay and northern Argentina, to Chile's Atacama Desert—the driest place on earth.

The continent is rich in mineral resources. Exports include iron ore, manganese, copper, silver, mercury, gold, and emeralds, as well as the nitrates and phosphates used to make fertilizers. South America has very little coal, which has limited heavy industrialization in most countries. Oil and hydroelectric power are the primary sources of energy. South America exports hardwoods, beef, coffee, maize, cacao beans, cotton, and fresh fruits and vegetables, mostly to the United States.

Sugarloaf Mountain (Pão de Açúcar) is a towering rock landmark rising 1,300 feet above the blue waters of Guanabara Bay, Rio de Janeiro. Visitors who take the six minute cable-car ride to the top enjoy spectacular views of the city.

Caribbean Sea
LESSER ANTILLES
COSTA RICA
PANAMA
Gulf of Panama
Barranquilla
Maracaibo
Lake Maracaibo
Caracas
Port-of-Spain
TRINIDAD & TOBAGO
VENEZUELA
Orinoco
Guiana Highlands
GUYANA
Georgetown
Paramaribo
SURINAME
FRENCH GUIANA
Cayenne
NORTH ATLANTIC OCEAN
C. Corrientes
Medellín
Bogotá
Cali
Huila
COLOMBIA
Quito
Chimborazo
Guayaquil
ECUADOR
Putumayo
Japurá
Negro
Branco
Macapá
Marajó I.
Belém
Amazon
Manaus
São Luís
Fortaleza
Tocantins
Xingu
Tapajós
Madeira
Purus
Juruá
Marañón
Pta. Negra
Caatingas
Cape São Roque
Recife
ANDES MOUNTAINS
Huascarán
Selvas
PERU
Lima
BRAZIL
Sobradinho Reservoir
Parnaíba
Araguaia
Arinos
Guaporé
Mamoré
Salvador
Brazilian Highlands
São Francisco
Plateau De Mato Grosso
Brasília
Campos
Lake Titicaca
Illampu Peak
La Paz
BOLIVIA
Arica
Altiplano
Lake Poopó
Atacama Desert
Chaco
PARAGUAY
Paraná
Antofagasta
Llullaillaco Volcano
CHILE
Pilcomayo
Asunción
Itaipu Res.
São Paulo
C. Frio
Rio de Janeiro
Tropic of Capricorn
Serra do Mar
Cerro Ojos del Salado
Gran Chaco
Salado
Uruguay
SOUTH ATLANTIC OCEAN
L. Mar Chiquita
Pôrto Alegre
Lagoa dos Patos
ARGENTINA
URUGUAY
Lagoa Mirim
Rosario
Buenos Aires
Montevideo
Río de La Plata
Mount Aconcagua
Santiago
Pampas
P. Sur del Cabo San Antonio
PACIFIC OCEAN
Colorado
Bahía Blanca
Blanca Bay
Negro
San Matías Gulf
P. Valdés
Chiloé I.
Chubut
Archipelego de Los Chonos
L. Buenos Aires
San Jorge Gulf
C. Tres Puntas
FALKLAND Is. (ISLAS MALVINAS)
West Falkland
East Falkland
Grande Bay
Archipelago Reina Adelaide
Strait of Magellan
Punta Arenas
Tierra del Fuego
C. San Diego
Cape Horn
SCOTIA SEA
South Georgia
Central America
MEXICO
BELIZE
GUATEMALA
HONDURAS
EL SALVADOR
NICARAGUA
COSTA RICA
PANAMA
Caribbean Sea
Gulf of Mexico
PACIFIC OCEAN
80° 70° 60° 50° 40°
10° 0° 10° 20° 30° 40° 50°
90° 80° 70° 60° 50° 40° 30° 20°
0 500 1000 1500 2000 Miles
0 500 1000 1500 2000 2500 3000 Km

Belize

Status:	Constitutional Monarchy and Parliamentary Democracy
Area:	8,865 square miles
Population:	266,000
Capital:	Belmopan
Languages:	English, Spanish, Mayan
Currency:	Belize dollar (100 cents)

This former British colony changed its name from British Honduras to Belize in 1973 and became a fully independent nation in 1981. British troops remained in Belize until 1994 as protection from a possible invasion by neighbouring Guatemala. The troops were withdrawn when Guatemala recognized Belize as a sovereign state.

Belize is a small country with forest-covered mountains in the south and patchy savanna and forest in the north, dotted with lakes and marshes. The country has a swampy coastal plain, and the coral reef that lies offshore is the world's second longest after Australia's Great Barrier Reef. More than half the population lives along the coast, 50,000 of them in Belize City, the former capital. In 1970 Belizeans built a new capital city, Belmopan, 50 miles inland—safe from the hurricanes that frequently hit the coast.

Belize City is the country's principal port, exporting tropical hardwoods, coconuts, bananas, sugarcane, and fresh fish and lobsters from the local fisheries—products accounting for 65 percent of Belize's foreign trade. Tourism continues its rapid expansion, contributing to the country's foreign exchange. To lessen tourism's impact, the government has set aside some coastal land as conservation areas to protect the fragile mangrove forests and reefs from hotel and road construction and other developments.

Guatemala

Status:	Republic
Area:	42,042 square miles
Population:	13 million
Capital:	Guatemala City
Languages:	Spanish, Amerindian languages
Currency:	Quetzal (100 centavos)

Guatemala's landscape is distinguished by three major land regions. The Petén region in the northeast is a flat, low, limestone plateau covered in tropical forests, which hide impressive Mayan ruins. Not many people inhabit this remote area, but the government is encouraging logging and new farming settlements—a plan Guatemalan conservation groups oppose.

Most of Guatemala's population live in the highlands in the southern half of the country. The climate there is cooler, and rainfall is moderate. Farmers grow coffee on the lower hillsides (up to about 5,000 feet) and plant maize and beans at the higher elevations. Cardamom, a valuable spice, is an important crop along the southern edge of the highlands. This region also contains the country's main urban centres, including the national capital, Guatemala City.

Guatemala's third region, the Pacific coastal plain, boasts fertile volcanic soil and an abundance of water tumbling from the Sierra Madre range. Coastal farmers produce fruits, vegetables, cotton, sugarcane, rice, and beef for both local use and export.

Cash-poor and heavily populated, Guatemala supplements its agriculturally based economy with the mining of oil, nickel, lead, and zinc. Industrial workers produce processed foods, clothing, textiles, and traditional crafts for export.

Huge stepped pyramids with wide, steep, stone stairways are typical of the Mayan ruins hidden in the forests of northern Guatemala's Petén region and Mexico's Yucatán Peninsula.

Honduras

Status:	Republic
Area:	43,278 square miles
Population:	7.2 million
Capital:	Tegucigalpa
Languages:	Spanish, Indian languages
Currency:	Lempira (100 centavos)

Most of Honduras is mountainous, with several western peaks that rise to more than 8,000 feet. Oak and pine forests cover the foothills. Evergreen cloud forests grace the higher elevations. Nearly 60 percent of Hondurans live in small, scattered highland communities. Most are peasant farmers who own or rent small plots of land and produce just enough food for themselves, with a little extra to sell in local markets.

Narrow lowland plains run along the country's short Pacific coast and its longer Caribbean coast. Rich volcanic soil on the Pacific coastal plain supports large farms and cattle ranches. Farmers on the northern coast grow an abundance of bananas, which account for more than 30 percent of the country's exports. Honduras's only railroads snake through the northwestern coastal region, carrying bananas from the plantations to the port of Puerto Cortés. Coffee, sugarcane, beef, timber, and shrimp comprise the country's other major exports. Farmers grow maize and beans for local use.

Honduras has built few roads, and the interior of the country is largely undeveloped. Schools are few, especially in rural areas, and more than 40 percent of the population cannot read or write. About 15 percent of the people work in food processing, textile, furniture, and paper factories—industries situated in Tegucigalpa and San Pedro Sula, the country's two largest cities. Honduras abounds in minerals. Workers have mined only a small portion of the country's resources, such as silver, gold, lead, zinc, and cadmium.

Military dictators ruled Honduras for much of this century until 1981 when the Honduran people elected their first civilian government. It and the succeeding goverments have pledged to improve the country's living standards.

El Salvador

Status:	Republic
Area:	8,125 square miles
Population:	6.7 million
Capital:	San Salvador
Languages:	Spanish
Currency:	Colón (100 centavos)

El Salvador, the smallest of the Central American countries, has the third-largest population after Guatemala and Honduras. Nearly three-quarters of its people live in the country's central region—a wide rolling plateau with average temperatures of 73°F and about 45 inches of annual rain. Farms and ranches scattered across the plateau employ nearly half of El Salvador's workers. Small family farms grow beans, rice, maize, and other crops for home consumption and to sell at local markets. Many farmers also keep cows, pigs, and poultry. Most of the land belongs to large ranches raising beef and dairy cattle and to plantations of coffee—El Salvador's primary export crop. Plantations on the coastal plain grow sugarcane and cotton, which thrive in the hotter, wetter lowland climate. The Sierra Madre, a low mountain range created by ancient volcanic eruptions, forms El Salvador's northernmost boundary.

Most Salvadorans are mestizos (people of mixed Spanish and Indian ancestry), and the vast majority are poor. The wealthiest 2 percent of the population own most of the land in contrast to the nearly 20 percent who own none. This gulf between rich and poor led to a civil war that raged from 1980 to 1990. More than 75,000 people died, hundreds of thousands were left homeless, and the monetary drain on the country was enormous. Salvadorans are slowly rebuilding their country.

Nicaragua

Status:	Republic
Area:	50,193 square miles
Population:	5.7 million
Capital:	Managua
Language:	Spanish
Currency:	Gold córdoba (100 centavos)

Three distinct land regions divide Central America's largest country. The Pacific region consists of a fertile coastal plain, a range of hills and volcanoes, and a long depression containing Lake Nicaragua and Lake Managua—Central America's two largest lakes. The region enjoys a warm climate with ample rain from May to November. Local farmers cultivate cotton, sugarcane, and bananas for export and rice and vegetables for local consumption. The bulk of Nicaragua's people and industries inhabit this region, an area often hit by earthquakes.

The Central Highlands, although cooler than the Pacific region, also receive most of their rain between May and November. Highlanders primarily grow coffee—one of the country's major exports—and maize and beans for local consumption.

Nicaragua's third region is the flat, low-lying Caribbean coast where the climate is hot (average temperature of 80° F) and wet. More than 165 inches of rain fall each year in the dense tropical rain forest and coastal swamps and lagoons. Very few people live in this part of the country.

Costa Rica

Status:	Republic
Area:	19,730 square miles
Population:	4.3 million
Capital:	San José
Language:	Spanish
Currency:	Colón (100 centimos)

Coffee trees produce small white flowers and then bright red cherries that contain the coffee beans. Workers remove the soft flesh of the fruit and dry the beans in the sun before packing them for export.

Costa Rica is a republic and one of the most stable countries in Latin America. The president and the 57 deputies of the Legislative Assembly are elected every four years, and all citizens 18 years of age or older are required to vote. Local government oversees such basic services as fire fighting and access to water supplies.

Most of Costa Rica's terrain is mountainous, and high plateaux run northwest to southeast across the country. These highlands contain two large areas of very fertile land, surrounded by rugged peaks. Roughly three-quarters of Costa Ricans live in the highlands, many of them employed by the coffee plantations that produce the country's second most significant cash crop. Highlanders also grow maize, cacao beans, rice, potatoes, and beans. To the west, a narrow coastal plain runs along the Pacific shore. The coastal climate is ideal for growing bananas, Costa Rica's major export. Coastal farmers supplement their banana crops with sugarcane and tropical fruits. The Caribbean Lowlands to the east are hot and humid, with some of the world's richest rain forest vegetation and wildlife. The coast alternates between swamps and forests and long sandy beaches.

Although Costa Rica depends largely on agriculture, the country also produces fertilizers, cement, machinery, furniture, cosmetics, and pharmaceuticals and enjoys a healthy tourism industry.

Panama

Status:	Republic
Area:	29,158 sq. miles
Population:	3.2 million
Capital:	Panama City
Languages:	Spanish, English
Currency:	Balboa (100 cents)

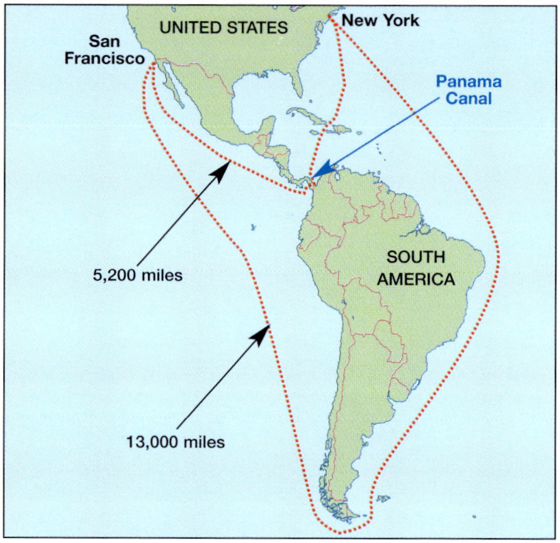

Narrow and S-shaped, Panama is the southernmost country on the isthmus linking North and South America. Bisected by the world's most famous canal, Panama is 450 miles long and 30 to 130 miles wide. Mountains run west to east across the country. The chain begins with Barú Volcano—an 11,400 feet peak near the border with Costa Rica—drops to the low rounded hills of the Canal Zone, and then rises again to 6,000 feet in the east. Very few people inhabit this forest-covered territory. More than 90 percent of the population lives in Panama's central region (near the canal) or on the Pacific coastal plain, where rich volcanic soil provides the country's most fertile farmland.

Panama City, at the canal's southern end, and Colón, at its northern end, are the country's largest cities and its centres of commerce and industry. Colón's Free Trade Zone allows companies to import and export goods without having to pay duties. Although not highly industrialized, Panama produces cement, beer, cigarettes, and processed foods. An oil refinery near Colón processes crude oil from other countries. Small farms grow subsistence crops of rice, maize, and beans. Larger farms and estates mass-produce bananas and other cash crops—sugarcane, coffee, and tobacco—for export to the United States and Europe.

The Canal

The Panama Canal, which links the Atlantic Ocean with the Pacific Ocean, is one of the world's most significant waterways. Built by the United States between 1904 and 1914, the canal allows an average of 36 ships to pass through it each day, cutting thousands of miles from the long trip around South America. On the first stage of

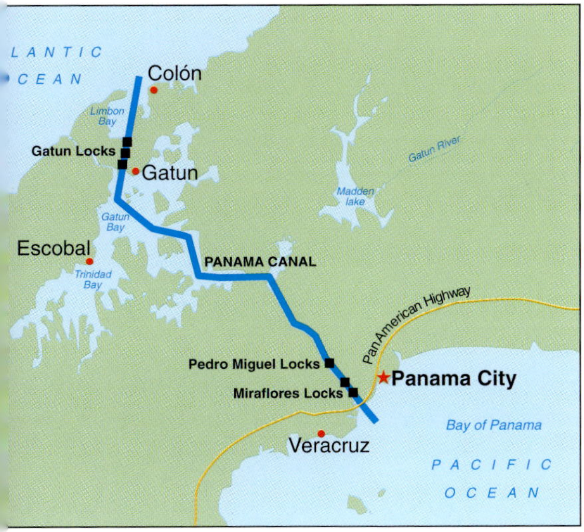

Far Left: This map shows just how important the canal is to ship operators. The 7 to 8 hour transit from the Pacific to the Atlantic saves 7,800 miles on a trip between New York and California—well worth the canal fee of about $30,000.

the 40-mile transit, a series of locks transports a ship 85 feet up to Gatun Lake. After crossing the lake, the ship enters the Gaillard Cut, a one-way channel just 160 yards wide that slices through the hills for more than eight miles. A second series of locks then lowers the ship to sea level again. After passing the city of Balboa, the ship sails under the Thatcher Ferry Bridge and heads into the Gulf of Panama.

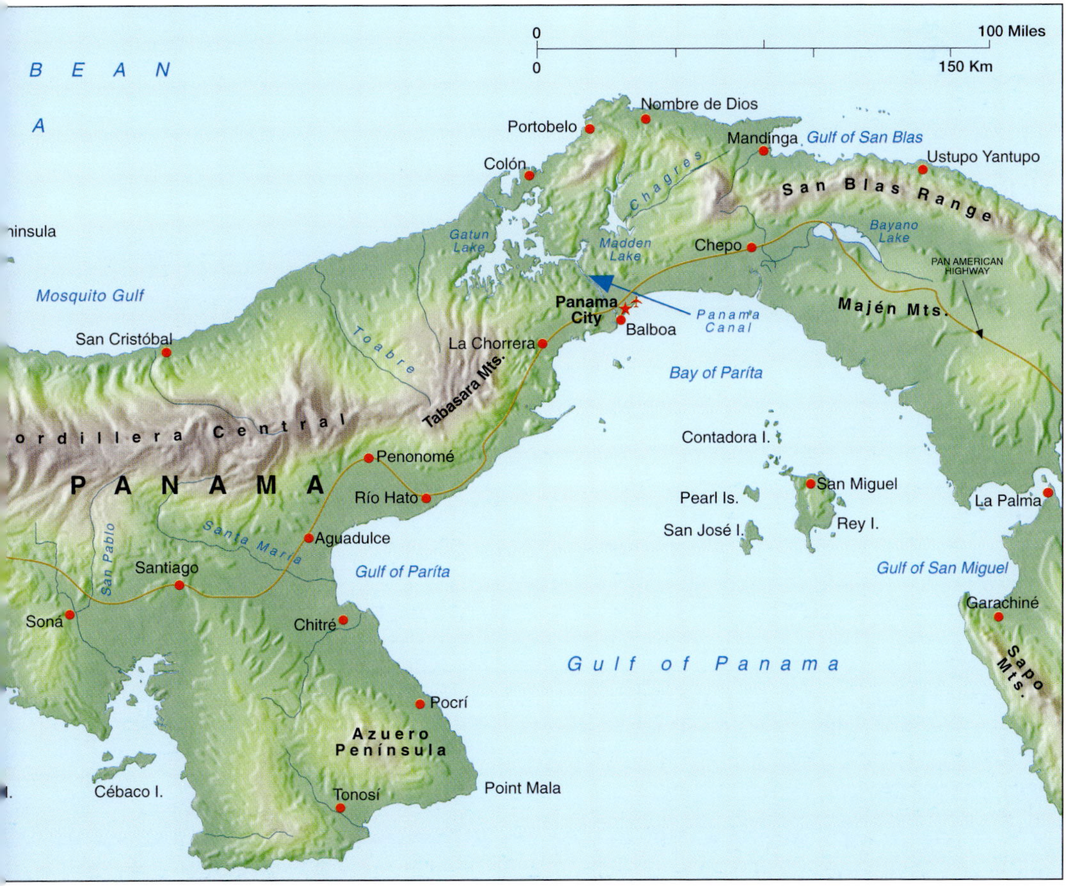

Colombia and Venezuela

Status:	Republic
Area:	439,734 sq. mi.
Population:	45.6 million
Capital:	Bogotá
Language:	Spanish,
Currency:	Peso (100 centavos)

Long coastlines on the Pacific Ocean and the Caribbean Sea cradle Colombia, South America's fourth-largest country. The rugged Andes Mountains dominate the western landscape, fanning across the country in three separate ranges. The Cauca and the Magdalena—Colombia's two largest rivers—flow through the valleys on either side of the central range. This vast highland region supports the country's richest farmland and many of its larger towns—Bogotá, Cali, Medellín, Armenia, and Manizales.

Colombia produces more coffee than any other country except Brazil. Farmers also grow rice, potatoes, rubber, sugarcane, and bananas. Abundant coal reserves and massive oil production bolster the economy. Colombia is also rich in platinum and gold and produces 95 percent of the world's emeralds.

Status:	Republic
Area:	352,143 sq. mi.
Population:	26.6 million
Capital:	Caracas
Languages:	Spanish
Currency:	Bolivar (100 céntimos)

Most of Venezuela's people live in the highland regions of the north and northwest and on the narrow coastal plain. A vast llano lies between the northern mountains and the Orinoco River. South of the Orinoco, a mixture of savanna and forest covers the rest of the country, rising to the Guiana Highlands in the southeast. The climate varies from a dry north to a very wet south.

Venezuela is the largest oil producer in South America. Petroleum and refined petroleum products account for 94 percent of its exports. The country also has rich reserves of iron, bauxite, copper, nickel, manganese, gold, diamonds, and coal. Rivers provide hydroelectric power for the steel and aluminium industries. Venezuelans also process sugar and manufacture textiles, furniture, leather goods, paper, chemicals, and light machinery.

Venezuelan soil is not very fertile, so much of the land, especially the llanos, is used for cattle ranching. Rice, corn, sorghum, coffee, sugarcane, cotton, and tropical fruits are the major crops in more fertile areas.

CARIBBEAN SEA
Point Gallinas
ARUBA
NETHERLANDS ANTILLES
Cape of La Vela
Ríohacha
Gulf of Venezuela
Coro
Santa Marta
anquilla
Sierra Nevada de Santa Marta
Maracaibo
Altagracia
Cabimas
La Tortuga Island
Margarita Island
GRENADA
TOBAGO
Dragon's Mouth
Caracas
Cumaná
Gulf of Paria
TRINIDAD
Valencia
Maracay
Lake Valencia
Barcelona
Matur'n
Serpent's Mouth
Lake Maracaibo
Barquisimeto
Trujillo
Perijá Mountains
Magdalena
Mérida
Valera
Llanos
Portuguesa
Tucupita
Amacura Delta
La Grita
Tovar
Mér'da Range
Orinoco
Ciudad Guayana
Cúcuta
Apure
San Fernando de Apure
Orinoco
Ciudad Bol'var
San Cristóbal
Caicara
Bucaramanga
Arauca
VENEZUELA
El Dorado
Cuyuni
Mountains
Orinoco
Sierra Guanay
Sierra Maigualida
Caura
Paragua
Caroni
Angel Falls
GUYANA
Magdalena
San Lucas Mountains
Puerto Ayacucho
Guiana Highlands
Auyán Mesa
La Gran Sabana
izales
Meta
Ventuari
Orinoco
Sierra del Zamuro
Santa Elena
MOUNTAINS
Bogotá
Llanos
San Fernando de Atabapo
Pacaraima Mountains
Cordillera Oriental
Maigualida Mountains
Guaviare
Uraricoera
San José
Parima Mountains
Macanal
Maroa
Caranaco
Guainia
Casiquiare Channel
Orinoco
COLOMBIA
San Carlos
El Carmen
Branco
Mitu
Vaupés
Yar'
Uaupés
La Tagua
Negro
Apaporis
Caquetá
Puerto Miraña
BRAZIL
Arica
Puerto Alfonso
Solimões (Amazonas)
RU
0
500 Miles
0
500
1000 Km

Guyana, Suriname, French Guiana

Guyana

Status: Republic
Area: 83,000 sq. mi.
Population: 768,000
Capital: Georgetown
Languages: English, Asian languages, Amerindian languages
Currency: Guyana dollar (100 cents)

Suriname

Status: Republic
Area: 63,039 sq. mi.
Population: 442,000
Capital: Paramaribo
Languages: Dutch, Sranan Tongo, English
Currency: Suriname guilder (100 cents)

French Guiana

Status: Overseas Department of France
Area: 34,749 sq. mi.
Population: 200,000
Capital: Cayenne
Languages: French, local languages
Currency: French franc (100 centimes)

These three locations on South America's northern coast have many similarities—hot, wet, tropical climates; average temperatures of 80°F; and average annual rainfall of 80 to 126 inches. Each has a narrow coastal plain, wherein lives the majority of the population. Savanna and woodlands merge into densely forested highlands farther inland.

Guyana began as a Dutch colony in 1581, coming under British control 250 years later (as British Guiana). The country gained independence in 1966 and became a republic in 1970. Most Guyanans are descended from African slaves and Asian labourers brought in to work the sugar plantations. The population also includes Europeans (mainly Portuguese) and Chinese. Guyana's economy depends entirely on exports. Sugarcane and bauxite each account for about 32 percent of the country's income, with rice, rum, gold, and diamonds comprising the balance.

Suriname, formerly Dutch Guiana, gained independence in 1975. Dutch is still the primary language, but people also speak English and a local patois called Taki-Taki. Children are required to attend school, and most of the population can read and write. Since the 1920s, Suriname has been the world's chief supplier of bauxite, but during the 1980s antigovernment guerrillas attacked the mines and processing plants, causing extensive damage. Farmers grow oil palms, rice, sugarcane, coffee, and tropical fruits on Suriname's fertile coastal plain. The government is helping to develop a fishing industry—primarily for shrimp.

French Guiana, an Overseas Department of France since 1946, has been under French rule since 1817. Most of the people are descendants of slaves brought to the territory in the 1600s and 1700s to work the sugarcane plantations. Later, the French built penal colonies, including the infamous Devil's Island offshore, to hold convicts sent from France. The country's economy is underdeveloped and depends on France for financial support. Guiana has iron, copper, silver, gold, lead, bauxite, and diamonds—but so far only gold is produced in any quantity. French Guiana is working with France to develop a shrimp fishing industry, and the country is also the site of the European Space Agency's launch facility.

Ecuador and the Galápagos Islands

Status:	Republic
Area:	109,483 sq. miles
Population:	13.4 million
Capital:	Quito
Languages:	Spanish, local Indian languages
Currency:	Sucre (100 centavos)

Spain ruled Ecuador from 1534 until 1822 and was responsible for many influences, including the country's name. Ecuador is Spanish for "equator"—the line of 0° latitude that runs across the country just north of the capital city of Quito.

Ecuador has three contrasting regions—a wide coastal plain, the mountains and high plateaux of the Andes, and an eastern lowland region sloping down into the Amazon Basin. The country also lays claim to the Galápagos Islands, which are located more than 600 miles to the west in the Pacific Ocean. Ecuador's coastal plain, 100 miles wide in places, supports a rich soil of mud and silt washed down from the Andes. The climate is hot and wet year-round. Plains farmers

Below: The marine iguana is just one of many unusual animals found on the Galápagos Islands. These prehistoric-looking creatures live on the rocky shores but feed on algae growing on rocks below sea level. The iguanas, giant tortoises, and unique birdlife of the islands inspired Charles Darwin's ideas on the evolution of life on earth.

harvest bananas, coffee, and cacao beans for export from the port of Guayaquil and rice and sugarcane for local consumption. Coastal shrimp are another significant export.

Ecuador's Andean plateaux and valleys have a cooler, temperate climate ideal for cattle ranching and growing grains. The haciendas provide a much-needed paycheque for local citizens. Workers in the industrial cities of Quito, Ambato, Riobamba, and Cuenca produce textiles, shoes, and other leather goods. These cities lie on the Pan-American Highway, which runs from Santiago, Chile, to the border between Mexico and the United States.

The eastern half of the country is covered in rain forest. This region is largely uninhabited, apart from small groups of Indians and the oil crews who are opening up the rich oil fields in the north. Oil has been Ecuador's most valuable export since the early 1970s. The country has become South America's second largest oil producer after Venezuela.

Thirteen volcanic islands and scores of rocks and reefs form the Galápagos Islands. Barren rock covers the shores, but dense forests blanket the inland mountains. The Galápagos Islands are famous for their unique animal life, including 500-pound giant tortoises and 5-foot-long marine iguanas. Naturalist Charles Darwin developed his theory of evolution after visiting the islands in 1835.

Peru

Status:	Republic
Area:	496,224 square miles
Population:	28 million
Capital:	Lima
Languages:	Spanish, Quechua, Aymara
Currency:	Sol (100 cénts)

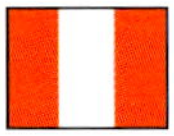

South America's third-largest country enjoys a variety of climates and scenery. Peru's coastal plain is a 100-mile-wide strip of desert with patches of scrubby vegetation moistened only by winter fog that rolls in from the sea. Yet this barren plain is home to 45 percent of the population, to the country's capital, to its largest farms, and to its primary industries. Desert farmers produce cotton and sugarcane for export and rice, fruits, and vegetables for city markets. They irrigate farmland with water from mountain streams, a resource shared with people in nearby cities.

Peru's nearness to the ocean influences several areas of the local economy. Fishing crews catch vast quantities of sardines and anchovies each year. Most of the catch is processed into fish meal and exported as animal feed. The southern coast supports iron ore mining, and oil fields dot the northern coast. Peruvians even mine offshore islands for guano (manure used as fertilizer), which is exported from the chief port of Callao, near Lima.

Approximately 40 percent of the population lives in the Andes Mountains, where plateaux at 10,000 to 15,000 feet above sea level break around towering peaks of 21,000 feet. Fertile soil and a temperate climate enable farmers to grow coffee on the lower slopes and grains and potatoes on higher ground. Large flocks of sheep, alpacas, and llamas graze in the grassy valleys. Peruvian mountains are also rich in minerals. The country exports great quantities of copper, lead, silver, gold, and zinc.

Peru's eastern landscape consists of the lower slopes of the Andes and the Amazon Basin's rolling plain, all covered in dense rain forest. The area is inhabited primarily by small groups of native Indians.

Above right: The Indians of the Peruvian highlands wear colourful traditional costumes of handwoven cloth made from the wool of llamas, alpacas, and guanacos. Warm clothing, a thick shawl, and an embroidered cap keep this young girl warm despite the cold of the high mountains.

Right: Andean villagers often sell handcrafted goods at the roadside. These women are selling decorative gourds, used to carry and drink water, and colourful handwoven clothes, rugs, and blankets.

Visitors travel from around the world to marvel at the ruins of Machu Picchu, an ancient Incan settlement perched above the Urubamba Valley, 7,875 feet up in the Peruvian Andes. The site is famous for its fine architecture and the terraced fields on the steep surrounding hillsides. Machu Picchu was discovered in 1911 by the American archaeologist Hiram Bingham.

Brazil

Status:	Federal Republic
Area:	3.3 million sq.mi.
Population:	182.8 million
Capital:	Brasília
Language:	Portuguese
Currency:	Real (100 centavos)

Brazil encompasses nearly half of the continent, sharing borders with every other South American country except Chile and Ecuador. Nearly as large as the United States, Brazil has far fewer people and much of its interior is uninhabited.

Northern Brazil consists of the vast Amazon Basin, which is bordered by the Guiana Highlands in the north and the Andes in the west. This huge area of hills and plains is warm and wet year-round. Covered by the world's largest tropical rain forest, northern Brazil embraces the world's greatest river system—the Amazon and its main tributaries, which flow for nearly 4,000 miles from the Andes to the Atlantic Ocean. The river is so big and so deep that ocean

going ships can easily navigate it for more than 1,000 miles inland.

The southern half of the country consists of the Brazilian Highlands—one of high plateaux and deep valleys. The climate is seasonal.

The south has cool winters and rain-drenched summers, perfect for the treeless savanna. Farmers graze cattle and sheep at the higher elevations and farm the fertile valleys and coastal plains. Roughly 80 percent of Brazil's population lives within 200 miles of the Atlantic coast. São Paulo, Rio de Janeiro, Salvador, and Recife—Brazil's major cities—lie on the country's southeastern coast.

Brazil produces more crops, timber, minerals, and manufactured goods than any other country in South America. Major commercial crops are coffee, cacao beans, soybeans, bananas, tobacco, sugarcane, maize, and oranges. Brazil raises beef cattle, horses, pigs, and sheep. The country is one of the world's chief exporters of iron ore, bauxite, beryllium, chrome, tin, manganese, magnesium, gold, and diamonds. Oil and gas wells along the coast produce fuel, as well as the raw materials for the country's petro-chemical industries. Brazil is the most heavily industrialized country in South America, and its exports include cars, aircraft, textiles, cement, chemicals, electrical goods, machinery, and paper.

Below: Iguazú Falls, on the border between Brazil and Argentina, consist of 275 separate waterfalls plunging 280 feet from a 2.5-mile-wide escarpment.

Bottom: Enormous open-pit iron ore mines scar the landscape at Belo Horizonte in the Minas Gerais province of southeastern Brazil.

Brazil

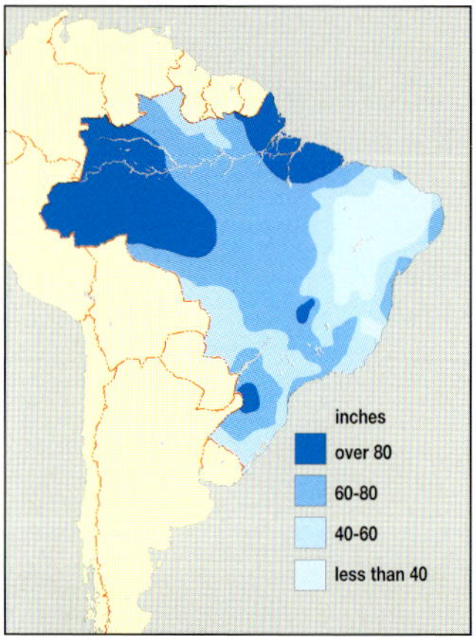

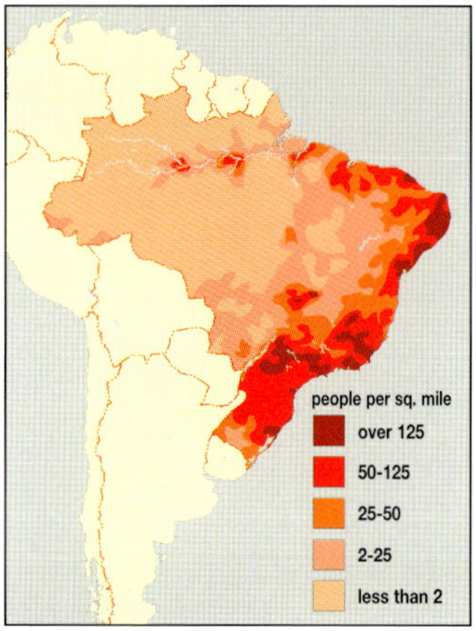

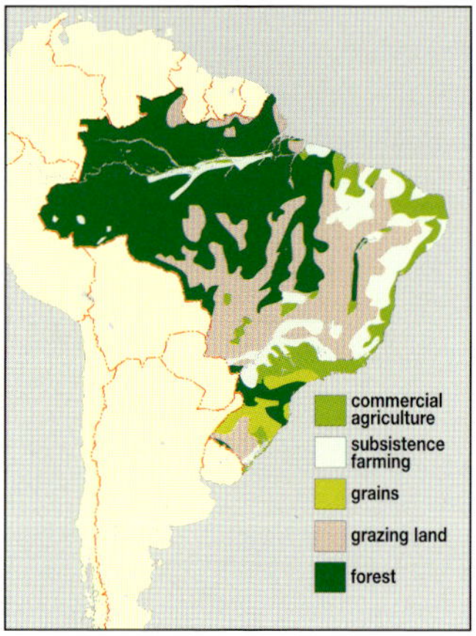

Left: Carnival time in Rio de Janeiro is one of the noisiest and most colourful spectacles in the world.

Below: The National Congress is one of many stunning modern buildings in the capital, Brasília, 3,500 feet above sea level on the central plateau. Work started on the city in 1957, and the government moved there from Rio de Janeiro in 1960.

Status:	Republic
Area:	424,162 sq. miles
Population:	9.1 million
Capital:	La Paz
Languages:	Spanish, Aymara, Quechua
Currency:	Boliviano (100 centavos)

The Cathedral of San Francisco overlooks this busy square in the Bolivian capital of La Paz. At 12,000 feet above sea level, La Paz is the highest capital city in the world.

Bolivia, like many of its South American neighbours, has three contrasting regions. The high plateaus of the altiplano dominate the west, surrounded by the snow-covered peaks of the Andes. The highland climate is cold and dry, with nighttime temperatures often falling below freezing. Despite the harsh conditions, most Bolivians live in this area. Herders raise llamas and alpacas for their wool on the sparse grasslands of the highlands. In the more fertile areas—around Lake Titicaca and the cities of Cochabamba and Sucre—farmers grow potatoes, maize, quinoa, wheat, and oca, an edible tuber. Coffee, cacao beans, beans, rice, cotton, and fruits comprise the major crops in the eastern lowlands.

The climate is humid in northern Bolivia where dense forests merge with the Amazon rain forest. Southern and central Bolivia enjoy gentle hills and wide valleys, and in the southeast, semi-arid grasslands merge with the Gran Chaco of Paraguay. Ranchers raise cattle on the drier plains. Nearly half of Bolivia's workers are employed as farm labourers, but the country is very poor, barely producing enough food for its own needs. Peasant farmers in many areas illegally grow coca, the source of cocaine.

Mines in the altiplano produce tin, copper, lead, tungsten, silver, and zinc. Large oil fields and natural gas fields lie beneath the eastern plains. Hydroelectric power stations on major rivers produce energy for the country's industries. Bolivia's principal exports are minerals (chiefly tin), natural gas, and textiles. The goods are shipped overland by road through Chile and Peru or south by river through Paraguay.

Paraguay

Status:	Republic
Area:	157,046 sq. miles
Population:	6.2 million
Capital:	Asunción
Languages:	Spanish, Guarani
Currency:	Guarani (100 céntimos)

The Paraguay River divides this landlocked country in two. A vast plain lies to the west of the river, rising gently from marshy bottomland near the river to the semi-arid Gran Chaco in Paraguay's northwest. Chaco vegetation is a mixture of coarse grasses, cacti, and thorny scrub—land best used for grazing cattle. A region of higher land lies east of the river, with alternating areas of grassland and hardwood forest. About 90 percent of Paraguayans live in this fertile eastern area. In addition to raising livestock, farmers grow maize, cassava, rice, and sugarcane for local use and tobacco, soybeans, and cotton for export.

Because Paraguay lacks a coast, the country's exports are shipped down the Paraguay River and on to the Atlantic Ocean, 1,000 miles away. The river, however, is so deep that 1,700-ton ships are able to sail upriver as far as the capital of Asunción.

Paraguay's chief energy source is hydroelectricity. And the country produces enough to export some to its neighbours. The gigantic Itaipu Dam on the Paraná River, built in partnership with Brazil, is the world's largest hydroelectric installation.

Status:	Republic
Area:	68,498 sq. miles
Population:	3.5 million
Capital:	Montevideo
Language:	Spanish
Currency:	Uruguayan peso (100 centésimos)

Uruguay, one of South America's smallest countries, is dwarfed by its neighbours, Brazil and Argentina. Its landscape consists of gently rolling long-grass prairies with ribbons of woodland growing alongside its rivers. Uruguay's highest point is just 1,640 feet above sea level. The climate is temperate, with warm summers and cool winters. Rain falls throughout the year. The country's many large rivers provide plenty of hydroelectric power, and the Paso de los Toros on the Río Negro has created the largest artificial lake in South America—the Embalse del Río Negro reservoir.

Uruguay's grasslands are ideal for grazing livestock. Local ranchers raise about 10 million cattle and 20 million sheep. Beef, wool, and leather goods are some of the country's main exports. The fertile soil of Uruguay's coastal plains supports a diversity of agriculture—wheat, rice, sorghum, maize, potatoes, and sugar beets—as well as milk and dairy products for the home market.

Most Uruguayans live in the coastal region—about half of them in the capital of Montevideo and the surrounding area. Beautiful beaches have helped boost tourism, a vital source of jobs and income. Uruguay has no mineral wealth, so machinery, cars and trucks, chemicals, and many other goods must be imported.

Well-developed educational, health, and welfare systems help Uruguay remain one of the most stable Latin American countries, despite some political unrest.

Chile

Status:	Republic
Area:	292,135 sq. mi.
Population:	16.3 million
Capital:	Santiago
Language:	Spanish
Currency:	Peso (100 centavos)

Chile is one of the world's most unusual countries in shape and climate. A narrow strip of land extending 2,600 miles from north to south, Chile's green bean shape averages only 110 miles wide. The country's northernmost point is well inside the tropics and yet contains one of the driest deserts on earth. Far to the south, Chile's Cape Horn lies at the tip of Tierra del Fuego and is a land of forests, glaciers, and rocky mountain peaks jutting into the wild Southern Ocean. The country's narrow width slivers into three contrasting landscapes. Steep, rocky cliffs dominate the western coastline. Just inland lies a fertile central valley—home to most of the country's population, agriculture, and industry. The Andes Mountains rise steeply in the east, separating Chile from neighbouring Argentina and Bolivia.

Chile enjoys one of South America's strongest economies, relying primarily on its significant mineral resources. The country is one of the world's chief producers of copper, and it also has large reserves of iron ore, lead, zinc, gold, silver, iodine, sulphur, and borax. Chile is one of the few South American countries with large coal deposits, although hydroelectric power and oil account for most of the country's energy supplies. Timber, manufactured goods, fruits and vegetables, fish, and by-products such as fish oil and fish meal also contribute to the local economy.

From 1973 to 1990, Chile was ruled by a military junta led by General Augusto Pinochet. In 1990 the country returned to democratically elected government, with a 120-member Chamber of Deputies and a 38-member Senate. Since the mid-1960s, all Chilean schoolchildren have had access to free primary education, and the country has one of the highest literacy rates in Latin America.

Above: An oil production platform sits off Punta Arenas in southern Chile. The oil fields in this region produce about half the country's fuel needs.

Below: Torres del Paine National Park in the Chilean Andes contains some of the finest scenery—and most demanding mountain climbing—in the entire Andes range.

Argentina

Status:	Republic
Area:	1.07 million sq. mi.
Population:	39.3 million
Capital:	Buenos Aires
Language:	Spanish
Currency:	Peso (100 australes)

South America's second-largest country is more than 2,170 miles long from north to south and 870 miles across at its widest point. Nestling into Chile's curved eastern border, Argentina covers most of the southern part of the continent. A varied landscape begins in the west with the Andes Mountains, whose highest peak, Aconcagua, towers over the region at 22,831 feet. The chaco in the northeast is damp and subtropical, with forested plains and swampy areas. The bulk of the country east of the Andes consists of rolling lowland plains. Flat and fertile, the pampas blanket most of eastern and central Argentina, from the dry west to the humid east where moist winds blow in from the Atlantic. South of the pampas lies the dry, windswept region of Patagonia and beyond that are the low mountains of the southern Andes and Tierra del Fuego, with their snow-capped peaks, ice fields, and glaciers.

Argentina's pampas boast large areas of fertile soil, a necessity for the country's agriculturally based economy. Farmers in the moist temperate regions produce wheat, maize, rye, soybeans, and linseed for export and fruit and vegetables for home consumption. In the drier regions, gauchos (cowboys) manage vast herds of beef cattle. Meat packing and food processing are primary industries, but

Like cowboys everywhere, the gauchos of the Argentinian pampas enjoy showing off their skill with horses.

Argentina also produces cars and trucks, iron and steel, cement, chemicals, textiles, and petroleum products. The country has few mineral resources apart from coal, iron ore, and uranium. Hydroelectricity provides about half of the country's energy. Coal and petroleum supply the rest. Locally mined uranium could be used for fuel rods should the country decide to use nuclear energy. Pine, larch, and oak forests in the flatland of Patagonia provide valuable timber for both local use and export, and Argentina's fishing crews catch hake, mackerel, anchovies, tuna, and squid.

Good schools and excellent medical services allow Argentinians to enjoy one of the highest standards of living in South America.

Atlantic Islands

The vast Atlantic Ocean is home to less than 100 islands, relatively few compared to the Pacific Ocean. Large islands lie close to the mainland. Smaller islands, most of them the tops of submarine volcanoes (some extinct, some still active), rise from the Mid-Atlantic Ridge. The islands are rugged and mountainous, with steep slopes ending in sheer sea cliffs. People who inhabit these remote islands make their living primarily from subsistence farming, fishing, and tourism—the Azores, Madeira, Canary, and Cape Verde Islands entertain many foreign visitors each year. Cape Verde in the North Atlantic is an important refueling stop for transatlantic ships and aircraft, and Ascension Island in the South Atlantic has a U.S. military base and a satellite tracking station. Most of these islands are overseas territories of Britain, Spain, and Portugal, and they rely financially on their parent countries for the essentials such as food and fuel. Cape Verde is an independent nation, which receives financial help from international aid organizations and from Cape Verdians who work abroad.

The Falkland Islands, 320 miles east of South America, rise from the South American continental shelf, rather than from the deep ocean floor. Low and windswept, the Falklands are covered in tussock grass and peat bogs. Islanders raise sheep for their livelihood. Mineral resources in the surrounding seas could also supplement the island's economy, but the industry has not yet been developed. Both Argentina and Great Britain claim ownership of this island group.

The Azores

The group consists of nine main islands spread over 400 miles of the eastern Atlantic. The Azores are rugged, with a temperate climate. Farmers grow bananas and subtropical fruits at the lower elevations and grains and temperate fruits higher up. Islanders fish for tuna and sardines to export. The islands also have a growing tourist industry.

Madeira

A warm, temperate climate and rich soil allow the islanders to grow sugarcane, vines, and both temperate and tropical fruits and vegetables. Grapes from the island's vineyards are processed into Madeira wine, a very popular export. Tourism is an important and growing industry.

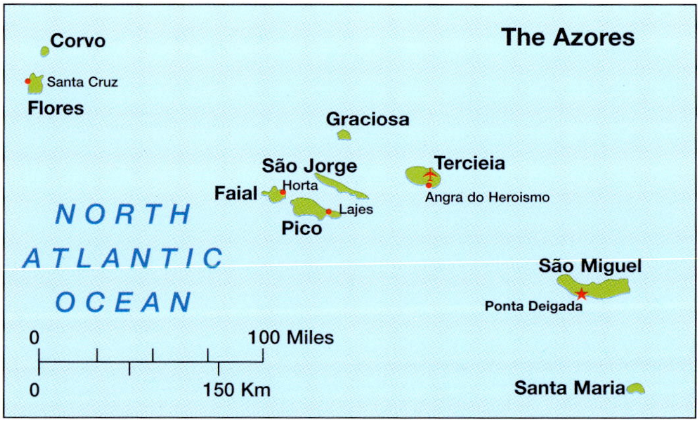

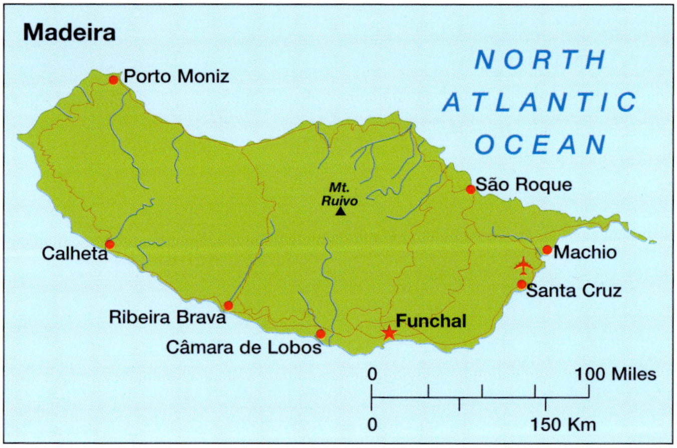

Newfoundland
C.Race
Grand Banks
Sable I.
Cape Cod
NORTH ATLANTIC OCEAN
Newfoundland Basin
Mid-Atlantic Ridge
Azores
North Eastern Atlantic Basin
Bay of Biscay
Mediterra
Cape de São Vicente
Cape Fear
Bermuda
Sargasso Sea
Canary Basin
Madeira
Canary Is.
Puerto Rico Trench
Cape Blanc
Caribbean Sea
Cape Verde Is.
Cape Verde
Senegal
Niger
Cape Verde Basin
Orinoco
Guiana Basin
Cape Orange
Sierra Leone Rise
Sierra Leone Basin
Cape Palmas
Guinea Basin
Guinea Rise
Romanche Fracture Zone
Amazon
Cape de São Roque
Ascension I.
Peru-Chile Trench
St. Helena
Angola Basin
Brazil Basin
SOUTH ATLANTIC OCEAN
Cape Frio
Mid-Atlantic Ridge
Walvis Ridge
Parana
Rio Grande Rise
Cape San Antonio
Tristan da Cunha
Cape Corrientes
Cape Basin
Gough I.
Argentine Basin
0 1000 2000 3000 4000 Miles
0 1000 2000 3000 4000 5000 6000 Km
Cape Tres Puntas
Atlantic-Indian Rid
Falkland Is.
Scotia Ridge
S. Georgia
Bouvet I.
Cape Horn
S. Sandwich Is.
Scotia Sea
Drake Passage

Atlantic Islands

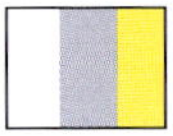

Canary Islands

Most of the islands in this group are rugged and mountainous. Only Lanzarote and Fuerteventura, nearest the African coast, are flat. Pico de Teide volcano on Tenerife erupted in 1909 and towers over the area at 12,156 feet. Fertile soil and irrigation procedures allow farmers to grow sugarcane, coffee, and tropical fruits on low ground and grains and temperate vegetables at the higher elevations. Tourism flourishes on the main islands.

The lowland and coastal areas of Tenerife are lush and fertile, but the island's mountainous interior is wild and rugged. Wind and rain have carved this rock pillar, standing like a sentry on the approach to Pico de Teide volcano.

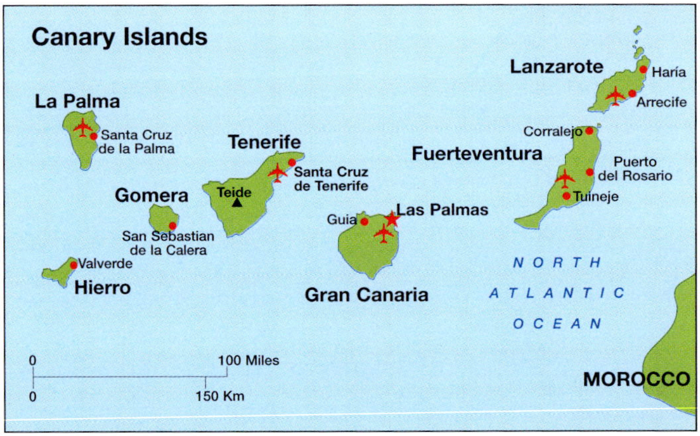

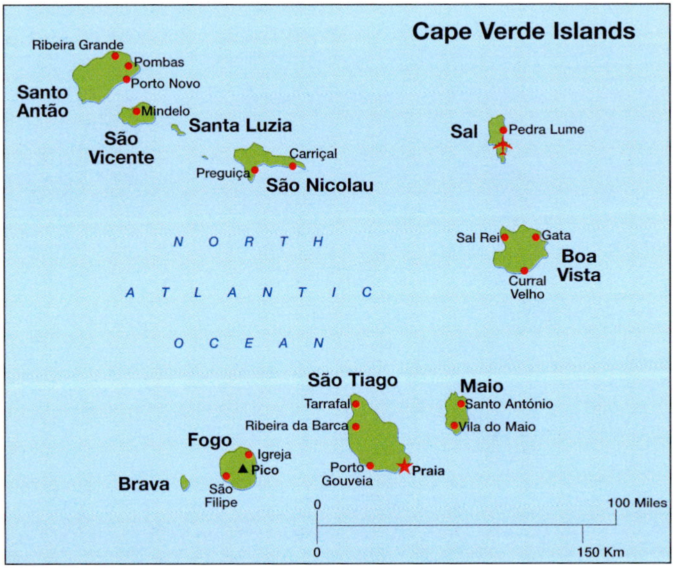

Cape Verde Islands

The islands are volcanic, mountainous, and very rugged. Cano Peak on Fogo Island is the highest point at 9,281 feet. The climate is arid, and much of the land is badly eroded. Local farmers grow maize, vegetables, and some fruits on land that has been improved by irrigation and by soil conservation programs. The islands' main exports are rum and fish (mainly tuna and lobster).

Falkland Islands

The Falklands consist of two main islands and nearly 200 smaller islands and islets. About half the population lives in the capital, Stanley. The remainder inhabits the outlying sheep stations. Since the war with Argentina in 1982, Britain has maintained a military garrison and air base on the islands.

Saint Helena Island

This mountainous island, 1,200 miles from the coast of Africa, is famous as the place where Napoléon Bonaparte died in exile in 1821. The island's small population lives by farming and by creating lace and flax for export. Saint Helena is the administrative centre for several smaller British Overseas Territories, including Ascension Island and Tristan da Cunha.

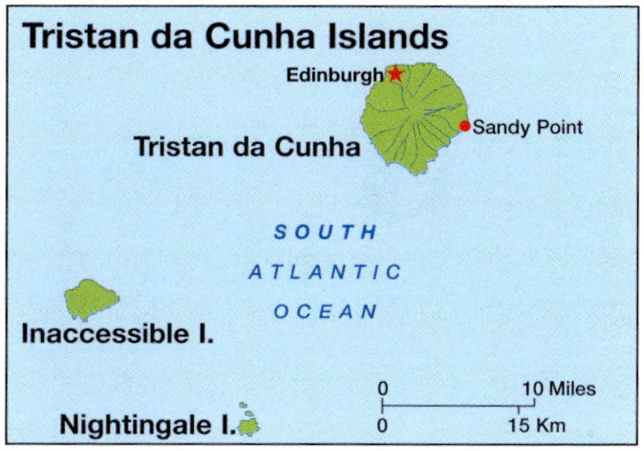

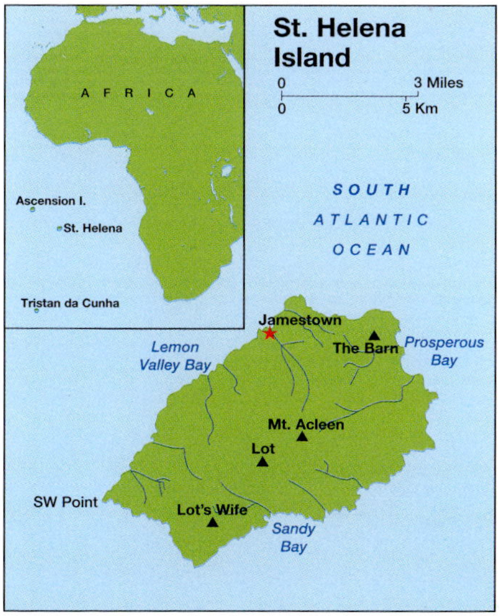

Tristan da Cunha Islands

The largest of these remote volcanic islands, Tristan da Cunha sits at the southern end of the Mid-Atlantic Ridge. The climate is mild and wet. Islanders grow vegetables and raise sheep and cattle. The entire population was evacuated in 1961 when a volcano erupted. Most returned in 1963.

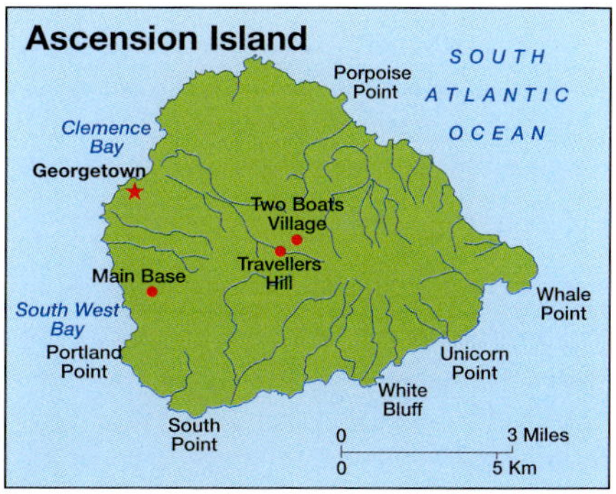

Ascension Island More than 700 miles northwest of Saint Helena, Ascension Island is most famous for the sea turtles that lay their eggs on its beaches each year. The inhabitants are mainly British and American. Many of them work at the satellite tracking station and the military airfield.

Europe

Europe is the second-smallest continent, yet it contains 40 independent countries. If you travelled the 925 miles from London, England, to northern Bosnia-Herzegovina, you would cross 10 countries each with its own history, traditions, and culture—that's 10 countries in the distance between Chicago, Illinois, and New Orleans, Louisiana.

With so many diverse nationalities packed into such a small land area, Europe has had a turbulent history. Over the past 2,000 years, great empires have come and gone. New countries have emerged, and old ones have disappeared. National borders have been redrawn time after time as a result of wars, alliances, and treaties.

Europe's landmass stretches 4,000 miles east to west and slightly more than 3,000 miles north to south. An abundance of bays, fjords, peninsulas, and inland seas have created a coastline that is nearly 38,000 miles long. The continent has a wide range of climates, soil types, resources, and scenery. It is one of the most densely populated and most productive regions in the world.

Europe has had an immense influence on the world despite its small size. Beginning in the fourteenth century, Europeans expanded their culture through art, music, science, medicine, navigation, industry, and technology. Intellectuals conceived many new ideas about economics, politics, and social justice. The world changed dramatically after World War II (1939–1945). Many European countries were devastated—their cities, industries, farms, and transport systems in ruins. It took many years to repair the damage. The United Kingdom, France, the Netherlands, and Belgium were also weakened by the loss of overseas territories as, one after another, their former colonies became independent nations. The United States and the Soviet Union emerged from the war as the world's superpowers.

Modern Europe continues to change. The former Soviet Union has fragmented into a dozen separate countries. But as one group separates, another develops. Major European countries have joined together as the European Union (EU, formerly the European Community). Its aim is to bring the people of Europe closer together culturally, technologically, and financially.

2000 Miles
3000 Km
Novaya Zemlya
Barents Sea
Kolguyev I.
White Sea
Gulf of Bothnia
FINLAND
EDEN
Lake Onega
Lake Ladoga
RUSSIAN FEDERATION
Rybinsk Res.
Baltic Sea
LATVIA
LITHUANIA
(RUSSIA)
BELARUS
POLAND
CH P.
UKRAINE
SLOVAKIA
RIA
HUNGARY
ROMANIA
CROATIA
BOSNIA-HERZEGOVINA
SERBIA and MONTENEGRO
BULGARIA
MACEDONIA
ALBANIA
GREECE
Crete
Black Sea
Caspian Sea
Aral Sea

Portugal

Status:	Parliamentary Democracy
Area:	35,514 sq. mi.
Population:	10.5 million
Capital:	Lisbon
Language:	Portuguese
Currency:	Euro (100 cents)

Overseas Territories
Azores
Madeira

Situated on the westernmost edge of the European continent, Portugal is 350 miles north to south and about 125 miles wide. It covers roughly one-sixth of the Iberian Peninsula, which it shares with its neighbour, Spain. The self-governing islands of the Azores and Madeira in the eastern Atlantic are all that remain of Portugal's once-vast overseas empire.

Northern Portugal is mountainous, with a mild damp climate and a short dry season. Farmers use the poor upland soil mainly for grazing sheep and goats and the forests for producing lumber and wood pulp. The hotter, drier, southern coastal plains are an area of flatland rising inland to the meseta—a region of dry highlands cut by broad river valleys. Portugal's most fertile land is found in the valleys and on the coastal plains.

Farmers grow mostly grains—corn in the north and wheat in the south. Other crops include beans for local use and olives, grapes, limes, oranges, and almonds for export. Portugal exports nearly half the world's supply of cork, as well as wine, turpentine, resin, and Atlantic sardines.

Portugal's main mineral resources are tungsten ore, copper ore, and coal. Lisbon and Setúbal have shipbuilding and repair yards, and the manufacturing centres around Lisbon and Porto produce processed food, leather goods, ceramics, glass, and textiles.

Status:	Parliamentary Monarchy
Area:	195,363 sq. mi.
Population:	44.1 million
Capital:	Madrid
Language:	Spanish
Currency:	Euro (100 cents)

Overseas Territories
Canary Islands
Ceuta Melilla

One of the oldest occupied territories in Europe, Spain has been inhabited for more than 100,000 years. Dry, scrub-covered meseta, lying at 2,000 to 2,500 feet above sea level, covers most of the central region. Numerous mountain ranges run across the middle of the country and along the north and south coasts. Prime farmland is found on the coastal lowlands of Valencia and Alicante, in the Ebro River Valley, and in the Guadalquivir Basin.

The inland climate is hot and dry in summer and cold in winter. Meseta farmers graze sheep and goats and grow barley and oats. Forestry workers produce lumber, cork, and resin. Farmers in the cool damp northern regions and in the warm mild-Mediterranean coastal areas produce wheat, barley, fruits, sugar beets, vegetables, cotton, and tobacco. Olive groves and vineyards cover vast expanses. Spain is the world's primary olive producer and one of the world's leading wine makers.

The northern cities of Bilbao, Santander, and Oviedo house the country's iron and steel, shipbuilding, automobile, chemicals, and cement industries. Spaniards mine copper, lead, zinc, silver, mercury, and other metals.

France

Status:	Parliamentary Democracy
Area:	212,934 square miles
Population:	60.7 million
Capital:	Paris
Language:	French
Currency:	Euro (100 cents)

Overseas Territories
French Polynesia
Mayotte
Wallis and Futuna Is.
New Caledonia
Kerguelen

Overseas Departments
Guadeloupe
Martinique
French Guiana
Réunion

France is one of the largest countries in Europe, extending about 600 miles north to south and 600 miles east to west. Fertile plains and rolling hills dominate northern France. The hard granite moors of Brittany jut into the Atlantic Ocean. The capital city of Paris stands in the middle of a huge saucer-shaped hollow called the Paris Basin. Western France is covered in flat plains, rimmed with sandy beaches that attract tourists to the Atlantic coast. Most of France's inland borders are mountainous. The Pyrénées separate France from Spain in the southwest. To the southeast, the Alps form a barrier between France and its neighbours Switzerland and Italy. The lower wooded Vosges and Ardennes Mountains mark France's borders with Germany and Belgium in the east and northeast.

France's Massif Central boasts beautiful scenery, opulent chateaus, and three of the country's great rivers—the Loire, the Seine, and the Rhône. Several large industrial centres (Clermont-Ferrand, Limoges, St. Étienne, and Lyon) have developed where these rivers flow into the northern lowlands. France's other important industrial centres lie near Paris, in the Nord-Pas-de-Calais and Lorraine coalfields, and close to the ports of Le Havre and Dunkerque on the English Channel. France has to import most of its coal and oil, but 70 percent of the country's power derives from its nuclear power plants. Mountain rivers and the world's largest tidal power station, at the mouth of Brittany's Rance River, supply energy for France's surging hydroelectric power.

France is the world's fourth-ranked industrial nation following the United States, Japan, and Germany. The country produces vast quantities of steel and aluminium and is a leading manufacturer of cars, locomotives, aircraft, turbines, and other machinery. Electrical goods, chemicals, pharmaceuticals, and textiles comprise the remainder of its industrial exports. France is also Europe's leading agricultural nation. Sixty percent of the land supports crops and livestock. Northern farmers produce grains, beets, beef, veal, poultry, and dairy products. Mediterranean farmers grow fruits and vegetables. Many French tend grapes to make wine.

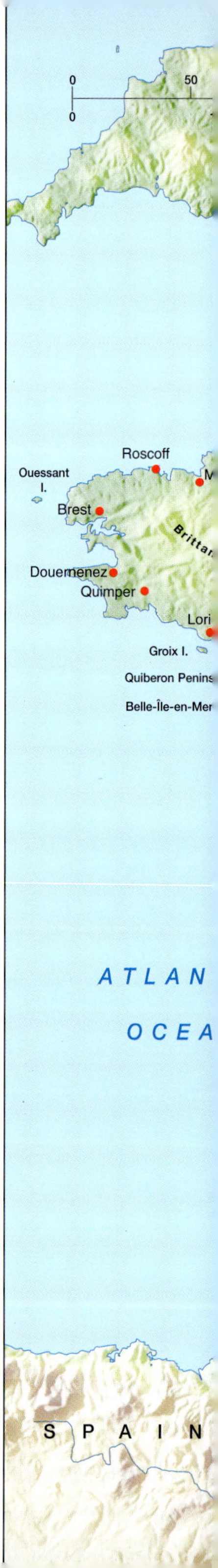

UNITED KINGDOM
150
200 Miles
200
300 Km
Strait of Dover
ENGLISH CHANNEL
Dunkerque
Calais
Gravelines
St.Omer
Boulogne
Roubaix
Hazebrouck
Lille
Montreuil
Douai
Arras
Valenciennes
BELGIUM
GERMANY
Abbeville
Bapaume
Cambrai
Somme
Ardennes
Hirson
Cap de la Hague
Cherbourg
Seine Bay
Fécamp
Dieppe
Amiens
St. Quentin
Charleville-Mézières
LUXEMBOURG
Valognes
Le Havre
Bolbec
Montdidier
Argonne Plateau
Carentan
Rouen
Beauvais
Compiègne
Reims
Meuse
Moselle
Elbeuf
Seine
Louviers
Caen
St. Lô
Lisieux
Evreux
Mantes-la-Jolie
St. Denis
Marne
Verdun
Metz
Normandy Hills
Granville
Argenteuil
Paris
Meaux
Châlons-sur-Marne
Pont à Mousson
St.-Malo
St. Germain-en-Laye
Versailles
Île-de-Paris
Nancy
Mont-St.-Michel
Argentan
St.Dizier
Toul
Strasbourg
Dinan
Rambouillet
Wassy
Fougères
Chartres
Seine
Fontainebleau
Alençon
Vilaine
Rennes
Mayenne
Nemours
Troyes
Épinal
Vosges
Vitré
Laval
Sens
Colmar
Le Mans
Orléans
Montargis
Langres
Langres Plateau
Mulhouse
Redon
Loir
Gien
Auxerre
Saône
Blois
Belfort
Basel
Vesoul
Angers
St. Nazaire
Loire
Tours
Loire
FRANCE
Avallon
Besançon
Nantes
Saumur
Dijon
Vierzon
Cholet
Dôle
La Chaux de Fonds
Cher
Bourges
Nevers
Autun
Châtellerault
Pontarlier
Bressuire
Châteauroux
Le Creusot
Chalon-sur-Saône
La Roche-sur-Yon
Loire
Lons le Saunier
SWITZERLAND
Poiters
La Châtre
Jura Mountains
Les Sables-d'Olonne
Montceau les Mines
Niort
Moulins
St.Claude
Lake Geneva
Montluçon
Mâcon
Île de Ré
La Rochelle
Civray
Lapalisse
Bourg-en-bresse
Rochefort
Île d'Oléron
Villefranches
Chamonix
Limoges
Clermont-Ferrand
Lyon
Villeurbanne
Royan
Cognac
Angoulême
Isère
Grave Point
Chambery
Nontron
Le Mont-Dore
Barbezieux
Ambert
Vienne
St.-Étienne
Val d'Isère
Lesparre-Médoc
Voiron
MASSIF CENTRAL
FRENCH ALPS
Pauillac
Tulle
Annonay
Étang de Carcans
Blaye
Périgueux
Mauriac
Tournon
Grenoble
Bourg
Brive-la-Gaillarde
Yssingeaux
Isère
ITALY
Murat
St. Flour
Romans-sur-Isère
Bordeaux
Libourne
Bergerac
Souillac
Aurillac
Le Puy
Valence
Dordogne
Arcachon
Figeac
Prives
Marmande
Marvejols
Cévennes
Étang de Cazaux
Mende
Gap
Durance
Lot
Cahors
Espalion
Montélimar
Garonne
Villeneuve-sur-lot
Villefranche
Rhône
Étang de Biscarresse
Rodez
Tarn
Florac
Mimizan
Agen
Alès
Orange
Millau
Maritime Alps
Moissac
Castelsarrasin
Carmaux
Avignon
Carpentras
Montauban
Monte-de-Marsan
Condom
Albi
Le Vigan
Apt
Verdon
Monte Carlo
Adour
Gaillac
Verdun
Nîmes
Tarascon
Dax
Graulhet
Lodève
Nice
Durance
Auch
Toulouse
Draguignan
Antibes
Biarritz
Bayonne
Montpellier
Arles
Cannes
Castres
Aix-en-Provence
Mirande
Muret
Mazamet
Étang de Berre
St.Raphael
St. Jean-de-Luz
Sète
Brignoles
Béziers
Carcassonne
Aude
Rhône Delta
Marseille
St.Tropez
Pau
Tarbes
Garonne
Bandol
Hyères
Narbonne
Mediterranean
Toulon
St. Gaudens
La Seyne-sur-Mer
Lourdes
PYRÉNÉES
Foix
Limoux
Gulf of Lion
Sea
Perpignan
Prades
ANDORRA

United Kingdom and Ireland

Status:	Constitutional Monarchy
Area:	94,548 square miles
Population:	60 million
Capital:	London
Languages:	English, Welsh, Gaelic
Currency:	British pound (100 pence)

The United Kingdom of Great Britain and Northern Ireland comprises a group of islands separated from mainland Europe by the English Channel, the Strait of Dover, and the North Sea. England, Scotland, the principality of Wales, and Northern Ireland comprise the country's four political divisions.

The United Kingdom's landscape is quite varied. Mountains and moors dominate the north. Rolling hills and fertile plains cover the southern and eastern lowlands. The rugged peaks and calm mountain lakes of the Scottish Highlands, England's Lake District, and Snowdon in northern Wales attract many tourists. Upland farmers graze sheep on the high ground and grow grain, hay, and fodder crops at the lower elevations. Depending on soil and climate, farmers grow wheat, barley, oats, vegetables, peas, beans, sugar beets, fodder crops, and fruit. Large dairy and beef herds graze on the rich lowland pastures. Agriculture employs only 1 percent of the country's workforce, but farming is highly mechanized and very productive.

The United Kingdom's early economy depended on heavy industries such as coal mining, steel, machinery, automobiles, chemicals, textiles, and pottery. Industrial centres developed in northern England and Scotland, in the western Midlands, and near the ports of London, Liverpool, Glasgow, and Belfast. Modern manufacturing such as light engineering, electrical goods, computers, biotechnology, and food processing have developed in parts of the United Kingdom where the older industries have declined. Although the country's imports exceed its exports, the economy is bolstered by banking, by insurance, by other financial services, and by tourism.

Status:	Republic
Area:	27,135 square miles
Population:	4 million
Capital:	Dublin
Languages:	English, Gaelic
Currency:	Euro (100 cents)

Southern Ireland's lush green countryside and rich pastures have earned the country its famous nickname—the Emerald Isle. Separated politically from Northern Ireland in 1921, southern Ireland first became the Irish Free State. In 1949 it was renamed the Republic of Ireland (Eire in Gaelic).

The central part of the country is low-lying, with peat bogs and clusters of low rounded hills called drumlins. Low rugged mountains rise to about 2,500 feet in the north and west. Southwestern Ireland's long ridges of hard sandstone jut out to sea like fingers, creating long sea inlets and natural harbours. Ireland's hills, lakes, and coastal scenery attract many visitors each year.

Nearly 70 percent of the country is farmland. Atlantic winds carry plenty of rain, and the climate is cool and mild. Farmers raise large dairy herds in the country's southern and midland regions. Smaller herds of beef cattle graze in the east and west. Primary crops are wheat, oats, potatoes, and sugar beets. Farmers also grow barley for cattle feed and to make beer. The Irish enjoy excellent fishing opportunities and export fish, lobster, prawns, and shellfish. Ireland's manufactured goods include machinery, textiles, fine glassware, and electronic equipment. The island's main manufacturing centre is a vast government-supported industrial estate near Shannon airport.

United Kingdom
Overseas Territories
Anguilla
Bermuda
British Antarctic Territory
British Indian Ocean Territory
British Virgin Islands, Cayman Islands, Montserrat, Turks and Caicos Islands
Falkland Islands
Gibraltar
Pitcairn, Henderson, Ducie, and Oeno Is
St. Helena, Ascension, Tristan da Cunha
South Georgia and South Sandwich Is
0 50 100 150 200 Miles
0 100 200 300 Km
LANTIC
CEAN
Shetland Is.
Foula
Lerwick
Fair Isle
Orkney Is.
Kirkwall
Cape Wrath
John o'Groats
Thurso
Noss Head
Butt of Lewis
Stornoway
Lewis
Outer Hebrides
St. Kilda
North Uist
Harris
South Uist
Barra
North Minch
Moray Firth
Fraserburgh
Peterhead
Inverness
Skye
Spey
Don
Dee
Aberdeen
Loch Ness
Rhum
Mallaig
Ben Nevis
Grampian Mts.
Montrose
Coll
Tiree
Mull
Oban
Tay
Dundee
Perth
Firth of Tay
Firth of Lorne
Jura
Forth
Firth of Forth
Edinburgh
Islay
Glasgow
Clyde
SCOTLAND
Holy I. (Lindisfarne)
Arran
Firth of Clyde
Ayr
Tweed
The Cheviot
Cheviot Hills
Nith
Malin Head
Tory I.
Rathlin I.
North Channel
Aran I.
Gweebarra Bay
Londonderry
Sperrin Mts.
Donegal
Donegal Bay
NORTHERN IRELAND
Belfast
Lough Neagh
Lower Lough Erne
Sligo
Armagh
Lough Conn
Lough Allen
Upper Lough Erne
Achill Head
Dundalk
Dundalk Bay
Lough Mask
Lough Ree
Lough Corrib
Athlone
Galway
Galway Bay
Aran Is.
IRELAND
Bog of Allen
Liffey
Dublin
Wicklow Mts.
Lough Derg
Shannon
Carlow
Wicklow Head
Loop Head
Limerick
Barrow
Tipperary
Galtymore
Galty Mts.
Waterford
Wexford
Wexford Bay
Dingle Bay
Killarney
Cork
Hook Head
Greenore Point
Caha Mts.
Cork Harbour
Bantry Bay
Bantry
Old Head of Kinsale
Mizen Head
CELTIC SEA
St. George's Channel
Stranraer
Solway Firth
Carlisle
Tyne
Newcastle upon Tyne
Durham
Tees Bay
Lake District
PENNINES
Tees
Middlesbrough
Swale
Isle of Man
Douglas
Walney I.
Flamborough Head
Bridlington Bay
IRISH SEA
Leeds
Ouse
Kingston upon Hull
Spurn Head
Preston
Liverpool Bay
Liverpool
Manchester
Sheffield
Anglesey
Holyhead
Caernarfon Bay
Snowdon
Wrexham
Dee
Trent
Derby
The Wash
Welland
Norwich
WALES
Wolverhampton
Birmingham
Peterborough
Coventry
Cardigan Bay
Aberystwyth
Severn
Cambridge
Northampton
Cam
Ipswich
Stour
Wye
Cardigan
Cheltenham
Cotswold Hills
ENGLAND
Colchester
Carmarthen
Gloucester
Oxford
London
Mouth of the Thames
Swansea
Cardiff
Thames
Reading
Canterbury
Bristol Channel
Bristol
North Downs
Dover
Lundy
Ilfracombe
Salisbury
Folkestone
Exe
South Downs
Southampton
Dungeness
Bude
Exeter
Bournemouth
Brighton
Beachy Head
Selsey Bill
Isle of Wight
Dartmoor
Lyme Bay
Plymouth
Portland Bill
ENGLISH CHANNEL
Star Point
Land's End
Penzance
Isles of Scilly
Alderney
Channel Is.
Guernsey
Jersey
FRANCE

Norway and Denmark

Status:	Constitutional Monarchy
Area:	125,050 square miles
Population:	4.6 million
Capital:	Oslo
Language:	Norwegian
Currency:	Norwegian krone (100 øre)

Norway stretches 1,100 miles north to south, but its coastline has so many bays, headlands, and fjords that the country's shoreline is more than 2,100 miles long. The northernmost third of the country lies inside the Arctic Circle, and Hammerfest is Europe's most northerly city. In midsummer, northern Norway sees nearly 24 hours of daylight, giving the country the nickname of Land of the Midnight Sun. More than 150,000 small islands, rocks, and reefs are scattered along Norway's Atlantic coast.

Norway is a mountainous country, and 80 percent of it is more than 500 feet above sea level. The only area of lowland occurs around Oslo in the south. Because Norway has few large alluvial plains, Norwegian farms average only about 40 acres. Farmers grow barley and potatoes and raise pigs, beef, and dairy cattle. The climate is cool in summer and cold in winter, but some farmers are able to grow fruit trees on sunny hillsides.

Forestry and fishing are Norway's traditional industries, but the country's abundant hydroelectric power has enabled Norwegians to build many manufacturing plants. Modern industries include lumber and wood pulp, metal goods, paper, processed food, engineering parts, and ship and boat building. Norway also has one of the world's largest merchant shipping fleets. Norway's already high standard of living grew after the country discovered oil and gas fields beneath the North Sea in the 1960s. The country's most significant industry is now the production and export of oil and natural gas.

Status:	Constitutional Monarchy
Area:	16,637 square miles
Population:	5.4 million
Capital:	Copenhagen
Language:	Danish
Currency:	Danish krone (100 øre)

Danish Overseas Territories
Greenland, Faeroe Islands

Nearly surrounded by water, Denmark consists of the low-lying Jutland Peninsula and 482 islands. The country's only link to the mainland is its 43-mile-long border with Germany that runs across the neck of the peninsula. Most Danes live on Sjaelland, Fyn, Lolland, Falster, and Bornholm, but about 100 of the smaller islands are also inhabited.

Nearly 70 percent of Denmark's land area is given over to agriculture. Danish farmers best utilize their fertile soils and mild climate by concentrating on high-value food products such as butter, cheese, bacon, and ham. Most farmers grow barley, green fodder crops, and root crops—used chiefly for animal feed. About 60 percent of the country's food production is exported as meat and dairy products, mainly to the United Kingdom and Germany. Fishing fleets based in West Jutland and on Greenland and the Faeroe Islands catch sand lances, cod, herring, and Norway pout. Factories in Jutland process much of the catch for export.

Denmark's only natural resources are oil and gas from beneath the North Sea and granite and kaolin (a fine white clay) from the quarries on Bornholm. Industrial centres around Copenhagen and other big cities import raw materials, turning them into lucrative products such as machinery, food-processing equipment, silverware, furniture, textiles, chemicals, and pharmaceuticals.

0 100 200 300 Miles
0 100 200 300 400 500 Km
NORWEGIAN SEA
NORTH SEA
Skagerrak
Kattegat
Gulf of Bothnia
Gulf of Finland
Gulf of Riga
BALTIC SEA
NORWAY
SWEDEN
FINLAND
RUSSIA
ESTONIA
LATVIA
LITHUANIA
(RUSSIA)
POLAND
GERMANY
DENMARK
North Cape
Kjelvik
Berlevåg
Båtsfjord
Lebesby
Hamningberg
Vadsø
Varanger Fjord
Sørøya
Hammerfest
Kistrand
Porsangen
Polmak
Tana
Kirkenes
Vanna I.
Ringvassøy I.
Alta
Karasjok
Kvaløy I.
Tromsø
Skibotn
Finnsnes
Vesterålen
And Fjord
Hadsel
Harstad
Narvik
Lofoten
Vagan
Svolvær
Vest Fjord
Sørfold
Bodø
Beiarn
Rognan
Mo
Vega
Mosjøen
Brønnøysund
Grane
Vikna
Kjølen Mts.
Folda Fjord
Namsos
Grong
Snåsa
Fro Fjord
Steinkjer
Frøya I.
Levanger
Trondheim
Kristiansund
Halsa
Surnadalsøra
Ålesund
Sunndalsøra
Stranda
Røros
Norddal
Dombås
Dovre Mts.
Galdhopiggen
Sande
Orkla
Glåma
Fåberg
Lillehammer
Voss
Myrdal
Fagernes
Hamar
Bergen
Gjøvik
Lågen
Kongsvinger
Uskedal
Long Mts.
Oslo
Skjotd
Haugesund
Dalen
Drammen
Sarpsborg
Horten
Stavanger
Fredrikstad
Otra
Oslo Fjord
Bygland
Larvik
Evje
Egersund
Arendal
Kristiansand
Mandal
Hjørring
Jammer Bay
Lim Fjord
Ålborg
Nissum Bay
Ålborg Bay
Viborg
Holstebro
Randers
Silkeborg
Ringkøbing
Århus
Horsens
Copenhagen
Esbjerg
Fan I.
Odense
Main I.
FYN
SJAELLAND
Rømø I.
Svendborg
LOLLAND
FALSTER
BORNHOLM
Rønne
Åland
Hiiumaa
Saaremaa
Gotland
Öland
L. Peipus
Daug

Sweden, Finland

Status:	Constitutional Monarchy
Area:	173,730 square miles
Population:	8.9 million
Capital:	Stockholm
Language:	Swedish
Currency:	Swedish krona (100 øre)

Sweden is a land of beautiful lakes, snow-covered mountains, and rushing water. The country's population is small compared to its land area, and Swedes enjoy a very high standard of living. Northwestern Sweden's mountainous terrain is dotted with hundreds of small glaciers. A broad, forested plateau sloping down from the mountains to the Gulf of Bothnia dominates northeastern Sweden. Hydroelectric power stations perched on the plateau's many rivers provide more than 60 percent of Sweden's energy. High-voltage power lines carry the electricity to the industrial areas of central and southern Sweden. The remainder of Sweden's energy is from nuclear power stations, but Sweden has decided to phase out nuclear energy by 2010.

A broad low-lying region of woodlands and lakes stretches across southern Sweden from Göteborg to the capital city of Stockholm. Natives and tourists flock to this area to camp, hike, and fish. Much of Sweden's manufacturing industry is located around Göteborg in the west and Stockholm and Eskilstuna in the east. Vast reserves of iron ore, copper, gold, lead, and other metals cover much of the Inner Northland. The country is a leading exporter of iron and steel, cars, aircraft, ball bearings, electrical equipment, and household appliances. Sweden also boasts the world's second-largest shipbuilding industry.

Swedish agriculture is concentrated in the fertile lowlands at the country's southern tip. Modern, highly mechanized farms specialize in meat and dairy produce. Farmers grow barley, oats, and hay for animal feed and grains, fruits, and vegetables for human consumption.

Status:	Republic
Area:	130,560 square miles
Population:	5.2 million
Capital:	Helsinki
Languages:	Finnish, Swedish
Currency:	Euro (100 cents)

Finland's capital, Helsinki, lies farther north than any other capital city except Reykjavík, the capital of Iceland. Most of Finland is low and flat. Two-thirds of the country is below 650 feet. Finland's highest point—in the far northwest—is only 4,357 feet above sea level.

Finland has three principal landscapes—the Upland District, the Lake District, and the flat Coastal Lowlands. Peat bogs and forests of pine, spruce, and birch cover the northern uplands, give way to treeless Arctic tundra in the far north. Very few people other than the nomadic Sami (also called the Lapps), along with their reindeer herds, live this far north. South central Finland is a lowland region of bogs, dense forests, and more than 60,000 lakes. Almost one-tenth of the country is covered by water. The lakes are shallow and fill the hollows in the thick layer of clay left behind by ice age glaciers. Coastal plains, 40 to 80 miles wide, extend along the Gulf of Bothnia and the Gulf of Finland.

Finland's forestry workers provide lumber, plywood, wood pulp, and paper for export. The country also mines copper, nickel, iron, zinc, chromium, and other useful metals. Engineering and shipbuilding are Finland's second-largest industries, followed by glass, chemicals, and textiles. Farmers on the coastal lowlands raise dairy and beef cattle, poultry, and pigs. They also grow wheat, barley, and vegetables.

0
100
200
300
0
200
400 Km
BARENTS SEA
NORWEGIAN SEA
WHITE SEA
RUSSIA
R
FINLAND
SWEDEN
NORWAY
ESTONIA
LATVIA
LITHUANIA
Utsjoki
Inarijärvi
Lotta
Enontekiö
Kiruna
Torne
Vittangi
Kittilä
Sodankylä
Pelkosenniemi
Ounasjoki
Gällivare
Torne
Rovaniemi
Jokkmokk
Övertorneå
Kemijoki
Kiule
Tornio
Kemi
Boden
Luleå
Sorsele
Arvidsjaur
Skellefte
Piteå
Hailuoto
Oulu
Oulujoki
Oulujärvi
Dikanäs
Storuman
Raahe
Åsträsk
Skellefteå
Kajaani
Vuokatti
Lycksele
Vilhelmina
Ume
Hällnäs
Lövånger
Dorotea
Sukeva
Alanäs
Hoting
Bygdeå
Pyhäjärvi
Iisalmi
Kokkola
Hotagen
Umeå
Jakobstad
Offerdal
Gåxsjö
Ådalsliden
Nykarleby
Kuopio
Outokumpu
Indals
Joensuu
Östersund
Örnsköldsvik
Vaasa
Lapua
Gulf of Bothnia
Kramfors
Håsjö
Seinäjoki
Varkaus
Äsarna
Härnösand
Jyväskylä
Kaskinen
Klövsjo
Sundsvall
Linsell
Ljusnan
Sysmä
Gnarp
Ljusdal
Tampere
Lillhärdal
Heinola
Hudiksvall
Pori
L. Ladoga
Los
Särna
Kouvola
Bollnäs
Hämeenlinna
Rauma
Söderhamn
Lahti
Anjalankoski
Forssa
Mora
Hyvinkää
Kotka
Höljes
Rättvik
Gävle
Porvoo
Leksand
Gävle Bay
Naantali
Turku
Åland
Falun
Helsinki
Gulf of Finland
Klar
Appelbo
Borlänge
Ekenäs
Mariehamn
Västerdalälv
Hangö
Arvika
Uppsala
Kopparberg
Västerås
Karlstad
Örebro
Stockholm
L. Peipus
Karlskoga
Eskilstuna
Södertälje
Hiiumaa
Strömstad
Katrineholm
Vänern
Saaremaa
Motala
Norrköping
Uddevalla
Lidköping
Vättern
Trollhättan
Linköping
Gulf of Riga
Gotland
Gränna
Göteborg
Boras
Huskvarna
Västervik
Mölndal
Jönköping
Visby
Vetlanda
Mälilla
BALTIC SEA
Varberg
Emån
Växjö
Kattegat
Borgholm
Halmstad
Kalmar
Öland I.
Tingsryd
Helsingborg
Karlskrona
Kalmar Sound
Kristianstad
Malmö
Hanö Bay
Ystad
Trelleborg
Bornholm

Estonia, Latvia, Lithuania

Estonia

Latvia

Lithuania

The three small countries known as the Baltic States—Estonia, Latvia, and Lithuania—cluster along the eastern shore of the Baltic Sea. Russia, Belarus, Poland, and the small territory of Kaliningrad (part of the Russian Federation) border the countries on the inland side. Before World War I , the Baltic States belonged to the Russian Empire. When the war ended in 1918, the three states gained independence. In 1940 during World War II, the Soviet Union (a successor to the Russian Empire) seized the three countries. After 50 years under Soviet control, Lithuania declared independence in 1990. Estonia and Latvia broke free the following year.

The three states have very similar geography. The land is flat and low-lying, with large areas of coniferous forest dotted with marshlands, peat bogs, and lakes. The climate is cool and mild at the coast, but farther inland—and in the north—the summers are short and winters are long and very cold.

Estonia's main resources are oil shale, which provides fuel for power plants, and phosphates, which are used to make fertilizer and other chemical products. Shipbuilding, engineering, chemicals, and textiles are the country's primary industries.

Latvia produces telephones and other electronic equipment, railroad cars, machinery, and household appliances. The country has no coal, oil, or gas reserves and imports most of its energy supplies from Estonia.

Lithuania has some oil and gas and a large nuclear power plant near the town of Ignalina. The country imports crude oil, processing it into fuels and other chemical products. Lithuania's factories produce industrial machinery, ceramics, glass, and textiles.

All three countries have fishing fleets and forest-based industries that create lumber, wood pulp, paper, and wood products such as furniture. Farmers in the Baltic States raise beef and dairy cattle, pigs, sheep, and poultry. Essential field crops are rye, oats, sugar beets, potatoes, and other vegetables. Most farmers grow fodder crops, and many specialize in growing flax, which is used to make linen and linseed oil.

Status:	Constitutional Monarchy
Area:	15,768 square miles
Population:	15.8 million
Capital:	Amsterdam
Language:	Dutch
Currency:	Guilder (100 cents)

The Netherlands—historically known as Holland—is one of Europe's smallest countries and is also one of the most crowded. Each square mile of land supports almost 1,200 people, compared to 277 per square mile in France and 76 per square mile in the United States. Despite this high population density, the Dutch people have one of the highest standards of living in Europe. International trade, many diverse industries, and a very efficient farming system all help support excellent state-funded education, health, and social services.

Nearly one-third of the country's land area is below sea level. The highest point, Vaalser Berg in the Southern Uplands, rises to just 1,053 feet above sea level. This lack of elevation has led people to name the Netherlands and neighbouring Belgium the Low Countries. The country's southern delta region is formed by the Maas, Rhine, and Schelde Rivers, which empty into the North Sea. Huge earth-filled dams, called dykes, prevent the North Sea from flooding vast areas of reclaimed land called polders. Dutch engineers are world leaders in land reclamation and in designing flood and sea defenses.

Farms occupy nearly 70 percent of the Netherlands, and farmers concentrate on high-value produce such as butter and cheese, flower bulbs, and tomatoes and other vegetables grown in greenhouses. Potatoes, sugar beets, and wheat grow in some areas.

The Netherlands has both oil and natural gas but imports large quantities of crude oil to feed the large refineries at Rotterdam. Imported raw materials support the manufacturing industries clustered around the busy ports of Amsterdam and Rotterdam—the gateways to Europe's inland waterways.

Belgium

Status:	Constitutional Monarchy
Area:	11,787 square miles
Population:	10.3 million
Capital:	Brussels
Languages:	Dutch, French
Currency:	Euro (100 cents)

Belgium, like the Netherlands, is densely populated and enjoys a high standard of living. Most of the country is flat and low-lying, rising gently to the forested hills of the Ardennes region on Belgium's borders with France and Luxembourg. Reclaimed polders along the coast provide the best cropland, while farmers in the higher inland regions concentrate on livestock and dairy farming. Belgium's main crops are wheat, barley, oats, sugar beets, flowers, vegetables, and hops (used to make the country's famous beers).

Excellent roads, railroads, and waterways link Belgium's manufacturing areas with Europe's main trading ports in the Netherlands. Belgian industries import raw materials for production of exports, such as textiles, glassware, metal goods, and electrical products. Luxury goods include lace and chocolate. Eighty percent of Belgium's energy is nuclear power, one of the highest percentages in the world.

Belgium was a founding member of the European Union. Many of the EU's governing bodies are headquartered in the capital city of Brussels alongside the command centre of the North Atlantic Treaty Organization (NATO) and other international organizations.

Status:	Federal Republic
Area:	137,830 square miles
Population:	82.5 million
Capital:	Berlin
Language:	German
Currency:	Euro (100 cents)

Germany is among the world's leading trade nations, is a major international finance centre, and is one of the most powerful partners in the EU. Before World War II, Germany was a single country, but at the end of the war the Allied Powers—Britain, France, the United States, and the Soviet Union—divided it in two. The Federal Republic of Germany (West Germany) remained allied with western Europe, while the German Democratic Republic (East Germany) became part of the Communist bloc, controlled by the Soviet Union. The two German states were reunited in 1990.

Western Germany's industry is modern and efficient, and the people have long enjoyed a very high standard of living. By contrast, eastern Germany's industries were badly run-down and inefficient. Since reunification, Germany is investing a great deal of money in eastern Germany's modernization.

Germany lacks abundant natural resources. Large coal deposits lie beneath the western Ruhr Valley—the country's main industrial region—and small oil and gas fields dot the northern lowlands, but Germany imports most of its necessary raw materials and energy. The country's economic strength rests on modern industries turning out high-quality manufactured goods such as cars, trucks, trams and buses, machine tools, printing presses, precision instruments, and electronic equipment. Germany also exports many chemical and pharmaceutical products.

Northern Germany is a flat lowland plain with patches of fertile farmland and sandy heathland. Farmers grow barley, oats, rye, potatoes, and sugar beets. Central Germany consists of rolling uplands and small, fertile river valleys, where farmers concentrate on producing grapes and hops. Cattle, pigs, horses, poultry, and sheep graze throughout the country, but Germany's best pastureland is in the southeast. In southern Germany the land rises toward the spectacular Alps. Forested mountains, beautiful lakes, picturesque castles, and medieval towns draw thousands of tourists to southern Germany each year.

- Mostly forested land
- Mostly cropland
- Grazing land mixed with cropland
- Major urban-industrial centre

Germany

0
50
100 Miles
0
50
100
150 Km
Sylt
Flensburg
Flensburg Fjord
Schleswig
Husum
Eckernförde
Fehmarn
Burg
Kiel Bay
Kiel
Rendsburg
Heide
Helgoland
Mecklenburg Bay
NORTH SEA
Neumünster
Lübeck Bay
Itzehoe
Cuxhaven
East Frisian Is.
Bad Oldsloe
Lübeck
Wismar
Rostock
Elmshorn
Ahrensburg
Norderstedt
Norden
Schortens
Bremerhaven
Wilhelmshaven
Buxtehude
Hamburg
Schwerin
L. Schwerin
West Frisian Is.
Emden
Nordenham
Leer
Varel
Winsen
Bucholz
Lüneburg
Bad Zwischenahn
Oldenburg
Papenburg
Bremen
Delmenhorst
Soltau
Weser
Verden
Walsrode
Uelzen
Elbe
Ems
Cloppenburg
Vechta
Meppen
NETHERLANDS
Lingen
Nienburg
Celle
Salzwedel
Wittenberge
L. Dümmer
L. Steinhude
Wolfsburg
Nordhorn
Bramsche
Wunstorf
Hannover
Aller
Rheine
Osnabrück
Minden
Stendal
Rathenow
Enschede
Gronau
Melle
Braunschweig
Wolfenbüttel
Burg
Ahaus
Teutoburg Forest
Bielefeld
Hameln
Hildesheim
Salzgitter
Magdeburg
Emmerich
Coesfeld
Münster
Detmold
Bad Harzburg
Osterwieck
Halberstadt
Rhine
Bocholt
Haltern
Gütersloh
Holzminden
Harz Mts.
Wernigerode
Goch
Hamm
Lippstadt
Paderborn
Osterode
Wesel
Dinslaken
Dortmund
Duisburg
Essen
Menden
Marsberg
Göttingen
Nordhausen
Eisleben
Krefeld
Hagen
Arnsberg
Münden
Mönchen-gladbach
Düsseldorf
Wuppertal
Korbach
Sondershausen
Kassel
Mühlhausen
Remscheid
Lennestadt
Solingen
Eschwege
Cologne
Bergisch-gladbach
Siegen
Bad Hersfeld
Aachen
Düren
Marburg
Bonn
GERMANY
Alsfeld
Eisenach
Gotha
Erfurt
Monschau
Fulda
Werra
Thuringian Forest
Neuwied
Giessen
Wetzlar
Fulda
Suhl
BELGIUM
Mayen
Koblenz
Friedberg
Prüm
Daun
Rhone Mts.
Taunus Mts.
Wiesbaden
Frankfurt am Main
Coburg
Rhine
Hanau
Offenbach
Vianden
Mosel
Hunsrück
Bingen
Mainz
Aschaffenburg
Schweinfurt
Main
LUXEMBOURG
Trier
Darmstadt
Würzburg
Main
Bamberg
Kitzingen
Wertheim
Saar
St Wendel
Worms
Steigerwald
Ludwigshafen
Mannheim
Saarbrücken
Kaiserslautern
Fürth
Nuremberg
Landau
Heidelberg
Jagst
Ansbach
Roth
Pirmasens
Neumarkt
Karlsruhe
Heilbronn
Pappenheim
Franconian Jura
Pforzheim
Ludwigsburg
Stuttgart
Aalen
Baden-Baden
Heidenheim
Donauwörth
Danube
Offenburg
Tübingen
Reutlingen
Lahr
Neckar
Black Forest
Schwabian Jura
Ulm
Augsburg
Rotweil
Rhine
Lech
Biberach
FRANCE
Freiburg
Memmingen
Landsberg
Munich
Weingarten
Kempten
Basel
Schaffhausen
Konstanz
L. Constance
Bregenz
Dornbirn
Feldkirch
Reutte
Bavarian Alps
SWITZERLAND
ALPS
Finsteraarhorn
Inn
BALTIC SEA
Sassnitz
Rügen
Stralsund
Pomeranian Bay
Anklam
Oder Lagoon
Güstrow
L. Kummerow
Neubrandenburg
L. Plau
Waren
Parchim
L. Müritz
Neustrelitz
Prenzlau
Eberswalde-Finow
Oder
POLA
Falkensee
Berlin
Fürstenwalde
Brandenburg
Potsdam
Frankfurt (an der Oder)
Luckenwalde
Eisenhüttenstadt
L. Schwieloch
Guben
Wittenberg
Lübben
Dessau
Bernburg
Cottbus
Finsterwalde
Forst
Elbe
Halle
Delitzsch
Spremberg
Lauchhammer
Neisse
Hoyerswerda
Weissenfels
Leipzig
Döbeln
Meissen
Görlitz
Zeitz
Borna
Bautzen
Dresden
Weimar
Jena
Gera
Chemnitz
Freiberg
Rudolstadt
Greiz
Zwickau
Saalfeld
Aue
Ore Mts.
Plauen
Hof
Kulmbach
Selb
CZECH REPUBLIC
Bayreuth
Weiden
Amberg
Schwandorf
Cham
Bohemian Forest
Regensburg
Straubing
Ingolstadt
Passau
Landshut
Inn
Waldkraiburg
Braunau
Salzach
Salzburg
Rosenheim
Hallein
Kufstein
AUSTRIA

Switzerland

Status:	Federal Republic
Area:	15,942 sq. miles
Population:	7.1 million
Capital:	Bern
Languages:	German, French, Italian
Currency:	Swiss franc (100 rappen)

Mountains cover nearly three-fifths of Switzerland. The snow-capped Alps in the south include 15,203-foot Monte Rosa and the dramatic 14,691-foot Matterhorn. The forested Jura Mountains rise in the north to 5,518 feet. Most Swiss people live on the Mittelland—a central plateau of rolling hills, broad river valleys, and beautiful lakes such as Lake Geneva, Lake Lucerne, and Lake Constance.

Switzerland is poor in natural resources. Mountain rivers provide hydroelectric power, but all other fuels and industrial raw materials must be imported. The Swiss have made up for this lack of resources by specializing in the production of high-quality, high-value precision-engineering goods such as clocks and watches, machine tools, scientific instruments, microscopes, and laboratory equipment. Swiss factories also produce glassware, textiles, chemicals, pharmaceuticals, and luxury foods such as chocolate and cheese. Switzerland spends more on imports than it earns from its exports but makes up the difference with a thriving tourist industry—nearly 12 million visitors a year—and the country's world-famous international banking and insurance businesses.

Farmers in the more fertile valleys grow grains, potatoes, sugar beets, vegetables, and fruit. Many farmers also raise beef and dairy cattle. Those in the south take advantage of their nearness to the mountains, grazing their animals on the high alpine pastures in the summer and herding them back to the sheltered valleys for the winter.

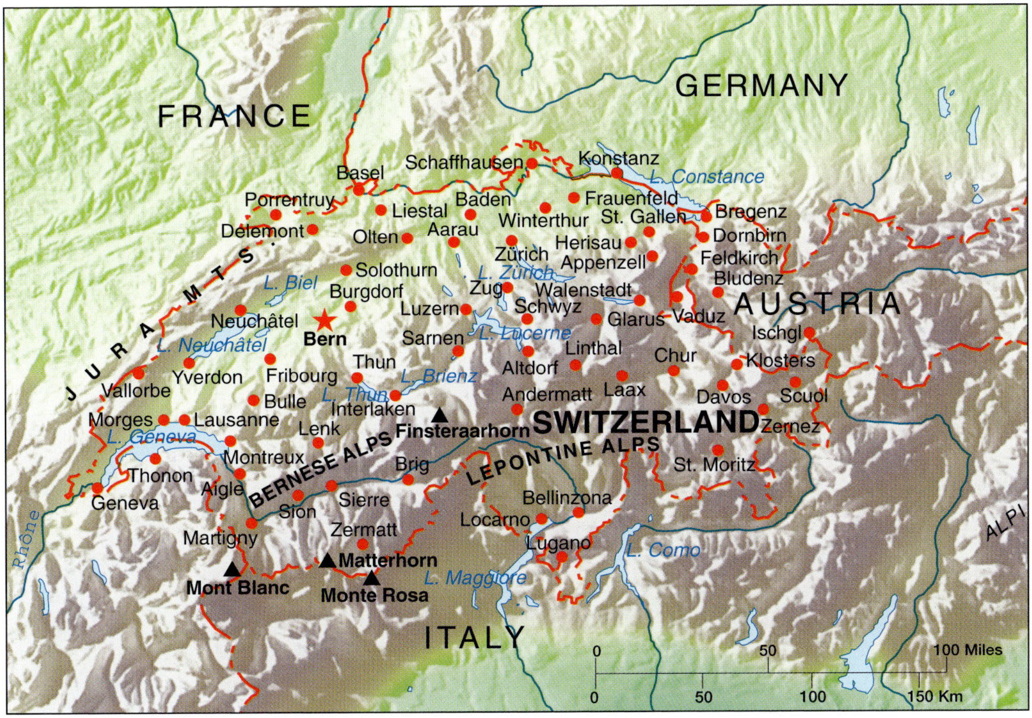

Austria

Status:	Federal Republic
Area:	32,378 sq. miles
Population:	8.1 million
Capital:	Vienna
Language:	German
Currency:	Euro (100 cents)

Austria's Alps attract thousands of winter sports enthusiasts every year.

The jagged Austrian Alps and their foothills cover most of western, southern, and central Austria. At 12,470 feet, the Grossglockner towers over this mountainous area. Central Europe's longest river—the Danube—flows through northern Austria's fertile valleys and past the forested hills that border the Czech Republic. Eastern Austria is a broad fertile plain that slopes gently eastward and merges with the great plain of Hungary.

Austria's farmers utilize only about 20 percent of the land, but modern methods and machinery allow them to meet three-quarters of the country's food needs. Meat and dairy production, grains, sugar beets, potatoes, fruits, and vegetables contribute to both the local and export markets. Forests cover about 40 percent of the country. Strict conservation laws control lumber companies, allowing them to produce a steady but replaceable supply of sawed lumber, pulp, and paper.

Graphite, magnesite, and iron ore are Austria's most valuable mineral resources. Hydroelectricity generated by mountain rivers accounts for two-thirds of Austria's energy needs. The balance derives from imported fuels and small local oil and gas fields. Most of the manufacturing industries are located in the Danube Valley and around Vienna, where factories produce iron and steel, cars, tractors, machinery, electrical goods, plastics, chemicals, textiles, ceramics, and processed foods. Like most alpine countries, a thriving tourist industry based on winter sports and cultural attractions such as historic Vienna and the famous Salzburg Festival bolsters Austria's economy.

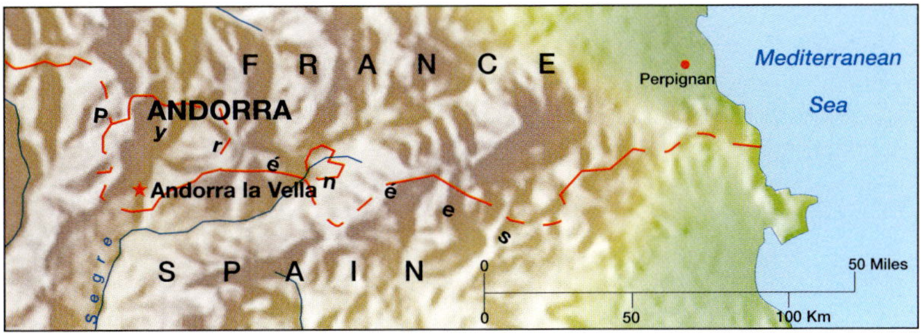

Andorra

Status:	Co-principality
Area:	174 sq. mi.
Population:	64,000
Capital:	Andorra la Vella
Languages:	Catalan, French, Spanish
Currency:	Euro (100 cents)

Monaco

Status:	Constitutional Monarchy
Area:	1.0 square mile
Population:	32,000
Capital:	Monaco
Languages:	French, Monegasque
Currency:	Euro (100 cents)

Vatican City

Status:	Sovereign State of the Holy See
Area:	0.2 sq. miles
Population:	900
Capital:	Vatican City
Language:	Italian
Currency:	Euro (100 cents)

Andorra

Andorra sits on the French-Spanish border, high in the Pyrénées Mountains. Beginning in 1278, the Spanish Bishop of Urgel and the French Comte de Foix (later the French president) became the country's joint heads of state. When Andorra adopted its first constitution in 1993, these co-princes lost most of their power. An elected council with a modern constitution governs the country.

Tourism drives Andorra's economy. Visitors can buy luxury items without paying high duties.

Monaco

Tucked into the Mediterranean coast, Monaco lies nine miles east of the French city of Nice. The capital, also named Monaco, perches on a rocky headland, overlooking the Port of Monaco. Monte Carlo's casinos, luxury hotels, opera house, and famous beaches are just minutes away. Monegasques—natives of Monaco—comprise only 14 precent of the population. French citizens account for nearly half the population, and Italians number about 16 percent. The Grimaldi family has ruled Monaco since 1308, but in the past it accepted protection from and partial control by Italy, France, and Sardinia. Modern Monaco is an independent country with close ties to France.

Some Monegasques work in light industry, but Monaco's economy depends on tourism and banking. Extremely low taxes have encouraged foreign corporations to relocate to Monaco, and many of the world's wealthy and famous people have built lavish homes along the sun-drenched coast.

Vatican City

The walled enclosure of Vatican City lies on the west bank of the Tiber River in the middle of the city of Rome, Italy. The Vatican is the home of the Holy See—the Roman Catholic Church's governing body. Vatican City is also one of the world's great cultural treasure houses, containing museums, galleries, libraries, St. Peter's Basilica, and the Vatican Palace where Michelangelo's famous paintings grace the ceiling of the Sistine Chapel. The pope is head of state, but Vatican City also has a civil administration run by a governor and a Pontifical Commission.

Status: Republic
Area: 23 sq. mi.
Population: 27,000
Capital: San Marino
Language: Italian
Currency: Euro (100 cents)

San Marino, the world's oldest republic, nestles on top of Mount Titano, a limestone peak on the eastern edge of the Apennine Mountains about 12 miles southwest of the Italian port of Rimini.

Many San Marinese work in tourism, hosting two million visitors each year. Other locals labour on small farms, in limestone quarries, or in factories producing leather goods, ceramics, and textiles.

Status: Republic
Area: 124 sq. mi.
Population: 397,000
Capital: Valletta
Languages: Maltese, English
Currency: Maltese lira (100 cents)

The tiny island country of Malta, 60 miles south of Sicily, comprises three inhabited islands—Malta, Gozo, and Comino—and three small uninhabited islands. Formerly a British colony, Malta became independent in 1964.

Low limestone hills cover most of Malta. The soil is thin and dry, and farmers can raise only small crops of barley, wheat, potatoes, grapes, and citrus fruits. The Maltese have to import most of their food and also the fuel and raw materials for the islands' manufacturing industries—ship repairs, textiles, and electrical goods. Most Maltese work in the shipyards, in construction, or in tourism.

Status:	Constitutional Monarchy
Area:	62 square miles
Population:	34,000
Capital:	Vaduz
Language:	German
Currency:	Swiss franc (100 centimes)

Liechtenstein

Roughly the size of Washington, D.C., Liechtenstein lies between Austria and Switzerland. A narrow strip of fertile land in the country's northwest runs along the Rhine River. Farmers use this lowland area to raise beef and dairy cattle and to grow grains, vegetables, and fruits—including grapes for wine production. Southeastern Liechtenstein is mountainous and nearly covered with pine forests. Before World War II, Liechtenstein was a farming country. The modern economy is highly industrialized, specializing in machinery, scientific and medical instruments, pharmaceuticals, ceramics, and textiles.

From 1815 to 1866 the country was part of the German Confederation but kept its independence. Liechtenstein remains a monarchy, ruled by the House of Liechtenstein, but also has a constitution and an elected government.

Status:	Constitutional Monarchy
Area:	1,000 square miles
Population:	465,000
Capital:	Luxembourg
Languages:	French, German, Letzeburgish
Currency:	Euro (100 cents)

Luxembourg

The Grand Duchy of Luxembourg shares borders with Belgium, France, and Germany. Wooded hills in the north merge with the Belgian Ardennes. Fertile lowlands in the southern two-thirds of the country provide rich agricultural land where farmers grow barley, wheat, oats, and potatoes and raise pigs and cattle. Luxembourg's main industries are located in the south. Iron ore supplies the primary raw material for a huge iron and steel industry. Luxembourg's workforce also produces chemicals, plastics, synthetic fibres, and computer equipment.

Luxembourg was a founding member of the EU. The country also headquarters both the European Court of Justice and the European Coal and Steel Community. Luxembourg's history traces back to the Holy Roman Empire of the Middle Ages and includes periods of rule by Spain, Austria, France, and the Netherlands. The country gained its independence in 1867.

Italy

Status:	Republic
Area:	116,320 square miles
Population:	57.7 million
Capital:	Rome
Language:	Italian
Currency:	Euro (100 cents)

Italy's distinctive long, boot-shaped peninsula stretches 685 miles southward from the Alps to the Mediterranean Sea, reaching almost to the northern coast of Africa. Italy shares borders with France, Switzerland, Austria, and Slovenia and is bound by three seas—the Tyrrhenian Sea to the west, the Ionian Sea in the south, and the Adriatic Sea on the east. Italy's territory also includes the large islands of Sardinia to the west and Sicily, just off the toe of the boot.

The Alps in the far north provide Italy with magnificent scenery and fine skiing resorts that support a thriving winter tourist industry. Alpine rivers supply hydroelectric power to the large northwestern industrial centres of Milan, Turin, and Genoa. Just south of the mountains, the land levels out onto the North Italian Plain—Italy's only large lowland area. Farmers in this fertile region grow wheat, barley, rice, vegetables, fruits, and tobacco. The Po River and its tributaries provide the extra water needed to irrigate the rice fields in summer. Large numbers of tourists visit Venice and Verona in the northeast and Bologna and Florence farther south in the Apennine foothills.

The Apennine Mountains snake down the peninsula like a backbone, curving from west to east and back again. Italy's highest northern mountains run along the country's Adriatic shore. Broad coastal plains lie to the west. Farther south the mountains hug the Tyrrhenian coast, creating spectacular cliffs and headlands south of Naples. Historic Rome, the ruins of the ancient cities of Pompeii and Herculaneum, the Bay of Naples, and the island of Capri attract thousands of tourists to Italy's western coast. Italy also boasts Europe's only active volcanoes—Vesuvius just inland from Naples, Mount Etna on Sicily, and Stromboli and Vulcano on small islands off the north coast of Sicily.

Southern Italy has a hotter, drier climate than the north. Most of the farmers are smallholders or tenants working farm plots on large estates. They graze sheep and goats on the dry uplands and grow olives, grapes, tomatoes, fruits, vegetables, and flowers—most of which they export to northern Europe.

Italians mine sulphur and mercury, and the quarries at Carrara produce some of the world's finest marble, but the country imports most industrial raw materials, fuel oil, and coal. Italian power is 80 percent thermal and 20 percent hydroelectric. Major iron and steel centres have developed in Taranto, Naples, Piombino, and Genoa. Italians manufacture vehicles, motorcycles, aircraft, ships, military equipment, power tools, electronic goods, household appliances, and textiles—especially fashion and sportswear. Petrochemical plants produce industrial chemicals, fertilizers, plastics, synthetic fibres, and rubber.

Far left: Venice is built partly on the Italian mainland and partly on 120 small islands off the northeastern coast. The city's canals, spanned by hundreds of bridges, are its roads and streets.

Left: The Fountain of Neptune in Rome's Piazza Navona was created in the mid-1600s by the sculptor Gian Lorenzo Bernini. It is one of more than 300 beautiful fountains that adorn the Italian capital.

SWITZERLAND
AUSTRIA
HUNGARY
SLOVENIA
CROATIA
BOSNIA-HERZEGOVINA
DINARIC ALPS
ALPS
MONACO
ITALY
CORSICA
SARDINIA
SICILY
TUNISIA
MALTA
Gozo
APENNINES
ADRIATIC SEA
LIGURIAN SEA
TYRRHENIAN SEA
MEDITERRANEAN SEA
SICILIAN CHANNEL
IONIAN SEA
Monte Rosa
Matterhorn
Corno Grande
Vesuvius
Mt. Etna
Lake Maggiore
Lake Como
Lake Lecco
Lake Garda
Lake Trasimeno
Lake Bolsena
Lake Varano
Ticino
Oglio
Po
Adige
Piave
Panaro
Reno
Arno
Tiber
Pescara
Liri
Ofanto
Tanagro
Bradano
Tirso
Côte d'Azur
Gulf of Genoa
Gulf of Venice
Gulf of Gaeta
Bay of Naples
Gulf of Salerno
Gulf of Manfredonia
Gulf of Taranto
Gulf of Squillace
Gulf of Catania
Gulf of Gela
Gulf of Asinara
Gulf of Orosei
Gulf of Cagliari
Strait of Bonifacio
Bolzano
Pieve di Cadore
Trento
Borgo
Udine
Trieste
Arona
Lecco
Bergamo
Rovereto
Bassano
Treviso
Portogruaro
Biella
Monza
Milan
Crema
Brescia
Vicenza
Venice
Garlasco
Pavia
Lodi
Verona
Padova
Turin
Valenza
Voghera
Cremona
Lendinara
Chioggia
Alessandria
Piacenza
Mantova
Rovigo
Adria
Porto Tolle
Tortona
Parma
Novi Ligure
Ovada
Salsomaggiore
Carpi
Cento
Ferrara
Comacchio
Reggio
Modena
Mondovì
Savona
Genoa
Pontremoli
Bologna
Ravenna
Carrara
La Spezia
Massa
Forlì
Rimini
San Marino
Pesaro
Viareggio
Lucca
Pistoia
Empoli
Florence
Pisa
Montevarchi
Sansepolcro
Iesi
Ancona
Livorno
Volterra
Siena
Arezzo
Cortona
Fabriano
Osimo
Macerata
Perugia
Cape Corse
Capri
Elba I.
Piombino
Norcia
San Benedetto
Bastia
Grosseto
Terni
Teramo
Giglio I.
Pescara
Rieti
Civitavecchia
Vasto
Termoli
Peschici
Vieste
Ajaccio
Avezzano
Rome
Agnone
Isernia
Foggia
Bonifacio
Latina
Benevento
I.Asinara
Bari
Olbia
Ponza Is.
Naples
Melfi
Altamura
Alghero
Sassari
Ischia
Salerno
Potenza
Brindisi
Taranto
Nuoro
Agropoli
Senise
Lecce
Gallipoli
Oristano
Tricase
Scalea
Castrovilla
Belvedere Marittimo
Rossano
Cosenza
Cagliari
San Pietro
Amantea
Crotone
Catanzaro
Stromboli I.
Vibo Valentia
Salina I.
Lipari I.
Lipari Is.
Vulcano I.
Nicotera
Palmi
Messina
Reggio di Calabria
Trapani
Palermo
Alcamo
ISOLE EGADI
Mazara del Vallo
Catania
Caltanissetta
Agrigento
Ragusa
Siracusa
Pantelleria I.
0 50 100 150 Miles
0 100 200 Km

Poland

Status:	Republic
Area:	124,807 sq. miles
Population:	38.7 million
Capital:	Warsaw
Language:	Polish
Currency:	Zloty (100 groszy)

Poland's landscape is dominated by the Great North European Plain, a vast expanse of flat land extending from northern Germany, across Poland, and into neighbouring Belarus and Ukraine. Soil quality is poor in northern Poland, and forests cover much of the countryside. Rich soil and the country's major farming regions lie in central and southern Poland. The Sudetic and Carpathian Mountains form Poland's jagged southern border.

Most Polish farms are small family businesses. Not highly mechanized, the farms cover almost two-thirds of the land, producing huge quantities of rye and potatoes.

Lesser crops include barley, oats, wheat, sugar beets, and other vegetables. Many farmers also raise pigs, beef and dairy cattle, and sheep.

Poland's only coastline is a short expanse on the Baltic Sea with a well-developed fishing industry. Primary catches are cod and herring, much of which is processed in the ports of Szczecin, Gda´nsk, and Gdynia—either frozen or canned for human consumption or turned into animal feed. The ports house ship repair yards, container terminals, and bulk cargo facilities for handling exports of coal, grain, and metal ores.

Southern Poland sits on one of the world's most abundant reserves of hard coal and lignite, a soft brown coal. Polish workers also mine copper, silver, lead, zinc, and nickel. Iron and steel production in Katowice forms the backbone of Poland's industrial sector. Metal-based industries include ships, cars, aircraft, and railroad stock. Lód´z is the hub of the country's textile industry, and Plock, near Warsaw, is the centre of Poland's petrochemical industry.

Status:	Republic
Area:	30,448 sq. mi.
Population:	10.3 million
Capital:	Prague
Language:	Czech
Currency:	Koruna (100 haléru)

Czech Republic

From 1918 to 1992, the Czech Republic was part of the Communist country of Czechoslovakia. Communist rule ended in 1989 when Václav Havel, a playwright, led the nonviolent Velvet Revolution, which toppled the old regime. In its place the Czech people adopted a democratic system with an elected government. The two factions of the old state—the Czechs and the Slovaks—could not agree on how to proceed, and on January 1, 1993, they separated into two nations called the Czech Republic and Slovakia. Good health and educational services enable the two states to have a higher standard of living than many of the former Communist states.

The Czech Republic is divided into the highland region of Bohemia in the west and the Moravian lowlands in the east. Farmers in both areas produce wheat, sugar beets, rye, hops, potatoes, and other vegetables. Summers are warm, but the winters are long and cold. Mines in the highlands produce uranium, lead, zinc, copper, mercury, and tin. Czech factories produce steel, machinery, cars, clothing, and leather goods, much of which is exported to western Europe.

Status:	Republic
Area:	18,923 sq. mi.
Population:	5.4 million
Capital:	Bratislava
Languages:	Slovak, Hungarian, Czech
Currency:	Koruna (100 halierov)

Slovakia

Slovakia comprised the eastern one-third of Czechoslovakia until the two countries gained independence in 1993. The forested Carpathian Mountains dominate northern Slovakia. The rest of the country is mainly lowland, sloping south to east to merge with the Hungarian Plain. Several of Slovakia's rivers flow into the Danube, which marks the country's border with Hungary.

Slovakia's climate is temperate, with cold winters and hot summers, especially in the lowland areas. Farmers tend grains, beets, potatoes, and other vegetables. Pigs are common farm animals, as they are in many eastern European countries, but Slovak farmers also raise beef and dairy cattle, sheep, and poultry. Slovakia's main natural resources are iron ore, copper, lead, zinc, mercury, and perlite—a volcanic rock that is crushed and used to make plaster, cement, and some types of insulation. Factory workers make vehicles, machinery, chemicals, plastics, and paper. Coal-burning and hydroelectric power plants provide the country's energy.

Status:	Republic
Area:	35,919 sq. mi.
Population:	10.1 million
Capital:	Budapest
Languages:	Hungarian, German
Currency:	Forint (100 fillér)

Hungary

Two large lowlands dominate the Hungarian landscape—the Little Plain in the northwest and the Great Plain in the southeast. A line of low hills separates the two plains, stretching from Lake Balaton and the Bakony Forest to the Northern Highlands on the Hungarian-Slovakian border. At 45 miles long, Lake Balaton is central Europe's largest lake and a popular tourist resort.

Some of Europe's most fertile soil covers Hungary's plains, and the country's spring rains and long hot summers are ideal for growing wheat, corn, beets, potatoes and other vegetables. Upland farmers tend grapes for wine. Those in drier, sandy areas raise cattle, pigs, and poultry.

Factories in Hungary's main industrial regions around Budapest and Miskolc produce trucks and buses, machinery, chemicals, textiles, leather goods, and canned foods. Hungary has some natural gas and large deposits of bauxite—the principal ore of aluminium—but has to import most of the fuel and raw materials it needs for industry.

Czech Republic, Slovakia, Hungary

Prague, straddling the Vltava River, is one of Europe's oldest and most beautiful cities. The Charles Bridge, lined with statues of the Christian saints, is a local attraction in this City of a Hundred Spires.

Status:	Parliamentary Democracy
Area:	7,819 sq. mi.
Population:	2 million
Capital:	Ljubljana
Languages:	Slovenian, Serbo-Croatian, Italian
Currency:	Tolar (100 stotins)

Slovenia

Slovenia is a small mountainous country bordered by Italy, Austria, Hungary, and Croatia. It has a short stretch of Adriatic coastline to the southwest. Visitors are attracted to the country's mountain lakes, coastal resorts, limestone caves of Postojna (the largest European caverns), and the medieval capital, Ljubljana.

Slovenes farm about one-quarter of the land, growing grain, potatoes, beets, hops, flax, and fruit trees. Cattle, pigs, sheep, and horses graze on another one-quarter. About 40 percent of the country is covered in trees—conifers on the high ground, with chiefly beech and oak at the lower elevations. Slovenia's mines produce mercury, bauxite, copper, antimony, zinc, and iron ore. Manufactured goods include vehicles, chemicals, textiles, and electrical goods. Slovenial became the first of the former Communist bloc countries to join the EU in January 2007.

Status:	Parliamentary Democracy
Area:	21,830 sq. mi.
Population:	4.4 million
Capital:	Zagreb
Languages:	Slovenian, Serbo-Croatian, Italian
Currency:	Croatian kuna (100 lipes)

Croatia

Croatia has two distinct climates split east to west along the Dinaric Alps. A large lowland region called the Pannonia Plains extends eastward to the Serbian border, and a contrasting region of limestone mountains extends southward along the coast. The Dinaric Alps and the resorts along the spectacular Dalmatian coast once attracted huge numbers of overseas visitors. Civil war has severely damaged this valuable tourist industry.

Thick black soil on Croatia's lowland plain provides some of the best farmland in Europe, producing large crops of grains, beets, cotton, sunflowers, olives, fruit, hemp, and flax. Local resources include coal, oil, natural gas, and bauxite. Before the civil war, Croatia's well-developed industries produced machinery, chemicals, cement, paper, lumber, electrical goods, and textiles. The people of Croatia are rebuilding their cities, industries, and infrastructure. Croatia hopes to join the EU in 2010.

Events of the Conflict in the Former Yugoslavia

1990 Slovenia and Croatia hold the first multiparty elections in the Yugoslav republics. Macedonia and Bosnia-Herzegovina hold their own multiparty elections later in the year.

1991 Croatia and Slovenia declare independence. War breaks out between Croats and ethnic Serbs living in Croatian territory.

1992 In January, Macedonia declares independence. Bosnia-Herzegovina declares independ ence in April. Bosnian Muslims and Bosnian Croats begin fight ing. Reports of ethnic cleansing of non-Serbs cause the UN to impose economic sanstions. Serbia and Montenegro form a new Yugoslavia.

1993 International negotiators present the Vance-Owen peace plan, which would divide Bosnia into ethnic provinces. The plan is rejected.

1994 Continued fighting provokes UN and NATO ultimatums; Bosnian Muslims agree to a truce with Bosnian Croats and the Croatian government. A cease-fire is negotiated.

1995 The cease-fire is broken six weeks early. In October, after thousands from both sides have been killed, all parties agree to a truce. The Dayton Peace agreement is signed in November. The United States and NATO agree to supply peacekeeping forces.

1997 Slobodan Milosevic becomes president of the federal republic of Yugoslavia (Serbia and Montenegro).

1998 In Kosovo, a Yugoslav province, Serbian police attempt to crack down on ethnic Albanians. In February, Yugoslav forces enter Kosovo. Under threat of NATO action, Yugoslav troops withdraw in October.

1999 After peace talks between Serbia and Kosovo fail, the UN begins an air strike against Yugoslavia. In May, Milosevic and others are indicted by the International Criminal Tribunal for the Former Yugoslavia (ICTY).

Slovenia, Croatia, Bosnia-Herzegovina

Status:	Democracy
Area:	19,741 sq. m.
Population:	4.2 million
Capital:	Sarajevo
Language:	Serbo-Croatian
Currency:	Marka (100 pfenniga)

Bosnia-Herzegovina

Bosnia-Herzegovina borders Croatia to the west and north. Serbia is to the east, and Montenegro is to the south. The country is nearly landlocked, with just one 12-mile-long stretch of coast near the mouth of the Neretva River. The northern region, Bosnia, is mountainous and thickly forested. Herzegovina, the smaller southern section around the city of Mostar, consists of low hills and flat farmland. The country's coastal climate is mild, but the inland regions have short hot summers and bitterly cold winters with heavy snow.

Before the civil war, Bosnia had a thriving tourist industry of skiing, hunting, fishing, and river kayaking. Vast forests, large reserves of iron ore and coal, and abundant hydroelectric power enabled Bosnian industries to produce vehicles, machinery, textiles, and electrical goods. The country's farmers grew wheat, corn, fruits, vegetables, and tobacco. Much of Bosnia's industry and agriculture were devastated by the war, but efforts are under way to repair the damage.

Status:	Republic
Area:	39,448 sq. mi.
Population:	10.6 million
Capital:	Belgrade (Serbia) and Podgorica
Languages:	Serbo-Croatian, Albanian, Hungarian
Currency:	New dinar (100 paras)

Serbia and Montenegro

Serbia and Montenegro are the two former republics of Yugoslavia that act as a joint independent state. The two countries have three contrasting landscapes. Fertile lowlands cover the northern part of Serbia. The plains drain into the Danube River, which flows east into neighbouring Romania through a spectacular gorge called the Iron Gate. Central and southern Serbia are mountainous and include parts of the Dinaric Alps and the Balkan Mountains. Roughly one-quarter of Serbia is covered in forest—firs and pines on the mountain slopes, with oak and beech on the lower ground. The third region, Montenegro in the southwest, consists of a limestone plateau with typical karst scenery and shrub vegetation. The coastal region has hot, dry summers and cool winters. Inland, the climate is more extreme. The mountains have cool summers and very cold winters, while the northern plains have hot, dry summers and cold winters.

Status:	Republic
Area:	9,927 sq. miles
Population:	2 million
Capital:	Skopje
Language:	Macedonian
Currency:	Macedonian dinar (100 dari)

Macedonia is a country of wooded mountains, rising to 9,068 feet in the Korab range on the Albanian border. Most of the land is drained by the south-flowing Vardar River. Ancient Macedonia included parts of Greece and Bulgaria and was the centre of the great Kingdom of Macedonia. Macedonia was in turn part of the Roman, Byzantine, and Ottoman Empires. In 1945 Macedonia one of the six republics of Yugoslavia. Modern Macedonia declared its independence in 1991.

Macedonia's farmers supply most of the country's meat, dairy products, cereals, vegetables, and fruit. They grow cotton and tobacco for home use and for export. Mines produce a wide range of metal ores and some coal, but Macedonia depends on imported oil and gas to fuel its manufacturing industries.

Albania, Greece

Status:	Republic
Area:	11,100 sq. mi.
Population:	3.2 million
Capital:	Tiranë
Language:	Albanian
Currency:	Lek (100 qintars)

Status:	Parliamentary Republic
Area:	50,950 sq. mi.
Population:	11 million
Capital:	Athens
Language:	Greek
Currency:	Euro (100 cents)

Albania is a small country on the Adriatic Sea, cut off from its neighbours by high, rugged, inland mountain ranges. For nearly 500 years Albania was part of the Turkish Ottoman Empire. In 1912 Albania broke free from Turkish rule and declared its independence. From 1928 to 1939, Albania was a monarchy ruled by King Zog. After World War II, it became a Communist republic. In 1992 the Albanian people elected their first non-Communist president.

Albania is the poorest country in Europe. Most of the people are farmers, growing corn, grapes, sugar beets, olives, potatoes, and grains and raising livestock. Albania is reasonably rich in resources, yet the country's industries are poorly developed. Albanians mine oil, gas, bitumen (used for surfacing roads), copper, iron, nickel, and large reserves of chrome—the country's most lucrative export.

Fast-flowing mountain rivers generate hydroelectric power, and extensive hardwood and softwood forests supply the raw materials for lumber, plywood, pulp, and paper factories.

Mainland Greece occupies the ragged southern end of the Balkan Peninsula, which juts more than 300 miles into the Mediterranean Sea. The country is bordered by Albania, Macedonia, and Bulgaria in the north and by the Ionian Sea to the west. Turkey and the Aegean Sea lie to the east. Greece also includes more than 2,000 islands, most of them scattered across the Aegean side of the mainland. Some islands in the Dodecanese group lie barely 10 miles off the Turkish coast.

Crete is the largest island, at 3,200 square miles. More than half a million people live on Crete. With their Mediterranean climate, picturesque villages, spring flowers, and beautiful scenery and beaches, the Greek islands attract more than 10 million tourists each year.

Greece is mostly dry, scrub-covered mountains, rising to 8,256 feet in the northwest. Mount Olympus, famous from Greek mythology, towers over the eastern central portion of the country, reaching 9,573 feet. Narrow strips of lowland follow the coast, and several small fertile valleys dot the Macedonia and Thrace regions north of the Aegean Sea. Most Greeks live near the coast and have done so for generations. The country's numerous inlets and bays support Greece's long tradition as a seafaring nation. The country has one of the world's largest merchant fleets, and shipping is a significant source of income.

Byzantine buildings overlook the sea at Monemvasia on the Aegean coast—one of the southernmost towns of mainland Greece.

Greece produces small amounts of bauxite, lead, zinc, chrome, nickel, and silver, but the country does not have the large energy resources needed for smelting, so most of the ore is exported. Farming provides the bulk of jobs and income. Farmers grow wheat, corn, tomatoes, olives, grapes, citrus fruits, cotton, and tobacco. Food processing plants create canned olives, olive oil, and dried grapes (sultanas and raisins) for export.

Romania

Status:	Republic
Area:	92,042 sq. miles
Population:	22.5 million
Capital:	Bucharest
Language:	Romanian
Currency:	Leu (100 bani)

Romania, like many of its neighbours, has recently become a democratic republic after more than 50 years of Communism—24 of them under the rule of Nicolae Ceausescu. In 1989 the Romanian people, backed by the army, overthrew Ceausescu's regime in a short but violent revolution. The people adopted a new constitution in 1991.

Romania is a mountainous country, but the elevations are not so extreme as to inhibit travel. The Transylvanian Plateau in the country's centre consists of rolling hills and fertile farmland 1,000 feet to 2,000 feet above sea level. Around it a great arc of mountains,the Moldovian Carpathians and the Transylvanian Alps, snakes south from the Ukrainian border and then goes westward into Serbia. The lower Bihor Mountains in the northwest complete the highland ring encircling the plateau. Outside the mountain ring, lowlands stretch clear to the country's borders. The western lowlands merge with the plains of Serbia and Hungary. The eastern plains slope down to the Black Sea and include the marshes and lakes along the lower Danube River.

The fertile soil of the central plateau and plains provides abundant grains, beets, oilseeds, fruits, and vegetables. Farmers with rich pastures raise pigs, sheep, and dairy cattle. Romania produces enough food for local needs and exports surplus grains, fruits, and wine to neighbouring countries. Forests cover about one-quarter of the land, providing raw materials for house and furniture construction and for the paper industries. Hydroelectric power and natural gas supply much of the nation's energy, but Romania also imports coal and oil. The country's mineral resources include copper, lead, zinc, aluminium ore, and sulphur. Factories concentrated around Bucharest in the south make vehicles, machinery, textiles, furniture, and food products.

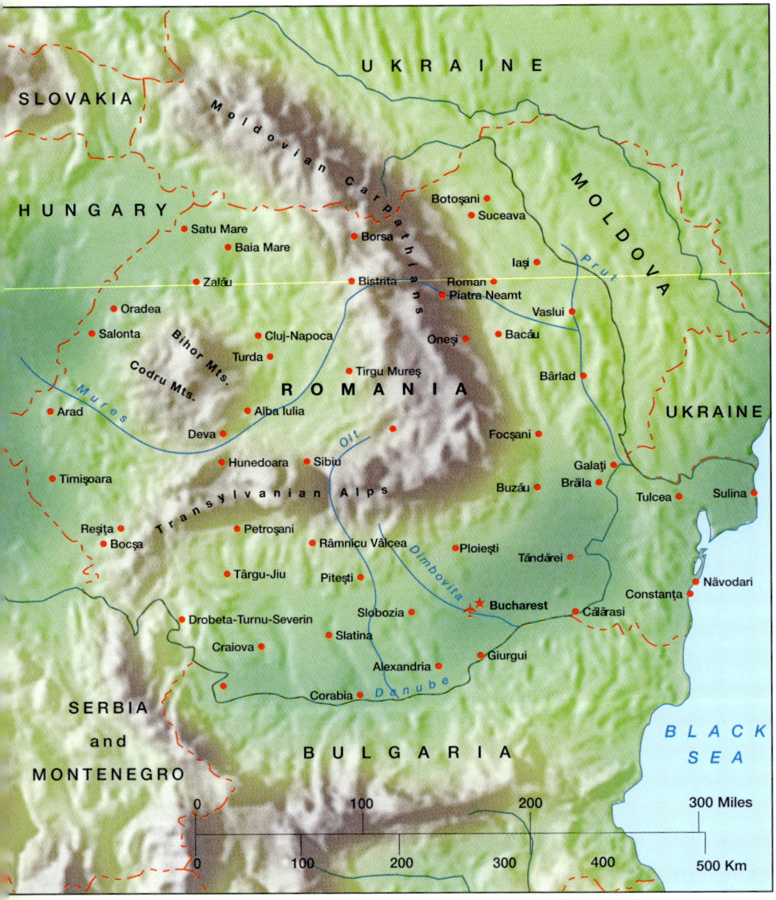

Status:	Republic
Area:	42,822 sq. miles
Population:	8.2 million
Capital:	Sofia
Language:	Bulgarian
Currency:	Lev (100 stotinki)

East-west bands of lowlands and mountains separate Bulgaria into four distinct land regions. The fertile Danube Valley stretches across northern Bulgaria. The Balkan Mountains march across the country's middle, rising to about 6,500 feet in the west and gradually descending toward the Black Sea. To the south lies the broad fertile Maritsa River Valley. And south of the Maritsa, the land rises again to the Rhodope Mountains, which separate Bulgaria from Greece and Turkey.

Hot summers and cold winters characterise the Danube Valley, where farmers grow wheat, barley, corn, beets, and vegetables. The Maritsa Valley is milder, with damp winters and warm, dry summers. Farmers in this region cultivate grapes, rice, sunflowers, grains, and tobacco. Bulgarian farmers produce more than just edible crops. The fragrant petals of the country's roses contain a sweet-smelling oil—attar of roses—that is sold to perfumeries all over the world.

Agriculture and tourism drive Bulgaria's economy. Mines in the Rhodope Mountains produce iron, copper, lead, and zinc, but Bulgaria is very short of fuel and has to import energy for its industries.

Belarus

Status:	Republic
Area:	80,154 sq. mi.
Population:	9.8 million
Capital:	Minsk
Languages:	Belarussian, Russian
Currency:	Belarussian ruble (100 kopeks)

Belarus has changed hands often. The country was once part of the Mongol Empire, then a portion of Lithuania, then a section of Poland. In 1918 the country achieved its independence but was invaded by Russia the following year, becoming one of the original Soviet Union members. Belarus gained its independence again in 1991 but maintains close ties with Russia.

Most of Belarus is a vast, flat plain. A line of low hills runs through the middle of the country, but the highest point is only 112 feet above sea level.

Southern Belarus contains Europe's largest area of marshes and peat bogs—the famous Pripyat Marshes. Forests cover about one-third of the land—birch and pine in the north, with ash, oak, and hornbeam in the warmer south.

Belarussian factories produce trucks and tractors, machinery, computers, household appliances, pulp, paper, fertilizers, and industrial chemicals. Belarus trades many of its goods to Russia, receiving energy supplies and raw materials in return. Farms cover nearly half of the country. Many farmers concentrate on cattle, pigs, sheep, and goats. The remainder grow grains, beets, potatoes, flax, and hemp.

Most of Belarus is a vast, flat plain. A line of low hills runs through the middle of the country, but the highest point is only 112 feet above sea level.

Southern Belarus contains Europe's largest area of marshes and peat bogs—the famous Pripyat Marshes. Forests cover about one-third of the land—birch and pine in the north, with ash, oak, and hornbeam in the warmer south.

Belarussian factories produce trucks and tractors, machinery, computers, household appliances, pulp, paper, fertilizers, and industrial chemicals. Belarus trades many of its goods to Russia, receiving energy supplies and raw materials in return. Farms cover nearly half of the country. Many farmers concentrate on cattle, pigs, sheep, and goats. The remainder grow grains, beets, potatoes, flax, and hemp.

Moldova

Moldova is a small republic sandwiched between Ukraine and Romania. Most of the country is hilly, especially in the centre where it rises to 1,400 feet. The hills give way to a broad flat plain in the south. Moldova has virtually no mineral resources and no oil or gas, but it has extremely fertile soil and a mild climate.

Status:	Republic
Area:	13,012 sq. mi.
Population:	4.3 million
Capital:	Chisinau
Languages:	Romanian, Russian, Ukrainian
Currency:	Moldavian leu (100 bani)

Ukraine

Status:	Republic
Area:	233,089 sq. mi.
Population:	47.8million
Capital:	Kiev
Languages:	Ukrainian, Russian
Currency:	Hryvnia (100 kopiykas)

Ukraine produces about 8 percent of the world's barley.

Covering more than 230,000 square miles, Ukraine is the largest country lying within Europe. Russia is bigger, but it stretches into northern Asia, so it spans two continents. Ukraine consists mainly of plains, called steppes, with low hills separating the major river valleys—the Dniester, the Bug, and the Dnieper, all of which flow into the Black Sea.

Ukraine has abundant peat, coal, and natural gas but has to supplement its meager oil reserves with imports from neighbouring countries. Its major industrial regions in the east and south house coal fields and iron ore mines. Ukraine is also one of the world's chief producers of manganese. Modern Ukrainian factories include chemicals, plastics, and food-processing.

Russian Federation (European Russia)

Status:	Federation
Area:	6,592,819 sq. miles
Population:	146.5 million
Capital:	Moscow
Language:	Russian
Currency:	Russian ruble (100 kopeks)

Russia is the largest country in the world. Even after losing 14 of the 15 republics that comprised the former Soviet Union, Russia is still nearly twice the size of the United States. The Russian Federation stretches 6,000 miles from the borders of Norway, Finland, and the Baltic States in the west to the Pacific Ocean in the east. It extends almost 2,800 miles from the Arctic Ocean to the borders of Kazakhstan, Mongolia, and China.

Russia traces its history to the medieval Slavic state of Kievan Rus, which covered most of modern Ukraine, Belarus, and European Russia. Mongol invaders from central Asia destroyed Kievan Rus in the thirteenth century. In the 1300s, a new state called Muscovy took its place and was succeeded in the 1700s by the Russian Empire. The Russian Revolution of 1917 ended imperial rule, replacing it with a Communist government, which remained in power until 1991.

Russia's vast land area consists of four main regions—the European Plain (European Russia), which extends as far as the Ural Mountains; the West Siberian Plain between the Urals and the Yenisey River; the Central Siberian Plateau between the Yenisey and Lena Rivers; and the East Siberian Highlands.

Most of European Russia lies on the European Plain, bounded by the Carpathian and Caucasus Mountains in the south and by the Urals in the east. Mount Elbrus is Russia's highest peak at 18,510 feet. Climate and vegetation vary greatly from north to south. Treeless tundra dominates the Arctic zone. South of the tundra lies a forested belt of pine, spruce, and fir called the taiga, which merges southward into mixed forests of birch, oak, elm, and maple. Fishing and herding reindeer are traditional occupations in these harsh northern regions. In the forested zones, farmers grow potatoes and flax and raise livestock. The steppes stretch across the southern part of the country, containing the rich black and brown soil that makes Russia the world's foremost producer of barley, oats, wheat, and rye. Farmers in the warmer southern region bordering Ukraine and the Black Sea grow a variety of vegetables, as well as subtropical crops such as tea and citrus fruits.

Large coal fields operate near the capital city of Moscow, in the northern Urals, and on the Russian-Ukrainian border. Oil fields in the Urals, the Arctic, and the Caucasus Mountains provide fuel and raw materials for Russia's petrochemical industries. Huge iron ore deposits along the Ukrainian border support the country's iron and steel industries. Russia also has vast reserves of most other minerals, but many are located in remote areas, far from European Russia's manufacturing centres, which are located in Saint Petersburg, Moscow, Kursk, Nizhny Novgorod, and Volgograd. To compensate, Russia imports fuel and raw materials from many of the states along its western borders.

Russians enjoy a traditional winter pastime—fishing through holes in the ice on a frozen lake at Zagorsk.

Africa

Africa is the second-largest continent by land area (11.7 million square miles) and the third largest by population (771 million people). The continent is a patchwork of more than 50 countries, each with many different people, languages, and customs. Africa's population is spread unevenly across the land. The desert countries of Libya and Mauritania have only about 7 people per square mile, while Nigeria, the most crowded country, supports 319 people per square mile.

The continent stretches 5,000 miles north to south—from the warm shores of the Mediterranean Sea to the cold stormy waters off the Cape of Good Hope—and 4,700 miles west to east, from the Atlantic coast of Senegal to Somalia, which juts into the Indian Ocean. Three major mountain ranges skirt the continent. The Atlas Mountains rise to 13,671 feet in the northwest. Africa's highest peak, Mount Kilimanjaro, at 19,341 feet, towers over East Africa's high plateau. The Drakensberg Mountains rise 11,425 feet above sea level in eastern South Africa and Lesotho.

The Great Rift Valley, Africa's most spectacular landscape feature, is a huge crack in the earth's crust that cuts through the continent for 4,300 miles from the Red Sea to Malawi. Africa embraces some of the world's most noted water features. Lake Victoria, covering 26,828 square miles, is in area the world's second-largest freshwater lake after Lake Superior. The Nile, snaking along for 4,160 miles, is the world's longest river. The Victoria Falls on the Zambia–Zimbabwe border rushes around three islands before plunging 350 feet.

Africa has vast forest resources, as well as huge reserves of copper, diamonds, gold, and petroleum. But most African countries lack the money and skilled workers needed to build and run factories. South Africa, Egypt, Morocco, Algeria, and Nigeria are the only African countries with well-developed industries. Most African families depend on subsistence agriculture, growing just enough to feed themselves. Farmers in more fertile areas often grow cash crops for export. Large-scale plantations, owned mostly by multinational companies, produce cacao beans, coffee beans, cashews, cloves, bananas, vanilla, tea, cotton, and sugar.

Wildebeest thunder across the open grasslands of South Africa's Rooipoort Game Reserve.

MEDITERRANEAN SEA
Persian Gu
RED SEA
Gulf of Ade
INDIAN OCEAN
Gulf of Guinea
TIC
N
Mozambique Channel
ALGERIA
TUNISIA
LIBYA
EGYPT
MALI
NIGER
CHAD
SUDAN
ERITREA
DJIBOUTI
ETHIOPIA
SOMALIA
BURKINA FASO
BENIN
TOGO
GHANA
NIGERIA
CAMEROON
CENTRAL AFRICAN REPUBLIC
Bioko
EQUATORIAL GUINEA
São Tomé and Principe
GABON
REPUBLIC OF THE CONGO
Cabinda
DEMOCRATIC REPUBLIC OF THE CONGO
UGANDA
KENYA
RWANDA
BURUNDI
TANZANIA
Zanzibar
SEYCHELLES
Comoros
Mayotte
ANGOLA
ZAMBIA
MOZAMBIQUE
MADAGASCAR
ZIMBABWE
NAMIBIA
BOTSWANA
SWAZILAND
LESOTHO
SOUTH AFRICA
1000
1500
2000 Miles
2000
3000 Km

Morocco, Algeria

Status:	Constitutional Monarchy
Area:	172,413 square miles
Population:	31.6 million
Capital:	Rabat
Languages:	Arabic, Berber, French, Spanish
Currency:	Dirham (100 centimes)

Status:	Republic
Area:	919,591 square miles
Population:	32.9 million
Capital:	Algiers
Languages:	Arabic, Berber, French
Currency:	Algerian dinar (100 centimes)

Morocco is bordered by the Atlantic Ocean to the west and the Mediterranean Sea to the north. The two coastlines are separated by a rocky headland that juts toward Spain to form the narrow Strait of Gibraltar. Well-watered fertile plains stretch along the coasts, where farmers produce wheat, barley, corn, sugar beets, beans, fruits, and vegetables. Major landowners control about one-third of the farmland and account for 85 percent of all the crops produced. Most Moroccan farmers get by on a few acres, raising crops and tending sheep, goats, and dairy cattle. Morocco is one of Africa's leading fishing nations. Sardines, mackerel, and tuna are caught and then canned for export or converted into animal feed or fertilizer.

Morocco has about two-thirds of the world's reserves of phosphate rock, which is mined and exported for making fertilizer and other chemical products. The country also has reserves of iron ore, copper, lead, and zinc, but most of the country's energy is based on imported oil.

Casablanca, Morocco's main manufacturing centre, produces cement, chemicals, fertilizers, paper, plastics, leather goods, and processed foods.

Farmers' wives wash freshly picked cotton on the banks of the Oued Grou River at Rabat, Morocco.

Nearly half of Algeria's people live in cities and towns on the narrow coastal plain bordering the Mediterranean Sea. Here the climate is warm, with mild winters and up to 30 inches of rain each year. Farmers in this region grow cereal grains, vines, olives, fruits, and vegetables and raise sheep, goats, and cattle. About 30 percent of Algerians work in factories in Algiers, Annaba, Constantine, Skikda, and other cities on or near the coast. These manufacturing centres produce iron and steel, construction materials, textiles, phosphate fertilizers, and refined petroleum products. The country is rich in oil and natural gas, but political unrest has prevented the government from making full use of these resources. As a result, many thousands of Algerians go abroad, many of them to France, to find work.

The Atlas Mountains rise steeply behind the coastal plain, separating the mild northern region from the hot dry Sahara Desert,

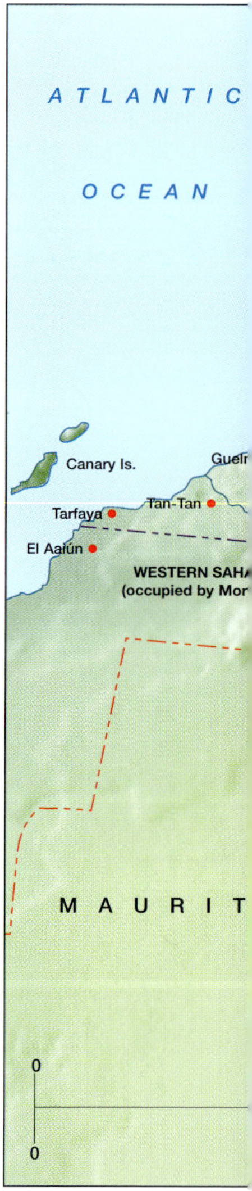

which covers 80 percent of the country. The northern Sahara is mainly sand. To the south and east, it is bare rock and boulders. Less than 3 percent of Algerians live in the desert. A few are oil field workers, and some live in scattered oases where dates and cereal grains can be grown. The remainder are nomadic Tuareg people who speak the Berber language and travel between the region's sparse grazing areas with their camels, sheep, and goats.

A natural rock arch in the rugged Tassili Mountains of southern Algeria.

Tunisia

Status:	Republic
Area:	63,170 square miles
Population:	10 million
Capital:	Tunis
Languages:	Arabic, French, English
Currency:	Tunisian dinar (1,000 millimes)

Tunisia's northern landscape consists of low mountains with patches of cork oak and evergreen woodland. The Atlas Mountains lie near the Mediterranean coast of this North African nation, and the Tabassah Mountains, part of the same Atlas range, lie farther south. Farmers grow wheat and other grains in the Majardah River Valley and in additional fertile lowlands between the two ranges. A vast, dry, grassy plain lies south of the mountains and is dotted with salt lakes and pans. Beyond the plain lies the Sahara Desert.

Tunisia's most productive region is the narrow plain along its eastern coast, where fertile soil and winter rains yield excellent crops of grains, citrus fruits, grapes, melons, and olives. Olive groves cover nearly one-third of the country's farmland, making Tunisia the world's fifth-largest producer of olives and olive oil.

Phosphates and oil are Tunisia's major mineral resources. Both are exported in large quantities. The country's manufacturing centres supply textiles, clothing, paper, steel, construction materials, and processed foods to both local and export markets. Tourism is fast becoming one of Tunisia's most important industries. Although Tunisia suffers frequent droughts and dwindling oil reserves, the government devotes nearly half the national budget to education, health care, and other social services.

Status:	Republic
Area:	679,359 square miles
Population:	5.8 million
Capital:	Tripoli
Languages:	Arabic, Berber
Currency:	Libyan dinar (1,000 dirhams)

The Sahara Desert blankets nearly 95 percent of Libya. Vast sand dunes cover much of the country's northern half, gradually giving way to stone-covered desert that rises to a rugged mountain range in the south. Libya's climate is hot and dry, receiving less than two inches of annual rainfall. Of the few Libyans who inhabit this desert area, most live in scattered oases and grow dates, grains, and vegetables. Some work in the desert oil fields. The rest are nomadic herders constantly on the move in search of grazing land for their camels, sheep, and goats.

Most of Libya's people live in towns and villages on the Mediterranean coastal plain, where they enjoy fertile soil, mild temperatures, and up to 16 inches of rain each year. Farmers in this region grow wheat, barley, potatoes, dates, and citrus fruits and raise cattle, sheep, and poultry. Most Libyan farms are small family businesses, so the country imports much of the food it needs to feed its rapidly growing population.

Oil, Libya's principal mineral resource and its most significant export, accounts for about one-quarter of the country's total economic production. Libyans also mine iron ore, lime, gypsum, sulphur, and some natural gas.

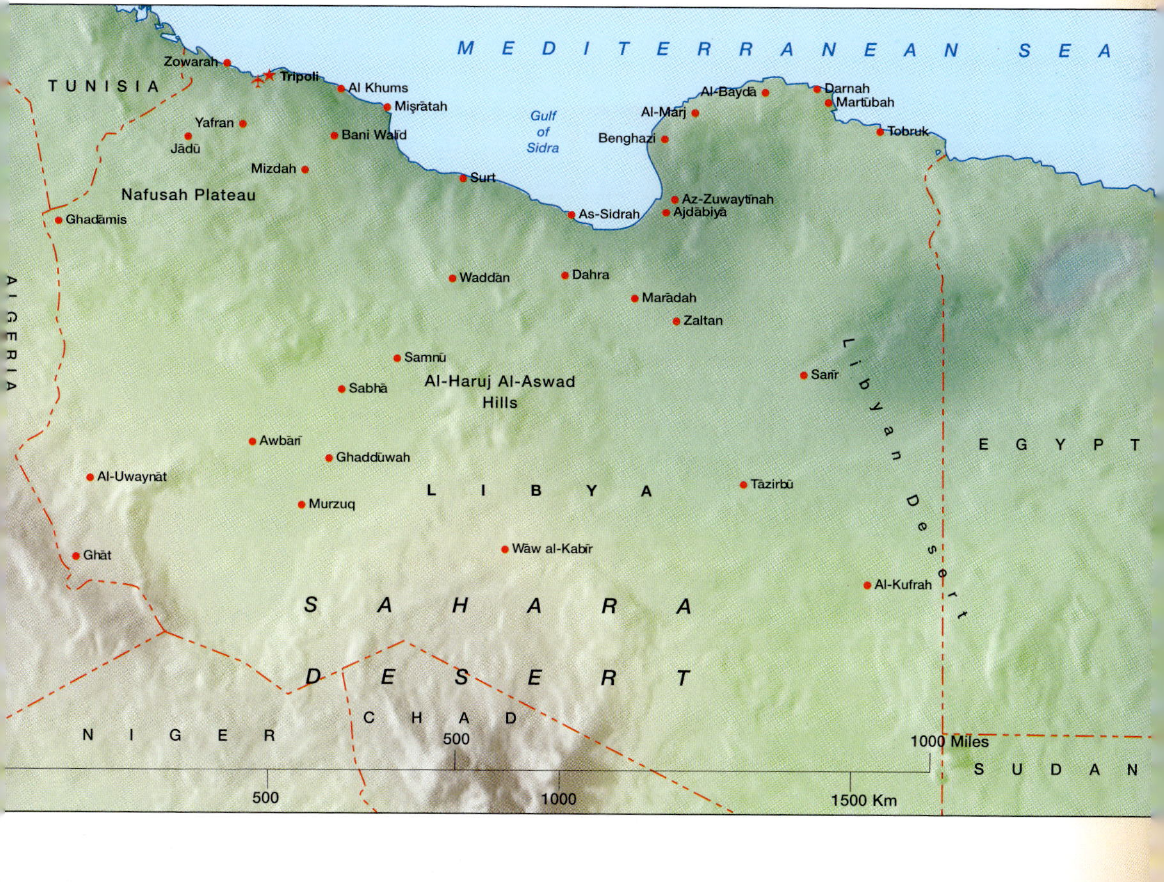

Egypt

Status:	Republic
Area:	386,660 square miles
Population:	74.9 million
Capital:	Cairo
Language:	Arabic
Currency:	Egyptian pound (100 piastres)

Egypt has the second-largest population in Africa (after Nigeria), and its capital, Cairo, is the continent's most populous city, housing 13 million residents. About 99 percent of Egyptians live on just 4 percent of the land—consisting of the narrow fertile valley of the Nile, the Nile Delta, and the banks of the Suez Canal.

The Nile River has enabled Egypt to become one of Africa's leading nations. Farmers in the Nile Valley produce nearly all of Egypt's home-grown food including corn, rice, potatoes, wheat, oranges, tomatoes, and sugarcane. These farmers also tend Egypt's most valuable cash crop—high-quality, long-fibre cotton that is exported worldwide. Dams and reservoirs hold back the Nile's waters and provide year-round irrigation.

Sand and rock deserts interspersed with a few salt marshes claim the rest of this North African country. Scattered oases house small communities that grow date palms and vegetables and rear sheep and goats. The deserts are also home to the Bedouin people. Some still follow the traditional nomadic way of life, although many have settled and become farmers.

Egypt is not rich in mineral resources, but petroleum and natural gas, iron ore, manganese, and phosphates are vital exports and provide fuel and raw materials for the country's industries. Cairo and the main port of Alexandria house the country's principal manufacturing centres. Factory goods include petrochemicals, textiles, chemicals, steel, fertilizers, and metal and

food products. Cairo is also a major financial centre and the launching point for millions of tourists who visit the country's spectacular ancient monuments—the pyramids, the Sphinx, and the Valley of the Kings.

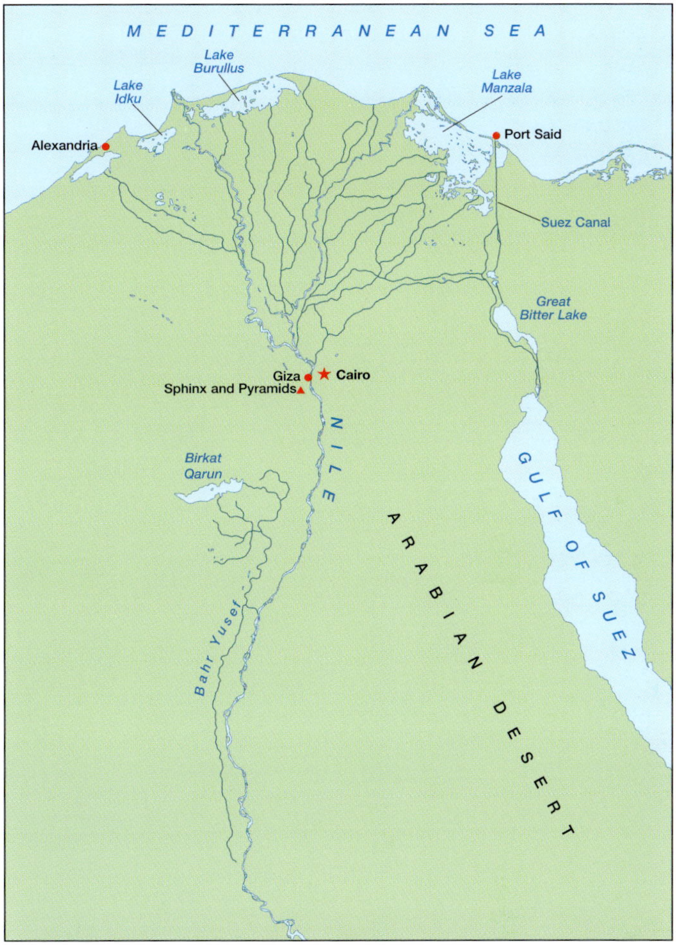

Right: The Nile Valley and its vast river delta are one of the world's most fertile regions. This great river irrigates almost six million acres of farmland in Egypt and three million acres in neighbouring Sudan.

Above: The felucca is the traditional boat of Nile fishers and traders.

Right: The Sphinx and the great pyramids at Giza are among the most identifiable sights of the ancient world.

Sudan

Status:	Republic
Area:	967,494 square miles
Population:	35 million
Capital:	Khartoum
Languages:	Arabic, English
Currency:	Sudanese dinar (100 pounds)

Africa's largest country by area, Sudan is a land of contrasts. Northern Sudan is mainly desert, with less than 4 inches of annual rainfall and daytime temperatures consistently above 100°F. The central region is a vast grassy plain that gets slightly more rain. Southern Sudan is hot and humid with 40 inches of rain each year and temperatures averaging 80°F. This southern region is covered in dense forests and swamps that merge with the tropical rain forests of the Democratic Republic of the Congo and the Central African Republic.

Like Egypt to its north, Sudan depends on the Nile River. About 80 percent of its people live in rural areas, most of them farming the valleys of the Nile and its main tributaries—the White Nile and the Blue Nile. But the valleys are not productive enough to feed everyone. Infertile soil leaves many farmers struggling to grow enough food to feed their families. The remaining 20 percent of the population live in Sudan's major cities—the capital city of Khartoum, Omdurman (the biggest city), Wad Medani, Port Sudan, and Juba. Small factories and service industries provide jobs for a majority of the city dwellers.

Agriculture accounts for 40 percent of Sudan's economy. Cotton and gum arabic are the principal exports. Sudanese farmers plant millet, sorghum, sugarcane, and vegetables and produce meat and dairy products for local consumption. Miners extract chromium, gold, gypsum, and oil. Urban factory workers make cement, fertilizers, textiles, and leather products for local and international markets.

Eritrea, Ethiopia

Eritrea

Status:	Independent State
Area:	45,405 sq. miles
Population:	4.4 million
Capital:	Asmara
Languages:	Tigrinya, Tigre, Arabic, English
Currency:	Nakfa (100 cents)

After periods of rule by Italy, Britain, and Ethiopia, Eritrea fell into a bitter civil war in the 1980s and early 1990s. Eritrea formally declared itself, as well as the Dahlak Archipelago in the Red Sea, free of Ethiopia in 1993. But the constant conflicts and a succession of severe droughts have devastated this new East African country. Three-quarters of the people depend on foreign food aid, and the country's illiteracy rate is high.

The government in the capital of Asmara is attempting to rebuild Eritrea's economy by supporting traditional textile and leather industries and by developing fishing and tourism. Highland farmers grow sorghum, cotton, teff, coffee beans, tobacco, and citrus fruits. The land is not very productive, however, and rainfall is erratic. Salt mines in the arid Danakil Depression in the hot, dry eastern region produce the country's most valuable export.

Ethiopia

Status:	Federal Republic
Area:	426,371 sq. miles
Population:	74.2 million
Capital:	Addis Ababa
Languages:	Amharic, Arabic
Currency:	Ethiopian birr (100 cents)

Rugged mountains and high fertile plateaux veil western Ethiopia, where the highland climate is usually a mild 60°F. Droughts occur and the people are poor, but enough rain falls during most summers for farmers to produce sufficient wheat, corn, sorghum, and teff to feed their families. Most farmers also raise cattle, sheep, goats, and chickens. The richest farmland is in the southwest, where farmers grow commercial crops of oilseed, sugarcane, and coffee beans—the country's biggest export. The Great Rift Valley, which runs north to south through the country, splits the highland region in two. Eastern Ethiopia consists of hot, dry, lowland plains where rainfall seldom exceeds 15 inches, and the temperature averages 80°F.

Status: Republic
Area: 8,958 square miles
Population: 721,000
Capital: Djibouti
Languages: Arabic, Afar, Somali, French
Currency: Franc (100 centimes)

Djibouti is very small, extremely poor, and depends almost entirely on the fact that it has one of the best harbours on Africa's eastern coast—at the nation's capital, also called Djibouti, on the Gulf of Aden. The port is the end point for a railroad built in 1917 by the government of Ethiopia to link Addis Ababa, Ethiopia's capital, to the coast. A large proportion of Ethiopia's foreign trade passes through the port, providing Djibouti with its primary source of income.

More than 90 percent of Djibouti is desert. Its barren coastal plain suffers one of the hottest, driest climates on earth, with less than five inches of annual rainfall and average temperatures around 90°F. Hilly terrain rises to nearly 5,000 feet in the country's north and west, meeting Ethiopia's highlands at the border.

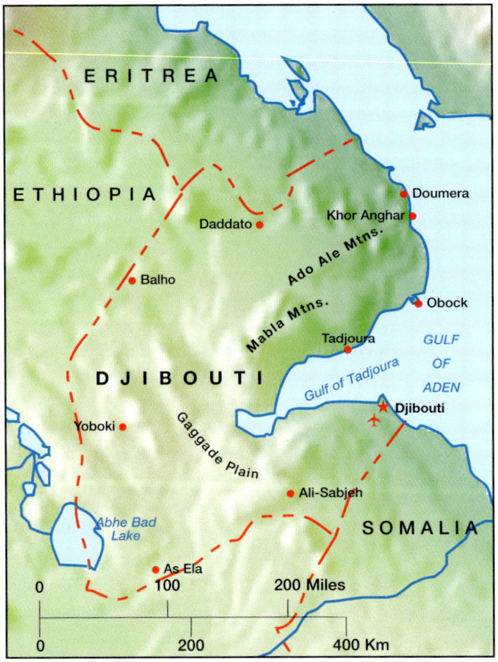

Status: Republic
Area: 246,201 square miles
Population: 10.7 million
Capital: Mogadishu
Languages: Somali, Arabic, English
Currency: Shilling (100 cents)

Somalia, like so many other African countries, gained independence in 1960 after nearly 100 years of shared colonial rule between Britain and Italy. But independence did not bring peace. For the last 30 years, Somalia has been torn apart by civil war, conflict with Ethiopia, and severe droughts that have killed nearly half a million people.

Somalia is a hot, dry East African country, covered almost entirely in dry savanna grassland. A low mountain range lies across northern Somalia, where average temperatures reach 100°F and annual rainfall can be as little as 3 or 4 inches. Central and southern Somalia feel almost wet by comparison. Annual rainfall in these low, flat regions can exceed 12 inches, and temperatures range from 64°F to 100°F.

Most of the country is too dry and infertile for farming. Two-thirds of Somalis are nomadic herders—grazing their sheep, goats, cattle, and camels wherever they can find enough pasture. In the south, the Jubba and Shabeelle Rivers provide water for irrigation and enable farmers to grow corn, sorghum, cotton, bananas, citrus fruits, and sugarcane. Somalia's main exports are animal hides and leather goods, bananas, and livestock—most of which Saudi Arabia purchases. The country has to import much of its food, the bulk of its manufactured goods, and all of its oil and petroleum.

After nearly 25 years of intense fighting and severe starvation, Somalia allowed in U.S. forces, which hoped to keep the warring factions apart and to ensure that desperately needed food and supplies would reach the starving people. The following year, the United Nations took over the operation, but in 1995 the peacekeepers withdrew, unable to stop the fighting.

Somali nomads draw water for their camels from a deep well in the Ogaden Desert on the country's border with Ethiopia.

Western Sahara, Mauritania

Status:	Disputed Territory
Area:	97,344 sq. mi.
Population:	200,000
Capital:	El Aaiún
Languages:	Arabic, Moroccan
Currency:	Dirham (100 centimes)

Western Sahara, formerly Spanish Sahara, lies on Africa's northwestern coast. Most of the country is barren desert dotted with wadis (dry streambeds) that fill briefly after occasional rainstorms but dry out almost immediately. The Saharawi people are mostly Arab and Berber nomads who roam the desert with their herds of camels, sheep, and goats. The inland desert soil is too dry and infertile for agriculture, although small farms on the coast manage to grow grains and vegetables. Fishing crews along the coast catch and dry fish for export to the Spanish-owned Canary Islands, 70 miles off the African coast. Western Sahara's one asset is its huge reserves of phosphate rock, an ingredient in fertilizers. The deposits southeast of the capital of El Aaiún are the largest in the world. The valuable minerals are one of the reasons neighbouring states have tried to take control of the country.

Status:	Republic
Area:	395,954 square miles
Population:	3.1 million
Capital:	Nouakchott
Languages:	Arabic, Poular, Wolof, Soninke, French
Currency:	Ouguiya (5 khoums)

Mauritania bridges two worlds—the Arab world to the north and black African world to the south. Most of the northerners are of Arab and Berber descent who speak Arabic and follow the Islamic faith. A large proportion of black Africans, many of whom are Christians or followers of traditional religions, inhabit southern Mauritania. The country was a French colony from 1903 until it achieved independence in 1960. Military leaders ruled Mauritania until 1991, when the country adopted a new constitution and democratic elections.

The vast sand plains and rocky highlands of the Sahara Desert dominate most of the country. The Sahel, a belt of low, arid plains covered in sparse grass and scrub, stretches across Mauritania's southern border. Most of the people living in the Sahel region are nomadic herders. Black Africans, most of them settled farmers, are concentrated in the southwest where the fertile soil of the Senegal River and its tributaries affords premium crops of millet, corn, beans, rice, and dates. Coastal fisheries provide another important source of food and export income. High-grade iron ore mined near Fdérik is Mauritania's most valuable mineral resource. Most of it is exported to Europe. Fish, iron ore, and copper exports do not earn enough to support the economy, and Mauritania depends heavily on foreign aid, much of it from France.

Sand dunes in the Sahara.

Canary Is.
(Spain)
MOROCCO
Disputed border
Hagunia
El Aaiún
Farcia
Semara
TLANTIC
OCEAN
Cabo Bojador
Bu Craa
ALGERIA
Guelta Zemmur
Bir Mogreïn
WESTERN SAHARA
Dakhla
SAHARA
Imilili
Fdérik
Mount Ijill
Bir Gandus
Tichla
Adrar Hills
Güera
Nouâdhibou
Cape Blanc
Ouadane
Atar
Chinguetti
Akjoujt
Cape Timiris
Nouamrhar
MAURITANIA
Coppolani
Nouakchott
Tidjikdja
Tîchît
MALI
Boutilimit
Tiguent
Aleg
Rosso
Bogue
Saint-Louis
Kaédi
Guérou
Kiffa
Ayoûn el Atroûs
Néma
Sénégal
Mbout
Sélibabi
SENEGAL
500
1000 Miles
500
1000
1500 Km
BURKINA FASO
NIGER

Mali, Burkina Faso

Status:	Republic
Area:	478,838 square miles
Population:	13.8 million
Capital:	Bamako
Languages:	French, local languages
Currency:	CFA franc (100 centimes)

Mali is a land of plateaux and plains, hot sand, and mild tropics. Northern Mali, which the Sahara Desert partly covers, receives very little rain and often reaches temperatures over 110°F at midday. The central region spans the Sahel, which is populated mainly by nomadic herders. Southern Mali enjoys a tropical climate of 80°F temperatures and annual rainfall of about 35 inches—most of it falling between July and October.

Southern Malians farm the land, growing corn, millet, cassava, sorghum, rice, and yams on the fertile soil along the Senegal and Niger Rivers. But even in the south, life is extremely hard. Very few farmers can afford tractors, modern tools, or fertilizers, and most of them struggle to grow enough food for their families.

When there is enough rain, farmers in the south grow peanuts, cotton, and sugarcane for export, and fishing crews catch carp, catfish, and perch from the main rivers for export to neighbouring countries. Mali has large reserves of iron ore, gold, copper, bauxite, uranium, manganese, phosphates, and salt, but only salt, phosphates, and a small amount of gold are excavated. Radical investment is needed to develop these resources. Manufacturing provides jobs for about 10 percent of Mali's people, who produce textiles, leather goods, processed foods, and cement. The country depends heavily on foreign aid, especially from France, which ruled Mali until independence in 1960.

Status:	Republic
Area:	105,792 square miles
Population:	13.8 million
Capital:	Ouagadougou
Language:	French
Currency:	CFA franc (100 centimes)

Surrounded by Niger, Mali, and the coastal states of Côte d'Ivoire, Ghana, Togo, and Benin, Burkina Faso is one of the poorest and least-developed countries in Africa. Formerly the French colony of Upper Volta, this West African country gained independence in 1960 and later changed its name to Burkina Faso, meaning "land of the honest people."

The landscape consists mostly of wooded grasslands that rise to 2,300 feet above sea level in the west. The soil is poor and the climate is dry, especially in the north where most of the people herd livestock. Cattle, sheep, and goats account for almost half of Burkina Faso's export earnings, and much of the livestock goes to its southern neighbours. River valleys in the south provide the best cropland. Farmers grow millet, corn, sorghum, rice, and beans for their families and cotton, peanuts, and shea nuts for export—primarily to France.

Burkina Faso's people belong to many ethnic groups, embrace a wide variety of languages, beliefs, and customs, and live in very distinct homes and villages. Most of the rural people live in extended family groups or clan communities, but as in other poor countries, people are moving away from the country and into the towns in search of jobs. Many young men have found work in factories or on coffee bean and cacao bean plantations in Côte d'Ivoire and Ghana. Poverty and a lack of social services have led to a short life expectancy, a high infant mortality rate, frequent epidemics, and illiteracy. Less than 30 percent of the children attend primary school, and less than 1 in 10 of the people can read and write.

An aerial view of a village in central Mali. The houses are typically square, with mud-brick walls and flat roofs. Circular mud-brick silos with thatched roofs contain stored grain.

Niger, Chad

Status:	Republic
Area:	489,189 square miles
Population:	12.9 million
Capital:	Niamey
Languages:	French, Hausa, Djerma-Songhai, Fulani
Currency:	CFA franc (100 centimes)

The Sahara Desert covers three-quarters of Niger, one of the hottest, driest countries on earth. Sand and stony plateaux blanket most of the land, which rises to a central mountain region with peaks to 6,300 feet. The desert sees little rain, and temperatures often exceed 120°F. Small groups of nomadic Tuareg and Fulani people graze livestock in the desert during the short rainy season from July to September, moving to the thinly wooded savanna in the dry months. The savanna enjoys up to 22 inches of rain annually and is home to the Hausa, Djerma-Songhai, and Kanuri peoples, who are mostly settled farmers. Only 3 percent of the country is cultivated, but nearly 90 percent of the labour force works in agriculture. Farmers grow cassava, millet, sorghum, beans, and rice as food crops and cotton and peanuts for export. Most exported crops are grown in the southwest, on the Niger River's floodplain. Nigerien farmers also export livestock, meat, and animal hides. Repeated droughts in the last few decades have damaged Niger's fragile farming economy and have caused widespread suffering.

Niger's principal industry is uranium mining, but a drop in world demand during the 1980s reduced the resource's value. Nigeriens also mine phosphates, iron ore, and tin. Factory workers in cities such as Niamey, Agadez, Maradi, and Zinder process food and create textiles, leather goods, and cement. But with no railroads, few good roads, and inadequate communication between regions, industrial development is very limited. The country has large foreign debts and depends heavily on foreign aid.

Status:	Republic
Area:	495,753 square miles
Population:	9.1 million
Capital:	N'Djamena
Languages:	French, Arabic, Sara
Currency:	CFA franc (100 centimes)

Chad is a large landlocked country with few natural resources, a harsh desert climate, and little productive farmland. Ravaged by droughts and famine, it is one of the world's poorest countries. The country is torn by conflicts between the nomadic herders of the northern desert and the many different ethnic groups of the south, most of whom are farmers.

Most of Chad consists of a huge depression edged by mountains in the north, east, and south. Lake Chad, in the west, is all that remains of a huge lake that once filled most of the depression. Lake Chad varies in area from about 4,000 square miles in the dry season to nearly 10,000 square miles during the rainy months from May to October. Farmers around its shores rely on the lake's seasonal flooding to irrigate their rice and corn crops. Fishing on Lake Chad and on the Chari and Logone Rivers is an important source of food and income.

About 80 percent of the people live in the south, where up to 50 inches of annual rain enable farmers to grow millet, rice, sorghum, and cotton—the country's principal export crop. Chad's few mineral resources include oil, uranium, and natron, a sodium carbonate mineral mined near Lake Chad. But development is hampered by a lack of roads, railroads, and equipment. Chad has developed little industry and has to import most of its food and energy. France and the United States provide financial aid, and many international charities have donated food, tents, and medical aid during the worst droughts.

Nomadic Tuareg on camels and on foot make their way through the dusty scrub landscape of a valley in the Air Massif in north central Niger.

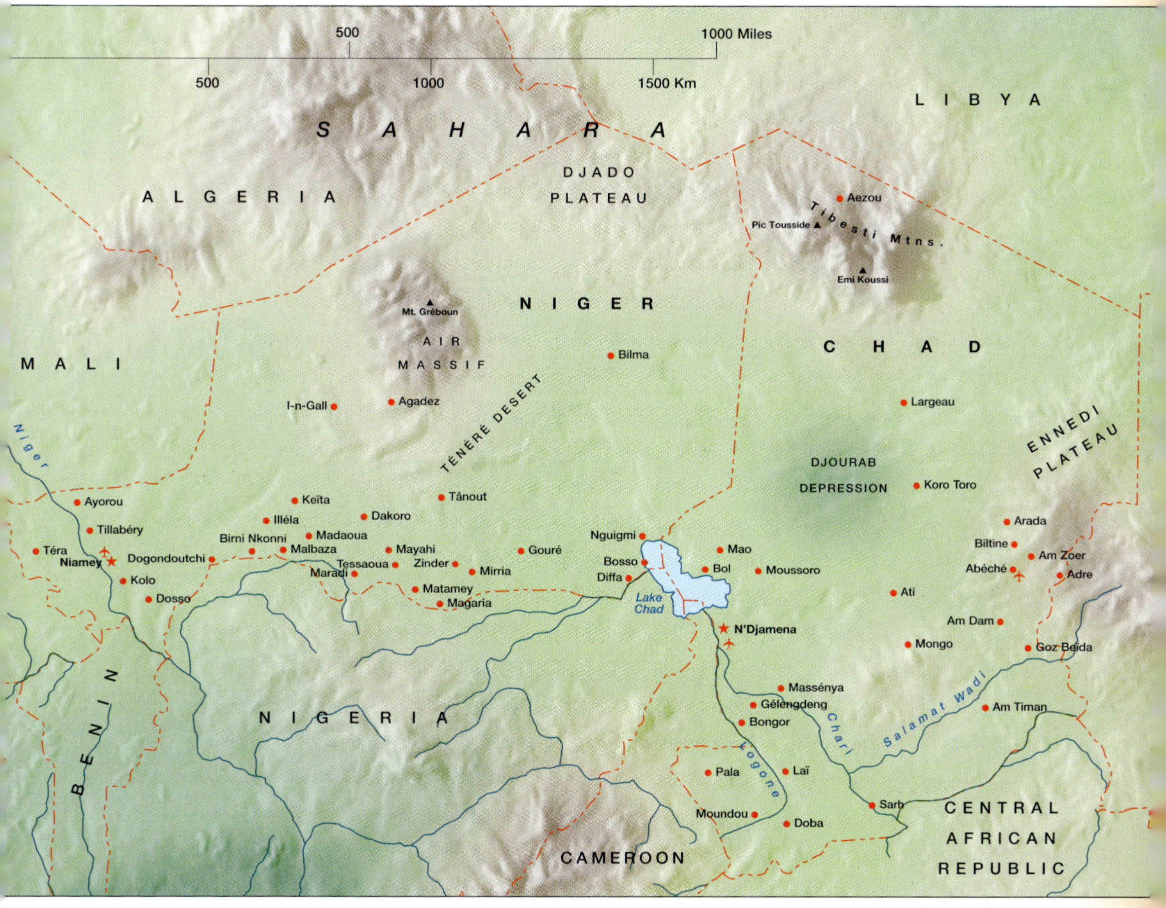

Senegal, Gambia

Senegal

Status:	Republic
Area:	75,954 square miles
Population:	10.6 million
Capital:	Dakar
Languages:	French, Wolof, Sengal-Guinean, Mandé dialects
Currency:	CFA franc (100 centimes)

Senegal, shaped like a lion's head and looking as if it is devouring Gambia, includes the westernmost point on mainland Africa. Low plains dominated by wooded savanna cover most of the land. Rainfall and vegetation vary from north to south. Annual rainfall is about 15 inches in the sparsely wooded grasslands of the north. Southern Senegal is more densely forested and receives as much as 50 inches of rain each year. Northern portions of the country have suffered from erosion, so Senegal's government has enlisted international aid for tree-planting projects to protect these semi-arid areas.

Nearly all of Senegal's people are black Africans, and about 85 percent are Muslims. The largest ethnic groups are the Wolof, Fulani, Serer, Toucouleur, Diola, and Mandingo. Each group has its own language, cultural traditions, and housing and clothing styles. Farmers in the more fertile south grow sorghum, millet, and beans for local use. Nuts are exported whole or to be processed into oil. Farmers along the country's main rivers are able to irrigate their land to produce cotton.

Senegal has a thriving fishing industry, and urban factory workers produce textiles, food products such as peanut oil and processed fish, chemicals, and consumer goods. Golden beaches attract a growing number of tourists each year, but economic benefits are not shared by most of the population. Senegal's people remain poor. Only 10 percent can read and write. There are very few doctors, and epidemics occur frequently.

Gambia

Status:	Republic
Area:	4,363 square miles
Population:	1.5 million
Capital:	Banjul
Languages:	English, Mandinka, Fula, Wolof
Currency:	Dalasi (100 butut)

Buried in Senegal like an earthworm, Gambia is barely 180 miles long east to west and is only 30 miles at its widest, north to south. The capital, Banjul, at the mouth of the Gambia River, is a busy port and the country's only large town. Mangroves and swamps line the coast and the riverbanks. Sparse forest and savanna dot the rest of the landscape.

Gambia is a poor country, with very little fertile land and no mineral resources. Farmers grow tropical fruits in the west and sorghum and rice on the higher ground north and south of the river. Peanuts are Gambia's main cash crop and principal export. The country also derives some income by transporting goods overland from Banjul to Senegal, Mali, and Guinea.

Beautiful beaches of silver sand, backed by palm groves full of colourful birds, are beginning to attract large numbers of international tourists to Gambia—providing this poor country with an important new source of income.

Guinea-Bissau

Status:	Independent State
Area:	13,946 square miles
Population:	1.6 million
Capital:	Bissau
Languages:	Portuguese, Crioulo
Currency:	CFA franc (100 centimes)

Guinea-Bissau is a small, very poor West African country that gained independence from Portugal in 1974 after an 11-year war. In addition to its mainland territory, Guinea-Bissau includes the Bijagós Islands clustered off its coast. The country's capital, Bissau, is the principal port and largest city. Many long inlets along the country's coast allow boats to reach towns and villages miles inland.

Guinea-Bissau is mostly flat. Swamps and mangroves line the coast and inlets, providing fertile soil on which farmers grow rice. Farther inland the land rises to a plateau a few hundred feet above sea level. Farmers grow peanuts and cashews for export. Corn, yams, and beans are cultivated for local markets. Many inland farmers also raise cattle and poultry. Fish is the country's only other export, but nuts and fish alone cannot support the economy. More than 60 percent of Guinea-Bissau's income is from foreign aid. To restart the economy, Guinea-Bissau's government is encouraging investment in roads and machinery.

Guinea, Sierra Leone

Guinea

Status:	Republic
Area:	94,927 square miles
Population:	8.8 million
Capital:	Conakry
Languages:	French, Fula, Malinké, Susa
Currency:	Guinea franc (100 centimes)

Guinea looks like a boomerang, extending inland from its short West African coastline in a wide arc that supports many landscapes. The coastal strip is marshy, backed by a narrow plain that rises to a central plateau called the Fouta Djalon. Upper Guinea, an area of grassy savanna, stretches across the country's northern edge. The forested hills of the Guinea Highlands dominate the southeast.

Despite its many resources, Guinea is a poor country that has suffered from inadequate government since gaining independence from France in 1958. It has a rich cultural tradition, but education and health services suffer from lack of funding, and economic improvements have been slow.

Lowland crops include rice, cassava, and bananas. Farmers in the savanna grow coffee beans, cacao beans, corn, and millet and raise cattle. Guinea's commercial growers produce bananas, coffee beans, cacao beans, palm oil, and peanuts. Guinea has about one-third of the world's bauxite reserves and pulls enough ore from the earth to comprise nearly 95 percent of the country's export earnings. But bauxite mining is hampered by inadequate roads, railroads, and equipment.

Sierra Leone

Status:	Republic
Area:	27,699 square miles
Population:	5.3 million
Capital:	Freetown
Languages:	English, French, Mende, Temne, Krio
Currency:	Leone (100 cents)

The country takes its name from Sierra Lyoa, or the Lion Mountains, the name that fifteenth-century Portuguese seafarers gave to the country's mountainous headland. The outcropping shelters the capital city of Freetown and forms the world's third-largest natural harbor. British abolitionist Granville Sharp founded Freetown in 1787 to provide a home for freed slaves.

Sierra Leone's coast is a 25-mile-wide bed of swamps that rise gently to a grassy savanna with scattered trees. Hills and plateaux cover the country's eastern region. The temperature averages 80°F, and rainfall varies from 150 inches at the coast to 80 inches in the highlands. Even with abundant rain, the gravelly, sandy soil is not very fertile, but farmers manage to grow rice, cassava, sorghum, and millet for their own tables and coffee beans, cacao beans, peanuts, and ginger for export. Forest hardwoods and Atlantic fish round out the country's vital resources. Mineral exports dominate the economy, accounting for 80 percent of the country's income. Sierra Leone is one of the world's leading diamond producers and exports bauxite and rutile—an important source of titanium.

Liberia

Status:	Republic
Area:	43,000 square miles
Population:	3.6 million
Capital:	Monrovia
Languages:	English, local languages
Currency:	Liberian dollar (100 cents)

Liberia, from the Latin for "free land," was founded in 1816 by the American Colonization Society as a settlement for freed U.S. slaves whom the society had returned to Africa. Gaining independence in 1847, Liberia is the only country in black Africa that has never been under colonial rule. Slave descendants comprise just 5 percent of the population. The other 95 percent consists of many local African ethnic groups—the Kpelle, Bassa, and a dozen smaller groups—each with its own language, culture, and traditional territory.

Swamps and mangroves fringe the coast. Inland are grassy plains and the highlands that border Guinea and Côte d'Ivoire. Liberia's climate is hot and humid, with marked wet and dry seasons. About 75 percent of the people work in agriculture, growing cassava, rice, sugarcane, and fruit and raising sheep, goats, pigs, and poultry. Most of the produce is used rurally, so Liberia must import food to feed its city dwellers. Large estates, mostly foreign-owned, cultivate the export crops—coffee beans, cacao beans, and rubber. Liberia's miners dig large quantities of iron ore for export. Shipping, insurance, and other financial services help support the economy. Education and health services are better than in most West African countries, but there are shortages of teachers and doctors, especially in rural areas.

Côte d'Ivoire, Ghana

Status:	Republic
Area:	124,502 square miles
Population:	18.2 million
Capital:	Yamoussoukro
Language:	French
Currency:	CFA franc (100 centimes)

Côte d'Ivoire—the Ivory Coast—was named by fifteenth-century French seafarers who traded for ivory in the plentiful jungles of West Africa. The territory was a French colony from 1893 until it gained independence in 1960. Côte d'Ivoire has been the country's official name since 1986.

The land has four distinct regions—a coastal strip of sandbars and lagoons, a belt of tropical rain forest 95 to 185 miles wide, a broad wooded savanna in the north, and highlands in the west. The country's climate ranges from hot, wet, and humid near the coast to mild, dry, and variable in the hills.

More than 60 ethnic groups, practicing an abundance of languages and cultures, inhabit Côte d'Ivoire. Most of the people are farmers who live in small villages and produce cassava, corn, rice, and yams for home use and coffee beans, cacao beans, sugarcane, palm oil, cotton, pineapples, and rubber for export. Industries include oil refining, textiles, timber, fishing, and processing of sugar, palm oil, and fish products. After 1960 Côte d'Ivoire built on the French legacy of roads, railways, industrialization, and strong educational and health services, becoming one of West Africa's strongest economies. Even so, falling world prices and reduced financial aid from France have caused economic difficulties. Although the official capital since 1983, Yamoussoukro shares some governmental functions with the former capital of Abidjan.

Status:	Republic
Area:	92,100 square miles
Population:	21.8 million
Capital:	Accra
Languages:	English, Twi, Fanti
Currency:	Cedi (100 pesewa)

Fifteenth-century Portuguese explorers found this West African country so rich in gold that they dubbed it the Gold Coast. After periods as a Portuguese, a Dutch, and a British colony, Ghana became in 1957 the first black African colony to achieve independence.

Ghana's altitude changes very little from its coast to its northern border with Burkina Faso. Dense rain forests cover the southwestern region and provide valuable tropical hardwoods such as mahogany for export. Grassy savanna covers much of rest of the country. Confined by the Akosombo Dam, Lake Volta in east central Ghana is one of the largest artificial lakes in the world. The dam provides hydroelectric power for Ghana's towns and a large aluminium smelting plant at Tema. Ghana also exports electricity to Togo and Benin.

Ghana, like Côte d'Ivoire, went through a period of prosperity, but political changes and falling prices for cacao beans—the country's principal export—and other agricultural products have left the country with huge debts. Ghana must continue to develop industries such as food processing, textiles, timber and furniture making, cement, and mineral exports.

Ghana's education system is one of the best in black Africa, and state-funded health services keep life expectancy and infant mortality rates close to the average for the continent.

Togo

Status:	Republic
Area:	21,927 sq. mi.
Population:	5.1 million
Capital:	Lomé
Languages:	French, Ewe
Currency:	CFA franc (100 centimes)

Just 365 miles north to south and less than 90 miles across at its widest, Togo is one of Africa's smallest countries. Formerly part of German Togoland and once a United Nations trusteeship administered by France, Togo gained independence in 1960.

The Togo Mountains dominate the country's western edge then angle across the centre, dividing the country in two. South of the hills, a plateau covered in grasslands and hardwoods slopes down to a coastal plain dotted with swamps and palm forests. To the north, rolling savanna and thorny scrub extend to the Burkina Faso border.

Most of the people are small-scale farmers who grow cassava, millet, corn, rice, yams, and beans to feed their families. Larger farms produce coffee beans, cacao beans, peanuts, palm oil, and cotton for export. Livestock and fishing contribute to the food supply. Phosphates, mined in the southeast, are Togo's principal mineral export.

Benin, Nigeria

Status:	Republic
Area:	43,483 square miles
Population:	6.2 million
Capital:	Porto-Novo
Language:	French
Currency:	CFA franc (100 centimes)

Looking somewhat like a turkey drumstick, this former French colony in West Africa gained its independence in 1960 and changed its name from Dahomey to Benin in 1975. Porto-Novo is the capital city, but Cotonou, the largest city and principal port, is the main business, cultural, and administrative centre.

Sandy beaches and lagoons extend along the short coastline. No natural harbours exist, so ships must anchor offshore or alongside two long jetties built out to sea at Cotonou. Most of southern Benin is flat and forested, with areas of marshland. Savanna grasslands in the north rise to hills 2,000 feet above sea level in the northwest. The south is hot and humid throughout the year, while northern Benin enjoys a seasonal climate with a cooler, drier winter.

The Beninese are descended from a variety of ethnic backgrounds, and many follow traditional animist religions. About half the population works in agriculture. Farmers in the sparsely populated north herd livestock or grow cotton—the country's most significant export. Some southern farmers grow just enough to feed their families, but others produce palm kernels—the country's most valuable food export—as well as coffee beans, cacao beans, tobacco, and shea nuts. Benin produces some gold, oil, and limestone but has little industry and depends largely on foreign aid, principally from France.

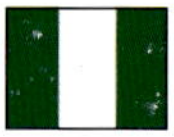

Status:	Republic
Area:	356,668 square miles
Population:	113.8 million
Capital:	Abuja
Languages:	English, Hausa, Yoruba, Igbo
Currency:	Naira (100 kobo)

Nearly 114 million people live in Nigeria, making it Africa's most populous country. Abuja, in the country's centre, was chosen as the new capital in 1991, but the former capital city of Lagos—the largest city south of the Sahara—is Nigeria's commercial and industrial hub.

The Niger and Benue Rivers cut this West African country into three triangles. High grassy plains fill the upper triangle, dropping to the flat, fertile lowlands of the Sokoto River in the northwest and the dry, sandy Chad Basin in the northeast. Highlands south of the Niger and Benue rise to about 1,900 feet in the west and to more than 5,000 feet on Nigeria's eastern border. Forested lowlands extend about 100 miles inland from coastal swamps and lagoons and from the huge fan-shaped delta of the Niger. Nigeria's rainy season extends from April to October. The remainder of the year is considered the dry season. Rainfall and temperature vary considerably, from 150 inches of rain and 80°F at the coast to less than 30 inches and 105°F in the north.

Nigeria is home to more than 250 ethnic groups, the largest of which are the Hausa and Fulani in the north, the Yoruba in the southwest, and the Igbo in the southeast. About 75 percent of Nigerians live in rural areas and depend on agriculture, but Nigeria also has a large urban population living in cities such as Lagos, Ibadan, Kano, Enugu, Kaduna, Zaria (home of the country's largest university), and Port Harcourt—the country's second port after Lagos.

Petroleum is Nigeria's principal resource and the economy's mainstay. Most of the oil fields are in the southwest and in offshore waters. Tin and columbite (used in steel making) are mined in the central highlands. Miners also extract coal, gas, iron ore, lead, and zinc. Nigeria's coastal waters, lakes, and rivers produce an abundance of fish, and the lowland forests yield valuable timbers. These resources support a range of industries including oil refining, food processing, and the production of cement, chemicals, fertilizers, textiles, and steel. Most farms in Nigeria are small family businesses that raise crops and livestock for local use. Larger farms concentrate on export crops—the most important being cacao beans, palm oil, peanuts, and rubber.

Cameroon

Status:	Republic
Area:	183,568 square miles
Population:	16.6 million
Capital:	Yaoundé
Languages:	English, French
Currency:	CFA franc (100 centimes)

After World War I (1914-1918), the League of Nations declared the former German protectorate of Cameroon a trusteeship that France and Britain would govern. In 1960 French Cameroon achieved independence. A year later, the southern portion of British Cameroon voted to join the new republic, while the northern section became affiliated with Nigeria.

A range of hills and mountains runs along Cameroon's western edge, from Lake Chad in the north to Mount Cameroon, the country's highest point at 13,353 feet above sea level. A forested plateau in the country's middle drops to dry savanna in the north, tropical rain forest in the south, and a coastal plain in the southwest. Annual rainfall ranges from 400 inches in the west to 15 inches in the north.

Climate and terrain determine how people live. People on the savanna—Hausa, Fulani, and related groups, most of whom are Muslim—herd livestock and grow grain. The Bamileke inhabit the western highlands, while the Doula, Ewondo, and Fang occupy the central and southern areas. Most are settled farmers, growing cassava, corn, and yams for their families and bananas, coffee beans, cacao beans, cotton, rubber, and peanuts for export. Petroleum for oil processing and bauxite for making aluminium are important mineral exports. Good transportation systems, hydropower from the Sanaga River, a deepwater port at Douala, and a broad range of manufacturing industries contribute to the country's economic health.

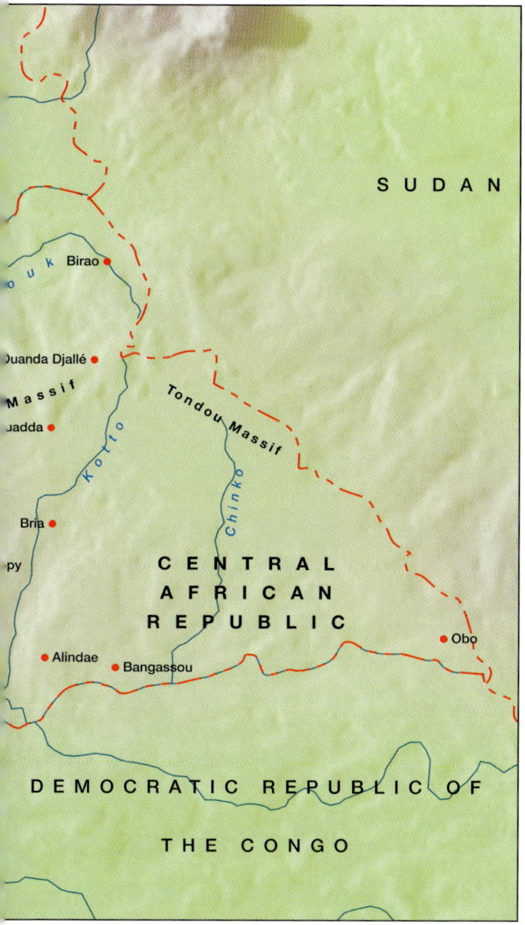

Central African Republic

Status:	Republic
Area:	240,533 square miles
Population:	3.9 million
Capital:	Bangui
Language:	French, Sango
Currency:	CFA franc (100 centimes)

This landlocked country in Africa's middle was formerly a French colony. It achieved independence in 1960, but the following years were turbulent. David Dacko, the country's first elected president, was forced from office in 1966 by Jean-Bedel Bokassa. Bokassa ruled for more than a decade as a self-crowned emperor but was deposed in 1979 by Dacko's supporters, who put Dacko back in charge. Several years later, Dacko was overthrown by the military. The Central African Republic has returned to democratic rule under a new constitution. But with few roads, no seaport, and very little industry, the country is one of the poorest and least developed in Africa. It still relies heavily on financial aid from France.

Tropical savanna grasslands, 2,000 to 3,000 feet above sea level, cover most of the country. Rain forests lie in the south, and dry savanna is on the country's borders with Chad and Sudan. The country's low altitude keeps the average temperature near 80°F and annual rainfall at about 54 inches.

Most Central Africans are farmers who take advantage of the mild climate to grow enough food for themselves. People only keep cattle in areas where there are no tsetse flies, because the flies transmit deadly diseases to cattle, horses, and humans. Coffee beans, cotton, and sisal—the principal cash crops—are exported by ship through Bangui, the capital and principal river port. The country also exports tropical hardwoods, diamonds, and some gold, but most of the country's mineral resources lie untouched.

Equatorial Guinea, São Tomé and Príncipe, Gabon

Status:	Republic
Area:	10,830 sq. mi.
Population:	521,000
Capital:	Malabo
Languages:	Spanish, Fang
Currency:	CFA franc (100 centimes)

Equatorial Guinea consists of two sections—a small territory called Mbini (formerly Río Muni) on the West African mainland and five offshore islands. The capital and largest city, Malabo, is on the biggest island, Bioko. Portugal claimed the territory in 1472 but gave it to Spain in 1778. Equatorial Guinea gained its full independence in 1968.

On the mainland, a narrow coastal plain covered in mangroves bounds a dense tropical rain forest. The soil is poor, and the mainland population of about 320,000 survives by subsistence farming, by growing coffee beans, and by harvesting tropical hardwoods, notably okoumé.

The islands are made of volcanic rock, which provides fertile soil. Farmers on the islands grow cassava, yams, and bananas as food crops and bananas, coffee beans, and cacao beans for export. Fishing and forestry contribute to the economy.

Status:	Independent State
Area:	371 sq. mi.
Population:	169,000
Capital:	São Tomé
Language:	Portuguese
Currency:	Dobra (100 centavos)

The tiny country of São Tomé and Príncipe consists of two main islands and several smaller ones in the Gulf of Guinea, about 180 miles west of Gabon and Mbini. São Tomé accounts for nearly 85 percent of the country's land area and is home to 95 percent of the population. Most of the remaining 5 percent live on Príncipe, 80 miles to the northeast. The country gained its independence in 1975, after 500 years of Portuguese rule. About 70 percent of the people are Creoles—people of mixed black African and European ancestry. Mainland Africans, Cape Verdians, and Europeans comprise the remainder.

The capital city of São Tomé is the largest urban area, the principal port, and the country's centre for trade. A hot, humid climate and rich volcanic soil provide an excellent agricultural base. Cacao beans, coffee beans, coconuts, copra, and bananas are the major export crops.

Status:	Republic
Area:	103,347 sq. mi.
Population:	1.4 million
Capital:	Libreville
Languages:	French, Fang, Eshira
Currency:	CFA franc (100 centimes)

Gabon in West Africa is one of six African countries that straddle the equator. Libreville—the capital and main port—lies just north of this imaginary line. Gabon achieved independence in 1960, after 50 years as a French colony.

Sandy beaches, lagoons, and swamps line the 550-mile coast. Inland, dense tropical rain forests blanket the land, rising to rolling plateaux and hills. The climate is hot and wet, with average temperatures around 80°F and about 100 inches of annual precipitation.

Gabon is one of Africa's least populated countries. People are unevenly distributed, mainly inhabiting villages along the coast and river valleys, where they grow cassava, yams, bananas, and mangoes. Many also fish the rivers and coastal waters and hunt in the forests. The land is not very fertile, so Gabon must import most of its food. The country is one of Africa's richest in terms of natural resources. Its many forests yield high-quality woods such as mahogany, ebony, and okoumé. Oil fields in the south also garner foreign income.

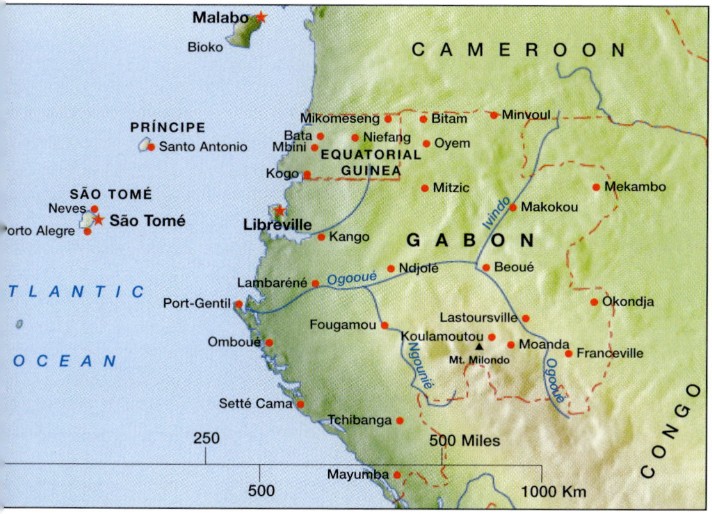

Republic of the Congo

Status:	Republic
Area:	132,046 sq. mi.
Population:	3.9 million
Capital:	Brazzaville
Languages:	French,Lingala, Kilkongo
Currency:	CFA franc (100 centimes)

For centuries the Republic of the Congo's coastline was an abundant source of slaves and ivory for European traders. In 1883 the territory became a French protectorate, and in 1910 it joined Chad, the Central African Republic, and Gabon as part of French Equatorial Africa. Congo achieved independence in 1960 and, after four decades of political turmoil, is developing into a modern multiparty state in central Africa.

The country's narrow coastal plain backs up to the 2,500-foot high Mayombe Highlands. Beyond the highlands lies the broad, fertile Niari River Valley. Grassy upland plains fill the centre of the country, and dense forests and swamps cover much of the north. Congo's climate is hot and humid.

An unusually high proportion of the population are urban dwellers—nearly half the people live in Brazzaville, Pointe-Noire, and other southern and coastal towns.

Larger farms, mostly state owned, produce coffee beans, cacao beans, and sugarcane for export. Petroleum is the principal commercial export, followed by lead, potash, and zinc.

The Democratic Republic of the Congo, Uganda

Status:	Republic
Area:	905,351 sq. mi.
Population:	56 million
Capital:	Kinshasa
Languages:	Swahili, Lingala, Kikongo, French
Currency:	Congolese franc

The Democratic Republic of the Congo—formerly Zaire—is a vast country in central Africa that is joined to the coast by Cabinda, a narrow land corridor between Angola and the Republic of the Congo. Belgium ruled the country from 1885 until it gained independence in 1960. Since then ethnic violence, army mutinies, attempts by the mineral-rich Shaba region (formerly Katanga) to break away, and political and economic crises have plagued the country.

One of the world's largest tropical rain forests covers most of the northern part of the country. Conditions are hot and humid year-round, averaging 90°F and more than 80 inches of annual rain. The 2,900-mile Congo River and its tributaries—together forming more than 7,000 navigable miles—provide the principal transportation routes for most of the country. Railways in the south link mining areas to the river ports and to the seaport at Matadi.

The country's people speak more than 200 languages. and The country produces half the world's cobalt, ranks sixth in copper production, and is the leading producer of industrial diamonds.

Status:	Republic
Area:	93,066 sq. mi.
Population:	27.6 million
Capital:	Kampala
Languages:	English, Swahili
Currency:	Ugandan shilling

Europeans arriving in this small, landlocked country in the 1850s found one of the richest kingdoms in Africa. Made a protectorate of Britain in 1894, Uganda gained its independence in 1962. Until 1986 civil unrest and military uprisings caused great hardship and economic strife, the worst of which occurred under Idi Amin Dada from 1971 to 1979. In the early 1990s, a stable government supported by the people enabled Uganda to start rebuilding its economy and to attract foreign investment.

Most of Uganda is a high plateau that lies 3,000 feet above sea level, with thick forests in the south and savanna in the drier north. The extreme northeast is semi-desert. The Virunga and Ruwenzori ranges in the southwest provide spectacular scenery, with Mount Stanley's snow-capped peak rising to 16,763 feet. Lakes Victoria, Albert, Kyoga, and many others cover nearly one-fifth of the country.

The decades of conflict have severely damaged Uganda's health and educational services—a problem intensified by rapid population growth and the highest incidence of AIDS in Africa. Agriculture dominates the economy. Farmers grow cassava, corn, beans, yams, and bananas as food crops. Larger farms and plantations grow coffee beans (the principal cash crop), tea,

cotton, and sugarcane for export. Mines near Kasese in the southwest produce copper, Uganda's main mineral resource. The ore is sent by rail to Jinja for smelting and on through Kenya to the port of Mombasa. The Owen Falls Dam at Jinja provides hydropower for the town's manufacturing industries.

Kenya

Status:	Republic
Area:	224,081 square miles
Population:	32.8 million
Capital:	Nairobi
Languages:	Swahili, English
Currency:	Kenyan shilling (100 cents)

Top: The Masai are a nomadic, livestock-herding people with a rich culture of song, dance, and storytelling.

Above centre: Nairobi, Kenya's national capital, is a sprawling city of almost 850,000 people. This view shows the modern office blocks along Government Road, one of the city's principal thoroughfares.

Above: The twin peaks of Mount Kilimanjaro, just over the border in Tanzania, dominate the scenery of Kenya's southern border region.

The former colony of Kenya gained independence in 1963 after 20 years of violent opposition to British rule. Since independence, internal conflicts have continued to damage the country's economy. In 1992 the government allowed multiparty elections for the first time in 25 years. Population growth and droughts have also increased Kenya's problems.

From a narrow coastal plain, Kenya's landscape rises quickly to the 4,000-foot plateau that covers much of the country. In the west, the land rises even higher, to the 13,000-foot Kenya Highlands, which the Great Rift Valley splits in two. Along Kenya's borders with Ethiopia and Somalia is a dry semi-desert region that supports very few people—mostly wandering livestock herders. More than 85 percent of Kenyans live in the southwestern highlands, where the altitude and a cool, moist, sunny climate combine with fertile volcanic soil to provide good growing conditions for both tropical and temperate crops. Farmland is split just about evenly between subsistence crops, such as corn and wheat, and cash crops, such as coffee beans and tea, which account for nearly half the country's export earnings. Farms on the tropical coastal strip produce sisal, cashews, sugarcane, and cotton for export. Kenya used to grow enough food to feed all its people, but the population has grown so fast that large amounts of food must be imported.

Kenya's industrial products are processed foods, paper, textiles, chemicals, and cement. Imported oil is processed at a refinery at Mombasa, and there are several vehicle assembly plants. World-famous national parks and a magnificent coast support a thriving tourist industry.

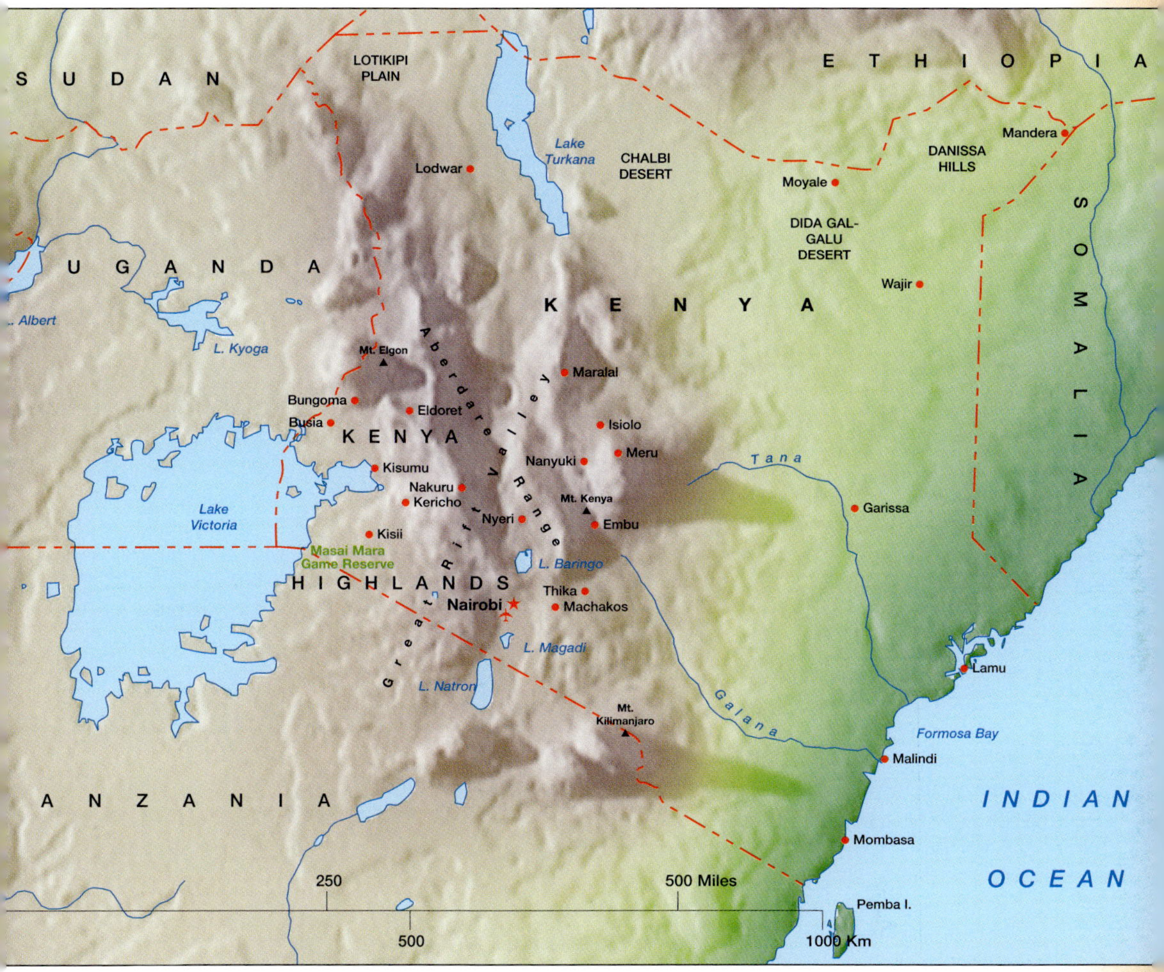

Right: Eager tourists get their first close-up view of elephants in the Masai Mara Game Reserve in southwestern Kenya. Tourism provides employment for 40,000 Kenyans and is an important source of income for the country.

Tanzania, Rwanda

Status:	Republic
Area:	364,900 square miles
Population:	38.4 million
Capital:	Dodoma (Dar es Salaam)
Languages:	Swahili, English
Currency:	Tanzanian shilling (100 cents)

Tanzania formed in 1964 when the mainland state of Tanganyika banded politically with the East African island of Zanzibar. A rolling plateau of savanna grassland, 3,500 feet above sea level, covers most of mainland Tanzania. Mangroves fringe a narrow coastal plain in the east. Northern Tanzania is hilly and home to Mount Kilimanjaro, Africa's highest peak, which rises to 19,341 feet on the border of Tanzania and Kenya. Lake Victoria dips into the country's northwestern corner, and Lake Tanganyika—the world's longest freshwater lake—forms part of the western border. Zanzibar, 23 miles offshore, is the largest coral island off the coast of Africa. Tanzania's climate ranges from 70°F and 24 inches of rain in the central highlands to 90°F and 58 inches annually at the coast.

Agriculture accounts for about two-thirds of Tanzania's income. Rural farmers raise cassava, corn, bananas, and vegetables, often having just enough to feed their families. Larger farms, mostly government owned, produce coffee beans, tea, cotton, cashews, and tobacco for export. Cloves are Zanzibar's most important export.

Tanzania's miners excavate small amounts of diamonds, gold, tin, iron ore, and coal, but the country is not highly industrialized. Factories produce processed food, textiles, fertilizers, paper, cement, and other goods, mostly for local markets. Spectacular wildlife, beautiful scenery, and unspoiled beaches attract growing numbers of tourists.

Status:	Republic
Area:	10,170 square miles
Population:	8.6 million
Capital:	Kigali
Languages:	Kinyarwanda, French, English
Currency:	Rwanda franc (100 centimes)

Rwanda's history and politics are closely linked with those of its central African neighbour, Burundi. After World War I ended, the League of Nations placed this former German colony under Belgian control. At that time, it formed the northern half of the Ruanda-Urundi territory. But the country was bitterly divided by ethnic conflict between the small but dominant Tutsi people and the much larger Hutu group—subsistence farmers with no political or economic power.

In 1962 the two parts of Ruanda-Urundi separated into independent nations—Rwanda and Burundi—but the conflict continued. In the mid-1990s, 500,000 Rwandans were massacred. Hundreds of thousands of refugees fled first to Burundi, then into neighbouring Tanzania and the Democratic Republic of the Congo as Burundi also collapsed into civil war.

Rwanda is small and very poor, and it is home to many more people than the land can support. But Rwandans continue to develop their country. Tin and wolframite—the principal ore of tungsten—account for one-quarter of Rwanda's exports. Coffee beans, tea, and pyrethrum, an insecticide made from chrysanthemums, comprise the rest. The valleys are fertile, even though the higher land is badly eroded, and the country has great potential to attract tourists—especially to Volcanoes National Park in the Virunga Mountains, where rare mountain gorillas can still be seen.

Status:	Republic
Area:	10,745 sq. mi.
Population:	7.3 million
Capital:	Bujumbura
Languages:	Kirundi, French, English
Currency:	Burundi franc (100 centimes)

Burundi, like its northern neighbour Rwanda, has been devastated by civil war for several decades. Hundreds of thousands of Tutsis and Hutus have been killed, wounded, or driven from their homeland.

Most of Burundi's people are poor subsistence farmers who grow cassava, corn, beans, and yams and raise cattle for milk and meat. Farmers on more fertile land grow coffee beans, tea, and cotton for export. Robusta coffee beans, used to make instant coffee, are grown on land up to 4,500 feet above sea level. The more valuable arabica coffee beans, sold as whole beans or ground coffee, are grown at higher elevations. Fishing on Lake Tanganyika provides an important source of food for local markets.

Angola, Namibia

Status:	Independent State
Area:	481,351 square miles
Population:	14.5 million
Capital:	Luanda
Language:	Portuguese
Currency:	Kwanza (100 lwei)

Angola is a large, sparsely populated country on the western coast of southern Africa. Its territory includes the tiny province of Cabinda in the northwest, which is separated from the rest of the country by the Congo River and the Republic of the Congo's narrow land corridor to the coast.

Portuguese slave traders established colonies on Angola's coast in the sixteenth century, and later colonists cultivated sugarcane and tobacco for the European market. Angola won its independence from Portugal in 1975 after a long and bloody war, but the principal rebel armies continued fighting until the early 1990s.

Grass-covered plateaux, 4,000 to 6,000 feet above sea level, cover most of the country, with a range of hills in the west dropping sharply to a narrow coastal plain. In the hotter, wetter north, thick forests merge with those of the Democratic Republic of the Congo. In the south, the savanna gives way to stony desert and scrub.

Decades of war have left Angola's railroads and mines in ruins and the country poor and heavily in debt. But a stable government has many resources with which to jumpstart the economy. Most of Angola has ample water and fertile soil, especially in the river valleys. The coastal waters teem with fish. The mining regions hold huge reserves of iron ore and some of the world's richest diamond deposits, and Cabinda is rich in oil. Most of Angola's farmers grow cassava, corn, bananas, and sugarcane as food crops, but a rejuvenated economy could restore the country's once-strong exports of coffee beans, cotton, sugarcane, corn, and fruits.

Status:	Independent State
Area:	318,259 square miles
Population:	2 million
Capital:	Windhoek
Languages:	English, Afrikaans, German
Currency:	Namibian dollar (100 cents)

Namibia, formerly called South-West Africa, won independence in 1990 after 75 controversial years under South African control. Before South Africa controlled it, Germany had ruled the territory as a protectorate for 31 years.

With only five people per square mile, Namibia is one of the most sparsely populated countries in Africa. Dry rolling grasslands, 3,000 to 6,000 feet above sea level, blanket most of the country's interior. The Namib Desert—home to the world's largest sand dunes, some of which stand more than 1,200 feet high—covers the 80-mile-wide coastal strip, while the Kalahari Desert dominates the country's southeast. The narrow Caprivi Strip in the extreme northeast, ceded to Germany by Britain in 1893, provides Namibia with a land corridor to the Zambezi River.

Namibia is not fertile, but farmers in the central uplands and northern areas are able to grow corn, millet, and vegetables, and there is sufficient grass for grazing cattle and sheep. Coastal fisheries provide employment and an important source of food, but excessive fishing has caused catches to diminish. Mining dominates Namibia's economy, with gem-quality diamonds, copper, zinc, lead, silver, gold, and the world's most productive uranium mine providing much of the country's export income. Tourism is a growing industry with great potential for future development. Etosha Game Park in the northwest contains all the principal big game species and attracts many visitors each year.

Seafarers had good cause to name this the Skeleton Coast. There was little hope of survival for anyone shipwrecked here.

Zambia

Status:	Republic
Area:	290,583 square miles
Population:	11 million
Capital:	Lusaka
Languages:	English, Nyanja, Tonga, Beruba
Currency:	Kwacha (100 ngwee)

Zambia in south central Africa became an independent nation in 1964. From 1924 to 1953, it was the British colony of Northern Rhodesia, and from 1953 until 1963 it formed part of the Federation of Rhodesia and Nyasaland, along with Southern Rhodesia (Zimbabwe) and Nyasaland (Malawi).

A vast undulating plateau that lies 4,000 feet above sea level covers most of Zambia. The southern part is drained by the Zambezi River and its principal tributaries, the Kafue and the Luangwa. Lake Kariba, formed by the Kariba Dam on the Zambezi, is Africa's second-largest artificial lake. Generators in the dam supply power to both Zambia and its southern neighbour Zimbabwe. Victoria Falls, upstream of the dam, is one of the world's great tourist attractions. The Chambeshi River, which flows into the marshlands around Lake Bangweulu, and the Luapula River, which flows north from the lake and then joins the Congo, drain Zambia's northern region. Most of the plateau is savanna grassland, with forested valleys full of mopani trees. The Muchinga Mountains rise to 7,000 feet near the border with Malawi.

Zambia's economy is almost completely dependent on one commodity—copper—which accounts for nearly 90 percent of the country's income. Exports of lead, zinc, cobalt, and other minerals account for most of the rest. Zimbabwe, Mozambique, and South Africa provide rail access to seaports. Kitwe in north central Zambia is the country's mining centre and, like the capital city of Lusaka, is attracting many poor rural people in search of work. Rapid urban population growth is straining the country's inadequate educational and health systems.

Zambia's farmers grow corn, millet, sorghum, cassava, and beans as staple food crops, while some of the larger farms on fertile valley soil produce tobacco, fruit, cotton, and sugarcane commercially. Some farmers raise cattle in the south, but tsetse flies prevent livestock raising in the north.

Victoria Falls, named for Queen Victoria by the British explorer David Livingstone who discovered them in 1855, plunge more than 300 feet into a narrow gorge on the Zambezi River in southern Zambia. The constant roar and clouds of spray earned the falls their local name—Mosi-oa-Tunya—"the smoke that thunders."

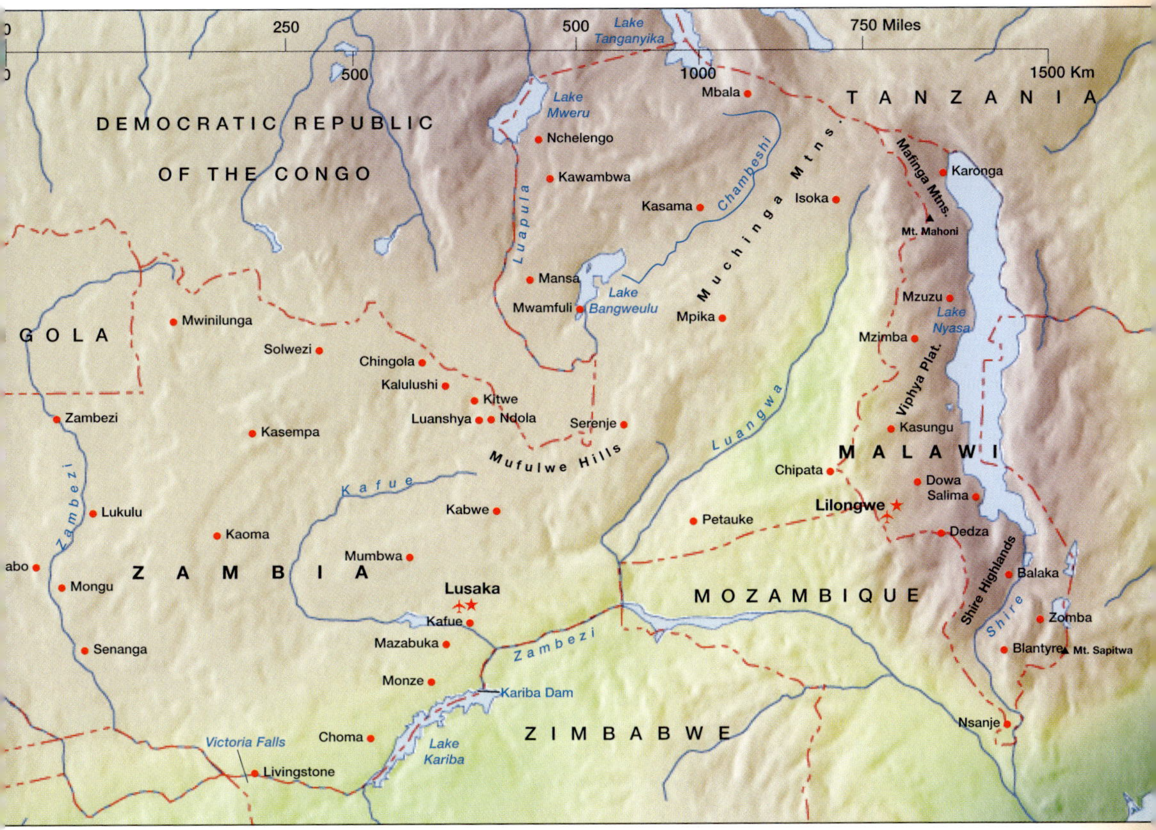

Status:	Republic
Area:	45,745 sq. mi.
Population:	12.6 million
Capital:	Lilongwe
Languages:	Chichewa
Currency:	Kwacha (100 tambala)

About 520 miles long and 100 miles wide, Malawi sits at the southern end of Africa's Great Rift Valley on the western and southern shores of Lake Nyasa. Rich volcanic soil and lake sediment provide some of the most fertile farmland in Africa, but only one-third of the land is suitable for farming. To the west and south, the land rises steeply to about 4,000 feet. Mount Mulanje, Malawi's highest peak, reaches 9,843 feet in the south.

The climate in the valley bottom is hot and humid, averaging about 75°F. Malawi's highlands are cooler at 55° to 65°F. Annual rainfall ranges from 60 inches in the north to 33 inches in the south. A warm, wet season occurs from December to March. Malawi's cool, dry season extends from May to October.

More than half the country's people live in the south, primarily in the capital city of Lilongwe and in Blantyre—the country's principal business and industrial centre. Both cities are overcrowded, having seen rapid growth in the 1980s, with the influx of more than one million refugees from Mozambique's civil war.

Despite its fertile land, Malawi remains very poor. Government policies favor large commercial farms that produce tea—the predominant cash crop—and cotton, tobacco, sugarcane, and peanuts for export. The country's lack of roads and machinery has kept it from developing a timber industry—another possible source of income.

Mozambique, Seychelles, Comoros, Réunion

Mozambique

Status:	Republic
Area:	309,494 sq. mi.
Population:	19.5 million
Capital:	Maputo
Language:	Portuguese
Currency:	Metical (100 centavos)

Mozambique, in southeastern Africa, has fertile land, minerals, forests, and hydroelectric power. Yet life expectancy there is among the shortest in Africa, infant mortality is among the highest, malnutrition is widespread. The causes lie in the country's recent history. Mozambique gained independence in 1975 after 400 years as a Portuguese colony and after a bloody 10-year war. A civil war that continued until the mid-1990s added to the devastation.

A wide coastal plain with many port cities covers half the country, rising inland to low plateaux and then to highlands and mountains on the borders. Forests in the north contain ebony, ironwood, and other valuable timbers. Lowland plantations produce cashews, coconuts, cotton, and sugarcane for export. Inland farmers harvest cassava, corn, and vegetables.

Natural resources include gold, diamonds, uranium, iron ore, copper, bauxite, coal, and offshore gas. The economy also depends on foreign aid and on payments from neighbouring countries for railroad access to the harbours at Maputo, Beira, Quelimane, and Pemba.

Seychelles

Status:	Republic
Area:	174 sq. mi.
Population:	76,000
Capital:	Victoria
Languages:	English, French, Creole
Currency:	Seychelles rupee (100 cents)

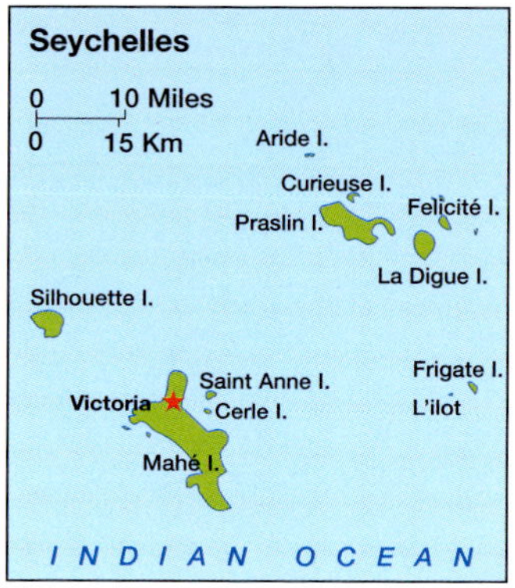

The Seychelles comprise about 115 islands. Almost 90 percent of the people live on the main island, Mahé. The economy depends mainly on tourism. Small farms produce some food for local use, but most of the islands' food is imported. Tea growing and tuna fishing also contribute to the economy.

Comoros

Status:	Republic
Area:	861 sq. mi.
Population:	812,000
Capital:	Moroni
Languages:	French, Arabic
Currency:	CFA franc (100 centimes)

The Comoros Islands became independent from France in 1975, following a referendum. The country is poor, with most of the people dependent on subsistence farming. Vanilla, cloves, and ylang-ylang—a perfumery essence obtained from the flowers of a native tree—are the islands' only significant exports.

Réunion

Status:	Overseas Department of France
Area:	969 sq. mi.
Population:	700,000
Capital:	Saint Denis
Languages:	French
Currency:	French franc (100 centimes)

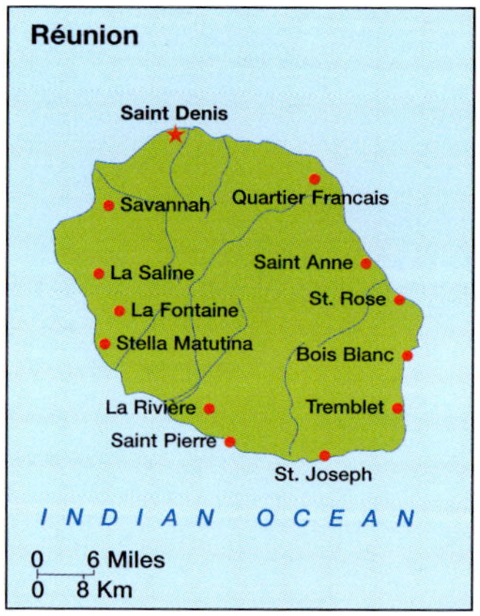

Réunion has been an Overseas Department of France since 1946. Before that it was a French colony for 300 years. The island's principal exports are vanilla, tobacco, tea, and perfumes.

Madagascar

Status:	Republic
Area:	226,656 sq. mi.
Population:	18.4 million
Capital:	Antananarivo
Languages:	Malagasy, French
Currency:	Malagasy franc (100 centimes)

Madagascar is actually one large island and many tiny islands separated from the southern African mainland by the Mozambique Channel. The main island lies about 250 miles off the coast.

Mauritius

Status:	Republic
Area:	788 sq. mi.
Population:	1.2 million
Capital:	Port Louis
Languages:	English, French, Creole
Currency:	Mauritian rupee (100 cents)

This remote country is in the Indian Ocean consisting of one large island and about 20 smaller ones. It gained independence from Britain in 1968 and declared itself a republic in 1992. Sugarcane plantations long ago replaced all the native vegetation. Sugarcane is still an important export crop, but the island economy has diversified to include tourism, fishing, tea growing, manufacturing of clothing, and banking.

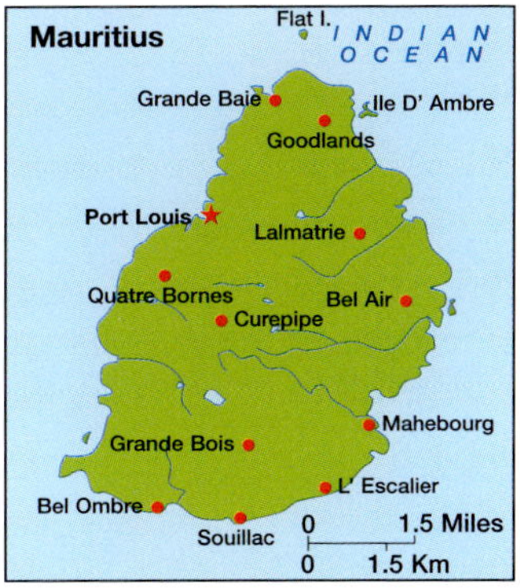

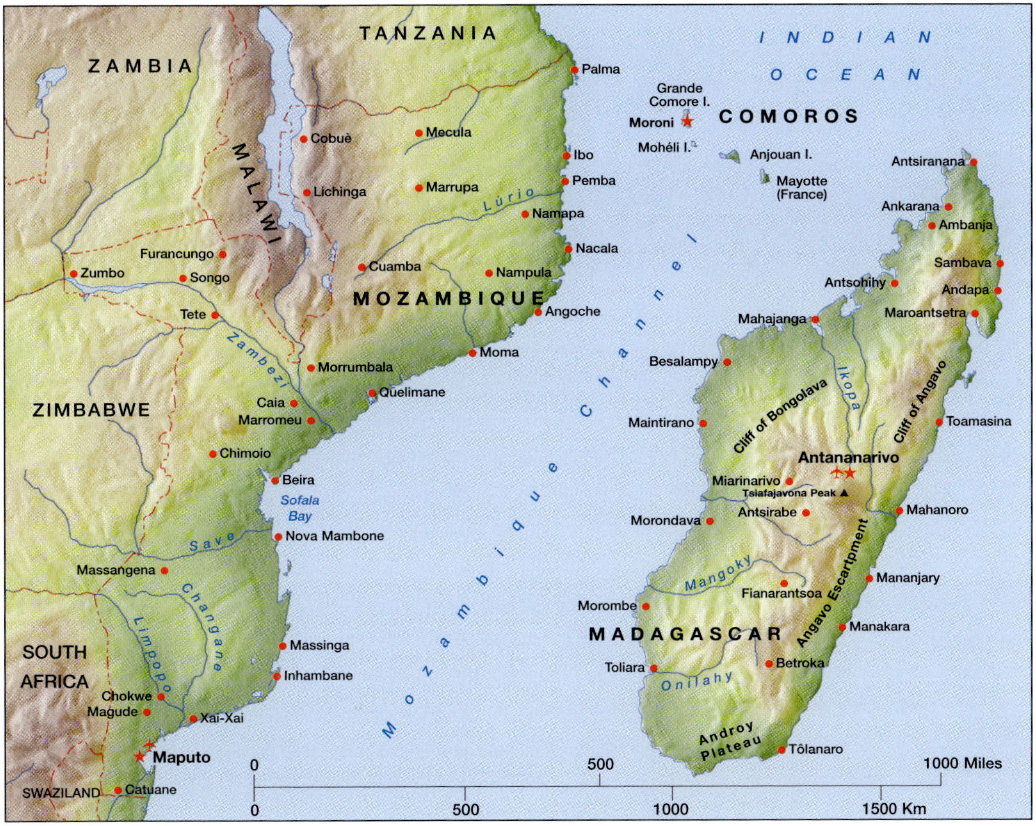

Botswana

Status: Republic
Area: 224,606 sq. mi.
Population: 1.8 million
Capital: Gaborone
Languages: Setswana, English
Currency: Pula (100 thebe)

This large, landlocked country in the centre of southern Africa achieved independence in 1966 after 71 years as the British protectorate of Bechuanaland. It is one of Africa's most thinly populated countries, with just seven people per square mile. Dry rolling plateaux about 3,000 feet above sea level cover much of the country. Low hills rise in the east and northwest. A huge depression in the north receives the waters of the Okavango River, which flows south from the Angolan Highlands. In the rainy season, the waters spread out to form the vast Okavango Swamps that teem with wildlife. Tiny Lake Ngami is all that remains in the dry season. Streams flowing eastward from the marshes evaporate in a large salt basin called the Makgadikgadi Pans. The Kalahari Desert covers much of central and southwestern Botswana.

Most of Botswana's people live in small rural villages in the eastern half of the country, where they farm and raise cattle. Corn, sorghum,

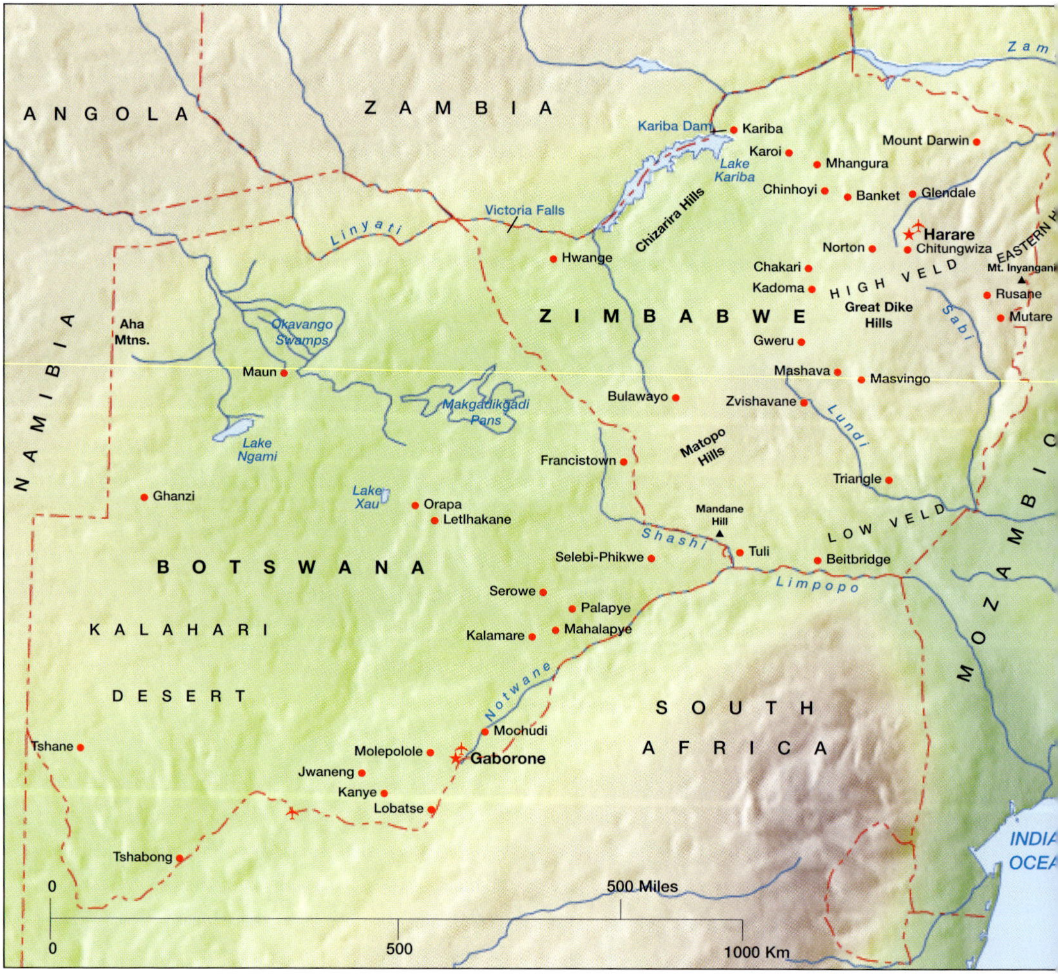

and millet are the principal food crops, but the land is not very fertile, so Botswana imports food from its neighbours. Livestock comprises the core of Botswana's agricultural economy. The country exports beef and leather, and the production of leather goods is one of the few manufacturing industries.

The discovery of minerals in the 1970s enabled Botswana to grow from one of Africa's poorest nations to one showing rapid economic improvement. Diamonds from the mines at Orapa and Jwaneng account for 80 percent of export earnings. The remainder is mostly copper from Selebi-Phikwe and coal from the east. Botswana's principal economic partner is South Africa. Botswanan exports headed to sea travel by rail through South Africa, and South African investments have long supported Botswana's mining industries. South Africa also provides jobs for thousands of Botswanans.

Status:	Republic
Area:	150,873 square miles
Population:	12.9 million
Capital:	Harare
Languages:	English, Shona, Ndebele
Currency:	Zimbabwean dollar (100 cents)

Zimbabwe's journey to independence began in 1965, when the ruling white minority unilaterally declared independence from Britain rather than accept black majority rule. International political pressure, trade sanctions, and a long guerrilla war finally forced the white minority to concede. Zimbabwe gained independence under black majority rule in 1980.

Located in southern Africa, Zimbabwe has four natural regions. The High Veld, a 4,000-foot rolling plateau, runs southwest to northeast across the country. Large farms in this area, many of them still owned by white farmers, produce Zimbabwe's principal export crops—tobacco, cotton, sugarcane, and tea. A narrow ridge called the Great Dike stretches for 300 miles across the highlands. The dike consists of igneous rocks that were forced up through the surrounding rocks as molten magma. These rocks contain platinum, nickel, chromite, and other minerals, which account for about 20 percent of the country's exports. The Low Veld consists of sandy plains in the valleys of the Lundi, Sabi, and Limpopo Rivers. The Eastern Highlands rise to 8,507 feet at Mount Inyangani near the Mozambican border. Hot, wet summers and cool dry winters make some of the High Veld farms very productive, but most black Zimbabwean farmers work small plots on the less fertile Low Veld and manage to grow just enough corn and millet to feed their families.

Coal from the Hwange region and hydroelectric power from the Kariba Dam provide ample energy for Zimbabwe's well-developed industrial districts in Harare and Bulawayo. Iron and steel, automobile assembly, textiles, chemicals, and the processing of agricultural products such as leather, tobacco, soybeans, and sunflower seeds drive the country's industrial sector. Zimbabwe exports goods by rail through South Africa and Mozambique. Tourism also contributes to a balanced economy that supports efficient educational and health systems.

Left: The Okavango Swamps in northern Botswana attract ecotourists and birdwatchers from all over the world.

Lesotho, Swaziland

Status:	Constitutional Monarchy
Area:	11,718 sq. mi.
Population:	2.1 million
Capital:	Maseru
Languages:	English, Sesotho
Currency:	Loti (100 lisente)

This small mountainous country is completely surrounded by South Africa and depends on that country for most of its food, manufactured goods, energy, and employment.

Dominating much of the country are the high plateaus and peaks of the Moloti and Drakens-berg ranges that rise to 11,425 feet at the summit of Mount Ntlenyana on Lesotho's eastern border. Flat plains at about 5,500 feet encompass western Lesotho. The country's altitude affords Lesotho a mild, damp climate, with temperatures around 70°F in January—the heart of summer—and 35°F in the winter month of July.

Farmers tend corn, sorghum, barley, beans, peas, and other vegetables. Cattle, sheep, and goats supply milk and meat for the table and provide wool for export. Lesotho's eastern highlanders are less settled. Men and young boys spend months in the hills riding on ponies as they move their livestock from place to place in search of grazing land.

Status:	Monarchy
Area:	6,703 sq. mi.
Population:	1.0 million
Capital:	Mbabane
Languages:	Siswati, English
Currency:	Lilangeni (100 cents)

The tiny kingdom of Swaziland is bordered on three sides by South Africa and on the fourth by Mozambique. Mountains clad in dense pine forests cover much of the country's western edge. To the east, the land drops through rolling grassy savanna to a flat, rather dry lowland plain. Several large rivers flow across the plain, providing ample water for irrigating farmland and for generating hydroelectricity.

Swaziland has abundant resources. The western highlands contain one of the world's largest asbestos mines, huge reserves of iron ore, and deposits of tin and gold. Swaziland's miners also excavate barite, kaolin, and coal. Natural forests and some of the largest plantation forests in Africa supply the raw material for wood-pulp factories and sawmills. Large farms on the fertile savanna and on irrigated land in the lowland plains grow sugarcane, rice, cotton, tobacco, and citrus fruits for foreign markets. Meat and animal hides are also significant exports. Manufacturing—mainly processing agricultural and forest products—comprises nearly 25 percent of total productivity.

Traditional Swazi farmers in rural areas grow corn, millet, beans, and other crops and raise livestock. Cattle, representing wealth and status, have a special importance in Swazi culture and are rarely killed. Rural culture and social traditions remain strong even though many Swazi people live in the urban centres and work in offices and factories.

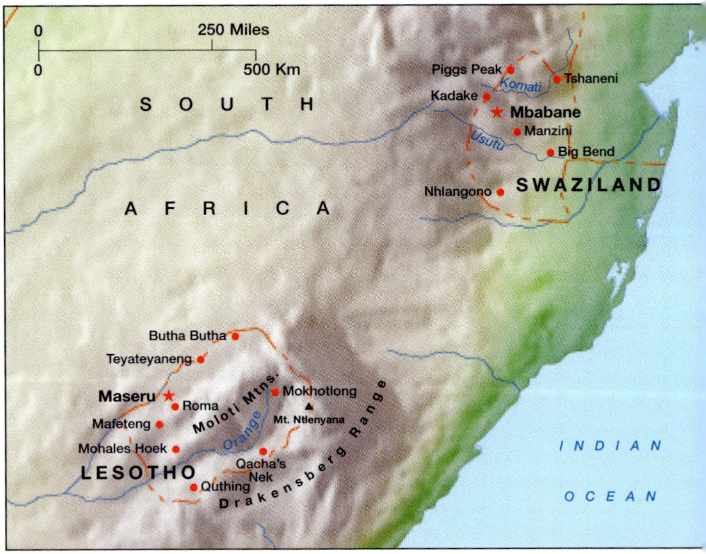

Status:	Republic
Area:	471,444 square miles
Population:	42.6 million
Capital:	Pretoria (administrative), Cape Town (legislative), Bloemfontein (judicial)
Languages:	English, Afrikaans, Zulu, Xhosa, Ndebele, Sesotho, Tswana
Currency:	Rand (100 cents)

South Africa is the richest, most highly developed country in Africa. It covers barely 4 percent of the continent's land area and is home to only 6 percent of its people, yet it produces 50 percent of Africa's minerals and 40 percent of its manufactured goods. It also generates about 70 percent of the continent's electricity.

The country's history has been one of conflict—from the first wars between Dutch settlers and the Xhosa people, through the Boer War (1899–1902) between Britain and the Afrikaner Orange Free State and Transvaal. In 1948 the white majority introduced apartheid, a policy of segregation that fueled a long struggle for black majority rule. The struggle culminated in the election of the nation's first black president, Nelson Mandela, in 1994.

South Africa's landscape is as diverse as its history. Most of the interior consists of an undulating plateau called the veld. The High Veld contains Africa's richest goldfields and much of its best farmland, where farmers cultivate corn, wheat, potatoes, and fruit.

In western South Africa lies the lower Middle Veld—cattle-ranching country. The northern Transvaal region consists of rolling grasslands where farmers grow corn, tobacco, and fruit. The Great Karroo Mountains in the south and the Drakensberg Mountains to the east separate South Africa's veld from its narrow coast. The Namib Desert borders the Atlantic coast in the extreme west, and the Kalahari Desert takes up the northwestern corner along the border with Botswana. South Africa's spectacular scenery, 16 national parks, and hundreds of game

Top: In Swaziland, the huge reeds that grow along riverbanks and in marshes are made into thatching, baskets, and many other goods.

Centre: Cape Town is one of the world's most beautiful cities, with fine avenues, elegant shops, and parks. Its thriving waterfront serves cargo ships that arrive from all over the world.

Bottom: On a calm day, the Cape of Good Hope looks tranquil, but it was earlier called the Cape of Storms.

reserves attract millions of tourists each year.

Much of South Africa's prosperity comes from the country's wealth of minerals, particularly diamonds, gold, silver, platinum, iron ore, copper, manganese, and uranium. Gold earns the most export money, accounting for nearly one-third of the country's income. Oil is the only major mineral resource the country lacks, but South Africa has vast coalfields and has developed the process of creating fuel oil from coal. Coal provides 80 percent of the country's energy. The remainder is hydroelectric and nuclear power.

South Africa's exports consist primarily of minerals and agricultural products such as wool and wine. Manufacturing industries—concentrated in the Witwatersrand region and around the chief ports of Cape Town, Port Elizabeth, East London, and Durban—produce goods mainly for the domestic market. These goods include processed foods, textiles, iron and steel, paper, chemicals, automobiles, furniture, and domestic appliances. South Africa also plays a major role in the trading activities of neighbouring countries. Most of the imports and exports of Lesotho, Botswana, and Swaziland and about half the goods travelling to and from Malawi, Zimbabwe, and the Democratic Republic of the Congo cross South Africa by rail and pass through South Africa's seaports.

Top: Gold has long been one of South Africa's many valuable mineral exports.

Centre: Black rhinos in Kruger National Park are among the great sights for visiting tourists.

Bottom: With a total population of more than 1.7 million, Johannesburg and its surrounding suburbs and townships form the largest metropolitan area in South Africa.

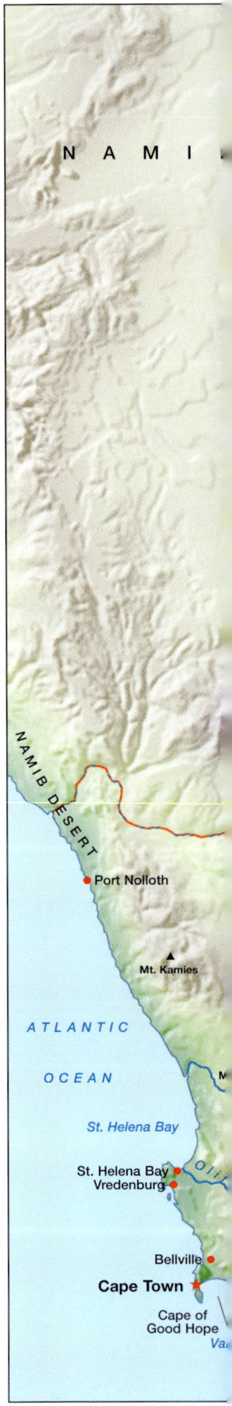

ZIMBABWE
BOTSWANA
KALAHARI
DESERT
MOZAMBIQUE
SWAZILAND
LESOTHO
SOUTH
AFRICA
INDIAN
OCEAN
Messina
Sibasa
Louis Trichardt
Duiwelskloof
Giyani
Phalaborwa
Pietersburg
Lebowakgomo
Thabazimbi
Water Mtns.
Limpopo
Mogalakwena
Olifants
Pilgrim's Rest
Rustenburg
Mafikeng
Pretoria
Nelspruit
Middelburg
Carletonville
Soweto
Johannesburg
Vanderbijlpark
Vereeniging
Vryburg
Klerksdorp
HIGHVELD
Kuruman
Kathu
Asbestos Mtns.
Harts
Vaal
Utrecht
Maputo
Newcastle
Welkom
Upington
Orange
Kimberley
Madder
DRAKENSBERG
Tugela
Richard's Bay
Prieska
Hopetown
Bloemfontein
Riet
Mt. Hexrivier
Pietermaritzburg
Durban
De Aar
Gariep Dam
Aliwal North
Port Shepstone
Margate
Carnarvon
Umtata
Queenstown
Great Kei
Cradock
Beaufort West
Graaff Reinet
Butterworth
Great Fish
Sundays
Groot
Great Karroo Mtns.
East London
Oudtshoorn
Grahamstown
Uitenhage
Swellendam
George
Port Elizabeth
0
250
500 Miles
0
200
400
600
800 Km

Northern and Western Asia

The northern and western sections of the Asian continent comprise a vast region that covers 6,800 miles of territory. This part of Asia stretches from the deserts of the Arabian Peninsula in the extreme southwest across the snow-covered mountains of Kyrgyzstan and Tajikistan in western central Asia. The region includes the grassy steppes of Asian Russia and the ancient forests of Siberia (part of Russia). In the far Russian north lies the frozen tundra of the Chukchi Peninsula, which is lashed by the icy waters of the Arctic Ocean and the Bering Sea.

Northern and western Asia also exhibit some of the world's most extreme climatic conditions. For example, the desert interior of Oman in the Middle East is one of the hottest places on earth, with temperatures often exceeding 120°F and sometimes soaring well above 130°F. At the other extreme lies the Central Siberian Plateau, where, far from the moderating effects of the oceans, winter temperatures average –50°F and often plunge to –85°F and below.

The northern and western sections of Asia are also sparsely populated. Deserts dominate the Middle Eastern countries of the west, where populations tend to congregate in the coastal regions, in the cooler highlands farther inland, and in the main river valleys. The deserts of the Middle East are largely uninhabited, except for small groups of nomadic Bedouin.

The landscapes of western central Asia rise from the dry grasslands bordering the Caspian Sea to the windswept glaciers and peaks of the Pamir Mountains and the Tian Shan (mountains). Most of the people live near the shores of the Caspian Sea or in the foothills of the mountains, where rivers provide water for homes and for irrigating fields.

The least populated parts of northern Asia are in Asian Russia. Most of the people live in mining and industrial areas near various cities—Yekaterinburg and Chelyabinsk at the southern end of the Ural Mountains, Novosibirsk and Irkutsk in southern Siberia, and Vladivostok along the coast of the Sea of Japan. The people of the far northern forests and tundra are mainly reindeer herders, trappers, and fishers.

Farmers in the more fertile areas of northern and western Asia produce a variety of grain crops, vegetables, and fruit. Some regions grow vines for wine making, while others raise mulberry trees to provide food for silkworms. Cotton and flax are important nonfood crops in some areas, and the great forests of northern Asia produce vast quantities of lumber, plywood, pulp, and paper products. Rivers are an important source of hydroelectric power.

Oil and natural gas are the principal natural resources of the Middle East—one of the world's leading oil-producing regions. Russia also has vast reserves of both oil and gas and also extensive coalfields. Northern Asia probably has more untapped reserves of minerals than any other region in the world. Miners in the Pamir Mountains, the Tian Shan, the Ural Mountains, and the upland zones of southern Siberia produce iron, copper, lead, zinc, tungsten, tin, gold, and many other minerals. These deposits feed the region's heavy industry and manufacturing centres.

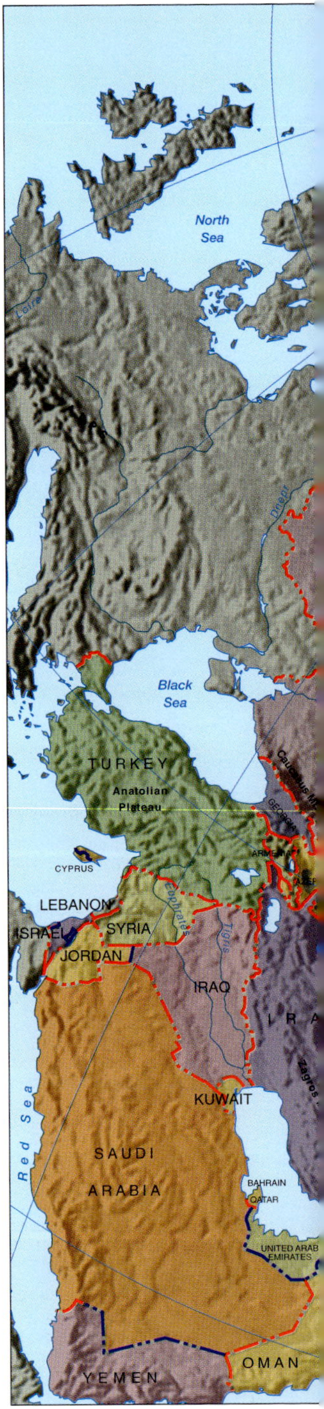

ARCTIC OCEAN
Norwegian Sea
Svalbard
Barents Sea
Franz Josef Land
Severnaya Zemlya
New Siberian Is.
Novaya Zemlya
Kara Sea
Laptev Sea
East Siberian Sea
Bering Sea
Chukchi Peninsula
Kolyma Lowland
Kamcha.
Sea of Okhotsk
Central Siberian Plateau
West Siberian Plain
RUSSIA
URAL MOUNTAINS
Lower Tunguska
Angara
Lena
Yenisey
Ob
Irtysh
Ishim
Tobol
Ural
Amur
L. Baikal
Sayan Mts.
Manchurian Plain
KAZAKHSTAN
Aral Sea
Turanian Plateau
Syr Darya
L. Balkhash
UZBEKISTAN
TURKMENISTAN
KYRGYZSTAN
TAJIKISTAN
AFGHANISTAN
Hindu Kush
Altai
Gobi Desert
Tian Shan
Tarim Basin
Kunlun Shan
HIMALAYA
Great Basin
Sea of Japan
Yellow Sea
East China Sea
South China Sea
Arabian Sea
Indus
Ganga
0° 20° 40° 60° 80° 100° 120° 140° 160° 180°
0 1000 2000 Miles
0 1000 2000 3000 Km

Turkey

Status:	Republic
Area:	299,158 sq. mi.
Population:	73.3 million
Capital:	Ankara
Language:	Turkish
Currency:	Turkish lira (100 kurus)

Turkey, one of the few countries that spans continents, forms a bridge between Europe and Asia. The European portion of the country, called Thrace, comprises just 3 percent of Turkey's total landmass and sits on the southeastern tip of the continent. The remainder of the country covers a broad peninsula known as Anatolia or Asia Minor.

Mountain ranges along the country's northern and southern shores border Turkey's two plateaux. The Taurus Mountains dominate the south and almost completely hide the western plateau from the sea. The Pontic and Küre Mountains lie along the shore of the Black Sea. The country's coastal regions enjoy hot summers and mild winters, but inland Turkey is a land of extremes, with very hot, dry summers and bitterly cold winters. Less than 10 inches of rain falls each year, and parts of the land are semidesert.

Farmers on the plateaux and in the southern mountains raise sheep and goats. Those in the more fertile western valleys and northern plains grow cotton, tobacco, and olives for export and wheat, fruits, and vegetables for local markets.

Turkey's economy, long reliant on agriculture, is developing around other means of revenue. Miners in eastern Turkey excavate chromite—the country's most valuable mineral export—as well as copper, borax, and coal. Factory workers manufacture motor vehicles, chemicals, metal, wood, and leather goods. Textiles and clothing account for about one-third of all manufactured exports. Tourism is Turkey's fastest-growing industry, enticing visitors to the historic city of Istanbul, to a wealth of ancient monuments, and to the sunny resorts along the southern coast.

Status:	Republic
Area:	3,572 sq. mi.
Population:	0.9 million
Capital:	Nicosia
Languages:	Greek, Turkish
Currency:	Cypriot pound (100 cents) Turkish lira (100 cents)

A small island in the eastern Mediterranean Sea, Cyprus has been divided since 1974, when Turkish forces took command of the island's northern section. The intervening years have been harsh, and the relatively poor inhabitants of the Turkish sector rely heavily on aid from Turkey. Cypriots of Greek origin remain in control of the more prosperous south, where the economy thrives despite the conflict. Repeated United Nations (UN) efforts have failed to bring about a settlement, although an uneasy standoff has replaced the bitter fighting. Only Turkey recognizes the northern section as a separate country.

Cyprus is a scenic land with a pleasant climate. Mount Olympus, the highest peak, rises to 6,403 feet in the centre of the Troodos Mountains, which dominate central and western Cyprus, while the rugged limestone mountains of Kyrenia parallel the northern coast. The broad fertile Mesaoria Plain lies between the two ranges, spanning the country from Morphou in the west to Famagusta in the east.

Farmers in the north raise sheep and grow grains, grapes, olives, vegetables, and citrus fruits. Southern farmers benefit from better soil and ample water for irrigation. Their crops include fruits, salad crops, early vegetables, and flowers for export to mainland Europe.

The rocky shoreline near Paphos on the southwestern coast of Cyprus is associated with Aphrodite, the Greek goddess of love and beauty.

Syria

Status:	Republic
Area:	71,498 sq. mi.
Population:	18.6 million
Capital:	Damascus
Languages:	Arabic, Kurdish, Armenian
Currency:	Syrian pound (100 piastres)

More than 2,000 years ago, ancient cities such as Palmyra were important trading centres on the caravan routes linking Asia, Africa, and Europe.

Western and central Syria can be divided into three principal land regions. A narrow coastal plain along the Mediterranean Sea has rich soil and a mild, moist climate. Winds blowing in across the water provide about 40 inches of annual rain, allowing coastal farmers to grow a variety of crops without the need for irrigation. Inland from this plain and running south to the Jordanian border lie the rugged Anti-Lebanon and Jebel Druz Mountains, whose west-facing slopes catch the moisture carried by the prevailing winds.

To the east of the mountains lies another, less-fertile plain. Farmers here rely for irrigation on the mountain streams and the Orontes River, which flows northward through a series of gorges and broad valleys. Most Syrians live in the plains regions bordering the mountains. The capital city of Damascus, near the country's southeastern border, houses more than one million residents, and the populations in Aleppo, Homs, Hamah, and the coastal city of Latakia each exceed 150,000. Much of the remaining population live in small towns and villages that dot the countryside.

Cotton and wheat dominate Syria's cropland, supplemented by barley, sugar beets, olives, other fruits and vegetables, and tobacco.

Status:	Republic
Area:	4,015 sq. mi.
Population:	3.8 million
Capital:	Beirut
Languages:	Arabic, French, English
Currency:	Lebanese pound (100 piastres)

Lebanon became the scene of renewed and deadly fighting in July 2006, when Israel launched a major military campaign against the Lebanon-based Shia Muslim armed group Hezbollah, sparked by the movement's capture of two Israeli soldiers. This small Arab country at the eastern end of the Mediterranean Sea has long sandy beaches backed by a narrow coastal plain. Beyond the plain, the land rises steeply to a double range of rugged mountains running north to south, parallel to the coast. The Lebanon Mountains form the first range, rising to 10,131 feet above sea level. The land then dips into the deep Bekáa Valley before rising again to the Anti-Lebanon Mountains on the border with Syria.

Hot dry summers, mild wet winters, and rich soil provide favorable farming conditions on the coastal plain. Winter rains falling on the Bekáa Valley support a second fertile farming region. Apples, peaches, oranges, lemons, grapes, and cherries are Lebanon's most valuable crops.

Israel

Status:	Republic
Area:	8,130 sq. mi.
Population:	6.7 million
Capital:	Jerusalem
Languages:	Hebrew, Arabic, English, Yiddish
Currency:	Shekel (100 agorot)

Four contrasting regions comprise Israel's landscape. A narrow fertile coastal plain fronts the Mediterranean Sea. Its northern section broadens around the Qishon River in the Plain of Esdraelon, where farmers grow grain, cotton, and vegetables. South of the Qishon, the drier Plain of Sharon supports the country's citrus farmers but must be irrigated.

The rolling hills of Galilee dominate north central Israel. Rich dark soils and plentiful rainfall sustain highly productive commercial gardens, where farmers grow vegetables and flowers for both local use and export.

The Jordan River Valley, running north to south from the Sea of Galilee to the Dead Sea, marks much of Israel's border with Jordan. Lying 1,300 feet below sea level, the Dead Sea is the lowest point on the earth's surface. It has no outlet and is the world's saltiest inland sea, providing Israel with a source of bromine, potash, and salt. The Jordan Valley is dry and not naturally fertile. Irrigating near the river and draining the marshy area north of the Sea of Galilee have created more fertile agricultural land.

The State of Israel was created in 1948 from part of the former territory of Palestine. Neighbouring Arab countries and displaced Palestinians oppose the new state, and Israel's short history has been one of constant wars. Signs of peace are often ruined by acts of terrorism by both parties.

Status:	Constitutional Monarchy
Area:	37,738 sq. mi.
Population:	5.7 million
Capital:	Amman
Languages:	Arabic, English
Currency:	Jordanian dinar (1,000 fils)

The Hashemite Kingdom of Jordan does not have the oil wealth enjoyed by some neighbouring Arab states. Its developing economy is based on the service industry, agriculture, and mining and is also supported by foreign aid.

The country has three principal land regions. In the west lies the Jordan River Valley. The land is not very fertile, but farmers are able to grow fruits and vegetables on fields irrigated by river water. To the south, the land rises to the Transjordan Plateau, a rolling upland region containing many of Jordan's largest cities and towns and most of its best farmland. Barley, wheat, citrus fruits, olives, and vegetables are the principal crops covering the northern plateau. The southern plateau region is very dry, supporting only small crops of wheat and olives. Northeastern Jordan lies on the Syrian Desert, which sees less than 10 inches of rain annually, and summer temperatures soar to 120°F. Few people live here apart from small groups of nomadic goat and sheep herders.

Many Jordanians work in neighbouring countries. About 70 percent of those who remain in Jordan work for the government, for the military, or in various service industries such as education, banking, or the hotels and restaurants that support the growing numbers of tourists visiting the country's ancient sites.

Fertilizers, cement, and refining of imported oil comprise Jordan's only large-scale industries. Smaller factories in the plateau towns produce leather goods and textiles, processed food, pharmaceuticals, and some chemicals. Power for these industries comes from imported oil.

The barren wilderness of the desert surrounds Mount Ramm (5,755 feet) in southwestern Jordan.

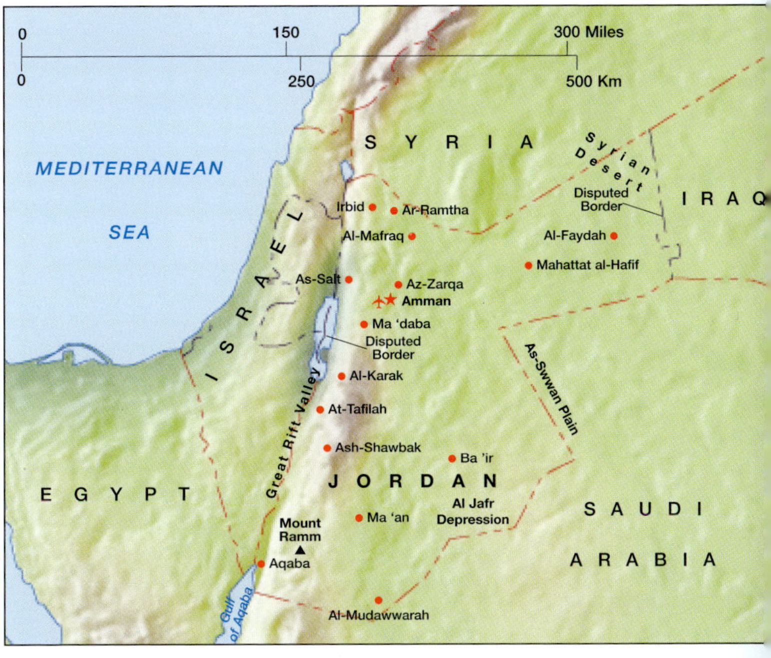

Iraq

Status:	Democracy
Area:	169,235 square miles
Population:	26.5 million
Capital:	Baghdad
Languages:	Arabic, Kurdish
Currency:	Iraqi dinar (1,000 fils)

Iraq has been the battleground of a variety of forces vying for power since the US-led invasion which toppled the government in 2003

Insurgents have targeted civilians, Iraqi security forces and international agencies. Tensions between Shia and Sunni Muslims

have spilled over into brutal sectarian violence, prompting fears of civil war. Coalition and Iraqi troops have faced armed rebellions and guerrilla-style attacks.

The government of national unity and the US-led coalition forces are struggling to establish control; thousands of civilians have been killed and security forces are under constant threat from well organised rebels

Violence and sabotage are hindering international efforts to revive an economy shattered by decades of conflict and international sanctions

Iraq is split in three by the Euphrates and Tigris Rivers—waterways that once supported the world's oldest known civilization. Farming communities occupied Sumer, in what would become southeastern Iraq, about 3500 B.C. The great city of Babylon—at the heart of the Babylonian Empire—flourished on the Euphrates's fertile banks from about 2200 B.C. until 539 B.C., when it was overthrown by Persian invaders.

The Zagros Mountains dominate northeastern Iraq, rising to more than 10,000 feet above sea level as they extend toward northern Iran and southeastern Turkey. Bitterly cold winters and just 15 inches of annual rainfall create a harsh environment for the local people.

Dry, rolling hills cover the northern plains between the Tigris and Euphrates Rivers. Farmers in the small, scattered villages grow wheat and barley on the productive soil that collects in the hollows and valleys. Sheep and goats graze on the surrounding dry grasslands. Southward from the capital city of Baghdad is an area between the two great rivers that provides Iraq's most fertile farmland. Farmers on the great southern plain grow grains, rice, fruit, and vegetables, irrigating their fields with water from the Tigris and Euphrates through a complex system of dams, channels, and control sluices. The two rivers meet at Al Qurnah, forming the Shatt al Arab. This channel flows southward to the Persian Gulf, where its delta forms Iraq's only stretch of coastline. Some of Iraq's most productive oil fields lie in this region, between the city of Basra and Iraq's border with Kuwait. Southeastern Iraq is a vast area of marshland and swamps.

Desert covers most of southwestern and western Iraq in a wilderness of sand dunes and bare limestone rock that stretches deep into Syria, Jordan, and Saudi Arabia. As in most deserts, there are no permanent rivers, just wadis (dry river channels) that briefly fill after a rainfall but dry out again almost immediately. The land is empty except for groups of Bedouin nomads and their camels, sheep, and goats.

Iraqis manufacture natural gas, phosphates, sulphur, cement, iron and steel, textiles, ceramics, chemicals, and household goods, but oil has been the country's economic mainstay for many years. Oil revenues helped improve schools, hospitals, roads, and the irrigation systems used to water the farms of Iraq's southern plains.

Much of that progress, however, was destroyed by war. A conflict with neighbouring Iran, from 1980 until 1988, and the Gulf War, which followed Iraq's invasion of Kuwait in 1990 by Saddam Hussien, left Iraq's roads, bridges, oil refineries, factories, phone system, and parts of the main cities in ruins.

In the post-Saddam years, attacks by insurgents on Iraq's oil infrastructure have cost the country billions of dollars in lost revenues.

In the north, the Kurdish community has now broken away to create a semi-autonomous region of its own

Muslim pilgrims sit in the quiet shade of the ornately decorated Pilgrimage Shrine in Karbala.

Iran

Status: Republic
Area: 630,577 sq. mi.
Population: 70.7 million
Capital: Tehran
Languages: Farsi (Persian), Arabic, Azeri-Turkish, Kurdish, Baluch
Currency: Iranian rial (10 dinars)

Iran is an ancient land with a history dating back 5,000 years. Around 550 B.C., Iran (then known as Persia) was the centre of an empire stretching across southwestern Asia, southern Europe, and part of North Africa. For much of the twentieth century, powerful shahs (kings) ruled the country. The last shah, Mohammad Reza Pahlavi, was forced into exile in 1979 by an Islamic revolution that brought to power the religious leader Ayatollah Ruhollah Khomeini. The ayatollah died in 1989, and more moderate politicians took charge of the government.

Fundamentalist clerics still have enormous influence in Iran's affairs. Women in particular have felt the effect. The rise of fundamentalism swept away all signs of modernization, such as free speech, relaxing of traditional dress codes, and relaxing of the strict rules governing women's lives. While Iran's large cities have schools, hospitals, and other amenities, most small rural communities have few of these benefits, and most houses do not have running water or electricity.

A desert plateau, 3,000 feet above sea level, dominates central and eastern Iran. North of the plateau, the rugged Elburz Mountains tower over a narrow coastal plain bordering the Caspian Sea. Mount Damavand, Iran's highest peak, rises to 18,984 feet in this range. West of the plateau, the broad Zagros range forms a mountainous barrier between Iran and Iraq. Lesser mountain ranges ring the eastern and southern margins of the plateau. Iran's central desert area is one of the driest, most barren places on earth. Few people live there. A narrow coastal plain on the shores of the Caspian Sea and a small fertile lowland area at the head of the Persian Gulf provide Iran's only good agricultural land. Farmers supplement the principal crops of wheat and barley with lentils, cotton, sugar beets, fruits, vegetables, and tea. Farmers use less fertile land to raise cattle, sheep, and goats. Water is always in short supply in the south. The Caspian coastal plain is the only region that enjoys plentiful rain and a mild climate. Many of Iran's cities depend for their water on a labyrinth of tunnels and reservoirs that tap underground water supplies and catch what little rain falls inland.

Oil and gas are Iran's most important natural resources. The country is one of the world's top ten oil producers, and its gas reserves are second only to those of Russia. But Iran's war with Iraq from 1980 to 1988 and continuing internal political instability have greatly reduced its oil exports. The country supplements its economy by mining copper, chromite, iron ore, lead, and zinc. Factory workers manufacture machines, cement, chemicals, petroleum products, processed foods, textiles, and leather goods. Fishing fleets roam the Persian Gulf and the Caspian Sea in search of tuna, sardines, shrimp, carp, salmon, and sturgeon—a huge fish whose eggs yield the tiny, crunchy delicacy called caviar. Most of the fish is consumed locally, but the caviar is a valuable export.

Iran has come under strong pressure from the US since President George W Bush declared it part of an "axis of evil" in 2002. That pressure intensified after the US-led war against Iraq, with Washington accusing Tehran of attempting to develop nuclear weapons and of trying to subvert US efforts in Iraq. Iran, which is building its first atomic power station with Russian help, says its nuclear ambitions are peaceful.

Two worlds meet in the Iranian desert—with oil wells of the industrial age towering over a livestock herder whose way of life goes back thousands of years.

Saudi Arabia, Kuwait

Status:	Monarchy
Area:	829,996 square miles
Population:	25.6 million
Capital:	Riyadh
Languages:	Arabic, English
Currency:	Saudi riyal (100 halalas)

Saudi Arabia is the largest country in the Middle East, but more than 95 percent of its land is desert. A vast rocky plateau stretches across the country's middle. This area is dotted with oases—the most fertile of which support farming communities that grow dates, melons, vegetables, wheat, and other crops.

A broad area of sand dunes called An-Nafud lies north of the plateau, merging with the stony Syrian Desert on Saudi Arabia's borders with Jordan and Iraq. South of the plateau, bare rock and patchy vegetation meet a seemingly endless sea of sand dunes. This is the Rub al-Khali (Empty Quarter)—the largest unbroken expanse of sand on earth. Most of the desert's inhabitants are nomadic Bedouin herders who travel constantly with their camels, goats, and sheep to find grazing land.

Roughly three-quarters of the population live in urban areas, such as the capital city of Riyadh in east central Saudi Arabia and in Jidda, Al-Maqnah, and the Islamic holy cities of Mecca and Medina. More than 1.5 million pilgrims make the journey to Mecca every year.

Saudi Arabia is the world's leading oil producer. Thirty years of multibillion-dollar oil revenues have allowed the government to fund a massive modernization program—building schools, colleges, hospitals, airports, and seaports and investing heavily in new industries and agricultural improvements.

Status:	Constitutional Monarchy
Area:	6,880 square miles
Population:	2.7 million
Capital:	Kuwait City
Languages:	Arabic, English
Currency:	Kuwati dinar (1000 fils)

Tiny Kuwait is dwarfed by its enormous neighbours, Iraq and Saudi Arabia, but this small wedge of land on the northwestern shore of the Persian Gulf accounts for about one-tenth of the world's known oil reserves.

Rainfall is sparse, and most of Kuwait consists of flat, stony desert, where temperatures rise to 104°F in summer. Farmers are able to take advantage of a small coastal strip with milder conditions and a little more rain, but much of the country's food must be imported.

R A Q
I R A N
NAFUD
SERT
Rafha
Umm Qasr
Ar-Rawdatayn
Sabiyah
KUWAIT
Kuwait City
Hawalli
Ash-Shaqaya Peak
Al-Ahmadi
Mina ' Su'ud
Al-Wafrah
Qasr
MAZHUR
DESERT
Al-Mish 'ab
Qana
AD DAHNA DESERT REGION
Jubail
Buraydah
Az-Zilfi
Ad-Dammam
BAHRAIN
P E R S I A N
G U L F
Al-Khubar
Al-Mubarraz
QATAR
Marah
Riyadh
Na 'jan
UNITED
ARAB EMIRATES
Halaban
Zalim
Disputed
Border
S A U D I
A R A B I A
RUB AL-KHALI
Al-Bahah
As-Sulayyil
OMAN
ar
MA PLAIN
ASIR
Disputed
Border
Mount Sawda
Najran
Jaza'ir
Farasan
Y E M E N
0
250
500 Miles
0
500
1000 Km

Bahrain, Qatar

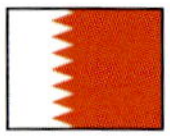

Status:	Emirate
Area:	268 sq. mi.
Population:	754,000
Capital:	Manama
Languages:	Arabic, English
Currency:	Bahraini dinar (1,000 fils)

Bahrain is a cluster of more than 30 islands in the Persian Gulf, about 20 miles off the eastern tip of Saudi Arabia. The country's capital city, Manama, sits at the northern end of Bahrain Island—the largest and most populated island of the group. A paved causeway provides a direct link to the Saudi Arabian mainland.

Desert covers most of the islands. Oil revenues have turned the country into one of the richest in the world. Bahrainis have a very high standard of living. Education is free, and the country has hundreds of schools, including two universities. Health services are excellent, and the people enjoy a healthy diet of fish, rice, vegetables, and fruit—especially dates.

Rainfall is sparse, averaging just three inches annually, but numerous freshwater springs and wells provide plenty of water for domestic use and for irrigation of the fertile farmland found on northern Bahrain Island. Oil refining is the main industrial activity. Bahrain is the major banking centre for the Persian Gulf region.

Status:	Emirate
Area:	4,247 sq. mi.
Population:	628,000
Capital:	Doha
Languages:	Arabic, English
Currency:	Qatari riyal (100 dirhams)

The tiny Arab nation of Qatar occupies a rocky desert peninsula that juts into the Persian Gulf. Saudi Arabia and the United Arab Emirates are Qatar's mainland neighbours. Discovery of oil in the 1940s transformed Qatar from a poor nation of camel herders, subsistence farmers, and pearl divers into a wealthy urbanized nation with free education and health services and a very high standard of living.

Oil revenues paid for desalination plants to provide fresh water for homes, hotels, offices, and industrial areas and enabled the government to sink many deep wells to provide water for irrigation. Qatari farmers meet most of the country's vegetable needs and provide some of its grain and fruit, but meat, dairy products, and many manufactured goods are imported. The government owns most of Qatar's industries, which range from oil refining and petrochemicals to commercial fishing, fertilizer production, and plastics.

Status:	Federation of Seven Emirates
Area:	32,278 sq. mi.
Population:	2.8 million
Capital:	Abu Dhabi
Languages:	Arabic, English
Currency:	UAE dirham (100 fils)

Above: One of the many large oil storage facilities in the United Arab Emirates

Right: A traditional bazaar (market) in Abu Dhabi

The United Arab Emirates is a federation of seven independent states bordering the southern shore of the Persian Gulf. The member-states and their capital cities, from west to east, are Abu Dhabi, Dubayy, Ash Shariqah, Ajman, Umm al Qaywayn, Ras al Khaymah, and Al Fujayrah. Abu Dhabi is the federation's capital and second largest city. Dubayy is the largest urban area and the federation's principal port and business centre. Formerly a British protectorate, the seven countries were once called the Trucial States. Six of the states gained independence in 1971 and were joined by the seventh, Ras al Khaymah, the following year.

The countries that formed the United Arab Emirates, like its neighbour Qatar, used to be dependent on camel herding, fishing, trading, and subsistence farming. Life for its people changed dramatically with the discovery of oil in the 1950s. The modern federation has one of the world's highest standards of living.

Yemen

Yeman

Status:	Republic
Area:	203,850 square miles
Population:	21.5 million
Capital:	Sana'a
Language:	Arabic
Currency:	Yemeni riyal (100 fils)

Yemen occupies the southwestern corner of the Arabian Peninsula. Yemen's territory includes the Red Sea islands of Kamaran and Perim and Socotra Island in the Arabian Sea.

Yemen consists of rugged mountains in the west and a desert in the east that spreads northward into Saudi Arabia's Rub al-Khali. Temperatures are very hot and humid along the narrow coastal plain, but the country enjoys cooler, milder conditions in the highlands, where fertile valleys provide Yemen's best farmland. Yemenis cultivate crops in the highlands and on scattered desert oases, and they graze sheep, goats, and camels in the drier desert areas. Fishing crews ply the abundant waters along the coastline.

A large oil refinery at Aden processes oil from Yemeni fields in the northwest, as well as oil from other Persian Gulf states.

The minaret of a mosque overlooks the town of Raydah in the western part of Yemen.

Oman

Status:	Monarchy
Area:	82,000 square miles
Population:	3 million
Capital:	Masqat
Languages:	Arabic, local dialects
Currency:	Omani rial (1000 baizas)

Oman curves around the southeastern corner of the Arabian Peninsula, exposing a long coastline on the Arabian Sea and a short stretch of coastline facing Iran across the Gulf of Oman. The narrow Strait of Hormuz, off Oman's northernmost tip, guards the entrance to the Persian Gulf. Much of the world's oil is shipped through this narrow seaway.

Similar to its neighbours, Oman is mostly desert. One of the earth's hottest areas, the country often sees temperatures rise to 120°F, sometimes soaring above 130°F. Rainfall is meager.

Most of the people wear traditional dress and nearly all are devout Muslims.

IRAN
Strait of Hormuz
OMAN
Persian Gulf
Gulf of Oman
Disputed Border
Shinas
Suhar
Khabura
Al-Masna 'ah
Dank
Barka'
Masqat
Qurayyat
AL HAJAR
Nizwa
Sur
UNITED ARAB EMIRATES
SAUDI ARABIA
WAHIBA SANDS
Khaluf
Masirah
Gulf of Masirah
Hayma'
Duqm
Disputed Border
OMAN
Sawqirah Bay
Thamarit
Khuriya Muriya Bay
AL-QARA Mts.
Khawr Rawri
Mirbat
Taqah
Salalah
Rakhyut
Min 'ar
Tarim
Al-Ghaydah
Sayhut
ARABIAN SEA
0
250
500 Miles
0
500
1000 Km
SOCOTRA (Yemen)

Russian Federation (Asian Russia)

Status:	Federation
Area:	6,592,819 square miles
Population:	146.5 million
Capital:	Moscow
Language:	Russian
Currency:	Russian ruble (100 kopeks)

Climate and vegetation define four broad zones that stretch west to east across Asian Russia. The extreme northern reaches support a bleak landscape of mosses, shrubs, and dwarf trees called tundra. The soil is permanently frozen, and winters are long and harsh. Summers offer a brief respite, during which the soil's surface thaws and some vegetation grows—enough to feed reindeer, hares, lemmings, and ptarmigan and the wolves, foxes, stoats, owls, and hawks that hunt them.

Dark coniferous forests of pine, fir, and spruce lie south of the tundra, merging into deciduous forests of birch, oak, aspen, and maple. Deer, elk, beavers, brown bears, and squirrels are typical forest animals. Rolling grassy plains called the steppes stretch across Russia south of the forests. Thick dark soils in this region provide Russia's best farmland. The steppes offer little cover from predators. Animals able to survive here are those that burrow—hamsters, susliks, lemmings, and marmots—and the eagles and buzzards that patrol the skies. Deserts and mountains dominate Russia's southern edge, forming natural borders

Asian Russia—east of the Urals—is almost three times the size of the country's European segment. Russia is a sparsely populated land of plains, plateaux, and forests. A train journey from Moscow to Vladivostok takes seven days and passes through eight time zones.

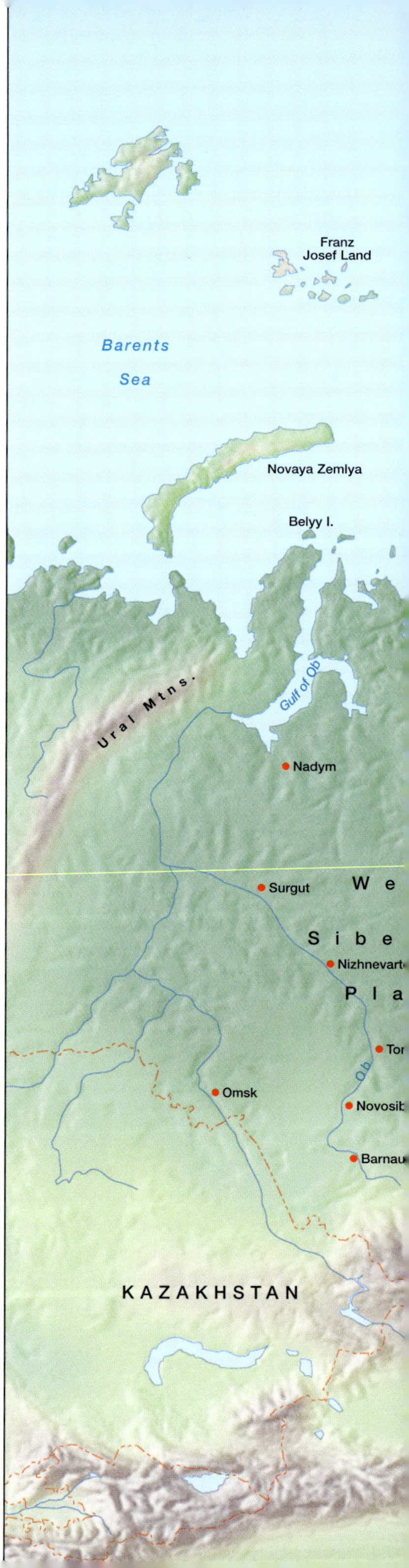

ARCTIC OCEAN
Wrangel I.
Saint Lawrence I. (U.S.)
Bering Strait
Bering Sea
Gulf of Anadyr
Mys Shmidta
Chukchi Peninsula
Pevek
Ayon I.
Anadyr
East Siberian Sea
New Siberia I.
Komsomolets I.
Kotel'nyy I.
New Siberian Is.
Lyakhovskiye Ostrova
Bol'shevik I.
Bilibino
Nizhnekolymsk
Srednekolymsk
Koryak Mountains
Kolyma Mountains
Kolyma
Indigirka
Laptev Sea
Novosibirsk
Korf
Karagin I.
Bol'shoy Begichev I.
Tiksi
yrranga Mtns.
Palana
Kamchatka Peninsula
rth Siberian Lowland
Cherskiy Range
East Siberian Highlands
Lena
Oimyakon
Magadan
Verkhoyanskiy Khrebet
Petropavlovsk-Kamchatskiy
Okhotsk
Central Siberian Plateau
Udachnyy
Sangar
Sea of Okhotsk
Yakutsk
Nyurba
Mimyy
Dzhugdzhur Range
Kuril Islands
Lower Tunguska
Tura
Lensk
Aldan
RUSSIA
Sakhalin I.
Neryungri
Badzhal'skiy Mtns.
Komsomel'sk na-Amure
Amur
Tatar Strait
Sikhote-alin Mtns.
Angara
Bodaybo
Ust'-Ilimsk
Tynda
Yuzhno-Sakhalinsk
noyarsk
Zeya
Ust'-Kut
Bratsk
Bratsk Reservoir
Yablonovyy Range
Shimanovsk
Soya Strait
Khabarovsk
Vyazemskiy
Blagoveshchensk
Lake Baikal
Nerchinsk
Yenisey
Chita
Baley
Ust-Ordinskiy
Ulan Ude
Angarsk
Irkutsk
Aginskoyo
Borzya
Abakan
Sayan Mtns.
Munku-Sardyk
Spassk-Dal 'niy
Ussurlysk
Kyzyl
Kyakhta
Vladivostok
Nakhodka
JAPAN
Sea of Japan
MONGOLIA
CHINA
NORTH KOREA
SOUTH KOREA
0
500
1000
1500 Miles
0
500
1000
1500
2000
2500 Km

with its huge southern neighbours—Kazakhstan, Mongolia, and China.

Asian Russia has three major land divisions—the West Siberian Plain, the Central Siberian Plateau, and the East Siberian Highlands. The Urals form a long, narrow north-south barrier between European Russia and the westernmost Asian Russian landform—the West Siberian Plain. East of the mountains, the West Siberian Plain stretches for nearly 1,000 miles. The northern section of the plain is low and marshy. In the southern section, farmers use the fertile soil to raise barley, oats, rye, potatoes, sugar beets, fruits and vegetables, and fodder crops for beef and dairy cattle. The plain also contains rich oil and gas fields, and miners take out coal, iron ore, lead, and zinc from deposits along the mountainous southern edge. Omsk, Novosibirsk, Tomsk, and Novokuznetsk are the main manufacturing centres of the West Siberian Plain.

The Central Siberian Plateau lies east of the Yenisey River. The topography ranges from 2,000 feet above sea level to 11,451 at the top of Munku-Sardyk, the tallest peak in the Sayan Mountains. Forests cover much of the land. The plateau lies in the heart of the huge Asian landmass, far from any moderating effects of the ocean. In winter it is one of the coldest places on earth. January temperatures in northeastern Siberia average below –50°F and can plunge to –90°F. Few people live in this region's far north, but industrial cities such as Krasnoyarsk and Irkutsk have developed in the south, where miners extract gold, nickel, tungsten, tin, and other minerals.

Beyond the Lena River, the land rises to the East Siberian Highlands—a vast empty wilderness of pine forests and mountain ranges. The highlands stretch unbroken to the Chukchi Peninsula, which faces the United States across the narrow Bering Strait, and to the leaf-shaped and volcanic Kamchatka Peninsula that partly encloses the Sea of Okhotsk. Inhabitants of this region cluster around the inland city of Yakutsk, around Khabarovsk on the Amur River, and around the industrial city and seaport of Vladivostok on the Sea of Japan's northwestern coast.

Oil pipelines run for hundreds of miles across the forested landscape, carrying crude oil from the Siberian oil fields to European Russia, where demand for energy is greatest and where the largest refineries are located. The zigzag construction allows the pipeline to expand and contract without cracking as temperatures rise and fall.

Right: Vladivostok, on the southeastern coast of Siberia, is Russia's most important Pacific seaport. Shipyards, fish canneries, and factories producing mining equipment and other heavy machinery are the principal employers.

Below: A huge roll of heavy packaging paper is hoisted off the production machine at a paper mill in Siberia.

Kazakhstan

Status:	Republic
Area:	1.05 million sq. mi.
Population:	15.4 million
Capital:	Astana
Languages:	Kazakh, Russian
Currency:	Tenge (100 tiyn)

One of western Asia's largest countries, Kazakhstan ranks ninth in the world in land area. In 1991 Kazakhstan gained its freedom from the Soviet Union after 70 years under Communist rule. Since becoming an independent republic, Kazakhstan's government has built a new capital, Astana, near the centre of the country. Almaty, the former capital, lies close to the border with China and remains Kazakhstan's largest city and principal commercial and cultural centre.

Kazakhstan extends almost 1,800 miles east to west, up to 900 miles north to south, and boasts a variety of landscapes. Dry lowland plains wrap around the northern tip of the Caspian Sea. The Karagiye Basin, between the coastal town of Aqtau and the Turkmenistan border, is the lowest point in the country at 433 feet below sea level. Rolling steppes cover much of northern Kazakhstan, and sandy deserts dominate the country's southern region. The rugged Altai Shan (mountains) rise on the country's northeastern border with Russia, and the Tian Shan form the southeastern border with Kyrgyzstan and China. Rivers rising in the mountains feed Lake Balkhash, the largest lake in the country at 6,670 square miles.

The dry grassy plains that cover much of the country are not well suited to farming. Most Kazakhs were traditionally nomads, travelling with the sheep, goats, camels, cattle, and horses that provided their transportation, food, and materials for clothing and shelter. The traditional Kazakh home was a portable tentlike structure, called a yurt, made of thick felt mats covering a frame of bent poles. Some Kazakhs still live as their ancestors did, but most rural villagers live in houses.

Prime farmland lies in northeastern Kazakhstan where farmers sow barley, wheat, cotton, and vegetables and graze sheep, and beef and dairy herds. During the Communist era, Kazakhstan's government greatly expanded agricultural production by irrigating dry western lands with water from feeder rivers to the Aral Sea. While this enabled some farmers to grow rice, grain crops, and vegetables, the Aral Sea shrank by 70 percent. These irrigation projects left much of the former sea glistening with salt pans and littered with the rotting hulks of stranded fishing boats.

Kazakhstan is rich in mineral resources. Miners in the northeast extract coal, while those in the central and eastern regions mine copper, zinc, iron, lead, tin, titanium, vanadium, thallium, and other valuable minerals. Oil and gas are pumped from fields beneath the Caspian Sea.

Factories in the principal industrial towns of Almaty and Shymkent in the southeast and Karaganda and Pavlodar in the northeast provide textiles, chemicals, leather goods, machinery, electrical goods, and food products.

A Kazakh horseman looks across the rolling forests and grasslands that supported his nomadic ancestors and their livestock for thousands of years.

Uzbekistan, Turkmenistan

Status: Republic
Area: 172,742 square miles
Population: 26.9 million
Capital: Tashkent
Languages: Uzbek, Russian
Currency: Uzbek som (100 tijuns)

Uzbekistan lies in western central Asia and shares borders with Kazakhstan, Kyrgyzstan, Tajikistan, Turkmenistan, and Afghanistan. The latter is the only one of Uzbekistan's neighbours that wasn't a former Soviet republic.

The vast barren wilderness of the Kyzyl Kum Desert fills the country's centre. Few people, apart from workers in scattered mining settlements, live in this region. Farther west, dry grasslands and deserts border the Aral Sea, merging with the arid plains and plateaux of Kazakhstan and Turkmenistan. Most inhabitants of western Uzbekistan live in small towns and villages clustered along the banks of the Amu Darya (River) and its tributaries.

About 80 percent of the Uzbeks are farmers, a fact that concentrates the population in southern and eastern Uzbekistan. The land in these areas rises to meet the Tian Shan and the Pamir Mountains. The region's rich soil and mountain streams support fertile crops such as rice, grains, vegetables, melons, and cotton—the country's principal export crop. Sheep and dairy cattle are significant livestock, supplying mutton and milk for the country's traditional dishes. The high-quality wool of the Karakul sheep is another important export.

Uzbekistan's miners extract coal, copper, gold, petroleum, and natural gas. Industrial contributions include textiles, chemicals, farm machinery, and fertilizers. Traditional craft workers in rural areas create carpets, shawls, jewelry, ceramics, wood products, and metal goods.

Status: Republic
Area: 188,456 square miles
Population: 5 million
Capital: Ashkhabad
Languages: Turkmen, Russian, Uzbek
Currency: Turkmenistan manat (100 tenge)

Dominated by the large, central Kara-Kum Desert, Turkmenistan is ringed by Kazakhstan, Uzbekistan, Afghanistan, Iran, and the Caspian Sea. The country's landscapes include low coastal plains hugging the Caspian Sea, mountains along the border with Iran, and the broad Amu Darya Valley forming the northern boundary with Uzbekistan. The Kara-Bogaz Gol, a deep gulf near the Caspian shore, is the country's lowest point at 102 feet below sea level. Summers are very hot, with temperatures reaching 120°F. Winters are bitterly cold. Thermometers hover near zero for many weeks. Rainfall is scarce, providing just a few inches annually to most of the country.

Small settlements are located at desert oases, but most Turkmen live by water—near the coast of the Caspian Sea, beside the 750-mile long Kara-Kum Canal, or in the irrigated highland river valleys. Farmers in these regions grow grains, vegetables, and grapes for local consumption, but more than half the cultivated land in Turkmenistan is committed to cotton, the country's principal crop. Many farmers supplement their crops by raising sheep, camels, pigs, and horses.

Turkmenistan's chief natural resources are oil and gas. The mining industry provides copper, lead, mercury, gold, and other minerals, including limestone and sand for Turkmen homes. Factories—concentrated around the capital city of Ashkhabad and in the city of Chardzhou—produce textiles, glassware, petrochemical products, and cement.

Right: An Uzbek elder wears the traditional wound cloth headdress known as a termez.

Far Right: A Turkmen woman wears a traditional costume of brightly patterned fabrics, a headdress, and handmade jewelry.

Kyrgyzstan, Tajikistan

Status:	Republic
Area:	76,641 square miles
Population:	5.3 million
Capital:	Bishkek
Languages:	Kyrgyz, Russian
Currency:	Kyrgyz som (100 tyin)

Status:	Republic
Area:	55,251 square miles
Population:	6.3 million
Capital:	Dushanbe
Languages:	Tajik, Uzbek, Russian
Currency:	Tajik somoni (100 diram)

Kyrgyzstan is a small, landlocked country high in the Tian Shan and the Alai Mountains of western central Asia. Rugged and inhospitable, three-quarters of the country sits more than 5,000 feet above sea level—most of it covered in glaciers and snowfields. Pobedy Peak, Kyrgyzstan's highest summit, towers 24,406 feet over the eastern border with China. Winter temperatures often fall to –20°F in the mountains. Sheltered valleys and lowlands experience warm, dry summers and cold winters. Rainfall is minimal, so the country taps mountain rivers for water to use on crops, in homes, and by the industrial sector.

The people of Kyrgyzstan once wandered across the lowlands and foothills, grazing their sheep, goats, pigs, cattle, and horses. Few people still follow the traditional nomadic ways, but livestock continues to be vital to the economy. Farmers grow cotton, rice, fruits, sugar beets and other vegetables, and mulberry—a tree whose leaves are used to feed silkworms.

Kyrgyz miners extract the country's reserves of coal and minerals such as uranium, mercury, lead, gold, and zinc. The country also holds untapped oil reserves. Manufacturing industries, concentrated mostly around the capital city of Bishkek, use these resources to produce textiles, machinery, domestic appliances, and electronics. The government is expanding the industrial sector and attracting foreign investors, making Kyrgyzstan one of the fastest-growing economies among former Soviet republics.

Tajikistan, like its neighbour Kyrgyzstan to the north, is a rugged, mountainous country. Half of its land reaches 10,000 feet above sea level. The Pamir Mountains to the southeast form a border with Pakistan. The Zeravshan, Turkestan, and Alai Mountains dominate central and northern Tajikistan. The country's valleys and lowlands experience long, hot, dry summers and cool winters. Both urban and rural populations rely for water on the country's rivers. Irrigation projects in eastern and northern Tajikistan support the country's agriculture.

Cotton is Tajikistan's most significant commercial crop, but farmers also grow many fruits, vegetables, and grains. Cattle, chickens, and sheep provide meat, milk, eggs, wool, and leather, and domesticated yaks

graze on the high mountain slopes. Some farms specialize in growing mulberry trees for silkworm farms, while others harvest eucalyptus, geraniums, and other plants whose oils and fragrances are used to make perfumes.

A huge dam at Nurek on the Vakhsh River supplies hydroelectric power to a large aluminium refinery atf Dushanbe. The Nurek Reservoir provides water for the cities and farms of western Tajikistan. Tajik miners extract antimony, lead, tungsten, uranium, and zinc, and the country possesses large gold and silver reserves. Unlike neighbouring Kyrgyzstan, economic development in Tajikistan has suffered throughout the 1990s from internal conflict and civil war.

A few Kyrgyz families still follow the traditional ways, living in tentlike yurts and constantly moving from pasture to pasture with their livestock. The yurt, made of felt, is warm, comfortable, and immensely practical in the rugged conditions.

Georgia, Armenia

Status:	Republic
Area:	26,911 square miles
Population:	5 million
Capital:	Tbilisi
Languages:	Georgian, Russian, Armenian
Currency:	Lari (100 tetri)

Status:	Republic
Area:	11,506 square miles
Population:	3 million
Capital:	Yerevan
Languages:	Armenian, Russian
Currency:	Dram (100 luma)

Georgia broke away from the former Soviet Union in 1991. The country's independence has been marred by ethnic conflicts between the dominant Georgians, who comprise 70 percent of the population, and the peoples of South Ossetia, Abkhazia, and Adjaria who demand self-government for their regions. Years of unrest have damaged the country's economy and have slowed development.

Mountains dominate northern and southern Georgia. The broad, fertile Kura River Valley in central Georgia and the western lowland plains bordering the Black Sea provide excellent farmland. These areas have hot summers and mild winters and receive ample rainfall.

Farmers in the western plains grow citrus fruits, tea, and tung trees, whose seeds yield valuable oil used in paints and varnishes. Wheat, barley, and vegetables are the main crops farther inland. Many farmers also cultivate flowers and herbs for the perfume industry. Mulberry trees support a thriving silk industry. The soil on sunny hillsides produces grapes for making wine. Large forests in the mountainous regions provide raw materials for lumber and plywood factories.

Georgia's miners excavate many minerals, but food processing remains the country's primary industry, and food products are its main export. Coastal resorts along the Black Sea attract large numbers of tourists, many of them from neighbouring Russia.

Nestled between Georgia, Azerbaijan, Iran, and Turkey, this tiny state is the smallest of the 15 former Soviet republics and one of five that declared independence in 1991. A mountainous plateau, 5,000 feet above sea level, covers most of the country. The plateau is dissected by deep river gorges and is dotted with towering peaks reaching higher than 12,000 feet above sea level. Armenia also boasts more than 100 lakes. Forests of beech, oak, and hornbeam blanket parts of Armenia's eastern mountains. Short grasses and scrub cover much of the rest.

Low rainfall in the valleys combined with short hot summers, very cold winters, and a lack of investment have kept agricultural productivity quite low. Farmers grow wheat, barley, potatoes, walnuts, and quinces and other fruits on fertile black soil in the valleys, but farming is most productive on irrigated land in the Araks River Valley on Armenia's borders with Turkey and Iran.

Vanadzor, Gyumri, and Yerevan in the northwest and Kapan in the southeast are important manufacturing centres. Hydroelectric power stations on fast-flowing rivers such as the Hrazdan provide power for the country's main industries—machinery, chemicals, electronics, and textiles. These industries, along with the copper, lead, and zinc produced by Armenia's miners, account for about two-thirds of Armenia's economic production.

Turkish-style bathhouses nestle among modern apartment blocks in the old sector of the Georgian capital of Tbilisi.

Azerbaijan

Status:	Republic
Area:	33,436 square miles
Population:	8.5 million
Capital:	Baku
Language:	Azeri Turkish
Currency:	Azeri manat (100 qepik)

Azerbaijan is divided into three distinct land regions. The Greater Caucasus Mountains run east to west near the country's northern edge, separating Azerbaijan from Georgia and Russia and marking a line between the continents of Europe and Asia. Rocky highlands rise in the west and southwest. Between the two highland regions, a broad, lowland plain slopes down to the Caspian Sea. The small autonomous republic of Naxçivan, which is geographically separate but still belongs politically to Azerbaijan, lies beyond Azerbaijan's southwestern border and is surrounded by Armenia.

Oil fields near the capital city of Baku and beneath the Caspian Sea provide Azerbaijan's principal source of income. The country also extracts aluminium, copper, iron, and salt. Factories in the main industrial centres of Baku, Gäncä, Säki, Xankändi, and Naxçivan produce aluminium, machinery, chemicals, textiles, cement, and timber products.

Azerbaijan depends heavily on its waterways. Hydroelectric stations use river water flowing from the surrounding mountains to power much of the country's industrial sector. Rivers also irrigate farms on the dry central plain, where rainfall is generally minimal. Lowland farmers grow grains, cotton, vegetables, fruits, and tea. Those in the upland regions raise sheep, goats, and cattle and grow fodder crops for winter animal feed.

Southern and Eastern Asia

The southern and eastern sections of the huge Asian continent comprise a land area that contains almost every kind of landscape imaginable, every climatic extreme on earth, and a kaleidoscope of peoples with widely different languages, religions, lifestyles, and economic conditions.

Southern and eastern Asia stretches west to east for more than 3,700 miles from Pakistan to the Pacific coast of China. North to south covers 4,000 miles from China's northern border with Russia to the tropical islands of Indonesia. Mount Everest, the world's highest mountain, towers 29,028 feet above sea level in the eastern Himalayas, while some of the world's deepest ocean trenches plunge six and a half miles below sea level off Japan and the Philippines.

Vast rolling steppes, high plateaux, and huge deserts dominate the western and northern parts of the region. To the south and east, densely forested mountains and hills cover much of the land. Some of the world's mightiest rivers—the Ganges, the Brahmaputra, the Mekong, the Chang (Yangtze), and the Huang He (Yellow)—pass powerfully through the region, crossing fertile coastal plains and broad deltas to reach the ocean.

The peoples and lifestyles of southern and eastern Asia are as varied as their landscapes. Mongolia's livestock farmers graze their sheep and cattle on vast plains. Rice farmers in the mountains of the Philippines plant their crops on small steep hillside terraces constructed 2,000 years ago. Factory workers in many southern Asian countries work from dawn till dusk for very low wages. And hunger, water shortages, and inadequate health and educational services are a fact of life for millions. But alongside the nations with less in the way of services are some of the world's most powerful and dynamic economies. Japan is one of the world's leading manufacturers of cars, electronic goods, textiles, and household appliances. Farther south are other world-ranking industrial and commercial centres, including Taiwan, Singapore, and Hong Kong (part of China).

In addition to economic powerhouses, there are population powerhouses in southern and eastern Asia, too. India and China together are home to 37 percent of the world's population. With the populations of Indonesia and Bangladesh added in, these four nations alone account for 43 percent of the world's people—but they all inhabit a combined land area that represents just 8 percent of the earth's total. These sorts of contrasts make southern and eastern Asia among the most complex areas of the world.

0
1000
2000 Miles
0
1000
2000
3000 Km
MONGOLIA
Altai Mtns.
GOBI DESERT
CHINA
Hokkaido
Sea of Japan
JAPAN
Honshu
NORTH KOREA
SOUTH KOREA
Shikoku
Kyushu
Yellow Sea
East China Sea
RYUKYU IS.
PACIFIC OCEAN
TAIWAN
Macau
Hong Kong
BHUTAN
BANGLADESH
MYANMAR
Hainan I.
LAOS
VIETNAM
Bay of Bengal
South China Sea
Luzon
THAILAND
PHILIPPINES
CAMBODIA
Mindanao
Sulu Sea
Gulf of Thailand
Andaman Sea
Celebes Sea
BRUNEI
IRIAN JAVA
MALAYSIA
Singapore
Celebes
Banda Sea
SUMATRA
KALIMANTAN
INDONESIA
Java Sea
Flores
Timor
JAVA

China

Status:	Republic
Area:	3,705,390 sq. mi.
Population:	1.3 billion
Capital:	Beijing
Language:	Mandarin (numerous dialects)
Currency:	Yuan (100 fen)

China has by far the largest population of any nation in the world, with more than 1,300 million people. It is also one of the world's largest countries by land area. China's vast territory is also enormously varied in topography and climate. The rugged Tian Shan, the Pamir Mountains, and the Karakoram Mountains rise in the west, forming a high, cold, rocky barrier between China and Kazakhstan, Kyrgyzstan, Tajikistan, and Pakistan. The eastern part of the Tian Shan range extends across northwestern China becoming the Mongolian Uplands—a dry, high desert region with few inhabitants. The Gobi Desert's stony expanse forms part of this arid plateau. Daytime temperatures in the deserts can soar past 100°F in summer, plunging to –30°F during the icy winter nights.

North and east of the highlands lie large areas of loess—fine, yellowish soil formed from the clay deposits left behind by glaciers, then blown around and dumped in thick layers by the wind. The soils, though fertile, are soft and easily eroded. One of China's great rivers, the Huang He (Yellow

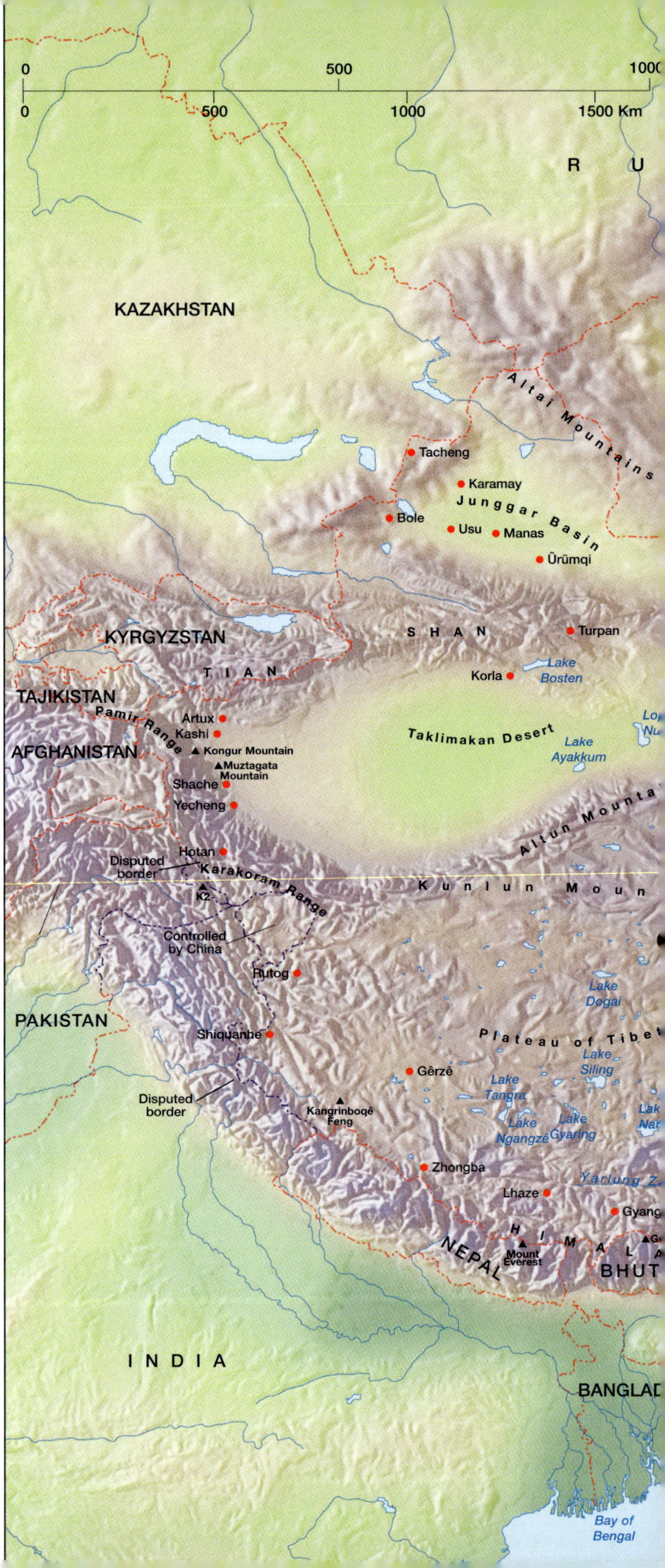

Mohe
Gulian
Mangui
Aihui
Amur
Argun
Yitulihe
Nenjiang
Yichun
Hegang
Jiamusi
Shuangyashan
Qitaihe
Jixi
Lake Khanka
Manzhouti
Hailar
Suihua
Qiqihar
Anda
Daqing
Harbin
Mudanjiang
Arxan
Greater Hinggan Range
Manchurian Plain
Changchun
Jilin
Yanji
Huaide
Siping
Hailong
Tiefa
Hunjiang
Tieling
NORTH KOREA
Fuxin
Fushun
Beipiao
Chaoyang
Jinzhou
Anshan
Dandong
Chifeng
AbagnarQi
Erenhot
Chengde
Jinxi
Korea Bay
Bayan Obo
Zhangjiakou
Hohhot
Qinhuangdao
Dalian
Beijing
Wuyuan
Tangshan
SOUTH KOREA
Gulf of Chihli
Weihai
Yantai
Longkou
Shandong Peninsula
Baotou
Xinzhou
Tianjin
Baoding
Dongying
Shijiazhuang
Hengshui
Jinan
Qingdao
YELLOW SEA
Linhe
Dongsheng
Mu Us Desert
Huang He
Xinzhou
Taiyuan
Wuhai
Yan'an
Gobi Desert
Mongolian Uplands
Anxi
Yumen
Zhangye
Shizuishan
Yinchuan
Wuzhong
Handan
Tai'an
Rizhao
Linyi
Lianyungang
Zliengzhod
Shangqiu
Kaifeng
Xuzhou
Yancheng
Linfen
Houma
Zhoukou
Hancheng
Pingliang
Yuncheng
Zhengzhou
Luoyang
Weinan
Xi'an
Baoji
Tianshui
Lanzhou
Bengzbu
Nantong
Fuyang
Wuhan
Wuhu
Shanghai
Nanjing
Hefei
Jiaxing
Hangzhou
Yuyau
Shaoxing
Ningbo
Xinyang
Suizhou
Qin Ling Mtns.
Qilian Mountains
Da Qaidam
Delingha
Tianjun
Koko Nor
Golmud
Xining
I A
N G O L I A
H I N A
Hanzhong
Nanyang
Shiyan
Xiangfan
Anqing
Wuhan
Mianyang
Denyang
Daxian
Yichang
Shashi
Jiujiang
Jinhua
Haimen
Nanchong
Wanxian
Huaying
Enshi
Jinshi
Lake Dongting
Nanchang
Lake Poyang
Quzhou
Chengdu
Fengcheng
Shangrao
Lishui
Fuling
Jishou
Changsha
Xinyu
Fuzhou
Yingtan
Wenzhou
Chongqing
Xiangtan
Shaowu
Luzhou
Bozhou
Zunyi
Nanping
Wuyi Mtns.
Fuzhou
Jinggangshan
Sanming
Taiwan Strait
Yong'an
Putian
Shuicheng
Guiyang
Anshun
Duyun
Zixing
Chenzhou
Ganzhou
Longyan
Quanzhou
Xiamen
Nan Ling Mtns.
Zhangzhou
Shaoguan
Meizhou
Zhaotong
Guilin
Zhaojue
Dukou
Hechi
Chao'an
Shantou
Qujing
Dongchuan
Guangzhou
Zhaoqing
Shenzhen
Jiangmen
Zhuhai
Hong Kong
Kunming
Bose
Litang
Yulin
Macau
Nanning
Yuxi
Maoming
Pingxiang
Qinzhou
Beihai
Zhanjiang
SOUTH CHINA SEA
Haikou
Danxian
Hainan I.
Gulf of Tonkin
Hongqizhen
Daxue Mountains
Jinsha
Nu
Gongga Shan
Yulongxue Shan
Baoshan
Diancang Shan
Wandiogzhen
Lancang
MYANMAR
VIETNAM
LAOS

A goatherd tends his flock near Yangchou in China's Eastern Lowlands, with the hills of the Mongolian Uplands rising in the distance.

River) flows across this region. The river takes its name from the huge amounts of yellow mud that stain its waters. Little rain falls in northern China, and the winters are long and very cold. Average January temperatures drop well below freezing. Farmers in the north concentrate on hardy crops like winter wheat, corn, and millet.

The towering Himalayas and the lofty Plateau of Tibet dominate southwestern China. The Himalayas contain the world's highest peak, Mount Everest, which at 29,028 feet is a legendary mountain to climb. Most of the plateau consists of bare rock, gravel, and snow fields, but farmers are able to graze hardy yaks on the sparse mountain pastures and to grow vegetables and grains in some of the sheltered valleys and low-lying areas.

China's Eastern Lowlands form a long narrow north-south belt of hilly country dissected by broad river valleys such as the Chang (Yangtze). The lowlands support much of China's most productive cropland. Farmers grow wheat, rice, and vegetables, and raise cattle, pigs, and poultry. These lowlands also contain some of China's largest coalfields and iron ore deposits. Extensive forests wedged between the lowlands and the Pacific Coast supply premium timber for construction projects. Just beyond the trees, the coast is dotted with several natural deepwater harbours.

A small, circular lowland called the Sichuan Basin, on the eastern edge of the Plateau of Tibet, provides a second important agricultural region. The climate here is mild, and the hilly land is broken up with fertile valleys. Most farmers cultivate terraced fields to make the best use of every available acre. Primary crops are rice, corn, potatoes, cabbage, apples and pears, sugar beets, soybeans, and tea. Nonfood crops include rubber, cotton, and tobacco.

Steep wooded hills and rocky mountains cover most of southeastern China. Much of the land is too steep for farming, but the valleys contain good cropland, and the wide delta of the Xi Jiang (West River) southern China's principal waterway, supports deep, fertile soil. Southeastern China enjoys a tropical climate with mild winters, hot summers, and plentiful rainfall. Farmers here grow many varieties of grains, vegetables, and fruits and tend large herds of cattle, sheep, goats, pigs, chickens and ducks. China's farmers raise about one-third of the world's pigs, using them not only for their meat but also for their manure, which is an excellent fertilizer.

Roughly one-fifth of the world's population lives in China, but the people are distributed unevenly. Only about 10 percent of the population live in western China, settling in the valleys and foothills that ring the mountainous western and southern borders. The deserts and plateaux of west central China appear even emptier, with less than five people per square mile. People along these borderlands—subsistence farmers and livestock herders—include a mix of ethnic Chinese and several minority ethnic groups such as Kazakhs, Mongols, Uygurs, Manchus, and Tibetans.

Eastern China is much more densely populated, with up to 1,000 people per square mile. About 80 percent of the eastern inhabitants live in small farming villages scattered across the land. Many of these farming communities belong to a cooperative system, in which a large group of members decides which crops and livestock each family farm will produce. After the harvest, part of the crop is sold to the government, and part of it goes to the community for sale or distribution. Any surplus can be eaten by the family or sold in the local market. Farming is not highly mechanized, and the people work long hours, often using simple hand tools. Horses, oxen, handcarts, and bicycles are common transportation options. Most rural families live in single-story houses of mud or clay brick, with a thatch or tile roof. There are few luxuries, but most homes have electricity, and most villages have schools, libraries, and community centres.

China also has some of the world's largest and most crowded cities. Shanghai has nearly 12 million people, Beijing supports 10 million, and more than 30 other cities house at least one million people each. Most major Chinese cities have built large, new apartment complexes alongside the older houses. Living units are small, but most people have enough income to meet their needs, and all have access to education, health care, and community services. City dwellers work in manufacturing, in shops, in service industries, in transportation, in education, and in government administration. Shanghai is the principal manufacturing centre, followed by Beijing, Tianjin, and Shenyang in the north; Guangahou, Hangzhou, and Wuhan in the south; and Chongqing and Chengdu in east central China. Factory workers produce industrial and farm machinery, vehicles, textiles, fertilizer, cement, chemicals, and household goods such as sewing machines, televisions, and furniture. China has developed many hydroelectric plants that provide 20 percent of its power needs. The remainder comes from vast coalfields in the north and northeast and large oil fields in Manchuria, near Tianjin, and on the Shandong Peninsula. Miners also extract huge quantities of iron ore, tungsten, antimony, lead, and tin.

The mountain ranges, forests, and deserts that encircle most of its western and southern borders cut off China from western Asia and Europe. The Pacific Ocean formed a natural barrier between China and the developing world of North America. This geographical separation combined with an ancient Chinese policy of discouraging contact with other countries, meant that the country's culture, traditions, and internal politics remained unaffected by world events well into the nineteenth century.

Powerful dynasties (ruling families) governed the Chinese Empire from the third century B.C. until the eighteenth century when a dramatic rise in the population and a succession of failed harvests led to widespread suffering and political unrest. Wars with Britain and Japan in the nineteenth century hastened the empire's collapse, and in 1912 China's last emperor abdicated. China became a chaotic republic, ruled by army generals, powerful regional governors, and local warlords. After almost 40 years of civil hostilities and a long war with Japan, the Communist leader Mao Zedong took control in 1949, founding the People's Republic of China.

Morning exercise in Shanghai. All over China, millions of people start their day with ancient Chinese exercises called taijiquan. The exercises promote relaxation, deep breathing, and a sense of harmony.

Since Mao's death in 1976, his successors have continued to insist on total government control, but they have also recognized the need for economic growth. They have encouraged foreign investment and have increased world trade. The government has set up special economic zones where foreign firms can establish businesses in China. The government also continues the staggering task of modernizing China's agriculture, industry, infrastructure, and urban areas.

Hong Kong, Macau

Hong Kong lies at the mouth of the Zhu Jiang (Pearl River) about 90 miles southeast of Guangzhou. It comprises a mountainous peninsula jutting from mainland China, and 235 islands—the largest of which is Hong Kong Island, the territory's capital and commercial centre.

Leased to Britain in 1898, Hong Kong was returned to Chinese rule with great ceremony in 1997. It forms an important part of modern China's expanding economy. Most of its people work in banking and financial services, tourism, international trade, and manufacturing—sending watches, textiles and clothing, electronic equipment, and plastic goods all over the world.

The tiny territory of Macao, including the nearby islands of Coloane and Taipa, lies about 40 miles west of Hong Kong. Portuguese traders settled in Macao in 1557, and for the next 200 years the city and its port dominated the international trade in silk, spices, and other goods. A treaty with China recognized the settlement as Portuguese territory in 1887. Portugal returned Macao to Chinese rule in 1997. More than 90 percent of Macao's people are Chinese. Most of the rest are Portuguese.

Macao's thriving capitalist economy benefits China, which supplies virtually all Macao's food, fresh water, and energy needs and buys manufactured goods from the region. Tourism and light industry are Macao's main economic activities. Factory workers produce textiles and fireworks, which are exported to China and countries all over the world. Hotel staff, restaurant workers, and taxi drivers support a successful tourist industry. Around six million tourists visit Macao each year—almost 80 percent of them from Hong Kong.

The view across Hong Kong's busy harbour, from Hong Kong island to Kowloon on the mainland.

Status:	Republic
Area:	13,969 sq. mi.
Population:	22.7 million
Capital:	Taipei
Languages:	Mandarin Chinese, Taiwanese
Currency:	New Taiwan dollar (100 cents)

The 250-mile-long island of Taiwan lies astride the Tropic of Cancer, about 90 miles off the Chinese coast. It has a warm, moist climate through most of the year, with heavy monsoon rains between June and August. Mountains extend along the whole length of Taiwan, dominating the central and eastern parts rising to 12,000 feet in places. Evergreen forests of camphor, hemlock, and cork oak cover the lower slopes of the mountains, with cedar, larch, and pine forests taking over higher up.

Along the western coast, low rolling hills slope down to a broad, fertile plain and provide Taiwan's only large area of lowland. Most of the population live in the towns and cities of the west, where most of the island's agriculture also takes place. Taiwan's principal crops are rice, maize, bananas, citrus fruits, asparagus, sweet potatoes, and other vegetables, sugar cane, and tea. Chickens, ducks, and pigs are the most common livestock. Coastal fishing crews bring in shrimp, tuna, and other fish for the local markets.

Taiwan is not rich in mineral resources, but the island's miners produce modest quantities of coal, copper, gold, silver, sulphur, and salt. Limestone quarries produce hard stone for building houses and roads, and oil and gas wells contribute to the country's energy needs. Most raw materials, however, are imported. Manufacturing industries in the larger towns produce electronic goods such as computers, calculators, television sets, and radios. They also make textiles and clothing, plastics, toys, and a wide range of forest products—bamboo, lumber, plywood, paper, and wooden furniture.

Mongolia

Status:	Republic
Area:	604,826 sq. mi.
Population:	2.4 million
Capital:	Ulaanbaatar
Languages:	Mongolian, Kazakh, local dialects
Currency:	Tughrik (10 mongo)

Mongolia, sandwiched between Russia and China in eastern central Asia, is the world's largest landlocked country. Spanning 1,500 miles from east to west and nearly 800 miles from north to south, it is larger than Alaska. It is one of the world's most sparsely populated countries, with an average of less than four people per square mile. It is a harsh, rugged country of mountain ranges, upland plateaux, windswept plains, and deserts. Mongolia's climate is typical of a highland region far from the softening influence of the sea. Summers are short and often hot, with temperatures up to 100°F. Winters are long, windy, and bitterly cold, with temperatures dropping to 55°F. Heavy snowfalls are common in the mountainous regions.

Mountains and high steppes dominate northern Mongolia. The Altai Shan (mountains) rise above 14,000 feet on Mongolia's border with China, the Hangayn Mountains stretch across the country's middle. The densely forested Hentiyn Nuruu extends northeast from the capital city of Ulaanbaatar to the Russian border. A high undulating plateau dotted with lakes and forests covers northwestern Mongolia. The country's largest body of water, Uvs Nuur, has an area of more than 1,300 square miles. Lower plains of semi-arid grassland cover the east, gradually becoming more arid as they merge with the barren expanse of the Gobi Desert, which stretches across much of Mongolia's border with China.

The country's people boast a long history of herding livestock. Traditionally nomadic, they constantly shifted their cattle, horses, sheep, goats, and camels from one grazing area to another. Their homes were circular tentlike structures, called yurts, that were made of thick felt mats fixed over a frame of bent poles.

Herding livestock and the nomadic lifestyle, as the principal farming activity in Mongolia and a mainstay of the economy. Most of the population has settled in small villages that dot the vast grazing lands. Mongolians raise more than 20 million head of

Mongolian men sitting outside a traditional yurt making felt.

livestock—about half of them sheep. Cattle, wool, hides, and dairy products comprise the country's principal exports. Mutton, beef, milk, and cheese form the basis of the national diet. In the country's hilly north, farmers plant grains and vegetables in the fertile black soil.

From 1921 to 1990, Mongolia was a Communist state dependent on the Soviet Union for financial assistance. Mining and manufacturing grew rapidly during this period, eventually contributing as much to the country's economy as agriculture did. When the Soviet Union broke apart, Mongolia's financial aid dried up. The country continued to develop its mining interests, producing coal, oil, iron ore, copper, molybdenum, tin, gold, lead, and other minerals. Factory workers made textiles, glass, ceramics, timber products, and other goods. But economic growth has faltered and the country has been unable to continue modernizing its industries and transportation systems without the additional funding.

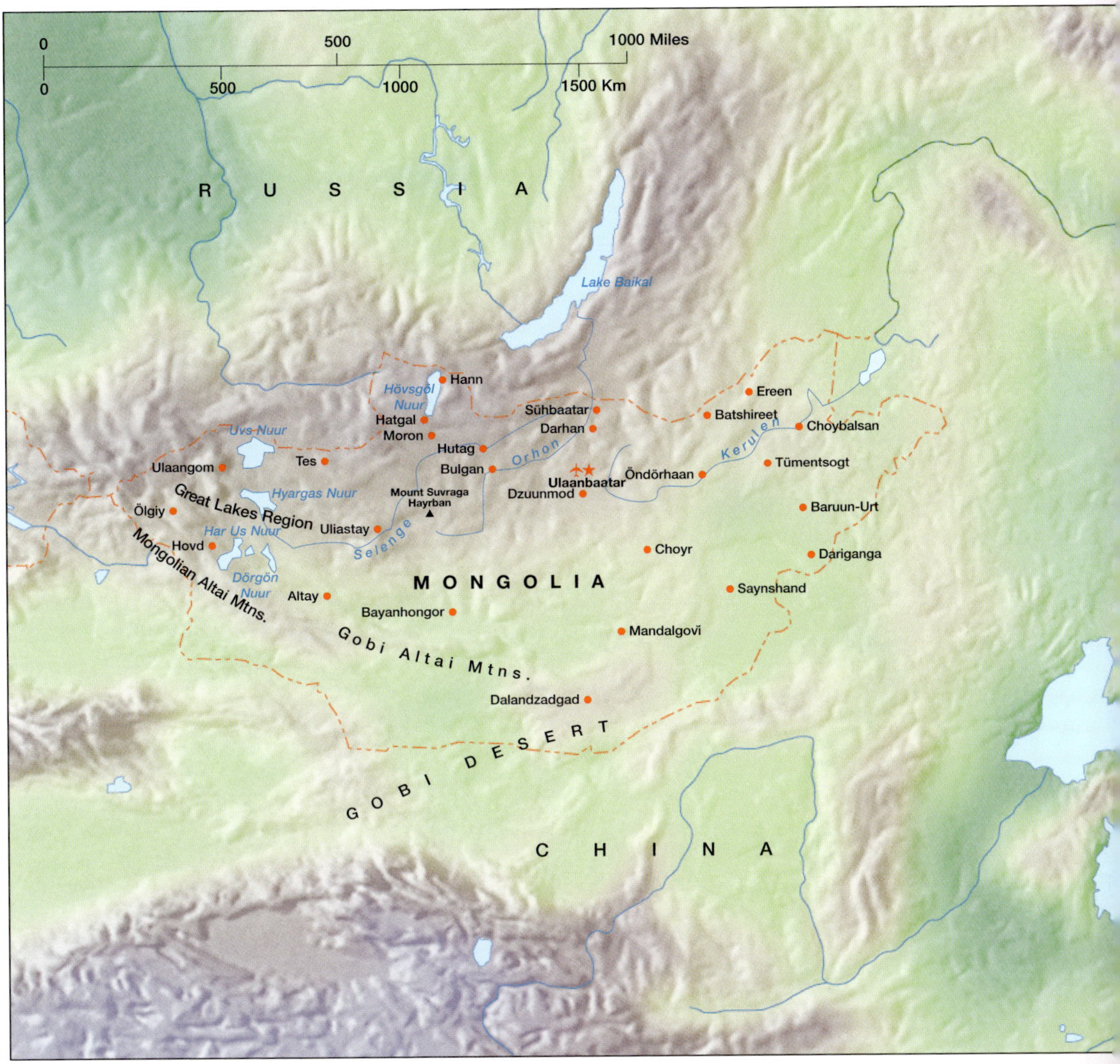

North and South Korea

Status:	Republic
Area:	46,541 square miles
Population:	22.9 million
Capital:	Pyongyang
Language:	Korean
Currency:	North Korean won (100 zeuns)

Three distinct land regions divide North Korea. A broad plain subdivided by low hills parallels the western coast, providing most of North Korea's best farmland. Government-organized cooperatives divide the land into farming communities of up to 300 families. Each family works a section of the land, earning a portion of the harvest and a small income. The bulk of the produce is given to the government for distribution to the cities. Principal cooperative crops include rice, corn, millet, potatoes, and other vegetables. Most farmers also raise chickens and pigs.

Monsoon rains and winter snows provide 30 to 60 inches of precipitation each year, enough to meet the needs of both rural and urban populations. Roughly half the North Koreans reside in this western region—about two million of them in the capital city of Pyongyang. The country's industrial strength is based on mining, iron and steel, machinery, chemicals, and textiles. Miners dig copper, iron ore, lead, zinc, and tungsten, much of it for export to China, Japan, and Russia.

Forested mountains cover central North Korea. The country's largest region has a small population and virtually no agriculture. Residents support their families by mining many of the country's raw materials and by cutting timber for construction, furniture, and plywood and paper production.

A narrow band of coastal lowlands face the Sea of Japan. About one-quarter of the country's people live in the area, farming North Korea's second most productive farmland area.

Status:	Republic
Area:	38,324 square miles
Population:	48.2 million
Capital:	Seoul
Language:	Korean
Currency:	South Korean won (100 chon)

South Korea has two principal land regions. Wide flat plains separated by ribbons of rolling hills form a broad band around the western and southern coasts. Central and eastern South Korea is covered in densely forested mountains. The fertile, well-irrigated coastal plains support most of South Korea's agriculture. In sharp contrast to state-run North Korea, southern farms are almost entirely small, privately owned family businesses. The farmers supplement the primary crop of rice with barley and a great variety of vegetables, including white radishes, onions, cabbages, sweet potatoes, and fruits such as apples and oranges. Farmers in the mountain regions cultivate every spare foot of land possible. They terrace the hillsides, farm the valley floors, and plant crops in the few small areas of lowland along the eastern coast. South Korea's large fishing fleet catches a variety of seafood for local and international markets.

About three-quarters of South Koreans inhabit the coastal plains, where manufacturing and service industries provide about 75 percent of the country's jobs. In the 1950s, North Korea dominated the peninsula's industrial force. South Korea invested heavily in both traditional and high-tech industries, overtaking North Korea as a major producer and worldwide exporter of iron and steel, ships, cars, machinery, chemicals, and tires. The country also manufactures and exports computers, audio and video equipment, cameras, household electrical goods, textiles, and clothing.

0
50
100
150 Miles
0
50
100
150
200 Km
CHINA
Hoeryong
Aoji
Unggi
Najin
Musan
Puryŏng
Hamgyŏng Mtns.
Yonsa
Ch'ŏngjin
Paegam
Kyŏngsŏng
Chonggang
Chasŏng
Huch'ang
Sinp'a
Hyesan
Orang
Hwap'yŏng
Manp'o
Kapsan
Changjin
Nangnim Mtns.
Kanggye
P'ungsan
Hwadae
Lake Sup'ung
Ch'osan
Hoch
Usi
Kop'ung
Lake Changjin
Mandŏk
Kimch'aek
Sup'ung
Kangnam Mtns.
Tanch'ŏn
Iwŏn
Taegwan
Songwŏn
Puckch'ŏng
Myohyang Range
NORTH KOREA
Sinŭiju
Sinp'o
Ch'ŏngch'ŏn
Taedong
Ch'ŏlsan
Sŏnch'ŏn
Ch'ŏngju
Hamhŭng
Chŏngp'yŏng
Ka I.
Puktae Range
Yodŏk
Sinmi I.
Mundŏk
Sunch'ŏn
Hŭngdŏki
P'yŏngsŏng
SEA OF JAPAN
Korea Bay
P'yŏngyang
Wŏnsan
Chŭngsan
Sŭngho
Chunghwa
Imjin
T'ongchŏn
Namp'o
Songnim
Hoeyang
Ch'o I.
Kŭmgang
Kosŏng
Anak
Sariwŏn
Sin'gye
Ich'ŏn
Kimhwa
Kansŏng
Songhwa
Changyŏn
Tosan
Sokch'o
Kumch'ŏn
Yŏnch'ŏn
Pukhan
Yanggu
Paengnyŏng I.
T'aet'an
Haeju
Ongjin
Panmunjom
Tongduch'ŏn
Yangyang
Uijŏngbu
Kap'yŏng
Taebaek Mtns.
Kangnŭng
Kanghwa I.
Kuri
Hongch'ŏn
Seoul
Tonghae
Ullung I.
Inch'ŏn
Sŏngnam
Chongsŏn
Kyŏnggi Bay
Ansan
Anyang
Han
Wŏnju
Tŏkchŏk Is.
Suwŏn
Samch'ŏk
Chech'ŏn
T'aebaek
Ch'ungju
Han
Ulchin
Sŏsan
Onyang
Yech'ŏn
P'yŏnghae
Ch'ŏngju
Yŏngyang
SOUTH KOREA
Sobaek Mountains
Anmyŏn I.
Taech'ŏn
Kum
Taejon
Sangju
Yŏngdŏk
YELLOW SEA
Naktong
Kunwi
Kunsan
P'ohang
Kimch'ŏn
Chŏnju
Kimje
Taegu
Ulsan
Koch'ang
Hamyang
Miryang
Yonggwang
Chinju
Masan
Kwangiu
Somjin
Pusan
Imja I.
Muan
Korea Strait
Mokp'o
Namhai I.
Kŏje-Do
Taehŭksan Is.
Kohung Peninsula
Tolsan I.
Chindi
Haenam Peninsula
Tsushima
Chin I.
Kŭmo I.
Tsushima Strait
Ch'o I.
Kŏ-zaki
Soan Is.
Cheju Strait
Iki
Cheju
Cheju I.
JAPAN

Japan

Status:	Constitutional Monarchy
Area:	145,869 square miles
Population:	126.7 million
Capital:	Tokyo
Language:	Japanese
Currency:	Yen (100 sen)

Four large islands—Hokkaido, Honshu, Shikoku, and Kyushu—account for nearly 98 percent of Japan's land area. These islands lie in a 1,180-mile-long arc off the Asian mainland, facing Russia, North and South Korea, and China across the Sea of Japan and the East China Sea. Japan's remaining 2 percent of land includes about 4,000 smaller islands. Some nestle near the coasts of the main islands. Others, such as the Izu, Daito, Bonin, and Volcano Islands, reach far into the Pacific Ocean. And the Ryukyu Islands extend like a string of pearls from Kyushu Island southwest almost to Taiwan.

Japan's islands lie above one of the most geologically active sections of the earth's crust. Far beneath the island chains, a section of seabed is dragging another down and beneath it. As the seabed grinds, earthquakes—1,500 each year— jolt Japan's landscape and people. Most quakes are minor tremors, causing little or no damage, but every few years a large earthquake strikes, causing extensive damage and casualties. The earthquake of January 17, 1995, rocked the industrial city of Kobe at the southern tip of Honshu Island. The quake destroyed at least 103,000 homes, killed more than 5,000 people, injured 27,000, and left one-fifth of the city's population homeless.

Volcanoes are another geologic component of Japanese life. The islands are actually the tops of a huge range of volcanic mountains rising from the Pacific seabed. More than 150 large volcanoes peek above the ocean's surface, and about half of them are still active (capable of erupting). Mount Fuji, an inactive volcano, forms Japan's highest summit, rising to 12,388 feet above sea level on Honshu Island.

Bridges, water, cherry blossom, and varicoloured foliage are the classic components of traditional Japanese formal gardens.

CHINA
RUSSIA
NORTH KOREA
Sea of Okhotsk
SEA OF JAPAN
PACIFIC OCEAN
JAPAN
Korea Strait
Tsushima Strait
Tsugaru Strait
Bungo Channel
Wakkanai
Rishiri I.
Esashi
Nayoro
Mombatsu
Kitami Mtns.
Rumoi
Asahikawa
Kitami
Abashiri
Shibetsu
Ishikari
Otaru
Sapporo
Kutchan
Tomakomai
Obihiro
Kushiro
Hidaka Sammyaku
Imagane
Muroran
Urakawa
Cape Erimo
Esashi
Hakodate
Fukushima
Seikan Tunnel
Ohata
Aomori
Hirosaki
Hachinohe
Odata
Kuji
Akita
Morioka
Miyako
Kamaishi
Sakata
Tsuruoka
Ishinomaki
Yamagata
Sendai
Ou Range
Sado
Niigata
Fukushima
Nagaoka
Aizu-Wakamatsu
Kōriyama
Kashiwazaki
Iwaki
Tok Is.
Nanao
Jyoetsu
Shinano
Nagano
Toyama
Hitachi
Kanazawa
Komatsu
Japanese Alps
Maebashi
Utsunomiya
Mito
Tsuchiura
Fukui
Oki Is.
Urawa
Tokyo
Punabashi
Kawasaki
Mount Fuji
Yokohama
Yokosuka
Tsuruga
Gifu
Matsue
Tottori
Yonago
Yokkaichi
Oda
Chugoku Range
Lake Biwa
Nagoya
Shizuoka
Kyoto
O Island.
Masuda
Amagasaki
Tsu
Okayama
Kobe
Osaka
Hamamatsu
Toyota
Tsushima
Hagi
Nara
Hiroshima
Takamatsu
Tokuyama
Yamaguchi
Sakai
Izu Islands.
Shimonoseki
Ube
Kitakyushu
Niihama
Tokushima
Kumano
Matsuyama
Goto Is.
Fukuoka
Kochi
Susaki
Muroto
Beppu
Oita
Sasebo
Nagasaki
Kumamoto
Nakamura
Nobeoka
Amakusa Is.
Yatsushiro
Minamata
Akune
Miyazaki
Sendai
Miyakonojō
Kagoshima
Nichinan
Makurazaki
Kanoya
Osumi Is.
0
250
500 Miles
0
350
700 Km

Spectacular mountains, rolling hills, and precious forests cover much of Japan, providing stunning scenery for the country's many visitors. Nearly 70 percent of the land is mountainous, so Japan's 128 million people tend to concentrate near the coasts, where narrow plains provide space for urban development. Flat land is so scarce that many of Japan's large industrial cities sit on shore land that has been pumped dry. The most heavily inhabited areas lie along the Pacific coast of Honshu Island, where major cities, industrial centres, and ports have developed around deep sheltered bays. Tokyo's metropolitan area houses more than 12 million people, and the surrounding area holds another 6 million. Osaka's residents number nearly 10 million. Other major urban areas include Yokohama, Nagoya, Osaka, and Kyoto—each home to several million people.

Despite its small size, Japan has one of the world's strongest economies. The country's gross domestic product (GDP) is second only to that of the United States. Japan has achieved this rank with relatively few natural resources. Japanese miners extract small quantities of coal, lead, tin, zinc, manganese, silver, and other minerals, but Japan imports most of

Top: Downtown Tokyo is noisy, colourful, and busy at all hours of the day and night.

Centre: Tokyo shoppers examine the latest goods on display in a downtown electronics store.

Left: Japan's famous "Bullet trains" are part of a rail transport system the operators proudly claim is the most reliable and punctual in the world.

its copper and aluminium and nearly all the coking coal and iron ore used in its huge iron and steel industry. Japan produces steel for its own use as well as manufacturing steel sheets, rolls, pipes, and wire for export.

About one-quarter of Japan's workforce is employed in manufacturing industries. Cars are among the country's principal exports. More than eight million of them are produced annually. Japan is also the world's leading shipbuilder and a major supplier of heavy machinery, such as cranes, turbines, machine tools, and electrical equipment. Factory workers create cameras, watches, scientific instruments, audio and video equipment, computers, calculators, washing machines, and many other household goods. Textiles, ceramics, paper, and wood products are also exported, and the country's petrochemical industries—using oil and natural gas as raw materials—produce a wide range of plastics, and synthetic fibres for the textile trade.

More than half the Japanese are employed in one of the service industries—working as healthcare providers, teachers, bank tellers, insurance agents, telephone operators, and hotel and restaurant workers. Many work as tour guides for the country's thriving tourist industry.

Japan's climate varies a great deal from north to south. Residents of Hokkaido experience cool summers and bitterly cold winters, often with thick snowfalls. Honshu has warm, humid summers and winters that get more mild the farther south on the island one travels. As the southernmost large island, Kyushu enjoys a warm, temperate climate, with hot summers and mild winters. Most of Japan receives ample rainfall to meet the needs of both city dwellers and farmers. Only Hokkaido's eastern side has a markedly dry climate.

Japan has a rich and complex theatrical tradition dating back many centuries.

Japan makes productive use of its relatively sparse farmland. Farmers have boosted productivity by irrigating, by terracing the hillsides, by choosing high-yield crop strains, and by using large amounts of fertilizer. Rice is the country's most significant crop and the basis of its national diet. Japanese farmers grow many varieties of vegetables and fruits, and many raise poultry, pigs, and cattle. Some farmers specialize in nonfood crops such as tobacco, and mulberry trees, whose leaves are used to feed silkworms. Japan's agriculture sector produces almost 70 percent of the country's food needs. The remainder is imported.

With a long coastline and hundreds of bays and inlets, Japan has a long tradition of fishing and the largest fishing fleet in the world—estimated at more than 400,000 vessels. Traditional fishers with small boats work the coastal waters, while the large modern deepsea trawlers, seiners, and squid-catchers roam the oceans. Fish has long been Japan's principal source of animal protein, and nutritionists believe that the combination of rice, fish, and vegetables in the Japanese diet has long protected the population from the high incidence of heart disease seen in other developed countries.

Pakistan, Afghanistan

Status:	Federal Republic
Area:	307,375 square miles
Population:	161.1 million
Capital:	Islamabad
Languages:	Punjabi, Urdu, Sindhi, Pashtun, Baluchi, English
Currency:	Pakistan rupee (100 paisa)

Pakistan emerged as a country in 1947, when India gained its independence from Britain. A large section of the Indian subcontinent became the predominantly Hindu state of India. The other, smaller section became the Islamic state of Pakistan, home to a population that was 95 percent Muslim. Pakistan then consisted of West Pakistan and East Pakistan, two Muslim territories located nearly 1,000 miles apart. Civil war led to a breakup in 1971, and East Pakistan gained independence as Bangladesh. West Pakistan became simply Pakistan.

The dry, barren Baluchistan Plateau blankets most of southwestern Pakistan. With less than five inches of annual rainfall, the area supports little vegetation. Few people inhabit the region apart from scattered settlements of sheep and goat herders. In northern Pakistan, the land rises to the rugged mountains of the North-West Frontier province, where the Khyber Pass links Pakistan with neighbouring Afghanistan. Farther east rises the world's second-highest peak, K2 (also known as Godwin Austen), which towers 28,250 feet on the Himalayan border with China.

Stretching northward and eastward from the Arabian Sea, the Thar Desert reaches deep into India along several river valleys. Farmers have been able to tap into the area's rivers to irrigate parts of the desert for cultivation. The lowlands of the Indus River and its principal tributaries dominate the Punjab and Sind provinces of eastern Pakistan. Over millions of years, these rivers have deposited thick layers of silt, forming a broad, fertile alluvial plain. Even here, in Pakistan's wettest region, annual rainfall rarely exceeds 20 inches. The farmers of these plains channel the rivers into extensive irrigation systems, which allow the farmers to grow wheat, rice, chickpeas, vegetables, and fruits. Cotton and sugarcane are the country's primary nonfood crops.

Most of Pakistan is underdeveloped. Two-thirds of the people live in farming villages with few modern amenities. The country is short on schools and teachers as well as on hospitals and medical staff. Despite government efforts to improve educational standards, less than 50 percent of school-age children attend classes and only about one in four Pakistanis can read and write.

Manufacturing employs about 15 percent of the population, mostly in the urban centres of Karachi, Hyderabad, Lahore, Multan, Rawalpindi, and Peshawar. Factory workers produce textiles and clothing, processed foods, fertilizers, and cement. Along the coast, many Pakistanis work in the fishing industry, catching shrimp, sardines, shark, and other fish for local and foreign markets.

Magnificent scenery of Mount Nowshak, Northeast Afghanistan.

Afghanistan is a rugged, mountainous, landlocked country. Its people belong to more than 20 ethnic groups, and power struggles among them have led to constant political unrest. In 1973 a military coup replaced Afghanistan's monarchy with a republic, but further unrest led to occupation by Soviet troops. Since the Soviet withdrawal, internal conflicts have continued, and some have been extremely violent and disruptive.

Rolling plains and plateaux stretch across northern Afghanistan, supporting sheep and goat herders on sparse grasslands. The soil is fertile, but annual rainfall rarely exceeds seven inches. Farmers cultivate the river valleys, diverting water to their fields through irrigation channels.

The high mountains of the Hindu Kush fill central Afghanistan, rising to more than 20,000 feet near the Pakistani border. Many Afghanis live in the high, cold valleys of this region. The farmers grow grain and vegetables using hand tools and centuries-old farming methods and graze livestock on the sparse hillside pastures. The farmers grow grain and vegetables using hand tools and centuries-old farming methods and graze livestock on the sparse hillside pastures.

Afghanistan has little industry, and most of its rich mineral deposits lie undeveloped because of their remote locations. The country has developed two valuable minerals for export—natural gas and the stone lapis lazuli.

Status:	Republic
Area:	251,772 sq. mi.
Population:	26 million
Capital:	Kabul
Languages:	Pashtu, Dari
Currency:	Afghani (100 pue)

Nepal

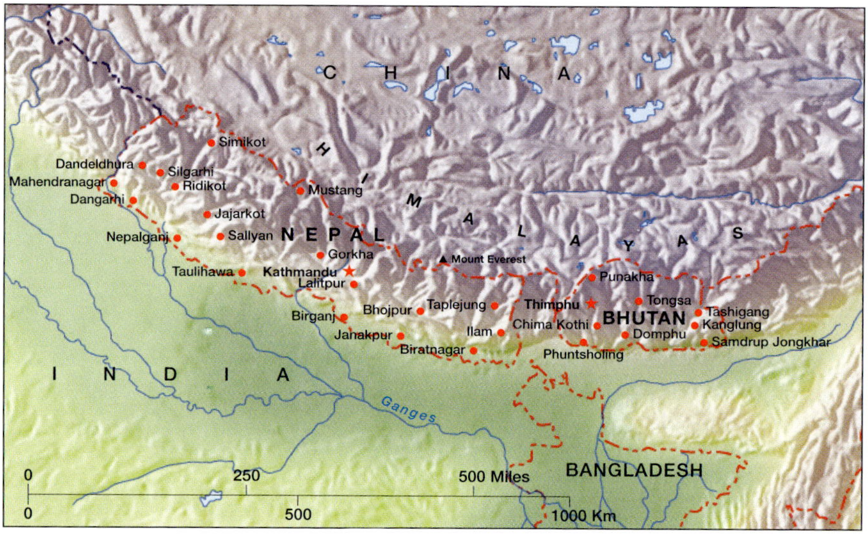

Status:	Constitutional Monarchy
Area:	56,826 sq.mi.
Population:	26.3 million
Capital:	Kathmandu
Languages:	Nepali, many local dialects
Currency:	Nepalese rupee (100 paisa)

The remote mountain kingdom of Nepal lies in the Himalayas, sandwiched between China and India. More than 80 percent of the country is covered by these towering mountains and by the hills and valleys of a lesser range, the Mahabharat Mountains, that lies to the south. The broad fertile Tarai Plain stretches west to east across the southern edge of the country, along the border with India.

Nepal's mountainous terrain and lack of roads make communication difficult, especially for the 55 percent of the population that lives in the mountain regions. The economy is underdeveloped, and there are few schools or hospitals. A government program begun in the 1950s to improve health and educational services has raised the country's literacy rate from 5 percent to about 20 percent.

Nearly all of the Nepalese depend on agriculture for their income. People in the high mountains raise sheep and longhaired yaks. The animals' milk is a fundamental part of the local diet, and their wool is woven to make clothes and blankets. Some crops in this area cling to the terraced hillsides, but much of the original forest has been cut for firewood causing the hillsides to wash away. Farmers at the lower elevations benefit from better soils, a mild, cool climate, and summer rains. They harvest rice, corn, millet, wheat, and vegetables and herd cattle, oxen, sheep, and goats. Most Nepalese farmers work small family plots and manage to produce just enough food for their own needs, with a small surplus to sell or trade.

The Tarai enjoys a hot, wet climate, with ample moisture and fertile soil. Farmers in the plain grow grains, vegetables, sugarcane, and nonfood crops such as jute and tobacco. Some sections of the Tarai are covered in jungle and swamp, teeming with wildlife such as crocodiles, elephants, leopards, rhinoceroses, and tigers.

Nepal's mineral resources—coal, iron, copper, and gold—are undeveloped because of their remote locations. The country has little industry apart from craftwork. Nepal's hope for the future lies in its huge potential for hydroelectric power from Himalayan rivers. With international funding Nepal will be able to build several giant power stations and to sell the electricity to the industrial regions of northern India.

Status:	Absolute Monarchy
Area:	18,147 sq. mi.
Population:	2.4 million
Capital:	Thimphu
Languages:	Dzongkha, English
Currency:	Ngultrum (100 chetrum)

The tiny mountain kingdom of Bhutan lies between India and Tibet—formerly an independent country but since the 1950s an autonomous (self-governing) region of China. Like neighbouring Nepal, Bhutan has three major land regions. The high Himalayas dominate the north—cold, windy, with ice-covered peaks and large areas of bare rock. Herders raise goats and yaks on the rough, windswept mountain pastures. South of the main Himalayas the land consists of low mountains and rolling hills, densely covered with ash, oak, and poplars. Good soils and the milder, damper climate of the sheltered valleys allow farmers there to grow wheat, barley, rice, and vegetables. Some of the lower south-facing hills are hot and humid, and that same climate extends across the rolling plains and broad river valleys that cover the south of the country. Farmers in this fertile tropical area grow rice, bananas, and citrus fruits, and miners in the south produce coal, much of which Bhutan exports to India.

With aid from India, Bhutan is modernizing its road system, improving its agriculture, and developing industries such as food processing for export. A hydroelectric power station has been built to supply the capital, Thimphu, and others are planned.

Below: A young Buddhist monk collects alms (donations, usually of food or drink) in the streets of his village. Most young Bhutanese men spend at least two years in a monastery.

Bottom: Terraced rice paddies at Kanglung in eastern Bhutan.

Bangladesh

Status:	Republic
Area:	55,598 square miles
Population:	125.7 million
Capital:	Dhaka
Languages:	Bengali, English
Currency:	Taka (100 poisha)

Elephants are still widely used to haul logs in the forests. Handlers reward these strong, intelligent animals with a refreshing scrub in the river after a hard day.

Bangladesh consists almost entirely of a flat alluvial plain, formed over millions of years by the meandering and frequent flooding of the country's three major rivers—the Ganges, the Brahma-putra, and the Meghna. They flow through Bangladesh to the Bay of Bengal. Most of the country lies less than 50 feet above sea level, making Bangladesh the world's most flood-prone country. Heavy monsoon rains from May to October often cause the rivers to burst their banks, and cyclones sweeping in from the Bay of Bengal can drive inland enormous volumes of water. These awesome storms have devastated entire villages and left hundreds of square miles of crops rotting under several feet of muddy, salty water.

Bangladesh is one of the world's most heavily populated countries, with more than 2,200 people per square mile. It is also a very poor country. More than 80 percent of Bangladeshis live in rural areas and grow rice, wheat, beans, vegetables, and jute—the primary nonfood crop. The soil is fertile and the government has made efforts to improve farm yields with fertilizers, better varieties of seed, and more modern farming methods. But with so many mouths to feed, most Bangladeshis do not have enough to eat.

Typical rural homes are built of bamboo and thatch. Only a third have electricity, running water, or sanitation. The cities are bursting, with millions of people living in makeshift homes in sprawling shantytowns. Health and education services do not begin to meet the country's needs.

Jute factories—Bangladesh's only large-scale industrial employers—process the plant's fibre into ropes and sacking. Fishing boats that ply the coasts and rivers provide an important source of food, allowing Bangladesh to export large quantities of shrimp and prawns.

Sri Lanka

Status:	Republic
Area:	25,332 sq. mi.
Population:	19 million
Capital:	Colombo
Languages:	Sinhala, Tamil, English
Currency:	Sri Lankan rupee (100 cents)

Droplet-shaped Sri Lanka is a beautiful island of wild animals, coastal plains, and forested mountains reaching to 8,000 feet in the south. Once a British colony named Ceylon, the island is famous for its Ceylon tea, which it exports and consumes locally in great quantities.

Two major ethnic groups dominate life and politics in Sri Lanka. The mostly Buddhist Sinhalese comprise 74 percent of the population and largely control the government. The predominantly Hindu Tamil make up 18 percent of the country's inhabitants and feel their lack of political power has led to fewer opportunities. Outbreaks of fighting between the rivals have torn the island for nearly 50 years.

Sri Lanka's economy is based on farming. About half the labour force works the land, growing rice, rubber, tobacco, coconuts, and tea—Sri Lanka's most valuable export. Another 10 percent work in processing plants or textile factories. The country's service industries of government offices, communications, and transportation employ 35 percent.

Maldives

Status:	Republic
Area:	116 sq. mi.
Population:	300,000
Capital:	Malé
Language:	Dhiyehi
Currency:	Rufiyaa (100 laari)

More than 1,000 coral islands make up the Maldives. They stretch in a 475-mile-long chain in the Indian Ocean. One of the world's smallest countries, the island group sits off India's southwestern tip, covering little more than 100 square miles. Just over 200 of the islands are inhabited. Many are tiny atolls that barely break the ocean surface. Some of the islands lie so low in the water that ocean experts fear they eventually may submerge altogether.

Maldivian livelihoods depend on fishing, tourism, and farming. Thousands of boats head to sea each day, pulling in bonito and tuna for local consumption and for export—primarily to Sri Lanka and Japan. Glistening white beaches and a hot, sunny tropical climate attract large numbers of visitors each year.

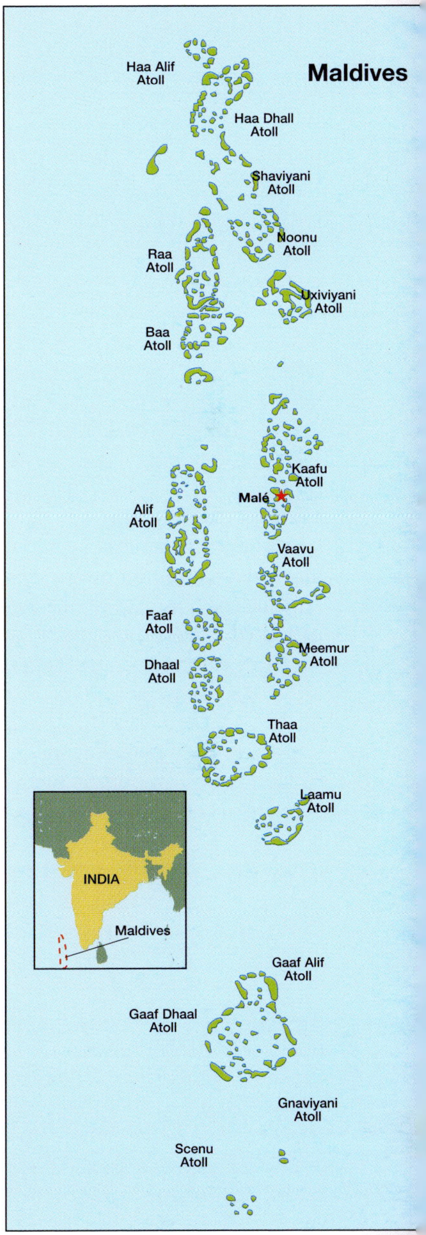

India

Status:	Federal Republic
Area:	1,269,340 sq. mi.
Population:	1.1 billion
Capital:	New Delhi
Languages:	Hindi, English, Telugu, Bengali, Marathi, Urdu, other regional dialects
Currency:	Rupee (100 paisa)

India is the world's seventh-largest country but is second only to China in population. Over one billion people—one-sixth of the world's people—live in India.

Long before humans lived there, the Indian subcontinent had a remarkable and spectacular history. Along with South America, Africa, Antarctica, and Australia, India once formed part of a vast supercontinent, called Gondwana, that was situated far south of its current location. When Gondwana broke apart more than 200 million years ago, India drifted northward, crossed the equator, and crashed into the landmass that would become Asia. India ploughed so hard into Asia that it buckled and crushed a 1,500-mile long, 200-mile-wide section of the earth's crust, pushing it five miles into the sky. The result of that geological collision is the Himalayas—the world's tallest mountain range, which marks India's borders with China, Nepal, and Bhutan.

The huge diamond-shaped subcontinent—2,000 miles from north to south and 1,000 miles across at its widest—contains enough variety of landscapes and people to be several countries. Snow-covered mountain peaks and vast open plains meet deserts, high plateaux, and dense rain forests. India's people speak 14 major languages and more than 1,000 additional languages and dialects. About one-third of the population principally speaks Hindi—one of India's 14 official languages. English, a reminder of India's colonial connection to Britain, is still widely used in government circles and by the legal, academic, and scientific communities.

Over the centuries, India has been both a large sprawling empire and a collection of separate states. Colonists from Portugal, Britain, France, and the Netherlands arrived in the fifteenth and sixteenth centuries, but the British East India Company steadily established itself as the dominant power. The British government formally colonized India in 1805, and it remained under British rule until 1947. At that time, India was divided, or partitioned, into modern India, which is predominantly Hindu, and the primarily Muslim state of Pakistan. Border conflicts between the two states and religious conflicts both between the states and within each state have plagued the subcontinent ever since.

India itself can be divided into three major land regions. A northern strip of foothills and towering peaks in the Hima-layas supports India's highest summit, Kanchenjunga, which rises to 28,208 feet on the border with Nepal. Few

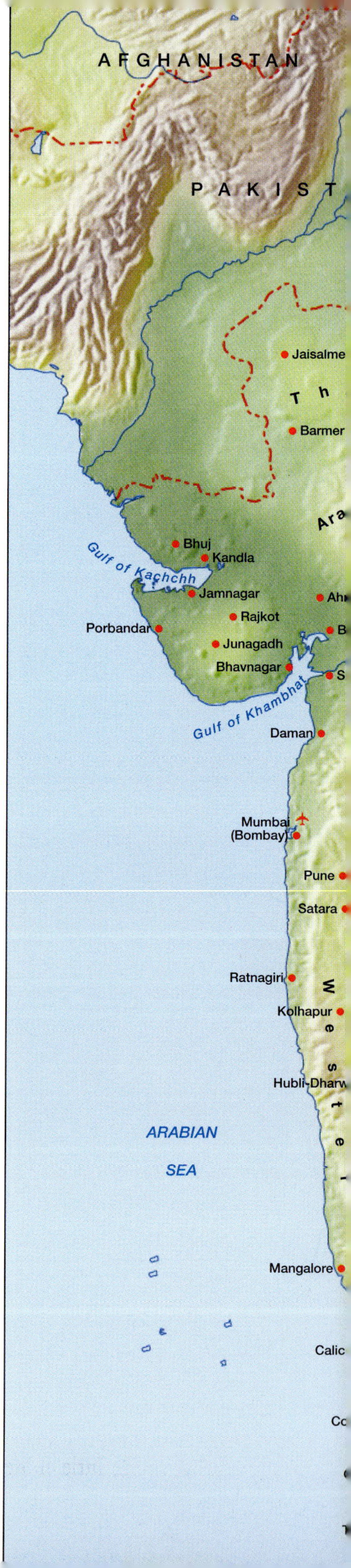

CHINA
HIMALAYA RANGE
NEPAL
BHUTAN
BANGLADESH
MYANMAR
INDIA
SRI LANKA
BAY OF BENGAL
INDIAN OCEAN
Andaman Is.
Kamet Peak
Nanda Devi Peak
Pathankot
Amritsar
Ludhiana
Chandigarh
Bhatinda
Patiala
Dehra Dun
Saharanpur
Muzaffarnagar
Bhiwani
Meerut
Delhi
Faridabad
Rampur
Aligarh
Mathura
Sitapur
Jaipur
Agra
Lucknow
Yamuna
Gomati
Kanpur
Faizabad
Gwalior
Ghaghara
Gorakhpur
Gangtok
Tawang
Itanagar
Shiliguri
Gauhati
Brahmaputra
Jaunpur
Bhilwara
Jhansi
Darbhanga
Kota
Allahabad
Varanasi
Chhapra
Ganges
Katihar
Shillong
Mirzapur
Patna
Munger
Bhagalpur
Rewa
Son
Bihar
Imphal
Sagar
Bhopal
Indore
Jabalpur
Aizawl
Dhanbad
Narmada
Bokaro
Navadwip
Satpura Range
Maikala Range
Lunglei
Jamshedpur
Howrah
Calcutta
Kharogpur
Raurkela
Chittagong
Nagpur
Hirakud Reservoir
Raipur
Baleshwar
Mouths of the Ganges
Aurangabad
Mahanadi
Chandrapur
Cuttack
Godavari
Puri
Nizamabad
Rayagartha
Brahmapur
Deccan Plateau
Koraput
Vizianagaram
Warangal
Eastern Ghats
Hyderabad
Gulbarga
Kakinada
Krishna
Adoni
Kurnool
Guntur
Bellary
Proddatur
Anantapur
Nellore
Penner
Madras
Pallavaram
Bangalore
Pondicherry
Salem
Cuddalore
Tiruppur
Coimbatore
Kumbakonam
Thanjavur
Madurai
Palk Strait
Tuticorin
Gulf of Mannar
0 500 Miles
0 500 1000 Km

Dramatic scenery in one of the many mountain passes in Kashmir.

people live in the high mountains, but villagers in the foothills graze sheep and goats on the mountain pastures and grow rice, wheat, and vegetables. Farmers in northern India grow rice on the fertile soil of the terraced foothills and cultivate fruit and nut trees. Above the terraces, the dry, rugged hills are crossed by ancient tracks that lead northward into China and westward into Pakistan. Far to the east, where India borders Myanmar (formerly Burma), greater rainfall allows upland farmers to raise wheat, barley, and rice. Parts of this region enjoy more than 300 inches of annual rain. The village of Cherrapunji holds the world record for a single year's rainfall—1,042 inches.

South of the mountains, a broad plain stretches from east to west across the continent ending in the hot and dusty Thar Desert. Only small groups of sheep and goat herders roamed the desert until 1986, when a new canal provided irrigation for crops and farmers were encouraged to settle there.

The tropical state of Gujarat, south of the desert and bordering the Arabian Sea, is one of India's principal cotton-growing regions. The country's great rivers—the Ganges and the Brahmaputra—dominate the central and eastern plains. Fed by runoff from Himalayan glaciers and snowfields, the rivers and their tributaries flow across broad fertile plains, meeting in Bangladesh before emptying into the Bay of Bengal. The rivers provide ample irrigation, allowing the plains' farmers to grow much of India's food. Rice covers the greatest percentage of India's cultivated land, but farmers also grow wheat, millet, sorghum, and many varieties of peas and beans. Local markets also brim with onions, cauliflower, aubergines, potatoes, apples, and bananas. Many farmers grow and sell tea, sugarcane, cotton, jute, tobacco, and rubber.

Farther south lies India's great triangular Deccan Peninsula, a huge plateau sloping gently from west to east. Rocky mountain ranges mark the plateau's edge. The steep, 5,000-foot Western Ghats overlook a narrow coastal plain on the Arabian Sea, while the 2,000-foot Eastern Ghats slope to a broader coastal plain facing the Bay of Bengal. On most of the Deccan, farmers grow grains and vegetables and raise large herds of cattle and buffalo for their milk and for their strength in pulling carts and ploughs. Western Deccan farmers take advantage of their wetter soil to grow mainly cotton and sorghum. Farmers in the drier eastern sector harvest millet, beans, sugarcane, and spices. India's southwestern coast enjoys a hot tropical climate with more than 120 inches of annual rain and abundant crops of peppers, mangoes, bananas, and coconuts.

Coastal inhabitants eat a great deal of fish, supporting a large portion of India's fishing industry. Vessels chug home at the end of the day bursting with prawns, mackerel, herring, sardines, shark, and Bombay duck—a small fish that is dried and used in many curried dishes.

About 70 percent of India's people reside in small rural farming communities, often numbering no more than 1,000 people. The remaining 30 percent live in towns and small cities. Only about 250 urban areas house more than 100,000 people, and just ten of them have more than a million people—the three largest being Calcutta (11 million), Mumbai (formerly Bombay) (10 million), and Delhi (7 million). But the urban population is growing quickly. Improved health care has allowed people to live much longer, and the rural poor are flocking to urban areas in search of jobs. Many are disappointed and end up in overcrowded slums or on the streets.

Although India's major cities are among the most crowded urban environments in the world, recent government health and education programs have had considerable success. Since the 1950s, life expectancy has increased by 25 years, as new hospitals and clinics have been built. Teams of health workers have visited thousands of rural communities giving advice on childcare, nutrition, hygiene, and sanitation. The government has also invested in schools, teachers, books, and public television services, all of which have led to a dramatic rise in India's literacy rate. About half the population can read and write—more than twice as many as in the 1950s, when these programmes began.

From June to September, warm winds blow in from the southwest carrying moisture from the Indian Ocean. This moisture falls as torrential rain and often causes flooding in low-lying areas like the Ganges Delta. The Bay of Bengal is also prone to hurricanes. These devastating storms have destroyed coastal villages, have killed livestock, and have buried precious crops under several feet of muddy saltwater.

India's industries have grown rapidly since independence. More people are employed in the textile industries than in any other sector. Mumbai and Ahmadabad in the west are the principal cotton centres, wool processing is based in Punjab in the far northwest, and jute factories are concentrated around Calcutta. Textiles and clothing are among India's principal exports. Iron and steel plants at Bhilai, Bokaro, Durgapur, and Raurkela in the eastern Deccan process local iron ore with locally mined coal to supply steel for factory-made cars, bicycles, railroad parts, household appliances, and other metal goods. Factory workers in cities such as Delhi, Ahmadabad, and Hyderabad manufacture electrical goods, lace, decorative wood and leather goods, fine brassware, and food products for both local and overseas markets. India's chemical plants produce pharmaceuticals, dyes, fertilizers, and industrial chemicals. India meets more than half its energy needs with local resources. Power stations burn Deccan coal and use oil from wells off the coast near Mumbai and onshore in Assam. Another 35 percent is hydroelectric power from major river stations, and the remainder is nuclear power.

Camel driver, Rajasthan, western India.

Houses, temples, boats, and people crowd every inch of the Ganges riverfront at Varanasi, in the north-central Indian state of Uttar Pradesh. To Hindus, the Ganges is the most sacred river in India.

Myanmar (Burma)

Status:	Republic
Area:	261,228 sq. mi.
Population:	50.7 million
Capital:	Yangon
Languages:	Burmese, English, several local dialects
Currency:	Kyat (100 pyas)

Myanmar has a 1,650-mile-long coastline on the Bay of Bengal and shares its land borders with Bangladesh, India, China, Laos, and Thailand. The country changed its name from Burma in 1989, but many Burmese, who oppose the government, still use the old name.

Myanmar is a land of mountains, dense tropical rain forests, and great river valleys. The low-lying Arakan Yoma range in the west overlooks a narrow fertile plain fronting the Bay of Bengal. This highland region runs north through the Chin and Naga Hills along Myanmar's border with India. Clothed in dense tropical forests, the hills hold much of the world's teak The high peaks of the Kumon range—rising to 19,296-foot Hkakabo Razi in the far north—and the Shan Plateau's wooded hills separate Myanmar from China. To the east, the Tanen and Dawna Mountains dominate the country's borders with Thailand and Laos.

Three great rivers—the Irrawaddy, the Sittang, and the Salween—and their tributaries flow from north to south through Myanmar's middle. Low-lying hills separate the rivers from one another. Their broad, fertile valleys support the country's most productive farmland. Myanmar is a major producer of jade, rubies, and sapphires, which are exported worldwide.

Status:	Constitutional Monarchy
Area:	198,116 sq. mi.
Population:	61.8 million
Capital:	Bangkok
Languages:	Thai, Chinese, Khmer, Malay
Currency:	Baht (100 satang)

Thailand is a tropical South-east Asian country of forests, mountains, lakes, and rivers. Winters are mild, springtime is hot and dry, and summers are long, hot, and very humid. The climate is generally hot and sticky along the coasts but cooler and drier in the northern highlands.

About 75 percent of Thailand's people live in rural areas. Farming is the principal occupation, and rice is the dominant crop. Farmers also cultivate cassava, corn, soybeans, sugarcane, bananas, coconuts, and pineapples. Cotton, jute, and rubber are the chief nonfood crops.

Thailand also has considerable mineral wealth. Miners dig up zinc, copper, feldspar, kaolin, lead, limestone, and lignite. Buried in the sandbars of Thailand's shallow coastal waters are some of the world's richest tin deposits—making Thailand one of the world's leading suppliers of that valuable mineral. The country extracts natural gas from offshore wells in the Gulf of Thailand but otherwise is short of fuel and has to import most of the oil it needs.

Tropical hardwoods—especially teak—were one of Thailand's chief exports until unregulated cutting created mudslides, rock falls, and massive soil erosion. Enormous environmental damage and destruction of entire villages led the Thai government to halt hardwood cutting in 1988. The country focused on developing other industries, especially tourism and manufacturing. The capital city of Bangkok has become a major manufacturing centre, producing textiles, cars, electronic goods, cement, pharmaceuticals, paper, plywood, and agricultural chemicals.

Thailand's growing economy supports free primary schools and a large number of secondary schools and colleges. Nearly 90 percent of the population can read and write. But the drift of poor rural people to the cities and the continued presence of many Vietnamese refugees have placed great pressure on housing and other services.

More than 400 temples grace Thailand's capital, Bangkok, on the delta of the Chao Phraya River. Their intricately decorated walls and ornate spires are a major tourist attraction.

Vietnam, Laos

Status:	Republic
Area:	128,066 sq. mi.
Population:	83.6 million
Capital:	Hanoi
Languages:	Vietnamese, French, English
Currency:	Dông (100 xu)

Status:	Republic
Area:	91,429 sq. mi.
Population:	5.9 million
Capital:	Vientiane
Languages:	Lao, French, Vietnamese
Currency:	Kip (100 at)

Vietnam is a long, narrow, S-shaped country with a 2,140-mile-long coastline on the South China Sea. The country stretches 1,030 miles north to south and 380 miles west to east at its widest, although the central section is barely 30 miles wide.

France controlled Vietnam before World War II (1939-1945), but Japan occupied the country during the war. France's efforts to regain control after the war were defeated in 1954 by the Communist army of the Vietminh. Peace negotiators divided the country into Communist North and non-Communist South, but fighting soon broke out between the two nations and escalated into a full-scale civil war. The United States was deeply involved in support of South Vietnam but made a humiliating retreat when the two Vietnams declared a cease-fire in 1973. In 1975 the Communist regime unified the country.

Densely forested mountains cover northwestern Vietnam, continuing in a narrow mountain chain along the borders with Laos and Cambodia. Most Vietnamese live in two large river deltas that dominate eastern Vietnam. The Red River Delta in the north and the Mekong Delta in the south provide fertile farmland where Vietnamese farmers grow rice, maize, cassava, soybeans, vegetables, peanuts, coconuts, coffee beans, and cacao beans. Cotton, jute, rubber, and tobacco are the main nonfood crops. Fishing crews catch crabs, lobsters, shrimp, and squid off the coast. Apart from coal in the north, Vietnam has few mineral resources. Factory workers produce farm machinery, bicycles, cement, fertilizers, and textiles.

Laos, like its neighbour Vietnam, was formerly a French-controlled territory. The country threw off foreign control in 1954 but then suffered a long period of civil war before it emerged as an independent Communist state in 1975.

Mountains blanketed in dense, humid tropical rain forest cover the north of the country, while broad, fertile lowlands along the Mekong River dominate the south. Farmers in the highlands grow maize, rice, tobacco, and cotton. Lowland farmers harvest rice as their principal crop, along with vegetables, fruit, maize, and coffee beans. Most farmers also raise pigs, cattle, and poultry.

Laos is rich in natural resources but poor in infrastructure—the roads, refineries, and other operations that help export the resources. As a result, its deposits of gold, lead, silver, tin, zinc, and other minerals and its valuable stand of tropical hardwoods, gums, and resins have yet to be tapped.

Youngsters have fun wherever they live, and Vietnam's rivers provide a natural playground.

Cambodia

Water buffaloes are the "living tractors" of rural Asia, pulling carts and plows, hauling logs in the forests, and driving threshing machines, water pumps, sugar cane presses, and other machines.

Status:	Constitutional Monarchy
Area:	69,900 sq. mi.
Population:	14.8 million
Capital:	Phnom Penh
Languages:	Khmer, Chinese, Vietnamese, French
Currency:	Riel (100 sen)

Cambodia is a mainly lowland country in Southeast Asia, ringed by low forested hills along its borders with Thailand, Laos, and Vietnam. In the south, Cambodia has a short coast on the Gulf of Thailand.

The largest ethnic group in Cambodia are the Khmer, whose ancestors ruled a vast empire in Southeast Asia about a thousand years ago. The magnificent ruined temples of Angkor, capital of the Khmer Empire, are among the most spectacular ancient monuments in southern Asia.

The tradition of royal rule gave way in 1863 to French control as part of French Indochina. Cambodia became fully independent in 1954 but then suffered years of civil war.

Most of Cambodia's people are farmers, living in small lowland villages. With fertile soils, plentiful rain, and numerous rivers to provide water, most farmers grow two or even three crops of rice a year. Rivers, lakes, and warm offshore waters yield Cambodia's other main food—fish.

Malaysia

Status:	Constitutional Monarchy
Area:	127,317 sq. mi.
Population:	25.3 million
Capital:	Kuala Lumpur
Languages:	Bahasa Malaysian, English, Chinese, local languages
Currency:	Ringgit (100 sen)

Malaysia has two large but widely separated land areas. West Malaysia consists of the southern end of the long, paddle-shaped Malay Peninsula which also holds Thailand. East Malaysia, 400 miles away across the South China Sea, consists of the territories of Sarawak and Sabah on the northern side of the island of Borneo. (The other parts of Borneo belong to Indonesia or form the independent country of Brunei.)

The modern state of Malaysia was formed in 1963, when the Federation of Malaya and the British colonies of Singapore, Sarawak, and Sabah joined together. Singapore left the federation in 1965 to become an independent country.

Roughly 50 percent of the people of Malaysia are Malay, 35 percent are Chinese, and 10 percent are Indian. The rest, especially people in Sarawak and Sabah, belong to many smaller ethnic groups. This ethnic diversity gives Malaysia a rich and varied culture in which art, music, dance, drama, and sports play a part. Islam, Hinduism, Buddhism, Christianity exist side by side without conflict.

Much of Malaysia is covered in dense tropical forests. From the Thai border, a ridge of mountains runs down the Malay Peninsula, where 80 percent of the Malaysians live. The ridge forms a thinly populated inland zone that is separated from the densely populated coastal areas where the principal cities are located.

Rugged mountains dominate the interior of Sarawak and Sabah, while fertile plains line parts of the coast. The highlands of East Malaysia are famous for their dramatic limestone scenery. Towering rock outcrops loom out of the forest, and huge cave systems run for miles beneath the surface.

Malaysia's economy, one of the strongest economies in Asia, is based on agriculture, industry, and trade. The country produces half the world's palm oil and one-third of the world's rubber, as well as being a major producer of cacao beans, tobacco, coconuts, tea, peppers, pineapples, and other fruits. Malaysia's forests produce valuable hardwoods that are shipped worldwide as logs, boards, veneers, plywood, and furniture. Malaysia is the world's third-largest producer of tin and ranks as a major producer of oil and gas. Long-established industries produce textiles, rubber goods, timber products, and foodstuffs, while a host of new high-tech industries export electronic equipment, industrial chemicals, pharmaceuticals, and plastics, chiefly to Japan, Singapore, the United States, and Europe. This strong economic base gives most of Malaysia's people access to good educational and health-care services.

Old architecture of the secretariat buildings contrast with the modern city in Kuala Lumpur.

Singapore

Status:	Republic
Area:	239 square miles
Population:	4.4 million
Capital:	Singapore
Languages:	Malay, Mandarin Chinese, English, Tamil
Currency:	Singapore dollar (100 cents)

Singapore is a small country by area, but it is one of the economic powerhouses of Southeast Asia. The country consists of one main island (Singapore Island) and about 50 smaller ones that are clustered at the tip of the Malay Peninsula. The city of Singapore is the capital and one of the world's busiest seaports.

The skyline of the crowded, bustling capital is dominated by the high-rise towers of its commercial district. These structures rise above traditional shophouses, elegant apartment buildings, shopping malls, industrial districts, and the container terminals, warehouses, and repair yards that service the endless flow of ships.

Almost half the land is built on, and most of the rest consists of parks and other public spaces. Singapore's small amount of farmland produces fruit and vegetables for local use, but most of the island's food has to be imported. Water is piped in from Malaysia to meet the city's needs.

Like Malaysia, Singapore has a diverse population. About 78 percent are Chinese, 14 percent Malay, and 7 percent Indian. A small number of Europeans and Americans live in Singapore, where hundreds of international companies have offices.

Singapore's wealth comes from importing and exporting goods from all over the world. It also has a thriving manufacturing sector making electrical and electronic goods, textiles, clothing, cameras, scientific instruments, chemicals, plastics, and food products. Heavy industry consists of ship repairs and oil refining.

The wealth generated by Singapore's economy provides the people with some of the highest living standards in Asia.

Brunei

Status:	Absolute Monarchy
Area:	2,228 sq. mi.
Population:	374,000
Capital:	Bandar Seri Begawan
Languages:	Malay, English
Currency:	Brunei dollar (100 sen)

Brunei is a small W-shaped country on the northern coast of the island of Borneo, facing the South China Sea.

Formerly a British protectorate, Brunei achieved independence in 1984 and is ruled by a sultan (king) who is elected for life by a council of senior politicians. About 65 percent of the people are Malay and predominantly Muslim. Another 25 percent are Chinese and Christian. More than 70 percent of the population live in the towns and cities.

The mainstays of Brunei's economy are the oil and gas fields that lie beneath its coastal waters.

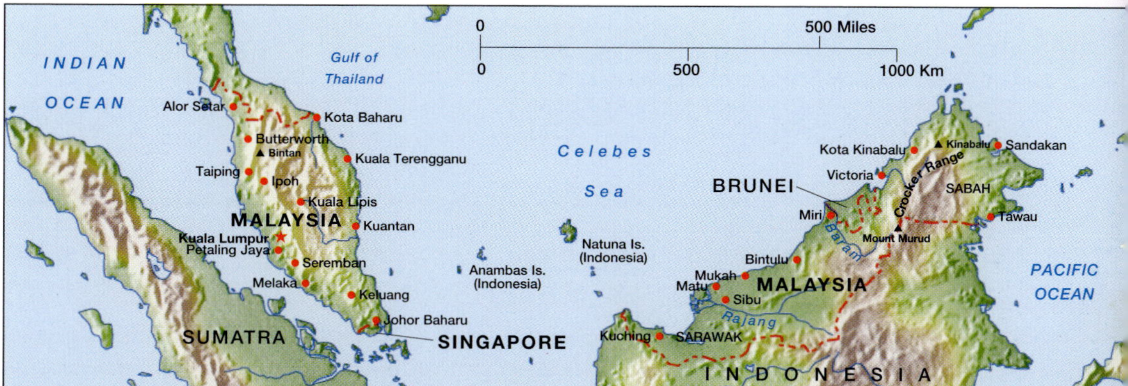

Philippines

Status:	Republic
Area:	115,830 sq. mi.
Population:	82.8 million
Capital:	Manila
Languages:	Tagalog, English, Spanish, Cebuano
Currency:	Filipino peso (100 centavos)

Modern buildings dominate the centre of Manila.

The Republic of the Philippines consists of more than 7,100 islands, set in the western Pacific Ocean between Taiwan to the north and Indonesia to the south. The island group extends 1,150 miles north to south, nearly 700 miles west to east, and has almost 11,000 miles of coastline. About 1,000 of the islands are inhabited. Most Filipinos live on the two largest islands—Luzon at the northern end and Mindanao in the south—and on the cluster of medium-sized islands called the Visayas that lie between them. About half the total population lives on Luzon, with the greatest concentration in and around the capital city of Manila.

The Philippine islands were formed by volcanoes, and more than 20 of them are still active. Mount Pinatubo, northwest of Manila Bay, erupted in 1991 in one of the most violent volcanic eruptions of the past century. Forests cover about half the total land area, providing the islands with a valuable resource. Philippine mahogany is exported worldwide, pine and bamboo are used for large- and small-scale construction projects. The cottonlike fibre that covers the seed pods of the kapok tree is harvested and exported for use as an insulation material and for stuffing furniture.

The Philippines population contains many different ethnic groups. Most Filipinos are descended from early immigrants from Indonesia and Malaya. Others are descended from more recent arrivals from China, India, Japan, Europe, and North America. A few large groups dominate the lowlands and cities of the main islands, but the mountainous regions are home to many smaller groups who speak more than 100 local languages and dialects and have their own distinctive traditions and cultures.

The islands' fertile volcanic soils and a hot, damp, tropical climate make the land very productive. Filipino farmers grow most of the food the country needs. Rice and maize are the staple food crops. Others include cassava, sweet potatoes, mangoes, and bananas. Cacao beans, coffee beans, pineapples, sugarcane, hemp, and tobacco are grown for use within the Philippines and also for export. Farmers also raise large numbers of cattle, water buffalo, pigs, goats, and hens. Most of the crops are grown on the plains, but the northern part of Luzon also contains some of Asia's most spectacular hillside rice terraces some of them built more than 2,000 years ago. As well as producing food, these remarkable fields are a major tourist attraction, along with the islands' stunning scenery, wild flowers and birds, and beautiful beaches.

Fishing is a major industry in this island nation. Fishing crews catch sardines, mackerel, tuna, and many other fish offshore, and crabs, shellfish, and sponges are harvested from the shallow coastal waters. Fish farmers raise shrimp and tilapia, a popular food fish, in artificial ponds constructed along the shores.

Mining and manufacturing are the fastest-growing sectors of the economy. Miners produce copper, nickel, and gold for export, but the islands also contain large reserves of chromite, lead, silver, manganese, and zinc that have yet to be exploited. Food processing is the largest industry. Newer industries include textiles, clothing and shoes, electrical and electronic goods, and furniture.

Babuyan Is.
Babuyan Channel
0
100
200 Miles
0
200
400 Km
Aparri
Laoag
Cordillera Central
Cagayan
Madre
Bangued
Vigan
Tabuk
Tuguegarao
Candon
Bontoc
Ilagan
Cauayan
Sierra
San Fernando
Mount Pulog
Bayombong
Baguio
Lingayen Gulf
LUZON
PHILIPPINE
SEA
Lingayen
Dagupan
San Jose
Baler
Zambales Mtns.
Cabanatuan
Palayan
Dingalan Bay
San Antonio
Polillo I.
Mt. Pinatubo
Caloocan
Quezon City
SOUTH
CHINA
SEA
Manila
Lamon Bay
Manila Bay
Laguna de Bay
Tagaytay
Lucbao
Daet
Pandan
Lake Taal
Lipa
Lucena
Catanduanes I.
Lubang
Batangas
Naga
Virac
Batangas Bay
Pasacao
Tiwi
Santa Cruz
Mayon Volcano
Lake Naujan
Legazpi
Sibuyan Sea
Claveria
Sorsogon
MINDORO
Trosin
San Bernardino Strait
Romblon
Sibuyan I.
San Jacinto
Laoang
San José
Odiongan
Masbate
SAMAR
Mindoro Strait
Busuanga I.
Dimasalang
Tablas I.
Calbayog
Dolores
Coron
MASBATE
Catbalogan
Culion I.
Kalibo
Visayan Islands
Roxas
Visayan Sea
Naval
Borongan
Tabango
PANAY
Tacloban
LEYTE
Guiuan
Bogo
Leyte Gulf
Pototan
Sagay
Palawan Passage
San Jose
Iloilo City
Baybay
Abuyog
Dumaran I.
Bacolod
CEBU
Canlaon
Panay Gulf
Cebu
Maasin
Talibon
Dinagat
General Luna
Puerto Princesa
NEGROS
BOHOL
Surigao
Palawan
Bais
Tagbilaran
Bohol Sea
Narra
Dumaguete
Camiguin I.
Diuata Mtns.
Tandag
Lazi
Butuan
Siquijor I.
Gingoog
Lianga
Dipolog
Cagayan de Oro
Agusan
Sulu
Bislig
Bugsuk I.
Malaybalay
Ozamiz
Balabac
Sea
Liloy
Tangub
Marawi
Valencia
Balabac I.
Lake Sultan Alonto
Pagadian
Baganga
Balabac Strait
MINDANAO
Tagum
Margosatubig
Illana Bay
Cotabato
Davao
Mindanao
Mati
Cagayan Sulu I.
Mt. Apo
Lunon
Moro Gulf
Zamboanga
Tacurong
Davao Gulf
Koronadel
Basilan I.
General Santos
Jolo I.
BORNEO
Celebes Sea
Sulu Archipelago
Tawi-Tawi I.

Indonesia

Status:	Republic
Area:	741,097 sq. mi.
Population:	225.3 million
Capital:	Jakarta
Languages:	Bahasa Indonesian, Dutch, English
Currency:	Rupiah (100 sen)

Indonesia consists of more than 13,600 islands strung out in a 3,100-mile chain across a vast expanse of tropical sea between the eastern Indian Ocean and the western Pacific Ocean. Many of the islands cover only a few square miles, but Indonesia also includes some of the world's largest islands. Sumatra, for example, is nearly 1,060 miles long, and Java is more than 620 miles long. Indonesia also includes the western half of the world's second-largest island, New Guinea, called Irian Jaya, and more than three-quarters of the world's third-largest island, Borneo, which makes up the province of Kalimantan. People inhabit about half the islands, but 80 per cent of the population live on Sumatra, Java, Kalimantan, Sulawesi, and Irian Jaya, with almost half the total population crowded onto Java.

Most of Indonesia's people are of Malay descent, but the population also includes Chinese, Papuans, Arabs, and Polynesians. Islam is the dominant religion, but millions of people on the smaller islands and in remote inland regions also follow ancient traditional beliefs. The largest cities are Jakarta, Surabaya, and Bandung (all on Java) and Medan on Sumatra. The majority of the nation's people, however, live in small rural communities.

The Indonesian islands are dotted with hundreds of active volcanoes. Mountains covered in dense rain-forest dominate the interior regions, while broad fertile plains fringe the coasts. Forestry workers extract

teak, ebony, and other valuable hardwoods from the forests—chiefly on Borneo and Sumatra. Rattan and bamboo are also harvested for making mats and furniture. Most village houses are made of these versatile materials.

Agriculture is the backbone of Indonesia's economy. The country's farmers benefit from rich volcanic soil, plentiful rain, and year-round sunshine, all of which allows them to grow a wide variety of crops. Large plantations on the main islands produce coffee beans, tea, sugarcane, palm oil, rubber, and tobacco as cash crops. Smaller farms grow rice as their main food crop, along with maize, sweet potatoes, cassava, bananas, and other fruits and vegetables. Rural farms are not highly mechanized. Most farmers use traditional hand tools, and ploughs and carts are pulled by oxen and water buffalo. Many farmers also raise pigs, goats, and poultry for the table. In coastal areas, sardines, anchovies, tuna, prawns, and shellfish provide the protein in people's diets.

Oil and natural gas fields on Java and Sumatra supply fuel to the islands and are also Indonesia's principal export. Tin, from islands off the northern coast of Sumatra, is the country's second major mineral export. Miners also extract smaller amounts of coal, copper, manganese, and nickel. Manu-facturing is a relatively small part of the economy, and is concentrated almost entirely on Java. Factory workers process food products for export and make textiles, glassware, rubber products such as car tyres, furniture, paper, and other wood products. Newer industries include car and truck assembly plants and petrochemical plants fed by the country's oil fields.

A young Indonesian villager heads for the paddy fields, protected from the hot sun by a wide hat made of woven bamboo.

Australasia, and Antarctica

Two enormous and hugely contrasting regions—Australia, and the great southern continent of Antarctica—lie in the Southern Hemisphere. Together they cover 40 percent of the earth's surface, yet between them they have a total population of barely 30 million people.

Australia is the only country to have an entire continent to itself. Separated from other land areas 200 million years ago, Australia became home to a unique collection of animals and plants, many of them found nowhere else on earth. Its original people, the Aborigines, arrived by canoe from Southeast Asia more than 40,000 years ago. These early peoples lived by hunting and gathering. In the 1600s, when Europeans first began to explore the Southern Hemisphere, about 300,000 Aborigines lived in Australia. Britain took control of the continent in the late 1700s, using it first as a place to send convicted criminals. It was not until the 1800s that the British began to explore the country, setting Australia on the road to become a leading industrialized nation.

The Pacific Ocean covers more of the earth's surface than all the world's land areas combined. It stretches more than 14,500 miles, from the islands of Malaysia in the west to the coast of Colombia in the east and from the Bering Sea off Alaska's shores in the north to the icy waters of Antarctica in the south. Almost lost within this vast expanse are between 20,000 and 30,000 islands—the exact number is unknown. Thousands are tiny coral islands and reefs that hardly break the ocean surface. Others, such as New Guinea and New Zealand, are among the world's largest islands.

Antarctica has no people, apart from a few thousand visiting scientists, and no year-round animal residents. In summer its shores and offshore islands teem with breeding seabirds, penguins, and seals. But in winter its vast, high, windswept plateau of snow and ice is broken in places by the jagged mountains that jut through ice up to two miles thick.

Papua New Guinea

Status:	Constitutional Monarchy
Area:	178,703 sq. mi.
Population:	5.9 million
Capital:	Port Moresby
Languages:	English, Pidgin English, Motu
Currency:	Kina (100 toea)

Papua New Guinea consists of the eastern half of the island of New Guinea and more than 600 smaller islands, including New Britain, the Bismarck Archipelago, Bougainville Island, the Louisiade Archipelago, and the D'Entrecasteaux Islands. Papua New Guinea's nearest neighbours are Indonesia, Malaysia, and the Philippines to the west and northwest and Australia to the south. In the late nineteenth century, parts of the region were controlled by Germany and later Britain. After World War I (1914-1918), the island became a mandated territory under the League of Nations. By the end of World War II (1939-1945), the United Nations (the league's successor) had declared it a trust territory to be administered by Australia. Papua New Guinea became independent in 1975 but maintains close ties to Australia.

Mountains that reach 8,000 to 14,000 feet above sea level dominate the interior of the main island. In between the mountains are steep river gorges. Tropical rain forests cover most of the land, but broad valleys and basins within the mountains provide large areas of rich soil that support most of the country's agriculture. Most of Papua New Guinea's people live in these highland valleys and basins, where the climate is cooler and healthier than it is on the coast.

Papua New Guinea's hot, humid coastal plains support a number of large towns—Wewak, Madang, Lae, and Popondetta on the north coast and Kerema, Kupiano, and the capital of Port Moresby in the south. However, swamps cover large parts of the coast, and few people live in these areas.

Most of Papua New Guinea's people live in small villages, where hundreds of dialects are spoken and where there is a huge variety of traditions and customs. Farmers on most of the islands grow taro, yams, and bananas in the wetter areas and sweet potatoes, coconuts, and other vegetables and fruits on the drier soils. Pigs and chickens provide meat for most families. Farmers on small holdings and on large plantations produce cash crops for export. The principal commercial crops are coffee beans, cacao beans, copra, and tea, with smaller amounts of peanuts, tobacco, rubber, and pyrethrum (used to make insecticides).

Forestry workers extract hardwoods for export as logs, sawn lumber, plywood, and veneers. These goods are destined mainly for Australia, Asia, and Europe. Fishers catch many species for the home and export markets, the most valuable export being skipjack tuna.

Factories in Port Moresby, Lae, Madang, Bulolo, and Goroka on the main island, in Kieta on Bougainville Island, and in Rabaul on New Britain process farm and forest produce and manufacture furniture, textiles, clothing, cement, and chemicals. Papua New Guinea has many large mineral deposits, but many are in inaccessible regions and so far have not been exploited. Natural gas fields around the Gulf of Papua produce energy for the country. The chief mineral exports are copper and gold from the world's biggest copper mine, which is located at Panguna on Bougainville Island. Japan, Germany, and Spain buy the bulk of the copper exports. Papua New Guinea is not wealthy, but its government is using the profits of its developing economy to improve access to healthcare and educational services.

Australia

Status:	Constitutional Monarchy and Federation of States
Area:	2.98 million sq. mi.
Population:	20.6 million
Capital:	Canberra
Languages:	English
Currency:	Australian dollar (100 cents)

Australia—the world's sixth largest country—is the only country to occupy an entire continent. It is also one of the most thinly populated countries in the world, with an average of only six people per square mile. But even that figure is misleading. Deserts, scrub, and dry grasslands cover nearly all of western and central Australia, and these arid and semi-arid regions support an average of only one or two people per square mile.

Most of Australia's 19 million people are concentrated along the southern and eastern coasts, where there is enough rainfall to support intensive agriculture and large urban areas. In fact, more than 80 percent of Australians live in cities and towns. Some of the largest cities are Perth in the southwest, Adelaide, Melbourne, and Sydney in the southeast, and Brisbane in the east.

Agriculture and mining are the mainstays of Australia's economy. They employ relatively few people but produce virtually all Australia's export goods. The two sectors are also the source of raw materials for many of Australia's industries.

About 65 percent of Australia's land is available for farming, but climate and terrain determine how farmers use the land. The western two-thirds of Australia consist of a vast, dry plateau. Deserts, unsuitable for any kind of farming, fill the central region and are surrounded by dry grasslands that extend to the coast. Livestock farmers raise sheep on these grasslands, primarily for their

Melville I.
Crocker I.
Bathurst I.
Van Diemen Gulf
Wessel Is.
Darwin
ARNHEM LAND
Groote Eylandt
Roper
Sir Edward Pellew Group
Gulf of Carpentaria
Wyndham
Kununurra
Victoria
Wellesley Is.
Cape York
Weipa
Great Barrier Reef
Coral Sea
Princess Charlotte Bay
Mitchell
Cooktown
Cairns
Gilgert
Innisfail
NORTHERN TERRITORY
Leichhardt
Flinders
Norman
Ingham
Townsville
Ayr
Burdekin
Tennant Creek
Mount Isa
Cloncurry
Charters Towers
Bowen
Mackay
Winton
Georgina
QUEENSLAND
Moranbah
AUSTRALIA
Alice Springs
Macdonnell Ranges
Diamantina
Thomson
Barcoo
Belyando
Yeppoon
Rockhampton
Gladstone
GREAT ARTESIAN BASIN
Moura
Bundaberg
Dawson
Maryborough
Fraser I.
Charleville
Todd
Ayers Rock
Roma
GREAT DIVIDING RANGE
Musgrave Ranges
Innamincka
Maroochydore
Dalby
Toowoomba
Brisbane
Oodnadatta
Warrego
Gold Coast
VICTORIA DESERT
Coober Pedy
Lake Eyre North
Goondiwindi
Lismore
SOUTH AUSTRALIA
Moree
Lake Eyre South
Barwon
Grafton
Bourke
Narrabri
NULLARBOR PLAIN
Leigh Creek
Mount Painter
Flinders Ranges
Woomera
Lake Torrens
Wilcannia
Tamworth
Port Macquarie
Eucla
Lake Gairdner
NEW SOUTH WALES
Dubbo
Maitland
Newcastle
Broken Hill
Darling
Orange
Bathurst
Gosford
Whyalla
Mount Remarkable
Port Pirie
Lachlan
Spencer Gulf
Mildura
Sydney
Port Lincoln
Gawler
Balranald
Murrumbidgee
Wollongong
Adelaide
Gulf Saint Vincent
Swan hill
Wagga Wagga
Canberra
Murray
Cooma
Kangaroo I.
Bendigo
Shepparton
Albury Wadenga
Bega
INDIAN OCEAN
VICTORIA
Mount Kosciuszko
Eden
Ballarat
Melbourne
Mount Gambier
Geelong
Warrnambool
King I.
Bass Strait
Flinders I.
Tasman Sea
Burnie
George Town
Mount Ossa
Launceston
Ossa
TASMANIA
Derwent
Hobart
1000 Miles
0 Km

Ayers Rock—Uluru in the native Aboriginal language—rises to 2,844 feet in central Australia. Caves along its flanks contain hundreds of ancient Aboriginal rock paintings.

wool, which is one of Australia's principal exports. Rainfall increases toward the southwest, allowing farmers to grow wheat, another important export. A small region south of Perth is wet enough to nurture crops of fruits and vegetables and to support dairy herds. In the northern part of the state of Western Australia, farmers graze herds of beef cattle.

The eastern one-third of Australia divides into two subregions—a central lowland region and the eastern highlands, which parallel the coast from Cape York to Melbourne. Farmers in the southern part of the lowlands raise cattle and sheep and grow wheat, barley, and vegetables. The Great Dividing Range dominates the eastern highlands. This region of hills and plateaux is not very high—the highest point is Mount Kosciuszko at 7,310 feet—but it separates rivers flowing into the hot interior from those that flow to the Pacific coast. More rain falls on the highlands than on any other part of Australia, and the region's fertile soil supports Australia's most productive farms. Farmers in the states of New South Wales and Victoria grow rice, wheat, barley, vegetables, sugarcane, oranges and other fruits, and grapes for making wine. Others specialize in beef and dairy produce. Farmers farther north, along the coast of the state of Queensland, concentrate on raising sugarcane and tropical fruits such as bananas and grapefruit.

Australia is one of the world's leading exporters of diamonds, lead, and bauxite (the principal ore of aluminium) and is a major supplier of iron ore, nickel, silver, tin, copper, gold, tungsten, and zinc. Australian miners also produce gypsum and asbestos, which are used for making construction materials, and uranium, which powers nuclear plants. Coal, oil, and gas fields provide much of Australia's energy needs and are supplemented by some of the world's biggest solar energy complexes.

Manufacturing and service industries provide more than three-quarters of the country's jobs. Many workers process farm products such as meat, dairy products, wool, sugarcane, and fruit for export. Factories produce furniture, textiles, clothing, shoes, household appliances and other consumer goods, while heavier industries include iron and steel, car manufacture, chemicals, and paper. Tourism is another important industry. Attractions like the Great Barrier Reef and Ayers Rock provide thousands of jobs and attract more than one million visitors every year.

Because of the country's successful economy, most Australians enjoy a high standard of living, with comfortable housing, well-developed social amenities, and excellent educational and health systems. In addition to supporting sports facilities of nearly every kind, the cities also cater to a wide variety of cultural tastes, with some of the world's finest opera houses, concert halls, theaters, and art galleries. Medical and educational support is also available to the 13 percent of tha population who live in the widely scattered mining settlements and sheep stations (ranches) of the interior, commonly called the outback.

More than 40,000 years ago, Australia's indigenous people, the Aborigines, arrived from Southeast Asia. They travelled by raft or canoe across the shallow seas that separated Asia and

Australia at that time. Numbering more than 200,000, they live mainly in rural areas of the states of New South Wales, Queensland, and Northern Territory. In recent decades, many young Aborigines have moved to the towns, but most are disadvantaged in terms of education, employment, and living standards. Many Aborigines feel a great sense of injustice at the treatment of their people, their ancient culture, and their ancestral lands by the overwhelmingly dominant European-descended population.

European settlement began with a British penal colony in New South Wales in 1788. But exploration and voluntary settlement developed rapidly through the nineteenth century, based principally on mining and sheep farming. The fledgling states of Australia joined together under a federal constitution in 1901. The British monarch is head of state and is represented in Australia by a governor-general.

Australia still has close links with Britain, but since the 1960s trade has become more and more focused on Asia, especially Japan and China, and on the United States. Partly as a result of this shift, many Australians believe the time has come for the country to break its historic ties with Britain and to become a republic. Another factor has been the change in Australia's population mixture. Historically, England, Scotland, Ireland, Germany, and the Netherlands supplied most of Australia's immigrants, but the country relaxed its immigration laws in the 1960s, and since then new waves of immigrants have arrived from Greece, Italy, eastern Europe, the Middle East, and Asia.

Sydney Harbour, with downtown office blocks forming a backdrop to the city's spectacular modern Opera House.

New Zealand

Status:	Constitutional Monarchy
Area:	104,452 sq. mi.
Population:	3.8 million
Capital:	Wellington
Languages:	English, Maori
Currency:	New Zealand dollar (100 cents)

New Zealand, separated from Australia by the Tasman Sea, lies almost 1,000 miles southeast of its giant neighbour. New Zealand's two main islands—North and South—and a scattering of smaller ones form the southernmost islands of Polynesia.

Volcanic mountains cover the central and western portions of North Island. The tallest peak is Mount Ruapehu, which rises to 9,175 feet above sea level. Thick layers of volcanic lava extend over much of the land, creating fertile soil. Geysers and bubbling mud pools attract millions of tourists and provide New Zealand with a valuable energy source. Holes drilled deep into the ground tap superheated steam, which is used to drive the turbines of geothermal power stations. Low hills in eastern North Island offer grazing for beef cattle, dairy herds, and sheep, while farmers in the region's coastal lowlands grow fruits and vegetables. Forests, sandy beaches, and sheltered inlets make the ragged northern peninsula a popular vacation area.

The larger South Island is dominated by the Southern Alps, which angle across the country from northeast to southwest. Snowfields and glaciers cover Mount Cook (12,349 feet) and other neighbouring peaks, which tower above forested slopes and beautiful lakes. Stunning mountain scenery attracts walkers and climbers from all over the world. Dense forests cover the western slopes of the Alps, which drop steeply to a narrow coastal plain. To the east, the mountains slope more gently to the broad, flat Canterbury Plains and to the rolling hills of Otago in the south. The Canterbury Plains provide New Zealand's only extensive lowland area, where farmers grow wheat, barley, oats, and fodder crops.

Lush grazing land in the east of New Zealand's North Island.

Cropland and pasture are New Zealand's greatest assets, supporting nearly 60 million sheep and about 8 million cattle. Mutton, lamb, beef, dairy produce, and wool are exported to Australia, Britain, Europe, Japan, and the United States and make up about half the country's export earnings. New Zealand farmers are also the world's principal suppliers of kiwi fruit. A thriving fishing industry hauls in crabs, lobsters, and shellfish for the home market and for export. New Zealand's forestry industry supports lumber, plywood, and paper factories.

Hydroelectric stations on rivers supply about 75 percent of New Zealand's energy needs. Geothermal energy, coal, oil, and natural gas provide the rest. New Zealand's modest reserves of iron ore, gold, silver, and tungsten are insufficient to support heavy industry, so iron and steel, industrial machinery, cars, buses and trucks, and oil are the country's principal imports. Factories concentrated around Dunedin and Christchurch on South Island and around Wellington (the nation's capital) and Auckland on North Island produce textiles, clothing, food products, furniture, metal goods, chemicals, and petroleum products.

The first settlers in New Zealand were the Maori, who arrived from islands elsewhere in Polynesia more than 1,000 years ago. The Maori make up about 15 percent of the population, with the remaining 85 percent being the descendants of British immigrants who began to arrive in the 1800s.

Te Kao
Great Exhibition Bay
Kaitaia
Bay of Islands
Russell
Whangarei
Dargaville
Bream Bay
Great Barrier I.
Hauraki Gulf
East Coast Bays
Takapuna
Auckland
Manukau
Thames
Waihi
North Island
Hamilton
Waikato
Tauranga
Matamata
Bay of Plenty
Te Araroa
Tikitiki
Te Awamutu
Otorohanga
Rotorua
Kawerau
Opotiki
Tasman Sea
Murupara
Matawai
Tolaga Bay
Kaimanawa Mtns.
Gisborne
Mokau
Taumarunui
Lake Taupo
Waitara
New Pymouth
Wairoa
Mount Egmont
Mount Ruapehu
Hawke Bay
Hawera
Napier
Hastings
Patea
Wanganui
Waipawa
NEW ZEALAND
Marton
Rangitikei
Palmerston North
D'Urville I.
Tasman Bay
Masterton
Motueka
Porirua
Upper Hutt
Lower Hutt
Wellington
Nelson
Karamea
Richmond
Cook Strait
Wairau
Blenheim
Granity
Buller
Westport
Awatere
Tapuaenuku
Clarence
Kaikoura
Greymouth
Runanga
Hokitika
Cheviot
Waipara
Pegasus Bay
Kaiapoi
PACIFIC OCEAN
Christchurch
Rakaia
Mount Cook
Rangitata
Ashburton
Southern Alps
Canterbury Bight
Canterbury Plains
Twizel
Mount Aspiring
Timaru
Wanaka
Waitaki
Milford Sound
Lake Wakatipu
Queenstown
Cromwell
Oamaru
Alexandra
South Island
Lake Te Anau
Kingston
Te Anau
Clutha
Roxburgh
Otago Harbour
Mosgiel
Dunedin
Milton
Winton
Otago Plateaus
Kaitangata
Riverton
Invercargill
Foveaux Strait
Bluff
Halfmoon Bay
Stewart I.
0
150
300 Miles
0
200
400 Km

Antarctica

Status:	Protected International Territory
Area:	5.4 million sq. mi.

Antarctica is a land of extremes. It is the highest, coldest, windiest place on earth. Although covered by water in the form of ice, Antarctica is a desert without a single tree in all its 5.4 million square miles. Seasonal birds such as penguins live on the continent when they breed and hatch their young.

The fifth-largest continent, Antarctica is almost one-and-a-half times the size of the United States but has no native people, no flag, no government, no farming, and no industry. Seven countries—Argentina, Australia, Chile, France, Great Britain, New Zealand, and Norway—have all claimed sectors of Antarctica. These claims fan out in pie-shaped slices from the South Pole to the coast and beyond. In 1961, all these countries set aside their territorial claims under the Antarctic Treaty, which preserves the continent for science alone and bans any form of military use, commercial exploitation, or environmental damage. Antarctica has no fixed population, but several thousand scientists and support personnel live there in the summer months. In winter, this number dwindles to less than a thousand, who carry out long-term research on climate studies.

Ice, averaging more than a mile thick, covers almost the entire continent. In a few places,

Summer on the Antarctic Peninsula, and the ice that covered the sea through the winter has broken up, littering the surface with wave-worn fragments. Only at this time of year can supply boats reach the scientific bases scattered around the edge of Antarctica.

0
1000
2000 Miles
0
1000
2000
3000 Km
ATLANTIC OCEAN
South Georgia
INDIAN OCEAN
SOUTHERN OCEAN
South Orkney Is.
Falkland Is.
Scotia Sea
ENTINA
Deception I.
Graham Land
Antarctic Peninsula
Weddell Sea
Palmer Archipelago
Palmer Land
George V Sound
Alexander I.
Charcot I.
Bellingshausen Sea
Peter I.
Ellsworth Land
Vinson Massif
Berkner I.
Ronne Ice Shelf
Coats Land
Dronning Maud Land
Lützow-Holm Bay
Amundsen Bay
Enderby Land
Edward VIII Bay
Mac Robertson Land
Prince Charles Mtns.
MacKenzie Bay
Amery Ice Shelf
Prydz Bay
EAST ANTARCTICA
SOUTH POLE
WEST ANTARCTICA
Thurston I.
Walgreen Coast
Amundsen Sea
Mt. Kirkpatrick
Mt. Markham
Transantarctic Mtns.
Queen Mary Land
Davis Sea
Vostok (Russia)
Knox Coast
Vincennes Bay
Mt. Sidley
Marie Byrd Land
Ross Ice Shelf
Siple I.
Roosevelt I.
Mt. Erebus
Victoria Land
Wilkes Land
Dalton Ice Tong
Ross Sea
Porpoise Bay
Terre Adélie
Oates Land
Cook Ice Shelf
Sturge I.
Balleny Is.
PACIFIC OCEAN
Macquarie Is.
Campbell I.
Auckland I.
TASMANI
Antipodes Is.
NEW ZEALAND

is a vast, smooth plateau of ice with an average elevation of 7,500 feet above sea level. The continent is lopsidedly centreed on the South Pole and is divided into two contrasting parts—West Antarctica and East Antarctica—by the Trans-antarctic Mountains. This range stretches across the continent from the Weddell Sea to the Ross Sea.

Mountain ranges, basins, glaciers, and plateaux dominate West Antarctica. If the ice melted, this region would be a confusion of islands and seaways. West Antarctica reaches northward toward South America as a long, narrow S-shaped peninsula that is an extension of the Andes Mountains. Near the base of the peninsula, Vinson Massif, Antarctica's highest peak, rises to 16,860 feet. West Antarctica is much younger and more geologically active than East Antarctica is. Mount Erebus, Antarctica's most active volcano, occasionally spouts lava at the Ross Sea end of the Transantarctic range, and Deception Island near the tip of the peninsula erupted several times in the late 1960s.

East Antarctica is geologically much older. It is also much larger, covering almost three-fourths of the continent. A huge ice dome pushes up between the Transantarctic range and the mountains that rise along coastal sections of the Southern Ocean (sometimes also called the shores of the Indian and Atlantic Oceans). In the dome's centre, the ice is more than 15,700 feet thick. In places, the weight of the ice has pressed the underlying land surface far below sea level. This enormous mass of ice contains 70 percent of the earth's fresh water.

Temperatures at the South Pole average –56°F and often fall below –90°F in the winter months. In 1983 scientists at Russia's Vostok Station, which sits 11,220 feet above sea level, recorded the world's lowest-ever air temperature of –128.6°F. High winds frequently sweep across the plateau and down the mountain slopes and glaciers of the peninsula. Winds of 70 miles per hour can blow for days at a time, but the windiest place on earth is Commonwealth Bay on the Antarctic Peninsula, where meteorologists have recorded gales of 200 miles per hour. Surprisingly, little new snow falls on Antarctica. Yearly total precipitation is about six inches—half the average for the Sahara Desert. The blizzards that often reduce visibility to a few yards are full of granular snow and ice grains that have been picked up, blown around, and dumped again, over and over.

Ice hides most of Antarctica's coastline, so maps generally show the outer limit of the permanent ice, including the huge ice shelves that partly fill the Ross Sea and the Weddell Sea. These shelves are up to 2,000 feet thick where they join the coast and 600 feet thick at their outer edge.

In summer, huge slabs break off and drift out to sea as tabular icebergs. One of the largest in recent years measured more than 200 miles long and 60 miles wide. In winter, the surface of the sea freezes, and thick pack ice extends up to 900 miles from the coast. In summer the ice breaks up into ice floes and wave-worn lumps called brash. Only at this time of year can supply ships reach the scientific stations around Antarctica's coast. The stations that are far inland, like Vostok and the U.S. Amundsen-Scott base at the South Pole, are supplied by air.

Only two kinds of flowering plants and tiny lichens, algae, and mosses manage to survive in Antarctica's harsh climate. Around the coast, penguins, skuas, petrels, and other seabirds arrive to breed in summer, and seals haul themselves out onto ice floes and beaches to give birth to their pups. By contrast, the Southern Ocean teems with life. Plankton (tiny floating plants and animals) and their larger relatives, the shrimplike krill, feed fish and baleen whales. Fish and squid, in turn, provide food for seals and toothed whales.

Geologists have found copper, manganese, zinc, chromium, lead, and other minerals in Antarctica, as well as thick coal seams exposed in cliff faces in the Transantarctic Mountains. But any such mining is forbidden under the Antarctic Treaty. Oil and gas fields may lie beneath the continental shelves around Antarctica and its fringing islands, but these, too, are out of reach.

Antarctica's value to humans does not lie in a few hard-to-reach resources but in its value as a unique natural laboratory. Glaciologists examine patterns of ice movement and the effects of global warming on the Antarctic ice sheets. Biologists study the sea and land life, including fish that have developed a natural antifreeze to prevent them from freezing in the icy sea. These and other studies continue to add to people's understanding of the natural environment.

After years of persecution which brought several species to the brink of extinction, many of Antarctica's whales are slowly recovering.

Adelie penguins dive into the water to hunt for fish.

Index

Index